RELATED STRANGERS

❖

STEPHEN G. WILSON

RELATED STRANGERS

JEWS AND CHRISTIANS
70–170 C.E.

❖

Fortress Press
Minneapolis

To Lloyd, Michel, and Peter

Scripture quotations are from the New Revised Standard Version Bible, copyright © 1989 by the Division of Christian Education of the National Council of the Churches of Christ in the United States of America. Used with permission.

Interior design: Graphic Composition, Inc.
Cover design: Ann Artz

Library of Congress Cataloging-in-Publication Data

Wilson, S. G. (Stephen G.)
        Related strangers: Jews and Christians, 70–170 C.E./Stephen G.
    Wilson.
            p.   cm.
        Includes bibliographical references.
        ISBN 0-8006-2950-7 (alk. paper)
        1. Judaism—Relations—Christianity.   2. Christianity and other
    religions—Judaism.   3. Judaism—History—Talmudic period, 10–425.
    4. Jews in the New Testament.   5. Bible. N.T.—Criticism,
    interpretation, etc.   6. Christianity—Early church, ca. 30–600.
    7. Christianity in rabbinical literature.   8. Rabbinical literature—
    History and criticism.   I. Title.
    BM535.W554   1995
    261.2′6′09015—dc20   95–32217
                                                                              CIP

The paper used in this publication meets the minimum requirements of American National Standard for Information Sciences—Permanence of Paper for Printed Library Materials, ANSI Z329.48-1984.⊗

Manufactured in the U.S.A.

99   98   97   96   95   1   2   3   4   5   6   7   8   9   10

CONTENTS

❖

PREFACE

I have many to thank who have in various ways helped in the production of this book. Some of the research was funded by grants from the Social Science and Humanities Research Council of Canada and by successive Deans of Arts at Carleton University. Two librarians at St. Paul University, Ottawa, gave me ready access to their remarkable collection, which has greatly aided my research. The production staff at Fortress Press have been gracious and helpful, and my wife, Jenny, has used her editorial expertise to save me from a number of errors. Alan Segal cast his critical eye over an early version of chapter 6. Steve Muir, a doctoral student at the University of Ottawa, kindly agreed to prepare the indexes. To all of them my heartfelt thanks.

Some works became available only at a late stage in the production of the manuscript. I have been able to inject them into the Notes but, regrettably, not always give them the full discussion they deserve. I am thinking particularly of J. T. Sanders's recent book and the volume edited by J. D. G. Dunn, which readers will no doubt wish to compare and contrast with mine.

I have dedicated the book to three colleagues and good friends—Michel Desjardins, Lloyd Gaston, and Peter Richardson—each of whom read the manuscript in its entirety and offered many useful suggestions as well as encouragement along the way. In addition, Peter Richardson was particularly helpful when I first began to formulate the project some ten years ago. I am especially happy to mention Lloyd Gaston in the year that he formally retires, and hope that retirement will not mean that he will put down his pen. They are but three of the many members of the Canadian Society of Biblical Studies who have been a source of constant stimulation and friendship during the last two decades. I think of them, too, with gratitude.

S. G. Wilson

ABBREVIATIONS OF MODERN SOURCES

❖

AbrN	Abr-Nahrain
AJA	American Journal of Archaeology
AJS	The Journal of the Association for Jewish Studies
ANRW	Aufstieg und Niedergang der römischen Welt
Anton	Antonianum
ATR	Anglican Theological Review
Bib	Biblica
BJRL	Bulletin of the John Rylands University Library of Manchester
BZ	Biblische Zeitschrift
CBQ	Catholic Biblical Quarterly
Cons.Jud.	Conservative Judaism
CSEL	Corpus scriptorum ecclesiasticorum latinorum
EJ	Encyclopaedia Judaica
ET	Expository Times
ETL	Ephemerides theologicae lovanienses
EvT	Evangelische Theologie
H.St.Class.Philol.	Harvard Studies in Classical Philology
HTR	Harvard Theological Review
HUCA	Hebrew Union College Annual
Int	Interpretation
JAAR	Journal of the American Academy of Religion
JANESCU	Journal of Ancient Near Eastern Studies of Columbia University
JBL	Journal of Biblical Literature
JBR	Journal of Bible and Religion
JECS	Journal of Early Christian Studies
JEH	Journal of Ecclesiastical History
JES	Journal of Ecumenical Studies
JJS	Journal of Jewish Studies
JQR	Jewish Quarterly Review
JRS	Journal of Roman Studies

JSJ	*Journal for the Study of Judaism in the Persian, Hellenistic and Roman Period*
JSNT	*Journal for the Study of the New Testament*
JSP	*Journal for the Study of the Pseudepigrapha*
JTS	*Journal of Theological Studies*
MGWJ	*Monatsschrift für Geschichte und Wissenschaft des Judentums*
NedTTs	*Nederlands theologisch tijdschrift*
Neot	*Neotestamentica*
NT	*Novum Testamentum*
NTS	*New Testament Studies*
Quest.Lit.	*Questions Liturgiques*
RB	*Revue biblique*
Rel.St.Th.	*Religious Studies and Theology*
RevExp	*Review and Expositor*
RFIC	*Rivista di Filologie e d'Istruzione Classica*
RHPR	*Revue d'histoire et de philosophie religieuses*
RSR	*Recherches de science religieuse*
SBLSP	*SBL Seminar Papers*
SecCent	*Second Century*
SJT	*Scottish Journal of Theology*
SL	*Studia Liturgica*
StPatr	*Studia Patristica*
SWJTh	*South Western Journal of Theology*
TDNT	G. Kittel and G. Friedrich (eds.), *Theological Dictionary of the New Testament*
TLZ	*Theologische Literaturzeitung*
TR	*Theologische Rundschau*
TRE	*Theologische Realenzyklopädie*
TS	*Theological Studies*
TU	Texte und Untersuchungen
TZ	*Theologische Zeitschrift*
USQR	*Union Seminary Quarterly Review*
VC	*Vigiliae Christianae*
VT	*Vetus Testamentum*
ZKG	*Zeitschrift für Kirchengeschichte*
ZKT	*Zeitschrift für katholische Theologie*
ZNW	*Zeitschrift für die neutestamentiiche Wissenschaft*
ZTK	*Zeitschrift für Theologie und Kirche*

ABBREVIATIONS OF ANCIENT SOURCES

❖

Abod. Zar.	*Abodah Zarah*
AC	*Apostolic Constitutions*
Acts Pil.	*Acts of Pilate*
AJ I, AJ II	*Ascent(s) of James*
Ap. John	*Apocryphon of John*
Aphrahat	
Dem.	*Demonstrations*
Apoc. Abr.	*Apocalypse of Abraham*
Apoc. Adam	*Apocalypse of Adam*
2 Apoc. Bar.	Syriac *Apocalypse of Baruch*
3 Apoc. Bar.	Greek *Apocalypse of Baruch*
1 Apoc. Jas.	*First Apocalypse of James*
2 Apoc. Jas.	*Second Apocalypse of James*
Apoc. Pet.	*Apocalypse of Peter*
Aristides	
Apol.	*Apology*
Asc. Isa.	*Ascension of Isaiah*
Athenagoras	
Diogn.	*Diognetus*
Leg.	*Legatio*
Auth. Teach.	*Authoritative Teaching*
b.	Babylonian Talmud
Bar.	*Baruch*
Barn.	*Barnabas*
B. Bat.	*Baba Batra*
Ber.	*Berakot*
1 Clem.	*First Epistle of Clement*
Chron. Pasch.	*Chronicon Paschale*
Chrysostom	
Adv. Jud.	*Adversus Judaeos*
Did.	*Didache*
Dio	Dio Cassius
Hist.	*Historia*

Diogn.	Diognetus
Eccl. Rabb.	Ecclesiastes Rabbah
Ep. Arist.	Epistle of Aristeas
Ep. Clem.	Epistle of Clement
Epiphanius	
Adv. Haer.	Adversus haereses
Mens. Pond.	Libellum de mensuris et ponderibus
Pan.	Panarion
Eusebius	
Hist. eccl.	Historia ecclesiastica
Life of Const.	Life of Constantine
Gen. Rabb.	Genesis Rabbah
Gos. Eb.	Gospel of the Ebionites
Gos. Eg.	Gospel of the Egyptians
Gos. Heb.	Gospel of the Hebrews
Gos. Naz.	Gospel of the Nazarenes
Gos. Pet.	Gospel of Peter
Gos. Phil.	Gospel of Philip
Gos. Thom.	Gospel of Thomas
Gos. Truth	Gospel of Truth
Great Pow.	Concept of Our Great Power
Hermas Sim.	Similitudes
Hermas Vis.	Visions
Hippolytus	
Haer.	Refutatio omniam haeresium
Hist. Aug. Hadr.	Historia Augusta Vita Hadrianus
Hul.	Hullin
Hyp. Arch.	Hypostatis of the Archons
Ignatius	
Eph.	Letter to the Ephesians
Magn.	Letter to the Magnesians
Phld.	Letter to the Philadelphians
Smyrn.	Letter to the Smyrnaeans
Irenaeus	
Haer.	Adversus haereses
Jerome	
Comm. Is.	Commentary on Isaiah
De vir. ill.	De viris illustribus
Ep.	Epistle
Josephus	
Ant.	Antiquities of the Jews
Ap.	Contra Apionem
Bell.	Bellum Judaicum
Vit.	Vita

Justin
   Dial.   *Dialogue with Trypho*
   I Apol.   *First Apology*
KP   *Kerygmata Petrou*
m.   *Mishnah*
Mart. Pol.   *Martyrdom of Polycarp*
Meg.   *Megilla*
Midr. Qohelet   *Midrash Qohelat Rabba*
   Rabba
Odes Sol.   *Odes of Solomon*
Origen
   Cels.   *Contra Celsum*
   Hom.   *Homilies*
Orig. World   *On the Origin of the World*
Pesaḥ   *Pesahim*
Pesiq. R.   *Pesiqta Rabbati*
Philo
   Conf. Ling.   *De Confusione Linguarum*
   Decal.   *De Decalogo*
   Flacc.   *In Flaccum*
   Migr. Abr.   *De Migratione Abrahami*
   Q. Gen.   *Quaestiones in Genasin*
   Som.   *De Somniis*
   Spec. Leg.   *De Specialibus Legibus*
   Vit. cont.   *De Vita Contemplative*
   Vit. Mos.   *De Vita Mosis*
Pliny
   Ep.   *Epistles*
   Pan.   *Panegyricus*
Plutarch
   Cic.   *Cicero*
Polycarp
   Phil.   *Letter to the Philippians*
Prot. Jas.   *Protevangelium of James*
Ps.-Clem. Hom.   *Pseudoclementine Homilies*
Ps.-Clem. Rec.   *Pseudoclementine Recognitions*
Ros. Has.   *Ros Hashana*
Sabb.   *Sabbat*
Sanh.   *Sanhedrin*
Šeb.   *Šebiʿit*
Šeqal.   *Šeqalim*
Sib. Or.   *Sibylline Oracles*
Sozomen
   H.E.   *Historia ecclesiastica*

Suetonius
   Claud.   *Claudius*
   Dom.   *Domitian*
Syn. Pray.   *Synagogue Prayers*
t.   *Tosephta*
Ta'an   *Ta'anit*
Tacitus
   Agric.   *Agricola*
   Hist.   *Historiae*
Tertullian
   Adv. Jud.   *Adversus Judaeos*
   Apol.   *Apologeticum*
   Haer.   *De Praescriptione Haereticorum*
   Marc.   *Adversus Marcionem*
   Scorp.   *Scorpiace*
Test. XII   *Testaments of the Twelve Patriarchs*
   T. Ash.   *Testament of Asher*
   T. Benj.   *Testament of Benjamin*
   T. Dan   *Testament of Dan*
   T. Gad   *Testament of Gad*
   T. Iss.   *Testament of Issachar*
   T. Jos.   *Testament of Joseph*
   T. Jud.   *Testament of Judah*
   T. Levi   *Testament of Levi*
   T. Naph.   *Testament of Naphtali*
   T. Sim.   *Testament of Simeon*
   T. Zeb.   *Testament of Zebulon*
Testim. Truth   *Testimony of Truth*
Theodoret
   Ep.   *Epistles*
   Haer. Fab.   *Haeritocorum fabulorum compendium*
   Comp.
Theophilus
   Autol.   *Ad Autolycum*
2 Treat. Seth   *Second Treatise of the Great Seth*
Tri. Trac.   *Tripartite Tractate*
Trim. Prot.   *Trimorphic Protennoia*
y.   Jerusalem Talmud
Yad.   *Yadayim*
Yebam.   *Yebamot*
IIQMelch   *Melchizedek* from Qumran Cave II

INTRODUCTION

❖

The first question that is likely to occur to anyone glancing at this book is, "Why 70–170 CE?" I should explain. There are several studies of the Christian view of Judaism in the New Testament period, some of them reaching to, but not beyond, 135 CE. Then there is the magnificent book by M. Simon, which covers the period 135–425 CE.[1] It has deservedly held the field for some forty-five years, and its major thesis—that Judaism thrived throughout this period—has been repeatedly confirmed. So, why should we give particular attention to the overlapping century? Partly because it has been neglected. When scholars address the issue of Jewish-Christian relations, it is not uncommon for them to pass rapidly from the evidence of the New Testament to that of the third or fourth century, where John Chrysostom's Antioch is a favorite place to linger. They do so, I suspect, because in both cases there appears more to discuss—so that studies that focus on the earlier period are weighted heavily toward the New Testament, and Simon's account rests primarily on evidence from the third century and beyond. Yet, it can be argued, the intervening period is the crucial era for Jewish-Christian relations. Once we move beyond Justin and Melito, their relationship settles into a fairly predictable pattern. Tertullian and others seem to do little more than sum up in rather wooden fashion what has already been fought out and decided. And from this point on the increasingly dominant rabbinic movement goes its own independent way. This is not to say that things became rigidly defined, and John Chrysostom (ah!) is sufficient witness to this. Yet there remained in the century we shall study a degree of variety and complexity in Jewish-Christian interaction that was to become increasingly rare. In addition, some of the best literature on this period comes in the form of discrete studies or collected essays. My aim is to provide a more sustained treatment than is currently available.[2]

A case could be made for including Jesus and Paul. I have not done so for several reasons. One is that it would have made a long book even longer, and in the interests of my own sanity and the patience of the reader I have not included them. Another is that they have been examined so thoroughly and scrupulously that there seems little new that one could say, except to side with one or another of the finely discriminating readings that are readily available elsewhere. Moreover, Jesus, I think, was wholly embedded in the Judaism of his day and thought he was going to precipitate the restoration of Israel. That he would found a religion called Christianity, which would become competitive with the Judaism he knew, was a thought that never entered his mind. Paul, with his obsession for converting Gentiles, set in place a number of changes that resonated through the succeeding centuries, but, in the last resort (Romans 9–11), he remained committed to Israel.

The end of the Jewish War has often been seen as a crucial turning point in Jewish-Christian relations, so that seemed a natural point to begin. The century that followed can be thought of as the tunnel period, where things looked one way at the beginning and rather different at the end. The chronological limits have not been strictly observed. Occasionally the discussion has spilled over at both ends, but only insofar as it might illuminate what was going on in between.

There is an added advantage to these chronological parameters. In traversing the century between 70 and 170 CE, we are forced to ignore the artificial divisions in both Judaism and Christianity between the canonical and noncanonical traditions. Our second chapter, which deals with the canonical Gospels and Acts, may seem to belie this, and it is rather long and necessarily engaged in the seemingly endless flow of debate about these texts. Lumping them together was initially a matter of convenience—and there are other ways of organizing the evidence—but in the end it proved fortuitous because it highlighted the differences between them. Chapter 3, on the somewhat neglected Jewish and Christian apocrypha, should at any rate provide appropriate balance.

It will be clear from the Contents that the discussion is heavily biased in favor of Christian evidence. This, sadly, is the way it must be. Our records for Judaism during this century are extraordinarily slim. We start at 70 CE, the date at which Josephus's historical surveys conclude. The Mishnah, which tells us something about one significant group of Jews, was not put into written form until around 225 CE. For the period in between we have to resort largely to surmise, extrapolating from Jewish and Christian sources what we can. Christian evidence is more helpful, but even then we face yawning gaps, both geographical and historical, in our sources. I suspect that our reconstructions look only vaguely like the historical reality, but a suspicion is all that it can be.

There have been attempts to reduce the story of Jewish-Christian relations to a core issue. Rosemary Ruether's fine study is perhaps the best known case in point, where it is argued that the disagreement over Christology held precedence.[3] It has been rightly criticized because, like all similar studies, it underestimates the extraordinary range of ideological and pragmatic reasons why Jews and Christians parted company. If I began with a conviction, it was that the story is far more complex and interesting than is suggested by the identification of any single issue as the key to all else. Not surprisingly, perhaps, it has been confirmed, but to a far greater degree than I first expected. This may seem dull, hardly a hypothesis, perhaps even an antihypothesis, yet it seems to be what the somewhat parlous evidence points us to.

Thus if I use the singular terms "Judaism" and "Christianity," or their equivalents, it is only because the plurals ring unmusically to my ears. In almost all instances the plural should be understood, as I think the context usually makes clear. I also use the phrase "Jewish-Christian *relations*" deliberately. I do not wish to belittle the tradition of Christian hostility toward Judaism that the sources display, and "The Origins of Christian Anti-Judaism/Anti-Semitism" would be a fair way of describing much of what they say. Yet, at least in the century we shall study, there are signs that Jews and Christians related to each other in ways that are not entirely captured in this negative way of defining them, and "Jewish-Christian relations" appropriately has a more neutral ring. I should add, in view of J. T. Sanders's recent book, that I use the term "relations" to include both relations and attitudes, both the way in which Jews and Christians interacted in practice and the way they viewed each other in theory.[4]

THE POLITICAL AND SOCIAL CONTEXT

1

❖

The primary aim in this chapter is to sketch the political and social factors that form the background to, and that may help to explain, the Jewish-Christian schism. Stated thus, it sounds deceptively simple. Yet we soon run up against a number of constraints, some imposed by the nature of the evidence and some by the nature of our topic. To begin with, the evidence for both Judaism and Christianity in this period is sporadic. Josephus's writings are scarcely a straightforward source of information for the period up to and including the Jewish War, but where his narratives leave off there is a dramatic decline in the range and quality of evidence for developments in Judaism. From this point on we have to rely heavily on scraps of literary and archaeological evidence, often as not from Roman or Christian sources. As an insignificant newcomer on the scene, Christianity left few traces in either Jewish or Roman sources. For evidence originating within the Christian movement we are better served, but it deals largely with internal matters and tells us only implicitly about their political and social history. The one historical source (Acts), as problematic in its own way as Josephus, also concludes at about the time the period we are interested in begins. And of course the paucity of evidence here, as elsewhere, means that what little we do have has been the object of extensive, sometimes overwhelming attention.

A second problem is that the evidence for the sociopolitical developments in the two traditions rarely reveals information about their relationship to each other, so that we often have to resort to speculation about what was inherently likely to have been the case. If, for example, we wish to consider the effect of the most traumatic events in Jewish history of this period—the Jewish War, the revolts under Trajan, and the Bar Cochba rebellion—on both the status of the Jews and on their relationship with Christians, we might naturally decide to start with what the traditions themselves

1

say. Yet aside from Josephus, other Jewish writings—the Pseudepigrapha and early rabbinic traditions—are notoriously reticent about the rebellions against Rome, as they are about most contemporary historical events, and what they have to say about Christians is obscure and allusive.[1] Christian sources might seem initially to be more promising, yet in the earlier writings references to the Jewish rebellions, apart from being scarce, are shaped by internal Christian concerns and often conflate the consequences of the two rebellions in Judaea. They thus provide little help in answering particular questions we may have in mind and force us back to the weighing of probabilities.

It is clear, thirdly, that a rapid sketch carries its own dangers. The most obvious, perhaps, is to speak of either Christianity or Judaism in the singular, as if they were homogeneous entities. As a form of shorthand it may be acceptable, but both traditions in reality exhibit an extraordinary range of practice and belief. This now commonplace assertion, it will become clear, finds ample support in subsequent chapters. At this stage we need only bear it in mind as we skate lightly over a century of Jewish and Christian history. It will help us, when the evidence is sparse, to resist the temptation to extrapolate universal claims from local occurrences.

As if the vagaries and constraints of the evidence were not enough, the discussion that follows is organized along both thematic and chronological lines in order to accomplish several aims. It is, as stated, focused primarily on sociopolitical issues. Yet within that broad compass there are specific topics that bear directly on the issue of Jewish-Christian relations and that can be most usefully subsumed under the rubric of this chapter. We shall therefore concentrate on two broad areas: first, the Jews and Rome, considering their place in society in general but with particular emphasis on the consequences of the Jewish revolts and on the major literary product of the period, the Mishnah; second, the Christians and Rome, concentrating especially on the legal and social standing of Christians in the Roman Empire and on the attempts by Christian apologists to explain and defend their tradition. Each of these has been the subject of extensive and fascinating debate in its own right, but our task will be to focus as clearly as possible only on those elements that bear directly on our theme.

THE JEWISH REVOLTS AND THEIR CONSEQUENCES

We turn first to the three Jewish rebellions. The focus will be quite precise and will largely ignore the intervening years until the following section of this chapter. This is a somewhat artificial division, but it is made for two reasons. The first is that the political ramifications of the revolts have as much to do with internal Jewish-Christian relations as with the relations of either group with Rome. The second is that two of these revolts have often been thought to have had a significant effect on the separation of Christianity from Judaism. In this way a central issue for our purposes can be brought to the surface from the start, and the arrangement has the additional advantage of providing a clearly focused aim to guide us through the burgeoning literature on the Jewish wars. Moreover, lurking behind our discussion, and to some extent shaping it, is an even more pointed question to which we shall subsequently return: Which of these rebellions had the more traumatic effect on Jewish-Christian relations?

The complex history leading to the sack of Jerusalem can, apart from an occasional backward glance, be left to one side. Our concern is with the outcome. There is a scholarly tradition that sees the defeat by the Romans in 70 CE as having led to almost total devastation and loss—the destruction of Temple and cult, a change in legal status, widespread confiscation of Jewish land, a dramatic worsening of economic conditions, and loss of political freedom.[2] This is not entirely unfounded and it is worthwhile briefly to summarize some of the more dramatic consequences:

—Thousands were held captive, sold as slaves, or slaughtered in the final siege (Josephus Bell.6.414–20; 7.118), resulting in a significant decline in the population.

—The destruction of the Temple and large parts of the city, two of the great unifying symbols of Judaism. This in turn led to cessation of the cult and the demise of the high-priestly office, but it also meant the disappearance of the nerve center of political and religious life in Judaea, as well as the place where, for many Jews, God supremely dwelt. The trauma is poignantly expressed in works such as 4 Ezra and 2 Baruch.[3]

—The disappearance of the Sanhedrin, the civic and political powers vested in it, and its symbolic role as the defender of Jewish freedom and independence, however limited by Roman authority. In effect, Judaea ceased to be a political entity.

—The appointment of more experienced Roman governors and an enlarged military establishment, thus tightening the Roman grip on Judaea.

—Economic havoc caused by the war, which led to considerable hardship, exacerbated by the awarding of lands to Roman veterans (Josephus Bell.7.216).

—Eligibility for the Temple tax extended (to young and old, men and women, slaves—Josephus Bell.8.218; Dio 66.7.2),[4] and the funds funneled into Roman coffers. The amount, estimated to be about the value of one week's wages for every taxpayer, became a considerable burden, especially in large households.

It is thus possible to paint a fairly bleak picture of the aftermath of the Jewish War. Yet it has been argued persuasively, most notably by G. Alon, that the outcome was far less devastating for Judaism than appears at first sight:[5]

—The final, drawn-out siege affected only Jerusalem and the surrounding lands, since the rest of Judaea had already been pacified.

—Diaspora Judaism was scarcely affected. True, there were skirmishes between Jews and Greeks in Antioch, Alexandria, and Cyrene (Josephus *Bell*.7.46ff., 409ff., 437ff.), but in the last resort the Romans always upheld the traditional privileges of the Jews. Agrippa II remained loyal to the Romans, for which he was duly rewarded, and the extended love affair between his sister, Berenice, and Titus shows that Jewish-Roman relations could proceed on one level!

—There is no evidence for a change in the legal status of Jews after 70 CE,[6] nor of persecution outside the context of the war. Some who surrendered or were captured may have lost their land:

> About the same time Caesar sent instructions to Bassus and Laberius Maximus, the procurator, to farm out [*apodosthai*] all Jewish territory. For he founded no city there, reserving the country as his private property, except that he did assign to eight hundred veterans discharged from the army a place of habitation called Emmaus, distant thirty furlongs from Jerusalem. (Josephus *Bell*.7.216)

This obscure statement by Josephus can scarcely mean that the emperor confiscated all of Judaea;[7] rather, it seems to mean that Vespasian sold off all lands (to Jews?) confiscated during the war and settled only a few foreigners in the vicinity of Jerusalem. In fact, it seems most likely that most land "remained in or reverted to private ownership after 70."[8]

—No ban was placed on rebuilding or repairing the Temple or on reviving the cult, though in the absence of tax funds the former could have occurred only with Roman support or Roman defeat. No attempt was made to stamp out Jewish observance in Judaea or the diaspora, and as far as the Romans were concerned the Temple cult could have continued, though it did not.[9] In general Jews continued to enjoy tolerance in religious matters.[10] No Jewish practice was banned and no foreign cult imposed.

—The Yavnean sages founded their academy with Roman approval.[11] Those who had been Pharisees had already developed a flexible view of the law, which eased the transition to postwar conditions.[12] Together with some of the surviving priests and aristocracy, they filled the vacuum in Jewish political life. Eventually the patriarchate and the Sanhedrin took over the role of the pre–70 high priest and Sanhedrin, though precisely when the Sanhedrin was reestablished and when the Romans granted them official recognition remains uncertain.[13] The restoration of civilian government was for the Romans a natural and necessary process, and they probably called on Jews who had been neutral or supportive during the war.[14]

In short, while we should not minimize the losses of the war, the Jews showed a remarkable resilience and were able to normalize their relations with Rome within a relatively brief period. In this they were aided by the tolerance and pragmatism of the Romans. Nor should it be forgotten that the Jews were sufficiently buoyant and uncowed to instigate the revolts under Trajan and Hadrian early in the second century.

About the revolts under Trajan in 115–117 CE, we know very little. The general picture, reconstructed from laconic literary allusions and fragmentary archaeological remains, is of a series of savage battles between Jews and Greeks in North Africa and Cyprus, which caused a dramatic reduction in the Jewish population there. The revolt spread either from or to Mesopotamia, but was nipped in the bud in Judaea.[15] The reconquest of Judaea might have been the ultimate aim of the rebels and thus explain the wanton destruction of the lands they hoped to leave behind, but this is mere surmise.[16] We know little of the causes or inspiration: some see the hand of displaced rebels from the Jewish War, others the influence of heightened messianic expectations.[17] The outcome was disastrous—decimation of the Jews in North Africa and their expulsion from Cyprus.

For the Bar Cochba rebellion we are better informed, and fortunately, since we have a particular purpose in mind, we can ignore many of the more controversial issues.[18] The precise nature and length of the preliminary stages of the revolt, whether the building of Aelia Capitolina and the ban on circumcision were causes or results of the rebellion, and the extent to which the Yavnean leaders supported or distanced themselves from the rebels are all issues that we can leave to one side. We have sufficient secure knowledge to allow us to assess the effects of the revolt on Jews and Christians, and the simplest way to proceed is by direct comparison with the Jewish War.

—Both the Jewish War and the Bar Cochba revolt were driven by intense nationalism and a theocratic vision. The desire to overthrow the Romans and reestablish Judaea as an independent kingdom was probably one of the few ideals shared by the various groups caught up in the Jewish War.[19] The Bar Cochba coins speak of the liberation of Jerusalem, an ambition that may not have been realized,[20] and give a significant position to Eliezer the priest. This expresses a central aspiration of the rebels—the restoration of Jerusalem and the Temple—and indicates that not all Jews accepted the results of the Jewish War with equanimity.

—If the building of Aelia Capitolina as a pagan city and the prohibition of circumcision (as part of a general ban on castration) either instigated or exacerbated the Bar Cochba revolt, as is arguable,[21] they are evidence for a degree of interference that has no parallel in the Jewish War. Then the local Roman officials were inexperienced and frequently corrupt, and the central authorities neglectful, but there were no imperial decrees to match those of Hadrian. Yet Hadrian may not have intended to provoke the Jews. His rebuilding of Jerusalem may have been welcomed by many Jews, and some may actively have encouraged his program of hellenization.[22] He was at any rate a compulsive builder and hellenizer, the most aggressive since Augustus, and doubtless saw Aelia Capitolina as a project that would enhance the stature of the province as well as his own reputation. The prohibition of circumcision may have been introduced during (rather than before) the rebellion, and may have been part of a general ban on all forms of castration, a practice that the Romans viewed as barbaric.[23] Yet whatever his intentions, and however wide his initial support, he provoked a significant group of Judaeans to resist.

—Bar Cochba was almost certainly recognized as a messianic figure.[24] Christian sources called him Bar Cochba (= "son of the star"; the original family name was Bar Cosiba) and assumed it referred to his messianic role (Justin *I Apol*.31.6; Eusebius *Hist.eccl*.4.6.2). Tradition has it that Akiba concurred in this claim (*y. Ta'an* 4.68d), a tradition that is significant even if fictional. Rabbinic literature later frequently calls him Bar Coziba (= "son of lies"), which expresses their disillusionment with all messianic rebels.[25] The evidence for similar messianic fervor in the Jewish War is slight. Menahem may have been a messianic pretender, but with only brief success (Josephus *Bell*.2.433–34). Some may have seen Simon ben Giora as a messianic figure, but the best evidence comes from his hour of defeat when he surrendered to the Romans in a quixotic gesture, dressed like a king (Josephus *Bell*.7.29–31, 153–55; cf. *Bell*.4.510).[26] Josephus's bias may have led him to minimize the importance of messianism, but the competing groups involved in the Jewish War nevertheless do not seem to have engendered messianic expectations in the way that the single dominant figure of the later rebellion did.

—This had direct consequences for Christians. In the Jewish War the Jerusalem Christians appear to have escaped before the worst fighting broke out (or, according to another theory, to have died supporting the rebel cause). Under Bar Cochba, Christians who would not deny Jesus, presumably when pressed to recognize Bar Cochba's messianic status, were executed.[27] There is no reason to deny Justin's report, and it concurs with other evidence for Bar Cochba's rigor in upholding the law, his encouragement of recircumcision of those who had undergone epispasm, and his ruthlessness with those who opposed him.[28] Further light on this matter may be shed by a cryptic passage in the *Apocalypse of Peter*:

> (8) They will promise that "I am the Christ who has come into the world." And when they have seen the wickedness of his deed they will follow after them. (9) And they will deny him whom they call the Glory of our Fathers, whom they crucified, the first Christ. . . .(10) But this liar was not Christ. And when they have rejected him he will kill with the sword and many will become martyrs. (11) . . . This is the house of Israel only. There will be martyrs by his hand. . . .(12) For Enoch and Elijah will be sent that they might teach

them that this is the deceiver who must come into the world and do signs and wonders and deceive. (13) And on account of this those who die by his hand will be martyrs and will be reckoned with the good and righteous martyrs who have pleased God in their life. (2:8–13)

The most recent commentary on this passage,[29] which dates it to ca. 132–35 CE, detects an allusion to the reaction of Jewish Christians to Bar Cochba: some Christians, presumably Jewish Christians (v.11) joined the cause of the false messiah (v.8), which amounted to a denial of Christ (v.9); when they realized that he was not the messiah they abandoned him and he in turn persecuted and killed them (vv.10–11); messengers are promised who will confirm that he is *the* deceiver and that these are the end times (v.12); the one-time defectors, now martyrs, will be counted among the righteous (v.13). If we follow this analysis it adds a few details to an otherwise bare account: that the Christians caught up in the Bar Cochba revolt were Jewish Christians; that they were persecuted not just because they were Christians but because they had initially supported the rebel actions and claims and then balked at accepting Bar Cochba as messiah (i.e., they were defectors); and that these events were seen by some Christians as definitive signs of the arrival of the last days. It is an attractive interpretation and fits well with the concern elsewhere in the work with signs of the end and false messiahs (1:2–5), those who die in their sins having not observed the laws of God (1:2), the fate of Israel (2:1–13), and the certainty of resurrection (4:1–13). In addition it illuminates one of the critical points of dispute between Jews and Christians: Jesus' messiahship. Earlier evidence, almost invariably from the Christian side (e.g., Acts), shows that messianic differences could lead to puzzlement and frustration that the Jews would not believe, but rarely to outright schism—precisely what we would expect since Judaism itself allowed for a considerable range of messianic convictions. The ominous change comes when an exclusive messianism was adopted, if only temporarily, by a significant number of Jews. Christian convictions then no longer met with indifference but with hostility.

—The rebellion was followed by a period of repression (ca. 135–38 CE) unparalleled in the earlier conflict. In addition to the massive losses, Jewish and Roman, and the virtual depopulation of Judaea (Eusebius *Hist. eccl.*4.6.1; Dio 69.14.1-2), the construction on the site of Jerusalem of a pagan city and a temple of Jupiter, which was begun in earnest after the rebellion, dispossessed all Jews settled in the Jerusalem area. Further, Jews were banned from the city and its environs except for one annual visit, the proscription of circumcision was rigorously pursued, and the province was renamed Syria-Palestina.[30] There is evidence in rabbinic literature for even more severe measures under Hadrian—a virtual outlawing of Jewish observance including, in addition to circumcision, Sabbath observance, the ordination of rabbis, and study of the Torah (*m.Sabb.*4.11; *b.B.Bat.*60.b;

*b.Sanh.*14a; *b.Ber.* 61b, etc.). Although this evidence does not include en-
forced participation in pagan worship, in all other respects Jews were being
compelled to live in a manner indistinguishable from Gentiles. It is precisely
in these circumstances that many locate the unusual rabbinic ruling that,
under severe persecution, all commands of the law could be ignored except
those pertaining to idolatry, incest/adultery, and murder (*b.Sanh.*74a;
*y.Šeb.*4.2). Most agree that this rabbinic evidence indicates serious persecution of Jews in Hadrian's time, but it is unclear whether these were war
measures during the rebellion or punishments after it, and many of the details are, at any rate, suspect. As Schäfer neatly puts it: the evidence becomes
more detailed the farther it is from the events.[31] Yet the traditions are too
deeply embedded to be entirely fictitious, and they seem to represent more
than a mere elaboration of the circumcision ban, though precisely what was
involved remains obscure. The prohibition of circumcision was sufficiently
effective and offensive that Antoninus, Hadrian's successor, apparently revoked it with respect to the Jews (Modestinus, *Digest* 48.8.11.1).[32]

—The role of the rabbinic leaders in all of this, as well as the extent of
the rebels' influence, remains unclear. Akiba may have been an exception in
supporting the rebels, and there is little other evidence for rabbinic involvement. Recent studies have emphasized that the conflict was essentially local,
confined to Jerusalem and the surrounding hills, and that it may not have
enjoyed much popular support beyond.[33] If so, it may have passed the Yavnean rabbis by. They would have had good reason to view with skepticism
and reserve one who called himself *Nasi* and to whom some ascribed messianic status, and Bar Cochba and his followers would certainly have been a
challenge to their institutions and to the authority that they were slowly
establishing among their fellow Jews.[34] Yet, for all this, it is possible that
while the military conflict was confined, the aims of the rebels, especially
with regard to Jerusalem and the Temple, expressed more widely shared
aspirations. Moreover, even if it is argued that the rebellion was not as important in the history of Judaism as has sometimes been thought, this does
not necessarily reduce its influence on the Jewish-Christian schism.

It is now appropriate to return to the question we posed briefly above.
Was it the Jewish War or the Bar Cochba revolt that was more significant
for the Jewish-Christian schism? The question can be phrased in this way
because we know nothing about the effects of the revolts under Trajan on
Jewish-Christian relations. Not only is our knowledge from the Jewish side
severely limited, but we know virtually nothing about the development of
Christianity in the affected areas during this period and absolutely nothing
about how they might have been affected by the Jewish rebellion.

It has frequently been asserted that the Jewish War was the fundamental
turning point in the relation between Jews and Christians. This view is associated with A. von Harnack and, more recently, with S. G. F. Brandon, but it

is often unthinkingly repeated. Von Harnack expressed it as follows: "It was the destruction of Jerusalem and the temple which seems to have provoked the final crisis, and led to a complete breach between the two parties."[35] In this view the Bar Cochba revolt was a mere coda and of no great significance in its own right. It is not, however, the only opinion to have been expressed. Marcel Simon's *Verus Israel,* the classic modern work on early Jewish-Christian relations, begins at the year 135 CE, in the conviction that it was a decisive watershed, though he thinks it should be viewed together with the consequences of the Jewish War. Others have emphasized the importance of 135 CE as a turning point, though they are also less interested in a comparison with the Jewish War.[36] Recently the issue has been taken up by J. D. G. Dunn, who has argued that 135 CE was decidedly the more important date for the Jewish-Christian schism.[37]

Our purpose at this stage is to focus on the sociopolitical evidence. Yet although the question can be simply posed, it cannot be so simply answered. The paucity of explicit statements on the matter makes the argument necessarily circumstantial and inferential. In addition, we are not comparing like with like. Some sixty-five years passed between the destruction of Jerusalem and the end of the Bar Cochba rebellion. Both traditions developed in various ways during this period, not always in reaction to each other and not always in response to the events of 70 CE, so the task of comparison becomes much more complex and subtle. Then again the effects of the Judaean revolts were not evenly spread. Jews (including Christian Jews) who lived in Judaea were more immediately and profoundly affected than those in the diaspora. And the different effects on Jewish and Gentile Christians must be borne in mind too.

The immediate impact of the Jewish War on Christians would have been slight. Some may have been caught up in the Roman conquest of Jerusalem, but it is probable that a significant number had already left for Pella and were able to regroup in Jerusalem after the war.[38] Jewish Christians would presumably have been subject to the *fiscus Judaicus* imposed by Vespasian after the war, yet this added financial burden had the compensation that they could enjoy the privileges and protection afforded the Jews. The defeat may have been ignominious for the Jews, but it did not change their official standing in the Roman Empire, and certainly not in any way that would have encouraged Christians to disengage from them.

The impact of the Bar Cochba rebellion on Christianity was surely more dramatic. The messianic nationalism was more blatant, the defeat more devastating, the repression more severe, the interruption of civil government more serious and, in all probability, the ignominy more lasting. These would have been enough to encourage Christians to put some distance between themselves and Jews. Although diaspora, and even Galilean, Jews were not directly involved, the actions of Bar Cochba would have created a negative image of Judaism in general, and Hadrian's brief repression during and/or after the rebellion presumably would have affected all Jews alike. By way of contrast, this was the age of the early Christian apologists (see below) whose purpose was essentially irenic, intent on putting their case to, and trying to find a niche in, Roman society. Above all, of course, the persecution and murder of Christians by the Bar Cochba rebels showed what could happen under the pressure of a messianic nationalism unrestrained by Roman rule. In addition, according to Eusebius, 135 CE marked a definitive change in the character of the Jerusalem church, for the prohibition against Jews entering Jerusalem necessitated the replacement of a Jewish by a Gentile line of bishops there (Eusebius *Hist.eccl.*4.5).

There is little doubt, therefore, when we weigh up both the known and the probable consequences of these two rebellions, that the second would have had a more traumatic effect on Jewish-Christian relations. Yet, as we noted, between 70 CE and 135 CE both Judaism and Christianity had changed as had the relationship between them. The more difficult question, therefore, is whether the Bar Cochba rebellion marked a radically new stage in Jewish-Christian relations or whether it was simply the last nail in the coffin of an already moribund relationship. One place to look for further information is in the literature that specifically reflects on this issue. Unfortunately we are here, as so often, better served by Christian than by Jewish evidence. We do have Jewish writings that react to the rebellions, but works such as *4 Ezra* and *2 Baruch* tell us only about the way Jews came to terms with their own history, and there is not even a hint of the way in which it might have affected their view of Christians.

Christian evidence is somewhat more informative, but tells us less than we might have expected: "The capture of Jerusalem by Titus and the burning of the Temple seem, so far as we can judge from the literature of the succeeding century and a half, to have made a surprisingly small impact on the Christian communities."[39] These events drew from the earliest Christian writers two main responses: a redefinition of their eschatological timetable (the Synoptic Gospels); and a focus on superior heavenly counterparts of the earthly city and Temple (John, Hebrews, Revelation). There is little direct reflection on their effect on Christian views of Judaism.

The author of *Barnabas* alludes clearly to the destruction of Jerusalem and the Temple, but for a specific and contemporary reason: the threat that the Temple would be rebuilt. This profoundly disturbs his convictions about the meaning of recent historical events and is one reason for his particularly negative account of Judaism. *Barnabas* marks something of a turning point. From then on the Jewish War and the Bar Cochba rebellion are never viewed neutrally, but appear only in the service of anti-Jewish polemic. Two things imprinted themselves especially clearly on Christian memory: the destruction of the Temple and the banishment from Jerusalem. They are often mentioned in the same breath and in a way that makes no clear distinction between them (*AC*5:25; Justin *I Apol.*47). Lampe's conclusion is that the events of the Jewish War were "remembered in association with, and to some extent only as a prelude to, the ever more final and crushing judgement of God executed in 135 against the opponents of the church's claim to be the authentic Israel."[40] It is interesting to note where Lampe puts the emphasis, confirming our argument above. Yet there is more to be said and, since many of the relevant texts will subsequently be discussed in some detail, we shall return to this matter in our concluding chapter.

JEWS, CHRISTIANS, AND ROMAN POLITICS

We must now loop back on ourselves and consider the political standing of Jews and Christians apart from the Jewish revolts. Of the political life of Judaism in the few decades after the war we know little. The attempt by Alon, among others, to reconstruct the history and governmental structures of this period has an initial plausibility, but he depends heavily, as he must, on the tangled evidence from rabbinic sources and tends to accept their view as normative.[41] A few useful insights have been gleaned by studying the shifts in Josephus's account of political and religious authorities from the earlier to the later writings, but we are still largely in the dark.[42]

Exactly how the Jews were governed after 70 CE remains obscure. Immediately after the Jewish War it is probable that surviving members of the old Judaean aristocracy, high priests and Herodians, continued in their familiar governing role, at least in judicial and legislative matters. It was normal for the Romans to encourage established aristocracies in the empire to perform the routine tasks of government and, although some of the Judaean aristocracy had been active in the rebellion, the survivors would have been the natural group to turn to. They were not the only survivors. The precursors of the rabbis, who had retreated with Roman approval to Yavneh during the siege, presented an alternative type of leadership. At first the two groups may have forged an uneasy alliance, perhaps by concentrating on separate spheres of activity. During the eighties, however, it seems that the influence of the prewar aristocracy began to decline, perhaps because of waning Roman support, and that the chief governing role passed increasingly into the hands of the rabbis and those priests who had joined them.[43] Some of the early rabbinic decisions, as plausibly recorded in their tradition, show them willing to fill the vacuum by taking upon themselves responsibility for the more urgent cultic matters, though this may reflect a period later than the immediate postwar years. One task they appear to have taken on, and which came to expression at about the time their role became more prominent, was the redefinition of the community in the light of postwar circumstances and their own new powers. It involved, in part, weeding out and anathematizing alternative (that is, nonrabbinic) forms of Judaism. It is quite probable that Christians were caught up in this process, but full discussion of this belongs to a later chapter.

During Domitian's reign two things in particular affected his relations with the Jews. First, he rigorously imposed the Jewish tax on those who "followed the Jewish way of life without professing Judaism" or who "denied their Jewish origin and thereby avoided paying the taxes levied on their race" (Suetonius *Dom*.12.2). The reference seems to be to tax evaders, that is, those who were eligible but not paying. The latter group are clearly Jews by birth, perhaps apostate Jews who had turned to paganism or Christianity, but more likely Jews who had given up active involvement in Jewish life and/or those who simply wanted to avoid the tax. The former group seem to be proselytes, who were eligible for the tax, but Judaizers/sympathizers could be included too.[44]

Secondly, he executed Flavius Clemens and exiled his wife Domitilla for "atheism" and "drifting into Jewish ways" (Dio 67.14.1–3). Some scholars have argued that these two were Christians, which is a possible understanding of the accusations since Christians were charged with atheism and could broadly be said to have adopted Jewish ways.[45] The issue is confused by Eusebius's also mentioning someone by the name of Domitilla:

> In the fifteenth year of Domitian, Flavia Domitilla, who was the niece of Flavius Clemens, one of the consuls of Rome at that time, was banished with many others to the island of Pontia as testimony to Christ. (Eusebius *Hist. eccl.* 3.18.4)

The two Domitilla are sometimes conflated, but the most that could be concluded from this would be that Domitilla was a Christian. Nothing indicates that this was true of Clemens too.[46] Most probably Dio's notice should be taken at its face value, that is, Clemens and his wife were Jewish sympathizers, not Christians.

There is a curious tension between these two snippets of information. In the one, taking up Jewish ways (as proselyte or sympathizer) resulted in eligibility for the Jewish tax; in the other, it led to banishment or execution. This may in part have had to do with rank. Clemens and Domitilla were Roman aristocrats, and their sympathies with Judaism would have been seen as a significant defection. Judaizers among the lower classes were probably of little interest to the imperial court except as potential taxpayers. It is possible, too, that while Judaizing was the formal charge the real motives were political. Clemens and Domitilla were the parents of Domitian's two designated heirs. At the best of times they were probably vulnerable but if, in the latter years of Domitian's rule, informers and rumors ran out of control,[47] they were even more likely to have become victims of court intrigue. This reading of events, when combined with the view that the tax measures were motivated by financial need and a desire for administrative efficiency and any abuses were the work of minor bureaucrats, has been used to exonerate Domitian from any suspicion of anti-Judaism. Toward the Jews, it has been argued, he remained essentially neutral.[48]

This argument, part of a broader move to rehabilitate the reputation of Domitian, is not entirely convincing, as M. H. Williams has argued. First, an obsessively interventionist administrator like Domitian is not likely to have been unaware of tax abuses that were sufficiently widespread to have been corrected by Nerva immediately upon his succession. It is significant, too, that the accusation against Clemens and his wife was one that was expected to stick and to produce the desired outcome whatever other political undercurrents may have been at work. Among the Roman upper classes, drifting into Jewish ways, especially by one of their own, would not have been viewed with equanimity. Like other foreign cults, Judaism was viewed with deep suspicion, not least because it appeared to challenge and undercut so much of what aristocratic Romans stood for and revered. That this view would have been shared by Domitian is suggested not only by his insistence that state cults be punctiliously observed, but also by the anti-Jewish strain in much of the literature written by his contemporaries and dedicated to him. Martial and Quintillian, for example, were imperial toadies, and it is likely that they expected their ridicule of the Jews to meet with imperial approval.[49] We must assume, then, that for some Jews at least life under Domitian would not have been without its stresses and strains. It did not amount to persecution. Presumably most Jews paid their taxes and were left undisturbed. Clemens and his wife, it should not be forgotten, were sympathizers, not Jews, and lived too close to the imperial throne for comfort. Moreover, Josephus is one example, even if an exceptional one, of a Jew who came to no harm under Domitian.[50]

Among the tax evaders mentioned by Suetonius, those who denied their Jewish origins could have included Jewish Christians who no longer wished to be identified as Jews. And, among those who lived like Jews without professing Judaism, Christians of various sorts might officially have been included. If not, however, they could have been unofficially swept up in Domitian's measure like many others (Judaizers, vegetarians, and so forth) whose lifestyle associated them with the Jews. Distinctions that were meaningful within these groups may not have much interested tax collectors who were determined to raise revenue. It is quite possible, therefore, that some Christians were forcibly associated with Judaism during Domitian's reign for the purposes of the tax.[51] This could have bred resentment, but a resentment that may have been stifled if Christians were periodically subjected to harassment *as Christians*. Association with Judaism would then have had advantages, since Christians could move under the protective umbrella of Judaism—precisely the situation that some think lies behind the reference to "those who call themselves Jews but are not" in Revelation 2:9; 3:9.

Was association with Judaism the only threat to Christians under Domitian? Not if we are to believe the traditions of Roman and Christian historiography in which Domitian is presented as a depraved and monstrous tyrant who unleashed a reign of terror over all his subjects, including the Christians.

In fact, in Christian memory he came down as a persecutor whose only equal was Nero (Eusebius *Hist.eccl.*4.26.9). This view of Domitian has recently been vigorously challenged, notably by L. L. Thompson.[52] He has shown conclusively that the image of Domitian has been distorted in a way that belies the complex and often contradictory evidence of his contemporaries. Yet it is unlikely that he can be whitewashed altogether. It may well be that Tacitus, Pliny, and Suetonius go overboard in their condemnation of Domitian in order to enhance the image of his successor, yet it is highly improbable that all their accusations, some of them quite specific, were concocted or distorted in tune with the needs of a later era. In fact, they give the impression of being too deeply rooted to be so lightly dismissed. That they waited until after his death to voice their opinions may well have been, as they claim, because it was unsafe to do so during his reign (perhaps only toward the end, as Suetonius implies). And it scarcely strengthens the case to note that those who wrote during Domitian's reign (Quintillian, Frontinus, Martial, for example) lavished him with praise. What else would we expect from writers who enjoyed or aspired to imperial favor? The reality, it would seem, like the evidence, was mixed. He was no tyrant, but no saint either.

More to the point, however, is his effect on the Christian movement. There is no doubt that later Christian writers depended on the Roman literary tradition that presented a negative portrait of Domitian and added to this information extrapolated from early Christian writings. Not only was he seen as oppressive and cruel, but he was pictured also as a megalomaniac who promoted his own divine status in new forms of imperial worship. It was this, in particular, which placed Christians on the spot. The evidence is indirect and ambiguous. Eusebius, quoting Hegesippus, speaks of attempts to wipe out descendants of David by Vespasian and Trajan (*Hist.eccl.*3.12, 3.32) and Domitian (*Hist.eccl.*3.19–20). The former, he says, led to persecution of the Jews after the war, but this is confirmed in no other sources. The incident involving Domitian is double-edged. On the one hand, the grandsons of Jude are freed because they seem to Domitian to be harmless yokels; on the other, their innocence encourages him to decree an end to the persecution of the church. It thus implies that there had been a persecution, but also that Domitian was not averse to changing his policy when faced with innocent Christians. That an emperor would scarcely have deigned to involve himself in such a piffling affair is an argument that can be countered by his reputation for paranoia and for meddling in administrative detail. Perhaps the whole account, or at least its imperial setting, is legendary. We cannot know.

More significant are hints in the correspondence of Pliny with Trajan (*Ep.*10.96–97), to which we shall shortly return. Christians had been brought before him on a variety of charges lodged (often anonymously) by the local populace. Pliny, uncertain how to proceed, writes (in 112 CE) for advice because he had not been present before at the trial of Christians. To some this implies that there had been no previous trials, but the more natural inference is that there had been but that he had no further information about them.[53] If so, it is improbable that they occurred in Rome, where Pliny was active (for a time as a prosecutor) during Domitian's rule, for he would surely have known about them. Perhaps they had occurred in Asia Minor, to which he was a newcomer. They could have occurred during the reign of Domitian. He also refers to Christians who, up to twenty years earlier (92 CE), had renounced their faith—clearly during Domitian's reign. He does not say why they did so, nor that they were forced. Yet the juridical setting in Pliny's account might suggest that it was in a similar setting that they had made their earlier declaration. Some Christians, only in Bithynia in this case, may thus have acceded to official pressure to renounce their faith during the reign of Domitian.

Other evidence is hard to come by and rests on inference more than fact. Three texts that are often assigned to the reign of Domitian may imply persecution of Christian believers.[54] 1 Clement, written ca. 95 CE, refers to persecutions (1; 5–7), and in reference to the past says, "We are in the same arena" (7:1). This is allusive, but it does suggest some form of harassment. 1 Peter 4:12–19 speaks of a "fiery ordeal" that any of his readers may suffer "as a Christian," which could point in the same direction. That both writers should also praise imperial government (1 Clem. 60–61; 1 Pet 2:13–17) is odd but not unthinkable. Revelation has, perhaps, been the mainstay of this form of argument. It refers clearly to one martyr (2:13) in the past, takes an unrelievedly hostile view of Rome (Rev 13; 17), and promotes an alarmist view of threats to Christians in the present. Yet it is not clear how much of this lies in the eye of the beholder. The threat could have been more perceived than real, engendered by an intense antipathy to the world, which Rome represented, rather than by any change in imperial policy. And the threat may have come more from within—Christians who compromised with the state cults (the Nicolaitans?)—than from political authorities without.[55] Nor should it be forgotten that Acts, which may come from the same period, takes a much more benign and positive view of the state and sees the political threat to come more from the Jews than from the representatives of Roman rule.

This evidence is not easy to assess. Clearly nothing points to an official, empire-wide persecution of Christians. It may even be that Domitian did not unduly promote the imperial cult, though on balance the contemporary evidence points in this direction. It would traditionally at any rate have been more prominent in the Eastern provinces, where most of this evidence originates. Moreover, local enthusiasm for the cult could have made things as awkward for Christians as any imperial decree.[56] The confluence of evidence for increased pressure on Christians during the reign of Domitian in some parts of the empire is suggestive, but more than this we cannot say.

Under Nerva Jewish fortunes may have improved. He is said to have deflated the imperial cult, discouraged informers, and corrected abuses of the Jewish tax. This is the minimum we can surmise from Dio (68.1.2—"no one was allowed to accuse other people of *maiestas* and Jewish life") and the coins stamped with *fisci Judaici calumnia sublata* which appear at the beginning of his short rule. One undeniable implication of these moves was that there were things in need of correction, which sheds some light on Domitian's rule. Relaxation of the tax rules would have favored some Jews (and perhaps irritated others).[57] Abandoning charges of *maiestas* and Judaizing may have been intended only to avoid exceptional and recent cases like that of Clemens and Domitilla, but the problem may have been more widespread. This no doubt would have pleased Jews, but the direct beneficiaries would have been Gentile sympathizers. Similarly, the tax reform may have benefited non-Jews (including Christians) if, as suggested above, many such had been swept up by zealous tax collectors. But if this pleased Christians, other decisions did not. Richardson and Shukster, putting together Nerva's reforms with some obscure rabbinic traditions and *Barnabas* 16:4, suggest more extensive action by the emperor on behalf of Judaism, including official support for the reconstruction of the Jerusalem Temple—policies that were carried over into the early years of Trajan's reign, but then quickly abandoned.[58] If so, and if this is what the author of *Barnabas* is reacting to, then it is clear that Roman support for the Jews could evoke deep resentment and alarm among Christians—though this Christian writer subsequently directs his vitriol at the Jews rather than the Romans.

It may be that in Domitian's time there was still genuine confusion about who Christians were (the book of Acts would be an interesting example, if it belongs here). During the early decades of the Christian movement they were, to outside eyes, largely indistinguishable from Jews and therefore treated as such. Some have connected the edict of Claudius (Suetonius *Claud.*25) with disturbances caused by Christians in Rome and have concluded that it was only they (and not the Jews) who were expelled. If so, it is the first example we have of Roman officials distinguishing between Jews and Christians—but the evidence is inconclusive. We can be sure that Nero knew the difference some fifteen years later when he singled out the Christians for a rather vicious bout of persecution, whether to deflect attention from his own involvement in the fire of Rome or more generally in response to the perceived misanthropy of Christian believers.[59] This confusion of Jews and Christians was to persist in various forms for some time. But by the time Pliny wrote to Trajan about legal action against the Christians (*Ep.*10.96–97) in the year 112 CE, there is no doubt about their distinct identity in Roman eyes. Not only were they distinct, they were outlawed. Simply to confess to the name Christian was in itself, and without reference to anything otherwise defined as a crime, a capital offense.[60] Pliny mentions three groups: those who confessed that they were Christians; those who denied that they were Christians; and those who had been Christians but had since defected. He was in no doubt that the first group should be executed (unless they were Roman citizens) and the second freed; it was about the third group that he sought advice, while implying his preference for setting them free. His task was complicated by an increasing flow of anonymous accusations. Trajan's reply was firm: Christians were to be executed unless they recanted, others to be let free; no charges were to be pursued on the basis of anonymous testimony; and Christians were not to be sought out.

It is unclear whether this was an innovation, though, as we noted above, Pliny seems to imply that such trials were not unheard of. We might then have expected more evidence for persecution of Christians in the interim. That it does not exist may be because Christians were an insignificant minority who did not draw attention to themselves, and because the Roman legal system was accusatory rather than inquisitorial in style and depended on the degree to which the victims gave offense to their fellow citizens (as Pliny's discussion with Trajan shows). Yet we should not forget that not all martyrdoms were recorded: no Christian sources, for example, record the fate of those Pliny sent to their deaths.

Yet it is clear from Pliny's account that the Romans had no interest in hunting Christians down. Opposition came mainly from local populations to whom Christians were deeply suspect and for whom they were a convenient scapegoat. When forced upon the attention of Roman officials, the outlook for Christians was grim, but the number so arraigned was relatively small and the majority seem to have been treated with an indifference that amounted to toleration.

Under Hadrian, in this respect, things remained much the same. In a rescript to Minucius Fundanus, proconsul of Asia, he addresses a situation where provincial officials had sent a petition to the governor attacking Christians. Hadrian, like his predecessor, seems to have been most concerned about preserving public order and due process. Strict legal procedures were to be followed, mob pressure and anonymous accusations avoided. Adversaries whose testimony proved false were themselves to be arraigned and severely punished. This would doubtless have provided some relief, since informers would have had second thoughts about starting proceedings that might have backfired on them. Neither the charges against nor the consequences for Christians are specified, and this has led some (beginning with Justin) to suppose that Hadrian was moving a step beyond Trajan by insisting that transgression of the standard laws and not mere profession of the name had to be proved. More likely, Hadrian was tightening up the procedures laid down by Trajan, rather than devising a new charter for Christians. For those who confessed the name Christian the fate was doubtless the same.[61]

However, during Hadrian's reign there were no known Christian martyrs, which might tell us something. It was also the time when the early apologists (Quadratus) were confident enough to begin addressing their defense of Christianity to the world at large, which perhaps reveals an expectation that things might take a turn for the better. Hadrian was an ambitious hellenizer and a restless traveler, and showed great curiosity about the lands belonging to his empire. This may have made him more thoughtful and receptive to "foreign" ideas and practices, but this we cannot say for sure.[62]

If Hadrian did try to revoke the simple confession of faith as a capital offense, he seems to have had little effect on his successors. For the rest of the century the political status of Christians seems to have changed little, but if anything for the worse.[63] Persecution and martyrdom of Christians continued throughout the second century for simple confession of the name, especially in the wake of natural disasters or temporary rejuvenation of the imperial cult.[64] Under Antoninus Pius (138–61 CE) and Marcus Aurelius (161–80 CE) a number of apologies were addressed to the emperor by leading Christian thinkers. One of their aims was to overturn the law that made mere confession of Christian belief a crime and thus find for themselves a legal niche in the Roman world. They did not succeed. A number of prominent Christians—Polycarp, Justin and his companions, the martyrs at Lyons—met their deaths at the hands of the Roman judiciary, and in the latter case (ca. 177 CE) the emperor Marcus Aurelius specifically decreed the death penalty, even for those who were Roman citizens. Throughout the period we are interested in, therefore, the legal and political position appears not to have changed.

The force of the law should not be exaggerated. For example, Ignatius, Polycarp, and Justin were all eventually martyred, but not before they had enjoyed long and distinguished careers as Christian leaders. Justin had, at least formally, addressed apologies to the emperor some fifteen years or so before his execution. Moreover, their fellow believers seem to have been left largely unscathed. In principle, all Christians could be arraigned, but for the majority it remained no more than a distant threat. One consequence, however, was that public evangelism was largely abandoned as Christians relied on more discreet, personal contacts to spread their message. Most Christian literature of the period was written for internal consumption. And even the apologists addressed themselves as much to Christians as to their ostensible imperial audience.

Apart from the two rebellions, which we know little enough about, we are hard-pressed for information about the Jews under Trajan and Hadrian. Trajan comes down in Jewish sources as the one who during the rebellion unleashed severe oppression on Judaea in the form of his general, Lucius Quietus, and as one who met a deservedly ignominious death in foreign lands.[65] Hadrian's accession may initially have been welcomed. He restored peace and promoted law and order, abandoned Trajan's Eastern conquests (which removed the threat to Mesopotamian Jews), had the hated Quietus removed and executed, and created the sense of a new beginning. Judaea appears to have prospered under his energetic and tolerant rule, and Alexandrian Jews found his protection and support. It may be, too, that he initially led the Jews to believe that he was in favor of rebuilding Jerusalem and the Temple.[66] Reflecting these early years (117–30 CE), he receives a good press in some Jewish sources.[67] But things took a turn for the worse around 130 CE. Not all Jews, at least those in Judaea, were satisfied, and the combination of their aspirations and Hadrian's new policies pushed them disastrously toward revolt.

If the lack of information about Judaism for the period 70–135 CE has already become something of a refrain, for the period that follows the situation is even worse. A glance at any of the standard histories indicates the scale of the problem by the extraordinary brevity of their accounts.[68] The breakdown in Jewish-Roman relations immediately after the Bar Cochba rebellion may have been severe, but it was also brief. As far as we can tell, Hadrian's successor, Antoninus, revoked the ban on circumcision as it applied to the Jews, which may indicate that some other proscriptions from the war years were relaxed too.[69] The rest of the second century seems to have been a period of rapprochement. The bloody rebellion gave each of them good reason to look for compromise. The general tendency of the Romans was to restore the antebellum situation as far as possible. Of course, Jerusalem was out of bounds and circumcision restricted to Jews (making proselytism problematic), though these were tacitly ignored from the third century on. In Galilee, for which we have the best evidence, the Jews were largely left to their own affairs, a situation that suited both them and the Romans, and there ensued a period of relative peace and stability, which provided an environment in which the rabbinic movement could grow and flourish.[70]

The early rabbis had been established at Yavneh, but just before or just after the Bar Cochba rebellion they moved to Usha in Galilee.[71] We do not know how widespread their influence was. There was at one time a tendency to assume that after 70 CE they rapidly established their hold over the Jewish community at large, but the available evidence suggests that this was a long-drawn-out process which went on well into the second century and beyond. The move to Galilee would have been something of a setback, and Goodman has shown that the process of establishing their authority even there took considerable time.[72] Their authority was mostly local, based on the "study houses" of leading rabbis, and was not institutionalized until the third century.[73] While some fourth-century traditions speak of the sending out of rabbinic emissaries to convey opinions and decisions worldwide, and also of the collection of a new patriarchal tax, it seems that these did not get under way until well after 138 CE, perhaps not until the fourth century.

Moreover, they would have come up against well-established and distinctive Jewish communities, and it would have taken some time to win them over to the rabbinic cause.

In the diaspora, in particular, there is no more reason to suppose that all synagogues came under rabbinic influence in the early centuries than there is to assume that all synagogues were governed by the same procedures and policies. The little evidence we have about early synagogues indicates that they were run by local leaders and not by representatives of the rabbis.[74] The reputation of the rabbis within Jewish circles was undoubtedly enhanced in the second half of the second century by such as the patriarch/*Nasi* R. Simeon III, who is said to have "succeeded in raising the dignity and prestige of his office as supreme head of the worldwide Jewish community above its pre-war level and thus laid the foundations for the almost autocratic rule of his son, R. Judah I, the greatest of the patriarchs."[75] Rabbi Judah I was wealthy, learned, and influential, but the more centralized control he represents takes us beyond our period. This development was presumably further encouraged by the reconstitution of the new, rabbinic-dominated Sanhedrin, but the dating of this is unusually obscure. There remains too the question of Roman recognition of these developments within Judaism. When did they formally accept the patriarchy and the Sanhedrin as the official voices of Judaism? This probably occurred, after a period of tacit approval between the wars, in the decades following the Bar Cochba revolt, but, again, precise dates cannot be assigned.[76]

THE JEWS IN ROMAN SOCIETY

The Social Context

Long before the second century the Jews had been granted a number of unusual concessions by the Romans—for example, the right to observe the Sabbath, to refuse military service, and to substitute prayers for the emperor in place of participation in the imperial cult. No other subject peoples were granted such concessions, and whenever they were officially challenged the emperors generally upheld them. Moreover, apart from the extension and diversion of the Temple tax after 70 CE and the brief persecution during the Bar Cochba rebellion, to the best of our knowledge the Jews enjoyed recognition as a venerable if eccentric people, who were governed most effectively by placation rather than confrontation. This did not necessarily make them widely liked, as the occasional outbursts of violence indicate. Their exclusivism was often noted, and it is probable that they were the object of popular suspicion and ridicule, as nonconformists commonly are. But the more extreme anti-Jewish sentiments were usually either the temporary expression of local political tensions, often sparked by resentment of the Jews' claim for both special privileges and civic equality, or the preju-

diced and often ignorant vituperation of a handful of the literary intelligent-
sia. Politically and socially the Jews were thus relatively secure—the adherents of a tradition of laudable antiquity, high morality, and intellectual
appeal. They were an accepted part of the landscape, viewed as much with
curiosity and respect as with suspicion and antipathy.[77]

Demographically the Jews were also in a strong position. Although there
was some decimation of Judaea after 70 CE, and even more extensively after
135 CE, the Jewish community as a whole thrived. Estimates typically put
them at some four to six million of a total population of sixty million in the
Roman Empire of the first two centuries.[78] The majority of these were diaspora Jews, who were largely unaffected by the events in Judaea and often
thoroughly integrated into their local communities. Following the Bar
Cochba rebellion the Jewish population of Judaea was decimated,[79] but they
remained the dominant group in Galilee and a significant presence in Mesopotamia. Beyond this they were a visible and often influential minority in
the towns and cities of the empire. Thus, if the Jews made up about six to
ten percent of the population in general, in areas where Jewish settlements
were more concentrated—Palestine, Syria, Egypt, and Asia Minor—they
would have been proportionally that much larger.

For the Jewish communities in these diaspora concentrations in this period we rely largely on archaeological and epigraphical evidence.[80] It is sporadic, often ambiguous, and reveals many local variations. Yet a few broad
conclusions can safely be drawn. The first is that Jews retained their identity,
lived according to their own customs and traditions, had communal gatherings in their own public buildings, and generally conducted themselves
publicly and distinctively as Jews. In the retention of their identity they
were tenacious, but they did not form exclusive communities cut off from
the culture around them. Some Jews held local, or even Roman, citizenship,
but this was not a prerequisite for social or civic activism. There is overwhelming evidence, especially from Asia Minor, that Jews were well integrated into the life of the cities. The presence of a large and impressive synagogue in the heart of Sardis and the active role a number of its members
played in local government is a particularly striking example.[81] The degree
of cultural integration that could occur is most famously shown in the art
of the Dura-Europas synagogue, with its liberal use of pagan themes in the
service of Jewish devotion.

Both of these elements—preservation of identity and integration into the
community—are illustrated by another prominent feature of synagogue life:
the presence of Gentile sympathizers or God-fearers, for which the much-
discussed Aphrodisias inscription is the best current example.[82] The fascinating list of God-fearers on a stone celebrating the establishment of a charitable soup kitchen, or perhaps a memorial building erected by a burial
society,[83] reveals a number of things. That Gentiles joined with Jews in the
erection of Jewish edifices shows not only a respect for the distinct identity

of the Jews but also the degree to which they were accepted and integrated into society (the list of God-fearers includes a wide range of professions and social classes). Some God-fearers in Aphrodisias related more intimately to the Jews than others, which is what we would expect from other evidence too.[84] The evidence from Aphrodisias is merely the most dramatic example of the association of diaspora Jews with Gentiles in this period.[85]

Jewish communal life, centered around the synagogue, had thus become a standard, sometimes prominent, feature of the ancient world. For the Jews it served many and varying functions: a place to meet, teach, study, eat, worship (even sacrifice), dispense charity, and put up travelers. For Jews the synagogue became increasingly a substitute for the Temple, but to outsiders it would, like the churches, have looked most like one of the collegia—the clubs or guilds that were a common feature of the ancient world.[86] For Christians, these Jewish communities and their active synagogue life would have loomed large, part of their foreground rather than background. Indeed it has been suggested that it is precisely in those places where the Jews appear to have been strongest and most integrated that Christianity struggled to find a foothold.[87]

It has become a commonplace to argue that all forms of Judaism at this time were hellenized, and there is an undeniable element of truth in this view. It is an understandable and demonstrably correct reaction to the notion of Palestinian/rabbinic Judaism as insulated, pure, undefiled by the Hellenistic world. But this does not alter the fact that diaspora communities were in many significant ways different from Judaism in the homeland.[88] First, they were less immediately subject to the decisions and influence of the rabbinic leaders. Second, while diaspora Jews displayed a number of common features, they would not have appeared entirely uniform. The inducements of local circumstance would have shaped and colored them in a variety of different ways, including ways that differentiated them from Palestinian Judaism.[89] Third, diaspora Jews were more exposed to, and open to the attractions of, Hellenistic culture. Not all synagogues were decorated like the one in Dura-Europas, but it is a dramatic example of the absorption and adaptation of non-Jewish culture. Fourth, in many synagogues in the diaspora Gentiles were a significant and visible minority presence, the majority of them intrigued by and compliant with Jewish ways but unwilling to face the social and physical (i.e., circumcision) disadvantages of full proselytization. It seems probable, therefore, that, while Palestinian Jews were undoubtedly influenced by Hellenistic culture, many diaspora Jews were influenced that much more.

The Literary Evidence

Apart from the two apocalypses that appeared in the first century fairly soon after the war (2 *Baruch* and 4 *Ezra*), and a few pseudepigrapha that are often vaguely dated to the "1st–3rd centuries CE," we rely for literary remains largely on the Mishnah. It was compiled somewhere around the end of the second century CE, but few would doubt that it uses a variety of earlier traditions, in some cases preformed collections, and bears the bold imprint of the final compiler, R. Judah the Prince. The Mishnah is not the most amenable source of information: it tells us about only one type of Judaism among others (Dura-Europas is a dramatically contrasting example) and about only one aspect of that type. Moreover, while it is invaluable as a partial expression of the vision of its final compilers, only with the greatest of caution can we use it to trace back the tributaries that eventually fed into the main stream.

The most sustained scholarly analysis of the Mishnah, that of J. Neusner, attempts to isolate within it three strands: pre-70 CE material; views developed between the wars (approx. 70–140 CE); and pre-Mishnaic reflections (approx. 140–200 CE).[90] The first period is of no immediate interest to us, and the second, according to Neusner, marks a preliminary and relatively insignificant stage when compared with what follows. However, between the revolts some changes were initiated that anticipated the concerns that came to dominate the later tradition: from holy Temple to holy people; from priest to sage; and from cultic sacrifice to loving-kindness and study of the Torah. The dominant concerns appear to be economic (especially agricultural) life, which was related to the Temple cult, and the cult itself. These emphases are further developed in the period leading up to the completion of the Mishnah.

We can broadly characterize the attitudes of those who produced the Mishnah in three ways. First, on the surface they show a remarkable lack of interest in historical events. In particular, the Jewish War and the Bar Cochba rebellion are virtually ignored apart from a few glancing allusions in the service of some abstruse legal discussion. It is as if they have collectively turned a blind eye to the most momentous events of their time.

Superficially this is plausible, yet, secondly, the very structure, themes, and attitudes of the Mishnah may be seen as an oblique yet profound response to the tragedies that beset the Jewish people. Faced with a Temple in ruins, banishment from their holy city, and the disruption of everyday routines, the rabbis appear to have created, by force of will and imagination, a fixed point in the turning world. For in their obsessive concern with sanctification, whether in daily life or Temple cult, and in their unflagging urge to demarcate and define, they try to create a fixed, stable, and ideal universe. It is a utopia, a world fully perfected and therefore fully at rest. In a context of unpredictable chaos it is a vision of predictable order. One of Neusner's definitions is as follows:

> The Mishnah tells us something about how things were, but everything about how a small group of men wanted things to be. The document is orderly, repetitious, careful in both language and message. It is small-minded, picayune,

obvious, dull, routine—everything its age was not. The Mishnah stands in contrast with the world to which it speaks. Its message is one of small achievements and modest hope. It means to defy a world of large disorders and immodest demands.[91]

Third, this imaginative tour de force was bred in almost total isolation from the Gentile (including the Christian?) world around it. True, there are Greek and Latin loanwords in the Mishnah, there is some overlap with Stoic ethics and the rhetorical conventions of the Hellenistic world, and perhaps some connection with Gentile converts during this period.[92] But in content the Mishnah has few parallels in the ancient world. It is singular in its obsessions and insular in its range.

But Neusner does not stop here. He wishes to make even more extensive and complex claims. He suggests, for example, that the Mishnah presents the entire and exclusive worldview of its framers, different from and opposed to other expressions of Jewish devotion common in their day, such as scriptural interpretation (midrashim) and prayers (the synagogue liturgy). Further, Neusner assumes that the silences of the Mishnah indicate not so much indifference as opposition. If it does not mention the two wars, then it opposes them; if it does not dwell on prophecy or eschatology, then it eschews them; if it barely mentions the messiah, then it is not messianic. In addition, he argues, what the Mishnah superficially does discuss is much less important than the deeply buried message that it does not. What it really wants to tell us is not what it ostensibly does tell us. Working from these presuppositions, Neusner makes sweeping claims about the profound philosophy that underlies the apparently mundane legal debates of the Mishnah. It is "a sustained philosophical treatise in the guise of an episodic exercise in ad hoc problem solving."[93] What it promotes is a metaphysic of stasis, a profoundly antihistorical worldview driven by a determination to keep things as they are.[94]

These more grandiose claims of Neusner have been subjected to a severe and caustic critique by E. P. Sanders.[95] He notes that, as a collection of legal debates and opinion, the Mishnah was neither the entire nor the exclusive expression of rabbinic piety. Legal documents, he argues, do not typically contain history or theology, and it is inconceivable that its compilers did not pray and study the scripture both privately and publicly like most other Jews. By the same token, silence does not signify dissent or even disinterest; rather, it reflects the natural constraints of the legal genre. And the grand philosophy of the Mishnah turns out under scrutiny to be an interpretation that is not even hinted at, let alone rooted in, the texts themselves.[96]

Some of these points are well taken, and Sanders would use them to undercut even the more modest summary we offered above. But here he may go too far. We may accept that there is a difference between legal debate, historical reflection, and theological speculation. But there is undeniably something odd about a collection of documents that includes tractates about priestly tithes, the shekel tax, and the conduct of sacrifices in the Temple when priests were a rapidly disappearing breed, the Temple tax had been expropriated by the Romans, the Temple destroyed, and the Jews banned from Jerusalem. The legal discussion and the historical realities seem almost never to meet. And this remains true even if we assume, as some do, that these tractates express a hope for the restoration of those things that have disappeared.

Similarly, the urge to define and demarcate, order, and control is certainly characteristic of legal writings and should not be inflated into a grandiose philosophy of stasis. Nor should we suppose that the two wars in Judaea hung like an oppressive cloud over the Jews for the whole of the second century. Life went on and, no doubt, memories faded. But while the tannaitic sages may have done other things than refine the law, this they obsessively did. And the limitations of this focus may in turn express a deliberate turning away from momentous and disruptive wars or merely from the routine political realities of Roman rule.[97] Some forms of Christian literature, as we shall see, move in a quite different direction.

THE CHRISTIANS IN ROMAN SOCIETY

The Social Context

We turn our attention now to the Christian community as a feature of the Roman landscape in the first two centuries: to consider their political, social, and economic standing and to assess the demonstrable or the likely impact of these factors on their relationship with the Jews.

The simplest of questions are often the hardest to answer. Estimates of the number of Christians, let us say ca. 100 CE and again ca. 200 CE, are extremely difficult to calculate. Generally we are better informed about the scatter than the density of early Christian communities, and scholars have been properly cautious about estimating absolute numbers. For the later date, 200 CE, we are offered anything from around 1 to 1.5 million, or 1.4 to 2.5 percent of the total population, usually reckoned to be around sixty million. Essentially this figure is reached by calculating backward from later evidence that is itself none too informative. For the year 100 CE we are even less informed. Something in the order of 100,000 to 250,000, or .14 to .35 percent of the total population, is about as close as we are likely to get, though, if anything, this may be on the high side. The evidence, like our conclusions, is frustratingly vague, but we can draw at least one conclusion from it: Christianity was a small and insignificant movement during the first hundred years of its existence and even some seventy years later, ca. 200 CE, it had advanced numerically in only a modest way.[98]

Despite legal constraints, occasional local pressure and a few dramatic martyrdoms, the Christian movement continued to expand. While by the end of the second century it was still not a massive presence, certainly not as significant as Judaism, yet compared with similar cults or sects its growth was remarkably sustained. Celsus, in a few notorious passages, ridicules Christianity for its appeal to the poverty-stricken, feebleminded, and superstitious in society.[99] There must have been an element of truth to this for the gibe to work, but it is an exaggeration. From as early as the time of Paul we find evidence that the church attracted the interest and devotion of at least some of the well-to-do. This is confirmed in the narrative of Acts, in which a number of important and influential people are portrayed as favorably disposed toward Christianity, and in Pliny's statement that the church in Pontus contained "every age, rank and sex, from the villages and the rural areas."[100] Yet it is probable that during most of the first two centuries the wealthy, the educated, and the upper classes were only a small percentage of the typical membership. They may loom rather large in the surviving evidence, as the literate and famous tend to do, but this belies their numerical importance. The last quarter of the second century was probably a period of transition in this regard, since the next century provides us with more examples of Christians from the upper echelons. To an outsider a more striking feature of the church, at least in the earlier period, would have been the unusual number and importance of women members, including those well born.[101]

Another feature of the Pauline era was to become a hallmark of Christianity up to the end of the second century: it was essentially an urban phenomenon. Christian believers in rural areas were not unknown, as the quotation from Pliny in the preceding paragraph shows, but from its earliest days the Christian movement had greater success in the towns and cities and, most especially, in those that already contained large and important diaspora Jewish communities. This, in turn, was no accident, because in the early decades a rich source of recruits for the Christian movement was found precisely in the synagogues: among the Gentile God-fearers or sympathizers who associated with the Jewish community but declined full proselytization.[102]

The communal structure of the churches has been subject to considerable discussion by those interested in the social world of the early Christian movement. The consensus is that the early communities organized themselves around a basic unit—the house church. Assuming a typical unit membership of twenty to thirty, by the end of the first century major areas of Christian expansion would have required several house churches to accommodate their members. What little we know of early Christian architecture suggests that the privately owned home remained the favored meeting place for some time and that it was not until around the last half of the second century that such homes were purchased, adapted, and enlarged to serve the communal and liturgical needs of expanding Christian communities. Purpose-built structures (early basilicas) were a feature mainly of the post-Constantine era.[103]

How would these house gatherings have appeared to the Romans? There were parallels at hand. Initially they might have seemed somewhat like the collegia, small clubs or guilds formed for a common social purpose (e.g., charitable distribution or burial arrangements) or for celebration of a common craft. But the analogy would have been, from the Christian angle, neither exact nor helpful: not exact, because important features of the house church had no parallel in the typical collegia—an intensely intimate and exclusive sense of belonging, an unusually catholic range of members, and a strong sense of being part of a universal church; not helpful, because Roman authorities were throughout this period deeply suspicious of new clubs and guilds. The older established guilds were allowed to continue, but requests for approval of new ones were almost invariably turned down. It was suspected that they not only distracted attention from official state cults but also encouraged political and social subversion. To be likened to a collegium would therefore have been both misleading and dangerous and, while it might have rendered Christianity more comprehensible in the popular mind, would have done little to enhance its reputation among Roman officials.[104]

Some Christian communities may have shared traits with the philosophical schools, and Justin, for example, specifically draws this analogy (*Dial*.8:1). This might have appeared presumptuous, but Galen accepted the point, even if he did think they promoted a third-rate system of thought. A more obvious comparison would have been with the synagogues.[105] For an originally Jewish sectarian movement the connection was natural enough. The things that distinguished a church from a collegium were often shared with synagogues: the sense of belonging to an intimate, exclusive, but also universal community. Even the defiance of normal societal boundaries— between Jew and Gentile, slave and free, male and female, adult and child— was found in less radical form in the diaspora synagogues. But the synagogues had distinct advantages: they were long-established, familiar, and politically acceptable to Roman authorities. In most cases their buildings and their officials had a prominence and a degree of integration with the local community that the Christians could not match. Moreover, after the early decades, there was little inclination on the part of either Christians or Jews to encourage the establishment of churches under the auspices of the synagogue.

The Literary Evidence

This is an appropriate place, finally, to consider a particular body of Christian literature that has a direct bearing on the issues raised above: Christian apologetic literature. Our brief survey will concentrate on two questions: What were the issues facing the Christians that elicited the early apologies;

and, How, in devising them, did they present their relationship with Judaism?

Some of the criticisms of Christianity in the first two centuries have been touched on above.[106] First, and perhaps most important, Christians were political and social misfits. Occasionally churches were likened to mystery cults, and some Christians (e.g., Justin) optimistically presented themselves as a sort of philosophical school, but whatever benefits accrued from such analogies were of relatively minor significance. As members of what, in outward appearance, was little more than an illegal association, Christians would automatically have been suspected of conspiracy and disloyalty, and it was precisely for such reasons that Roman rulers exercised tight control over the licensing of new collegia (e.g., Dio 52.36; Philo *Flacc.*4; Pliny *Ep.*10.33–34). Regular meetings, nighttime vigils, and a certain wariness in dealing with outsiders invited further misunderstanding. In addition, the rejection in the churches, at least in principle, of familiar social distinctions—Jew/Gentile, slave/free, citizen/noncitizen, male/female, rich/poor—challenged the established order and lent itself readily to accusations of subversion and disloyalty. To the Romans Christianity almost inevitably appeared as a movement that promoted disruption of the established order and dangerous social tendencies. So instinctive was the prejudice that throughout this period, once arraigned, mere confession of the name Christian was sufficient grounds for execution.

Yet, secondly, their challenge to accepted religious practice and belief was not negligible, even though it is hard to keep the political and religious elements apart. The emperor cult is a case in point: for Christians participation was an unacceptable public blasphemy; for Romans their refusal was a profound political insult.[107] Christians were regularly described as those infected with *superstitio*—what the Romans pejoratively referred to as sentimental, irrational, foreign, or novel religious impulses. They were also pilloried for being atheists, that is, those who did not accept the normal array of deities associated with everything from the household to the imperial court. Closely associated were accusations of magic and immorality. The miraculous powers ascribed to Jesus and his earliest followers were readily given a polemical twist, and both they and later Christian generations were charged with dabbling in magic. This reinforced another popular suspicion: that Christians worshiped in private to cover up their involvement in infanticide and orgiastic feasts.[108] This was not simply hostile speculation. For some it was confirmed by garbled snippets of early eucharistic ritual (consuming the body and the blood, the holy kiss, etc.) and the willful promotion of sexual promiscuity in some extremist sects.

Finally, there was the uncertain and troubled relationship with Judaism. As a Jewish sect they shared much in common with the parent tradition and, at least early on, there may have been something to be gained by seeking political protection under the umbrella of Jewish privilege. But things soon went awry. Jewish resistance to Roman rule, especially in 132–35 CE, made the Jews unwelcome bedfellows, quite apart from the antipathy aroused by Jewish harassment of Christians. But this left Christianity more vulnerable, struggling to find its own niche in Roman society—no easy task, as we have seen. In addition, when detached from Judaism, Christianity gave the unwelcome appearance of being an upstart cult no longer covered by the respected antiquity of Judaism. The dispute over who was the "true Israel" could certainly take a theological turn (see Justin and Trypho), but it also had profound political ramifications when those such as Celsus accused Christians of being a bastard child of Judaism. How to explain this relationship to a skeptical audience and in the face of a thriving and numerically superior Judaism was a constant and pressing issue for Christian writers throughout this period.[109]

In this largely unfriendly environment the apologists attempted to make the case for Christian belief and practice. They complained bitterly about Roman persecution for the mere confession of faith and argued that they should be charged only with specific and legally defined crimes—confident, as they were, that they were largely innocent.[110] Although they boasted of their citizenship in another, heavenly world,[111] they nevertheless insisted on their loyalty to the state and, in particular, to the emperor. Athenagoras is particularly obsequious, lacing his *Legatio* with flattering comments on the emperor's renowned wisdom, learning, and justice (2.6; 6.2; 16.2; 17.1; 31.3). While it was normal for an emperor to be reasonably well versed in the classics, it is hardly likely that he could be trusted to explore, of his own volition and without guidance, the scriptures of the Jews (9.1). His concluding comment can stand as a summary of the typical apologist's view:

> But do you, who by nature and learning are in every way good, moderate, humane, and worthy of your royal office, nod your heads in assent now that I have destroyed the accusations advanced and have shown that we are godly, mild and chastened in soul. Who ought more justly to receive what they request than men like ourselves, who pray for your reign that the succession to the kingdom may proceed from father to son, as is most just, and that your reign may grow and increase as all men become subject to you? This is also to our advantage that we may lead a quiet and peaceable life and at the same time may willingly do all that is commanded. (*Leg.*37.1–3)[112]

A step beyond this moderate and modest plea was taken by Melito, who had the temerity to suggest that there was something divinely providential in the coincidence of the rise of Christianity and the success of the Roman Empire (Melito in Eusebius *Hist.eccl.*4.26.7–11). Whether arguments such as these had much success we may doubt. The fact that successive generations felt compelled to reproduce and refine them suggests they were of little effect, and pleas to Marcus Aurelius did nothing to stop the execution of Justin and his associates or the Gallic martyrs. But they do, at any rate, give us some sense of how educated early Christian thinkers tried to secure an acceptable niche for the Christian movement in an unfriendly world and to allay the fears and suspicions that they inevitably aroused. Not all Christians took the same tack. Tatian, for example, bade his farewell to a Greco-Roman world of which he gave an openly negative assessment. But he was the exception.

The second cluster of charges were met head on. The accusation of atheism, for example, was parried by the observation that Christians were monotheists and that they had in addition a rich concept of the divine in their developing trinitarian thought.[113] The scriptural prophets provided superior supporting evidence, but the arguments of pagan poets and philosophers were also used when appropriate, even if some believed that they were ultimately beholden, and therefore inferior, to the great Israelite teachers such as Moses.[114] At the same time they could go on the offensive and expose the absurdities and contradictions of much pagan worship, again using the weapons provided by the prophets and by enlightened pagans who ridiculed their own religious traditions and practices.[115] The charge of magic was more difficult to counter since, as is now widely recognized, one person's magic was another's miracle. Charge and countercharge on this issue were common among rival religious groups, and much depended on the eye of the beholder.[116] One tack was to enhance the Christian claim by showing how various miracles were predicted in the scriptures and another was to bolster the superiority of Christian miracles by pointing to their dramatic and lasting effects.[117] Persistent rumors of incestuous and cannibalistic elements in Christian ritual were dismissed as fundamentally improbable in view of their high moral standards, based commonly on a conflation of Jewish and Christian teaching, their demonstrated care for the outcast and needy, and their well-known aversion to infant exposure, abortion, public executions, gladiatorial spectacles, and the like.[118] Indeed, Christian superiority and pagan inferiority could be demonstrated by their moral standards alone.[119] And when Justin details the Christian rituals of Baptism and Eucharist it may be precisely to demonstrate what did occur as distinct from what was rumored (*I Apol.*61–66).

The early apologists pursued no uniform line in dealing with their awkward and complex relationship to Judaism.[120] For example, Athenagoras, writing ca. 176–80 CE, simply ignores the Jews. For him they seem to be an irrelevance, and they appear in the argument only in the most residual fashion (e.g., via use of their scriptures, though these are now thoroughly Christianized). One of the first questions in *Diognetus,* by way of contrast, is why Christians do not worship like the Jews—posed, interestingly enough, as if it would have been one of the most obvious things to ask. The answer comes in the form of a sharp attack on Jewish worship as foolish, because it offers sacrifices to a God who does not need them, and impious because its various scruples and discriminations favor some foods/days/months over others, when God has created all things equal. This dismissive view of Jewish observance is reinforced by the claim that Christians abstain from "the general silliness, deceit, fussiness and pride of the Jews,"[121] and when the author claims that Christians have no special homeland, language, or customs he is not only claiming a special sort of citizenship for them but also contrasting them with the Jews, who were well known for their attachment to Judaea, Hebrew, and a range of distinctive customs (5.1–5).[122] The promotion of Christianity is thus bolstered by the denigration of Judaism. Much the same happens in Justin. In the *First Apology* this is done more by implication than by direct statement. The Jews are the enemy, denying Jesus and persecuting Christians (31,36) as the scriptures foretold (37–38). Despite their devastating defeats by the Romans (32,47) they do not understand their own fate, continue to refuse the gospel, and thus ensure that Christianity will become a predominantly Gentile movement (49,53,63). To the reader, including Roman officials if such there were, the implication is clear: the Jews are in an unenviable position, rejected by their God and deservedly defeated by their enemies. With them the Christians are not to be confused. What hovers in the background of the apologies comes to the forefront in the *Dialogue with Trypho*, where the question of the Christian relationship to Judaism is given lengthy consideration. Ostensibly it too could have been aimed at Roman officials (*Dial.*141), but this raises complex matters that we will leave for a later discussion.

Ignoring and denigrating Judaism do not exhaust the tactics of the apologists. Aristides, who divides the world into barbarians, Greeks, Jews, and Christians, dismisses the first two out of hand as incorrigible idolaters. The Jews by contrast are more advanced: they worship God and not his works, and they express his nature in their compassion and care for the needy (*Apol.*14). Express sympathy with certain fundamental features of Judaism is reinforced in striking fashion when the author presents the arguments for Christian possession of the truth, for they amount to little more than Jewish apologetic arguments lightly adapted for Christian use: a commitment to monotheism and to the virtuous life (*Apol.*15–16). Yet the Jews are not without fault: their various rituals, feasts, and scrupulous food laws can never be fully observed, and show them to be servants of the angels rather than God himself. A critical but not bitter note is struck, leading Rendel Harris to suggest: "If the Church is not in the writer's time under the wing of the Synagogue, it has apparently no objection to taking the Synagogue occasionally under its wing."[123] Yet this may well get things back-to-front for, despite the claim that Christians are truly a new people (*Apol.*16), the impression given by Aristides is not so much of a confident, independent Christianity condescending to recognize some preliminary truths in Jewish teaching, but rather of an offspring that has found no way beyond simple assertion of demonstrating its independence from or superiority to its parent tradition. The lack of rancor may well indicate a date before the Bar Cochba rebellion.[124]

A more subtle relationship with Judaism is presupposed in Theophilus's *Ad Autolycum*, written toward the end of the second century. There is no doubt that he was a Christian. He alludes to various parts of the New Testament, especially Paul and the Gospels (1.11,14; 3.19) and once refers specifically to the prologue of John (2.22). He refers to Christians by name and asserts that "only the Christians have held the truth" (2.33). Yet three features of his thought give him an unusual profile. First, despite his apparent knowledge of some Christian writings, he venerates and is more profoundly influenced by the Jewish Bible. Thus if Christians have access to the truth through the Holy Spirit, it is a truth found in the Jewish scriptures (2.33); if honoring the emperor can be encouraged by allusions to the New Testament, it is enjoined by quotation of the book of Proverbs (1.11); and if Christian morality has a basis in the Gospel record, especially Matthew, it is equally dependent on the Mosaic code (3.12–15). The prophets are inspired and reinforce the teaching of the law (2.34–35; 3.9,12–14), which is itself central and essential to Christian thinking. The Mosaic commands are the basis of Christian morality, even if a few of them (sabbath and taking the name of God in vain) have been abrogated by the example of Jesus (3.9). Second, Theophilus's understanding of the scriptures closely parallels that of Jewish interpreters such as the authors of *Bereshit Rabbah* and those whom Philo opposes in his *Questions on Genesis*. The meaning of the biblical account of creation is expounded at some length and almost entirely with ideas borrowed from the Jewish exegetical tradition. Third, and most striking, is the virtual absence of Christology in his defense of the Christian faith. Spirit, Logos, and Wisdom were concepts with rich potential, as Theophilus's predecessors had shown, but he uses them inconsistently and usually in service of a *theo*logy in which christological notions at best lie deeply buried (2.10,22). The revelation of the divine Logos in Jesus, for example, was seen as one of many similar events having no unique claim. The life and work of Jesus are never mentioned, though curiously he describes Adam, the generic human, in terms that echo the Lucan infancy narratives (2.24–25). Even allusions to the New Testament (e.g., echoes of Romans in 1.14) appear in service of a theology rather than the Christology that infuses the documents in which they originally appeared.

The emphasis on creation rather than redemption, on theology rather than Christology, led one writer to suggest that a pagan reader of *Ad Autolycum* could as easily have been converted to diaspora Judaism as to Christianity,[125] and another to remark that "one cannot be sure that he reflects Christianity rather than Judaism or if, indeed, there was a clear line between the two in his own mind."[126]

Where does Theophilus's ambiguity spring from and what does it tell us of his attitude toward Judaism? He was probably an anti-Marcionite, and this would have led him to place particular and positive emphasis on the Jewish God and scriptures, but this scarcely explains all the curious features of his thought. It has been suggested that Theophilus was a Jewish Christian. The overwhelming influence of Jewish ideas, the indifference to (and therefore "low") Christology, the fondness for the Gospel of Matthew, and the affinity with ideas that appear in the Pseudo-Clementines all point in this direction and certainly help explain some features of his thought. He was also, however, a man with an apologist's sensibilities. He was aware that Christianity was perceived as a novelty (3.1,4) and tries to counter this by appropriation of Jewish tradition (3.18,20,25) and by an extensive chronology of world history designed precisely to prove "the antiquity of our religion" (3.17–29, quote from 29). That he was reticent on christological matters, as to a lesser degree was Athenagoras too, may be because it was an especially difficult theme to put across to a pagan audience, whereas arguments about the nature of deity and standards of moral behavior covered familiar territory—not least because Jewish apologists and pagan philosophers had already paved the way. What this implies for Theophilus's view of Judaism remains unclear. It does not necessarily imply a positive relationship with contemporary Jews and might even be taken to show a casual disregard for them.[127] On the other hand, it could be argued that presenting the case for Christianity in such a way that an outsider could scarcely perceive the difference between the two faiths, and making positive use of borrowed material without denigrating the community where it originated, promotes, if only by default, a relatively positive image of Judaism. Perhaps, too, he continued to hope that the Jews would take what was for him the relatively small step toward Christian belief, for when he recalls the frequent calls for repentance addressed to the Jews he does not conclude, as others did, that they were now beyond the pale (3.11).

CONCLUSION

This leads us finally to a brief assessment of the preceding sections. How, vis à vis the Romans, did Jews and Christians compare?

1. The Jews had a significant numerical advantage. In the early decades, when the Christian movement was no more than an offshoot from Judaism, the difference was overwhelming, but even by the end of the second century there were three or four times as many Jews as Christians.

2. The Jews were by and large privileged and protected, whereas the Christians were outlawed as members of an illegal, immoral, and irreligious cult. When Rome took action against the Jews it was in response to Jewish provocation, and even extreme crises such as the Bar Cochba rebellion seem not to have disturbed the stable pattern of their relationship for long. In fact that rebellion probably had a far more profound effect on Jewish-Christian

than on Jewish-Roman relations. During the first two centuries Christians, by way of contrast, never attained official acceptance; they thus lived constantly under threat even though the full force of the law was felt only sporadically and usually in response to local antipathies.

3. In addition to being a privileged and familiar minority the Jews enjoyed a further overwhelming advantage: their sheer antiquity. Romans generally venerated what was ancient or well established. The fundamentals of Jewish belief, customs, and organization were thus accorded a degree of acceptance that the upstart Christian tradition could not match on its own.

4. Both communities established themselves most successfully in the towns and cities, in fact, largely in the same towns and cities. They were thus in direct competition, especially for the attention of sympathetic Gentiles. Christians could make their message appealing by offering full membership in their community without some of the obstacles involved in conversion to Judaism (e.g., circumcision), and in this way they probably had some success in recruiting from the outer edges of the synagogue communities despite their less enviable political position. This presumably caused the same resentment among Jews as did the occasional defection in the other direction among Christians.

5. Christians and diaspora Jews made inroads into, and were affected by, Hellenistic culture, but rabbinic Jews remained largely cut off from developments outside their own closed circles, including those taking place in Christian circles and among nonrabbinic Jews. Together with the observation above (point 4), this indicates that Christians had the least connection with that brand of Judaism which was eventually to become the most important.

6. In many other respects Jewish and Christian communities were not dissimilar. The social and economic range in their membership would eventually have been much the same. Initially the Jews had a greater percentage of the educated, the wealthy, and the privileged (e.g., Roman citizens), but by the second century this would have become less obvious. The cohesion, intimacy, and self-supporting charity of the typical synagogue would have been matched by the local church, and certain fundamental beliefs (monotheism) and ethical principles (the Decalogue) would, at least to an outsider, have looked much the same, as would their wariness of, and communal attempts to demarcate themselves from, the outside world. Christianity was less restrictive and much more active in its recruiting, and initially had more women in prominent positions than was typical of the synagogues. Yet even these differences may not have appeared so stark, since Jews encouraged Gentiles to associate with the synagogue and Christians soon reverted to a more patriarchal mode.

7. The rabbis who produced the Mishnah and the Christians who wrote apologies were minorities in their respective communities and their views may not initially have been widely shared. Clearly, too, their literary products belong to different genres with different aims. It is nevertheless inter-

esting to note the striking contrast that they make as two ways of dealing with the exigencies of life in the Roman world, one turning essentially inward, the other outward. Of course, Jews did not urgently need to write apologies in the way that Christians did, because their position was more secure. But they had written them before, and they did not do so now.

JEWS AND JUDAISM
IN THE CANONICAL NARRATIVES

2

❖

It is well understood that the canonical narratives tell us not only about the past, the time of Jesus and the early church, but also about the needs and pressures at the time of their composition. It is also apparent that while these narratives cover a lot of common ground, they are each marked by distinctive traits and special emphases. In order to gain some control over the vast amount of relevant material, each narrative is discussed here under a title that points to something particularly significant in shaping its view of Jewish-Christian relations. These are not intended to be exclusive, since the same concerns often crop up in more than one of the narratives. They will, however, help us to shape a discussion of what is often complex evidence and at the same time gain a sense of the way in which differing backgrounds, times, and places could profoundly affect the perceptions of early Christian writers. The chronological limits of this book would lead some to exclude the Gospel of Mark, since it would be reckoned that he wrote before the destruction of the Temple in 70 CE. But about this there is considerable disagreement, and many scholars have recently been inclined to date Mark after 70 CE.[1] At any rate, all agree that he wrote either immediately before or just after the conquest of Jerusalem and that his views were highly colored by eschatological convictions rooted in current events.

MARK: THE SHADOW OF WAR—APOCALYPSE AND CRISIS

Since Mark began to be read less as a historical record of the life of Jesus and more as an expression of the theology of the author and the needs of the readers, a phase introduced above all by the brilliant work of William Wrede,[2] interpretations of the Gospel have generally tended to relate it to tensions or conflicts within the Christian communities for whom it was composed. This is particularly true of Christology and the portrait of the disciples, which for good reason have been two of the most discussed of Marcan themes. The attitude of the author and readers to external forces has not been entirely ignored, but it has been neglected.

This is to some extent understandable. The question of political loyalty, for example, certainly obtrudes in the trial narrative and a few places elsewhere (12:13–17), but it can hardly be said to be a dominant or overriding concern. The portrait of Jews and Judaism, which is much more integral to the narrative as a whole, has been discussed, but mostly in connection with questions about the historical Jesus and his opponents.[3] Part of the reason for this may well be that the relevant material rarely appears at center stage of Mark's presentation; rather it tends to be the by-product of, or setting for, some other issue that animated the author a great deal more. But before we try to explain the evidence we must first set it out.

It has become traditional to divide Mark into two broad sections: the first covers Jesus' public activity as a wandering charismatic preacher and healer, mostly in Galilee and mostly to popular acclaim; the second describes the turn toward Jerusalem, dark intimations of suffering, and the climactic death of Jesus at the hands of Jewish and Roman authorities. These two halves of the story are framed by a brief prologue (1:1–13) and an even briefer epilogue (16:1–8).[4] Exactly where to divide the narrative is disputed, although 8:27 is commonly suggested, but undeniably there are contrasts that correspond roughly to these two phases of the Marcan story: from Galilee to Jerusalem, from synagogue to Temple, from reticence and riddle to openness and provocation, from dazzling miracle worker to suffering and crucified Messiah, from popular acclaim to official execution, and, for the disciples, from plodding ignorance to willful betrayal.

Within this framework appear a number of themes that patently bear on Mark's attitude toward Judaism: the people and the religious authorities, the law, and the Temple. In addition we shall briefly consider the miracles and the suffering of Jesus and his followers for any further light they may shed.

Leaders and People

Mark's portrait of the Jewish people and their leaders is, on the whole, consistent and uncomplicated.[5] The people at large are generally impressed with Jesus and enthusiastic about his activities. They recognize the novelty and authority of his teaching (1:22,27; 6:2; 11:18; 12:37) and respond with awe and praise to his miraculous deeds (2:12; 4:41; 7:37; 9:14). The sick press themselves on him in droves (1:32; 3:10; 5:24; 6:54–56), and he is constantly surrounded by large and enthusiastic crowds (1:45; 2:2,13; 3:19–20; 4:1; 5:21,24; 8:1; 10:1). So great are their numbers that he has to escape by boat or deliberately retreat with his intimate followers (2:2; 3:9; 4:1; 6:33,44–45; 7:24) and so great is his reputation that they come to him from far and wide, "from Judea, Jerusalem, Idumea, beyond the Jordan, and the region around Tyre and Sidon" (3:8).

Their assessment of Jesus is open and predictable. His teaching and deeds force them to ask, "Who then is this?" (4:41; cf. 1:27; 2:12; 7:37), and they take him to be Elijah, or a prophet, or even a messiah (6:15; 8:28; 11:8–10). Jesus responds in kind, teaching them "as was his custom" (2:13; 4:1,33; 6:2,34; 10:1, et al.) and extending his compassion through healing (1:34,39; 3:10) and feeding them (6:35–44; 8:1–8).

The overriding impression is one of mutual respect and enthusiasm. Yet the picture is a little more complex. When Jesus asks the people not to publicize his miracles, they disobey (1:44–45; 7:36). It is perhaps implied that they do not understand his urge to preach as well as to heal and to extend his work throughout Galilee and beyond (1:38–39). And while they are recipients of his public message they are excluded from the special teaching afforded to the intimate followers alone (4:11–12; 7:17; 10:10).[6] Yet neither of these detract substantially from the overall picture. That they do not understand the deeper intentions of Jesus, are not even privy to them, leaves them in no worse position than the disciples.[7] The disciples *are* given special instruction about the meaning of the miracles, Jesus' heavenly identity (9:1–8), and his coming death (8:31; 9:31; 10:45), but little good it does them. They remain puzzled (4:13; 7:18; 8:32–33; 9:10,32) and quarrelsome (9:33; 10:35–45) and in the end abandon Jesus to his fate (14:50,66–72).[8]

That Jesus was not received in his hometown (6:1–6) or by his immediate family (3:21) detracts somewhat from his enthusiastic welcome elsewhere, but it throws into greater relief the overwhelmingly positive response he got from others. A more significant exception is the transformation of the common people during the denouement, baying for Jesus' blood before Pilate (15:11–15) and mocking him as he hung on the cross (15:29–32).[9] This is unexpected and runs against the grain of the preceding narrative. But Mark offers an ameliorating aside: they were stirred up by the chief priests (15:11). Previously the authorities had been reluctant to move against Jesus for fear of the crowds (11:18; 12:12; 14:2), but now they succeeded in turning them against him.

This brings us naturally to the portrait of the religious authorities, which is as uniform in the opposite direction: almost without exception they tangle with Jesus, challenge his authority, and plot to kill him. The first allusion to them sets a tone that is scarcely to change: Jesus taught with authority "not as the scribes" (1:22). A number of different groups are named. The Pharisees dispute with Jesus over eating with the socially marginal, fasting, the sabbath, hand washing, seeking signs, divorce, and paying taxes (2:16,18,24; 3:6; 7:1–3,5; 8:11; 10:2; 12:13). They are associated with the scribes (2:16; 7:1,5), and with the Herodians (3:6; 12:13).[10] Only once do they appear in Jerusalem (12:13), and although they plot Jesus' death they do not subsequently appear.

The scribes are ubiquitous. They engage in controversy over healing and forgiveness (2:6), eating with the marginal (2:16), demonic/divine inspiration (3:22), hand washing (7:1,5). It is implied that they teach without authority (1:22), though their teaching is sometimes challenged and sometimes accepted (12:35; 9:11), and at one point they are roundly condemned for their public pretension and rapacity (12:38–40). They are, as we have seen, associated with the Pharisees but, unlike them, they are strongly linked to the Jerusalem establishment. They come from Jerusalem (3:22; 7:1), and when the scene shifts there they are routinely associated with the chief priests (10:33; 11:18; 14:1; 15:31) or the chief priests and elders (8:31; 11:27; 14:43,53; 15:1).

The chief priests (see also 14:10,55; 15:3,10,11), scribes and elders, high priest (14:53,60,61,63), and council (14:55; 15:1) make up the official opposition to Jesus in Jerusalem. The chief priests, the most frequently mentioned, take a leading role but usually in tandem with one or more of the others. To complete the picture, even the Sadducees get drawn in for one controversy (12:18–23).

Recent studies of the religious authorities in Mark have come independently to similar conclusions. First, they conclude that the authorities act as one. They are, in effect, one character. This is clear not only from the multiple interlinkages that the author explicitly points out—between the different groups and between the scenes in Galilee and Jerusalem—but also from the absence of any clear distinctions in the issues they dispute and the manner in which they oppose Jesus.[11] Second, there is an intensification of the opposition to Jesus as the narrative progresses. This can be detected through chapters 3 to 8: the plot to get rid of Jesus is mentioned early and hovers ominously in the background (3:6); the conflicts move from indirect confrontation with Jesus and the disciples (2:6–8) to direct confrontation with Jesus (8:11–13), and from legal issues (chaps. 2–3) to the issue of authority itself (chaps. 7–8). This, in turn, emphasizes that underneath specific disputes the fundamental issue is always the authority of Jesus over and against that of the leaders.[12] The more obvious intensification, however, comes with the shift from Galilee to Jerusalem, from verbal dispute to physical assault, from smoldering resentment to public execution. The drawn-out climax to the narrative intensifies and heightens the conflict, so that although in the end the Romans put Jesus to death, they are strangely passive and move reluctantly against Jesus only at the insistence of the Jewish authorities.[13]

There are, thirdly, apparent exceptions. Jairus, whose young daughter is brought back to life, and who clearly had a strong faith in Jesus' healing powers, is described as a "leader of the synagogue" (archisynagogos, 5:22,36,38). One scribe agrees with Jesus' definition of the greatest commandments and is described as being "not far from the kingdom of God" (12:34). The compliment is restrained: "not far from" suggests that the scribe has insight but is still an outsider. Yet it contrasts with an otherwise uniformly negative picture of the scribes and, for the reader, of course, confirms from within the scribal circle that Jesus is right. Joseph of Arimathea, who courageously retrieves Jesus' body and entombs it, is described as "a respected member of the council, who was also himself waiting expectantly for the kingdom of God" (15:43). If "member of the council" (*bouleutos*) means a member of the Sanhedrin, he must have been one of those who had just condemned Jesus ("the whole council" [*holon to synedrion*], 14:55; 15:1). Such a sudden change of heart is odd, and it may be that by "council" Mark means a local body rather than the Sanhedrin.[14] Either way he is a respected Jewish authority who shows sympathy and respect for, but not necessarily belief in, Jesus.

It might be thought that these exceptions soften the otherwise stark profiles sketched by Mark. Yet this is hardly the case. While the description of these three characters is sympathetic, none of them is said to have become a disciple. Moreover, precisely because they are rare exceptions, they tend to underline rather than to blur the consistency of all the other evidence. We must remember, in addition, as always with these narratives, that they were probably heard rather than read in the first instance. What would have impressed the original audience would have been the broad sweep and overall shape of the narrative—and in this case there can be little doubt about what the preponderant image of the Jewish authorities would have been.

Related to their role as actors in the story are the allusions to the Jewish leaders in the parables. Most clearly this occurs in the parable of the wicked tenants (12:2–12). A stream of servants sent by the master are either beaten or killed, and when he finally sends his beloved son and heir they seize him, kill him, and throw him out of the vineyard. As a result the master will destroy the tenants and give the vineyard to others. No doubt one important point for Mark was the allusion to destruction and transfer which, in the context of his story, can readily be seen as an allusion both to the destruction of the Temple and the mission to the Gentiles, and perhaps to their role as the new Israel. But in his editorial comment (v.12) he draws attention to the analogy between the wicked tenants and the religious authorities who "realized that he had told this parable against them." For Mark, the evildoers in the world of the parable are precisely parallel to the evildoers in the world of the Gospel.

In the parable of the sower, which draws us into the strange world of Marcan parable theory, the main point seems clear: the gospel will meet with differing, often negative, reactions, but the ultimate harvest will be huge. It is not unnatural to see this generalization reflected in the Gospel itself, in which case the Jewish leaders would be equivalent to the path from which the seed is immediately removed by the birds (= Satan) before it even germinates.[15] The passing allusion to Satan is interesting, since it could be the only place where the leaders are associated with Satan and the demonic world where yet another level of opposition to Jesus is played out. Yet it is an inference we have to draw and not one that the author specifically encourages, so that we cannot suppose it was important for him.

In two cases, at least, the parables mirror the Gospel: in the one the leaders are totally immune to the message and work of Jesus; in the other they are actively hostile toward him and his prophetic predecessors. In both cases an already gloomy portrait is darkened further.

The Law

In his portrayal of the common folk, but more especially their leaders, Mark seems animated and engaged. In his treatment of the law this is much less the case. A number of potentially interesting legal issues are touched on, and they are of considerable interest to those trying to gauge Jesus' approach to the law, yet Mark often casually passes them by or diverts our attention elsewhere.[16]

On two occasions disputes arise over the Sabbath (2:23–28; 3:1–6). In neither case is observation of the Sabbath overtly challenged, but the meaning of Sabbath observance is given an unusual twist. On the one hand, it is subject to humane and compassionate demands (3:4; cf. "the sabbath was made for humankind," 2:27), and on the other to christological authority ("the Son of Man is lord even of the sabbath," 2:28). The latter, in particular, challenges the Sabbath law as it was understood in Judaism, but the challenge is implicit.

The story of the rich young man reveals a similar stance. His claim to have kept all the commandments is not queried, but he is asked to divest himself of his wealth and to follow Jesus (10:17–22). The implication is that keeping the commandments is all right as far as it goes, but insufficient. Jesus requires radical acts of charity and discipleship. The proper use of wealth was an issue in several Christian communities, and this may be where their interest in the story chiefly lay.

The Mosaic rules for divorce are overturned, but by intensifying rather than liberalizing them (10:2–12). The absolute sanctity of marriage and denial of divorce is based on God's intent at creation (vv.6–8) and his declared will (v.9). The Mosaic rules are dismissed as a concession to human frailty and, although one part of the "Mosaic" writings is being used to interpret another, Moses' authority is to some degree undercut by Jesus and his understanding of scripture. Jesus' reported view, which was different from those generally found in Jewish and Gentile society, would have been of prime interest to Christians.

In the discussion with the sympathetic scribe (12:28–34) the two great commandments are endorsed, as they are generally in the early Christian movement (Rom 13:8–10). Their formulation in rapid succession by both Jesus (vv.29–31) and the scribe (vv.32–33) reinforces their significance. They are said to be more important than the sacrificial system (v.33), thus implicitly undercutting another part of the law, but this issue is lightly passed over. Other Decalogue commands are alluded to, endorsed, and extended. The honoring of parents is upheld against the weakening of this obligation in scribal tradition (7:9–13; cf. 10:19), although this stands in some tension with Jesus' abrupt dealings with his family (3:31–35). The prohibition against killing is extended into an obligation positively to do good (3:4).

The most pointed and informative discussion of the law arises in connection with Jewish purity rules (7:1–23). The initial dispute between Jesus, the Pharisees, and the Jerusalem scribes is over hand washing and associated purity rites (7:2–5). This is defined by Mark as a conflict between the commands of God and human teachings (7:8), a more general point that is illustrated by reference to the corban vow (7:9–13). Unexpectedly the argument turns to a new matter, not unrelated to the opening issue but not identical with it either: clean and unclean foods (7:14–23). The declaration that "whatever goes into a person from outside cannot defile," for "it is what comes out of a person that defiles," radically overturns the purity taboos of Judaism and most other societies in the ancient world. And Mark leaves his readers in no doubt what it means: "Thus he declared all foods clean" (7:19).

This discussion invites a number of observations. First, it sweeps away a whole raft of biblical prohibitions. Second, Mark informs his readers that the Pharisees and all the Jews follow the purity rules (7:3–4). That they needed to be told implies that they were Gentiles. Since we know, thirdly, that not all Jews practiced hand washing and the other purity rites, it seems that the author had a vague or limited view of Judaism, probably implying that he was a Gentile too.[17] The way in which he slips from hand washing to unclean foods as if they were both matters of scribal tradition (when the second was scriptural) suggests much the same thing.

At other points where the issue of ritual purity might have become an issue it is rapidly passed by (2:13–17) or ignored (5:21–43). The odd exception is 1:44 for, whether the witness is to or against and the object the people or the priests, it recommends fulfilling the Mosaic command. That the author saw no tension between this and 7:1–23 probably indicates that the issue was not acute, despite the aside in 7:19.[18]

It is a delicate matter to surmise what most interested the authors of the Gospels and their original audiences. One of the chief reasons is that they were constrained by the traditions they received. Jesus was a Jew and lived among Jews, and inevitably much of the tradition about him deals with Jewish matters. A Christian wishing to write about Jesus could scarcely be unaffected.[19] Thus when Mark relates a number of stories concerning legal or quasi-legal matters, it does not mean he was consumed by, or even much interested in, the question of the law per se. In general he is explicitly positive and implicitly critical about specific commandments, but it is usually some christological or ethical aspect that interests him more, especially as they applied to everyday issues of Christian life. A favorable view of the Decalogue, especially the two love commands, is evident, and he presents raw material that might be turned into a distinction between ethical and ritual obligations or between the surface and the inner meaning of commandments. But he leaves them up in the air. Where he could have focused on the law he often does not, and he seems ill-informed about the distinction between scripture and tradition even as he purports to define it. The overall impression is that he was largely indifferent to the matter, and probably therefore a Gentile writing for Gentiles, for whom the law was no longer an acute problem.[20]

Miracles and Passion

We noted earlier the way in which Mark divides into two major sections. With some simplification we can say that in the first Jesus is a miracle worker, in the second a suffering Messiah. This has been widely recognized and most commonly related to christological disputes in the Marcan churches.[21] But both of them could have been relevant to other contexts too. In the first half of the Gospel, Jesus' most prominent activity is performing miracles, even though it is his teaching that is more commonly referred to in the editorial summaries. There can be little doubt that Mark wishes to present him positively as a powerful and impressive figure, a sort of divine man.[22] This was important in the ancient world, where one of the sure signs of divine inspiration was the power to work what we loosely call miracles. It commonly became a point of dispute between Jews and Christians. Some of this may be reflected in the Gospel. The famous Beelzebub dispute (3:22–27) encapsulates the most common form of disagreement—not over what has happened but by whose power, God's or Satan's. Healing a paralytic rapidly turns into a dispute over forgiveness of sins and the appropriation of divine authority (2:2–12) and other healings embroil him in legal disputes (3:1–6). The Pharisees ask for a sign, presumably some sort of undeniably miraculous demonstration, though they are refused (8:11–13); yet one synagogue official is positively affected by his powers (5:21–24, 35–43). One undercurrent, therefore, in the presentation of the miracle-working Jesus may have been disputes with the Jews, though it has to be said that Mark does not jump at the opportunity to point this out beyond what he found in the tradition.

The suffering Messiah balances the image of the miracle worker and provides the opportunity for reflection on notions such as atonement and the conquest of death. In addition, however, Jesus' fate is seen as a paradigm for his followers. They must take up their cross and follow him (8:34–38), serve with the humility of the Son of Man (10:41–45), and suffer rejection and persecution (13:9–13). Councils, synagogues, governors, and kings (13:9) clearly refer to Jewish opponents and most likely to Romans too, following the pattern of Jesus' fate.[23] Thus when Mark brings his story of the suffering

Messiah into the present by linking it to current Christian experience, he expects hostility from the Jews or, at least, from Jewish officialdom.

The Temple

Jesus' attitude toward the Jerusalem Temple, as has been noted, is among other things a legal issue. It is convenient to consider it separately, however, since it leads us naturally into the apocalyptic convictions that heavily color Mark's story.

In the Temple incident (11:15–19) Jesus' criticism centers on corruption and misuse: corruption on the part of those in the Temple market, and misuse of a building intended for prayer. That it should have been a house of prayer for all nations and not just the Jews confirms Mark's universalism,[24] and the reaction of the authorities—alarm at the popular influence of Jesus' teaching—confirms a pattern found throughout the Gospel. Otherwise the significance of Jesus' action is not spelled out. Yet Mark artfully sandwiches the cleansing between the cursing of the fig tree (11:12–14) and its observed result (11:20–21). This ominous note, in which the fate of the Jews is probably prefigured in the fig tree, points beyond a mere religious protest to the ultimate fate of the Temple and its people.[25]

This is picked up in the little apocalypse. Jesus claims that of the great buildings around him, in context certainly including the Temple, "not one stone will be left here upon another; all will be thrown down" (13:2). What this might mean comes out in the notoriously obscure allusion to the desolating sacrilege (13:14) which, whatever precisely it might signify, is agreed by all to refer to some kind of desecration of the Temple around the time of its destruction. That Jesus prophesied the destruction of the Temple is, for Mark, clear. The subsequent denial that he said he would destroy the Temple and rebuild it (14:58, based on false testimony; cf. 15:29) presumably denies his personal involvement: the Temple will be destroyed, but not by him.[26] We thus have a fairly bleak view of one of the central symbols of Judaism, motivated in part by a reaction to corruption and misuse but colored above all by its imminent or recent demise.

This brings us to chapter 13, which more than any other exposes the circumstances at the time of writing. This is where Mark locates himself in the grand scheme of things and where he specifically urges the reader to take note of his meaning ("let the reader understand," 13:14). It is generally agreed that at the time of writing the events predicted in 13:3–13 (the birth pangs) had already occurred and those in 13:24–27 (the end itself) had yet to occur. The dispute is mainly over the allusions to the destruction of the Temple and its aftermath (13:2,14–23). Were they written before or after 70 CE, in anticipation or in the wake of the destruction? The allusion to a "desolating sacrilege" (13:14; cf. Dan 9:27; 11:31; 12:11; Macc 15:54,59) hardly clarifies matters: it can plausibly be related to the actions of Romans or Jewish rebels in the Temple, to Vespasian, or to an otherwise unidentified antichrist.[27] In terms of his own predictions Mark seems to stand, as it were, between vv.13 and 14, but that could still locate him before or after 70 CE, depending on the meaning of v.14.[28] For our purposes it does not matter, since it is widely agreed that Mark was written just before or just after 70 CE and that he was profoundly affected by the events of the Jewish War.

In chapter 13 he expresses two convictions. First, the signs of the end are not to be confused with the end itself: "the end is still to come" (v.7), these are "but the beginning of the birthpangs" (v.8), "the good news must first be proclaimed to all nations" (v.10), and the sufferings associated with the Temple desecration (vv.14–23) are not the same as the grand cosmic conclusion (vv.24–27). Together with the double reference to false prophets and messiahs (vv.6, 21–22) these indicate that the war had brought some Christians to a fever pitch, convinced that it was all over. To them Mark recommends caution. Yet he does so, secondly, while sharing many of their convictions. For him too the predicted or already experienced events associated with the Temple were a prelude to the end, which was, in turn, imminent (vv.28–30; cf. 1:15; 9:1; 14:62). For Mark the signs and the end should not be identified, but they should not be severed either. They are intimately, inexorably bound together.

The outlook for the Jews and their Temple is not good. Yet Mark is less interested in this, in drawing out a judgment on the Jews, than he is in the effect of the war on Christian eschatology. For him the Jewish War and apocalyptic convictions are inextricably entangled, and it is under their shadow that he writes.

Conclusion and Context

A story about Jesus will inevitably deal with Jews and Judaism if it is to have the slightest appearance of authenticity. Mark is no exception. Of course, the mere inclusion of material tells us something about Mark's interests; the more difficult thing is to gauge when he is actively and creatively responding to it.[29] Writing at the time of its imminent or recent demise, Mark predicts the destruction of a Temple whose misuse and corruption Jesus had earlier attacked. This is implicitly an assault on a central feature of Jewish life, but Mark is more interested in its implications for Christian eschatology.[30] The proper understanding of the law arises a number of times. The Marcan Jesus responds with a number of potentially consistent but haphazardly applied principles. Some of the issues were important within Christian communities, but there is little sense of immediate or intense conflict with Judaism over the matter. The one place where Mark lights up is in his portrait of the official opposition to Jesus. The common folk are receptive, if somewhat superficial, but the Jewish leaders oppose him implacably from the start and get their way in the end. The reader knows it is a pyrrhic victory, because Jesus is resurrected, the Temple destroyed, and the promised parousia about to occur. There is a hint of supersession in 12:9, which concurs with the predictions of a universal mission (7:24–30; 13:10; 14:9), but no developed theory of the relationship between Jews and Christians.[31]

How do we explain this? Two things in particular have a bearing. The first is the Gentile context. That the readers were Gentiles is almost universally agreed. It is probable that the author was too.[32] A strong case has been made for the origin of Mark among Christians living in Syria, possibly in the border regions between Tyre and Galilee.[33] As Gentiles, involved largely in a Gentile mission, they could have been indifferent to the Jewish law, except for those parts that had been absorbed into the Christian tradition. At the same time the borders of Judaea/Galilee would have been close enough to follow the course of and be affected by the Jewish War—which is, of course, the second crucial element. The breakdown of Jewish-Gentile relationships during the war might explain the consistently hostile picture of Jewish authorities and some of the pressures experienced by those whose lives were supposed to mimic that of their founder.[34] The fate of the Temple stirred up turbulent apocalyptic notions, and Mark himself thought the end was near. In this context, reflection on the long-term relationship between Christians and Jews was hardly to be expected.

MATTHEW: THE SHADOW OF YAVNEH— AUTHORITY AND PRAXIS

The title is intended to focus attention on two things: the intense conflict between Christian and Jewish authorities as they strove to define and control their respective communities, and the degree to which these conflicts followed what we may loosely call a Jewish agenda.[35] If we allow the truism that Jews were more concerned with orthopraxy and Christians with orthodoxy, and that this was as true after as before 70 CE, it is striking that the tension between Matthew and the representatives of Judaism frequently turns on matters of halakah or, more broadly, on doing the will of God, precisely the chief point of contention between other Jewish groups at that time. We cannot point to many precise parallels, in form or content, with early tannaitic traditions, but Matthew's manifest sensitivity about questions of law and ethics—much more obvious than in the other canonical Gospels—suggests a predominantly Jewish ethos.[36] This, like the truism above, is intended only to capture a distinctive emphasis, not to provide in either case an exhaustive definition. Of course, Matthew contains narrative that resembles haggadah, and there are places in the Gospel where disputes with the Jews hinge on matters of belief rather than practice.[37] But then we should no more think that Jews after 70 CE were not interested in haggadah, ethics, or questions of fundamental belief than we should that Christians were not concerned with right living.

When we speak of Jewish leaders trying to define and control their community after 70 CE we usually think of the term "Yavneh." The fashion of associating Yavneh with a tightly knit, powerful group of rabbis who rapidly and effectively imposed their vision of Judaism in the few decades after 70 CE—best exemplified in their introduction of the *Birkat ha-minim*—has been questioned in almost every particular. Rather, it is argued, the Yavnean rabbis were a minority, took a long time to formulate their vision and an even longer time to impose it, and, as a result, the *Birkat ha-minim* at first had only a marginal effect on Christians and no discernible effect on the Matthean community at all.[38] These are important correctives. There is nothing in Matthew that invites us to find an allusion to the *Birkat ha-minim*.[39] If we assume that Matthew was engaged in conflict with those post-70 Jews who *were* engaged in redefining and consolidating Judaism in the wake of the Jewish War,[40] a helpful though not essential assumption, we should not exaggerate their numbers or their influence. They may have been the majority in the Matthean setting, but they may also have been a minority within Judaism as a whole.[41] What is important for our purposes is that Matthew was actively engaged with Jewish rivals, that they were a force to be reckoned with, and that they largely set the agenda.[42]

It has often been noted that Matthew's Gospel combines a distinct Jewish flavor with a vitriolic strain of anti-Judaism. The Gospel opens with birth narratives that draw us into a world full of Jewish piety and expectation, but, unlike the Gospel of Luke, this continues through the Gospel without a break. Semitic phrasing (e.g., "kingdom of heaven" instead of "kingdom of God," "Father in heaven" instead of "God"), untranslated Aramaic (e.g., "rabbi," "Golgotha"), deep concern with Jewish law and custom, liberal quotation from the scriptures, and the tendency to hold up Gentiles as a negative example (5:47; 6:7; 18:17) all contribute to the Jewish tone.[43] Yet as early as the birth narratives the Jewish authorities plot against Jesus (2:4,16)—a hostility that continues throughout the narrative, comes to climax in the Passion, and extends to a plot to deny the resurrection (28:11–15). Even the more favorably disposed common folk turn against him in the end and call down a curse on themselves and their generation (27:24–25). The renowned Sermon on the Mount (Matt. 5–7) reads much like a Jewish ethic, and yet it stands in the same text that includes the ferocious polemic against the scribes and Pharisees (chap. 23). It is above all this profound ambivalence that we need to explain. But first we must look a little more at the details.

Law and Custom

There is little doubt that Matthew is the most sensitive of all the Gospel writers about the question of the Jewish law.[44] It is an issue that actively engages his editorial eye and on which he states what was presumably to him a clear theoretical position (5:17–20).[45]

In the discussion of grain-picking on the Sabbath (12:1–8) there are a number of differences from the parallel tradition in Mark 2:23–28 / Luke

6:1–5. In addition to the example of David, Matthew adds a further biblical precedent (priests on the Sabbath, Num 28:9), a prophetic dictum that holds mercy to be greater than cultic obligation (Hos 6:6; cf. Matt 9:13) and becomes the basis for declaring the disciples guiltless, and (with Luke) omits the potentially subversive claim that "the sabbath was made for humankind, and not humankind for the Sabbath" (Mark 2:27). The disciples' behavior is explained by reference to their hunger, and the dispute (like many in Matthew, with the Pharisees) seems to hinge on the interpretation rather than the status of the Sabbath. There is, of course, a potential threat from the christological claim that "the Son of Man is lord of the Sabbath," to which Matthew adds "something greater than the temple is here." In the following pericope (12:9–14), doing good on the Sabbath is christologically authorized, but it remains unclear what effect that has on the sabbath. Thus two things are enhanced in the Matthean account: on the one hand, the biblical justification of the disciples' behavior and the assertion of their innocence; on the other hand, the subversive christological conviction that ultimately sets Jesus over the law. The law is not broken; the Pharisaic interpretation is discarded, and Jesus is pronounced the supreme interpreter of the will of God. The tension is, as we shall see, typical of Matthew.[46]

As we have seen, the discussion in Mark 7:1–23 (= Matt 15:1–20) is particularly helpful in assessing Mark's view of the law. The same is true of Matthew, but for different reasons. Matthew has no equivalent to Mark's radical declaration, "Thus he declared all foods clean" (Mark 7:19b), nor to his statement that things from outside cannot defile (Mark 7:18b–19a). He also concludes the pericope by forcing the issue of hand washing to the fore (Matt 15:20, "to eat with unwashed hands does not defile"), thus confining the potentially subversive statement of 15:11 ("it is not what goes into the mouth that defiles a person, but it is what comes out of the mouth that defiles") to the issue of eating food with unclean hands rather than the eating of unclean foods.[47] The focus on Pharisaic tradition is enhanced by the addition of a polemic against these "blind guides" and the ominous threat that "every plant that my heavenly Father has not planted will be uprooted" (15:12–14). A number of things are at work here: attention is deflected away from the issue of foods toward the issue of hand washing, and the contrast between human traditions and the will of God deepened by explicit polemic against the purveyors of the tradition; at the same time Jesus' authority, already expressed in his clear and forceful distinctions, is reinforced by allusion to his "heavenly Father." Again, the law is preserved, Pharisaic traditions discarded, and Jesus' authority enhanced.

In his report of the conversation between the scribe/lawyer and Jesus (Matt 22:34–40 = Mark 12:28–31 = Luke 10:25–28), Matthew introduces two distinctive features. First, the story is abbreviated, omitting the relatively favorable praise of the scribe/lawyer as someone "not far from the kingdom of God" and the contrast between the core commandments and the sacrificial cult. Second, to the summary of the law in the two love commands he alone adds the conclusion, "On these two commandments hang all the law and the prophets" (22:40). The two features contribute to the same effect: a stark focus on Jesus' summary of the law and on his core hermeneutical principle. Consonant with other references to love (5:43–48; 7:12; 19:19), and similar to the emphasis on showing mercy (5:7; 9:13; 12:7; 23:23; cf. 12:11; 18:23–35; 25:31–46), this passage singles out love as the key to the meaning of the law.[48] The law itself is not challenged, but it is claimed that it can be properly understood from only one perspective, its weightiest command, which is routinely set over and against the interpretation of the scribes and Pharisees.

The Matthean Jesus' unique summary of his relationship to the Law and the Prophets (5:17–20), riddled as it is with ambiguities, has been exhaustively analyzed. It can plausibly be construed in more than one way, and the meaning we give to it is closely related to our understanding of the following antitheses (5:21–48) and to Matthew's other statements about the law—an argument that can rapidly become circular. For our purposes it is sufficient to distinguish two main lines of interpretation. According to the first, the Law and the Prophets are held to be eternally sacrosanct and Jesus' teaching/actions an expression, but in no way an abrogation, of them. According to the second, the preeminence of the Law and the Prophets finds its denouement in the death and resurrection of Jesus, whose own life and teaching become the new focus of authority. The way in which Matthew has shaped other debates about the law, despite their christological emphasis, strongly supports the first sense and, if so, suggests how we should read them and the antitheses. That is, if Jesus upholds the eternal validity of the Law and the Prophets in 5:17–20, the antitheses and other legal disputes cannot be read as an attack on the Law and the Prophets, but rather as a debate about their true meaning.[49]

From this brief look at the evidence we can construct a fairly consistent picture of Matthew's approach to the law: the law itself remains intact; Jesus' aim is to interpret it, to expose the true intention obscured by the current experts. It is clear that for Matthew—in contrast to Mark, for example—the law was an issue of keen and lively interest, and it is plausible to suppose that he and his readers were sensitive to the charge, probably voiced by Jewish opponents, that they were antinomian. The issue is important enough to be faced head on at the beginning of Jesus' "legal" teaching (Matt 5:17ff.). The potentially subversive force of christological claims is evaded or subdued: Jesus' teaching is not an attack on the law but an interpretation of it.

This way of holding together the validity of Jewish law with the novelty of Jesus' teaching had to be convincing mainly to Matthew and his readers rather than their Jewish opponents, though they may have had hopes for persuading some of their fellow Jews. What practical obligations underlay their view remains unclear. Presumably they sat lightly on hand washing and similar postbiblical traditions, but there is no reason why they should not have observed the sabbath and the food laws. Silence on the issue of circumcision has led many to conclude that it was practiced too.[50]

Leaders and People

The pattern of response by the common people is much the same in Matthew as in Mark. Broadly, the crowds are sympathetic to Jesus' teaching and miraculous deeds prior to the Passion. They follow him from town to town, observe his miraculous works, and testify enthusiastically to his exceptional authority and power.[51] Together with the disciples they can be the object of Jesus' instruction (Matt 23:1). For all this, and despite their admission that Jesus is the Son of David (21:15–16; but cf. 22:41–46), they are never brought wholly onto Jesus' side. Their response is sympathetic but limited, hovering between the belief of the disciples and the hostility of the authorities. When the Passion story begins, they succumb to the influence of the leaders (27:20), call vociferously for the release of Barabbas (27:21–23), and then, in Matthew's unique and notorious statement, publicly announce their responsibility ("the people as a whole" said, "His blood be on us and on our children!" 27:25). Compared with Mark, things go one step farther: not only are the crowds persuaded by the religious authorities to reject Jesus, they collectively and unwittingly call down judgment on themselves.[52] Quite apart from its subsequent tragic and unpredicted effects, the saying in 27:25 extends and intensifies Jewish culpability and throws into doubt the future of the Jews.

Matthew is notorious for his polemic against the Jewish leaders. Some distinctions are preserved, partly reflecting the original historical circumstances: chief priests and elders are most associated with Jerusalem, the Temple, and the Sanhedrin (16:21; 21:23; 26:3,47; 27:1,3,12,20; 28:11–12), while scribes and Pharisees are more commonly associated with the synagogues and tend to be antagonists in disputes over the law (5:20; 12:2,9,14; 19:3; 22:15; 23).[53] Yet, like Mark, Matthew tends to fuse the leaders into a single "character," which presents a united opposition to Jesus and his followers. The root traits of this collectivity are hostility and wickedness, which find expression in their lawlessness, hypocrisy, error, and spiritual blindness.[54] From the time of their first appearances, in league with Herod (2:3) and as the targets of John's apocalyptic threats (3:7–10), to their active involvement in the death of Jesus (chaps. 26–27), they are a constant and negative presence. The occasional positive notes in Mark are altered to remove all exceptions: the thoughtful conversation between a scribe and Jesus (Mark 12:28–34 = Matt 22:34–40) is replaced, Jairus becomes a "leader" (archon, Matt 9:18–26) rather than a "leader of the synagogue" (archisynagogos, Mark 5:22–38), and Joseph of Arimathea becomes a "disciple" rather than a "member of the council" (Mark 15:43 = Matt 27:57).

While he tends to tar the Jewish leaders with the same brush, Matthew clearly has a predilection for two groups in particular: scribes and Pharisees, together or alone. There are many more references to Pharisees in Matthew than in Mark, though Luke has approximately the same number. Scribes alone or scribes and Pharisees together, however, are Matthean favorites.[55] They are involved (21:45; 22:15; 27:62) in Jesus' death, but unlike the chief priests and elders who are largely confined to Jerusalem, they turn up at all stages of Jesus' public career. The relentlessly negative portrait of them strikes an unpleasant tone, but even so the ferocious attack in Matthew 23 comes as something of a surprise.[56] The level of animosity, unprecedented in Matthew, let alone the other Gospels, strongly suggests that the scribes and Pharisees stand for contemporaries with whom the author is in conflict—almost certainly Jews.[57] It is increasingly accepted that Pharisees and scribes (with some priests, landowners, and others) were the most influential groups involved in the reconstruction of Judaism after 70 CE, so that the line of connection between Jesus' opponents and Matthew's opponents would have been plausible and direct.[58]

Particularly worth noting are the issues over which Jesus and the Jewish leaders come into conflict. The role of the chief priests and elders is chiefly to facilitate Jesus' death—predicted in 16:21, plotted in 21:45, and enacted in Matthew 26–28. They are provoked by his teaching and actions, but that is not the main focus in their appearances. With the demise of the Temple and the Sanhedrin after 70 CE, their influence would have been significantly reduced (though not necessarily altogether destroyed). The conflict with the scribes and Pharisees, on the other hand, is almost exclusively over questions of praxis: common meals (9:11); fasting (9:14); the Sabbath (12:2,14); hand washing (15:1,12); divorce (19:3); civic obedience (22:15–16). The whole Sermon on the Mount could be characterized as an ethic of righteousness which exceeds that of the scribes and Pharisees (5:20), and the complaint in chapter 23 hinges on the question of their behavior, how their understanding of the law distorts its intent, inflates their reputation, and engenders hypocrisy, rapacity, and murder. Thus, with the group who represent his contemporary opponents Matthew's disagreement is largely over matters of praxis.[59]

And what is Matthew's purpose? It is to bolster Jewish Christians in their struggle with the synagogue and denigrate their opponents. The struggle was over substance or right teaching, but also over authority. Whose teachers had the right teaching and best understood the will of God? Matthew's perspective is that of a sectarian minority, tenaciously defending its version of Judaism over and against other minorities or the Jewish community at large. In these circumstances what we would expect is what we find: fierce antagonism and fullblooded rhetoric. The conflict was rooted in earlier traditions about Jesus, and Matthew of course uses these, but the driving force is the contemporary battle over common turf.

Synagogues and Churches

The Jewish and Christian authorities did not work in a vacuum. Behind them were communities, similarly organized in many ways but anxious to define boundaries and secure their sense of identity. Several hints in the Gospel suggest that they would have looked remarkably similar, with parallel organizations and many common beliefs. It was, paradoxically, precisely this similarity (and proximity) that exacerbated mutual antagonism. The situation has been aptly described by L. M. White as "a case of 'marginal differentiation,' where minutiae—or marginal features of faith and practice—are used to preserve a sense of difference between organizations that are otherwise substantially similar."[60]

Matthew's use of pronouns in the phrases "their/your synagogues" (4:23; 9:35; 10:17; 12:9; 13:54; 23:34) may not be unique, but it is repeated, emphatic, and suggests that he saw the opponents' Jewish synagogues as alien institutions (cf. 6:2,5; 23:6).[61] It is not clear whether "their" contrasts with "our" or with some entirely non-synagogue institution. Part of the answer lies in Matthew's unique and oft-noted use of *ekklesia* (16:18; 18:17), a community run by authoritative figures, Peter and the disciples, who hold the power to bind and loose (16:19; 18:19)—a power, it is often noted, that parallels that ascribed to rabbinic authorities in precisely these terms.[62] Communal discipline is encouraged (7:15–23; 18:15–18), and might even involve an ecclesial *synedrion* (5:22).

If the scribes and Pharisees represent current Jewish leaders, their Christian counterparts are the disciples and Peter. As they opposed the Jewish leaders in their day, so do the Christian leaders at the time of writing. The connection is made easier by reconstructing their image: as the prime recipients of Jesus' teaching (Matt 5–7; 9:37; 18; 28:16) they are, compared with Mark, less susceptible to ignorance and misunderstanding, more settled than itinerant, and functioning more as teachers than miracle workers and missionaries.[63]

The opposition have "their scribes" (7:28), but there are good scribes who are persecuted (23:34) and, strikingly, scribes of the kingdom of heaven (13:51–52). This strongly suggests that the *ekklesia* had its own scribes, as well trained and as skilled as those in "their synagogues." They may have been the source of the distinctive formula quotations and other biblical exegesis scattered throughout the Gospel.[64] The warning against titles of honor—rabbi, father, teacher—suggests that some Christian teachers had already begun to mimic synagogue usage (23:8–10). Devotional life in the *ekklesia*—almsgiving, prayer, fasting—follows that of the synagogue in everything but the element of public display (6:1–18).[65]

Of course, not everything would be paralleled. Christian baptism and the Eucharist would have set them apart (28:19; 26:26–30) as, no doubt, would the focus of their prayers and devotion. The very existence of the Gospel and its traditions in the community, with their strong christological bent, would have marked them out. Yet the evidence otherwise points to Christians who lived in an overwhelmingly Jewish environment in *ekklesiai* that looked and functioned very much like synagogues.

Christology and Temple

If questions of praxis dominate the Matthean conflict with Judaism, they do not exhaust it. There are several hints that christological issues played their role too. Stanton has noted that Matthew's repeated claim that Jesus is the "Son of David" is several times vigorously opposed by Jewish authorities in passages where the author's redactional hand is clear (2:1–6; 9:27–34; 12:22–24; 21:9,15). There is every reason to suppose that these relate to continuing Jewish opposition to Christian messianic claims. It is much harder to prove that Matthew anticipates the later Christian use of two messianic advents, one in humiliation and one in glory, to explain the obvious discrepancies between Jesus' life and Jewish expectation. Nowhere is the disagreement raised in this form, and the themes of humility and glory are not securely linked with the title "Son of David."[66]

It is possible, too, that the description of Jesus as "that impostor/ deceiver" (27:63–64) and the threefold accusation that he worked in league with the demons (9:34; 10:25; 12:24) connect with later evidence that Jews viewed Jesus as a magician and deceiver (Just.*Dial*.69; b.*Sanh*.43a,107).[67] The former arises in the context of Jesus' public healings, adumbrating the link between miracle and magic that is to recur frequently in the first two centuries. "Deception" is closely associated with the resurrection in Matthew, though in later writers it refers more broadly to the influence he had on his Jewish contemporaries.

The resurrection is singled out because the securing of the tomb (27:63–66) sets the scene for the Jewish plot to subvert Christian claims (28:11–15). The story of the bribing of the soldiers is interesting for a number of reasons. First, there is no reason to doubt Matthew's report that it was "told among the Jews to this day" and that it was a sore point between him and his Jewish contemporaries. Second, it draws attention to a belief that is rarely a point of contention between Jews and Christians elsewhere. The emphasis on resurrection is unique. Third, the casual use of "Jews," recalling Luke-Acts and John, suggests a certain distance between Matthew and his Jewish contemporaries, as if they were entirely separate entities.[68] Matthew makes no similar allusions in his birth narratives. This is surprising, because traces of a lively dispute about the virgin birth can be found in a number of Jewish and Christian sources. Perhaps the inclusion of the narratives is enough to signal that Matthew was aware that they could have, among other things, apologetic value, but this we can only surmise.

The themes of Christology and Temple are directly linked in the passing, but significant, claim that "something greater than the temple is here"

(12:6), and it is interesting that the accusation at Jesus' trial about destroy-
ing the Temple (26:59–63), derisively repeated later (27:40), is followed
immediately by the accusation about his messianic claims (26:63–64).[69] The
Temple accusations presumably relate both to the cleansing of the Temple
precincts (21:12–13) and the prediction of the Temple's destruction (24:2).
There is little that is distinctively Matthean here. Like Mark, he seems to
want to confirm that Jesus predicted the Temple's demise but deny that he
would personally be involved.[70]

The apocalyptic discourse in Matthew is very similar to that of Mark. It
is possible that he has introduced a clearer separation of the destruction of
the Temple and the coming of the end, though that hinges somewhat on
how we understand Mark.[71] At any rate, it is possible that he shared Mark's
eschatological concern. But Matthew goes one step farther. It is widely believed that he inserted an allusion to 70 CE in the parable of the wedding
feast: "He [the king] sent his troops, destroyed those murderers, and burned
their city" (22:7). Here the destruction of the Temple is seen as a judgment
on the Jews for refusing God's invitation and rejecting his messengers. The
same note may be struck in the puzzling passage in 23:37–39. The "desolate" house (v.38) presumably included the Temple, even if it also alluded
to Jerusalem or even the people of Israel as a whole. When it is suggested
that the Jews will greet Jesus at his parousia with the words "Blessed is the
one who comes in the name of the Lord," will they be recognizing him as
savior or as judge?[72] It is clear that Matthew associates the destruction of
the Temple with divine judgment on the Jews. Whether this was his last
word is a question to which the ambiguous 23:39 directs our attention.

Israel's Salvation

The evidence we have considered so far combines expressions of hostility
toward (other) Jews with a tenacious defense of Matthean Christianity as a
legitimate expression of Judaism. Where did this leave Israel? Had they been
irrevocably abandoned, or was there hope for their ultimate salvation? Did
the Matthean *ekklesia* consider itself to be the new or true Israel or part of
the old?

The contrast between the "heirs of the kingdom" and the "many [who]
come from east and west" (8:11) is primarily, in context (v.10 juxtaposes
the centurion and Israel), a contrast between the fate of Jews and Gentiles.
In other contexts the "weeping and gnashing of teeth" is a threat to all,
including Christians (13:42; 22:13; 24:51; 25:30), but that is not the point
here.[73] The aim is to offer a deliberately provocative reversal of Jewish expectation, not to set out in detail the fate of all Jews and Gentiles.

More telling is Matthew's summary of the meaning of the parable of the
vineyard: "The kingdom of God will be taken away from you and given to
a people [*ethnos*] that produces the fruits of the kingdom" (21:43). Although he goes on to note that it was the chief priests and scribes who

concluded that he was talking about them, the use of *ethnos* broadens the scope to include Israel as a whole, of whom the leaders are representative. By using the usual word for Gentile nations (*ethnos*) rather than God's people (*laos*), Matthew implies that the "people" is either a new entity altogether or, if a new Israel, then an Israel that includes Gentiles.[74]

It is natural to turn to the final Christophany for further guidance: "Go therefore and make disciples of all nations [*panta ta ethne*]" (28:19). The critical issue is whether *ethne* means Gentiles (excluding Israel) or nations (including Israel). The latter is rightly becoming the favored view and finds support in 24:9,14. In addition, two things need to be said.[75] First, the commission echoes the earlier, more restricted one (10:5–6) and, by way of contrast, emphasizes particularly the opening of the mission to Gentiles. It is the universalist thrust that most interests Matthew at this point.[76] Second, if the Jews are included in the final commission, they no longer have a special status. They are not the "people" anymore (21:43). This mission, unlike the earlier one, does not distinguish them from Gentiles and Samaritans; they are one among many "nations."[77]

For Matthew, it seems, Israel had lost her special status. On the one hand this meant that another "nation" had inherited the role, though precisely how Matthew would have articulated this if pressed is not entirely clear— perhaps as a new or true Israel, perhaps as an entirely different entity. On the other hand it did not exclude Jews from salvation. They were now on a par with all other nations, and, of course, the only salvation offered was through Christ. This is what we may surmise from scattered hints, but Matthew gives no sustained answer to the question.

Conclusion

All the indications point to Matthew's having been written by and for Jewish Christians who were in conflict with other Jews. They were probably outnumbered and outmaneuvered.[78] This was presumably not the only thing that defined their existence, but it clearly colored their world. It is, as we have noted, difficult to know whether these Jews represented the Yavnean rabbis or some other group. It is no easier to define precisely the relationship between Matthew's church and the synagogue. That it had broken away ideologically and organizationally from non-Christian Judaism seems clear. Equally clear is that the break was not yet a clean one, since the obsession with Jewish matters and the polemic against other Jews show that the ties were still strong. The casual use of "Jews" in 28:15, as of a distinct other, and allusions to the Christian *ekklesia* are the strongest evidence for a separate identity. Involvement in the mission to all nations, if it was under way, would also have distinguished them from vaguer forms of Jewish universalism.[79] But did Matthew see his *ekklesia* as a Christian *synagogos*, as one form of Judaism competing with others rather than a distinct entity moving in a different direction? And would this explain why the church mimicked

synagogue organization feature by feature?[80] Such questions have an ideological and a social component, and they are not unconnected. As to the
first he is, unfortunately, vague; as to the second, we can only guess. Sufficient for our purposes is the certainty that, whether uneasily in or recently
out, the Matthean community, in its Christian way, measured itself in terms
of the predominantly Jewish ethos with which it vigorously came into conflict, a conflict fueled by competing claims to authority.

This points back to the other half of our title, "authority and praxis."
Certain matters of Christian belief, especially Christology, are presented as
a source of contention between Christians and Jews. Other sources confirm
that this was so, thus indicating that Jews were concerned about matters of
belief. But the abiding impression of the Gospel is that the shots were being
called by the other side. For the Christians mimicked the Jews not only in
their organization but also in the emphases of their teaching. They may have
had a Christian view of the law and ethics, of how to do the will of God,
but it was a Christian view of an essentially Jewish phenomenon. It was
Judaism that set the agenda.

LUKE-ACTS: THE SHADOW OF ROME— SYNAGOGUE AND STATE

The most distinctive thing about Luke's account of the relationship between
Christians and Jews is its setting. His story is played out on a broad stage,
which involves the interests of a third party, the Roman state. When he describes the interaction of Jews and Christians, which is clearly complex and
of interest to him in its own right, we find him frequently glancing in the
direction of the Roman political and cultural scene. This is distinctive,
though not unique. The other Gospel writers are not unaware of political
issues, most obviously in their Passion narratives, which are so eager to
blame the Jews and exonerate the Romans. Luke has his own way of enhancing this tendency, as we shall see, and he is also the one who locates
the story of Jesus within the broad context of secular history (Luke 3:1–2).
Unique to Luke, however, is that he wrote Acts, and it is in this second
volume in particular that he transfers us from the world of Galilee, Judaea,
and Jerusalem to that of Asia Minor, Greece, and Rome. The stage broadens
as the story unfolds and, we might suspect, brings us increasingly close to
the sort of situation that Luke and his readers knew well.

Luke's "political" interest has of course been widely recognized and variously assessed—a matter to which we shall return. Our concern is with the
way in which it colors his perception of the Jews. Exactly what impression
Luke was trying to leave us with—and especially what he thought about
the future of the Jews—has been the subject of an impressive number of
recent works. New avenues of argument have been opened up and old ones
retrodden. This is partly because recalcitrant facts outweigh decisive evi-

dence. It is also the result of Luke's ambivalence, once described as follows: "On the one hand, he is unsystematic enough as a theologian and author that no statement about his work can stand without qualification. On the other hand, he is creative enough as a theologian and author to be able to assert contradictory motifs simultaneously and throughout the course of his two-volume work." It is not surprising to find this scholar concluding, with considerable wisdom, that "Luke-Acts is one of the most pro-Jewish and one of the most anti-Jewish writings in the New Testament."[81]

Leaders and People

Prior to the Passion narrative the Jewish people play the role now familiar to us from Matthew and Mark.[82] The common folk (designated by *laos* and *ochlos*) are, with one or two exceptions, favorably disposed toward Jesus. Impressed by the authority of his teaching and awed by his miraculous powers, they receive Jesus gladly and seek him out. The Jewish leaders—scribes, elders, Sadducees, and high priests, as well as the peculiarly Lucan groups, rulers (*archontes*), leaders of the people (*protoi tou laou*), and captains of the Temple (*strategoi*)—are largely hostile. Jealous of his popularity, suspicious of his motives, and determined to put him to death, they bring their machinations to a climax in Jerusalem. In various combinations the same leaders oppose the Christians in Jerusalem (Acts 1–5), Stephen (Acts 6–7), and Paul (Acts 22–28). Initially the Gospel pattern is repeated in Acts as the people respond to the apostles' preaching and healing, holding them in sufficiently high regard to frustrate the rulers' malign intentions (Acts 1–5). Thus far the pattern is familiar, known from the other Gospels, and now merely spilling over into Acts.

Yet there are at least four ways in which Luke expands and alters things. The first is by introducing a lengthy account of Jesus' rejection in Nazareth as the frontispiece to his public activities (Luke 4:16–30). Its peculiar prominence and favored Lucan themes have led many to see it as a miniature overview of the narrative to come. That the fulfillment of prophecy (especially Isaiah) and the actions of the Spirit frequently appear later on can hardly be coincidence. What then of the people's violent reaction and the allusions to the work of Elijah and Elisha among Gentiles? Do they adumbrate Jewish rejection and a turning to the Gentiles, thus providing a firm clue to Luke's intention?[83] That they do to some extent seems difficult to deny, especially since violent Jewish reaction to the inclusion of Gentiles occurs elsewhere (Acts 13:46–50; 22:21–22) and might explain its unexpected appearance here. The point is, however, muted. The incident occurs in Jesus' hometown, and the reaction of the people is uncharacteristic at this stage of the story. Elijah and Elisha illustrate the adage about the prophet without honor as much as the acceptance of Gentiles.[84] It is at any rate clear that at this stage in Jesus' career the crowd's behavior is an aberration.

This is not the whole story. For, secondly, Luke implicates the people in the death of Jesus more deeply than his fellow evangelists.[85] From the arrest (22:47), through the interrogation by Pilate (23:4,13,18,23), to the cruci-fixion itself (23:26,33)—in league with their leaders and Jewish soldiers (22:52; 23:36)—the crowds not only call for, but put into effect, Jesus' cru-cifixion. In the light of repeated declarations of his innocence by Pilate (23:4,14,22), Herod (23:15), and a centurion (23:47), their deed is the more malign. What is narrated in the Gospel is reinforced in the speeches of Acts, which speak openly of Jewish responsibility for the death of Jesus (2:14–39; 3:12–26; 4:9–12; 5:29–32; 10:24–44; 13:16–41).

Luke, typically, leaves some loose ends. The pronouns (they/them) from Luke 23:13 on are vague, some of the people lamented or stood silently by (23:27,35), the soldiers who mocked were probably Roman (23:36), and Pilate and Herod are implicated in the general conspiracy (Acts 4:27–28). Moreover, the leaders rather than the people are sometimes blamed (Luke 24:20; Acts 4:9–12; 5:29–32), an important distinction is made between Jerusalemites and others (Acts 13:16), and some mitigation is granted be-cause of their ignorance and the inexorable working out of the divine plan (Acts 3:17; 13:27). It is not a tidy picture, but the finer distinctions tend to get lost in the blanket claims about Jewish guilt.

This may be related, thirdly, to the monotonous depiction of "the Jews" as the enemies of the church, and especially of Paul, in the second half of Acts.[86] It is true that some Jews convert and that Gentiles oppose Christians too (Acts 16; 19), but the overwhelming impression is that it is the Jews who harass and conspire against them. Sometimes they are specifically called the "unbelieving Jews" (Acts 14:2), a distinction implicit when Jew-ish converts are mentioned in the same breath as hostile "Jews." Yet the sheer repetition of the phrase, here as in John, tends to project an indiscrim-inately negative image. It may well be that the enemies of Paul have colored Luke's perception of the enemies of Jesus.[87]

The fourth distinctive trait is Luke's depiction of the Pharisees. In the Gospel the evidence is mixed. They charge Jesus with blasphemy in re-sponse to christological claims, but their opposition more commonly hinges on halakic issues—eating with the outcasts, hand washing, fasting, and sab-bath rules.[88] Their piety is undercut in the parable of the Pharisee and tax collector (18:9–14) and perhaps in the parable of the prodigal son (15:11–24). They are lovers of money and hypocrites; they court public ac-claim and neglect the essential commands.[89] On the other hand they invite Jesus to eat with them (7:36–50; 11:37–54; 14:2–24), warn him against Herod's plot (13:31), and take no part in events after Jesus' entry into Jerusa-lem (after 19:39). If in the Gospel Luke veers toward the negative side, in Acts he veers toward the positive, even if a note of ambivalence remains. Not only are there Christian Pharisees, including Paul (15:5; 23:6; 26:5), but also non-Christian Pharisees, who publicly defend the church's right to be given the benefit of the doubt (5:34–39; 23:9). Moreover, Paul himself claims that the gist of his message—the resurrection—accords fundamentally with Pharisaic belief (23:6). Luke shares the negative strain with the other evangelists, but only he matches it with a more positive image. Sanders suggests the following explanation: the Pharisees in the Gospel link up with the conservative Pharisaic Christians in Acts 15:5 to represent a Jewish Christianity that Luke, like his apostolic predecessors, firmly rejects; the friendly non-Christian Pharisees in Acts give their imprimatur to the Christian claim that they represent the true Judaism. The first suggestion involves a strained interpretation of the more positive material in the Gospel and an excessively negative judgment on the Pharisaic Christians of Acts 15:5, but the second has been widely endorsed before and since.[90] That the Pharisees were a particularly significant group in post-70 Judaism and that Luke's claim for Christian legitimacy is tied closely to his defense of Paul add further nuances.

The Law and the Prophets

The question of Luke's view of the Jewish law, once neglected, has recently attracted considerable attention.[91] About a number of things there is broad agreement. First, Luke manifestly believed that what happened to Jesus and his followers was in fulfillment of scriptural prophecy (to include this broadly under law for now). From Luke 1 to Acts 28, the story is littered with quotations and statements designed to make just this point. Secondly, Luke writes approvingly of obedience to the law as an expression of Jewish or Jewish Christian piety. This is particularly clear in the birth stories and in the account of Jesus' followers in Acts.[92] Of these, thirdly, the most significant is Paul, who more than any other is held up as a paragon of legal obedience. With him it is not a matter of inference. Repeatedly and explicitly (sometimes absurdly, Acts 23:5) his actions and words demonstrate that he lived rigorously by the law and did nothing to discourage other Jewish Christians from doing the same.[93]

There remain, however, areas of dispute. The most important are Jesus' teaching on the law and the relation of Gentile Christians to the law. They are related to a third issue—the consequences for Christians, Jewish and Gentile, in Luke's day. This last is not a matter of drawing a simple line from the evidence in Luke-Acts to the implied circumstances of Luke's community. As often as not it is the reverse: assumptions about Luke's readership are used to control assessment of the literary evidence. Circular reasoning is to some extent unavoidable, not least because the evidence does not seem to point consistently in one direction—though even that is disputed! In an earlier work I argued that in Luke, Jesus' teaching on the Sabbath (6:1-11; 13:10—14:6), the chief commandments (10:25–28; 18:18–30), burying the dead (9:60), and divorce (16:18) implies that Jesus had challenged and superseded the law but never explicitly says this. At the same time, some sayings seem clearly to state the opposite (16:17). From this I concluded that the issue of Jesus and the law per se did not much agitate Luke, probably because he and his readers were Gentile.[94]

Esler reads the Gospel evidence in much the same way but draws quite different conclusions. He ascribes Luke's inconsistency primarily to his need to cater to both Jews and Gentiles in his mixed community, some of whom kept the law and some of whom did not. Thus, upholding the Sabbath law while disputing the scope of its application and at the same time asserting Jesus' authority over it would allow Jewish and Gentile Christians to draw congenial but opposite conclusions, since both observing and not observing the Sabbath were condoned. The potentially radical saying on divorce, which would have been a well-known feature of Christian teaching, is tamed by being placed next to a statement about the permanence of the law (Luke 16:17–18), thus demonstrating to Jewish Christians that Jesus did not undermine the law. This is one way to explain the evidence, though how it shows that Luke had an "extremely conservative" view of the law is, in the light of Esler's own discussion, beyond me.[95] Esler himself notes that Luke's strategy was flawed: it wouldn't wash, at least with Jewish Christians. They would immediately perceive, for example, that slipping in Luke 16:18 next to Luke 16:17 was "a fairly transparent evasion of the issue."[96] This points to a general problem when we posit more than one group of recipients: is it likely that each group would have been so broad-minded and carefully selective as to take up only what suited them and ignore what seemed to point in a quite different direction? And if Luke was treading so delicate a via media, would he not have been better served by being a bit more forthright, just as he is in Acts?

Klinghardt's somewhat eccentric view moves in the same direction. He also assumes a mixed church of Jews and Gentiles, both committed to the law in their own way. Christians were called to radical almsgiving and divestment of wealth, strict marital rules (Luke 16:18), and avoidance of self-justification. Jewish Christians would also have observed the law, while Gentile Christians were subject only to the legal requirements of the apostolic decree. Almsgiving brought a purity that supplemented (Jews) or compensated for (Gentiles) that brought by the law. Strict marital rules enhanced communal purity and would have been seen by Jews as akin to the rules for Jewish priests and by Gentiles as similar to the purity traditions in popular philosophical thought and pagan cults. These obligations were, in effect, additions to the law. Some traditional obligations were given a new twist. The Sabbath—which Jewish Christians would have observed in addition to Christian celebrations on Saturday evening—was associated with preaching in the synagogue. This, rather than the niceties of Sabbath law, was what held Luke's interest.[97]

Klinghardt surmises that this mixed, strongly Jewish Christian community was in the process of separating from Judaism but still expecting to gain converts among sympathetic Jews. For Jewish Christians and potential

Jewish converts the chief obstacle was not Jesus' role as interpreter of the law, but mixing with Gentiles. Luke tries to cater to both Jews and Gentiles. Klinghardt draws a direct line between groups in the narrative and groups in Luke's community: scribes are equivalent to non-Christian Jews, Pharisees to strict Jewish Christians, the crowds and the marginal to other Jewish Christians, and the God-fearers to the Gentiles. Luke himself stood closest to the crowds and the marginal.[98]

In my view this analysis slides too easily between the Lucan narrative and the Lucan community. We cannot assume that every historical group had a contemporary counterpart, and in this case the groups in the narrative are too loosely defined and too readily susceptible to more than one identification.[99] That Luke had an extraordinary interest in the proper use of wealth is undeniable. The passages that touch on this theme are impressive in number and often unique to Luke.[100] The rich Jewish tradition on almsgiving may well hover in the background, but Luke 11:33, which has a particular polemical sense in context, and vague associations in the story of Cornelius between almsgiving and acceptability in the eyes of God, are not sufficient to prove that Luke's overriding interest lay in the connection between almsgiving and purity.[101] If it was, he missed many an opportunity to make this known. The connection between strict marital rules and purity is even more tenuous since, being absent in the text, it has to be imported from elsewhere. It seems far more likely that Luke includes it not for the complex reasons surmised by Klinghardt, but because it was firmly lodged in the dominical tradition and early Christian practice. And if these connections are not persuasive, nothing demands—though neither does it entirely exclude—a mixed community, let alone one that was predominantly Jewish Christian.[102]

The issue of the Gentiles and the law can be dealt with more briefly.[103] It hinges on the interpretation of the apostolic decree (Acts 15:20,29). In a context where, it is universally agreed, a broad decision is taken not to obligate Gentile Christians to the law of Moses, does the decree nevertheless impose minimal legal obligations on Gentile Christians, equivalent to the biblical rules for "strangers in the land" in Leviticus 17–18, and thus draw them under the aegis of Moses? This is the most commonly held view, and a plausible case can be made for it. But it is also riddled with difficulties, which I have discussed at length elsewhere and which recent discussions have done little to dispel.[104] In my view it remains uncertain whether Luke and his readers would have seen the decree (which they surely obeyed) as a legal obligation based on Mosaic authority or as a customary obligation based on apostolic authority. This uncertainty should make us cautious about jumping to far-reaching conclusions about the church and Israel à la Jervell.

We can conclude this section with a few general observations. First, there is an element of ambiguity in Luke's description of Jesus' view of the law.

This opens it to more than one interpretation, depending in part on what sort of readership we assume. It remains my impression that Luke, unlike Matthew, for example, was not intensely interested in the issue.[105] Second, while Jewish Christians could have pointed to plenty of things in the Gospel, and more in Acts, to support their observance of the law, it does not follow either that this was a point Luke actively wished to make or that there were significant numbers of Jewish Christians in his community. He is most anxious to defend Paul's reputation. This was a particular problem, and it was probably one factor that colored his overall portrait of the Jews. Insofar as he generally approved of Jewish Christian adherence to the law, it was more probably based on his view that Jewish law was appropriate for Jews, Christian or non-Christian, but not for others.[106] Third, the Gentiles, who were by any reckoning part of Luke's community, would as Christians have been subject de facto to many biblical commands, especially those highlighted by Jesus (to love one's neighbor, for example). Whether they or Luke thought the apostolic decree summarized the Mosaic commands for Gentiles, thus extending their obligation in a very specific way, remains unclear.[107]

Jerusalem and the Temple

For Luke the Temple and the city are virtually indistinguishable. Their symbolic force and their ultimate fate are inextricably intertwined. They serve two functions, which are held in tension. On the one hand they provide the central location for the unfolding of salvation history, and on the other they are the place where Jesus and his followers are ultimately rejected. The first of these is apparent as early as the birth narratives (Luke 2:22–52) and continues as Jesus sets his face firmly toward Jerusalem in Luke 9:51. It is from Jerusalem that the message spreads into the world, as Luke programmatically states at the end of the Gospel and the beginning of Acts (Luke 24:47; Acts 1:8). The church initially enjoys considerable success in Jerusalem, and it is the apostles there who oversee the expansion of the movement at least as far as Acts 15. Jerusalem (more than the Temple in this case) is thus far the critical pivot of the narrative, the place where salvation events occur and from which they spread.

Yet there is a dark side too. Jerusalem is also the place where Jesus was rejected and crucified, Stephen martyred (Acts 6–7), and Paul arraigned (Acts 21–28). If it is the focus of salvation, it is also the focus of rejection. In this the Temple plays a specific role. Offenses against the Temple, predicting its destruction and polluting it with Gentiles, are charged to Stephen and Paul (Acts 6:11–15; 21:28; 24:5).

As a consequence, the fate of the city and Temple come to play an emphatic role in the Lucan writings. There are two prophetic warnings unique to Luke 19:41–44, which predicts their destruction because the people did not recognize the time of their visitation; and 23:27–31, which foretells a catastrophe far greater than his death, for which the women grieve. In both of these it is obliquely but firmly suggested that the destruction is related to the rejection of Jesus by his people. The obscure prediction in Luke 13:33–35 reinforces this theme if, as is likely, the forsaking of their "house" refers to the destruction of city and Temple and the greeting of "the one who comes" refers to Jesus' parousia.[108] The allusions to Jerusalem's killing of the prophets and refusal of Jesus' offer of broody care likewise bring together his fate with that of the city and Temple. It is widely agreed that these, together with Luke 21:20–24, were written after 70 CE, that the events they predict had already occurred. Luke 21:20–24 retains its position in the apocalyptic schema, as in the other Synoptics, but for Luke it was an event of the past and no longer coincident with the end. No connection is made here with the rejection of Jesus, but in association with the other passages it is natural to infer it.

Is this, then, Luke's last word, that the place so central to salvation has become a place of damnation? This is the usual view, but some have tried to find a glimmer of hope for the future.[109] When it is said that the people will greet Jesus with the words "Blessed is the one who comes in the name of the Lord" (Luke 13:35), some think it implies a recognition that leads to salvation—though in that case it says nothing about the fate of the city and Temple. More to the point, the temporal limitation of Luke 21:24—that Jerusalem will be trodden down "until the times of the Gentiles are fulfilled" (emphasis added)—is taken by some to imply ultimate redemption. In biblical prophecies, it is argued, destruction is followed by restoration and judgment by vindication (Deut 32; Zech 12:3; Ezek 39:23; Amos 9:13–14; Joel 13–14 [LXX]; 2 Apoc.Bar. 67–68). It is further suggested that since Luke does not substitute the church or Jesus as the new temple, as do other early Christian writers, the way is left open for its restoration as part of the restoration of Israel (Acts 1:6).[110] Finally, Jerusalem's role as the supreme meeting place between God and the world, the axis mundi, would have constrained Luke, we must suppose, from abandoning hope for it altogether.[111]

These are not strong arguments. We cannot assume that when Luke uses one half of a prophetic prediction it automatically carries with it the other. The connection is not inexorable, and we would require at least a broad hint from Luke to make it so. This he does not provide. And while it is true that Luke does not speak of a substitute temple, it would be rash to conclude that its restoration is included in the obscure statement by the disciples in Acts 1:6, a statement that Jesus both deflects and corrects. Indeed, the comments in Stephen's speech (Acts 7:44–50; cf. 17:24–25), whatever precisely they are saying about the existing Temple, do not encourage the notion of its restoration.[112] Finally, there is no doubt that Jerusalem was for Jews the axis mundi, and that Luke shares some of their sense of its centrality. But for him it is central to a salvation-historical process, which progresses and ends, we should not forget, in another axis mundi—Rome. All in all, these arguments rely too heavily on obscure hints and silence. If we follow Luke where he is explicit and follow the broad drift of his narrative, it is difficult to avoid the conclusion that for him the time for Jerusalem and its Temple was over. [113]

The Future of Israel

It is universally agreed that Luke wishes to present Christianity as an extension of Judaism. The notion suffuses his narrative, from the broad Jewish matrix in which the Christian movement is born, through constant references to prophetic fulfillment and the early Christians' faithfulness to their Jewish heritage, to specific claims that they are God's people (*laos*, Acts 15:14), a people with the distinctive name "Christian" (Acts 11:26; 26:28). The continuous history of salvation, stretching back to the patriarchs and broadening out to include the Gentile church, is a core Lucan theme.[114]

How Christianity related to the old Israel is disputed. That it was enfolded within, an extension of, or a substitute for Israel in the Lucan scheme is not finally clear. More vigorously contested in recent discussion is what this implies for the fate of the Jewish people. There is a simple enough reason for this—the evidence is ambiguous. In discussing Luke's view of Jerusalem and the Temple, we considered a number of the relevant sayings (Luke 13:35; 21:24; Acts 1:6). Given their obscurity and the broad narrative context in which they appear, they provide little hope of a bright future for Jerusalem or the Jews. The same can be said of the one other passage, Acts 3:19–20, which does speak of "times of refreshing" and the fulfillment of God's ancient promises but does not specify exactly what this entails. If it expresses hope for the Jews, then, as in Luke 13:35, the context suggests it will be a future not as Jews, but as Christian Jews, those who repent and recognize their Messiah. All in all, there seems to be little warrant for projecting from these disparate, obscure sayings a positive future for the Jews and nothing to suggest that Luke harbored an expectation for their salvation as Jews, as Paul perhaps did in Romans 11. Luke is not reluctant to make his views known, and on an issue as important as this he would surely have been clearer.[115]

But, then, some would argue that he is, in the other strain of evidence we must now consider—the speeches and narratives of Acts. It is undeniable that the Jews appear here in two guises, as converts and as opponents. It is to Jervell's credit that he has forced on our attention the scale of Jewish conversions in Acts.[116] Early in the narrative they are consistently numbered in thousands, and the Jews continue to respond positively to Christian preaching until the end. We might dispute whether the myriads of Acts 21:20 refer to the Jerusalem springtime or to later successes, and we might note that success among the Jews tends to decline as the narrative progresses, but the overall drift is clear. Equally clear is the routine depiction of the Jews as the enemies of the church. They constantly oppose, harass, and plot against the Christians, bend the ears of political authorities, and generally stir up trouble.[117]

These two features, Jewish opposition and Jewish conversion, tug in opposite directions, and how we weigh them tends to affect our interpretation of the final strand—Luke's programmatic statements, especially the one that draws the narrative to its conclusion. When Paul and his companions declare that as the result of Jewish opposition they will turn to the Gentiles (Acts 13:46; 18:6), it is clear that Luke is telling us something important about his perception of the course of events. Yet the mission to the Jews continues, if only with modest success. For the third and final time, Paul, backed up by Isaiah, makes the same declaration in Rome (Acts 28:26–28). What does Luke mean by this?

In favor of the view that it leaves the door open for the Jews are a number of observations. First, despite the earlier programmatic statements, the mission to the Jews continued with some success; the same pattern should be assumed here. Second, some Jews in Rome were "persuaded" (*epeithonto*, Acts 28:24), a verb that may not always carry the connotation of full belief but in this verse, as the opposite of *epistoun*, probably does. Jewish opposition here, as elsewhere, was not unanimous. Third, Isaiah 6 is used to explain Jewish unbelief, not to signal Jewish rejection. Fourth, the last part of Acts is concerned not so much with the progression of the Christian movement as with the fate of Paul. Fifth, when the penultimate verse (Acts 28:30) says Paul welcomed all who came to him, "all" includes Jews. Sixth, when Paul claims that he is on trial for the "hope of Israel" (Acts 28:20; cf. 23:6; 24:15; 26:6), this entails hope for their salvation.[118]

The opposite conclusion is reached by observing, first, that *epeithonto* normally means something like "positively disposed toward" rather than "fully accepting of," and could still carry that meaning here.[119] Second, despite the absence of Jewish opposition, Paul suddenly turns on them ("this people" v.27) with a quotation that holds out no further hope ("they will *never* perceive/understand," v.26, emphasis added); instead salvation will go to the Gentiles, who will listen (v.28).[120] Third, although Acts clearly is concerned with the fate and reputation of Paul, where Paul goes so goes the Christian movement, as earlier it had gone largely with Peter. It is Luke's way to write history biographically. Fourth, when Paul speaks of the "hope of Israel," which is associated with the resurrection, it is merely one of Luke's ways (however implausible) of associating Paul with the Pharisees and demonstrating that he was a faithful Jew. It does not carry with it, unless specified, hope for the salvation of the Jews. Finally, the position of the scene at the end of Acts gives it an air of finality. The Jews have believed, but in declining numbers. They, like Jerusalem, have had their turn. Now the gospel has reached Rome, the Gentile *axis mundi,* and the impetus of the narrative points inexorably to a Gentile future.[121]

The evidence is delicately balanced. If one scholar can conclude that

"Luke has written the Jews off," another can say that "since the only type of Christianity that Luke describes maintains its relationship with Judaism, it is a blind leap off the end of Acts to a Lucan church free from Judaism."[122] How we read Acts 28 depends on a number of factors. Does Jewish belief or Jewish opposition, both manifest elsewhere in the narrative, weigh the more heavily in the end? Is it important that belief declines and opposition increases as the narrative works to its conclusion? Is it significant that in speeches the Jews are almost invariably condemned, whereas in the narratives their response is divided?[123] How much of what Luke tells us belongs purely to the past, a description of the origins of a movement that is now rather different?[124] Or, to turn this round, what elements point to the future, that is, to Luke's present? To what extent would Luke's audience have affected the reception of his narrative? A wholly or predominantly Gentile Christian audience might have read it one way, but one with a significant Jewish Christian membership, another.

In the end it is the impetus of the narrative that seems to me to point in the direction of a largely Gentile future. The setting in Rome and the ringing declaration that the Gentiles will hear seem to point beyond the limits of the narrative to a time when the mission of the church will be addressed predominantly and successfully to Gentiles. Nothing encourages a hope for the Jews as Jews, and the time of mass conversions lies, according to Acts itself, in the past. It does not follow that Luke had any objection to Jewish Christians, that there were none in his community, or that he would have discouraged individual conversions. But the future lay elsewhere.[125]

Miracles and Magic

Like the other Synoptic Gospels, Luke contains several stories in which Jesus displays his miraculous powers. These are reinforced by the inclusion of many similar stories scattered throughout Acts. Like the Gospel stories, they are clearly designed to enhance the standing of the miracle workers, to show that they had access to divine inspiration. As noted above, there may not have existed any precisely defined notion of a "divine man," but it can scarcely be doubted that in the ancient world miraculous powers were widely considered to be evidence of intimacy with the divine. That it was true for the world Luke wrote within and for is indicated by the frequency and prominence of these stories.

In Acts there is apparently an additional purpose, since the miracles that are not ascribed to direct divine intervention (breaking down prison doors, Acts 12:1–11, for example) are worked through Peter and Paul. As has often been noted, they are almost exactly parallel in both type and number, none-too-subtly drawing to the attention of the reader that Peter and Paul were to be seen on a par. Precisely what Luke had in mind when he did this has been a matter of considerable dispute and involves complex questions which reach deep into the history and divisions of the early Christian movement. For the moment the broad purpose is all we need to note.

There is at least one other purpose, hinted at in the Beelzebul controversy in the Gospels (Luke 11:14–23 parallels), but quite explicit in Acts: the conflict between Jewish and Christian miracle workers.[126] On the periphery lies the conflict with Simon Magus (Acts 8:9–24), a Samaritan rather than a Jew, a famous and self-promoting magician who is overwhelmed by the signs and miracles worked by the apostles. Many standard themes appear—divine inspiration (v.10), competing talents (v.13), financial involvement (vv.18,20)—and Simon is decisively humiliated when he tries to muscle in on the powers of the Spirit. The Jewish "false prophet" and "magician," Bar-Jesus/Elymas, attempts to stall Paul's success with the proconsul Sergius Paulus (Acts 13:6–12). Nothing is said about Elymas's magical deeds, but he is exposed as a "son of the devil," an "enemy of all righteousness," and blinded by Paul's magical curse. The Christian is superior to the Jew, not only in prophetic insight but also in sheer magical power. More striking is the tussle between Paul and the seven sons of the Jewish high priest, Sceva (Acts 19:11–20). When these itinerant Jewish exorcists try to mimic Paul and cast out demons in the name of Jesus, they are leapt on by the possessed man, overpowered, and disbanded. After the news spreads throughout Ephesus, many of those who had previously practiced magic voluntarily and publicly burn their books. A more dramatic and decisive demonstration of the superiority of Christian over Jewish magic could scarcely be conceived.

Two things distinguish these stories from others in the New Testament. First, the conflict with Jewish magicians/exorcists is so open, direct, and dramatic that Luke's point cannot be missed. It is notable, second, that the two conflicts with Jewish magicians take place in public and not within the confines of a Christian or Jewish community. In one case the house of a proconsul and in the other the whole city of Ephesus provides the stage. Jewish-Christian conflict over magic and miracles is not an internal affair, but a public dispute in which they vie for popular and official acclaim. It is true that there are many miracle stories that bypass this theme, as there are other motives for relating them, but we would probably not go far wrong to suppose that Luke told these stories with an awareness of an aspect of Jewish-Christian conflict that reached up to and beyond his day.

The Political Context

The discussion of miracles returns us to our opening comments. A great deal of what Luke says about Jews and Judaism is colored by the broader social and political circumstances in which he wrote. This may sound trite, since the same could surely be said of any early Christian writing. It is, however, a matter of emphasis. In Matthew, for example, intense conflicts between Jews and Christians are circumscribed by the boundaries of church and synagogue. They are internal to the interests and agenda of these two groups, to the extent that some think they were still effectively subdivisions within one larger entity—Judaism. Luke, while inevitably covering some of the same ground and occasionally matching Matthew's rancorous tone, places the emphasis on different themes and the debate in a broader context. These are not unrelated, since the emphases reflect the context. Jews and Christians may still take aim at each other, but they do so while vying for the attention of political authorities. The debate has, as it were, become public. This impression comes largely from Acts, but then Luke did choose to write a second volume, and it provides important clues to his purpose.[127]

As a description of what Luke relates, this is hardly controversial. It is more difficult to know precisely in what way Luke reflects his own circumstances and the message he intended for his audience. It has long been assumed that he had a political purpose. Initially it was thought that he was attempting to present Christianity to the Roman world as a peaceable, respectable movement with no subversive intent. Thus political authorities and their judgment on representative Christians are cast in the most favorable possible light, in the hope of influencing their successors. One strand in this argument was the relationship to Judaism. While some proposed that Christians were presented as quite distinct from Jews, who were tainted by their recently failed rebellion, the majority thought Luke wished Christianity to be seen as the one legitimate form of Judaism and thus as a *religio licita,* deserving of all the privileges that the Jews themselves already enjoyed. In its different forms the argument ran into several difficulties. *Religio licita,* it has been noted, is not a Roman but a Christian concept—though that hardly alters the fact that Jews had privileges that Christians might well have envied. That disinterested Roman officials would scarcely have waded through so much irrelevant material in order to cull this political message and that, had they done so, they would have found the portrait of some of their predecessors to be distinctly unflattering, were observations that raised further doubts.[128]

The notion of Luke-Acts as an apology primarily addressed to the outside world is untenable. The manner in which Luke dedicates his books to "most excellent" Theophilus indicates that we should not entirely exclude from Luke's audience interested and educated people from the upper echelons of society.[129] Yet it is unlikely that they were the chief target, and most of the problems disappear if we assume, as is now more common, that Luke addressed his political message to Christians, to cultivate in them a sense of their identity and their place in the world, of the appropriate stance toward political authority, and the generally benign response it was likely to receive.[130]

According to Acts, this was not simply a two-way relationship between Christians and Romans. A third group, the Jews, were a critical element in the sociopolitical arena. Part of the way in which Luke constructed his posi-

tive political image of Christians was to construct a correspondingly negative image of the Jews. If Christians were peaceable and law-abiding, Jews
were troublesome and seditious.[131] There is a recognizable pattern to Luke's
description of this three-way relationship as it appeared in the public
sphere:

—Typically it is the Jews who stir up trouble for Christians and accuse
them before political authorities, arguing that they ignore the laws of the
Jews and defy the authority of Rome (e.g., Acts 17:6–7; 18:13; 24:12–13).
Ironically, Jewish machinations show them to be guilty of the very things
they hold against Christians.
—Christians protest their innocence of any charge based on Jewish or
Roman law (especially Acts 25:8). Often they claim that they are merely
promoting a form of common Jewish belief (Acts 23:6; 24:14–21; 26:23;
28:20).
—Roman officials consistently confirm Christian innocence in the face
of accusations by Romans (Acts 16) or, more usually, Jews. The extreme
expression of this is when Paul is sent to Rome not because he is guilty but
because he insists on a hearing before Caesar (Acts 26:32). The abiding
conclusion of Roman officials is that Christians were involved in an internal
squabble, matters concerning Jewish laws and customs that had no place in
a Roman court (Acts 23:29; 25:18–19).

The curious feature in this pattern is the Christian claim, acceded to by
Roman officials, that they were promoting a form of Judaism. It muddies
the otherwise clear attempt to enhance the positive image of Christians with
a negative image of the Jews. This, among other things, has led W. Stegemann to propose a more complex explanation of the political message of
Luke and to root it in a specific historical situation. In brief, he suggests
the following:

—That Luke wrote during the reign of Domitian. There was no official
persecution, but Gentile Christians, whom the Romans associated with Judaism (as in Acts), would be subject to two pressures: the extension of the
Jewish tax, and the charge of *maiestas* against the emperor leveled at Gentiles (like Clemens and Domitilla) who had taken up a Jewish way of life.
—That the separation between church and synagogue was long-
established. The Jews had every reason to keep their distance, viewing
Christians as a politically embarrassing messianic sect who pilfered from
the ranks of socially influential God-fearers, promoted a liberal view of the
law, and supported a substantial Gentile membership which threatened Jewish identity. To reinforce their separate identity, the Jews may well have denounced the Christians to state authorities.
—That Christians saw some advantage in being ranked with Jews, arguing that they were involved in an intra-Jewish squabble. They may have

been subject to the Jewish tax and to Rome's xenophobic suspicion of the Jews, but they might have deflected the charge of *maiestas* associated with their Judaizing and enjoyed the protection accorded the larger and better-established community of Jews.

The Christian dilemma was as follows: they wanted to be seen as Jews to avoid the charge of Judaizing, though not the sort of troublesome Jews that the Romans suspected them of being; the Jews wanted nothing to do with them and did everything to fan Roman suspicion. They were squeezed between synagogue and state. It is this dilemma that Luke reflects and tries to resolve by suggesting that Christianity was a peaceable form of Judaism, a claim that Christians made and Romans confirmed, that they were involved in nothing more than an intra-Jewish dispute, and that troublesome disturbances and church-synagogue separation were the responsibility entirely of the Jews.[132]

This is by far the most thoroughgoing and subtle analysis of Luke's political message, which, Stegemann believes, was aimed at Gentile Christians.[133] As a description of the political dilemma that Luke reflects it makes two significant advances: it takes precise account of the many different strands in the text that make up the interplay between Christians, Jews, and Romans; and it provides a concrete sociopolitical context for a text whose message has previously been only vaguely located in the last quarter of the first century. As we saw in chapter 1, Domitian's extension of the Jewish tax may have swept up Christians and others who seemed like Jews, and the charge of Judaizing had (in some cases) serious consequences. If Luke simply reflects a dilemma, then this is the best account of it we have.

If, however, Luke intends to recommend to his readers a particular form of action, what would that have been? It depends on precisely how we envisage their situation. If they had already been subjected to the Jewish tax, they may have tried to make the best of a fait accompli, that is, by paying the tax and claiming that they were to be treated as Jews and not as Judaizers. As a tactical ploy in a delicate situation it might have worked for a while. At any rate, it tossed the ball back into the Roman court. If, however, Christians were trying to initiate things—by requesting to pay the tax and to be treated as Jews—in the face of Roman resistance and Jewish objections, it would have been an uphill struggle. At an earlier stage (that depicted in Acts) it might have been difficult for outsiders to distinguish Jews from Christians, and Roman officials might well have judged their disputes to be *intra muros*. But by the time of Domitian, when Christians were ethnically and organizationally separate from the Jews and the Jews themselves publicly denied any association with Christians (the situation Stegemann envisages), would the Romans have been convinced? Would they have distinguished between non-Christians who Judaized and Christians who (against all observable evidence) claimed to be Jews? If they had been Jewish Christians, perhaps, yet according to Stegemann they were Gentiles. The ploy might have worked if the authorities wanted to settle a tiresome dispute and enlarge their tax base, but it would have been a gamble. Since we have no clear picture of what went on during the reign of Domitian, we can only speculate. But it seems more likely, on Stegemann's hypothesis, that Luke was responding to, rather than initiating, the association of Christians with Jews.[134]

Stegemann has taken us a long way, even if puzzling questions remain. From our perspective he has convincingly underlined the public, political context of Luke's account of the relationship between Jews and Christians. This does not exclude other motivations.[135] As we suggested above, Luke's treatment of the law suggests that he was countering a negative image of Paul spread by Jews or Jewish Christians. His pervasive assumption that Christianity was a legitimate extension of Judaism would have fostered a sense of identity as much as it would have demonstrated Christian antiquity to the Roman world. These are important, but Luke's distinctive approach is to project the relationship between Jews and Christians onto the public stage and in the presence of a third party. In so doing, of course, the dispute ceases to be *intra muros*. Christian enmity toward Jews becomes a public affair.

JOHN: THE SHADOW OF ORTHODOXY— FROM MESSIANISM TO DITHEISM

That the Gospel of John is obsessively christological is obvious to even the most casual reader. So, of course, are the other Gospels, in the sense that Jesus is the chief object of their attention. In John, however, Jesus' origin and identity, his relation to the Father and the Spirit/Paraclete, his descent to an uncomprehending world and ascent in glory are explored so extensively and so publicly that they cast all other persons and themes into the shade. Nor is it just a matter of extent. Johannine Christology, in the level of its profundity and subtlety, is of a quite different order than that of the Synoptics. It moves, as has often been noted, farther in the direction of later Christian orthodoxy than any other early document, so much so that it has been all too easy to retroject later disputes and definitions into it where they do not belong. It is partly in this sense that I use the word "orthodoxy" in the title above. I also intend an allusion to the common distinction between Judaism and Christianity in terms of orthopraxy and orthodoxy, practice and belief—a distinction that is convenient, though misleading if too rigorously applied. The term "orthodoxy" is thus designed to draw attention to the central issue on which Jewish-Christian debate in this Gospel turns: christological belief which, at least in the later redactions of the Gospel, had reached a fairly advanced stage. To put it another way, if in Matthew the agenda is set by Jews, here it is set by Christians.[136]

When looking at the Synoptic Gospels, it is to some degree possible to survey the relevant data before considering what might explain them. With John this is more difficult.[137] It is a much more uneven, layered text, notorious for its aporias and tensions. This has led to a multitude of reconstructions related to two main issues: the history of the text and the history of the community. As to the first, it has been surmised that the Gospel evolved in stages as the result of a long and complex process of composition. Following the accumulation of stories by the founder of the community, it is widely believed that a short signs source/gospel—containing accounts of Jesus' miraculous deeds and, perhaps, a Passion narrative—was composed. Subsequently, and partly in reaction to the simple theology of the signs gospel, the tradition was expanded—perhaps once, perhaps more than once—by the addition of increasingly sophisticated theological reflection in the form of discourses placed on the lips of Jesus. The author(s) at this intermediate stage is usually thought to have been the presiding theological genius responsible for the bulk of the Gospel as we know it. At a later, third stage, the Gospel was touched up by a final redactor with the addition of at least chapter 21 and perhaps more besides.

It is commonly believed, secondly, that the evolution of the document was related closely to the evolution of the community. This is of particular relevance because the evolution of the community is thought to have been affected more than anything else by its relationship to the synagogue. The most commonly accepted hypothesis divides this story into three stages too. The first Johannine Christians were Jews, who participated in the communal life of the synagogue and couched their evangelical message in terms that adapted and expanded Jewish messianic expectations. This would correspond roughly to the first stage of the Gospel, including oral reminiscences about Jesus (e.g., John 1:35–49) and a gospel of signs. No doubt many Jews thought them odd, but they had some success and were left to go about their business.

Then, secondly, came a traumatic rupture with the synagogue, which resulted in Christians who openly confessed their faith being expelled. This is reflected clearly in the allusions to believers', or potential believers', being cast out of the synagogue (*aposynagogos*, 9:22; 12:42; 16:2). Some may have been put to death (16:2; cf. 10:28, 15:18). Compounding the problem may have been believers who preferred to remain within the synagogue rather than openly confess their faith.[138] What caused this rupture remains obscure, but a plausible thesis is that as the Christology of the community moved increasingly in the direction of ditheism, with its bold claims about Jesus' divinity and intimate relationship to God, it broached the limits of what was acceptable to Judaism. The shift from messianism toward ditheism, which we shall consider further below, may give us one clue about a situation that otherwise remains obscure.[139] About one thing we can be sure: the Johannine community parted ways with the synagogue and established an independent community congruent with increasingly independent strains of thought and a sectarian mentality. The first edition(s) of the Gospel, reflecting past traumas and articulating new realities, appeared at this time.[140]

In the third and final stage, the community consolidated its position with increasingly bold christological claims cast in a starkly dualistic mode of thought, which expressed alienation from Judaism and the world at large. It also began to look inward, to tensions and disagreements arising within the community, some of which came to expression in the final redaction of the Gospel and the Johannine letters.[141] As internal divisions became more prominent, the problem of Judaism faded into the background, so that while it retains its place in the final redaction of the Gospel it goes unmentioned in the letters.

This thumbnail sketch is sufficient for our purposes. It highlights a universally recognized fact which is independent of the details of any particular theory: that the depiction of Jews and Judaism in John expresses the troubled history of the relationship between his community and the synagogue. If it is accepted that Johannine Christians were at one stage expelled from the Jewish community, there must have been a time before when they lived within it and a time after when they did not—and this gives us *in nuce* the three stages noted above. It is not essential to connect the expulsion from the synagogue with the *Birkat ha-minim*.[142] As has been noted, a curse on the *minim*, insofar as Christians thought it applied to them, would have made attendance at the synagogue and participation in the prayers difficult. That would have set up a situation more like that in Acts 18–19, where Christians left the synagogue of their own accord in response to Jewish hostility, which is not quite the same as Jewish authorities' expelling them on account of their christological beliefs, as in John. But this may be to require too precise a match between the different strands of evidence. At the least, the *Birkat ha-minim* was designed to make Christians and other heretics distinctly unwelcome, and its effects may have been different from time to time and place to place. That in one case Christians were forcibly expelled, whether or not by the use of a liturgical curse, need not be doubted.[143]

If there is general agreement on the picture sketched above, there is less agreement on the degree to which tensions with the synagogue were a live issue influencing the composition of the Gospel. Some think that the community was still essentially Jewish Christian, that the wounds of separation were not yet healed, and that this shows through at all levels of the text. At the other extreme are those who think the community was predominantly Gentile and the conflict with the synagogue so far in the past that it neither haunted them nor had any significant influence on the composition of the Gospel. The evidence of the text is ambiguous. When the Pharisees ask of Jesus in 7:35, "Does he intend to go to the Dispersion among the Greeks and teach the Greeks?" does it mean Jews or Greeks in the Jewish diaspora?

Even if the latter, the question is more rhetorical than predictive. The Greeks (*hellenes*) who come to worship in Jerusalem at Passover and ask to see Jesus (12:20–21) might be God-fearers, proselytes, or diaspora Jews. If Gentiles, they are mentioned only here, unless phrases like "other sheep that do not belong to this fold" (10:16) and "the dispersed children of God" (11:52) allude to them too. References to "their" or "your" law (8:17; 10:34; 15:35), "a festival of the Jews" (5:1; 6:4; 7:2), and the explanation of Jewish terms and customs (e.g., 1:38,41) give some support for a Gentile component in the community, but they could also be the language of a Jewish Christian conventicle which saw itself as entirely separate from the Jews. My impression is that the community was predominantly Jewish and that if there were Gentile members they did not loom large at the time of writing. The rupture with the synagogue lies in the past, perhaps the not-too-distant past, but the community already seems to be living physically and mentally at a greater distance from Judaism than, say, the Matthean churches.[144] At any rate, the conflict between Jesus and the Jews takes up such a sizable portion of the narrative and is so manifestly updated to reflect later conflicts that it is difficult to suppose that the issue lay entirely in the past.

The Jews and Related Groups

The term *Ioudaios/Ioudaioi* occurs seventy-one times in John, far more than in the Synoptic Gospels and matched only by the eighty occurrences in Acts. Many of these are neutral—references to Judaeans as distinct from Samaritans/Galileans/Gentiles, to Jesus' contemporaries, and to festivals and customs of the Jews.[145] Others are more positive, describing sympathetic Jews (11:19,31,33,36) and even asserting that "salvation is from the Jews"—presumably as distinct from the Samaritans (4:22).

More significant are the hostile uses of *hoi Ioudaioi* to refer to the enemies of Jesus and his followers. The most careful recent analysis comes up with thirty-seven uses of this kind.[146] Not everyone's tally would be precisely the same, but all would agree that approximately half of John's uses of the term have this sense. Typically "the Jews" in these passages view Jesus with suspicion and hostility, dispute with him, accuse him of demon possession and blasphemy, plot against him, and finally arrest him and have him put to death. There is a discernible pattern: in chapters 1–4 the Jews are suspicious but not especially hostile, and in chapters 13–17 they are alluded to only once (13:33). The bulk of the hostile uses are in chapters 5–12 and 18–19, of which the most intemperate are to be found in 8:31–59 with its summary judgment that the Jews are children of the devil (8:44).[147]

As to the Passion, there are ways in which the role of the Jews is diminished in comparison with the Synoptics: Romans are involved in Jesus' arrest (18:3,12); there is no official meeting of the Sanhedrin, in fact, hardly any Jewish "trial" at all; and there is less abuse of Jesus by the Jews. If in some ways John lessens, in others he heightens, their responsibility. He underlines Pilate's passive role, extending the pressure from the Jews with arguments ostensibly based on their own law (19:7) and on the political realities of Roman rule (19:12,15), and even has Pilate hand Jesus over to the Jews for crucifixion (19:16; but cf. 19:23,31). Most significant, however, is the insidious, indiscriminate use of "the Jews" in chapters 18–19 to describe those primarily responsible for Jesus' death. And whatever fine adjustments John makes to the Passion narrative, they scarcely diminish the unequivocal designation of the Jews as the murderers of Jesus elsewhere in the Gospel (8:40,44).

It is commonly noted that groups familiar from the other Gospels—scribes, Sadducees, Herodians—do not appear in John. Those that do—Pharisees, chief priests, rulers—appear less frequently and seem to be interchangeable with, and therefore subsumed under, the Jews. A good example occurs in chapter 9, where the terms "Pharisees" (9:13,15,16,40) and "Jews" (9:18,22) alternate while clearly referring to the same group (cf. 1:19,24; 7:32,35; 8:13,22). In John these groups lose much of their distinct identity and are swept up in the more comprehensive term "Jews," thus reinforcing their uniformity as a group.[148]

The picture is, however, not quite so clear as it might seem. Jesus and his disciples were of course Jews, but are spoken of as if they were different from "the Jews." Contrasted with the Jews are Galileans (also Jews, but not called such), who are initially receptive to Jesus' deeds and words (1:35–51; 2:22; 4:43–45; 7:47–52) and Samaritans, who accept him as savior of the world (4:39–42). The terms "Galilean" and "Samaritan" are less geographical than they are symbolic designations. They stand, over and against the hostile Jews, for those who accept and believe in Jesus.[149] Similarly, the term "Israel" carries positive connotations (1:31; 12:13), especially in the story of Nathanael (1:47–49), and by reverse in the description of the initially baffled Nicodemus, who is not a true teacher of Israel (3:10, though later references, 7:50–52 and 19:38–42, show him in a more positive light). To some extent it also contrasts with "the Jews" who reject Jesus.[150] On occasions "the Jews" are divided over the meaning of Jesus' message (6:52; 10:19–21); some, presumably Jews but not so designated, believe in him (7:31; 10:42); and even some of the "authorities" believe, but do not confess for fear of the Pharisees (12:41–43). Most unexpected are references to "Jews" who believe (2:23; 11:45; 12:11) and the puzzling reference in 8:30–31, which seems out of place in its immediate context.[151]

It is proper to recognize that *hoi Ioudaioi* are not always neutral or hostile. But the few allusions to an ambivalent or positive response to Jesus do little to balance the heavily negative use of the term, the more striking in view of the positive use made of the terms Galilean, Samaritan, and Israelite. Two attempts have been made to take the sting out of John's language. M. Lowe suggested that, with the possible exception of 18:20, the hostile uses always refer to inhabitants of Judaea in general or their leaders in particular.[152] This may be the case in 7:1; 11:7–8, and a few other passages (12:9,11; 19:20), but it scarcely makes sense of phrases like "festival of the Jews," which seems to have a broader sense, and "Jewish rites of purification" (2:6), which occurs during the wedding in Galilee. It has been noted, moreover, that since in the ancient world groups of people were commonly designated by their place of origin or principal deity, the translation "Judaeans" would neither narrow the sense of the term nor explain why they were selected for the role John assigns to them.[153] Von Wahlde's suggestion is that, with the exception of 6:41,52, all uses of *hoi Ioudaioi* refer to religious authorities rather than the common people.[154] In many contexts this appears to be the case, but it leaves a number of things unexplained, not least the way in which John deliberately uses a broad and inclusive term to designate religious authorities when several more precise terms (some of which he occasionally does use) were readily at hand.

Two further observations are pertinent. We must first take account of John's characterization of the *Ioudaioi*—the nature and significance of their role in the narrative. Even if the initial reference was to Judaeans or religious authorities, we have to ask why they were singled out for such unrelentingly negative treatment and how this distinctive and dominant use of *Ioudaioi* colors all the other uses in the Gospel. That is, there is a distinction between referent and sense, between the quotidian and the symbolic use of a term. We must take account, secondly, of the circumstances in which the Gospel was received. Given that *Ioudaios* was a term familiar to Jews (especially in the diaspora) and non-Jews for designating the Jews as a whole, would that not most likely have been the sense conveyed by John's use of the term?[155] And this would have been true even though many Johannine Christians were themselves Jews, because by the time of writing, non-Christian Judaism had become to them something totally other, an alien entity. Thus if we bear in mind that the Gospel was by almost any reckoning produced outside of Judaea, that it reflects tensions between Christians and Jews that arose long after the time of Jesus, and that in typically Johannine fashion the term *Ioudaioi* comes to have as much a symbolic as a quotidian sense, there is every reason to think that the term has shifted decisively from a local to a universal plane of meaning. *Hoi Ioudaioi* have become the Jews in general.

Law, Temple, and Festivals

John deals with the law in typically distinctive fashion. There is first the core assertion in the prologue—"The law . . . was given through Moses; grace and truth came through Jesus Christ" (1:17)—which is immediately reinforced by a claim about the exclusive revelation of the Father through the Son (1:18). This we might consider to be John's primary statement of principle on the matter, in which the superiority of Christ is asserted at the expense of Moses and the law. The law is not so much criticized as subordinated.

The sense in which this subordinate role is to be understood, secondly, is suggested in the statements about the predictive role of Moses, the law, and the prophets. They "write" of Jesus Christ and bear witness to him (1:45; 5:39,45–47), and the actions of Moses anticipate the lifting up of the Son of Man or Jesus' feeding of the multitudes (3:14; 6:32). Here Moses and the law have a positive but secondary role.

In some places, thirdly, John reports controversy over specific legal obligations. One concerns his self-testimony (8:17–18) and another the observance of the Sabbath (5:1–18; 7:19–24; 9:13–17). It is striking that while these stories start out looking like the sort of controversy familiar from the other Gospels, the interest rapidly shifts from legal to christological issues. There are precedents in the Synoptics, but in John the shift is quite pronounced. He seems little interested in the niceties of legal obedience. He does at one point turn the law against itself by claiming that it allows breaking of the Sabbath in exceptional circumstances (7:19–24), but in general this is not the mode of argument he prefers. For him the disputes are a springboard for christological assertion. Thus Jesus is attacked "because he was not only breaking the Sabbath, but was also calling God his own Father, thereby making himself equal to God" (5:18); the healed blind man tangles with the authorities about Jesus' identity (9:18–34), which leads to further christological revelations (9:35–41); and the dispute over Jesus' self-testimony (8:12–20) and his claim to be the Son of God (10:31–38), while containing allusions to the law, are concerned primarily with his identity and authority.

Disputes over Moses and the law are designed to undergird Jesus' claims. At the same time the antagonists in each case are the Jews. It is they who do not understand their own law (5:45–47; 10:34) or keep it (7:19), who think they are disciples of Moses but do not recognize that the scriptures point to Christ (9:28–29). In fact, the Mosaic law becomes "your law" (8:17; 10:34) or "their law" (15:25), not the law of Jesus or his followers. The Jews are, once again, the foil.

Analogous is the story of the cleansing of the Temple (2:13–22). When the Jews query Jesus' action and ask for a sign, they get the enigmatic reply: "Destroy this temple, and in three days I will raise it up." They are incredulous, but do not understand that Jesus spoke of his body and resurrection. Jesus' attack on the Temple, which had both political and legal ramifications, is here given a radical christological twist. He has, in effect, taken its place, as he does that of the Passover lamb (19:32–36).

Similar are the several occasions when Jesus' discourses take place during Jewish festivals. Not only do the discourses imply that Jesus is the true source of all the benefits symbolized in the feasts, but epithets that formerly were attributed to the Torah are now claimed by him: living water (4:10–15); life (5:39–40); the bread of life (6:25–59); and light (1:4; 3:19; 8:12; 9:5). And if, as many think, wisdom/Torah speculation hovers close beneath the surface of the prologue, the Logos/Jesus figure would appear to inherit their roles here.

In John the law is subordinated to Jesus.[156] Even when debates are initiated in legal terms, John rapidly shifts the ground. The opponents are not allowed to debate on their terms, because their terms are of no interest to John—a striking contrast with Matthew. He is interested only in Christ. The law may point to Christ, but that is its sole remaining function, and not one that looms large in John's world. At best it points away from itself to the superior revelation through Christ.[157]

Christology and Dualism

It will by now be clear that the key to John's view of Judaism and his judgment on the disputes between Christians and Jews lies in his Christology. This is widely acknowledged. Whichever passage we turn to, when Jesus disputes with the Jews the focus is almost entirely on his origin and identity. Other matters, such as the law, are peripheral, useful only insofar as they contribute to the overriding christological theme.

As noted above, many think that two or more layers of Christology are embedded in the Gospel, reflecting different stages of debate with the synagogue. The first we may call messianic. The debate over the blind man (9:18–35) puts it in a nutshell: confession of Jesus as Christ leads to exclusion from the synagogue (9:22). Yet this may not have been the earliest experience if, as many think, Christians initially had some success in presenting their messianic beliefs to the Jews. John 1:19–2:11, in which titles with messianic potential are ascribed to Jesus, is often thought to contain the nucleus of this approach. Concepts such as Mosaic prophet, the eschatological Elijah, Lamb of God, Son of God, Messiah, and King of Israel can in different ways be connected to various messianic currents and eschatological expectations in Judaism, even if they have been transformed, in some cases virtually beyond recognition.[158]

Part of that twist may be the emphasis John places on the signs Jesus performed as evidence of his messiahship (7:31; 9:16; 11:47; 20:30–31), especially if we connect the introduction of an elementary signs source/gospel with this stage of development. It is frequently noted that in extant sources the Jews did not typically associate signs with the Messiah. It may be that the expectation of signs that *were* associated with the coming prophet and the general Hellenistic tendency to ascribe miraculous powers to influential figures colored popular messianic expectation. Further impetus may have come from the Christian connection of messiahs and signs in their apocalyptic tradition (Mark 13:22).[159] However that may be, it is clear that John thought messianic disputes were central to the debate with the Jews and that part of the argument rested on the authenticity of Jesus' signs.

Subsequently, at about the time of the break with the synagogue a further development is detected. Here the debate centers around Jesus' divinity and his relationship to the Father. Ashton has conveniently discussed these under three headings: equality with God (5:17–18); superiority to Abraham (8:58–59); and Son of God (10:34–36). The claim to divine status occurs precisely in confrontation with the Jews, and while the Johannine view is hardly typical of any known form of Judaism, it is nevertheless deeply rooted in Jewish soil and finds vague counterparts in heterodox Jewish speculation.[160] Controversy over the "two powers in heaven," which provoked such a strong reaction from the rabbis, is perhaps the most obvious example, pointing not only to currents of thought analogous to Johannine Christology but also to the sort of reaction it could expect to elicit in "normative" Jewish circles.[161] At this point Johannine Christology moves beyond the stretching and adaptation of messianic characters toward a definition of Jesus' divinity that is well on the way to ditheism. Father and Son (and Spirit) are separate but so intimately related that the Son shares essentially in the divine being. Nothing states this more clearly or profoundly than the Logos Christology of the prologue (1:1–18), but in one form or another it runs through all the other discourses too.[162]

Related to this is the Jewish response. They accuse Jesus of being a deceiver (*planos,* 7:13,47), of being a Samaritan and possessed by the devil (8:48,52). These are charges that find echoes in the other Gospels (Matt 27:63) and in many other early Christian texts. We might expect them to be related in part to his miraculous deeds, but in John they are not. They are, in context, a response to his claims about himself and his relationship to God.

At some point John's Christology is melded with his dualistic worldview. This might be because John had dualism in his blood, but rejection by the synagogue and the world at large may well have encouraged him to cast his thought in starkly dualistic terms. In this way the spurned and isolated Johannine group, like other sectarian communities, could find sense and justification for their position.[163] The Logos Christology, with its emphasis on a singular creation, is perhaps not a natural bedfellow for dualism, but it is clear that John wishes to hold them together even, indeed, in the very Logos hymn itself (1:1–4). Christology and dualism are not merely associated, they are intertwined, as the debate with the Jews in 8:12–58 clearly shows. And this brings us back to our theme.

That Johannine dualism was provoked by a deteriorating relationship with Judaism is a plausible but unprovable hypothesis, but its effect on John's view of the Jews is manifest. The Jews are associated with the negative side of the contrast, with unbelief, darkness, and the world. This reaches its peak in the notorious assertion of the Johannine Jesus that the Jews are liars and children of their father, the devil (8:44). It was this strain of Johannine thought that elicited the famous comment of Bultmann:

> The term *Ioudaioi*, characteristic of the Evangelist, gives an overall portrayal of the Jews, viewed from the standpoint of Christian faith, as the representatives of unbelief (and thereby, as will appear, of the unbelieving "world" in general). The Jews are spoken of as an alien people, not merely from the point of view of Greek readers, but also, and indeed only properly, from the standpoint of faith: for Jesus himself speaks to them as a stranger and correspondingly, those in whom the stirrings of faith or of the search for Jesus are to be found are distinguished from the "Jews" even if they are themselves Jews.[164]

In the end, therefore, John's view of the Jews is woven tightly into his overall theology. They epitomize everything that is dark and diabolical, that belongs to the unbelieving and antagonistic world. Hostility toward the Jews is thus lifted to a new and more insidious plane.[165]

CONCLUSION

The canonical Gospels and Acts clearly illustrate one characteristic of Jewish-Christian relations in this period: a variety of causes and a diversity of outcomes. This is not to deny the overlap between them. They were, after all, writing about the same figure and dependent on similar traditions—and this applies even to the eccentric Gospel of John. And, of course, the first three were in some way literarily interrelated. It is no surprise, therefore, that they cover many of the same themes. More interesting, however, are the shading and nuances that distinguish them.

Mark's view of Judaism combines a sense of immediate hostility toward Jewish authorities, who persecuted Jesus and his followers, and an absence of any long-term projections. In Matthew the conflict with the synagogue centers on halakic matters, which were of greatest concern to Jews, though christological disagreements play their role too. In John this pattern is reversed: halakic issues fade into the background or become subservient to a Christology which dominates the Gospel and which is the critical point of divergence between Christians and Jews. Luke, on the other hand, projects the Jewish-Christian dispute onto another and more public stage, where the two of them vie for the attention and support of a third party, the Romans.

We have thus emphasized a different constellation of factors that controlled each author's views of Judaism. These are not simply heuristic tools, pegs on which to hang the discussion, though they serve that purpose well. Nor are they intended to be exclusive, in the sense either that other factors are to be ignored in, or that their explanatory force is to be confined to, any one author. But they do take us to the heart of the four authors' views of Judaism and help to explain why their accounts of the same basic theme have such an individual flavor.

Two things in particular help to explain this: cultural background and compositional context. Mark and Luke were probably Gentiles. This is why they were largely indifferent to the question of the law as a point of Jewish-

Christian dispute, even if (for Luke especially) it continued to impinge on internal Christian affairs. In Mark the problem of Judaism was largely swallowed up in the political crises and foreshortened perspectives caused by the Jewish War. Luke, writing at a later date and in another (largely diaspora) context, was affected by a different sort of political pressure—welcomed by neither Romans nor Jews, synagogue nor state, Christians desperately needed to find a niche in which to secure themselves.

Matthew, a Jewish Christian, represented a community in intense competition and conflict with the early rabbinic movement. Their communal organizations were similar, with the church mimicking the synagogue, and they locked horns over issues that deeply concerned them both. It is the best example we have in this period of an intramural conflict—close, intense, tussling over agreed common ground—even if the precise location of the Matthean churches on the boundaries of rabbinic Judaism remains obscure. John's community had also been deeply affected by conflict with the synagogue, though whether in the immediate or distant past is hard to tell. Though predominantly Jewish Christian, it was at the time of writing organizationally and mentally more removed from Judaism than Matthew. It was also in conflict with other Jewish Christians, some of whom chose to retain their affiliation with the synagogue with whatever compromises that involved. The particular interest of John's Gospel is that, according to many scholars, we can trace in it a progression in Christian relations with the synagogue—from mild-mannered internal debates at the beginning to radical separation and bitter polemic at the end.

The approach to miracles follows a similar pattern. Mark promotes Jesus as a powerful worker of miracles, without suggesting that it routinely brought him into conflict with the Jews. Matthew brings the issue into play by echoing the later Jewish charge that Jesus was a magician and deceiver, and by associating the Jews directly with a plot to cover up the resurrection. Luke, in Acts, brings the conflict between Jewish and Christian miracle workers into the open, where they contend for outside recognition and public approval. John incorporates the performance of signs into the broader debate over messiahship, in which the antagonists are always the Jews.

The distinction between leaders and people, clearest in Mark and Matthew but increasingly blurred in Luke and John, may suggest a lingering hope for the Jews, but other evidence is less than clear about their long-term fate. Mark has the least to say, since he does not look much beyond the immediate future. Matthew and Luke give the impression that the time of the Jews as an elect and favored people (and of their Temple and city) was over. They were now on a par with the Gentile peoples, subject to the gospel as individuals but with no collective privilege. John says nothing directly on the matter, but the implications of his polemic against the Jews and his association of them with the evil forces of the world are not the least bit optimistic.

APOCRYPHA

3

❖

Neglected sources of information pertinent to our theme are to be found in the apocryphal literature of the Christian tradition and in Christian adaptations of Jewish apocryphal writings. A seminal essay on the latter was published by J. H. Charlesworth in 1981,[1] but his lead has not since been followed. And although individual Christian apocrypha, such as the *Gospel of Peter* and *5 Ezra,* have been brought into the debate, there exists no survey of all the texts that might have a bearing on the question of Jewish-Christian relations.[2]

Any survey of this material faces a number of difficulties. First, many of the texts cannot be securely dated. It is not uncommon, for example, for texts in the recent edition of the Old Testament Pseudepigrapha to be dated as vaguely as "the first century BC to the first century AD," or "the first to the fourth century AD."[3] We shall concentrate on those texts that are widely agreed to belong to the first two centuries CE, but there is rarely unanimity on such issues. It is even more difficult, secondly, to posit a particular geographical setting. Designations such as "either Egypt or Syria-Palestine" are properly agnostic, but they do not help us to gain a sense of local peculiarities or of genetic connections. This relates, thirdly, to the questions of authorship and influence. By whom and for whom were they written? Were they widely read, or was their influence confined to one geographical area or even to a small group of literate Christians? Questions such as these are a lot simpler to ask than to answer, although it could be argued that this is only an acute form of a problem faced in any reconstruction of early Christianity, whether we focus on canonical or apocryphal, literary or archaeological, theological or social data.

An additional, and perhaps more insidious, danger arises when we bundle writings together purely for our own convenience, driven by the particular questions we have in mind and, more often than not, an urge to discover thematic connections. In the process we run the risk of creating an artificial sense of the coherence and influence of a group of texts that are only a group because we have arbitrarily made them into one. Perhaps the best we can do in these circumstances is to be aware that we are involved in a heuristic process which imposes on, as much as it draws from, the texts themselves. It is some small relief that these texts exhibit a diversity that naturally resists procrustean treatment and helps to curb our more heavy-handed impulses.

CHRISTIAN APOCRYPHA

Christian apocryphal writings of interest to us can be loosely clustered according to their content or their genre. Based on what we find elsewhere, we would expect three aspects of Jesus' life to be a matter of contention between Christians and Jews: his birth, his miraculous powers, and his trial and crucifixion. To some extent we are not disappointed. The *Protevangelium of James,* traditionally labeled an infancy gospel, seems concerned above all to glorify Mary, the mother of Jesus, and to promote sexual asceticism.[4] It was a popular text, at one time a serious candidate for inclusion in the canon, and was probably composed ca. 150–200 CE.[5] It contains an implicit defense of the miraculous conception of Jesus against the charge that his mother was an adulteress or fornicator. The argument follows two lines: first, Jesus' miraculous birth is retrospectively guaranteed by the prior and miraculous conception of Mary as the result of divine intervention (chaps. 2–5); and second, Joseph is pointedly described as an aging widower with children from a previous marriage, thus presumably explaining the stories about Jesus' siblings (9:1–2) and yet again protecting his mother's reputation for purity.

The canonical birth stories, which are freely drawn on in the *Protevangelium,* invited skepticism and doubt, and most such reactions that have come down to us are attributed to Jews. That is not the case here, and it is noticeable that the Jews are generally portrayed positively—skeptical, perhaps, but willing to listen and to recognize miraculous occurrences (16:1–2; 19:1–3). However, it is difficult not to catch a whiff of the broader debate about Jesus' entry into this world and a response to some of the more common reactions it provoked.

Yet to see the *Protevangelium* as nothing more than a fantastic extension of the canonical infancy narratives springing from a common piety would, it has recently been argued, miss much of the point. The often dismissive classification of it as an "infancy gospel," so it is claimed, ignores the main point of the text, which is to appropriate Jewish (that is, biblical) history for Christian hermeneutical purposes. If the births of Mary and Jesus parallel each other they also deliberately echo the biblical stories of Joachim and Susanna (LXX Daniel), Hannah (1 Samuel), Abraham and Sarah, and Zacharias

(2 Chronicles). As such the text is better labeled according to its own self-designation, *historia* (*Prot. Jas*.1.1; 25.1), namely, a typological reading of the Jewish bible which stresses the continuity between Christianity and Judaism. It thus expresses a form of *Heilsgeschichte*, whose roots might be seen in at least two problems that vexed the second-century church: the threat of Marcionism, with its rejection of the Jewish bible; and the need to assert their antiquity—which they did by appropriating Jewish traditions—to ward off the charge that they were a novel, unrooted, and unwelcome addition to the Roman scene.[6] If this reading between the lines is plausible (there is no direct evidence in the text for these motives), it reveals an additional interest in Judaism: the *Protevangelium* responds not only to Jewish skepticism about the birth of Jesus, but also to Roman suspicion about the cultural credibility of Christianity. To counteract Jewish rumors it enhances the Christian story; to counteract Roman suspicions it leans heavily on the Jewish tradition.[7]

The question of Jesus' birth arises in another second-century text, the *Acts of Pilate*.[8] The Jewish elders argue that Jesus was born of fornication, that his birth meant the death of other children in Bethlehem, and that his parents fled to Egypt because the Jews despised them (2:3–4). Other Jews, twelve in number but otherwise largely unknown (despite the list of names), deny the charge of fornication by asserting that Joseph and Mary were betrothed. The elders dismiss them as born Gentiles, proselytes to Judaism and disciples of Jesus, but they affirm their Jewish birth and are prepared to swear to it on oath (2:5). Pilate, so it is claimed, believes the Twelve. Although the main charge of Jewish antagonists here, as elsewhere, has to do with fornication/adultery, the reference to other deaths and the flight to Egypt add an additional twist to the hostile reading of the nativity stories.

When we move from Jesus' birth to his childhood, the apocryphal narratives are less informative about Judaism. The *Infancy Gospel of Thomas* promotes two main characteristics of Jesus: that he was a performer of stunning miracles and a purveyor of arcane and profound wisdom.[9] The rather crude miracles seem to be motivated as much by petulance and arrogance as by compassion, but the main interest is in the demonstration of miraculous power per se—"that he is something great, a god or an angel" (7:4). The presence of Jews is incidental, part of the narrative setting. Similarly, the Jews are sometimes the foil to Jesus the dazzling teacher, but only as the contemporaries who would most naturally be his audience. There is apparently not much interest in pointedly focusing on the Jews. Yet we may occasionally catch echoes of second-century debates. For if the Jews are sometimes antagonists (2:3,5) or console Jesus' victims (8.1), on other occasions they praise Jesus and recognize his excellence and wisdom (19.5). When Jesus' Jewish contemporaries are made to concede that he is divinely inspired, this might be related to the later, well-documented dispute between Christians and Jews about the derivation of his miraculous powers and teaching. But such disputes occurred not only with Jews, as Celsus clearly demonstrates, and the early Christians, like most of their contemporaries, enjoyed stories of the miraculous for their own sake. In the absence of any more specific evidence we can only conjecture that disputes with the Jews might have been a factor too.

Jesus' crucifixion at the hands of the Romans was profoundly awkward for early Christian believers. It elicited ridicule from the Jews and suspicion from the Romans. The canonical Passion narratives, which contain a generous portion of fiction, react by placing the blame for Jesus' death on the Jews and exonerating the Romans. It is widely recognized that this tendency becomes increasingly pronounced as we move from the earlier to the later canonical Gospels. The trajectory continues into the apocrypha, but with some added effects. The second-century *Acts of Pilate,* which we have already drawn on, transforms the defense before Pilate into a broad apology for Jesus, most especially against Jewish attacks. Apart from the question of his birth, which we looked at above, the following accusations are leveled: that he broke the law (1:1); that he was a sorcerer (1:1; 2:1,5,6) and blasphemer (4:1–2); that he claimed to be god and king (2:5–6; 4:1–2); and that he threatened to destroy the Temple (4:1–2). All in all, they see him as a malevolent, godless deceiver, worthy of death. One example will suffice to show how the various accusations are lumped together: " . . . that he was born of fornication, and is a deceiver, and claims to be the Son of God and a king" (2:5). The pedigree of these charges lies in the canonical tradition, but some were perpetuated in Jewish circles as well.

Any ambivalence or uncertainty, such as we observe in the "canonical" Pilate, disappears from view. Now he is a clearheaded and determined opponent of the Jews. "His blood be upon us and our children" is quoted three times (4:1; 9:4; 12:1; cf. Matt 27:25), and Pilate constantly attempts to deflect the Jews from their evil intent and to insist on Jesus' innocence before Jewish law. The question of guilt before Roman law does not even arise. In one of the more fantastic exchanges Pilate even uses a thumbnail sketch of Jewish history to accuse Jesus' Jewish opponents of sedition and rebellion (9:2)! As regards Pilate, who presumably represents Romans in general, the picture is consistent: he is an adamant supporter of Jesus and colludes in his death only after extreme and cunning political pressure from the Jewish authorities. The rift between the Jews and the Romans, already apparent in the canonical narratives, is now absolute.

Yet the Jews themselves present no uniform reaction. When Jesus' mother is vilified, twelve Jews testify on her behalf (2:4–5), and when the authorities call for Jesus' crucifixion, some Jews weep in sorrow (4:5). Following the accusations before Pilate, Joseph of Arimathea, Nicodemus, the twelve who defended his mother, and "many others" testify to his good works (12:1). The Jews are apparently divided: some are sympathetic and supportive, others go along with his condemnation.

Most astonishing, however, is the sudden transformation in chapters 14–16, when the Jewish authorities begin to have second thoughts. When a priest, a teacher, and a Levite from Galilee report that they witnessed Jesus' ascension (14:1–2) the high priests remain doubtful, repeating the rumor reported in Matthew that the disciples had bribed the guards and stolen the body (14:3). Nevertheless they decide to check the story. It is confirmed by Nicodemus, using the analogy of Elijah (15:1; cf. 16:6). They then call upon Joseph of Arimathea as a witness to Jesus' resurrection (15:2–6), a student of "rabbi" Simeon to confirm the announcement of messianic prophecies at his birth (16:2), and the three Galileans (now called "rabbis") to confirm his ascension (16:3–6).

It is striking that virtually every imaginable Jewish leader is named in this brief section—priests, Levites and high priests, teachers and rabbis, elders and rulers of the synagogue—not to mention "all the people." It seems as if every Jew in sight is called upon as a witness. Equally striking are the concluding words:

> And all the teachers said to all the people of the Lord: "If this is from the Lord, and it is marvellous in your eyes, you shall surely know, O house of Jacob, that it is written: Cursed is every one who hangs on a tree [Deut 21:23]. And another passage of scripture teaches: The gods who did not make the heaven and earth shall perish [Jer 10:11]." And the priests and the Levites said to one another: "If Jesus is remembered after fifty years he will reign for ever and create for himself a new people." Then the rulers of the synagogue and the priests and the Levites admonished all Israel: "Cursed is the man who shall worship the work of man's hand, and cursed is the man who shall worship created things alongside the creator." And all the people answered: "Amen, amen." (16:7)

> And all the people praised the Lord God and sang: . . . "The Lord will not forsake his people for his great name's sake, for the Lord has begun to make us his people." (16:8)

The context does not make it clear whether the assessment of the priests in 16:7 is a form of faith or of grudging realism. Is it significant that the assessment of Jesus' impact is kept to themselves and not announced to all the people? And are the curses announced to the people either side of this assessment to be read negatively, as a reaction to the people's belief, or are they a tacit admission of his divinity because he has been resurrected, has not perished, and cannot therefore be thought of as the work of man's hands? It is difficult to be certain, but the broader context of chapters 14–16, in which representative Jewish authorities testify on Jesus' behalf, encourages a positive sense. Even a negative understanding of the response would be confined to the leaders, since it is clear that the people respond with enthusiasm.

What exactly is being implied in chapters 14–16 remains uncertain. So great is the contrast with the preceding chapters, where the Jewish leaders generally lead the opposition to Jesus, that some have argued that they are from another hand.[10] From the text as it stands, however, the following conclusions can tentatively be drawn. First, although there is residual resistance from the high-priestly group represented by Annas and Caiaphas, significant Jewish authorities, including those (rabbis, rulers of the synagogue) contemporary with the time of composition, confirm the reality of Jesus' resurrection and ascension and his creation of a "new people" (the fifty years having long passed). Secondly, the "new people" seems to be the church, made up of those who "remember" Jesus and implicitly including Jews while not mentioning Gentiles.

Perhaps the "new people" are the same as those who say that "the Lord will not forsake his people for his great name's sake, for the Lord has begun to make us his people." Yet the latter could be a Jewish remnant or a revived Israel standing alongside those who remember Jesus. That, at least, would seem to be the more natural meaning in context. Given the vagueness of the final chapter it would be rash to impose a two-covenant scheme on it, but the text as it stands might just bear it. The clear reference to Christians as a "new people" may in the context refer to Jewish Christians. Other grounds have been suggested for this: the favoring of Matthean tradition, and the ebionite tendency which countered the charge of Jesus' illegitimacy with an allusion to Joseph's paternity.[11] This would provide a coherent setting for the narrative, but the evidence is tenuous at best.

Some of the same themes can be found in the surviving fragment of the second-century *Gospel of Peter.*[12] It deals with Jesus' Passion and, as in the *Acts of Pilate,* the exoneration of the Romans is further extended. This is effected chiefly by presenting them as bystanders: Herod takes over the role of judicial authority from Pilate (1–5), and the Jews rather than the Romans become the perpetrators of the crucifixion (6; 21; 25). Pilate colludes with the Jews by providing troops to guard the tomb (29–31) and by imposing silence on the soldiers who witnessed the resurrection (43–49), but he is otherwise entirely removed from the action, publicly declares his innocence (46; cf. 1), and intervenes with Herod on behalf of his (and Jesus') friend Joseph in an attempt to retrieve Jesus' body for burial (3). Among those who witnessed the events at the tomb and recognized that "In truth he was the Son of God" (47) are the centurion and soldiers provided by Pilate. Thus the Romans are present but marginal, participants against their better judgment but concerned to preserve civil order and, until silenced, willing confessors of the divinity of Jesus.

The depiction of the Jews works manifestly in the opposite direction. They, and Herod, initially refuse to wash their hands of responsibility; rather, they willingly take charge of Jesus' crucifixion (1–2). Not only the leaders but the people have a part in the action—the ubiquitous "they" who control events from 5 to 20. Then "the Jews" remove him from the cross

(21) and hound his followers (26; 50–52). At the same time, they recognize that their evil deeds have brought the judgment and the end of Jerusalem near (25), thus acceding to the widespread Christian tendency to link responsibility for the death of Jesus to the fall of Jerusalem. It has also been pointed out that echoes of the canonical tradition are transposed in their present context to give a clearly anti-Jewish tone.[13]

Then a few cracks appear in the uniform flow. A division between leaders and people appears when the "scribes, Pharisees and elders" entreat Pilate to guard the tomb because "all the people" are beginning to read the signs anew: "If at his death these exceeding great signs have come to pass, behold how righteous he was" (28). Witnessing the empty tomb and the angelic appearances are a centurion, Roman soldiers, elders and scribes, and a crowd from Jerusalem (31; 34). Do those described as "of the centurion's company" (45), who report to Pilate that Jesus truly was the Son of God, include the elders and scribes as well as the Romans? Possibly, but the language is vague and the actors difficult to pin down. The "all" who beg for a cover-up are presumably Jews (perhaps only the elders, 38), as distinct from the centurion and soldiers whose silence is desired (47; 49), and it is they who make the most outrageous claim of culpability: "It is better for us to make ourselves guilty of the greatest sin before God than to fall into the hands of the people of the Jews and be stoned" (48). That is, they recognize the truth about Jesus and the consequences of denying it, but still they proceed. The leaders and the people are distinguished in this verse and elsewhere, but not consistently. Any amelioration of the generally negative portrait of the Jews is ambiguous and slight.[14] The overwhelming impression of the fragment is of Jewish connivance and consent, of a Jewish impetus that drives events while the innocent Romans stand by.

J. Denker has proposed a purpose and setting for the *Gospel of Peter* which, if plausible, would be of considerable interest to us. He thinks it is a Jewish Christian product (ca. 100–130 CE) designed to persuade Jews of their culpability in Jesus' death, but at the same time to encourage them to repent and convert. Despite the anti-Jewish strain (and it is that, and not pro-Roman), the author holds out hope for the salvation of individual Jews. To achieve this, the gospel deliberately counters Jewish calumnies about Jesus' death and resurrection and promotes practices (Sabbath, fasting) that encourage positive relations with the Jews. Unfortunately, at critical points the evidence is never sufficient to sustain the argument. To prove that there is opposition to Jewish polemic, Denker draws heavily on parallels in the rabbinic tradition and in the *Toledoth Jesu*, which are late and notoriously difficult to date. To demonstrate that recommended Christian practices had a pro-Jewish intent he forges dubious links between disparate items of Christian evidence.[15] Any notion that the *Gospel of Peter* was intended to persuade and convert Jews runs up against the manifestly anti-Jewish strain in the fragment we have. Apart from the fact that it is an extension of a trend observable in the canonical Gospels, we can only guess at what might have motivated the author. But that it was intended to win over Jews seems inherently unlikely.[16]

Still in the gospel genre, but much less focused and informative, are the so-called Jewish Christian gospels. Ancient reports about them are confused, but generally it is agreed that three separate gospels circulated in the second century: the *Gospel of the Nazarenes,* the *Gospel of the Ebionites,* and the *Gospel of the Hebrews.*[17] Their titles, original language, and content remain unclear and only one, the *Gospel of the Hebrews,* is actually named— the other two being modern labels of convenience. Moreover, we know their content, if at all, only from a few scraps preserved by other writers. Like most other evidence about the Jewish Christians these texts tell us more about internal Christian disputes than about Jewish-Christian relations. The *Gospel of the Nazarenes* is closely related to the Gospel of Matthew and tells us nothing additional about the relation to Judaism.[18] The omission of the genealogies and birth stories in the *Gospel of the Ebionites* may have been because they were irrelevant to a Christology that was both adoptionist and distinguished the human Jesus from the semidivine Christ (sayings 4–6),[19] but it would certainly reflect one of the well-documented areas of dispute between Christians and Jews. Opposition to the cult and sacrifices (saying 6) probably reflects a post-70 mentality, but has its parallels in Judaism and deep biblical roots. It would run afoul only of those to whom the restoration of the cult was central to the restoration of Israel, as may have been the case with the compilers of the Mishnah. The designation of the task of the twelve as a "testimony to Israel" echoes canonical Gospel tradition. Whether it was intentionally restrictive in a second-century context and what it says about a continuing mission to the Jews can scarcely be surmised on the basis of a few scraps of evidence. Perhaps we can only say that it is not qualified by any allusion to limited successes or the obduracy of the Jews.

James is a central figure in the *Gospel of the Hebrews* (saying 7), sharing sympathetically in Jesus' fate and becoming the chief witness to the resurrection. He was, we might note, from a Jewish point of view one of the more acceptable representatives of Christianity. When Jesus gives his linen cloth to the servant of a priest (saying 7), some see it as a counter to Jewish skepticism about the resurrection, but this is at best implicit.[20]

All in all, these gospel fragments provide us with lean pickings. If there were three, and if they are properly labeled Jewish Christian, they give some sense of the diversity and persistence of this form of Christianity. Two of them (*Gos.Eb.,* and *Gos.Heb.*) share traits with one strain of the Pseudo-Clementines and, like them, indicate both affinity with as well as divergence from Judaism. Positions are taken that would bring them closer to Judaism than other forms of Christianity, and there is little if any distinctively Christian polemic against Judaism. The absence of any emphasis on legal praxis, often thought to be the hallmark of Jewish Christians according to other sources, could be because they were associated with more liberal forms of hellenized Judaism,[21] or it could simply reflect the paucity of our sources.

The *Gospel of Thomas* may also belong here. The history and meaning of this text remain highly controverted.[22] One theory, not without its merits, is that the *Gospel of Thomas* used as one of its sources a Jewish Christian gospel.[23] If so, and if this element could be isolated, it would perhaps add to the meager stock of Jewish Christian traditions we have mentioned above. Yet neither the arguments nor the identifications have carried the day. What they have done, however, is to point to a few sayings that may indicate an attitude toward Judaism by the compiler of this miscellany.[24] Saying 14, for example, appears to undercut four things precious to Jewish observance: fasting, almsgiving, prayer, and dietary rules. Sayings 6 and 27 may point in the same direction:

> His disciples asked him: Do you want us to fast? And how shall we pray [and] give alms? What diet should we observe? Jesus said: Do not lie and what you abhor, do not do; for all things are manifest in the sight of heaven. (6)

> If you do not fast to the world, you will not find the kingdom; if you do not keep the Sabbath as Sabbath, you will not see the Father. (27)

Jesus' answer to the disciples' inquiry in saying 6 is evasive, but perhaps points to broad moral obligations that should supersede a concern for such things as fasting and diet. The enigmatic saying in 27 could be read as an ascetic reinterpretation of the obligation to fast and keep the Sabbath, though this is easier for the first than the second half of the saying and the latter has, improbably, been taken to be a call for more dedicated Sabbath observance.

Three other sayings have a decidedly anti-Jewish ring to them:

> His disciples said to him: Twenty-four prophets spoke in Israel, and they all spoke of you. He said to them: You have abandoned the living one before your eyes, and spoken about the dead. (52)

> His disciples said to him: Is circumcision useful or not? He said to them: If it were useful, their father would beget them from their mother [already] circumcised. But the true circumcision in the Spirit is useful in every way. (53)

> His disciples said to him: Who are you that you say these things to us? [Jesus said to them]: From what I say to you, do you not know who I am? But you have become like the Jews; for they love the tree [and] hate its fruit; and they love the fruit [and] hate the tree. (43)

The first of these appears to subordinate the testimony of the scriptures to Jesus in favor of his own living testimony, while the second flatly denies the usefulness of physical circumcision, preferring true circumcision in the Spirit. The third, in language that echoes the Fourth Gospel and Acts, likens the uncomprehending disciples to the archetypally uncomprehending Jews, just as saying 39 castigates the Pharisees and scribes in the manner of the Synoptics. In saying 12 James is given a central and elevated role similar to that in the *Gospel of the Hebrews.*[25]

It is difficult to weigh this evidence. It is, first, a minor theme and should not be exaggerated. Moreover, some of the material may simply echo the language of the canonical Gospels, and other parts can be tied in with the view of Judaism typical among Gnostics (for example, saying 27). Yet there appears to be more than that here—a hostility toward various forms of Jewish observance and a casual disregard for the Jews that are not common in other gnostic writings. Perhaps they indicate that at some stage, if not at the time of composition, the groups through whom these traditions were transmitted experienced some conflict with the Jews.

The Christian *Odes of Solomon,* some of the best surviving examples of early Christian hymnody, are generally joyful and optimistic in tone and are infused with an aura of piety and intimacy between the devotee and the Lord (Jesus and/or God).[26] Christian in content, but based on Jewish models, they occasionally allude to themes relevant to our discussion. Ode 10:6 speaks of the Gentiles (presumably Christian) who have "become my people." Jews are not mentioned, and the intent might be polemical. In Odes 28 and 31 Christ speaks of his grace and fortitude in the face of persecution and death at the hands of an anonymous "they/them"—a group identified by actions that rely more on echoes of the Psalms than on allusions to the Passion stories. "They" would include Jews even if it includes Romans as well. It is striking, therefore, that in Ode 31:12–13 Christ suggests that he bore his death "that I might save my nation and instruct it. And that I might not nullify the promises to the patriarchs, to whom I was promised for the salvation of their offspring." Who is meant by "offspring" cannot be said for sure. It could be the Christian community or the original people of God, but without further indication is most naturally taken as the latter. The purpose of Jesus' Passion here seems to be the redemption of Israel, or at least a remnant, and perhaps indicates a Jewish Christian ethos. If so, it would fit with a number of positive expressions of hope for the salvation of the Jews that we have discovered elsewhere.

In an earlier chapter we considered a passage from a second-century apocalyptic writing, the *Apocalypse of Peter,* when considering Christian reactions to the Bar Cochba rebellion.[27] It was widely read and respected in the early centuries, probably largely because of its detailed speculations about the afterlife, things such as rewards and punishments, and the classification of sinners. More interesting for our purposes is the close association in chapters 1–2 of three themes: the appearance of false messiahs (1:5); the persecution/martyrdom of Christians and their eternal reward (2:11–13); and the fate of Israel (2:1–7). In the last of these it is said that the fig tree (= Israel, 1:7) will be rooted out as it ceases to bear fruit. This will occur in the last days, which, it is implied, have now arrived. Israel, that is, is cut off and rejected. These three themes fit persuasively with Christian experience during the Bar Cochba rebellion. The condemnation and rejection of the Jews, themes found frequently enough elsewhere, here gain an added intensity and animus from the pressured political situation.

It has been suggested that the same circumstances might have inspired another early Christian apocalypse, 5 Ezra, which has come down to us as the first two chapters of the Jewish apocalypse 4 Ezra. We shall consider this text more fully below, but at this stage note that the dominant concern is the replacement of Israel by the "coming people," that is, the church. Most striking, and the surest indication of Christian authorship, is the radical rejection of Israel that precedes the transfer of divine affection to a new people. The repeated allusions to and intense concern with this theme suggest a specific historical crisis, the most obvious being the Bar Cochba rebellion. The pervasive image of a mother (probably = Jerusalem) who loses one son but gains another (2:10,15,17,31) has been connected to the aftermath of the rebellion, when Jerusalem was overrun and the Jews expelled.[28] When in 2:6–7 it is said that the mother (= Jerusalem) is "brought to ruin" and the people "scattered among the nations," the author could be alluding to the ravaging of Jerusalem by Rome and the expulsion of the Jews in 135 CE. The hardship and persecution of the "coming people" (2:23ff.) and the eternal reward to those who remain faithful (2:43ff.) could be words of comfort to those Christians threatened during the rebellion. Indeed, if it is not pushing the metaphor too far, when the new people are said to have the same mother (Jerusalem) we could connect this to the takeover of the Jerusalem church by Gentile bishops ca. 135 CE.[29] Obviously there are dangers in pressing the details of apocalyptic language for historical allusion, but in this case the fit between text and (proposed) context is remarkably coherent. Thus it may well be that these two early Christian apocalypses confirm our other observations about the critical significance of the Bar Cochba period.

Finally we turn to the few surviving fragments of the *Kerygma Petrou*.[30] This document has been routinely defined as an example of early Christian apologetic. Paulsen thinks it shares some elements with that genre, but insists also on its kerygmatic character and thinks it was primarily addressed to Christians rather than outsiders.[31] It is usually dated to the first half of the second century and probably originated in Egypt. A prominent theme in a number of fragments is monotheism and idolatry. The essential message is that there is one God, defined by terms of negation (invisible, incomprehensible, etc.) and contrasted with empty idols. But these themes, used widely in (and perhaps borrowed from) Jewish apologetic, are given a decidedly anti-Jewish twist. The Gentiles worship idols and in their ignorance deny the existence of the Creator. But the Jews are no better for they, who presume to know the true God, in fact worship "angels and archangels, the months and the moon" (fragment 2a). A classic Jewish characterization of

Gentiles is thus turned back upon themselves. And if Clement of Alexandria is right, and the author of the *Kerygma Petrou* excuses the Gentiles on the ground of ignorance and thinks they worship the same God as the Christians but in a different way, this would merely add salt to the wound.[32]

The attack on Gentile and Jewish forms of worship has at its root a strong sense of Christian distinctiveness and superiority:

> Learn then, ye also, holily and righteously what we deliver to you and keep it, worshipping God through Christ in a new way. For we have found in the scriptures, how the Lord says: "Behold, I make with you a new covenant, not as I made [one] with your fathers in Mount Horeb." A new one has he made with us. For what has reference to the Greeks and Jews is old. But we are Christians, who as a third race worship him in a new way. (fragment 2a)

It is worth quoting this in full because it contains one of the clearest assertions of a Christian sense of self-identity and the way in which this is bolstered by denigration of the alternatives. It is true that the issue arises in a comparison of three different forms of worship.[33] But ultimately the stark contrast between the old and the new (forms of worship, covenant) and the self-designation "third race" extend to a more comprehensive claim. Christians are a new, distinctive and superior people of God.

What this implies for immediate relations with the Jews remains unclear. Fragment 3 speaks as follows:

> If now anyone of Israel wishes to repent and through my name to believe in God, his sins will be forgiven him. And after twelve years go ye out into the world that no one may say: "We have not heard."

The main point seems clear: the disciples are to preach to Jews first and then to Gentiles in order that all may be without excuse.[34] But did the initial mission to Israel cease or continue after twelve years? In the surviving fragments there is no other hint of an interest in continuing contact with the Jews, though this would not be incompatible with the strong sense of identity and superiority expressed there. But in view of its sense in the immediate context, it would seem rash to press this statement for an opinion on the larger issue of an ongoing Jewish mission.

Clearly the group considered the Jewish scriptures as one source of authority (fragment 6), but this was an almost universal Christian stance. They have a hidden and obscure sense (as *parabole* and *ainigma*) as well as an open and self-evident meaning (*authentikos, autolexei*) which is available to Christians. The scriptures point uniformly to Christ, to "his coming, his death, his crucifixion and all the rest of the tortures which the Jews inflicted on him, his resurrection and his assumption to heaven." The reference to the Jews' involvement in Jesus' death comes only in passing but it reflects a widespread Christian perception, found in other apocryphal writings and elsewhere. When in fragment 1 it is claimed that Jesus is called both Law (*nomos*) and Word (*logos*), the two terms are used positively rather than antithetically. The precise meaning is not clear, but it may well be a shorthand way of expressing Christianity as the fulfillment of the aspirations of both Hellenism (represented by *logos*) and Judaism (represented by *nomos*).[35] This would certainly fit with the statements about Jewish and Gentile forms of worship, usurped and superseded by Christianity, as it would with the generally hostile references to Judaism.

In summary, in those Christian apocrypha that contain pertinent material, a number of themes stand out. First, there is Christian response to Jewish skepticism about Jesus' conception and birth, either indirectly by glorifying his mother or directly by calling on twelve worthy and persuasive Jewish witnesses. Second, Jewish culpability in the death of Jesus is mentioned in passing in the *Kerygma Petrou* but is prominent in the *Gospel of Peter* and the *Acts of Pilate*. It is reinforced by shrinking the role of the Romans almost to the point of invisibility. The motive here, as elsewhere, is not simply to castigate the Jews but also to appeal to the Romans for acceptance as a pacific and venerable group. At the same time, thirdly, the Jews are seen to have been rejected as God's people and their place taken by a new people, a third race of Christians. This is quite unambiguous, but discussed somewhat philosophically, in the *Kerygma Petrou*. But in two apocalypses, the *Apocalypse of Peter* and *5 Ezra,* the claim to the inheritance of Israel is marked by a bitter rejection of the Jews which, in turn, may well spring from the tensions associated with the Bar Cochba rebellion. In the *Gospel of Thomas* (but only here), fourthly, we find rejection of forms of Jewish piety and denigration of the Jews as the typically ignorant.

Yet, fifthly, the picture is not always so negative. In some documents, like the *Protevangelium of James* and the *Infancy Gospel of Thomas,* the Jews are portrayed fairly positively. In the *Gospel of Peter* and the early part of the *Acts of Pilate* they have a more ambivalent role, but it does seem that they are not uniformly depicted as opponents. The *Odes of Solomon* contain at least one statement that points to the future salvation of the Jews, or at least some of them. The ending of the *Acts of Pilate* provides emblematic examples of Jews, leaders and common people, who respond positively to the message about Jesus, indeed, who become key witnesses to his resurrection and ascension. Whether they are all thought of as Christian converts, or whether some respond sympathetically but remain Jews—a sort of two-covenant notion—is unclear, but the latter would not be out of line with some other early Christian evidence we have seen.

CHRISTIAN ADAPTATIONS OF JEWISH APOCRYPHA

As noted at the beginning of this chapter, few have attempted to extend Charlesworth's work on the sense of self-identity revealed in the Christian additions to Jewish apocrypha. We will attempt to supplement his observations and to place the results in the broad context of early Jewish-Christian relations.[36] The contribution of the Christian editors varies from text to text. In the first place, it might be noted, their interest in and preservation of the original Jewish writings was probably the thing that guaranteed their survival, given the increasing disinterest in them in the Jewish community (which Christian use of them might have encouraged). Sometimes the text is supplemented simply by adding chapters, in the case of 4 Ezra, at the beginning (5 Ezra) and the end (6 Ezra). Occasional interpolations are more common. Some are blatantly Christian, others more subtle and difficult to delimit. An important principle of interpretation for all of them, however, is that we should look for the Christian meaning not only in the identifiable additions, but in the text as a whole. We need to ask not only about the meaning of the interpolations, but about the way they affect the reading of the resulting texts *as Christian products in a Christian context*. That is, we must try to imagine how Christian readers or auditors would have interpreted originally non-Christian writings in their adoptive setting. Sometimes, no doubt, the original meaning would have been acceptable; but at other times it would have needed considerable transposition to get a satisfactory Christian sense.

A good place to begin is with 5 and 6 Ezra.[37] The original Jewish document, 4 Ezra, is usually dated ca. 100 CE and is a response to the traumas of the Jewish War. The questions it posed, for example about the righteousness and faithfulness of God, are rarely directly answered but rather become the basis for broader theological reflection. The two Christian sections were probably added in the second or third century, but that would not necessarily be the time of their composition. They could have circulated independently before being attached to the Jewish apocalypse. In particular, 5 Ezra, which has an affinity with Matthew and with Justin's *Dialogue,* is often dated to the second century. Moreover, as we have seen above, there is a good case for dating it to the immediate aftermath of the Bar Cochba rebellion. Allusions to the persecution of Christians, the ravaging of Jerusalem and the expulsion of the Jews, as well as the bitter schism between the church and Judaism, all point persuasively to this period.

Whatever the precise historical background, the most important issue from the author's point of view is that the old people have been abandoned and a new people have taken their place. "My people," "a coming people," and "these others" are all used to refer to God's current people in direct contrast to sinful "Israel" (1:25, 35–37; 2:10–11, 33–34, 41): Christians, that is, have replaced Jews as the people of God. They were so chosen from the beginning (2:41), and they will obey the law and the prophets (1:36; 2:40).

This particular theme sets up something of a tension with the Jewish apocalypse to which it is attached. In 5 Ezra the contrast is between faithless

Israel and the new (Christian) people, sometimes depicted as the "other nations" (1:24); in 4 Ezra God's chosen people Israel are contrasted with the faithless but victorious and prosperous nations (3:28–36; 4:22–25; 5:23–30; 6:55–56). In the one Israel is the villain, in the other the victim.

How would a Christian audience have put the two together?[38] Certainly, the reflections on the tragedy of the Jewish War in 4 Ezra turn on themes that were of abiding interest to Christians as well as Jews: God's faithfulness to his people; the pervasiveness and consequences of sin; and eschatological reward for the righteous.[39] It is also clear that judgment would bring joy to only a few, the faithful remnant, and not to the whole of Israel (7:47; 8:1–3, 15–16; 12:34). Moreover, the blending of messianic and Son of Man traditions lent itself readily to Christian glossing (7:28–30; 13:1–58), especially the reference to the death of the Messiah, and the call for repentance which would lead to salvation after death (14:34–35) fits a Christian as well as it fits a Jewish context. Yet the basic contrast, a faithful if reduced Israel set over and against the nations, remains.

The most obvious move would have been for Christians to have identified themselves with the remnant who were expected to survive judgment. The shift from current people, as opposed to Israel, to faithful remnant of Israel would not perhaps have seemed so great. This coincides with the insistence in 5 Ezra that the two peoples share the same mother. In fact it would have held together two of the overriding convictions of 5 Ezra: rejection of Israel and yet continuity with her.[40]

They must have treated 6 Ezra somewhat along the same lines. Here, in a series of oracles, the enemies of God's people (Rome and Asia, 15:43–63) are denounced and their punishment assured (15:5; 16:8). But not all God's people will be delivered. The faithless will be condemned (15:27), and deliverance will come only to "the chosen people" (16:73), "those who fear the Lord" (16:71) or who "keep my commandments and precepts" (16:76). There is little specifically Christian content in these two chapters, though the allusion to forced consumption of idol food (16:68–69) accords better with Roman treatment of Christians than of Jews. But again the notion of faithful survivors was readily susceptible to Christian adaptation. If we are right in thinking Christians made some such hermeneutical leap, it would be a good example of one way in which originally Jewish material could be adapted.

If the relationship with Judaism is unquestionably the dominant concern, there are hints of a broader sense of self-definition too. When Christians are said to be from "other nations" or "another nation" (1:24), they are also implicitly contrasted with the Gentiles in general who remain ignorant of God (2:7,28). They are, that is, a sort of tertium genus set over and against the Gentiles as well as Jews. It is never so clearly stated, but it is nevertheless implied.

What type of Christianity would most likely have produced such a document? We can, of course, only surmise, but the parallels with and dependence on Matthean tradition, together with the overriding concerns of the text, strongly suggest a Jewish Christian environment. It was they, after all, who were most profoundly traumatized by the Bar Cochba rebellion, even though its effects were felt more widely too.[41]

Another text with Christian interpolations can be fairly firmly dated to the same period—4 Baruch. Originally a Jewish composition, it reflects upon the destruction of Jerusalem and exile of the Jews and expresses hope for a restoration and return. Ostensibly set during the first destruction, it refers in fact to the Jewish War and the Bar Cochba rebellion. Restoration, it is predicted, will occur sixty-six years after the destruction (5:29; 7:28–29) which, allowing for some imprecision, points to the period of the Bar Cochba rebellion.[42] To the original eight chapters a ninth was added by a Christian, probably by the mid-second century, describing Jeremiah's vision of the coming Son of God, which he imparts to his followers Baruch and Abimelech.

The Jewish text appeals to the Jews to turn from foreign ways, especially idolatry and mixed marriages (7–8), and to prepare for the return to Jerusalem, that is, the gathering of Israel and the restitution of the cult. This projected future is understood realistically rather than symbolically and is reinforced by the expectation of the resurrection of the righteous.[43] In its original form we can imagine it's being produced before, or during the early stages of, the rebellion, when Jewish hope still ran high and a successful outcome was imaginable. As such, like some of its apocalyptic predecessors (Daniel), it would have encouraged the resurgent nationalism that led to or was already being expressed in the Bar Cochba rebellion.[44] After 135 CE it would have borne little relationship to reality.

What, then, would it have meant to Christians who apparently continued to use it after this date? One suggestion is that it was intended as an offer by Christians to Jews to renounce Judaism, to be baptized and believe in Jesus, and thus to regain the right to enter Jerusalem.[45] Another was that it was written by one group of Jewish Christians to bring hope and encouragement to another.[46] Both of these are necessarily speculative, and neither of them is implausible. Yet another possibility presents itself too: that Christians interpreted the text after 135 CE in terms of what was then manifestly the historical reality. The Jews had been expelled from Jerusalem and the Christians had not, even though they had to replace the Jewish bishops with Gentiles. Might they have identified themselves as those enjoying the restoration and return? That is, the Jews, because of their sins (1:1,8; 3:7), experienced destruction and exile; Christians, as those who inherited the promises to Israel, experienced restoration and return. This would certainly be in line with many other instances where Christians saw themselves as God's new people who inherited the promises of salvation, the corollary often being that the Jews inherited only the threats of condemnation and judgment.

Another echo of the Bar Cochba period might also be found in the story of
Jeremiah's martyrdom at the hands of his fellow Jews (chap. 9), since this
seems to have been the experience of at least some Jewish Christians during
this period.

Around the same time the *Apocalypse of Abraham* appeared.[47] It is commonly dated around the end of the first or the beginning of the second
century. Originally a Jewish work, it was subject to a few Christian additions
whose dates remain a matter of dispute. Some of the glosses seem to reflect
the interests of the much later Slavic Bogomils (20:5,7; 22:5), who favored
the text. One of them, however, may come from an earlier period. In an odd
and obscure vision (29:4–13) a "Man" arrives on the scene who is worshiped by Azazel (the devil), the heathen, and by some of the Jews. Other
Jews resist and insult him. The original allusion is thought to have been to
the demands of the emperor cult under Domitian and his successors and
perhaps, more specifically, to the attempt by Domitian to extend the Jewish
tax. Such assertions of imperial prerogative, despite a generally lenient policy toward the Jews, could still put added pressure on them. In response,
the emperor is portrayed as a heathen and blasphemous son of the devil.

A Christian editor subsequently made a clumsy attempt to give the vision
a christological twist. Instead of being from the heathen (v.4), the man becomes a son of Abraham (v.9), and instead of being a son of the devil (v.6)
he becomes the servant or savior of God (vv.8,10). The heathen worshipers
thus become the multitude of Gentile believers and the divided Jews those
who react to Christ.[48] The Christian interpretation overlays rather than replaces the original, and the result is confusion and inconsistency.

This interpolation might be early enough to indicate Christian adaptation of the work in the second century, though this is by no means certain.
There are a number of themes that Christians would have found congenial.
That Israel had been defeated by the Gentiles and their cult destroyed because of their sins was a familiar enough Christian view of the outcome of
the Jewish War. The cryptic references to defilement of the cult by idolatry
and murder (25–27) may originally have had historical referents, but their
present obscure form would have been enough to confirm a common Christian reading of these events. Cosmological speculation, the origin and purpose of evil and its Satanic progenitors, and the certainty of eschatological
judgment are all themes that could have appealed to Christians as much as
to Jews. If it is true that "individual retribution after death and the future
restoration of the nation are envisaged,"[49] both of these could have been
readily adapted for Christian use by the familiar move of appropriating the
promises rather than the threats.

There is some dispute, as there is with other texts, about whether *3 Baruch*
is a Christian work that uses Jewish traditions or a Jewish work with Christian additions.[50] There are two versions, Greek and Slavonic, and surprisingly the Slavonic is in places (chap. 4) less Christianized than the Greek.

Signs of Christian editing have been found in 4:3—6:15, but they are clearer in chapters 11–16 (especially 13:4; 15:4; 16:2). They are sufficiently light to suggest a Jewish original with Christian interpolations, possibly dating from the second century. Like many other apocalyptic texts of this period, the starting point is the catastrophe of the Jewish War and the destruction of the Temple, but this leads to reflection on wider issues in a manner that deflects rather than answers the initial problem. The seer undergoes what has been called the "apocalyptic cure," in which the revelation of heavenly mysteries allays the doubts and fears provoked by mundane events.[51] On the basis of his vision a rough-and-ready answer for others can also be surmised: hope for the reconstitution of the people centered around the Land and the Temple is to be replaced with an individualized eschatology, in which the archangel Michael daily offers up in a heavenly temple the prayers and deeds of God's faithful servants. The earthly realm moves to the heavenly, and the collective to the individual.

A close reading of the text, in which the vine that leads astray (4:8–16) is identified with the vineyard (= Israel, or Jerusalem) of 1:2, might suggest a final rejection of Israel as a people.[52] The connection might seem too subtle, but the same point would have been made in 16:2, whose reference to those who are "no nation," "a people without understanding," would have been most naturally taken by Christian readers to allude to the Jews. It was they, after all, who openly claimed to be a special nation, and they would readily have been identified with the last of the three groups who use Michael as an intermediary: the empty-handed who receive punishment (following the virtuous and semivirtuous who receive their due reward, chaps. 12–15). The emphasis on individual recompense would have been well suited to a Christian rereading. What is striking on either a Jewish or a Christian reading of the text is the absence of a renewed or new collectivity to take the place of the old one.

The Martyrdom and Ascension of Isaiah is more thoroughly Christianized than many of the texts we are considering. The second half (chaps. 6–11) is wholly Christian, as is one section (3:13—4:22) of the first five chapters too. The Jewish substratum is usually dated no later than the first century CE, and could be much earlier.[53] The Christian material, partly because it is more extensive than in other documents, can be more securely dated to the end of the first or the second century CE.[54]

It has recently been suggested that the complete work emanates from a Christian prophetic school that claimed to have taken heavenly trips and to have seen the descent and ascent of the Beloved—claims that other Christians, who shared their interest in prophetic and charismatic experience, firmly rejected. The author promotes his view by recalling Isaiah's experience as a precedent.[55]

Thus the two Christian additions, in which Isaiah foretells the coming of Christ and his church, are conflated with the story of Isaiah's original rejection and martyrdom at the hands of his fellow Jews. In the first of these, a thumbnail sketch of Jesus' career includes an allusion to his death at the hands of the "children of Israel," a familiar enough theme but one that is quickly passed over here. In the later vision Jesus' death is attributed to demonic forces, and Israel is said to have acted out of ignorance (9:14; 11:19)—part of the larger scheme in which Jesus' true nature remains hidden throughout his descent and earthly life and is revealed only during his ascent.[56] This may not exonerate the Jews, but it does place their actions in a broader context and confine them to a specific historical situation.

The rest of 3:13—4:22 paints a pessimistic picture clustered around two themes. First is corruption in the church, especially among its leaders: false prophecy, love of money and vainglory, fornication, and contention (3:21–31). The themes are conventional, but they may express intense conflict between the author's group and the leaders of the Christian majority. Second is the appearance of Nero redivivus, the son of Beliar/Satan, whose divine pretensions will attract many and reduce the number of faithful believers (4:1–13). The church is thus threatened from within and without, and only a minority (of which the author is a part) will survive to enjoy the imminent return of the Lord (3:21; 4:14–22). The immediate threat, it should be noted, comes not from the Jews but from the Romans. It is they who are the current manifestation on earth of demonic forces.

The final vision of Isaiah describes in some detail life in the heavenly spheres which the faithful can look forward to, and this no doubt was part of its attraction to Christian readers. At the same time, a detailed prophecy of Jesus' descent and ascent (chaps. 10–11) takes the opportunity to provide an eccentric version of the virgin birth: Jesus descends through the heavenly world incognito, is born two months after Mary's impregnation by the Holy Spirit, but then breast-feeds in the normal fashion so that people will not realize he is divine! This version seems designed more to fit into the writer's broader scheme of Jesus' incognito descent and incarnation than to counter the usual doubts about his conception.

The interweaving of Christian and Jewish material results in a book congenial for Christian readers beyond the group it may originally have been written for. The prophet's visions are essentially Christian in content: he sees the future role of the Beloved, his descent, earthly life, and ascent (1:4–6; 3:13–20; 10:7—11:33). Biblical texts had been regularly scoured for predictions about Jesus, but what they offered was often oblique at best. The apocryphal Isaiah, by contrast, foresees his heavenly and earthly existence in considerable detail. The martyrdom of Isaiah (5:1–16), who is rejected by his fellow Israelites, affords a parallel to the martyrdom of Jesus (3:13–14; 11:19–21) and thus confirms what typically happens to God's faithful servants. The details of the heavenly world and the relation between demonic and earthly forces were themes of increasing interest to Christians as well as Jews. The appearance of a Neronian antichrist figure spoke to the pressures that Christians could experience under Roman rule, especially during an upsurge of the emperor cult. Whether this alludes to a particular situation, such as the reign of Domitian, or to a more generalized fear based on past experience, is unclear. This document thus blends Jewish and Christian material into an attractive amalgam, useful beyond its original setting. Unfortunately, its allusions to matters that interest us are made only in passing.

The same sort of easy adaptation can be found in the so-called synagogue prayers lodged in the *Apostolic Constitutions* 7–8.[57] In their present form they are Christian but clearly have Jewish roots. Some of them recall specific Jewish prayers—prayer 4, for example, is close to the Kiddush (the prayer of sanctification) in the Jewish prayer book—but such parallels are not essential to the case for their Jewish origin. Much of the content is distinctly Jewish, the Christian additions are obvious and often clumsily break the flow, and if they had been Christian in origin we would have expected more specifically Christian content than we have. The place of their origin is not known, though Egypt and Syria have been suggested, and the Christian adaptation could have been as early as 150 CE.[58]

Most of the Christian additions consist of phrases like "through Jesus Christ," the simplest expedient for putting the prayers to Christian use. Jesus was revealed to Abraham (12:62), identified with Wisdom (5:4–8), indeed the mediator of all things from creation on. He can be seen as human or divine (1:8; 5:6; 7:15). God is identified clearly as his father (1:2; 4:41; 9:7), but without a particularly adoptionist ring. The virgin birth is asserted (5:4,21; 6:2), but more as part of a general creedlike confession than as a matter of particular contention. A third figure, the Spirit/Paraclete, also regularly appears to complete a loose Trinitarianism (7:15; 8:2; 9:9). The Christian additions would of course have been anathema to Jews,[59] but their removal leaves prayers that Jews as well as Christians could use.

In the Christian additions three significant themes emerge. In 7:15, a prayer of thanksgiving, the Christian praises God because he has "delivered us from the heresy of the Christ-murderers." Judaism, it seems, is a heresy and the Jews the killers of Christ. The words are strongly polemical, picking up a theme we find again and again in Christian sources, but they appear here only in the prayers. This does not lessen their force; indeed the ease with which they are casually dropped in might reinforce it. Second, a somewhat similar tone is set in prayer 5, which praises God for his redemptive deeds on behalf of Israel, including the giving of the law, especially the Sabbath as an opportunity for reverence toward God (5:13–19). The editor then rather clumsily inserts praise for the superiority of the Lord's Day, which for the Christian has taken the place of the Sabbath (5:20–24; cf. 5:7). The Christian feast is not only different from, but preferable to, the Jewish. The gift of the Law is praised, only for it to be replaced in the new order of things.

There is, thirdly, the emphasis on the people of God. Human beings can be presented as citizens of the world in the manner of the wisdom tradition (3:18–19; 11:2–4; 12:35) and the righteous and devout praised on account of these very virtues (2:5,8). Yet constant reference is made to "our fathers," the patriarchs (1:6; 2:2; 15:3; 16:4), and 4:12 speaks of "Israel, your earthly assembly out of the Gentiles." Who is this Israel, and to whom do the patriarchs belong? Certainly 4:12 could in isolation refer to the Jews, perhaps especially diaspora Jews, but in view of other claims made in the prayers it is likely that the Christian editor is appropriating the entire heritage of Judaism, including their status as God's favored people.[60] In 5:8 this is unambiguous: "For by him [Christ] you brought the Gentiles to yourself, for a treasured people, the true Israel, the friend of God who sees God." Confirmation is found in the phrase "your people who have believed in Christ" (13:8; cf. 14:6) and in the way in which the apostles are added to the righteous patriarchs and prophets in 16:12. Thus, when the history of Israel is recalled together with the blessings afforded by God, the Christians now see it as their past, their tradition, the guarantee of their favored status (5:9–19; 6:4–12; 7:2–6; 9:10–16; 12:53ff.).

The borrowing of Jewish liturgical material was not an innocent act, a mere matter of convenience. With it went the wholesale appropriation of the Jewish heritage, selective (as in the case of the Sabbath) when need be. Judaism is dismissed, curiously, as a heresy and the Jews as the killers of Christ. In what precise environment this radical appropriation took place is not known. It might seem natural to suppose that the move was first made by Jewish Christians, who had the easiest access to synagogue prayers. Yet 5:8 and 4:12 seem to imply that these Christians were conscious of their Gentile origin, and we know that both Gentile and Jewish Christians were capable of claiming the heritage of Israel.[61] At any rate, we can be sure that at one stage there was sufficiently close contact with a living Judaism for the borrowing to have taken place. In the form we have them the prayers are designed for use in a Christian setting, to confirm their sense of identity and tradition. They indicate distance from, but not indifference to, contemporary Judaism, and they certainly do not encourage any hopeful or positive attitudes toward the Jews.

Some of the same attitudes can be found in the *Sibylline Oracles,* some of which may have been composed before the end of the second century.[62] Books 1 and 2 reveal heavy Christian editing of a Jewish underlay, and can be dated to ca. 150 CE in Asia Minor. There is a considerable emphasis on eschatology, including the role of Christ as judge (2:241–44), but also on mundane matters such as usury (2:267–70), the treatment of widows and orphans (2:275), and sexual misdemeanors (2:279–82). These may simply be the repetition of conventional ethical themes or may reflect specific problems known to the writer.

"Israel" is blamed for the maltreatment and crucifixion of Jesus, and as a result experiences the wrath of the Most High (1:360–75). The language is stronger and the theme more prominent than in the synagogue prayers:

> Then indeed Israel, with abominable lips
> and poisonous spittings, will give this man blows.
> For food they will give him gall and for drink
> unmixed vinegar, impiously, smitten in breast and heart
> with an evil craze, not seeing with their eyes
> more blind than rats, more terrible than poisonous
> creeping beasts, shackled with heavy sleep.
>
> (1:365–72, trans. Collins)

In part we are dealing with rhetorical excess, much as we find in Melito, but there is no avoiding the intent: the Jews are pilloried as the murderers of Christ and the victims of God's wrath.[63] One expression of this wrath is the destruction of Jerusalem (1:387–400), described in the immediately following lines, where the Jews "reap the bad harvest," "since they committed an evil deed." The two things are not specifically tied together, but there is no doubting the implication: the destruction of Jerusalem was a punishment for the death of Jesus. When it says that the Hebrews will be scattered and driven from their land (1:395–96) the author may, like some other early Christian writers, be conflating the results of the Jewish War (destruction of the Temple) and the Bar Cochba rebellion (expulsion from Jerusalem).

Not only do they lose their land and their Temple, they also lose their inheritance, for when the Jews stumble the Gentiles come in and become God's new shoot from among the nations (1:345, 383). Perhaps they, like other Christians, saw themselves as the true Israel, as when reference is made to the "faithful chosen Hebrews" who will enjoy eschatological triumph (1:174). But if so, it is not an emphatic theme.

Eschatology and ethics, even when borrowed from Judaism, were readily absorbed by Christianity. Some of the ethical material—for example, 2:39–153, which quotes from *Pseudo Phocylides*—gives a broad and humane flavor to the text. A form of liberal universalism has been detected in the claim that God will save pious people "in all respects" (2:28, 48–52).[64] Salvation comes, that is, through good living, or through the intercessory prayers of the righteous (2:330–38). Within this context the Christians appear confident in their identity as a Gentile community, as members of the pious faithful. But they boost this confidence with castigation of the Jews.

Sibylline Oracles 4 contains traces of an updating sometime in the second century (1–48, 102–72, possibly 173–92), but the additions, like the original, were of Jewish origin. Collins states emphatically that "there is no trace of Christian redaction in *Sibylline Oracles* 4."[65] But he also notes that the promotion of baptism (162–65), the rejection of Temple worship (5–12, 17–30), and the pervasive *Naherwartung* find their closest parallels among the Ebionites and Elkesaites, concluding that "they were presumably written in Jewish baptist circles, of a kind similar to those Christian sectarian movements and perhaps historically related to them."[66] Whether this means that this oracle could have been used by these Christians at an early stage remains a matter of speculation, but even in the absence of specific Christian additions it is not inconceivable. How this could happen is shown in *Sibylline Oracles* 5, a document composed ca. 100 CE and entirely Jewish in content with the exception of one intrusive line alluding to the crucifixion (257). With this evidence that Christians used the work, we can see how easily it could have been adapted for their needs. The messianic passages were wide open to Christian use (108–10, 155–61, 256–59, 414–25), but reflections on the destruction of Jerusalem and the subsequent appearance of Nero redivivus (93–110, 150–51, 160–61, 397–413), and on the restored heavenly Jerusalem which the faithful will inhabit (249–55, 420–27) were also of immediate appeal.

Sibylline Oracles 6 is a short Christian hymn, whose date of composition remains uncertain.[67] It contains one hostile reference to the Jews as being from the "land of Sodom," who did not perceive their God when he appeared, and insulted and persecuted him at the point of his death (22–25). As a result they are promised "great affliction." The insulting association of Jews with Sodomites is clearly, as in other oracles, motivated primarily by their complicity in Jesus' death.[68]

Sibylline Oracles 7, an obscure poem that may come from the second century, is a Christian text with no evidence of a Jewish substratum, even though it dwells in part on "Jewish" themes. A connection with either Jewish Christians or Gnostics has been suggested but is hard to demonstrate, and this makes dating it all the more difficult.[69] Among the oracles directed against the nations, one envisages a time of restoration when God will "set up your race as it was before you" (145), which might be yet another example of Christians' taking over the role of God's chosen people. More interesting is the allusion to the false prophets of the last days "who putting on the shaggy hides of sheep, will falsely claim to be Hebrews, which is not their race" (134–35). This "may well be used in a spiritual sense or merely be an allusion to Rev. 2:9, 3:9,"[70] but if it has any more specific meaning, might it refer to the same problem detected in Revelation? That is, does the poet have a particular reason to single out Gentile Judaizers as a threat to his community? There is enough evidence elsewhere to suggest that the possibility cannot be dismissed out of hand.[71]

Sibylline Oracles 8 falls into two halves: 1–216, which is mostly Jewish (except 131–38, 194–216), written around 175 CE; and 217–500, a later, Christian addition (ca. 175–300 CE).[72] In general it is the Romans who loom large in the first author's mind. With the exception of a brief encomium on Hadrian (131–38), the sentiment is intensely anti-Roman; the Romans are the power to be reckoned with and will be subject to God's judgment in the last days. The author, of course, like his Christian adapter, identifies with

God's ultimate victory in the end times. In the later, Christian section the Jews appear, not by name but by clear implication, in a passage that retells the Passion. They are presumably the "lawless and faithless men" (287) who stab him "on account of their law" (296), but the description lacks the color and animus we found in 1.360–75. One of the consequences of Jesus' appearance is the dissolution of the laws that were given to humanity on account of their disobedience (300–1) and the setting aside of sacrificial cults (332–34). This would presumably include the Torah and the sacrificial cult of the Jews, but the perspective is broader, including Gentile laws and cults too. There is thus a sort of leveling effect in which the Jews, their law, and their cult are seen as one example of a broader human phenomenon. The precise focus on Jews found in other sources is absent.

We turn, finally, to the *Testaments of the Twelve Patriarchs*.[73] These documents present us with a rich mixture of Jewish and Christian sentiment. The common view is that, originally Jewish writings, they were adopted and edited by Christians, probably sometime in the second century. Jervell detects the work of a Jewish Christian editor working as early as 100 CE, but a date later in the second century is favored by many.[74] De Jonge has argued that they are essentially Christian documents, composed ca. 175 CE, but incorporate a considerable amount of Jewish material.[75] Either way we are dealing with documents that were used in Christian circles in the second century, and it is their final form rather than various hypothetical stages of composition that are of interest to us. And, as with the other literature we have surveyed, it is important that we read the whole text in order to understand how Christians might have understood it.

The Christology of the *Testaments* is haphazard rather than thoroughly worked through. The Incarnation is emphasized (*T.Sim.*6:5–7; *T.Naph.*8:3; *T.Ash.*7:3), as is the reality of Jesus' mundane life (*T.Ash.*7:3), and his descent into Hades and ascension are alluded to in *T.Benj.*9:2–5. The messianic material, as is well known, is not always consistent. Sometimes there is talk of two separate messianic figures, Levi the priest and Judah the king (*T.Jud.*1:6; 24:1–6; *T.Levi*18:1–11), at other times of one figure who combines both roles (*T.Dan*5:10; *T.Gad*8:1; *T.Benj.*4:2). Presumably Christians identified the Messiah with Jesus, a conventional Christian gesture. Unusual, however, is the repeated claim that the Messiah teaches, renews, and keeps the law (*T.Levi*16:3; *T.Dan*6:9; *T.Benj.*11:2; *T.Jud.*24:1,3; *T.Naph.*4:5; *T.Levi* 18:1ff.). This presents Jesus as a figure entirely congenial to Judaism even though, as prophesied, many of them reject him, and even though it would not have been welcome in some Christian circles.[76]

This picture is somewhat modified, however, when we place it in the context of the Torah-piety that pervades the *Testaments*, the repeated emphasis on keeping the law as the proper response to God, and the guarantee of his beneficence. This in turn is reinforced by connecting it to the concept of a universal, natural law, much in the manner of diaspora Judaism

(*T.Levi*13:1–3, 19:1–3; *T.Jud.*26:1; *T.Dan*6:9–11; *T.Jos.*11:1; *T.Benj.*10:3). The ethical ideals, a major concern in the instruction given by the patriarchs to their descendants, appeal correspondingly to universal moral virtues shared by Jew and Gentile alike. It is noticeable, accordingly, that distinctive Jewish precepts (such as circumcision and food laws) are not mentioned. And thus although adherence to the law is constant, it is placed in a broader context, which would have eased its absorption into the Christian tradition. For there was nothing exceptionable about Jesus or Christians adhering to the law when understood in this broadly universalist, ethical sense.

Repeatedly in the *Testaments* the descendants of the patriarchs are warned about the consequences of their transgressions (*T.Levi*9:10, 18:9; *T.Dan*5:5, 6:6; *T.Benj.*9:4, 10:4; *T.Jud.*23:2; *T.Naph.*4:1). Many of these echo traditional prophetic castigations against a disobedient people. One particular outcome is, however, specifically mentioned: the destruction of the Temple and the scattering of the Jews (*T.Levi*10:3–5, 15:1–3, 16:1–5; *T.Iss.*6:2–4; *T.Zeb.*6:6; *T.Benj.*5:12–13; *T.Ash.*7:1–3). These echo the language used to describe the destruction of the first Temple, but there is little doubt that Christians would find in them a reference to the disastrous experiences of the Jews under the Romans. The twin themes of Temple destruction and scattering of the people may suggest that, like other Christians of this time, they casually conflated the consequences of the Jewish War and the Bar Cochba rebellion. In *T.Levi*10:3–5, 16:3–5 destruction and scattering are seen to be the outcome of the Jews' rejection of Jesus and complicity in his death, a theme that crops up elsewhere too (*T.Levi*4:4; *T.Benj.*3:8). Yet unlike many other instances in which this forms more or less the last word on the fate of the Jews, in the *Testaments* it is interwoven with a more positive message.

This brings us to the most important theme of the *Testaments* for our purposes: their view of the salvation of Jews and Gentiles. They are properly mentioned together because many of the passages that speak of the one speak of the other too. The many statements about the salvation of Israel have been conveniently classified by de Jonge into three types: first, the salvation of the righteous patriarchs (*T.Zeb.*10:2; *T.Benj.*10:4–11); second, the description of Israel's fate in terms of a sin-exile-return pattern (*T.Iss.*6; *T.Levi*10:14–15; *T.Zeb.*9–10; *T.Ash.*7); and third, the protection and survival of the descendants of Levi and Judah (*T.Sim.*7:2–3; *T.Jud.*22; *T.Dan*5).

Many of the passages that speak of the salvation of Israel include the Gentiles as well.[77] In these instances there is invariably some form of christological allusion too, and thus a fairly consistent view that the salvation of the Gentiles comes about with the appearance of Christ. With the Jews this is not so clear: sometimes their salvation seems to come through obedience to God's commandments, sometimes only through Christ. The following two passages illustrate the point:

But you, if you walk in holiness before the face of the Lord, you will again dwell safely with me, and all Israel will be gathered to the Lord. (*T.Benj.* 10:11)

For the Lord will raise up from Levi someone as a high priest and someone as a king, God and man. He will save all the Gentiles and the tribe of Israel. (*T.Sim.*7:2)

It is difficult to retrieve a precise picture of the mode of Israel's salvation from this, even though there is no doubt about the author's profound interest in it. If we assume that the Christian writer was using a Jewish source, it might be argued that the nonchristological promises of Israel's salvation are the result of editorial oversight and should be interpreted by the more specifically Christian assertions. But in principle we must take the whole document at its face value, especially if it should turn out, as Jervell has argued, that the salvation of the Gentiles is presented as if it were self-evident, whereas the salvation of the Jews appears to be a matter of lively and anxious concern.[78] Nor should we necessarily interpret all the future promises in a Christian fashion. Perhaps the author believed that Christians, Jewish or Gentile, would be saved by Christ and the bulk of the Jews through God's original promise.

Apart from the interweaving of the future salvation of Jews and Gentiles, the most striking characteristic of the *Testaments* is their unrestrained universalism. Ultimately it is "all Israel" and "all the Gentiles" who will be saved, even if it is not clear precisely how this will occur (see the two sample passages above). Such breadth of vision is rare in the early Christian world; indeed, it runs counter to much of the evidence that we have considered in this chapter alone. Israel is neither rejected nor replaced by a "new people" or a "third race." This is the closest thing we have to Paul's universalist vision in Romans 11, though there are no signs of direct influence. It is, on one reading, also similar to the two-covenant notion detected in *Barnabas,* the Pseudo-Clementines, and perhaps elsewhere too.

It is worth highlighting a few points in conclusion. First, when a Jewish text was adapted for Christian use it would have been possible in some instances to absorb the original Jewish substratum effortlessly. In other cases this was doubtless more difficult. If we are to understand how they functioned as Christian texts, however, we cannot concentrate only on the obvious Christian insertions. We have to imagine how Christians would have understood whole texts after they had taken them under their wing, that is, when they were seen as Christian and not as Jewish works.[79]

The simplest way, secondly, to adapt a Jewish writing for Christian use was to introduce christological allusions. This happens in all the texts we have looked at, and is the surest sign of Christian influence. Sometimes the allusions are intrusive, clumsily breaking the flow of the passage, but sometimes they fit smoothly into the context. Messianic concepts were readily taken over even with a specifically Christian twist. The virgin birth crops up twice, but does not seem a matter of contention with Jews. Jesus' death, on the other hand, while it can be attributed to demonic forces, is usually associated directly and acrimoniously with the Jews.[80]

It is clear, thirdly, that some Christian editors thought that an immediate consequence of Jewish involvement in the death of Jesus and subsequent refusal of the gospel was the events of 70 and 135 CE. In addition to being "Christ murderers," they condemned themselves to a series of catastrophic events, which demonstrated their reprobation.[81] Equally clear, fourthly, is that the long-term prospects for the Jews is, in many texts, not much better. They lost their status as God's chosen people and were rejected. Their place was taken by a new people, who inherited their role as God's special elect.[82] The Bar Cochba rebellion, as we have found elsewhere, had a particularly significant effect, pushing one or two writers toward a radical rejection of Israel.

We have, fifthly, one remarkable text which, while containing reflections on the judgment of Israel and allusions to current historical disasters, has as its overarching theme the universality of salvation, for Jews and Gentiles alike (Test.XII). The unusual breadth and generosity of this vision singles it out among other works we have considered in this chapter, though not from all other early Christian evidence we shall consider.

Sixthly, in a number of texts the keeping of God's law is retained as a Christian ideal. This may be due to Jewish Christian influence, but it may also be because the keeping of the law had, as in diaspora Judaism, come to be understood in terms of broad human ideals, as much suited to the Gentile as to the Jew. If so, the transition of this ideal into Christian circles becomes the more readily explicable.[83] And, finally, it is possible that we have one allusion to Gentile Judaizing (Sib.Or.7).

CONCLUSION

The literature we have just surveyed is often neglected as a source of information about Jewish-Christian relations. Yet that should not be so. There is no reason to suppose that these Christian writings and adaptations were any less popular or influential than those that eventually made their way into the canon. The very existence of the New Testament and other conventional collections such as the so-called Apostolic Fathers gives to them a prominence that may belie their influence in the second century. If historically apocryphal writings have been considered somewhat peripheral, then we need to place them back firmly on center stage, where they belong just as much as other literature from the period.

In doing so we achieve at least three things. First, we find confirmation and expansion of a number of insights into Jewish-Christian relations that we find in the more familiar sources: responsibility for the death of Jesus, the significance of the Bar Cochba rebellion, and, above all in this case, the Christian appropriation of Jewish traditions and titles are only some of the more obvious examples. We also find confirmation, secondly, of the wide range of Christian reactions to Judaism, which the rest of our evidence also amply conveys. The story of Jewish-Christian relations, we find yet again, is neither simple nor uniform.

But above all, thirdly, we give prominence to voices that might otherwise go unheard. A number of the apocrypha present the Jews in a neutral or modestly positive fashion. The *Odes of Solomon*, however, and more especially the *Acts of Pilate* and the *Testaments of the Twelve Patriarchs*, promote an image of the Jews and an expectation for their future salvation that, in their generosity and optimism, are rarely matched. These views, as much a part of second-century Christianity as any others, are all too easy to underestimate or ignore.

SUPERSESSION: HEBREWS AND *BARNABAS*

4

❖

The theme of supersession crops up in the vast majority of early Christian writers. In most cases it forms part of a larger argument, as in Justin's *Dialogue* or the Gospels of Matthew and Luke, and it crops up in a number of places in our discussion. In two documents, however, it is an overriding obsession: the Epistle to the Hebrews and the *Epistle of Barnabas*. Because of their obsessive nature and because the theme is of central significance for Jewish-Christian relations, it will be instructive to consider them together, to compare and contrast both what they say and why they say it.

THE EPISTLE TO THE HEBREWS

"The struggle with Jewish tradition is omnipresent in the NT but nowhere do we find a clear rupture with Judaism. Paradoxically enough, it is the writer of Hebrews who—while passionately arguing along Jewish lines—moves furthest in the direction of the breach with Judaism which was later to take place."[1] So concludes one of the most recent studies of Hebrews pertinent to our theme. Even if we do not accede to every nuance, the statement nevertheless sharply delineates the radical view of Judaism which this most enigmatic of New Testament writings presents. Almost every study of Hebrews comments on its view of Judaism in some way or another and, given the content of the letter, it would take a particularly obtuse commentator to overlook it. Yet it is often relegated to passing comments or brief asides and is rarely the object of sustained attention. Lehne, whom I have quoted, concentrates on the cluster of issues associated with covenant and sees them as the overarching theme of the book. As a result, she is more alert to the issue than many. W. Klassen, one of the few to have focused directly on the view of Judaism in Hebrews, poses an interesting question about how Jews would have reacted to Hebrews and concludes, rather too sanguinely, that they would have found little to disturb them.[2] The more relevant question, since Hebrews was undoubtedly intended for the eyes and ears of Christian readers, is what view of Judaism it would have encouraged among them; and the answer, it would appear, is a more negative one than many have been inclined to find.

Hebrews has been loath to give up its secrets and has resisted the advances of many an interpreter.[3] There are a number of reasons for this. We do not know by whom or to whom it was written. It does not conform to any single literary genre: calling itself a "word of exhortation" (13:22), it has an epistolary conclusion but is often thought to be more like a sermon or meditation. It can be read in the light of a multitude of intellectual and religious traditions—Hellenistic Judaism (especially Philo), Qumran, early Christianity, Gnosticism, middle Platonism—but neither together nor alone have they been able to provide a complete or consistent understanding of it. Thus in form, as in content, Hebrews presents a unique, creative, often puzzling, blend. Add to this a subtle, allusive style of argumentation and it is hardly surprising that it has spawned widely divergent interpretations. And for a document that reflects at some length on priestly and cultic matters, it is exceptionally odd, whether we date it before or after 70 CE, that it alludes solely to the biblical account of the tabernacle and not to the Herodian Temple and its cult—even if only to note their demise.

Compounding the problems inherent in the text has been the scholarly tendency to set out the interpretative options in terms of stark alternatives. Thus, for a time, those who thought the primary aim of Hebrews was to avert a relapse into Judaism (mainly Anglo-Saxon scholars) were arrayed against those who thought it was to overcome a general lassitude caused by the delay of the parousia, persecution, and waning enthusiasm (mainly German scholars). Similarly it has been claimed that the basic intellectual impulse of Hebrews is either temporal/eschatological or spatial/Neoplatonic, as if they were mutually exclusive alternatives. Again, the demonstrable alternation in Hebrews between theological reflection and practical exhortation (sometimes conveniently labeled thesis and paraenesis) has almost inevitably led to the claim that the one or the other gets to the very heart of the author's message. One advance in recent scholarship has been the recognition that setting out the alternatives in this fashion is not only unjustifiably rigid, but also demonstrably false.

In fact, the last of these antinomies—thesis versus paraenesis—provides us with a convenient peg on which to hang our consideration of the message and context of Hebrews. The paraenetic sections contain a number of hints about the present and past circumstances of the recipients and a few about the author. They are oblique and elusive, but they do give us something to go on.

To what extent we can supplement them by reading between the lines of the theological sections is a matter of some dispute. Most attempts to do so involve mirror reading, which proceeds on the assumption that the views of the recipients were different from (often opposite to) those of the author. The assumption is by no means secure. Authors sometimes had reason to dwell on things that they held in common with their readers as well as on those over which they differed; the difficulty is to gauge which is which. Then again, not all texts are properly categorized in either of these ways. Some texts are an expression of an author's own obsessions and interests rather than a conscious attempt to chide or encourage the recipients. And even when the situation of the readers is in mind, there is no guarantee that it has been fully understood. Writers can be ill-informed, prejudiced, or simply muddled.[4]

These are valid warnings against naive and overeager attempts to reconstruct the situation of the readers from the text of the writer. When all is said and done, however, they encourage us to be alert and cautious rather than to abandon the procedure altogether. If we were to do so, the bulk of Hebrews (about two-thirds) would have to be disregarded and we would be left with the paraenesis alone. Yet the very structure of the work discourages this. The text does not divide neatly into two consecutive parts; rather, the two components, theology and exhortation, constantly alternate and intermingle. It is inherently unlikely that they are unconnected, and there is a prima facie case for considering them equally important for reconstructing the views of the recipients as well as those of the sender. Thus, while trying to avoid a procrustean approach, the more mutually supportive our understanding of the two components of the text, the more satisfying and persuasive it is likely to be.

This is not entirely a matter of surmise. In one section of paraenesis the author makes it clear that he considers the theology of the readers to be defective. They are like children, who can digest milk but not meat; indeed, even their understanding of the basic elements of the faith is in question. They have become "dull in understanding," and what the author has to say to them is going to be "hard to explain" (5:11—6:3).[5] Here theology and paraenesis are intimately linked, and it is quite clear that the theology of the author is intended to correct and advance that of the readers. Similarly, in a brief paraenetic interlude between reflections on Christ and the angels, the readers are exhorted to "pay greater attention to what we have heard, so that we do not drift away from it" (2:1), where "what we have heard" seems to include the speculative as well as the pragmatic aspects of the tradition.

That the author had firsthand knowledge of the recipients on which to base his comments is implied when he urges that they pray that he will be "restored" to them (13:19) and announces that he expects to see them with or without Timothy in the near future (13:23). Some have plausibly surmised that he was a member (and leader) of the recipient community, currently separated by sickness or imprisonment; if so, then presumably he had at one time had a reasonably accurate picture of what was going on there.

Paraenesis

And what was going on there? First, in the most general terms: drifting away (2:1), sluggishness (6:12), shrinking back (10:39), weariness and loss of heart (12:3), "drooping hands" and "weak knees" (12:12)—that is, a certain anomie and lassitude, which has led to reduced enthusiasm and commitment. This could express declining interest among third-generation Christians, which had no specific cause. But it might also have been caused by disillusionment—for example, with the delay of the parousia—or by external political pressures.

This brings us, secondly, to the closely connected and repeated calls for perseverance. Struggles and trials are to be endured like parental discipline, which will lead to the "peaceful fruit of righteousness" (12:3–11). The readers are to hold to their confession in the time of need (4:14–16), to hold on to the hope that brings the great reward (10:35–39). In nurturing the "diligence" that will allow them to inherit the promises, they are to be like those before them who had patience and faith (6:11–12)—exemplary Christian (cf. 13:7) or Israelite predecessors. The latter are called on in the impressive roll call of Israelite heroes in chapter 11, examples of the faith that is "the assurance of things hoped for, the conviction of things not seen" (11:1).[6] Among them were Enoch and Noah, Abraham and Moses, kings and prophets. All of them had faith, but in the end none of them obtained the ultimate promise revealed only in Christ (11:39–40). All underwent a severe testing of their faith, but as the list comes to a climax it is striking that the emphasis falls increasingly on external threats—persecution, imprisonment, rejection, destitution, and death (11:32–38).

An unmistakable note is struck here. The persistent call for endurance implies that something was threatening their stability and commitment. What that was is not immediately clear. Endurance could have been invoked to counter disappointed expectations. The failure of the promised parousia to arrive could have led to doubt and despair. Equally it could have been caused by external pressures, such as persecution and harassment. The two come together in chapter 10: an exhortation to endurance and confident hope (10:35–36) is preceded by an unambiguous allusion to persecution (10:32–34) and followed by the assurance that the Coming One will not delay (10:37–38). Where does the center of gravity lie? In this chapter, the eschatological theme seems secondary. It is introduced as both a promise and a threat: the end will come, and soon; do not be like those who are lost because they "shrink back."

Some insight into what may lie behind these exhortations is provided in passages that speak directly about the experience of the readers:

> But recall those earlier days when, after you had been enlightened, you endured a hard struggle with sufferings, sometimes being publicly exposed to

abuse and persecution, and sometimes being partners with those so treated. For you had compassion for those who were in prison, and you cheerfully accepted the plundering of your possessions, knowing that you yourselves possessed something better and more lasting. (10:32–34)

In your struggle against sin you have not yet resisted to the point of shedding your blood. (12:4)

Remember those who are in prison, as though you were in prison with them; those who are being tortured, as though you yourselves were being tortured. (13:3)

Remember your leaders, those who spoke the word of God to you; consider the outcome of their way of life, and imitate their faith. (13:7)

A number of conclusions can be drawn. First, that the addressees are Christians of some long standing. Their "enlightenment" lay some time in the past. They are not neophytes—a point confirmed by the author's observation that they ought to be feeding on "solid food" not "milk," to be teachers rather than learners (5:11–14). Secondly, they have undergone quite severe persecution—harassment, abuse, imprisonment, and confiscation. Not all were victims, but all were associated by sympathy and compassion. Some of their leaders may have been martyred, if "outcome" (*ekbasis*) in 13:7 means death rather than result.[7] Most of this occurred in the past, and it might be argued that it is recalled simply to bolster flagging spirits in the present. However, the constant calls for perseverance, the exhortation to comfort the imprisoned and tortured (13:3) and bear the abuse that Jesus also endured (13:13), suggest that a threat of the same order looms again. Nor should we forget that Timothy, and perhaps the author too, had recently been in prison. The past is remembered as a heroic era of resistance because it is directly relevant to the present.

The identity of the persecutors, thirdly, remains unspecified. It is just possible that they were Jewish authorities who had instigated the harassment of Jewish Christians. There is some evidence that this occasionally took place, but it is more likely that the allusion is to Roman persecution.[8] Imprisonment and confiscation sound more like the actions of state authorities, even if they were confined to occasional local outbursts.[9] Two events in particular have been connected with the statements in Hebrews: the expulsion of the Jews from Rome by Claudius in the forties and the victimization of Christians by Nero in the sixties.[10] Since in Hebrews it is clear that the readers had been persecuted *as Christians,* the first of these would require us to suppose that Christian Jews were one, if not the only, victim of Claudius's action, a popular interpretation based on very little but supposition.[11] Nero's notorious assault on the Roman Christians in 64 CE, which involved public torture and burnings, is a more obvious allusion (Tacitus *Annals* 15.44). It cannot be dismissed on the basis of Hebrews 12:4, since the readers may have belonged to a group that suffered severe harassment but not death,[12] or that had immigrated to Rome after the persecution.[13] Persecution could, of course, have occurred elsewhere, and Rome is not the only possible location, but it gains further support from the probable allusion to the martyrdom of leaders of the Roman church (13:7) which would coincide, in addition, with the vaguely dated traditions about the martyrdom of Peter and Paul (*1 Clem*.5–6).

In this connection we must add the references to apostasy. The two most striking passages are as follows:

> For it is impossible to restore again to repentance those who have once been enlightened, and have tasted the heavenly gift, and have shared in the Holy Spirit, and have tasted the goodness of the word of God and the powers of the age to come, and then have fallen away, since on their own they are crucifying again the Son of God and are holding him up to contempt. (Heb.6:4–6)

> For if we willfully persist in sin after having received the knowledge of the truth, there no longer remains a sacrifice for sins. . . . Anyone who has violated the law of Moses dies without mercy "on the testimony of two or three witnesses." How much worse punishment do you think will be deserved by those who have spurned the Son of God, profaned the blood of the covenant by which they were sanctified, and outraged the Spirit of grace? (Heb.10:26–29)

The sentiment of these two passages is identical: those who have enjoyed the benefits of Christianity but then "fall away" or "persist in sin" place themselves beyond God's mercy. They, like Esau, will find no opportunity for repentance (12:16–17). The verbs employed are unusually strong—crucifying, spurning, profaning, outraging, holding up to contempt. What provoked this colorful language and the categorical denial of repentance? Surely something more catastrophic than the day-to-day shortcomings that burden the average conscience. To have judged the routine sins of his fellow Christians in this way would have required a self-righteous insensitivity, which the rest of the book belies. Most obviously the allusion is to the ultimate sin—apostasy or defection—and this accounts also for the severity of judgment.[14] The vivid warnings are surely not entirely hypothetical. Some Christians, even if not from this particular group, must have defected in order for the threat to have arisen and the uncompromising conclusion to have been drawn; and the writer may not have been as confident as he claims to be that his readers would not succumb (6:9). This could have been in the recent or the more distant past, but in any case well enough remembered to have seared itself onto the consciousness of the community.

What precisely would have been meant by defection is not clear. For Gentile Christians it would have meant returning to their pagan way of life or defection to the synagogue; for Jewish Christians it would most likely (but not certainly) have meant a return to the synagogue, many of whose obligations they may well have carried over into their Christian existence at any rate.

All the many references we have considered so far point most clearly in the direction of state harassment of Christians, past and present, which has led to defections and may lead to more. Entirely consistent with this is the hint that some Christians have absented themselves from communal meetings (10:25; cf. Ignatius *Magn.*9:1; *Phld.*4:1; *Barn.*4:10), which could look worryingly like the first step toward a more serious defection. Their reluctance (if this is the proper way to read 13:12–14) to be marginalized, to live "outside the camp" and to accept the ridicule and abuse that this involved, points in the same direction.[15] The distinction between the readers and other local Christians in 10:25, and the greeting to "all your leaders" in 13:24 have plausibly been taken as hints that the author is addressing a house church (or group of house churches) that is only one segment of the total Christian community in the vicinity.

The connection between external pressure and flagging enthusiasm is readily understandable. Ostracism, harassment, and persecution posed threats that it would have been inhuman not to fear on a purely physical and social level. Equally, however, they could have punctured once-buoyant hopes, creating a profound disjunction between their christological and eschatological convictions and the harsh reality they routinely faced. The world was not as it should have been.[16]

The picture we have built up from the paraenetic material is so far fairly consistent. There is, however, one puzzling exception:

> Do not be carried away by diverse and strange teachings. For it is good for the heart to be made firm with grace, not foods, whose observers were not benefited. We have an altar from which those who serve the tabernacle have no right to eat. (13:9–10)[17]

The problem according to this cryptic statement is not persecution but "strange teachings," part of which at least presumably had something to do with foods.[18] An allusion to participation in pagan cult meals or eating meat offered to idols (see 1 Cor 8–10) is possible, but one would expect it to have evoked a greater note of alarm. It may be that some form of extreme (from the author's viewpoint) eucharistic theology is being repudiated, but if so the allusion is so oblique as to be impenetrable.[19] Far more likely is an allusion to some form of Jewish observance. "Observers" in Heb 13:9, literally "those who walked" (*hoi peripatountes*), is a term used elsewhere to denote religious observance (Mark 7:5; Col 2:6; Acts 21:21) and recalls the Jewish use of halakah (literally, "walk") to refer to observance of the law. "Those who serve the tabernacle" (v.10) must, in context, be the priests of the Jewish cult that has already been the subject of a lengthy discussion. Some form of Jewish observance, which some Christians are tempted to, or already do, participate in makes the best sense.[20] A form of kashruth or an ascetically inspired abstention from food could be in mind, although some argue that Jewish fellowship meals in the diaspora synagogue (cf. Josephus *Ant.*14.214ff.) fit the language better.[21] It is certainly possible that such synagogue meals had taken on the religious hue of similar meals organized by other voluntary associations. Much depends on how exact the author intends to be. "To observe foods" and (implicitly) "to make the heart firm" are often thought to imply consumption rather than abstention, and to be an odd way of referring to the restrictions of kashruth or ascetic piety.[22] But this may be to demand greater precision than the language is intended to bear. "Observing" foods, an odd phrase without precise parallel, is vague enough to refer to consumption or abstention, in fact, to any sort of special dietary regulation. And there is surely nothing untoward in the notion of abstention (as much as consumption) nurturing the heart or soul. It is in fact a commonplace notion in ascetic piety.

The tone is not the same as with the passages on defection. "Observing foods" seems to be on a par with the (probably Jewish) food, drink, and baptisms alluded to in 9:10: they are bodily regulations, of temporary value but unable to perfect the conscience or strengthen the heart. The superior altar from which the representatives of the old cult are excluded (13:10) is the Christian alternative—perhaps a form of the Eucharist, or perhaps simply the benefits brought by Christ's earthly and heavenly cultic activity.

In the paraenetic sections, most of the evidence about the recipient community clusters around what we might call a Roman or political problem—persecution, perseverance, apostasy. This passage deals with an apparently different set of issues: Christian participation in Jewish practices, specifically Jewish meals, which provokes the author sharply to contrast Jewish and Christian claims. Both aspects conveniently point us to the more reflective portions of the text, which present us with a theology that is at the same time articulated largely in terms of, but also radically contrasted with, the traditions of Judaism.

Theology

Viewed broadly, four features of the theology of Hebrews are particularly striking: it is overwhelmingly christological in its focus; it draws frequently, and in ways unlike any other early Christian writing, on scriptural, especially cultic, analogies; it routinely and starkly contrasts Christianity and Judaism to the detriment of the latter; and it blends in an unusual way the temporal eschatological scheme of the early Christian tradition with the spatial, Neoplatonic contrast between the heavenly and earthly realities.

The Christology of Hebrews is eclectic. Many titles are used that are familiar from other Christian sources—Son, Christ, Lord, firstborn.[23] The frequency of their occurrence probably indicates a degree of routinization, but there is no reason to think that they could not still express the grandeur of christological conviction, even if the casual combination of titles and assertions does not (at least from a later perspective) amount to a fully thought-out position. Hebrews 1:8–9 is a good example: Is Jesus God (v.8) or not (v.9)? One reason for this is that the author's main interest and most distinctive contribution lie elsewhere—in the creative interaction with Jewish scripture and traditions. In the opening chapters Jesus' superiority to the angels is emphatically asserted. As God's glory and image, he had a cosmic role in creation and has been exalted on high (1:1–4). The angels, on the other hand, are servants of God's Son (1:5–6) and of human beings (1:14), inferior to both. They mediated God's original message to Israel, now superseded by the Lord, his followers, and the gifts of the Spirit (2:2–4). Jesus' temporary incarnation and humiliating death achieve several goals: defeat of the devil and death (2:9,14–15); perfection through suffering (2:10); expiation of humans' sin, and empathy with their trials (2:11,14,17–18). The objects of this salvation are the "brothers and sisters" of Jesus, the "descendants of Abraham" (2:11–16)—that is, they are humans not angels, and they are Christians, not Jews.[24] There is a clear hierarchy presupposed and expressed in these opening chapters: Jesus is superior to human beings and human beings to angelic beings.

It has been suggested plausibly that the author is challenging some sort of angel Christology that the readers found attractive.[25] It could have included a tendency to see Jesus as one of the angelic horde, even if a decidedly superior one, and the salvation he brought as effective chiefly in the angelic world. Thus we might explain the emphasis on Jesus' superiority to the angels, and on human beings as the object of his salvation (2:16). Many strains of speculation about angelic and other heavenly beings are known to us from the Judaism of this time: intermediaries, such as Wisdom or Logos; heavenly travelers, such as the Son of Man; angelic leaders, such as Michael and, most interestingly, Melchizedek. Among Christian Jews or Gentile Christians influenced by Jewish speculation, a christological development along these lines would be perfectly understandable, though it is not immediately demonstrable. The emphasis in Hebrews on the reality and effect of Jesus' death could mean that the readers devalued it, but it may be mainly a way of reinforcing the view that it was human (not angelic) beings whose experience he paralleled and of anticipating the cultic/expiation themes of later chapters.

In 3:1—4:13 Jesus and his followers are compared to Moses and the Israelites. Moses was faithful, but in the end only a servant in God's house; Jesus was faithful, but as a son, and thus worthy of the greater glory (3:2–6). An equally unsophisticated comparison is made between the Israelites of the wilderness generation and the Christian readers. The Israelites, through disobedience, lost the promise and did not enter God's "rest"; the promise and the "rest," therefore, remain open for those who are faithful in Christ, who can become a new pilgrim people.[26] But for them, too, it can be lost through disobedience. It is interesting to note that Moses is praised but superseded, whereas Israel is castigated and superseded. The outcome is the same even though the estimation is somewhat different. Some have suggested that the author might be reacting to a Moses-Christology among the readers. The emphasis is, however, mostly on Israel rather than Moses, and on Moses as a faithful leader rather than as a proleptic prophet. If there is a reaction to anything, it is more likely to have been to the high estimate Jews and Jewish Christians place on Moses as lawgiver or, as in this case, as founding patriarch.

In 4:14—5:10 we are given an anticipation of the themes that are to dominate the theological reflections throughout the rest of the letter, and that mark the most distinctive contribution of the author to early Christian thought: the order of Melchizedek, the high priest, the new covenant, the heavenly cult. The subtle interweaving of these makes for a dense and complex argument, the gist of which is sufficient for our purposes.

Melchizedek, an obscure character in Genesis, became the focus of considerable speculation in early Judaism and is depicted variously as a heavenly, priestly, archangelic figure.[27] We can conclude without doubt that Jewish speculation provides the immediate context for these chapters, and yet there is no precise parallel to the particular analogies or the overall scheme that the author develops. The promise to Abraham was doubly secured: it was based on God's promise and confirmed by God's oath. Abraham was faithful, but God himself was the guarantor (6:13–20). Yet Abraham himself acknowledged the superiority of Melchizedek, described by the author as "king of righteousness . . . king of peace. . . . Without father, without mother, without genealogy, having neither beginning of days nor end of life, but resembling the Son of God" (7:2–3). As such he founds an unprecedented, non-Levitical priestly line, of which Jesus is the inheritor. The Levitical line is thus annulled, the law abrogated (7:16–19), and Jesus' superiority boldly asserted: his priesthood is guaranteed by God's oath, while theirs is not; his is eternal, theirs ever-changing; his sacrifice is singular and perfect, theirs repeated daily (7:22–28).

Having demonstrated Jesus' unorthodox route to the priesthood, the author launches into an intricate characterization of Jesus as the great high priest (8:1—10:18). Using the covenant and the rituals of the Day of Atonement as his main foils, the author gives full rein to the two main motifs of his argument: what Jesus has unequivocally, once and for all, achieved; and what in Judaism has consequently, irrevocably, been surpassed.

The covenant established by Jesus is declared superior: it is based on better promises; it is new, and the previous one thus old (8:6,13); it is ratified by his death and the sprinkling of his blood (9:15–22). Despite the promise in Jeremiah 31:31–34, which is fully quoted, no other contemporary Jewish or Christian writer dwells on this theme so lengthily or draws the lines of contrast so sharply. The same tone continues in the comparison of the old and new tabernacles. The new is superior to the old because it is heavenly, not earthly, rests on the sacrificial blood of Jesus, not that of animals, and is done once and for all, not again and again (8:1–5; 9:25–26; 10:2–11).

As the inaugurator of the new covenant and the celebrant in the new tabernacle, Jesus is portrayed primarily as expiator and intercessor, the one who gives himself willingly as a sin offering (2:10–18; 9:11–28; 10:1–18) and thus becomes pioneer and intercessor on behalf of his followers (4:14—5:10; 6:19–20; 7:11—8:7; 10:19–22), to whom he brings forgiveness, the transformation of the inner person, and the possibility of perfection.[28] The argument works by a constant shifting between two poles, both of which are essential to the author's case: Jesus' sacrificial death on earth and his inauguration of the new covenant in heaven. As Attridge puts it: "As the heavenly character of Christ's act is thus subjected to symbolic interpretation, the evaluation of the earthly pole of the earth-heaven antithesis undergoes a dramatic transformation. Surprisingly, Christ's 'heavenly' act is ultimately seen to be an earthly one, done in and through the bodily sacrifice."[29] The two planes of activity are held firmly together, and the traffic between them runs in both directions. What occurs on earth is simultaneously played out in a different key in heaven; and what happens in heaven has tangible effects on earth.

At the same time, this contrast between the heavenly and earthly is blended with a more traditional eschatological scheme. Some have argued that the author is deliberately supplementing, and thus correcting, the eschatology of his readers: their traditional temporal/futuristic eschatology is supplemented by his more spatial/realized, "Alexandrian" eschatology.[30] A blend of this sort, which emphasizes what has been achieved and is available as well as what is to come, could be designed to encourage those troubled by the delay of the parousia. That this was an issue may be implied by 10:37–38 (cf. 9:28; 10:25), and it is possible to imagine how it could have caused or exacerbated a general decline in enthusiasm. But there is little in the text that directly suggests that it was a major theme and, as we noted above, what there is could be designed to goad flagging spirits rather than bolster a disappointed expectation.

There is, finally, a constant thread in the christological argument that needs to be singled out: the radical contrast between old and new, good and better, sketch and reality, earthly and heavenly, spiritual and physical, outer and inner, repeated and unique.[31] The terms of contrast vary considerably, but they all serve the same purpose: to assert the superiority of Christianity and the inferiority of Judaism. With specific reference to the cultic section, the following table of contrasts has been drawn up:

Old Covenant	New Covenant
Many mortal priests with genealogy	— One high priest lives forever
Appointment by fleshly command-ment/law, in weakness	— By word of oath perfected forever
Offer for their own sins	— Sinless, blameless
Daily earthly ministry	— Superior heavenly ministry
Patterns of heavenly things	— The very heavenly things
Holy places made with hands	— Heaven itself
Figures of the "real"	— God's presence
Many offerings	— Once-and-for-all offering
Many (annual) entries	— One entry
Continual services	— Climax of ages
Limited access, barriers	— Access to the "real"
No final purgation	— Sins definitively removed
Sacrifice of animals	— Sacrifice of himself
Animal blood	— Christ's own blood[32]

A number of things are worth noting. The first is that the author returns repeatedly to favorite terms that show where his heart lies, most notably the comparative adjective "better/superior" (*kreitton*), which can be used to compare Jesus with the angels (1:4) or the readers with apostates (6:9), but is usually reserved for comparing the means and the outcome of Jewish and Christian ways of salvation (7:7,19,22; 8:6; 9:23; 10:34; 12:24). Most telling is the attribution of superior aspirations to the ancient Israelite worthies (11:16,35), only to conclude they did not receive what they hoped for because God planned something better in Christ. The use of terms such as "first" covenant as compared with the "new" or the "second" (8:7,13; 9:15; 10:9) runs in the same vein. The contrast between first/second and old/new could in principle be neutral, an expression of temporal order that allows that both elements have intrinsic value. But in this case it is not; their purpose is to elevate the new and denigrate the old.

This becomes clearer, secondly, when directly negative comments are borne in mind: the commandments of the law are "weak and ineffectual" (*asthenes kai anopheles*), a mere shadow, which cannot bring perfection and which will be abolished (*atheteo*) or annulled (*anaireo*) in favor of the new (7:18; 10:1–2,9); while sacrifices, food rules, and lustrations are merely "outward" and temporary, awaiting the greater and more perfect things to come (9:8–11). It is important to note, thirdly, that "the comparisons he draws have to do not with peripheral matters but with things at the centre: covenant, promises, law, approach to God."[33]

It is true that key figures from Israel's past are portrayed positively. Moses was faithful, even if the Israelites were not (3:1–18); Abraham persevered and obtained a promise (3:13–20); the galaxy of heroes showed faith and hope and function as a model for Christian believers (11:1–40). For some this ameliorates the overall tone.[34] Yet we cannot ignore the persistent drift of the argument: Moses was inferior to Jesus, as servant to son (3:5), and the Israelites did fall away; Abraham was subjected to Melchizedek, whose priestly line Jesus triumphantly fulfills (7:1ff.); the old heroes had faith, but they did not receive the promise, "since God had provided something better so that they would not, apart from us, be made perfect" (11:40)[35]. Similarly, if the old covenant is recognized as foreshadowing the new, it is *only* a shadow or sketch, which is then comprehensively overtaken (8:5).

The logic of the argument is at times explicitly from solution to problem: we have a new high priest, a new sacrifice, a new covenant, therefore there must have been something wrong with the old ones (e.g., 7:11; 8:7,13). Emphasis on the positive pole of Christian conviction can lead to the following kind of comment:

> The detailed comparison of the old and the new covenant is not an indication of the polemical anti-Jewish character of the letter to the Hebrews, because for him this represents simply a part of the hermeneutical method by means of which he seeks to make clear to them the irrevocable guarantee of the promise which has been subjected to questioning.[36]

This raises an important point that needs to be considered in relation to any potentially anti-Jewish material in early Christian documents. Is it merely a by-product of Christian self-assertion? Clearly, it is important to distinguish between the unrelieved polemic of a frontal attack and the casual sniping that can accompany ruminations on a Christian theme. But in the case of Hebrews the judgment of those like Grässer, quoted above, is not, I think, adequate. The author of Hebrews knew enough about Judaism to know what he was doing, and the positive christological case he makes could have been made, in principle, without the gratuitous denigration of things central to the Jewish tradition. It is not as if the negative comments about Judaism are a minor, surreptitious theme: they are explicit and implicit throughout, take up as much space as the more positive assertions, and seem to loom equally large in the writer's mind. Cumulatively they give the impression that Judaism (Christian or non-Christian) was an immediate threat.

It is sometimes argued that there is no polemic against Judaism because it is not Jews, but Christians (perhaps Jewish Christians), who are addressed.[37] We can concede that the immediate audience was Christian and that the negative strain was, in the broadest sense, secondary. But there is no reason why we should restrict the terms "polemic" and "anti-Judaism," by definition, to situations of head-on conflict. Polemic and anti-Judaism do not require the immediate presence of the target; they can appear in an entirely Christian environment. And there can be little doubt that the negative impulses of the author would have encouraged his readers—who, whatever else we say about them, must have had some knowledge of Judaism—

to form a clear and unambiguous judgment: Judaism is defunct, because it has been surpassed.

To summarize, we find the following: on the one hand, paraenesis, which deals largely with persecution, perseverance, and apostasy; and on the other hand, theological reflection, which is obsessively christological, cultic, and invidiously comparative. In the one, the Christian community is trying to come to terms with life in an unfriendly Roman environment; in the other, to define itself over and against Judaism.[38] This is the dilemma of Hebrews: not just how to give proper weight to theology and paraenesis, but how to explain why they appear to operate in two different worlds. And if, as we have argued, all the signs are that both elements are to be taken equally seriously, the dilemma is sharpened all the more. Can they be brought together?

Context

Traditionally, of course, we would start by trying to pinpoint the author and addressees. The author remains anonymous, and nothing but speculation can be used to unravel his identity. The destination of the work is a little less obscure. The arguments for Rome, the most popular option, are cumulative and generally persuasive:

> Possible allusions to the actions of Claudius and Nero (see above)
>
> Greetings from "those from Italy" (13:24), which most naturally means those abroad greeting Italy rather than those in Italy greeting those abroad[39]
>
> Timothy (13:23) had probably been in Rome (though elsewhere, of course) in the sixties
>
> Leaders (*hegoumenoi,* 13:7,24) was a term popular in Rome (*1 Clem.*1:3; 12:26; *Hermas Vis.* 2.2.6, 3.9.7)
>
> *1 Clement,* a Roman document, cites Hebrews (*1 Clem.*36:2–5; Heb 1:3–13), and Rome remained a main witness to Hebrews in the second and third centuries
>
> Points of connection with 1 Peter, perhaps also a Roman document[40]

Individually the arguments can be challenged, but cumulatively they seem to add up to something. Does this conclusion advance our understanding? R. E. Brown thinks it does. Having argued that the Roman church originated in Jerusalem, that it was conservative and Jewish in inclination, and that it saw itself as a replica of the Israelites of the exodus period, he suggests that they may have devised a cult modeled on the exodus period, a desert cult for a pilgrimage people, something between purely spiritual worship and the full cult of the Jerusalem Temple. This would have allowed them to come to terms with the destruction of the Temple and to have an alternative to the grandly public pagan cults of Rome. In addition, these conservative Jewish Christians probably had "the concomitant tendency to fit Jesus into an uninterrupted schema of salvation history, subsequent to the angels and Moses as revealers of God's will."[41]

This is an attractive attempt to imagine the context of Hebrews in a post-70 setting. That an inadequate Christology is combated seems to me persuasive, not only because it makes good sense of the author's theological predilections but also because it is quite clearly implied in 5:11—6:2. The intermediate cult is another matter, because it is not clear precisely what Brown has in mind. An "earthly sanctuary of a peculiarly Christian character" and a "visible replacement for the Jewish levitical cult . . . ," which nevertheless has no actual tabernacle, do not add up to anything to which I can give even an imaginary form. Brown also underplays the allusions to persecution and apostasy.[42]

A different kind of consistency is discovered by B. Lindars, who argues that all the allusions are to tensions that arose between church and diaspora synagogue. First came the initial separation from the synagogue, which included persecution by Jewish authorities in the past (especially 10:32–34).[43] Then a continuing sense of sin, exacerbated by the absence of Jewish atonement rituals and of Christian means of accommodating postbaptismal sin, led Christians to return to the synagogue and renew their solidarity with Judaism (apostasy, etc.). Finally, they are now being encouraged to accept the author's cultic Christology and to leave the synagogue once again, with all the attendant bitterness and pressures that this would have involved (which explain the current persecution and call to perseverance).[44]

Lindars's complex reconstruction tries to take account of most of the allusions in Hebrews, but it still leaves a lot of loose threads. Is it likely, for example, that Christians would so readily have returned to synagogues that had treated them as roughly as 10:32–34 seems to imply? And do the descriptions not fit Roman rather than Jewish harassment? Forgiveness of sin could be one of the issues addressed, but what exactly did Christians have to gain by returning to the synagogues? Lindars assumes a pre-70 date and speaks vaguely of diaspora synagogue meals, which gave a sense of solidarity with what transpired in the Jerusalem Temple—an interesting suggestion if we knew anything useful about celebration of the Day of Atonement in the diaspora before or after 70 CE. But we do not.[45] A more significant reason for return to the synagogue would at any rate seem to be required.

There seem to be two ways of explaining the evidence as we have unraveled it so far.[46] The first is to think of a community or house church of Jewish Christians, probably in the diaspora, with two defining characteristics: first, a set of underdeveloped Christian (especially christological) beliefs heavily influenced by their Jewish background, which tended, from the author's point of view, to diminish the uniqueness and efficacy of Christ.[47] This may have gone hand in hand with a positive assessment of Judaism and its place in the covenant.[48] The second characteristic is experience of persecution and harassment, which defined them as political and social pariahs, and in some cases threatened their lives. This in turn created a sense of tension between theological conviction and everyday reality, perhaps exacerbated by the delay of the parousia. In the past they had survived intact, but in the present they had begun to buckle. Some had defected back to Judaism (and thus raised the question of the limits of divine mercy),[49] while others had taken the first steps toward reassociation—withdrawing from Christian gatherings and sharing Jewish dietary rules/meals. Judaism provided political legitimacy and protection, and it might not have seemed so strange to the christologically unsophisticated to think of expressing their Christian beliefs once again in a synagogue context. Theological inclination, nagging doubts, and political pressure could all have edged them in the same direction.[50]

Before the Jewish War there would also have been the attractions of the Temple cult. Despite attacks on sacrificial cults by both Jewish prophets and pagan philosophers, it remains true that for most Jews and Gentiles such forms of worship were familiar, routinely accepted, and their attraction never entirely overcome.[51] A setting such as this could explain both the cultic slant of Hebrews, as it competed with attractive alternatives, and the absence of any reference to the destruction of the Temple.[52]

A date after 70 CE would require a somewhat different reading. The dashing of Christian eschatological expectations, tied somewhat to these events in the early traditions, would have increased uncertainty and doubt. The loss of the cult and its associated benefits, we know, caused depression and confusion among Jews, and no doubt among some Christian Jews too. Hebrews could be seen as bringing reassurance and comfort to those so troubled—a pastoral aim that might also have encouraged a tactful silence about the fate of the Temple. This sets up something of a tension with our earlier analysis. Why would these Christians wish to return to a Judaism that now lacked one of the things they treasured? One answer would be that political pressures were strong, another that the priestly Christology is being used as a lure.

A second, and rather different, way of understanding Hebrews would be to assume that the readers were Gentile Christians with a strong interest in and attraction for Judaism: that is, Gentile Judaizers. One scholarly tradition has argued that the recipients were Gentiles, but this has usually gone hand in hand with a minimizing of the Jewish themes, sometimes by interpreting them in a gnostic direction.[53] Others have noted that when we talk of Jewish Christians as the recipients we should also include Gentile Christians associated with their communities, though one gets the sense that they were minor players and are mentioned for the sake of completeness.[54] If, however, we think of them for the sake of argument as the dominant group among the recipients we can make good sense of a great many themes in Hebrews. In some respects, for example christological beliefs, they may have been indistinguishable from Jewish Christians, and so some of what we said about Jewish Christian readers would apply to Gentile Judaizers too. But can we be more specific? The conclusions we have drawn about Judaizers elsewhere, though admittedly from four different times and places, are quite illuminating in this context:

—They sought haven in the synagogue because of persecution (Revelation).

—They defected to the synagogue, abandoning the church (Justin) under Jewish or Jewish Christian pressure.

—They believed the covenant could be shared between Jews and Christians (*Barnabas*).

—They insisted that the Jewish scriptures be the basis for Christian belief and practice, and may have worshiped separately (on the Sabbath, with a special Eucharist) from other parts of the Christian community (Ignatius).[55]

Persecution and perseverance, apostasy, and a drift toward the synagogue are all found in Hebrews. While persecution is a common enough theme, Justin provides a specific allusion to apostasizing, which is rare in early Christian literature. Christians who claimed that they and the Jews could share the same covenant would be just the sort to provoke the radical supersessionism we find in Hebrews, including the deliberate assertion of the establishment of a new (rather than renewed) covenant. Similarly, biblical literalists could have caused some of the problems, christological as well as cultic, that Hebrews addresses, as they could also have encouraged the following of a Jewish way of life (including food rules). That their particular interests led to separate gatherings and a challenge to the leadership of the church parallels the situation in Hebrews remarkably well. A further advantage is that we could now explain why a book so dominated by Jewish themes is, on one reading at least, addressed to Gentiles. The evidence for Gentile readers is not, I think, ineluctable; but for those to whom it is, Gentile Judaizers would be a happy fit.[56] In addition, if these Gentile Christians had formerly been God-fearers, their affinity with the synagogue would have lent support to any more specific reasons they might have had for returning there.

There is, then, a significant confluence of themes. But can we imagine a time when Gentile Christians would have chosen to nestle up to, in some cases even join, the synagogue? A date before 70 CE would fit, when the Temple was still standing and the cult thriving. Immediately after 70 CE, with the Temple destroyed and the city in ruins, would not have been an auspicious moment and would not explain why the cultic theme is so important to the author. In our consideration of *Barnabas* we shall review the theory of a Jewish revival under Nerva (ca. 96 CE) which, with imperial support, focused on a rebuilding of the Jerusalem Temple. If this view can be sustained, such a context would make good sense of Hebrews too: a renewed interest in the Temple and its cult, and a reinvigorated Judaism, which would have looked all the more attractive to Gentile Christians already inclined to view it sympathetically. There might be a problem with the date, since it is widely agreed that *1 Clement,* usually dated ca. 96 CE, "quotes" Hebrews. This may be so, but, as Attridge points out, the date for *1 Clement* is very insecurely based on supposed allusions to a supposed persecution of Christians under Domitian. *1 Clement* could in fact come from any time up to 140 CE.[57]

Either version of our interpretation would fit well with P. Lampe's sketch of Roman Christianity in the first two centuries.[58] From an early stage the community was marked by its Jewish and God-fearing origins, a tradition that was perpetuated by Gentile Christian tradents (*1 Clement, Hermas*). The Gentile ex–God-fearers were a majority, but Jewish Christians survived for some time. The "weak" who are mentioned in Romans 14 were interested in Jewish food laws and feasts (Rom 14:2,5,15,20), which could be true of either Jewish or God-fearing Christians.[59] The Neronian persecutions indicate that most Christians were not Roman citizens (crucifixion was for non-citizens), and this would effectively have labeled Christians as dangerous outsiders. Judaism, with its higher percentage of citizens and its special rights, would have looked an attractive haven. The problem of wealth sharing, alluded to in Hebrews 13:5, becomes a more prominent issue in *1 Clement* and *Hermas*.

THE EPISTLE OF *BARNABAS*

The author of *Barnabas* cannot be identified and, as with Hebrews, there are few internal hints about where it was sent from or to. It is most commonly argued that it originated in Alexandria, since it was popular in Egypt at an early stage and uses a mode of scriptural interpretation (allegory/typology, based on a special *gnosis*) thought to have been particularly favored there. An equally strong, perhaps stronger, case can be made for a Syro-Palestinian provenance, but in neither case are the arguments compelling, and it would be a mistake to base an interpretation on them.[60]

We are, however, not entirely bereft of information about the writer and his audience, as long as we do not assume that the letter is addressed to an ideal rather than a specific community and that the personal references are entirely fictional.[61] The author, who has recently met with the recipients (1:3), presents himself with some ambivalence. On the one hand he insists that he is one of them, an equal rather than an authoritative teacher; and on the other hand he clearly believes he has a superior understanding of the present times and of the teaching appropriate to them (1:1–5,8; 4:9; 6:5; 21:7). He makes it quite clear, in fact, that he hopes to improve their knowledge, that he writes to them in simple terms in order that they may understand (1:5; 4:1; 6:5; 13:7). There is a hint of condescension and unease. Expressions of humility and equality may be no more than a rhetorical device to ease the reception of the letter, but they may also be an expression of genuine uncertainty about his standing and the sort of hearing he was likely to get.

It is apparent that the author and his readers were Gentiles. Certainly Jewish Christians, like Gentile Christians, could have said that Jesus had saved them from error, darkness, and death and that the universal promises associated with Abraham or the Isaian servant were fulfilled in him (14:5–8). Two statements, however, point decisively to their Gentile origin:

> . . . that we might not shipwreck ourselves by becoming, as it were, proselytes to their law. (3:6)[62]

> Before we believed in God, our heart's dwelling-place was corrupt and weak, truly a temple built by human hands, because it was full of idolatry and was the home of demons, for we did whatever was contrary to God. (16:7)

The use of the first-person plural assumes an identity of the author with the readers, and the description of them as proselytes and idolaters indicates their Gentile origin, though both statements would be consistent with their having been God-fearers.

The author's thinking is shot through with powerful eschatological convictions. Scattered throughout the work, the references are too frequent to be a mere formality. The present age is an evil age, controlled by the evil one (2:1,10; 4:1,13), but time is running out and the last days are here (4:3,9; 16:5; 21:3), preceding the certain judgment (15:1–3; 21:6). Christian existence, which entails pain and suffering (7:11), is characterized by a tension between current reality and future expectation (4:1; 6:19; 11:8). The writer's sense of urgency is unmistakable, and it was presumably either shared by his readers or something he wished to inculcate in them. That certain pressures were beginning to affect them is presumably why he explicitly says, at the beginning and end of the letter, that he writes in order to cheer them up (1:8; 21:9).

A few other snippets of information come to light. Some members of the community were apparently sufficiently well-off or influential to help out others who were not (3:1–3; 21:2). A warning against overconfidence may suggest that some thought they could relax because they were irrevocably called (4:13). And, in two striking parallels with Hebrews, it is suggested that some were dropping out of communal gatherings (4:10), while others might even have abandoned their faith after having enjoyed knowledge of the way of righteousness (5:4).

One way of posing the central enigma of *Barnabas* is to ask why a group of Gentile Christians (writer and readers), living with intense eschatological expectations, with some members lapsing or withdrawing, should be so obsessed with things Jewish. For even the most cursory look shows that reaction to Jewish beliefs and practices dominates the letter. Quite apart from the substance of each chapter, to which we shall return, the centrality of this concern is indicated by the pervasive use of contrasting pronouns: we/they, them/us, ours/theirs (2:9–10; 3:1–3,6; 4:6–8,14; 5:1; 8:7; 10:12; 13:1–6; 14:1,4–5,6–8).[63] The author does not use the term "Jews," and most of the references to "Israel" are to the distant past (5:2; 6:7; 9:2; 11:1; 12:2) or to the time when Jesus and his disciples worked among them (5:8; 8:3). The distinctive way he chooses to refer to Jews, past and present, is by pairing pronouns. For there is never any doubt who the contrasted entities are—Christians and Jews—nor that the latter are presented in negative and hostile terms. References to a "new law" or a "new people" (2:6; 5:7; 7:5; cf. 6:14) could in some contexts imply that the "old" had some sort of meaningful existence or even value. In the light of what he explicitly argues about the past, however, this cannot have been intended here, and the choice of terms is probably inadvertent.[64] More in tune with the overall drift of the argument is the description of Christians as "another type" (*allon typon*) of people (6:11).

Included among the many failings of the Jews is the supreme misdeed, responsibility for the death of Jesus (5:11–13; 6:7; 7:5; 8:2; 12:5). By this means they filled up the measure of their sins, and the responsibility is theirs alone. This by now traditional Christian theme is expressed here with stark simplicity. Only Jews come into the picture.

It will be convenient in our consideration of the main themes of *Barnabas* to divide the material into two main blocks. First, there are the chapters in which the author probes the origin and purpose of Jewish observances: fasting, circumcision, food rules and the Sabbath (3; 9; 10; 15 respectively). Second, there are those that cluster around two themes crucial for understanding the date and purpose of the epistle: the Temple and its associated rites (2; 7; 8; 16); the covenant and the land (4; 6; 13; 14).[65]

Jewish Observances

In chapter 3 the Jewish practice of fasting is both ridiculed and radically reinterpreted. Even the most extreme abnegation—"if you bend your neck in a circle and put on sackcloth and lie in ashes"—is unacceptable. This is what God says to the Jews ("them" v.1), apparently to no avail. Christians ("us" v.3), on the other hand, are to pursue justice, mercy, charity, and respect for all (vv.3,5). Since they are the ones who will "believe in all purity [*akeraiosyne*]," the implication is that they achieve purity or guilelessness not through Jewish ritual but through moral commitment—a view reinforced by the concluding statement that they should not wreck their faith by taking on Jewish obligations ("becoming proselytes to their law," v.6). One way of contrasting Jewish and Christian practice was to fast on different days of the week (*Did.*8:1), but our author allows no such compromise.

He insists on a radically different practice expressed, ironically, in precisely those terms that Jews would have used to express their own sense of moral obligation.

If anything, the rejection of circumcision in chapter 9 is even more radical. That other peoples circumcised (v.6) was used against the Jews by pagans and Christians alike, and the moral understanding of it as implying more deeply the circumcision of heart and ears (vv.1–3) is found in biblical, Jewish, and other Christian writings too.[66] Abraham's circumcising of his contemporaries is not condemned, but it is justified, in an argument original to the author, only as a harbinger of the cross (vv.7–8). But that Abraham "looked forward in the spirit" to Jesus scarcely moderates the devastating accusation that the Jews had always misunderstood circumcision "because an evil angel 'enlightened' them" (v.4)—in effect, a demonizing of the covenantal rite. It was common enough to believe that evil demons could inspire human behavior and polemicists could, in extremis, label their opponents or their opponents' teaching diabolical (John 8:44; Gal 3:1; Rev 2:9; 3:9; Ignatius *Eph.*10:3; 17:1; Polycarp *Phil.*7:1). Gnostics, too, viewed the whole of creation, including the Jewish scriptures, to be the work of the (sometimes evil) Demiurge. But 9:4, with its precise focus on the rite of circumcision, has no exact parallel.[67]

If one tack was to moralize and another to demonize, a third was to "christologize" the Jewish law. With a unique hermeneutical twist, the author interprets Abraham's circumcision of ten, eight, and three hundred men as a foreshadowing of Christ and his cross (vv.7–8). But barely, if at all, does this take the sting out of v.4, for the institution of circumcision is here given only one positive interpretation: it pointed to Christ.[68]

The author returns to allegorical moralizing in his discussion of Jewish food laws (chap. 10). Again, following a tradition already established by Jews and Christians, the Mosaic food laws, in what they allow as well as disallow, are understood to have force only when radically reinterpreted.[69] What is forbidden refers to forms of immoral behavior, and what is allowed to a spiritual focus on the Lord and his word. It is only the Jews who cannot grasp or understand this, who insist that they refer to actual foods. The Sabbath, too, is removed from the realm of routine observance and understood as an eschatological parable (chap. 15). The weekly Sabbaths are replaced by the eschatological Sabbath, which will come after six thousand years (vv.3–6), for in these present evil times the Sabbath cannot be sanctified (vv.6–7). Christians at any rate have their own day of celebration, the eighth (Sunday), on which they celebrate the resurrection and ascension of Jesus, which anticipates the end of the age (v.9).

By the use of allegory and typology the author thus translates the standard and most visible of Jewish observances to a different plane. The mode can vary between the ethical, the eschatological, the demonological, and the christological, but the end result is the same. Jewish observance is reinterpreted and, ultimately, discarded. Some of the arguments are novel, others merely rework familiar Jewish and Christian themes. It is conceivable that these issues arose only because they appear in the scriptures that Christianity had taken over from Judaism, and because there was some discomfort that manifest commands were being ignored.[70] In this case the discussion would be largely internal to the Christian community and would bear only tangentially on the Jewish-Christian debate. There are no clear indications in the four themes we have considered so far. With the other two, however, it is a different matter.

Temple

It is striking that the first issue raised, after the preliminaries of the opening chapter, is the sacrificial cult. It was easy enough for the author to tap the widespread skepticism about sacrificial cults expressed by Greeks, Jews, and Christians alike—that they were inappropriate and ineffectual and deflected attention from more important forms of worship. With quotations from the prophets and psalms (the LXX of Isa 1:11–13; Jer 7:22–23; Ps 50:19), he insists that love of one's neighbor, avoidance of false oaths, and a broken and humble heart are the forms of worship God really desires. To these familiar themes, however, the author gives his own twist. The abolition of sacrifice was intended not just to point to more acceptable forms of devotion, but "in order that the new law of our Lord Jesus Christ, which is free from the yoke of compulsion, might have its offering, one not made by man" (v.6). In what is probably an allusion to the freely offered sacrifice of Jesus' death, it is clear that a contrast with Jewish sacrifice is intended. It is not merely reformed; it is replaced. This is reinforced, secondly, with resort to the familiar contrast: they (the Jews) do not understand, they have gone astray; but we (Christians) ought to perceive what God says to us (vv.9–10). As usual, the contrast entails a takeover, in this case the of scriptures, which are now addressed to us for our understanding.

In tune with the apocalyptic note that opens the chapter, the final exhortation warns of the work of the devil: "We ought to give very careful attention to our salvation, lest the evil one should cause some error to slip into our midst and thereby hurl us away from our life" (v.10). The urgent tone invites us to consider whether this is more than an apocalyptic formality. Why is this the first topic to be broached, and why the warning about error creeping in when, on virtually all dates surmised for the letter, it was composed after the sacrificial cult in Jerusalem had ceased? Under what circumstances could Christians conceivably be in danger of forming erroneous views of the cult? This chapter invites the question, but it does not provide an answer.

Consistent with chapter 2, especially v.6, are the two later chapters that interpret the death of Jesus in terms of two sacrificial rituals, the scapegoat and the red heifer (chaps. 7; 8).[71] Intricate details of the scapegoat ceremony serve as a type of Jesus' crucifixion and his coming in glory. As to the first, the Jews are depicted as those who crucified, insulted, and spat upon Jesus, while at the time of the second they will recognize him, by his likeness to the scapegoat, as the Son of God (7:9–10). Here, as in the allusion to Isaac (7:3), the emphasis is on the inevitability of Jesus' suffering, as also that of his followers (7:11). In the following chapter the meaning of the sacrifice of the heifer and the sprinkling of its ashes for purification is explicitly spelled out: Jesus is the calf, the Jews those who killed him, the apostles those who sprinkled the good news of forgiveness. The scarlet wool and hyssop tied to a tree signify the cross and its healing powers. To Christians (us) the meaning is obvious (*phanera*), but to the Jews (them), obscure (*skoteina,* 8:7). The tradition of the Twelve being chosen to witness to the twelve tribes of Israel, it is worth noting, is affirmed (8:3). It seems to refer to the past, and did not do them much good if the obscure comment in the preceding verse is to be believed: "Then the men [= Jews] are no more; no more is the glory of sinners" (8:2). It could be a cryptic and bleak assessment of the fate of the Jews (cf. 5:12).[72]

The typological thrust of chapters 7 and 8 contributes to the Temple theme which crops up elsewhere,[73] but it also serves to reinforce the list of reasons given earlier (chap. 5) to explain why Jesus had to come in the flesh and submit to death: to effect forgiveness (v.1); to destroy death and proclaim resurrection (v.6); while preparing for himself a new people, to redeem the promise to the fathers by showing that he would execute judgment (v.7); to show his love for Israel by teaching, signs, and wonders (v.8); to show that he came to call sinners, not the righteous (v.9);[74] to reveal himself clearly to humankind (v.10); to complete the full measure of the sins of those who persecuted the prophets and put him to death (vv.11–12); to fulfill the prophecies of his death (5:13–6:7). This is the fullest exposition of Christology to which we are treated. The focus is clearly, perhaps anxiously, on the incarnation and crucifixion. Certainly it gives rein to the author's delight in finding ingenious proof texts, but some of the arguments work on a more reasoned level. He has firm views, but did he know or suspect that some of his readers were less convinced?

In considering the Temple theme, we turn finally to chapter 16, one of the most controverted and discussed in the letter. The opening is clear enough, if unusual. The familiar theme that God does not dwell in temples is given a particular twist (vv.1–2): the "wretched" Jews set their hope in a building rather than God, behaving "almost like the Gentiles [*ethne*]." Setting the Jerusalem Temple virtually on a par with pagan temples is a polemical demotion with few parallels in early Christian literature, and it sets the tone for what is to come. The critical statement is as follows:

(2) . . . You now know that their hope [in the temple] was in vain. (3) Furthermore, again he says: "Behold, those who tore down this temple will build

it themselves." (4) This is happening now [*ginetai*]. For because they went to war, it was torn down by their enemies, and now the very servants of the enemies will rebuild it [*nyn kai autoi [kai] hoi ton echthron hyperetai anoikodomesousin auton*]. (5) Again, it was revealed that the city and the temple and the people of Israel were destined to be handed over. For the scripture says: "And it will happen in the last days that the Lord will hand over the sheep of the pasture and the sheepfold and their watchtower to destruction." And it happened just as the Lord said.

The literary and historical issues are complex. Verse 4a, and perhaps verse 5, allude to the destruction of the Temple by the Romans in 70 CE. On this much almost all agree.[75] The problem lies with verse 4b, which clearly alludes back to the quotation from Isaiah 49:17 LXX in the previous verse.[76] It interprets the destroyers of v.3 as the enemy and the rebuilders as the "servants of the enemy" who are active "now." This appears to be a conscious effort to update the proof text and to find in it a contemporary meaning, thus differentiating it from the other temple material we have looked at.[77]

One manuscript (S, or Codex Sinaiticus) adds an extra *kai* in v.4, which changes the reference from one to two groups ("and now they and the servants of the enemies . . . ") but is still ambiguous. It could refer to Jews (*autoi*) and Roman servants (*hyperetai*) or to the Romans (*autoi*) and their servants (*hyperetai*), more probably the former.[78] Without the second *kai* the reference is to one group—"these [the very] servants of the enemy"— who could be Jews or Roman workers.[79] Thus the text of v.4b, in either form, offers no decisive identification of the builders, nor, therefore, of which temple is in mind.

We thus have a text that the writer believes has immediate relevance, which alludes to the destruction of the Jewish Temple in 70 CE and to a subsequent rebuilding of a temple by Jews, Roman workers, or both. The only way to unravel it seems to be to place it in the context of known events, though, as we shall see, that does not lead to much greater certainty.

The one temple construction we know about was Hadrian's temple to Jupiter, which replaced the Jewish Temple during the Bar Cochba period.[80] Most commonly the statement in *Barnabas* is thus seen as a comment on the planned, but not yet executed, pagan temple, which will be built by Roman underlings and which will be the ultimate judgment on the Jews' foolish trust in their Temple.[81] By allowing full force to the future tense of "shall rebuild" (*anoikodomesousin*, v.4b), and by arguing that *Barnabas* shows no knowledge of the outcome of the Bar Cochba rebellion, a date can be fixed somewhere near the beginning of the rebellion, ca. 130–32 CE.[82]

Following this general line of interpretation, an equally plausible alternative would be to date *Barnabas* 16 after the Bar Cochba rebellion when the building of the Jupiter temple had already begun. The future tense of "shall rebuild" is considerably weakened by the introduction of *ginetai* and *nyn*, and may at any rate be influenced by the same tense in Isaiah 49:17. While vv.3–4a refer to the Jewish War, the reference in the past tense to the handing over of the city, temple, and people in v.5 could refer to the aftermath of the rebellion, especially if one event associated with the rebellion—the building of the Jupiter temple—had just been mentioned. Admittedly, one might have expected clearer hints—a mention, for example, of the decree that banned Jews from Jerusalem—but clear hints are precisely what we do not have, whichever way we understand the passage.

Such interpretations would be consistent with the proof text from Isaiah, which identifies the destroyers with the builders. It has also been suggested that the brief and cryptic allusion is understandable if it is to a pagan temple: Christians would have had no interest in it, except insofar as it could be used in anti-Jewish polemic.[83] These arguments add marginally to a case whose strength is chiefly that it sets v.4b in the context of known events.

The case is, however, flawed. It introduces an intrusive reference to a pagan temple into a chapter that otherwise deals solely with the Jewish Temple and its spiritual Christian successor. The precise wording of v.4b, "rebuild it" (*anoikodomesousin auton*), would be an unnatural way of referring to a pagan temple. *Auton* must, in context, mean the temple that has been destroyed and "shall *re*build," which is the author's deliberately chosen term (the proof text in v.3 has "shall build"), most obviously refers to a reconstruction of the Jerusalem Temple.[84] If he was referring to the Jupiter temple, why did he not write something like "build" or "replace it," which would have made his point clearer?

An allusion to a rebuilt Jerusalem Temple is not without its problems. If v.4b alludes to an expected rebuilding of the Jewish Temple, it is curious that v.5 seems to return to the theme of vv.2–4a, which refer to the destruction in 70 CE, without more ado. Would not an expected rebuilding and an associated revival of Jewish hopes deserve more attention?[85] And is not the prophecy of v.5 in a sense contradicted, or at least shown to have limited duration, by the expected rebuilding of v.4b? Perhaps the argument is merely disjointed, as it often is elsewhere in *Barnabas* when proof texts are strung together in somewhat random fashion. Or perhaps the author deliberately surrounded his allusion to a worrying new development in Judaism with prophecies designed to assure his readers that nothing significant would come of it. It still seems most likely that we have an allusion to an expected reconstruction of the Jewish Temple by Jews, Romans, or both together.

Which brings us to another problem—finding evidence for an expectation that the Jerusalem Temple would be rebuilt. There is evidence, for example, that the Bar Cochba rebels (132–35 CE) wished to recapture Jerusalem and, perhaps, rebuild the Temple. There is no evidence that they achieved either, but there were doubtless times when temporary successes made their long-term ambitions look quite plausible. Alternatively, we might surmise that the earlier rebellions in Egypt under Trajan (usually dated 115–17 CE) were associated with similar hopes. It has been suggested that, like the Bar Cochba rebellion, they were fueled by a messianic fervor which included an expectation that the Temple would be restored.[86] Is it plausible to place *Barnabas* in the context of either of these rebellions? In principle, the prospect of a rebuilt Temple and a renewed Jewish state with messianic overtones would certainly have been enough to alarm some Christians and perhaps tempt others to jump on the Jewish bandwagon. But in neither case would it have been natural to describe the rebuilders of the Temple as the "servants of the enemy," that is, people working with Roman approval. To the contrary, if the Jews had achieved their ambitions, it would have been in the teeth of Roman opposition.

We require a situation where the Romans approved a plan to rebuild the Temple which, it was expected, would soon be put into effect by Jews, Romans, or the two in collusion. Only two have been plausibly proposed: under Nerva and under Hadrian.[87] In both cases the evidence is circumstantial. In principle it would have been an astute move, following the recent revolts in Egypt, for Hadrian to have mollified the Jews when he took over from Trajan. Reconstructing the Herodian Temple would have fitted his penchant for grandiose buildings, and the subsequent dashing of Jewish hopes once raised would be one plausible cause of the Bar Cochba rebellion. But this is entirely hypothetical. There is, in fact, little or no evidence that Hadrian, the more commonly mentioned in this context, encouraged or supported Jewish ambitions.[88] To the contrary, we know only that he fought the Jews savagely toward the end of his reign.

Richardson and Shukster have made a strong case for dating *Barnabas* 16 to the time of Nerva, but it too is inconclusive. It is known that Nerva corrected abuses of the Jewish tax, which perhaps shows that he was well-disposed toward the Jews; but there is not a single piece of evidence to connect him with a rebuilding of the Temple.[89] If anything can be extracted from the obscure quotations from Daniel in *Barnabas* 4:4–5, then Nerva is a more likely candidate for the "excrescent horn" than Hadrian.[90] Rabbinic sources about Trajan's Day and the Embassy to Rome can be brought into play, but they are notoriously treacherous when used in historical reconstruction.[91]

Despite these difficulties, it remains true that the text of *Barnabas* 16 implies a planned rebuilding of the Temple with Roman permission and that the historical evidence points to Nerva as perhaps the most likely to have approved this. This would not have been a matter of indifference to Christians, and perhaps we have here the answer to the question raised in connection with chapter 2: Why the concern with incipient error with regard to the sacrificial cult among Gentile Christians after 70 CE? A Judaism buoyed by hopes for a rebuilt Temple would have presented a serious challenge to a Christianity that thought of itself as the new Israel and of the destruction of the Temple in 70 CE as partial confirmation of this.[92] Some may even have been tempted to rethink their relationship to Judaism, and it is to them that we now turn.

Covenant

The second major theme, found in several chapters and with undeniably current references, is possession of the covenant. The opening salvo is in *Barnabas* 4:6–8:

> (6) I also ask you this . . . : be on your guard now and do not be like certain people; that is, do not continue to pile up your sins while claiming that your covenant is irrevocably yours, because in fact [*that the covenant is both theirs and ours*. (7) *It is ours, but*] those people lost it completely in the following way, when Moses had just received it. (7) For the Scripture says: "And Moses was in the mountain fasting for forty days and forty nights, and he received the covenant from the Lord, stone tablets inscribed by the fingers of the hand of the Lord." (8) But by turning to idols they lost it. For thus says the Lord: "Moses, Moses, go down quickly, because your people, whom you led out of Egypt, have broken the Law." And Moses understood and hurled the two tablets from his hands, and their covenant was broken in pieces, in order that the covenant of the beloved Jesus might be sealed in our heart, in hope inspired by faith in him.

As can be seen from the phrase in brackets, there is an important textual variation in vv.6–7. The translation follows C (Codex Hierosolymitanus) and the text in brackets follows L (Latin).[93] The sense is somewhat different in each case. In C the warning is against overconfidence, and in its favor is the reappearance of this theme in vv.10,13–14. In L there appear to be "certain people" who promote a joint covenant concept. In its favor is the immediate context, which clearly emphasizes the transfer of the covenant to Christians (v.8), the reappearance of the same theme in chapters 13–14, and the general tenor of the book, which emphasizes the transfer of all the privileges of Israel to the church. The stress on overconfidence later in the chapter would be a natural development of this—"the covenant is ours alone, but don't treat it lightly"—and may indeed explain the text of C as a revision, influenced by the immediate and more familiar context, of a point of view that a later scribe might have had some difficulty in understanding.

The comment in vv.6–8 follows a severe apocalyptic warning about pressures in the last days and, although the transition from vv.1–5 is somewhat abrupt, the indication is that this is a matter of lively concern to the writer. This is confirmed by the reappearance of the theme in chapters 13–14, which, quite apart from 4:6–8, show that the issue of covenant possession was still alive.[94] Who, then, were those who claimed that "the covenant is theirs and ours"? Not Jews, given the consistent use of contrasting pronouns throughout the letter: theirs/them = the Jews, and ours/us = the

Christians.[95] The speakers are, therefore, Christians. "Certain people" is vague and could in principle refer to Christians of a different sort from the writer and readers. Thus Jewish Christians could be in mind, though they appear nowhere else in the letter. All the indications are that the writer and readers moved in Gentile Christian circles, and it is most likely that the proponents of a joint covenant were Gentile Christians too. That is, they were Gentile Judaizers who not only held to a theory that allowed space for the Jews but, if 3:6 is any indication, were tempted to adopt Jewish practice as well. That is, if we tie 3:6 and 4:6 together, which seems reasonable, the problem concerns Gentile Christian Judaizers whose theory of a shared covenant could have the practical consequence of adopting Jewish ways. They may have been abetted by Jewish Christians, but the author's concern at any rate is with his Gentile brethren who might take, or already have taken, the same line.

It is important to emphasize this, since the opposite is commonly argued. Windisch argues that the author is concerned only with "judenfreundliche Theorie" not "judaisierende Praxis": motivated by the content of scripture and the continuing existence of Jews, he calls on anti-Jewish testimony collections to support the Christian claim.[96] Similarly, Wengst thinks the author's comments on Jews and Judaism are merely the dark foil to his own understanding of scripture, which is his primary concern. The Jews are a theoretical entity, not an immediate threat. The author, he thinks, is like those opponents of Ignatius who must prove everything from the archives (Ignatius, *Phld.*8:2).[97] Vielhauer declares that "the discussion about Judaism is entirely academic," but he recognizes that there was an intense inter-Christian theological dispute.[98] It does not follow, as Windisch and Wengst argue, that if it was a live issue it would have had to have been mentioned in the framing chapters (1;17;22). After all, the theme of covenant, broadly defined, on one reading makes up the substance of chapters 4–16.[99] Indeed, their view can be turned on its head: the obsessive concern with scripture is precisely because there was a perceived threat from Judaism and Judaizers. Moreover, they do not provide a convincing explanation of 3:6 or 4:6. Christian Judaizers may have been the immediate target, but behind them lay a Judaism whose attraction (and thus from the author's viewpoint, threat) was immediate and pressing.[100]

Faced with this, the author emphatically denies that the covenant could be shared: it belongs not to Jews but to Christians. Indeed, in a statement reminiscent in its radicalness of the discussion of circumcision (9:4), he asserts that it never had belonged to Jews. With heavy irony it is noted that Israel lost the covenant *eis telos*[101] before they ever possessed it in the first place. God gave the covenant to Moses, but Israel's immediate sin led to its simultaneous withdrawal (vv.7–8). In effect he argues, not that the covenant was once theirs but is now ours, but that it never was theirs and was always (in God's intention) ours. He does not think in terms of a new covenant, but of one covenant, never possessed by the Jews but reserved for Christians.

The same theme is reiterated in chapter 13, which opens with a question: "Now let us see whether this people [*houtos ho laos*] or the former people [*protos*] is the heir, and whether the covenant is for us or for them" (v.1). In answering this question the author introduces two analogies which lead to a terminological muddle. Rebecca's two sons represent two peoples, one of whom will dominate the other, and the greater of whom will serve the lesser. The reader is urged to understand "concerning whom he has shown that this people is greater than that one" (vv.2–3). When the sons of Joseph, Manasseh and Ephraim, are blessed by Jacob, it is the younger Ephraim who is blessed, signifying that "the greater will serve the lesser. Yet this one too shall be blessed" (vv.4–5). Jacob's action, the author concludes, shows that "this people should be first [*proton*], and heirs of the covenant" (v.6). The scheme seems to be as follows:

> This people = Christians, vv.1,3,6 (cf. this one, v.5)
> This people = the greater v.3, the lesser v.5
> This people = the first v.6, not the first v.1

There seems to be an inconsistency in the application of the various labels, and the inconsistency remains however we try to construe it.[102] Yet in the light of chapters 4 and 14 the burden of the passage is not unclear: Christians have taken over the covenant from the Jews. It is ours, not theirs; there is to be no sharing.

The inquiry continues in chapter 14, starting with a repetition of the story of Israel's loss of the covenant immediately after Moses had been given it (vv.1–4, cf. 4:6–8). In effect they never possessed it. Their loss was the Christians' gain: they became the "people of inheritance" (v.4) and received the covenant (v.5) because that was what God always intended from the start. As God's true people, they became a light to the nations and brought the message of salvation to the ends of the earth, thus fulfilling the role of the servant in Isaiah (vv.7–9). It is essentially the same with the promise of "the land flowing with milk and honey" (6:10–19). It is Christians who, as "another type" of people (6:11) and a new creation (6:14), will inherit this promise—if not in the present, then certainly in the future (6:18–19).[103]

The recurrence of the covenant theme, the allusion to Christians who favored the concept of a joint covenant, the uncompromising assertion of Christian inheritance, and the radical (and unbiblical) denial of the covenant to Israel—all of these suggest that the issue was not simply antiquarian, theoretical, or even scriptural, but an urgent and pressing matter which had already made disturbing inroads into the church.

This is not to deny the centrality of scripture in the arguments of *Barnabas*. The letter is littered with proof texts, exhortations to seek out a true understanding of scripture, and exegesis that the author considers decisive in settling an issue.[104] Indeed, it has been proposed that *Barnabas* effectively establishes a sort of Christian *Bet ha-midrash* to rival that of the rabbis and, even if this overemphasizes Jewish-Christian (as against intra-church) disputes, it nevertheless captures the centrality and pervasiveness of scriptural interpretation in this letter.[105] But scripture itself is not the sole and central issue. The agenda is set elsewhere, even if scripture provides the main terms in which it is discussed.

Conclusion

It is reasonable to connect the issue of the covenant with the one other that manifestly contains current allusions: the rebuilding of the Temple. If during the reign of Nerva (96–98 CE) Jewish hopes for a rebuilt Temple had been given imperial support, Judaism would have become both a serious competitor and a dangerous attraction. A reinvigorated Judaism would have dented the Christian sense of identity and cast doubt on its claim to be the people of God. At the same time, there were Christians who had begun to rethink their relationship with Judaism, who wished to create room for coexistence within a single covenant, and who were attracted to Jewish ways. Some may even have defected (5:4). The two issues, temple and covenant, could have been mutually supportive. This is not to say that the promised temple was the direct cause of Judaizing; but it would certainly not have discouraged it. If an external threat from a revived Judaism and an internal threat from Gentile Judaizers form the background to *Barnabas,* we can also account for the obsession with other Jewish themes throughout the work, for the fact that a Gentile Christian work has such an overwhelmingly Jewish agenda, and for the radical and uncompromising claims to which the author is driven.[106]

The extent of his obsession, the radicalness of his claims, and the general defensiveness and rancor of his tone would normally be thought to position the author of *Barnabas* on the margins of Christian opinion. There has, however, been one attempt to reclaim him for the Christian center. Several decades ago K. Thieme argued that the author of *Barnabas* took a moderate view of Judaism and held a firm but obscurely expressed hope for the ultimate salvation of the Jews. When he retells the incident of the golden calf (chapters 4;14) he is interested only in its "typical" features, and thinks the Jews lost the covenant only as long as they worshiped idols. The "amazement" that Jesus' persecutors will express at his parousia will signify recognition and conversion (7:9–10), and the blessing of Jacob applies ultimately to both Ephraim (Christians) and Manasseh (Jews) (13:5). Thus, Thieme argues, the author harbored the same hope as Paul and the whole New Testament that the Jews would be converted and saved, but could not express it too openly for fear of encouraging those who were already tempted to go over to Judaism (4:6).[107]

Paul's view (Rom 9–11) is, of course, something of an aberration, and *Barnabas* would be more in line with the drift of the New Testament if it condemned the Jews. Yet despite the uncompromising supersessionism of *Barnabas,* it is just possible that the author allowed for the conversion of the Jews and their participation in the exclusive covenant of the new people. It runs somewhat against the grain of the routine contrasts between "us" and "them," which we noted above, but it cannot be excluded in principle. In the end, however, the arguments do not carry sufficient weight. When the author says that the Jews lost the covenant *eis telos* (4:7), whether it is translated "finally" (so Thieme) or "completely," he seems to mean that they lost it once and for all and not merely for the duration of their idolatry. Their loss was permanent, not temporary, so that they did not have the advantages of being the covenant people even for the period prior to the coming of Christ. This, at least, is the sense of the surrounding arguments in chapters 4, 13, and 14: the covenant is, and always was intended to be, ours, not theirs. When Jesus' persecutors show "amazement" at his likeness to the sacrificial goat, it could as easily be a prelude to their condemnation as to their conversion, though, in fact, the text says nothing about either.[108] The allusion to Jacob's words to Joseph—"Yet this one too shall be blessed" (13:6)—is a more intriguing piece of evidence. In Genesis 48:18–19 it is clear that both sons, Manasseh and Ephraim, will be blessed but the younger will turn out to be the greater. The analogies developed in *Barnabas* 13:1–6 are, as we have noted, not entirely transparent or consistent. The author could be implying that the Jews (= "this one" = Manasseh) would enjoy an inheritance, even if a lesser one; but it might be that he thought of "this one" as Ephraim (= Christians), who would unexpectedly receive the inheritance. In view of the muddle in these verses and the overall tone of the letter, however, it would seem unwise to build too much on what may at most be an inadvertent implication of another, more important point, namely, Christians as the covenant people. In addition, we should note that other verses suggest a bleaker picture: "When they strike down their own shepherd then the sheep of the flock will perish" (5:12), and "then the men [who slaughtered Jesus] are no more, no more is the glory of sinners" (8:2). The first, an allusion to Zechariah 13:7, and the second, which is textually obscure,[109] may point to a rather unpromising future for the Jews—though we should not exaggerate them any more than the evidence noted by Thieme, given that in neither case do they appear to be in the forefront of the author's mind. Indeed, if anything, the view of Thieme is more likely to have been the sort of view held by the Judaizers than by the author of our text!

It should be noted finally, in view of our overall theme, that in *Barnabas* the voice of the author is not the only one to be heard. He had one view of Judaism and of Christianity's relationship to it, but some Christians known to him, the Gentile Judaizers, had another. The one involved radical rejection and appropriation, the other mutual accommodation. For the former we have, of course, the evidence of the whole text; for the latter only a few polemical allusions whose purpose is to suppress, not to inform. Yet this secondary voice is an important part of the record of Christian reactions to Judaism because, together with other evidence, it demonstrates that the views that Christians took of Judaism were far more diverse than the monochrome, negative portrait that was later to dominate the Christian tradition.[110]

What exactly the Judaizers believed can only be surmised. They seem to have supported a joint covenant, something to be shared, rather than two separate covenants. They could have found some support in Paul (Rom 9–11) and in the *Testaments of the Twelve Patriarchs*, but the closer analogy is in the Pseudo-Clementines:

> For on this account Jesus is concealed from the Jews, who have taken Moses as their teacher, and Moses is hidden from those who have believed Jesus. For, there being one teaching by both, God accepts him who has believed either of these. But believing a teacher is for the sake of doing things spoken by God. . . . Neither, therefore, are the Hebrews condemned on account of their ignorance of Jesus, by reason of Him who has concealed him, if, doing the things commanded by Moses, they do not hate him whom they do not know. Neither are those from among the Gentiles condemned, who know not Moses on account of Him who has concealed him, provided that these also, doing the things spoken by Jesus, do not hate him whom they do not know. (*Ps.-Clem.Hom.*8:6–7)

This startling statement, found in a weaker form in *Pseudoclementine Recognitions* 4:5, has been assigned to one of the earlier strata of the Pseudo-Clementines and dated to the late second or early third century.[111] It seems to propound a two-covenant theory, in which both are rooted in the same God but one revealed to the Jews through Moses and the other to the Gentiles through Christ. Equally valid and equally valuable, the parallel covenants are available to those who do not hate or oppose the other.

There are a number of themes in the Pseudo-Clementines that could broadly form the backdrop to this magnanimous view: the unity of God (*Ps.-Clem.Hom.*2:12; 3:59; 7:8; 9:23; 13:4), which in itself may be a reaction to gnostic or Marcionite views; the eternal and abiding value of the law, with the exception of the false pericopes (*Ps.-Clem.Hom.*8:6–7); and the succession Christology, which asserted that revelation had come through a line of prophets, culminating in Jesus. Yet still it remains a remarkably generous vision of salvation, which places Christianity and Judaism on a par. It is not precisely the same view as that of the Judaizers in *Barnabas*, who spoke of sharing one covenant rather than allowing for two covenants, but the underlying spirit is the same. What sort of view the Pseudo-Clementines represent is an open question. The passage quoted is normally assigned to an earlier source, which is labeled Jewish Christian. Yet in their final form the Pseudo-Clementines were produced by the Gentile church. Could it be that what we typically label "Jewish Christian" in the Pseudo-Clementines is in fact the product of Gentile Judaizers? The question can be asked, though hardly answered.

SUMMARY

A brief comparison of Hebrews and *Barnabas* reveals a number of similarities:

1. They share an obsession with Judaism, even though one probably and the other possibly were written for Gentile Christians.

2. The overriding intent in each case is supersessionary—to assert that Christians are the people of God. According to Hebrews the old Israel existed, even if its covenant, law, cult, and heroes were brought to an end and their inadequacies revealed by their superior Christian counterparts. In *Barnabas* the argument is more radical and uncompromising: Israel, in a sense, never was Israel; the covenant never was theirs but belonged, as God had always intended, to the Christians.

3. Temple and cult are important themes, though in Hebrews the high-priestly analogy carries a special significance. In both writings the sacrificial cult is subsumed under and surpassed by Christ's death. In *Barnabas* ethical and spiritualizing arguments reinforce the point, but they never achieve the theological sophistication and complexity of the arguments in Hebrews.

4. Hebrews develops a Christology that is in part designed to counter inadequate, Jewish-flavored christologies among its readers. The Christology of *Barnabas* may be in part an attempt to shore up those who had problems understanding the purpose of the incarnation and crucifixion.

5. The communities addressed share some similarities: members who were sufficiently well-off to be reminded of their obligation to share their wealth; loners who eschewed other Christian company; and, perhaps, defectors.

6. Both recognize suffering as an inevitable concomitant of Christian existence. In Hebrews external pressures seem more immediate, and the theme looms proportionately larger.

7. A plausible setting for both works can be surmised: late-first-century Christian communities which include a Gentile Judaizing element and face a revival of Jewish hopes for a rebuilt Temple. This is more directly evident in *Barnabas,* but may be proposed as an explanation of the curious combination of disparate features in Hebrews.

JEWISH CHRISTIANS AND GENTILE JUDAIZERS

$$5$$

❖

In this chapter we shall consider the two groups of Christians who, for quite different and often complex reasons, found themselves straddling, and thus inevitably blurring, the dividing lines between the Jewish and Christian communities. They were by virtue of their very existence subversive, posing a challenge to the sense of self-identity in both mainstream communities, a challenge that was taken up seriously if obliquely by the early rabbis (the *Birkat ha-minim*), but that was felt even more acutely by the less established and less secure Christian community.

JEWISH CHRISTIANS

As is well known, the evidence for Jewish Christian communities is slight, and often late and tendentious.[1] Yet the fascination with these groups, deeply rooted as they were in the Jesus tradition and intimately related to non-Christian Judaism, exerts a considerable pull and encourages attempts to shape the scraps of evidence into a coherent picture. There is, first, the problem of definition: are they better called Christian Jews than Jewish Christians, and what elements are the minimum necessary to justify the label? Clearly there must be "enough relation to Torah as covenant and commandments" to justify the label "Jew" and "enough relation to Jesus" to justify the label "Christian."[2] To distinguish them from Gentile Judaizers, we should add birth into a Jewish family or proselytization prior to conversion to Christianity. As a minimal definition this allows us to subsume a number of different groups that properly belong here and to use the common designation "Jewish Christian" without confusion.[3]

Most of our information about Jewish Christians has come down in two forms, each of them contentious: the reports of church fathers, who treat them as heretical sectarians; and Jewish Christian writings which purportedly lie embedded in later documents such as Epiphanius's *Panarion* and the *Pseudoclementine Homilies* and *Recognitions*.[4] A maximal and well-known use of the latter is offered by H. J. Schoeps, who, despite some acute observations on the difficulty of using the Pseudo-Clementines and the various sources reconstructed from them, still makes liberal use of them in presenting his counterhistory of the early Church.[5] The urge to fill in some of the historical gaps apparently strains successfully against his critical judgment. Recently it has been suggested that these sources, whose existence has in the past been widely accepted, cannot be isolated on linguistic or stylistic grounds and that they may well be entirely fictitious.[6] But if we allow for some linguistic and stylistic leveling when the various sources were incorporated into the preliminary version of the Pseudo-Clementines (the so-called *Grundschrift*) and accept, as most do, that the author used preexisting and thematically distinctive material, then questions about earlier (especially second-century) forms of Jewish Christianity cannot be dismissed.[7] It may not be possible to delineate the sources with great precision, but their general drift and the differences between them can be used to explore certain lines of development in the history of Jewish Christianity.

The reports of the church fathers have been subjected to similar critical scrutiny. It is known that they write with polemical intent, copy one another verbatim, conflate their sources, use false analogies, and confuse contemporary with ancient information.[8] Some have concluded that no useful information can be extracted from such a tangle of evidence. Their pessimism is understandable but not ineluctable, and in the end the debate hinges partly on a matter of attitude. If the evidence is approached with extreme skepticism, it is always possible to throw doubt on its reliability. If it is approached more positively, then, even though subjected to a properly critical and cautious analysis, it is possible to piece together the broad outlines of various Jewish Christian groups, as recent study of the Nazarenes suggests.[9]

Further contention surrounds the question of the size and influence of the Jewish Christian communities. In older histories of the Christian movement, it was commonly assumed that the Jewish Christians were thrown into disarray by the loss of their Jerusalem leaders, especially James, and by the dire consequences of the Jewish War. After this they became a minority with no central role or significance and rapidly faded into the heterodox fringes of the Christian movement.[10] It has recently become commonplace to assign a dramatically more important role to Jewish Christianity. The claims may vary, but they all point in the same direction (and the more they have been repeated, the looser and more sweeping they have become): that all early Christians were in some sense Jewish Christians; that they were the dominant force throughout the first century; and that they thrived in some areas (Transjordania and Syria) for many centuries, often remaining the dominant form of Christianity to be found in any particular locale.[11] The assumptions behind this commonly held view have in their turn been subjected to rigorous scrutiny in a series of papers by F. Wisse, who argues that the significance of Jewish Christianity has been vastly inflated and that something like the earlier consensus better fits the evidence.[12]

Pella Traditions

This leads us naturally to the traditions about the retreat of the Jerusalem Christians to Pella during the Jewish War, for any assessment of the survival and significance of Jewish Christianity must begin here. The historical reliability of these traditions has been challenged by a number of scholars, most recently G. Lüdemann and J. Verheyden,[13] but they have not been without their defenders.[14]

The main evidence comes from Eusebius and Epiphanius. Each of them speaks on occasion solely of the flight of the Jerusalem Christians to Pella:

> On the other hand the people of the church in Jerusalem were commanded by an oracle given by revelation before the war to those in the city who were worthy of it to depart and dwell in one of the cities of Perea which they called Pella. To it those who believed in Christ migrated. (Eusebius *Hist.eccl.*3.5.3)

> The heresy of the Nazoreans exists in Beroea in the neighbourhood of Coele Syria and the Decapolis in the region of Pella and in Basanitis in the so-called Kokaba, Chocabe in Hebrew. From there it took its beginnings after the exodus from Jerusalem when all the disciples went to live in Pella because Christ had told them to leave Jerusalem and to go away since it would undergo a siege. (Epiphanius *Pan.*29.7.7f.)

> After all those who believed in Christ had generally come to live in Perea, in a city called Pella of the Decapolis of which it is written in the Gospel . . . Ebion's preaching originated here after they had moved to this place and had lived there. (Epiphanius *Pan.*30.2.7)

Elsewhere both writers imply knowledge of a return to Jerusalem after the war:

> After James the Just had suffered martyrdom for the same reason as the Lord, Symeon, his cousin, the son of Clopas was appointed bishop. (Eusebius *Hist.eccl.*4.22.4)

> I have not found any written statement of the dates of the bishops in Jerusalem, for tradition says that they were extremely short-lived, but I have gathered from the documents this much—that up to the siege of the Jews by Hadrian the successions of bishops were fifteen in number. (Eusebius *Hist.eccl.*4.5.1–2)

> When the city was about to be taken by the Romans, it was revealed in advance to all the disciples by an angel of God that they should move from the city, as it was going to be completely destroyed. They sojourned as emigrants in Pella. . . . And this city is said to be of the Decapoli. But after the

destruction of Jerusalem, when they had returned … they wrought great signs. (Epiphanius *Weights and Measures* 15)[15]

Those who dispute the tradition of a flight to Pella rest their case essentially on the following main points: that all supposed allusions to the flight prior to Eusebius (Mark 13 = Luke 21, Matt 24; Rev 12:6,14; *Asc.Isa*.4:13; *Ps.-Clem.Rec*.1.37.2) are questionable; that the core tradition in Eusebius (*Hist.eccl*.3.5.3) speaks only of a flight and not a return; that this core tradition has no historical basis and is a theological construct of Eusebius; that later writers are all dependent on Eusebius and have no independent traditions; that flight from the city would have been impossible under the conditions of the siege; and that Pella was an unlikely refuge, since it was sacked by supporters of the Jewish rebellion.[16]

At first sight these arguments might seem overwhelming. They are in part convincing, but not at the crucial points that are required to support their conclusion. Several of the "allusions" to the Pella tradition are too vague to be convincing. Epiphanius does depend heavily on Eusebius and gives us little independent information. In *Hist.eccl*.3.5.3 Eusebius does speak only of a departure from Jerusalem, not a return, though Lüdemann, for example, presents no strong arguments for the notion that this is the "core" legend. Yet Wehnert has decisively demonstrated that the Pella story does not fit readily with other redactional emphases in Eusebius, in particular the notion of the departure of the apostles on a universal mission (not just to Pella) and of a line of continuity in the Jerusalem church (the election of James's successor and the list of Jewish Christian bishops). Moreover, if Eusebius had concocted this tradition, what possible reason would he have had for the arbitrary selection of Pella as the place of refuge? Everything in fact points to Eusebius's reporting traditional material in the Pella story, and, if so, there is good reason for finding a confirmatory allusion in *Ps.-Clem.Rec*.1.37.39.[17] For similar reasons it seems likely that the return from Pella after the war also rests on old tradition.

If this is so, there remain the pragmatic objections raised by Brandon and others—that flight during the war would have been impossible. In fact, Josephus indicates that rebel raids had different effects on different towns, and that it was possible for even sizable groups to flee Jerusalem up until the end of the siege.[18] Even so, the most plausible dates for the departure are between the death of James (62 CE) and the beginning of the war (66 CE). The execution of James and a general air of alarm encouraged by gloom-laden prophets and inexplicable portents (Josephus *Bell*.6.299–309; Tacitus *Hist*.5.13.1) would have been encouragement enough for Christians to make a move.[19] If so, then all the ostensible objections to a flight during the war become irrelevant.

It is of course inherently likely that the story of the flight and return has been stylized and dramatized in the telling. Many Jerusalem Christians, especially those most vulnerable because of their association with James, may have departed Jerusalem but not necessarily on the same occasion or for the same motives. Likewise, not all of those who fled necessarily returned to Jerusalem after the war, and those who did may have come back in dribs and drabs. If in fact some remained and others returned, this could have been grounds for a rift in the Jewish Christian movement at an early stage.

It is important to establish the likelihood of a flight and return in the face of Brandon's argument that most Jerusalem Christians stayed in the city, fought beside their fellow Jews, and were wiped out in the final siege, and that the few who survived outside of Jerusalem were essentially a spent force who drifted leaderless into Ebionism and other forms of sectarianism. Brandon thus sees the Jewish War as a deadly blow to the future of Jewish Christianity, and it is to his advantage that he can thus explain the remarkable silence in Christian sources about Jewish Christians and the Jerusalem leaders after 70 CE. Quite apart from the Pella tradition, Brandon's view was always an oversimplification. It assumed that the only significant Jewish Christian groups were closely tied to Jerusalem. It is highly probable, however, that Jewish Christians—some of them perhaps members of Jesus' family—were active in Galilee and its immediate environs from an early stage, and certain that other Jewish Christians originated in the diaspora. Jerusalem may have been an important part of their symbolic world, but their fate was not inexorably tied to its fate.[20]

Lüdemann is more modest in his claims, and it is important to note their limitations. He wishes to deny only the tradition of a wholesale flight of Jewish Christians to Pella. He does not deny that some may have fled, nor that there were links between prewar and postwar Jewish Christians—especially between the Jewish Christians of Pella and the Jerusalem community before the war—nor does he assume that a significant number of Jewish Christians were lost in the war.[21] In Lüdemann's view, therefore, there was probably no dramatic change in Jewish Christian fortunes during the war, at least none he is prepared to speculate about, and he is inclined to trace some continuity between the pre-70 and post-70 movements.

This reading of the evidence is supported by Eusebius's reference to the appointment of Jesus' cousin, Simeon, to succeed James as bishop of Jerusalem (*Hist.eccl.*3:11; 4.22.4). According to the first of these passages, this took place at the end of the war at a gathering of apostles, disciples, and the family of Jesus. The departure to Pella may thus have caused an eight-year gap in the Jerusalem leadership.[22] Further confirmation is found in Eusebius's reference to the fifteen Jewish Christian bishops of Jerusalem prior to 135 CE (*Hist.eccl.*4.5.1–2)—though it is difficult to know what to make of this number in view of Simeon's supposed martyrdom at a great age under Trajan (*Hist.eccl.*3.22.3).[23] But if we can thus assume that the Jewish Christians were not wiped out in the year 70 CE, we have yet to establish in what form and with what degree of influence they survived and in what manner they related to non-Christian Judaism.

Groupings of Jewish Christians

The various pieces of evidence for Jewish Christian groups ascribe to each of them characteristics that rarely correspond exactly with those of any other. One way of surveying them, therefore, is to treat them as discrete entities, carefully noting the characteristics of each group but resisting the urge to draw lines of connection between them. This has the appearance of rigor and the virtue of taking the evidence as it stands, but it has the disadvantage of leaving us with nothing more than a few scattered fragments of information. Not only does this make it difficult to build up any clear or coherent picture of the Jewish Christian movement, but it also ignores phenomena common to all the groups as well as clusters of characteristics that bind individual groups quite closely together. We shall, therefore, tentatively divide the evidence into three clusters—for which we shall use the labels Ebionite, Jacobite, and Nazarene—and attempt to provide a modest taxonomy of Jewish Christian groups up until the end of the second century.

Ebionites: As a name for a distinct group of Jewish Christians, the term "Ebionite" appears first in Irenaeus (*Haer.*I.26.2). He ascribes to them directly or by implication a number of characteristics: they denied the virgin birth, insisting that Jesus was the son of Mary and Joseph; they adhered to the commands of the Jewish law, including circumcision; they used only one Gospel, a version of Matthew; they rejected Paul as a lawbreaker and an enemy of Jewish and Christian truth; they had a distinctive way of interpreting the prophets so that they witnessed to Christian belief; they celebrated the Eucharist with water instead of wine; and they honored Jerusalem as the city of God, facing it when they prayed.

Later writers add little that is substantial to this list. Tertullian is the first to express the heresiologists' penchant for connecting all heresies with a founder by mistakenly supposing that theirs was a man called Ebion.[24] Origen (*Cels.*61) adds the interesting information that there were two groups of Ebionites (the label may in one case be false): one with a low Christology (as in Irenaeus) and one with an orthodox Christology. Epiphanius (*Pan.*29), who also knew of other Jewish Christian groups, which he tended to confuse with the Ebionites, expands on some of the things known from Irenaeus: that their commitment to purity involved avoidance of contact with non-Jews, ritual cleansing after intercourse, and abstinence from meat; that they celebrated the Eucharist with unleavened bread as well as water; that their interpretation of the prophets sometimes led to criticism or rejection of them; and that Paul's failed attempt to become a proselyte in order to marry a Jewish woman (he was originally Gentile!) fired his antipathy to Judaism.[25] Only in Epiphanius do we find that the Ebionites were obliged to marry, used Jesus as their exemplar in observing the law, accepted the abolition of sacrifice, and described their buildings as "synagogues" and their leaders as "elders" or "leaders of the synagogue."

Irenaeus was active around the last quarter of the second century. Like his successors, he probably had some firsthand knowledge of Jewish Christians, and the way he describes them implies that they had been in existence for some while. Epiphanius is the next most important witness (Origen we shall return to), but he comes almost two hundred years later and, despite knowing some Jewish Christians (not necessarily Ebionites) firsthand, he has a habit of conflating and confusing the groups and writings emanating from different Jewish Christian circles.[26] At any rate his information is substantially the same and merely adds a little flesh to the bare sketch in Irenaeus. Nothing he tells us contradicts what we find in Irenaeus and, if he has a discernible slant, it is to make the Jewish Christians look more Jewish in their commitments. It is difficult to know where to locate them. Following the main sources of information we could suggest Rome (Irenaeus), Egypt (Origen), or Transjordania (where Epiphanius got his sources).[27] Eusebius locates them firmly in Cochaba.

Can we push back beyond Irenaeus to discover anything about the Ebionites? There is little to go on. Justin appears to differentiate between two groups of unnamed Jewish Christians in *Dial.*48: those who accepted Jesus as the Messiah, but human; and, implicitly contrasted with them, those who agree with Justin, that is, in the preexistence of Jesus.[28] The first group could be linked, if tenuously, with the Ebionites on the basis of a common Christology. We could go farther and connect this "Ebionite" group with one of the Jewish Christian groups mentioned in the immediately preceding chapters (*Dial.*46–47), that is, those who kept the law strictly and who would not mix with Gentile Christians. The concern for purity rules fits the profile of the Ebionites, although it has to be admitted that the connection between *Dial.*46–47 and 48 is one that Justin does not make.

It remains possible that the term Ebionite (*ebionim* = the poor) was a self-designation of some early Jewish Christians.[29] Paul mentions "the poor among the saints at Jerusalem" in Romans 15:26 (cf. Gal 2:10). This could simply mean those who were materially poor,[30] but there was a strong tradition for using the term in the sense of "the pious" (who might also be materially poor). Thus in the Hebrew scriptures, the Qumran documents, and the New Testament it can have a broader sense—generally as a reference to a special form of piety and at Qumran as a self-designation.[31] It is thus possible, but not certain, that the term Ebionite had a long history, beginning in the apostolic era as a designation for certain Jewish Christian groups in Jerusalem and continuing with their successors, who, in turn, came to have a distinctive profile in the Christian world.[32]

The obscure Elkesaites shared a significant number of features with the Ebionites: they observed the law (sabbath and circumcision in particular are mentioned); they faced Jerusalem when they prayed; they rejected chastity and were obliged to marry; they rejected the apostle Paul (only in Eusebius); they venerated water (cf. the Ebionites' eucharistic water); and they had a low, if somewhat confused, Christology, which viewed the birth through Mary as merely one in a succession of incarnations and which claimed that Jesus was just as other men—thus, in one way or another, denying unique significance to the virgin birth.

The parallels are at first glance impressive, but the evidence for the Elkesaites is tangled indeed.[33] Apart from a brief notice in Eusebius (*Hist. eccl.*6.38), we depend essentially on Hippolytus (*Haer.*9.13–17) and Epiphanius (*Pan.*19 and 53), who appear to be independent witnesses. Hippolytus based his knowledge on a contemporary (ca. 220 CE), Alcibiades from Syria, who possessed a book supposedly revealed to one Elkesai early in the reign of Trajan (98–117 CE). Although Hippolytus claims to report the contents of the book, it is not clear whether we are getting the book itself or Alcibiades's interpretation of it. Epiphanius seems to have known the book of Elkesai but he introduces confusion by connecting the Elkesaites with even more obscure groups, the Ossaeans (Jewish?) and the Sampsaeans (Jewish Christian?), the latter of whom survived until Epiphanius's day. Elsewhere he connects them with the Ebionites (*Pan.*30.2.6; 30.16.7).

The key questions for us are whether the Elkesaites were originally a Jewish or a Jewish Christian group, and consequently at what point we date the Jewish Christian input. That Epiphanius makes them out to be more Jewish and Hippolytus more Christian is an interesting but not decisive observation. Of the traits they share with the Ebionites, anti-Paulinism and Christology are clearly Christian, though the others could as easily be Jewish. Of the remaining features, which find no parallel among the Ebionites, the theory of baptism for the remission of sins, and especially that of a second baptism open to those who, under severe persecution, deny their faith with the mouth but not the heart, are said to have a more Christian than Jewish ring to them. Thus some conclude that they were from the start a Jewish Christian group who absorbed various syncretistic or gnostic traits over time.[34] Yet the evidence for anti-Paulinism is found only in Eusebius, the baptismal tradition could have originated among the remnants of Baptist or Qumran circles, and the Christology could well be a later addition. From this some have concluded that they were a heterodox Jewish group originating sometime early in the second century who absorbed a few Christian traits through contact with Ebionites sometime in the late second or early third centuries.[35] The evidence scarcely allows a firm decision, but the upshot is that the Elkesaites are either evidence for an Ebionite-type Christianity early in the second century, or a confirmation in broad terms of Irenaeus's information about them around 200 CE.

Finally, a more tenuous connection with the Ebionites may be found in the *Kerygmata Petrou* (*KP*). This document is commonly thought to be embedded in the *Pseudoclementine Homilies* 2–3,11,17. The only mention of it, *Ps.-Clem.Rec.*3.75, is in a table of contents which many think fictitious. Strecker has provided the most detailed reconstruction of *KP* and dates its composition to ca. 200 CE in Syria,[36] but after a period of fairly wide acceptance his views have increasingly been challenged.[37]

If for the sake of argument, however, we assume both that Strecker is correct and that *KP* was recording traditions that circulated in the second century, what do we find? There are a few connections with the Ebionites: anti-Paulinism, in the form of a dispute between Peter and Simon Magus (= Paul);[38] an emphasis on purity rules; and criticism of the prophets in terms of the notion of "false pericopes." *Contestatio* 1:1 suggests that only the circumcised could inherit Peter's special teaching, which fits with other comments about Ebionite legalism, and the succession Christology of *KP* could (but need not) have been congruent with the Ebionites' reportedly low Christology. One difference is that the author of *KP* does not restrict himself to the Matthean tradition, but seems to be acquainted with more than one canonical Gospel as well as other New Testament writings. The elevation of Peter as the principal prophetic figure presumably would have been congenial to a number of Jewish Christian groups, but it is not found elsewhere in connection with the Ebionites.[39] Other traits suggest connections with the Elkesaites: the emphasis on baptism and lustrations; the use of oaths that call on the cosmic elements; and the distinction between male and female principles in the idea of the succession of true and false gnosis.[40] All in all, the evidence suggests some connection with Ebionite tradition, though the fit is not precise. The overlap with the Elkesaites, which is more with their non-Christian traits, may be because the author of *KP* knew Elkesaites who had already absorbed some Ebionite ideas.

One of the most distinctive traits of *KP* is its positive appraisal of Judaism. When Peter passes on his teaching, his model is Moses and the seventy elders, who were so successful that the Jews "to this day" maintain their monotheism and their distinctive ethical code. Not only this, they have also learned properly to harmonize the apparent contradictions of scripture and preserve the eternal values of the Mosaic Law (*Epistula Petri* 1:2–5). Judaism is not criticized, but rather held up as a positive example to be emulated. In line with this is a remarkable passage, which we looked at briefly in connection with *Barnabas*, and which speaks of the equality of the two covenants:

> For on this account Jesus is concealed from the Jews, who have taken Moses as their teacher, and Moses is hidden from those who have believed Jesus. For, there being one teaching by both, God accepts him who has believed either of these. But believing a teacher is for the sake of doing things spoken by God. . . . Neither, therefore, are the Hebrews condemned on account of their ignorance of Jesus, by reason of Him who has concealed him, if, doing the things commanded by Moses, they do not hate him whom they do not know. Neither are those from among the Gentiles condemned, who know not

Moses on account of Him who has concealed him, provided that these also, doing the things spoken by Jesus, do not hate him whom they do not know. (*Ps.-Clem.Hom.*8:6–7)

This statement, found in a weaker form in *Ps.-Clem.Rec.*4:5, is assigned by Strecker to *KP*.[41] It seems to propound a two-covenant theory, the one revealed to the Jews through Moses and the other to the Gentiles through Christ. Equally valid and equally valuable, the parallel covenants are efficacious for those who do not hate or oppose the other.

There are a number of themes in *KP* that could broadly form the backdrop to this unusually magnanimous view—the unity of God, and the eternal and abiding value of the law (with the exception of the false pericopes). Above all, perhaps, it is supported by the succession Christology, in which God is revealed through a series of holy prophets culminating in Jesus. The result is at any rate remarkable. Judaism and Christianity are placed on a par, two variants of the same revelation, the same "*Ur-religion*" that has existed since the creation of the world.

We cannot be sure where or when this view originated. Strecker assigns it to *KP* on the strength of its congruence with statements in the *Epistula Petri,* but it goes well beyond these in the boldness and generosity of its vision. However, even if we doubt the existence of *KP,* not to mention the presence of this passage in it, there is no reason automatically to assign it to some later period. It could represent a strain of Christian conviction that had deeper roots, and the parallel sentiment known to the author of *Barnabas* is one good reason for thinking this.

Between the groups we have discussed above there is not a precise match, and each of them bears some distinctive traits. This sort of variation is precisely what we would expect, as pockets of Jewish Christians developed their own beliefs and practices. There is sufficient common ground between them, however, to justify including them in the same broad category, which we might tentatively call an Ebionite cluster.

Jacobites: Turning to traditions that focus on the figure of James, we must begin with another writing reconstructed from the Pseudo-Clementines: *The Ascent of James.* We can be more confident of the existence of this source since it is quoted by Epiphanius in *Pan.*30.16.6–9 (commonly labeled *AJ I*) as well as forming the basis for *Rec.*1.33–71 (commonly labeled *AJ II*). It is usually dated ca. 150–200 CE and often associated with Pella.[42] Even among those skeptical of precisely defining its limits, it is agreed that we are dealing here with old and valuable Jewish Christian traditions with a distinctive flavor:[43]

1. The most pronounced feature of *AJ* is the central and undisputed role of James himself. "Our" James (69.1) is bishop of Jerusalem (66.2,5; 68.2). Ordained bishop by Jesus (43.3), he gives outstanding leadership to a thriv-

ing church and is recognized as *the* authority to whom others instinctively and properly turn (66.1; 69.8). Other apostles are mentioned, but they work outside Jerusalem and are of little immediate interest; other Christians appear in Jerusalem, but only as the shadowy backdrop to the central figure of James. And while such a picture runs counter to all other sources for this period and is largely fictional, it vividly illustrates the perspective of one group on the story of Christian origins.[44]

2. This dominant figure also has one overriding activity: preaching to the Jews. He is immensely successful, so that eventually there are more Christian than non-Christian Jews in Jerusalem (43.1; 71.1). Jesus is presented in 33–44 and 55–65 above all as the Mosaic prophet, and the Jews are said to accept the identification of the Mosaic prophet with the Messiah.[45] The one substantial disagreement is whether Jesus qualifies as this Messiah (43; cf. 50): it was agreed that the Messiah would come in the last days, but the Jews could not accept that he had already come in humility. Whether James's messianism involved any notion of preexistence remains unclear. Allusions to "the eternal Messiah" (43.1) and to Jesus' "assuming a Jewish body" (60.7) are tenuous evidence at best.[46] The only other dispute with the Jews comes with the charge that Jesus effected his resurrection by magic (42.4)— an analogous and more broadly based version of which we find in both rabbinic and other Christian sources.

3. Opposition to James follows on his success and eventually leads to his martyrdom (70.8). It comes in part from Jews, but above all from Paul (70– 71). Their dispute is ill-defined in the *Recognitions*,[47] but Paul is seen as the reason why James, himself an exceptionally devout Jew, could not win over the whole Jewish community to his side—a failure that leads ultimately to the destruction of the city and Temple. It seems to be the pre-Christian rather than the Christian Paul who is involved, but even this remains unclear.

4. God forewarned Israel about the demise of the Temple and the sacrificial cult that he had allowed as a concession to the ingrained idolatry of Israel (36–37; 64). It is replaced by baptism, which brings not only forgiveness but also physical protection during the disturbances of the Jewish War (39).[48] This anticultic strain does not seem to have been the prelude to more extensive criticism of the law. Circumcision is described positively (33.3–5), as is the giving of the law to Israel (35.2; cf. 60.4), the Passover is observed (44.1), and Jesus is received as a "teacher of the law" (62.3). To what extent this implies observance of the law by this Jewish Christian community remains, however, unclear.[49]

5. The call of Gentiles to replace the unbelieving Jews was predicted in the prophets, even though it might seem to go against the natural order of things (42; cf. 50), but it apparently did not begin until after 70 CE, when the Temple had been destroyed (64).

Here, then, we have firm evidence for a form of Jewish Christianity that is anti-Pauline but with a universalist strain, anticultic but with a legalist strain, and above all obsessed with James. Are there any earlier signs of such a group? The Epistle of James comes very close.[50] The publication of a pseudonymous work in the name of James clearly both depends on and attempts to enhance his reputation. This goes hand in hand with an implicit denigration of Paul. The discussion of faith and works in James 2:14–26, as a comparison with Romans 4:2ff. shows, has one target in mind—namely, Paul, but a Paul who is in fact fictitious, the product of rumor and gossip. Ironically, the key terms "faith" and "works" are used so differently by the two writers that there is nothing in this part of the Letter of James with which Paul could not have concurred. The real Paul would thus have agreed with the author of James. Yet even though the image of Paul, having passed through the rumor mill of Jewish Christian antagonism, was a caricature, it remains significant: first, because it indicates precisely the sort of distorted image of Paul that could thrive in Jewish Christian circles; and second, because the author intends to oppose Paul even if the Paul he knows bears only a tenuous relation to the historical figure.[51]

Other features of the letter also fit a Jewish Christian context. The attack on those who discriminate in favor of the rich in James 2:1–9 concludes with a quotation of Leviticus 19:18 as part of "the royal law" (v.8; cf. "the perfect law" in 1:25). The emphasis in the following passage on keeping "the whole law" (James 2:10ff.) could be expressing an extremely rigorous stance rare even in Judaism, though the immediate context does not make this clear.[52] Throughout the letter the emphasis is commonly said to be on ethical rather than ritual commands, although this distinction may have meant nothing to a Jewish Christian. The Christology of the epistle is notoriously unemphatic. The two references to Jesus as "Lord" (James 1:1; 2:1) and the obscure appellation "of glory" (also in 2:1) are about the sum of it and, as has often been noted, they could be deleted without affecting the sense of the epistle.[53] Finally, it is noteworthy that the epistle contains numerous echoes of the Gospel tradition, mostly with material from the Sermon on the Mount and mostly in its Matthean form.[54]

The Letter of James was composed sometime in the last quarter of the first century, in an environment in which Jewish traditions were familiar and the reputation of James the brother of Jesus considerable.[55] He is presented as a recognized authority and a teacher of practical ethics, and there is little doubt that the choice of pseudonym has polemical intent, insofar as it authorizes the modus vivendi of a Jewish Christian community and warns against falsehoods thought to have been propagated by the Pauline tradition. The parallels with the *AJ* source are strong: an emphasis on keeping the law, a modest Christology, anti-Paulinism, and, above all, invocation of the central and authoritative role of James. There are differences too: the anticultic and universalist strains in *AJ* are not found in the letter, unless the oblique address in 1:1 refers to the universal (including Gentile) membership of the church,[56] and dependence on Matthean tradition connects the letter generally with Jewish Christians and not specifically with *AJ*. But precise equivalence even within the same basic strain of Jewish Christianity is not to be expected if we allow for differences of time and place in composition. We are merely looking for clusters or groupings that allow us to make some taxonomic sense of the otherwise inchoate traces of the Jewish Christian movement. Thus, although the Letter of James and *AJ* share a great deal with the Ebionite tradition, they are distinguished by the emphatically central role of James.

Prior to the Letter of James and *AJ*, there is clear evidence that James played a major role in the early Christian movement. Partly (perhaps chiefly) because he was Jesus' brother he became a critical figure in the Jerusalem church, as is shown in both Acts and the Pauline letters (e.g., 1 Cor 15; Gal 1–2; Acts 15; 21). The dynastic connection is preserved according to the probably reliable tradition that Simeon, Jesus' cousin, succeeded James as bishop of Jerusalem (Eusebius *Hist.eccl.*3.22.3; 4.5.3; 4.22.4). The pivotal role of James is indicated by the *Gos.Heb.*7 in which he is the sole focus of attention in the postresurrection scenes (cf. *Gos.Thom.*12). In traditions attributed to Hegesippus—active in the second half of the second century and thought by Eusebius to have been a Jewish Christian—James is ascribed a threefold role: as the first and undisputed leader of the Jerusalem church; as a priestly figure who interceded for his people through his devotion and prayers; and as one whose widely renowned righteousness earned him the epithet "the Just" (Eusebius *Hist.eccl.* 2.23.4–18; 4.22.4; cf. Epiphanius *Pan.*29,78).[57] What these traditions share with the Letter of James and *AJ* is above all their focus on the figure of James. Apart from this they confirm the view of *AJ* that his dispute with the Jews was primarily over messianism (Eusebius *Hist.eccl.*4.22.9–10).

Nazarenes: From the Ebionite and Jacobite clusters we turn now to a third: the Nazarenes. The fullest description comes from Epiphanius (*Pan.*29) and, from those parts of his information we can trust, the following profile emerges: they used the Old and the New Testaments; they knew Hebrew and had one Hebrew Gospel; they accepted resurrection of the dead; they believed in one God, the creator, and his Son Jesus Christ; they observed the law; they originated among the Christians who fled from Jerusalem and were located in Pella, Cochaba, and Coele-Syria; they were hated and cursed by the Jews for their messianic beliefs.[58]

At around the same time, the mid to late fourth century, Jerome gives confirmation of this information based on personal contact with the Nazarenes: he knows of their Hebrew version of Matthew, parts of which he translated (*Devir. ill.*2 and 3), and confirms that they held to an orthodox Christology (*Ep.*112.13), including the virgin birth and divine sonship. In addition he quotes from a Nazarene commentary on Isaiah which provides interesting supplementary material: that they disputed the value of Jewish "traditions" (with reference to the errors of the scribes and Pharisees, *Comm.Is.*8:20–21; 9:1–4; 29:20–21); that they endorsed Paul and his Gentile mission, and thus presumably did not require Gentiles to keep the law (*Comm.Is.*9:1–4); and that they called for reconciliation with and repentance from the Jews (*Comm.Is.*31:6–9), thus harboring hopes for their conversion.[59]

In most respects the Nazarenes look like a mainstream Christian group. That they still kept the law singled them out (together with other Jewish Christians), and if they hoped for the conversion of the Jews, this would have been a more positive view than that held by most Christian groups from the second century on. On the other hand, they stand out from the Jewish Christian groups we have already surveyed by their endorsement of the Gentile mission, especially of Paul's role in it, and by their adherence to an "orthodox" Christology. Again, linking two separate pieces of information in Justin, we might suggest that if the Jewish Christians with the "orthodox" Christology (*Dial.*48) were the same as those who mixed with Gentiles and did not try to Judaize them (*Dial.*46–47), we would have a group that shared two of the important distinctive marks of the Nazarenes.

There is evidence to suggest that the Nazarenes we read about in the fourth century had a long history, possibly going back to the pre-70 period. Tertullian (*Marc.*4:8) confirms that the term "Nazarene" was an early as well as a current name for Christians, at least among Jews. More interestingly Eusebius (*Hist.eccl.*3.27.2–6) and Origen (*Cels.*61) know of two types of Ebionite, one with a low Christology and another with more "orthodox" views,[60] and Justin (*Dial.*48), as we noted above, mentions a similar division but without labeling the groups. Pritz has plausibly suggested that the more "orthodox" of the groups were Nazarenes and not, as Eusebius and Origen mistakenly supposed, Ebionites.[61]

Two other strands of evidence fill out the picture. In Acts 24:5 Paul is accused of being a ringleader of the "sect of the Nazarenes"—clearly in this context a name for all Christians. Was it a self-designation or a nickname given by outsiders, and does it reflect usage at the time of composition (ca. 90 CE) or at the time ostensibly being reported (ca. 55 CE)? It seems most likely that it was an early, Semitic self-designation of the Christian community, which was rapidly overtaken by the Greek term *Christianoi* (cf. Acts 11:26) as Gentiles came to dominate the movement.[62] This finds some support in the rabbinic traditions, where Jesus is referred to infrequently but fairly consistently as Jesus the Nazarene (*Jesu ha-notzri*; cf. *b.Abod.Zar.*6a; *b.Ta'an* 27b) and in those versions of the Jewish liturgical malediction against heretics (*Birkat ha-minim*) which extend or define the term "heretics" (*minim*) by the addition of the term "Nazarenes" (*notzrim*). The reference to Christians/Nazarenes in the synagogue malediction was probably neither early nor universal. It seems that it was added sometime in the second century, when it was felt necessary to add a specific reference to Christians to the more general term "heretic," and it may have been restricted to Eastern Jewish communities where the Jewish Christians were most numerous and threatening.[63]

This evidence suggests the following: that the term "Nazarene" was originally a general term for early Christians in Semitic circles; that it was soon superseded by the term *Christianoi* among the increasingly dominant Greek-speaking converts; that it lingered on in Jewish usage as a traditional term for Christians; and that it was preserved by one group of Jewish Christians as a self-designation because it had deep historical roots. The likelihood is that the Nazarenes, who are condemned as heretical sectarians in the fourth century, had their origins in those members of the pre-70 Jerusalem church who fled to Pella.[64]

Conclusions

We have provisionally identified three clusters in the extant evidence for Jewish Christianity: the Ebionites, the Jacobites, and the Nazarenes. When we view them in this way a number of things become apparent. First, these groups shared a number of things in common—a profound concern with the meaning of scripture, a tendency to favor the Gospel of Matthew, and observance of the Jewish law. Equally striking, however, are the differences between them. Plotted on a spectrum, the Ebionites would appear at one end, the Nazarenes at the other, and the Jacobites somewhere in between (if anything, shading more toward the Nazarenes, with whom their main disagreement lay in their estimation of Paul). The variety among, as well as within, these groups alerts us to the danger of speaking of Jewish Christianity as if it were a homogeneous entity, and this in turn suggests that they may have related differently to non-Christian Judaism.

It is possible that all three groups had their origins in the early church, and it is tempting to make more precise connections: The Ebionites with the more conservative Jewish Christians, normally thought to have opposed Paul at least in Antioch, Philippi, and Galatia; the more moderate Jacobites with those who upheld observance of the law but supported the Gentile mission; and the Nazarenes with Jewish Christians who endorsed Paul and his universal mission. The temptation to simplify categories and connections can, however, also mislead. Not all Jewish Christians lived in Judaea and, while there were many shades of opinion on matters such as the Gentile mission and Torah observance in the pre-70 period, it is also probable that Jewish Christian views on these and other matters continued to evolve for some time after.

F. Wisse's critique of the recent and increasingly influential tendency to see Jewish Christians as the dominant force during the first century and beyond, if not in numbers, then at least in policy and theology, is based on some acute observations. One tack he takes is to deflate the overall numbers of Christian adherents, which automatically deflates the Jewish Christian minority. Another is to point to exaggerations in Acts of missionary successes, to the absence of Jewish Christians in pagan and Jewish sources, but above all to Paul's anguished discussion in Romans 9–11 of the failure of the mission to the Jews. He has introduced a welcome note of skepticism to the debate and exposed the casually adopted but often unfounded assumptions of those who have overemphasized the significance of Jewish Christianity in the first two centuries. But he is also too quick to ignore or dismiss evidence that runs counter to his thesis. The range of evidence discussed above, the appearance of the *Birkat ha-minim* in the synagogue liturgy—directed at least in part against Jewish Christians—and the important evidence of Justin (*Dial.*46–48) for the existence of a number of different Jewish Christian groups apparently active in his day indicate that Jewish Christians survived in a variety of forms, and in sufficient numbers to be noted, throughout the period with which we are concerned.[65] The evidence seems to point neither to their rapid marginalization nor to their continuing dominance after 70 CE, but rather to their survival as a significant minority.[66]

How then did they relate to Judaism? About this we are not as well informed as we would wish, largely because our sources are more interested in internal Christian disputes than with the relationship of these groups to Judaism. Clearly, however, all Jewish Christians had one thing in common: they shared beliefs and lived a lifestyle that brought them significantly closer to Judaism than most Gentile Christians, with the exception of Gentile Judaizers. The single most consistent feature in the reports is that they were all committed to Torah observance in one form or another. This was often the main cause of dispute with other Christians as well as the feature of their lives that drew them closest to Judaism. Where opposition to Paul's supposed antinomianism, a low Christology, prayers facing Jerusalem, or a profound concern with the meaning of the scriptures are found, they usually express a Christian commitment, but they do so in a way likely to cause least offense to the Jews. The "we/they" language of *AJ* shows an awareness of separate identity, but it is accompanied by an anxiety to emphasize their Jewishness and to confine disagreement to a single issue, such as messiahship. Some of their views of scripture (the theory of "false pericopes" in *KP*, for example) would not have sat well with most Jews, but they would have seemed scarcely less heterodox to most Christians. The universalist strain as well as the rejection of the Temple cult have their broad parallels in the pseudepigraphic and rabbinic traditions even when the details and the motives differ.

The inclusion of the Nazarenes in the *Birkat ha-minim*—if it was added in the second century and if it includes Jewish Christians—indicates a degree of hostility that is otherwise rare in the surviving evidence. Of course, it may well tell us about the situation in only some locations. According to *AJ*, James meets with opposition from some Jewish authorities, but this may be a historical relic that does not reflect the experience of the writer.[67] An approximate parallel, seen from the other side, is Justin's angry reaction to Christian defectors who have abandoned their Christian beliefs and joined the synagogue, probably under the influence of Jewish Christians promoting observance of the Torah (*Dial.*47.4). In the one case Jewish Christians spark off hostility by their very presence among their fellow Jews, and in the other they precipitate defection to the synagogue among those who chose to take their recommendation of the Jewish way of life one radical and unexpected step farther.

Otherwise the most significant disagreement between Jewish Christians and their compatriots appears to have been over their conceptions of the Messiah. The Jews could agree that the Messiah had yet to come in glory (as in *AJ* and Justin's *Dial.*), but not that he had already come in humility.[68] In some sources this stands as the sole barrier between the Jews and Christian belief. Complicating matters was the figure of Paul, usually suspect for his antinomianism, but in *AJ* seen as the one who queered the pitch for James and seriously hindered the conversion and unity of Israel. Such a view seems to hold out little hope for the Jews, but it at least puts the blame not on the Jews themselves, as so commonly happens in the Christian tradition, but on the activities of a renegade Christian.

Going beyond *AJ* are two other strains of evidence. First, that the Nazarenes conversed with Jewish leaders over the meaning of scripture, organized their communities on the synagogue model, and, above all, clung to the hope of reconciliation with, and repentance by, the Jews. Exactly what was envisaged remains unclear. It is probable that they expected the Jews to be saved by conversion to Christian belief rather than by merely repenting as Jews, but we cannot be sure.

This modestly positive view of Judaism, whatever precise form it took, is found among those Jewish Christians who were closest to the Christian mainstream and, as we would expect, is expressed in terms of the conversion of the Jews. Far more radical is the view expressed in Ps.-Clem.Hom.8:6–7, in which Judaism and its covenant is placed on a par with Christianity as providing an equally valid and effective way of salvation. Perhaps not surprisingly it comes to expression in a strain of Jewish Christianity that was perhaps farthest from the Christian mainstream and closest to Judaism. But it was not without parallel, as the evidence of *Barnabas* has shown.[69]

GENTILE JUDAIZERS

We turn our attention now to the group who, coming from the other side, also straddled the Jewish-Christian divide: Gentile Christians who adopted in varying degrees the lifestyle of the Jews. In recent years a number of scholars have focused on these crossover Christians. For John Gager they are important evidence for his generally persuasive argument that in the Greco-Roman world Judaism, far from being universally mistrusted and vilified, was in both its beliefs and its practices often attractive to non-Jews.[70] Gager, like L. Gaston and others before him,[71] brought this observation to bear on the more specific issue of Jewish-Christian relations in the early centuries. For, so they have argued, Christian Gentiles were among those attracted to Judaism, and the reaction of ecclesiastical leaders to this situation was a major cause of anti-Jewish sentiment in the early church. Thus Judaizing was not, as had often been assumed, restricted to the first generation of Christians (approx. pre-70 CE), but remained an urgent and troublesome issue.

The plausibility of this thesis is enhanced by pointing to the classic example of Christian judaizing in Antioch in the time of John Chrysostom, which drew from him some of the most powerful anti-Jewish rhetoric in the history of the Christian West.[72] The question remains, however, whether the relatively clear picture from before 70 CE and after 200 CE also holds for the much more obscure period in between. We shall concentrate, therefore, on evidence that comes from this period and in which ostensible allusions to Judaizers are fairly specific. We shall ignore Ephesians at this point, because the most that can be said there is that Judaizers might lurk in the background.[73] That the intense concern with supersession of Jewish categories in Hebrews might be a response to Gentile Judaizers has already been argued, and we shall suggest that the hypothesis of Gentile Judaizing is one possible explanation of the distinctive positions taken by Marcion and Melito. In these three instances, however, it remains a hypothesis for which there is no direct textual basis. This leaves us with four pieces of evidence—found in Ignatius, Justin, *Barnabas,* and Revelation—which come from the same fifty- to sixty-year period.

In considering this evidence we shall have two aims in mind: first, an assessment of the evidence usually offered for the existence of Gentile Judaizers in this period, drawing attention to some relatively neglected material that may have a bearing on the issue; and second, the posing of a further question: What can we surmise about the motives of the Judaizers insofar as there is evidence for their existence? Can we go beyond vague statements about "the attractions of Judaism" to ask what specifically drew some Gentile Christians to the synagogue and its way of life?

The very term "Judaizer" requires brief definition. As New Testament scholars we use it most frequently and misleadingly of Jewish Christians who try to impose their practices on Gentile (usually Pauline) Christians. J. Gager, like M. Simon before him, adds to the confusion by using the term of both Jewish and Gentile Christians who choose a Jewish lifestyle. In practical terms, he argues, it amounted to the same thing and, at any rate, we often cannot distinguish between the two groups.[74] L. Gaston more sensibly argues that we should use the term Judaizer only in its ancient and technical sense, that is, of non-Jews who chose to live like Jews.[75] A Judaizer was by definition a Gentile, and it is Christian Gentiles of this sort on whom we shall focus.

Barnabas

We have already discussed *Barnabas* in considerable detail in chapter 4, and it will suffice briefly to recall that argument. The main texts are as follows:

> Do not continue to pile up your sins while claiming that the covenant is both theirs and ours [*he diatheken ekeinon kai hemon*]. (4:6)

> Now let us see whether this people or the first people have the inheritance, and whether the covenant is ours or theirs [*eis hemas e eis ekeinous*]. (13:1)

> But he [Christ] was made manifest in order that at the same time they might be perfected in their sins and we might receive the covenant through him who inherited it, even the Lord Jesus. (14:5)

The author and the readers of *Barnabas* seem to have been Gentiles (3:6; 16:7) and the identity of those who propound a shared covenant are thus most likely to have been Gentile Judaizers. If those who are in danger of shipwrecking their faith by observing the law (3:6) are the same as those who say that "the covenant is both theirs and ours" (4:6), then their theory of a shared covenant has a practical outcome: they adopt Jewish ways. This may well be in part a response to a newly resurgent Judaism which had high hopes, and imperial support, for a rebuilding of the Temple. The author of *Barnabas*, therefore, was faced not merely with a more generous theory about the place of Judaism than he inclined to, but with a powerfully attractive Judaism which had already made inroads among Gentile believers. This is why his response is so categorical and so extreme: not only do the Jews not share the covenant now; they never possessed it in the first place (4:7–8). It belongs solely to Christians and had been intended for them from the beginning.[76]

The Judaizers alluded to in *Barnabas* could have found some support for their position in Romans 11, if they had known it, and their view is not unlike the two-covenant notion of the Pseudo-Clementines as well as the attitude of the Christian author/editor of the *Testaments of the Twelve Patriarchs*. Their claim is not unthinkable on the lips of the Judaizers Ignatius encountered, though there is no hint of this in his letters. The separation between Judaism and Christianity, which Ignatius was also anxious to encourage, is no less radical in *Barnabas* than in Marcion, even though it leads to an entirely different outcome, and it will be argued elsewhere that one plausible explanation for Marcion's radical gospel is precisely the confusion caused by Judaizers in the early church.[77] These are interesting parallels but, if we are right to connect the themes of covenant and Temple, the generous theorizing and the Judaizing activities of those opposed by the author of

Barnabas can also be placed in a specific context: the attractions of a resurgent and officially supported Judaism.

Revelation

We turn next to some obscure references in the early chapters of the book of Revelation:

> I know your affliction and your poverty, even though you are rich. I know the slander on the part of those who say that they are Jews and are not, but are a synagogue of Satan. Do not fear what you are about to suffer. Beware, the devil is about to throw some of you into prison, so that you may be tested, and for ten days you will have affliction. (Rev 2:9–10)

> I will make those of the synagogue of Satan who say that they are Jews and are not, but are lying—I will make them come and bow down before your feet, and they will learn that I have loved you. (Rev 3:9)

There are three main suggestions about the identity of "those who say that they are Jews and are not." H. Kraft has argued that they were syncretistic Jewish Christians who compromised with the state and pagan cults, denied the salvific effect of Jesus' death and resurrection, and fled to the synagogue to avoid Roman persecution. He thus associates them with the Nicolaitans mentioned elsewhere in these early chapters.[78] The identification with the Nicolaitans is, however, problematic and it is difficult to imagine why the Romans would have persecuted them if they had been so willing to compromise.[79]

More common and more convincing is the suggestion that they were the Jews of Smyrna and Philadelphia and that the author, by denying them the title *Ioudaioi,* is claiming it for the Christians. The strongest arguments for this are: first, that they are called a "*synagogue* of Satan" (emphasis added), a curious nomenclature for any others than Jews; and second, that they may be implicated in the persecution and imprisonment of Christians (cf. 2:9–10, especially the reference to "Satan" in v.9 and "the devil" in v.10), an unlikely way for one Christian group to treat another. If they are Jews, then their "slander" could consist of their persecution, the accusations they laid, or their denial of the messiahship of Jesus. Two things are thus at work: a bitter reaction to Jewish harassment of Christians; and a desire to convince the outside world, for politico-social as well as religious reasons, that they were the true Israel.[80]

This is certainly plausible. There is evidence elsewhere that the author of Revelation saw Christians as the true Israel. The number of the saved in 7:1–8, explicitly related to the twelve tribes, clearly suggests this, however we relate it to the "great multitude" of 7:9–17.[81] The allusion to the mother of the Messiah and his people (chap. 12) and the vision of a new Jerusalem (chap. 21) also imply, if more obscurely, Christian inheritance of the promises to Israel.[82] Despite this, there is little in Revelation to indicate that the author wished to assume for his community the specific label *Ioudaioi*. A general claim to Israel's heritage is common enough in Christian writers at this time, but it is not usually expressed by the flat claim: "We are *Ioudaioi*." Indeed, most other Christians are at pains to distance themselves from "the Jews," even when they are claiming their heritage. Put in this way the claim would scarcely have been convincing to any of the parties concerned, and it remains odd that the author would claim that Jews were not Jews when they so manifestly were Jews.[83] It might be argued that an implicit Christian claim to be the true Jews is not essential to the argument that it is Jews that the author opposes. But this makes his denial of their Jewishness no easier to understand.

This points us to a third and equally plausible interpretation: that they were Gentiles. Taken at face value, this is the most obvious meaning of "those who say that they are Jews and are not." There is some evidence that the term *Ioudaioi* was used for Gentiles who observed Jewish practices. Dio Cassius, writing at the turn of the second and third centuries, says: "This title [*Ioudaioi*] is also borne by other persons who, although they are of other ethnicity, live by their laws."[84] Those who (in the author's eyes) falsely claimed to be Jews could, of course, have been non-Christian Gentiles, rather like those proselytes Justin refers to as being more active in persecution of the Christians than the Jews (*Dial*.122). Yet the connection between those who claimed to be Jews and those who persecuted is not inexorable in Revelation 2:9–10, and Gentile Christian Judaizers could be the group in mind.[85] Overwhelmingly the strongest argument for this is the evidence of Ignatius, who met Judaizers precisely in Philadelphia and at approximately the same time (see below).[86] Moreover the connection between the claim to be Jewish and the supposed persecution could also be understood differently. Could it not be that some Christians in Asia Minor were identifying themselves with the Jews in order to avoid official harassment, given that the Jews had a more stable and established position in the Roman world?[87] They would then not only be avoiding the fate that other Christians were expected to suffer (imprisonment, testing, and tribulation, Rev 2:10) but would also be allying themselves with those who might have been suspected of instigating harassment at other times. This would surely have been enough to call them (and implicitly the Jews too) a "synagogue of Satan." If, therefore, Judaizers are in view in Revelation, a further motive for Judaizing is implied: fear of persecution.[88] What exactly went on we cannot know. It might have been no more than a temporary expedient to relieve immediate pressure, and there is no suggestion that the Judaizers saw themselves as abandoning their Christian commitment altogether.[89]

Ignatius

The quality of Ignatius's evidence has admittedly been much debated. The spillover from his experience in Antioch, the heavy dose of Pauline language, and the intimate connection between his Christology and his predilection for martyrdom have often been given as reasons for querying any conclusions we might draw about the situation in Asia Minor that he ostensibly addresses. A recent commentator on Ignatius gives additional reasons for caution: the extent to which Ignatius's discussions reflect his attempt to define his own views rather than any concrete opposition to them; his use of conventional polemical language; and his overriding concern to meet the challenge to his ecclesiastical authority rather than engage with the views on which this challenge may have been based.[90] Some would thus doubt whether we can use Ignatius to discover anything significant about Asia Minor in general or any single community in particular. But while some of these observations are pertinent the conclusion is unduly skeptical, at least with regard to *Philadelphians*. We shall use two assumptions. First, that to those communities that he had visited (Philadelphia and Smyrna) Ignatius wrote about what he had observed there and did not simply transfer the problems of Antioch to Asia Minor. Second, that when he wrote to communities that he had not visited to warn them of similar problems (in this case Magnesia) he extrapolated from the situation he knew at firsthand to the one he was addressing at secondhand. It is thus legitimate for us to combine the information about Judaizers in the letters to Philadelphia and Magnesia and create a composite picture of the problem. Two passages are crucial:

> But if anyone expounds Judaism to you do not listen to him; for it is better to hear Christianity from a man who is circumcised than Judaism from a man who is uncircumcised. (*Phld*.6:1)

> For if we continue to live until now according to Judaism we confess that we have not received grace. (*Magn*.8:1)

From these passages we can conclude two things. First, that some (if not all) of the Judaizers were Gentile in origin.[91] That is the plain sense of *Phld*.6:1—those who "expounded" Judaism were uncircumcised. It seems highly unlikely that these were heterodox Jews or Jewish Christians who had eschewed circumcision, despite attempts to prove the existence of such groups.[92] While circumcision of proselytes was occasionally debated, it is clear that male Jews were, almost without exception, circumcised. Moreover, it is Gentiles, not Jews, who "Judaize" (*Magn*.10:3). Nor is it implied, as Schoedel has recently maintained, that Ignatius implicitly introduces a discussion of circumcision per se;[93] rather, the terms circumcision and uncircumcision in *Phld*.6:1 are simply a convenient way of referring to Jews and Gentiles. Whom Ignatius had in mind when, with grudging approval, he spoke of the circumcised expounding Christianity is unclear; but whether they were the early disciples, Paul, or Jewish Christians active in his day, they serve mainly as a rhetorical contrast to those who were the immediate and pressing problem—Gentiles who expounded Judaism.[94]

The phrase in *Magnesians*—"For if we continue to live until now [*mechri nyn*] according to Judaism"—may allow us to define this group more clearly. It could refer to earlier generations of Christians who had been closely tied to Judaism, but it seems to refer to the Judaizers of Ignatius's day, that is, Gentiles, who formerly (and presently) lived like Jews and expounded Judaism. Who then would these have been? Most obviously they would have been former God-fearers or sympathizers, who had been attached to the synagogue, had now joined the church, and had brought with them the predilections of their former existence.[95] Their Judaizing was not therefore something new, but merely an extension of their past practice. They did not come to know Judaism through Christianity, but brought a predisposition for Judaism to Christianity.

Can we say anything further? From the immediate context it is clear that "expounding" Judaism did not involve promoting Judaism in general. Rather, the Judaizers had a particular view of the scriptures, and were especially inclined to dispute any Christian beliefs that they could not find in them (*Phld.*8:1–2; 9:1); they probably observed the Sabbath instead of or in addition to Sunday (*Magn.*9:1); and they may have had a docetic Christology (*Phld.*3:3; 4:1) and a distinctive view (and separate celebration) of the Eucharist (*Phld.*4:1).[96] Three other general points may be made. First, Ignatius reproves the Judaizers for both expounding (*Phld.*6–8) and living according to (*Magn.*8–10) Judaism; in other words, the dispute seems to have been over both belief and practice. Second, the Judaizers were clearly part of the church rather than the synagogue community, sufficiently so that Ignatius initially found their arguments quite plausible (*Phld.*7:1; 11:1). The Christian community may have been split into factions (*Phld.*6:2–8:1), perhaps representing different house churches, but they were recognizably part of the same group. Third, what alarmed Ignatius most about the Judaizers was that they blurred the boundaries between Judaism and Christianity and thus compromised the distinctive identity of the latter (*Phld.*8:2; 9:1–2; *Magn.*10:2). This is the underlying motif of Ignatius's many particular objections, and it led him to place considerable stress on the distinctiveness of Christianity (*Phld.*8:2; 9:1–2).

Justin

In chapters 46–47 of his *Dialogue with Trypho*, Justin responds to a question about the status of Jewish Christians by outlining a number of different relationships between Jewish and Gentile Christians. Of these there are two types of Gentile Christians of particular interest to us, because they have apparently Judaized in different ways and with different consequences: one group who adopted Jewish customs while retaining their Christian beliefs, and another who adopted Jewish customs and then abandoned their Christian beliefs in favor of joining the synagogue (*Dial.*47:4). Both groups were Gentile,[97] and toward the first Justin shows a grudging acceptance. The apostates (and incidentally this is the clearest reference to such a group in early Christian sources) are condemned outright by Justin and declared irredeemable. Is Justin speaking of a situation that he knew about directly? The opening question by Trypho (*Dial.*46:1), like subsequent comments by both speakers, is conditional: "But if some people [*ean de tines*] . . . ," and it might be argued that he is speaking only hypothetically.[98] Yet the conditional is perfectly normal on the lips of partners in a dialogue, and could still refer to types of Christian known to both.

It might be supposed that Justin's account has here been unduly affected by his knowledge of apostolic tradition and that he has uncritically drawn conclusions about the present from documents that spoke only of the past. Yet the way in which he discusses the issue, and in particular the casual allusion to disagreements in the Christian community about how to evaluate and relate to Jewish Christians (*Dial.* 47:1–2), indicates most naturally a situation known to him firsthand. If so, then Justin implies that the Gentiles who Judaized did so under pressure from their Jewish Christian brethren (*tous de peithomenous autois,* 47:4), while of the defectors he says vaguely that they abandoned their Christian commitment "for some reason or another." Justin is also noticeably harsher in his judgment of those who propagate Jewish observance than of those Gentiles who succumb. Unfortunately, Justin tells us nothing of how these Judaizers related to non-Christian Jews, except in the case of the apostates, but his allusions nevertheless enrich as well as contrast with the situation implied by Ignatius.

Summary

In sum we may say, first, that there is an interesting spread of evidence for the existence of Judaizers in approximately the first half of the second century. Revelation and Ignatius point to Asia Minor, Justin to Rome, and *Barnabas* to Syria or Egypt. The problem seems to have been widespread in time and space.

Second, we can detect a variety of explanations for their attraction to Judaism. One would be the persuasive arguments of Jews or Jewish Christians (Justin), another the fear of persecution (Revelation). Ignatius's Judaizers seem to have transferred previous knowledge and habits gained as God-fearers to a new situation. The Judaizers of *Barnabas*, whose view of Judaism is the most generous, may in part have sprung from a resistance to the more dismissive attitudes of other Christians, but it was probably motivated also by the attractions of a newly confident Judaism at the turn of the century. It is as likely that these motivations are not mutually exclusive as it is that none of them presents a rounded picture of any of the particular local situations.

It is clear, thirdly, that Judaizing did not have the same consequences for each group. Rather, the evidence we have discussed indirectly confirms S. D. Cohen's recent classification of pagan sympathizers with Judaism into seven types, ranging from those who had no more than a vague admiration for some aspect of Judaism to those who became full and, if male, circumcised converts.[99] All of them can in the broadest sense be called Judaizers/sympathizers, but precisely what this meant in each case is not easy to define, not only because they would themselves have offered diverse descriptions of their degree of involvement with Judaism, but also because outsiders had their own standards of judgment. Judaizers could have been judged by Jews to be pagan but by pagans to be Jewish, whereas they may have seen themselves as no more than sympathetic toward certain Jewish customs. Among Christian Judaizers the variations run from those who provided vocal support for the Jews (*Barnabas*), through those who adopted Jewish customs and notions but remained in the church (*Barnabas,* Ignatius, and Justin), to those who attached themselves to the synagogue under duress (Revelation) or became full Jewish converts and abandoned the church (Justin).

The meager evidence available thus allows us to pry open the lid a little on one obscure aspect of early Jewish-Christian relations. Christian Judaizers were pushed and pulled toward Judaism for different reasons and in varying degrees. This would presumably have fostered in them a positive attitude toward Judaism, and we might suppose that, from the other side, some Jews would have made them welcome despite disagreements that would have made them more awkward bedfellows than non-Christian sympathizers. Unfortunately, as with the Jewish Christians, the accounts come down through the hands of their opponents and tell us about their relations with other Christians rather than with the Jews. In other, more "mainstream" Christians, they provoked profound suspicion of, and antipathy toward, the Jews. Of greatest concern was not so much the adoption of particular practices or beliefs, though these were certainly grounds for dispute, as it was the fundamental threat to Christian identity. This is most apparent in *Barnabas* and Ignatius, but it may well have been at work elsewhere too.

CONCLUSION

That Jewish Christians found themselves more closely allied to Judaism in belief and practice than some other Christians is hardly surprising, no more surprising than that they were eventually to be abandoned on both sides for being neither one thing nor the other. It is important to note, however, that they did not fade into complete obscurity after 70 CE. Moreover, not only were there several types of Jewish Christians, who can be differentiated according to their degree of affinity with mainstream Christianity, there is some suggestion that they differed in the breadth and generosity of their vision of the future of Judaism.

Gentile Judaizers presented the more radical challenge. It may often have been difficult, at least for an outsider, to distinguish between Jewish Christians and Christian Judaizers in terms of their respective beliefs and practices.

But whereas the practice of Judaism among Jewish Christians was understandable and acceptable even well into the second century,[100] the deliberate
adoption of Jewish ways among Gentiles posed a serious challenge to the
sense of identity, indeed to the very *raison d'être* of the Christian community.
The "Jewishness" of Jewish Christians could be seen as a hangover from the
past, even if it served as an uncomfortable reminder of the rapidly receding
Jewish roots of the Christian movement. The "Jewishness" of Judaizing
Christians lent credibility to what was supposed to be a moribund competitor and challenged the distinctiveness and supersessionary thrust of the
Christian claim. The denigration of Judaism that this could inspire in their
opponents is seen most clearly in Ignatius and *Barnabas*—that it was inferior and passé, that its rites and festivals were superseded, and that it did
not understand the true meaning of its own traditions. As Ignatius summarized it in one of the more implausible reverse claims in early Christian literature:

> It is ridiculous to profess Jesus Christ and to judaize; for Christianity did not
> believe in Judaism but Judaism in Christianity. (*Magn.*10:3)

JEWISH REACTIONS TO CHRISTIANITY

6

❖

Jewish response to the rise of Christianity can be traced directly in only a few sources. While we would like to have as much Jewish as we have Christian evidence in order to gain a balanced picture of their relationship, extant information is chiefly Christian in provenance. This accounts for an unfortunate, but unavoidable, imbalance in this or any other book that concentrates on the early period. Apart from the sociopolitical data reviewed in chapter 1 and information transmitted in Christian sources, evidence from the Jewish side can be discussed within the compass of a single chapter. By way of contrast, Christian evidence invites much more extensive consideration. Even here we are not as well served as we would like for, apart from what is lost completely, there is a fair amount of intriguing material that is known to have existed but is no longer extant—early dialogues between Jews and Christians, for example, or Jewish Christian gospels. But with Judaism the problem is infinitely worse, in some respects even disabling. Moreover, the period we have chosen to study, which is critical for the evolution of Jewish-Christian relations, provides particularly lean pickings. Josephus, one of the most important sources for the earlier period, ends his narratives more or less at the point at which we chose to begin (70 CE), and the rabbinic tradition that was evolving in the meantime makes its first extant appearance some fifty years after the point at which we chose to end (ca. 170 CE)!

In considering the Jewish evidence that is available, we shall be unavoidably drawn into one of the most complex and contentious issues of the period—the use of rabbinic sources. This can be cast in broad terms as a methodological problem that impinges on almost every discussion of early Jewish or Christian history, or more narrowly as it relates to the specific, rather sparse references to Jesus and the early Christians. To start with the latter: there are, even on the most optimistic count, very few allusions to

Christianity or its founder in rabbinic literature, and most of these are uncertain and obscure. The paucity and allusiveness of this material can be explained in a number of ways.

First, the rabbis (especially in their halakic vein) address themselves in a highly idiosyncratic fashion to a limited range of issues. One consequence is that they record little about contemporary historical events, such as the Jewish War or the Bar Cochba rebellion, which we would otherwise have expected to have made a considerable impact on their thinking. That the rise of Christianity is barely mentioned may thus be due to the limitations of the legal genre in which the Mishnah is cast, but also to the rabbis' broad indifference to historical events beyond their relatively small world.

In addition, all the while Christianity was numerically inferior and politically less respectable—which it was throughout the period we are concerned with—there would have been much less reason for Jews to concern themselves with Christians than the reverse. This is precisely what the evidence indicates: initially Christians were much more interested in Judaism than Jews were in Christianity, while Jewish allusions to Christianity increased from the third century on (though at no great rate), as Christianity burgeoned and became politically more powerful.

A third obstacle is that rabbinic traditions were censored by both Jews and Christians in the course of their transmission—by Christians out of hostility and a sensitivity to real or imagined Jewish slights, and by Jews as a means of self-protection. It is probable, therefore, that some allusions to Jesus or to Christians were excised from the tradition. Yet to move from this general statement, which would be widely conceded, to the identification of specific deletions is no easy matter.[1] Moreover, what survived the censors is often cast in such an obscure or enigmatic form that it is almost impossible to retrieve the original sense with any certainty.

It has been noted, fourthly, that the inherent problems of rabbinic traditions have been compounded by the simplistic or false assumptions that scholars have frequently brought to them. A common error, for example, is to assume that rabbinic Jews = Judaism, that is, that after the Jewish War the rabbis rapidly became the dominant and representative strain within Judaism—in effect, the mainstream. It is natural to fall into this trap in the absence of much nonrabbinic evidence for Judaism in this period, but it is a distortion, and we are now constantly reminded that in the first few centuries the rabbis were only one group among others and, in many places, not even the authoritative one. A related mistake is to treat Christianity and Judaism as homogeneous entities. Sometimes no distinction is made, for example, between Gentile and Jewish Christians, or between different Jewish Christian sects, whose interaction with Judaism may have varied considerably. Likewise there has been a tendency to ignore the considerable variety within post-70 Judaism. One aspect of this is the failure to recognize that hellenizing Jews, gnostic Jews, indeed any sort of nonrabbinic Jews, would have presented as much if not more of a challenge to the rabbis than did the Christians.

Even if we are alert to the drawbacks of the evidence and the weaknesses in its interpretation, there is still the broader methodological issue to confront: Of what value is rabbinic evidence, dating in its earliest written form from ca. 220 CE, for reconstructing Judaism in the first two centuries? There was a time when Jewish and Christian scholars blithely quoted rabbinic material without further ado, often disregarding the original context, accepting the ascriptions to particular rabbis and assuming that most of the material had been in circulation long before its written form. Due largely, though by no means solely, to the influence of J. Neusner and his students, this practice has been seriously called into question.[2] The ascription of sayings to particular rabbis has been shown to be unreliable, and it has been argued that rabbinic material should be considered as a whole and on its own terms, rather than as a depository of information on matters with which it ostensibly shows little concern. The effect, frequently, has been a sort of paralysis. Christian scholars in particular have become extremely hesitant to draw on rabbinic evidence for the pre-Mishnaic era and often find themselves at something of an impasse.[3]

When these reservations and critical procedures are taken into account, the effect frequently has been to remove the rabbinic evidence from consideration. J. Maier, for example, concludes that in the rabbinic tradition there is no tannaitic, and only a little amoraic, evidence for the Jewish view of Jesus and the Christians, and in doing so he aligns himself with the current majority view.[4] I do not find extreme skepticism to be any more justified than indiscriminate quotation. Speaking specifically of rabbinic traditions about the Pharisees, E. P. Sanders has recently commented that "there was no programmatic effort to retroject legal rulings to earlier sages"—a judgment that cannot necessarily be extended to rabbinic tradition as a whole (nor does Sanders suggest this), but that does put the brake on any tendency to sweep rabbinic evidence wholly to one side. Similarly, recent studies of Qumran halakah suggest that we should not too readily separate tannaitic traditions from the second Temple period.[5] Certainly there is not much to be culled from rabbinic sources, and what there is must be considered with great circumspection. There can be no going back to the days of wholesale and uncritical quotation. Yet there are points where rabbinic and nonrabbinic sources seem to coincide in their portrait of the Jewish view of Christians. This confluence could be mere coincidence, but it seems more likely that the two sorts of evidence are mutually reinforcing and provide us with at least a vague outline of the Jewish reaction to the Christian movement. In what follows, therefore, the procedure will be to concentrate on the rabbinic material that finds some nonrabbinic confirmation in order to see how the two sorts of evidence might illuminate each other.

In the following discussion we shall try to pull together the few but diverse strands of information: evidence for Jewish persecution of Christians; the supposed anti-Christian actions of the "council" at Yavneh; allusions to Jesus and Christians in rabbinic tradition; and, briefly in the conclusion, the views of Trypho and the Jewish informant of Celsus which we shall discuss more fully elsewhere. It is doubtful that the picture that emerges will be uniform, though that will be instructive in itself, and it will unavoidably be incomplete. But it will give us something to balance against the preponderance of evidence from the other side.

JEWISH PERSECUTION OF CHRISTIANS

Some controversy has arisen over the assessment of evidence for Jewish harassment of Christians. It has on the one hand been seen as confirmation of Tertullian's later judgment that the Jews were the *fontes persecutionum* (*Scorp.*10). In this view the Jews were unremittingly hostile toward Christians, encouraging and instigating persecution whenever possible and making use of their superior numbers and influence in the Roman world. They were always and everywhere opposed to Christians, and whatever they could not effect they goaded the Romans into doing on their behalf. This was at one time virtually an *opinio communis*.[6] In reaction there are scholars who have dismissed almost entirely the evidence for Jewish hostility toward Christians, suggesting that it is based on facile assumptions and an anti-Jewish bias.[7] There have been a number of more moderate and judicious assessments,[8] but in general the trend has been deflationary, playing down persecution as a factor in the souring of Jewish-Christian relations.

It is most useful to start with a consideration of the clearest body of evidence—that of Justin. Justin is inclined to attribute all opposition to Christians to the machinations of the Jews. According to him they sent envoys throughout the world to spread "dark and unjust tales" about both Christianity and its founder, not only among their fellow Jews but among the Romans too. But they did not stop at rumor-mongering. As in the past they had killed the prophets and Jesus, so now they cursed and killed the Christians. In this they were goaded by the extreme zeal of their own proselytes, who assaulted Christians with even greater enthusiasm than the Jews, and were constrained only by the force of Roman law. The Christians did not respond in kind, but rather prayed for their tormentors, confident that although they were sometimes cut down it was only to sprout again the more vigorously.[9]

Justin's charges are repetitive and, in broad outline, unambiguous. Like the equally frequent references to the cursing of Christians with which they are often associated (see below), they have a sense of immediacy and realism about them. But are they reliable? It is often suggested that Justin exaggerates and distorts, but a good case can be made for thinking that he is essentially correct. The references to killing could refer either to Jesus, to early

Christian victims (Stephen and the two Jameses, etc.) whose stories were known from the Acts of the Apostles, or to the victims of Bar Cochba's repression. That is to say, most of them lay in the past—a fact that Justin himself recognizes when he notes that the Romans constrain the Jews from such activity in the present (*Dial.*16:4).[10] The deaths of Stephen and James may have been aberrant, the result of momentary mob fury or personal animosity rather than any consistent policy of Jews toward Christians,[11] but they would have come down in Christian circles as evidence of exemplary Jewish hostility. The harassment and murder of Christians by Bar Cochba was for Justin, as we have seen, a particularly sore point, and it was sufficiently vivid and close to his own time that he was probably led to exaggerate its significance by tarring all Jews with the same brush.[12]

As far as we can tell, however, there is little reason to doubt that on some occasions some Jews took the opportunity to have Christians put to death.[13] It is important to note that this was uncommon. This was in part, as Justin suggests, because Jews were thwarted by the Romans. It is doubtful that during the period of Roman rule the Jews had the legal right to try or punish capital crimes, and for non-Jews the Romans would at any rate have insisted on the application of their normal legal procedures. It is significant that the least disputed case, during the Bar Cochba rebellion, occurred when Roman rule was temporarily overthrown. Also the combination of messianism and nationalism in the context of a temporarily successful rebellion was rare and presented for the Jewish Christians an unusual threat. It would be quite wrong to conclude from this that all Jews were straining at the leash to do away with Christians at the slightest opportunity. To the best of our knowledge Jews typically did not treat dissenters in this violent fashion, and most of them would have had no interest in such extreme action. Some would have chosen rather to debate with, harangue, or even proselytize the Christians, although most would probably have ignored them. Indeed, at a later date there are even examples of Jews harboring Christians who were under attack by the Romans.[14]

We may thus argue both that Justin is essentially correct and that he exaggerates by making sweeping judgments on the basis of a handful of incidents. This in turn alerts us to two different aspects of the problem: first, the actual incidence of violent deaths and, second, the degree to which they festered in collective Christian memory. If we are looking for factors that affected Jewish-Christian relations, the latter is as important as the former.

But if the Jews were directly responsible for the death of Christians only rarely, were they more often responsible for obstruction, harassment, and the encouragement of Roman suspicion? A vivid account of Polycarp's martyrdom, which occurred ca. 155 CE, relates how the mob gathered the wood for the execution, with "the Jews giving themselves zealously to the work as they were wont to do" and persuading the governor "not to allow the Christians to have the martyr's corpse but to reduce it to ashes" (*Mart.*

*Pol.*13:1; 17:1; cf. 18:1). There is little doubt that this account is affected by
the desire to make the death of Polycarp conform to that of Jesus, which
would thus include an exaggerated role for the Jews, but this does not entirely undercut its veracity. Some elements of the story have been considered
suspect—that Jews would frequent the theater or gather wood on the Sabbath—but it has been noted that the Jews of Smyrna may have been relaxed
about some matters of observance and that the actions may have been taken
by individuals rather than in any official capacity by the Jewish community
as a whole.[15] Despite the description of the Jewish actions as typical, they
may in fact reflect the local conditions in Smyrna more than anything else.

It is harder to say the same about some similar evidence. Writing around
the end of the first century, but about an earlier period, the author of Acts
repeatedly finds the Jews to have been behind the opposition to and ill-
treatment of Christians—stoning, flogging, detention, rumor-mongering,
and so on.[16] In addition Luke insists that the Jews frequently stirred up
Gentile opposition to Christian preachers by playing on the fears of the mob
or by bending the ears of the political authorities (Acts 13:50; 14:2–5,19;
17:5–6,13; 18:13; 24:5). There are exceptions, when Gentiles act alone
(Acts 16:16–24; 19:23–41) or when Jewish authorities give them the benefit
of the doubt (Acts 5:33–39), but the general impression is overwhelmingly
of opposition and obstruction, directed especially against Paul, and with the
frequent involvement of Gentile rulers.

Luke, like the author of the *Martyrdom of Polycarp,* modeled his heroes
(especially Paul) on the career of Jesus, and one consequence of this was an
emphasis on Jewish enmity. Both writers doubtless had a political agenda
too, like the Gospel writers before them. Blaming the Jews allowed for exoneration of the Gentiles, and currying favor with the Romans was something
that a numerically slight and politically suspect movement could not ignore,
especially when it was at the expense of their nearest rival. Luke may have
had a particular problem with Paul, and he may also have been responding
to a delicate political situation during Domitian's reign which included active Jewish opposition (see chap. 2). We must not forget that Luke is ostensibly describing the past rather than the present but, when all is said and
done, Luke seems to assume that Jewish opposition to Christianity was
widespread and normal and gives no indication that things had changed in
his own day. We must allow for exaggeration and stereotyping, but it is
doubtful that Luke was writing of things that were wholly false to the experience of his readers.

The evidence of the Gospels is more problematic. Predictions of the fate
of the disciples (Mark 13:9–13; Matt 10:17–25; Luke 21:12–17) and of the
opposition that can be expected from Jewish leaders (Matt 23:29–39; Luke
11:47–50; John 16:2) probably reflect the teaching of Jesus, have a strong
apocalyptic flavor, and may not always have been fulfilled. It has been noted
that what Christians expected to happen sometimes influenced their under-

standing of what had happened.[17] Yet there is some evidence for Jewish harassment of Christians in both Judaea and the diaspora (1 Thess 2:14–16; 2 Cor 11:23–27), in the early years at least, and there are grounds for thinking that Matthew and Luke were in part reflecting their own experience in these passages—Matthew responding to a tense and troubled relationship with contemporary Judaism and Luke to the contentious reputation of Paul and to the disputed public standing of the Christian movement.[18] Unlike Luke in Acts, Matthew does not imply that the Jews added to their own forms of harassment (flogging in the synagogues, pursuit from town to town, etc.) incitement of the Gentiles. Rather, he treats the two as separate. In the Gospel of John the Jews have become archetypal opponents, resisting Jesus and his followers at every turn, but the most vivid contemporary note is struck in allusions to the expulsion of Christians from the synagogues (John 9:22, 12:42). As we shall see, these are not helpfully associated with the *Birkat ha-minim*, but they almost certainly do reflect the immediate experience of at least one section of the Johannine community.[19] Where that community was located and to what extent the Jewish action was typical is difficult to know, but we can conclude that, in addition to other actions, excluding Christians from their synagogues was an effective way for Jews to express their disfavor and stifle recruitment to the churches.

What then can we conclude? There is sufficient evidence, from different periods and different places, to suggest that Jews did oppose Christians in a number of different ways and that this led to death and corporal punishment (rarely), expulsion, rumor-mongering, and the like. Christians were opposed by Jews and Gentiles. Jewish opposition was confined largely to the implementation of synagogue discipline, and while this could still be distressing for Christians toward the end of the first century (see Matthew and John), we would expect it to recede as the mission to the Jews died out and most Christians and Jews went their separate ways. From that point on the Jews could have got at the Christians only by influencing Gentile authorities. Several sources (Acts, Justin, and the *Mart.Pol.*) suggest that this did happen, and there is no reason to dismiss them out of hand.

On the other hand most of the evidence comes from Christian sources, and their biases and apologetic interests must always be allowed for. If they are read uncritically, we could easily arrive at a distorted sense of Jewish responsibility. Simon makes the following comment: "If we are to arrive at an accurate assessment, we must take account of local conditions, of the circumstances of the moment, and especially of personal considerations, all of which affected the adherents of the two cults. We ought not to talk too much about Judaism and Christianity, but rather about Jews and Christians, for to rely on general appearances might lead us to make some very false reconstructions."[20] The chief danger, as Simon sees it, is the tendency to simplify and generalize—precisely the problem that we have noted in a number of the early sources. Consideration of the chronological and geographical spread of the evidence and an assessment of its general plausibility will help to correct this.

If we conclude that there is plausible evidence for different kinds of Jewish harassment of Christians, but that some ancient and modern writers are inclined to exaggerate its incidence and significance, we have not said all. Just as important for Jewish-Christian relations is the effect on Christian attitudes (since almost all the evidence comes from the Christian side) that these distorted perceptions had. What was seen by Jewish authorities as disciplinary action may have been seen by Christians as persecution, so that it is not only what happened but also what was perceived to have happened that was important. How the reality was received, remembered, and manipulated had as profound an effect on the Christian communities as the reality itself. And thus while the conclusion that Jews did harass and obstruct Christians is significant, it may not be the most important thing that we have to consider.

THE YAVNEAN SAGES

It was for a time common to argue that after 70 CE the rabbis at Yavneh deliberately initiated a number of anti-Christian actions, which became one of the major causes, if not the major cause, of the Jewish-Christian schism. These rabbis were thought to have acted in concert, promulgating decrees in the manner of the councils of the later church, and it was assumed that their decisions immediately and universally took effect. Among the actions they initiated were the prohibition of Christian books, closure of the canon, banishment from the synagogue, cursing in the liturgy, and the commissioning of envoys to enforce their views. The broad context of these actions was certainly recognized, that is, the need to shore up the sense of identity and redefine the boundaries of a Judaism traumatized and thrown into disarray by the war against Rome. Yet the anti-Christian element still loomed large, as if Christianity presented the greatest threat to Jewish unity and survival.[21]

In recent works, however, there has emerged a largely persuasive consensus that the anti-Christian motives of the Yavnean rabbis have been considerably exaggerated and that the analogy with later church councils is seriously misleading. The linguistic and historical arguments are impressive, and the same conclusions have sometimes been reached simultaneously and independently.[22] It will be sufficient for our purposes to summarize and assess these arguments.

Prohibited Books

Rabbinic references to prohibited *sifre minim* ("heretical books") have been taken to refer primarily to "Christian books" (e.g., *t.Sabb.*13.5; *t.Yad.*3.4). These *sifre minim* are thought to cause severe contamination and thus provoke a severe response—such as destruction by burning. By implication these books and the people who produced them are the more reprehensible because, unlike pagan idolaters, they know God but deny him. However, surveys of rabbinic usage have shown unequivocally that *minim* is a general term for heretic and includes in its compass a considerable range of Jewish dissidents, for example, Gnostics, apocalyptists, and hellenizers. It does not refer solely, nor even mainly, to Christians. In fact, a later text (*y.Sanh.*10) lists twenty-four types of heretics to whom the rabbis objected. Thus the omnibus prohibition of heretical books may include Christian works, but only as one sort among others.[23]

The term *minim* is sometimes associated with *gilyonim*, the translation of which in *t.Yad.*2.13; 3.4; *t.Sabb.*13.5 is still disputed. Other rabbinic uses, such as *t.Yad.*2.2; *m.Yad.*3.4, suggest to some that it refers to the margins or blank spaces on a page,[24] or to collections of scriptural testimonies supporting a "heretical" viewpoint.[25] The connection between *gilyonim* and the *sifre minim* (cf. *b.Sabb.*116a–b) suggests, as has been noted, that something more important than margins or blank spaces is in mind. If the allusion is to collections of biblical excerpts, then gnostic writings could be in mind (whether Jewish or Christian?), but so could Christian testimony collections, which were apparently known to writers such as the author of *Barnabas* and Justin and may still have circulated after their time. The more specific reference to "gospels" still finds supporters (i.e., *gilyonim* = *evangelion*).[26] Yet Katz, who thinks that "gospels" is the probable rendering in some passages, nevertheless wisely concludes: "It is not without ambiguity and uncertainty. Any hard and fast conclusion is thus not possible."[27]

The same logic and the same uncertainties arise in discussion of *Seforim ha-Chizonim* ("outside books") in *m.Sanh.*10:1. The reference seems to be to noncanonical writings,[28] and this may have included heretical as well as nonheretical works. Among the former may have been Christian books, but there is no more reason here than elsewhere to assume that they were the primary, even less the sole, target.[29]

Closely related is the question of the closure of the canon at Yavneh. Moore argued that discussions of the canon at Yavneh were motivated more by the circulation and influence of Christian books than by disputes about the status of Jewish writings.[30] But this appears to be a considerable over-simplification. It has been noted, for example, that the canon was largely fixed before Yavneh, that there were plenty of other heretical works to worry about, and that there were many other internal factors that drove the process of canonization.[31]

We shall consider the broader issues in this debate more fully below, but for now we can make a few preliminary comments. First, the recent consensus is dependent on at least two related perceptions: that Judaism after 70 CE was not monolithic nor was Christianity its sole challenger. These provide an important corrective, because in previous studies the variety and dissidence in post-70 Judaism were underestimated and the threat from Christianity exaggerated.[32] Second, philological arguments are often critical, but the evidence for them rarely conclusive. There may be a consensus that *minim* meant "heretic" in general rather than "Christian heretic" in particular, the former probably including the latter, but rabbinic use of the obscure term *gilyonim,* for example, still leaves us floundering. That is, philological arguments alone cannot always settle the issue.

Third, it is agreed almost without exception that Christian works are to be included in the unacceptable writings censured by the rabbis. This is perhaps obliquely confirmed by Justin's statement that Trypho had read a Gospel, as if this was something unusual, and taken part in the dialogue in defiance of his own teachers (*Dial.*10:2–3; 38:1; 112:4). Fourth, these teachings were designed not to attack the Christians but to preserve the stability and purity of the Jewish community. They view the issues solely from a Jewish point of view and direct their discussions to a Jewish audience. The Christian writings targeted could have come from Jewish or Gentile Christian circles, and this brings us up against the familiar problem of dating. Are we dealing with first/second- or third/fourth-century conflicts here? It is hard to tell, though Justin's evidence may just tip the balance in favor of the former.

Jewish Envoys

Justin refers to Jerusalem envoys who traveled the diaspora and delivered letters warning against the emerging Christian heresy (*Dial.*17.1; 47.4). Since he imagines Jerusalem as their base, he seems to imply that the envoys began their activity before 70 CE, though most would in fact date them after the war.[33] The only certain thing is that Justin knew about them at the time of writing (ca. 160 CE), and it is possible that they were instituted much closer to his own time than the time of the Jewish War. If we accept a date after the war, Justin's comments still need to be placed in a wider context. He understandably concentrates on the anti-Christian motif, but if the rabbis did disseminate their views in the diaspora in this fashion it would certainly have been for a far wider range of purposes than simply countering the Christians—liturgical revisions (cf. *m.Ros.Has.*1.4), decisions on the canon, calendrical calculations, and the like. If there was a centrally organized form of anti-Christian propaganda, we might have expected it to be more clearly reflected in the rabbinic writings, where references to Jesus and to Christians are few and far between.[34] But there is nothing inherently improbable in the notion itself, especially when it is seen as part of a broader move to disseminate rabbinic views—mostly, it should be noted, to the diaspora communities about which very little is known.[35] Quite apart from any officially endorsed campaign, it is probable that a fair amount of vulgar anti-Christian sentiment circulated among the Jews and affected everyday opinion.[36]

Bans

The use of the mild, temporary ban (*Niddui*) or the more serious, excommunicatory ban (*Herem*) against Jewish Christians by rabbinic authorities has sometimes been assumed.[37] Yet there is little direct evidence for the use of a formal ban (*Niddui*) against dissidents with the aim of exclusion from the synagogue. In fact, the purpose was usually just the opposite—to bring them back under the wing of rabbinic authority. Rabbinic evidence for the use of excommunication (*Herem*) as a form of social control is too late for our purposes, and there is no suggestion that it was used against Christians.

Some early sources do allude to the removal of Christians from the synagogue (John 9:22; 12:42), but it is not said how this was done. What the author saw as expulsion may have been a form of self-exclusion; but if we accept the Johannine perspective, it was one that in all probability grew out of a local situation (wherever that may have been). That is, there is no more reason to doubt a serious rift between the Johannine community and the synagogue authorities than there is to assume that this was the experience of all Jews and Christians; again, however, we should not underestimate the way in which a few incidents, even if localized, could affect the more general Christian perception.

Avoidance of the *minim* and their idolatrous ways, expressed most polemically in *t.Hul.*2.20–21, is cast in the form of advice to the Jews. It is thus concerned with matters internal to the Jewish community. If Christians are included among the *minim*, and the following material (*t.Hul.* 2.22–24) suggests that they were the chief target here, then the recommendation is to avoid rather than engage with them.[38] It is the same kind of attitude that Justin reports in *Dial.*138:1, where Trypho is advised by his teachers to have nothing to do with Christians.

Liturgical Maledictions

The use of bans is sometimes associated with the best-known and most-discussed of the Yavnean policies, the introduction into the synagogue liturgy of a "benediction against the heretics" (*Birkat ha-minim*: in fact, a malediction). The story of its origin is told as follows:

> Our rabbis taught: Simon ha-Pakuli ordered the Eighteen Benedictions before Rabban Gamaliel in Yavneh. Rabban Gamaliel said to the sages: Is there no one who knows how to compose a benediction against the *minim*? Samuel Ha-Qatan stood up and composed it. Another year (while serving as precentor), he (Samuel Ha-Qatan) forgot it and tried to recall it for two or three hours. Yet they did not remove him. (*b.Ber.*28b–29a)

The Talmud does not quote the benediction at this point, though it may have been removed by censors. The most controversial version was found in the Cairo Genizah:

> For apostates let there be no hope, and the dominion of arrogance do Thou speedily root out in our days; and let Christians [notzrim] and heretics [minim] perish in a moment, let them be blotted out of the book of the living for ever and not be written with the righteous.[39]

The addition of this malediction is usually dated between 85 and 95 CE. Building on this, together with the Johannine references to expulsion from the synagogue (John 9:22; 12:42; 16:2) and frequent references in Justin to the cursing of Jesus and Christians in the synagogue (Dial.16; 35; 47; 93; 95; 96; 107; 108; 123; 133; 137), many have concluded that the primary, if not the sole, target of this curse was the Christians, and that it both expressed and exacerbated the seriousness of the Jewish-Christian schism.[40]

In recent discussions a number of important qualifications to this view have been made. First, the malediction probably existed before Yavneh and was revised rather than composed there.[41] Second, there is no single early version of the text available—perhaps because at this early stage there was no uniform version—but the much later text from the Cairo Genizah, which adds a reference to notzrim (= Nazoreans, i.e., Christians), has no special authority and represents a later expansion of the Yavnean version.[42] As is often noted, if the reference to Christians (notzrim) had been there from the start the malediction would most likely have been called the Birkat ha-notzrim. Third, the Yavnean version, which was directed primarily against heretics (minim), may have included Jewish Christians in that designation, but not exclusively or even primarily.[43] Fourth, the purpose of the malediction was not to exclude the minim from the synagogue, but rather to arouse the consciousness of the community and reinforce its rabbinic identity, to alert it to the danger of the minim and perhaps to call the minim back to the straight rabbinic path. Fifth, the references in the Fourth Gospel to expulsion from the synagogue thus envisage a situation different from that created by introduction of the Birkat ha-minim; indeed, it has recently been claimed that "it is time to recognize that the Birkat ha-minim has been a red herring in Johannine research."[44] If so, it is equally true that the Johannine evidence has been a red herring in trying to understand the Birkat ha-minim.

The overall drift of recent discussion has thus been to deflate the significance of the Birkat ha-minim for the Jewish-Christian schism. Christians may have been included in the category minim, but the Yavnean rabbis had many other problems on their hands as well. Insofar as they were included, the initial target would have been the declining Jewish Christian wing of the church and not the increasingly dominant Gentiles.

Two important assumptions lie behind this reconstruction. The first is that earlier interpreters consistently credited Christianity with too great a role in Jewish developments after 70 CE. This does not mean that they were altogether insignificant, but rather that the Yavnean sages were not obsessed with Christians and certainly not with them alone. Apart from promoting a number of complex and necessary adjustments to postwar conditions, they had also to deal with Gnostics, apocalyptists, hellenizers, and various other "nonrabbinic," but thoroughly Jewish, groups. Second, the influence of the Yavnean sages on Jewish thought and practice between 70 and 135 CE and beyond should not be overestimated. Their decisions were not imposed overnight, nor were they felt uniformly across all Jewish communities. The rabbinic account of the introduction of the *Birkat ha-minim* is thus a retrospective, punctiliar summary of what was in reality a lengthy process. The spread of their influence was gradual and almost certainly did not encompass all Jewish communities until well beyond the second century. This warns us against speaking of *the* Jewish reaction to Christians as other evidence does against speaking of *the* Christian experience of it.[45]

The first of these assumptions is challenged by A. Segal. He admits to much of the new consensus, but thinks that it involves a serious underestimation of the threat that Christianity posed to Judaism, and that the *Birkat ha-minim* was directed against Christians more than any other group. This is based largely on his subtle analysis of the "two-powers" controversy in rabbinic literature, which we shall consider below, although even here it is agreed that other groups could also have been in mind.[46] The difficulty here is to avoid circular arguments. Much of the evidence from the Jewish side comes from rabbinic tradition. The more important the Christians are assumed to have been the more allusions to them we are likely to find and vice versa; and, as we shall see below, evaluation of these traditions is fraught with difficulty. On the other hand, while we know that their relationship to Judaism was for many Christians of central importance, we cannot assume that the same was true for the Jews. It is often noted that in general it was a far more pressing matter for Christians to come to terms with Jews than Jews with Christians. W. Horbury has challenged the consensus too. He argues that from the early second century specific reference to Christians (*notzrim*) was added in some quarters, that it referred to Gentile as well as Jewish Christians, and that this concurs with a general pattern of hostility between Jews and Christians witnessed to elsewhere. Apart from the last point, however, much of his argument rests on evidence from the third and fourth centuries (and beyond) and relies rather heavily on supposition.[47] However, one important consequence of his argument is that we are warned against dismissing too lightly the evidence of Justin.

Justin is an important witness because his evidence is, relatively speaking, unambiguous and datable. His many references to the cursing of Christ and Christians seem to assume the existence of a practice that was, at least around 160 CE, widely known to Christians and Jews. It is described with a sense of immediacy, and at no point does Trypho protest or deny it. For some this evidence confirms the view that the *Birkat ha-minim* was directed mainly at Christians, certainly in the second century and probably at the time of its late first-century revision as well. For others Justin's evidence is too vague to be used with such confidence. It is noted, for example, that most of the references to the cursing of Christians are simply that. Only twice is this said to have occurred in the synagogues (*Dial.*16; 96) and, moreover, several refer to the blaspheming of Christ rather than of Christians (*Dial.*35; 47; 107; 137). In one place it is even specified that this was "after the prayers" rather than during them, as would have been expected in a reference to one of the Twelve Benedictions (*Dial.*137).[48] The key issue, therefore, is whether Justin refers to an officially endorsed malediction embedded in the synagogue liturgy or to a more intermittent, informal activity which he happened to have heard of.[49]

It is true that his references to the cursing of Christians are vague, but it is hard to know what they refer to if not to the *Birkat ha-minim*. An exact correspondence between the two is not to be expected. Unless Justin had firsthand knowledge of the wording of synagogue prayers—and he nowhere leads us to think that he had—a somewhat garbled account comes as no surprise. It is important too, even allowing for all the qualifications in recent discussions of the malediction, to note the consensus that Jewish Christians were included among the *minim*. A disparity between rabbinic intent and Christian perception could easily have arisen. The omnibus curse against Jewish heretics could have been understood by Christians to have been directed specifically against them even though that was not originally its sole purpose. Justin's mistake would then have been to assume that a curse designed for Jewish Christians, as one among other groups, was directed at all Christians and them alone.

Yet this may be too simple a conclusion. That Justin sometimes refers to the cursing of Christ rather than Christians is perhaps most simply explained by the similarity of *notzri* (Nazarene, i.e., Jesus) to *notzrim* (Nazarenes, i.e., Christians). The one could be misheard and misreported for the other, and Justin was presumably going largely on hearsay.[50] This would assume, of course, that *notzrim* was in the form of the malediction known to him.[51] Was this so, and was Justin therefore correct in thinking that in his day all Christians were included in the curse? There have been a number of hypotheses to explain variations in the wording of the prayer. Horbury has argued that the curse against the *minim* could have stood alone or have been combined with other targets—the wicked, pagan overlords, and Christians—as need dictated.[52] Pritz suggests that since most of the evidence for a curse against the Nazarenes comes from the East, it was only there that *notzrim* was introduced.[53] He assumes, however, that the term "Nazarenes" refers to Jewish Christians alone, and he does not accept a link between the evidence of Justin and the malediction.

A more interesting hypothesis is that *notzrim* was added to the malediction soon after the Bar Cochba revolt. Several scholars have argued that this was a crucial turning point. The refusal of Christians to recognize Bar

Cochba's messianic status, for which they were persecuted and killed, and the growing influence of a church that was increasingly Gentile (and therefore properly speaking not *minim*), led to a severe breakdown in relations and the introduction of a new and larger category into the malediction: *notzrim*—Christians in general.[54] Urbach independently suggests that of the four categories in later versions of the curse—apostates, arrogant nations, Nazarenes, and heretics—the apostates and Nazarenes would most naturally have been added in the aftermath of the Bar Cochba revolt.[55] Indeed, we might speculatively tie it to a more particular occurrence—the replacement of the Jewish leadership of the Jerusalem church by Gentiles. This, perhaps more than any other incident, would have brought home to the Jews the irrevocably Gentile direction of the Christian movement. Almost certainly, Gentile Christians were in a majority long before this, but the transfer of leadership would have been a highly symbolic event marking, from the point of view of the Jews, a significant break with the past. Combined with the ill will created by the conflict over Bar Cochba's messiahship, it could well have provided the motivation for expanding the terms of the malediction. This hypothesis—and it has to be stressed that this is all it is—has the further advantage of explaining Justin's evidence, because it would mean that in his day all Christians *were* included in the malediction—at least in the version known to Justin, which, of course, may not at this stage reflect universal synagogue usage.[56] It also reminds us again of the importance of the Bar Cochba revolt as a turning point in Jewish-Christian relations.

What can we conclude? Recent discussion of the *Birkat ha-minim* has tended on the whole to minimize its significance for the Jewish-Christian schism. This is in all probability correct. Christians were not the sole, or even the most important, group of heretics whom the Yavnean rabbis faced. At the same time, we should not underestimate the force of their innovation: Christian Jews were, apparently for the first time, included in a formal, liturgical malediction repeated regularly in some synagogues and approved by the Yavnean leaders. As with changes to Christian worship, we must reckon that material that appeared routinely in a liturgical setting would have had a more lasting and widespread effect than polemical tracts or arcane allusions in rabbinic debates. Its effect was probably exacerbated by Christians' exaggerating Jewish antipathy, and intensified following the inclusion of Gentile Christians in the benediction, perhaps in the aftermath of the Bar Cochba rebellion. It was thus not a negligible item in the souring of Jewish-Christian relations—as Justin, above all, amply shows.

JEWISH ALLUSIONS TO JESUS AND CHRISTIANS

Apart from specifically Yavnean material, is there any remaining evidence? In a famous passage of the *Antiquities* Josephus is supposed to have written the following:

> At this time there appeared Jesus, a wise man [*sophos aner*], *if indeed one should call him a man*. For he was a performer of startling deeds [*paradoxon ergon oietes*], a teacher of people who receive the truth with pleasure. And he gained a following both among many Jews and among many of Greek origin. *He was the Messiah*. And when Pilate, because of an accusation made by the leading men among us, condemned him to the cross, those who had loved him previously did not cease to do so. *For he appeared to them on the third day, living again, just as the divine prophets had spoken of these and countless wondrous things about him*. And up to this day the tribe of Christians, named after him, has not died out. (*Ant.* 18.63–64; italics added)

This short statement has been the object of a remarkable amount of attention. Every conceivable claim has been made on its behalf, ranging from those who consider it entirely spurious to those who consider it wholly authentic. A recent thorough review of the evidence has presented persuasive arguments for what has become an increasingly common conclusion: that it is an authentic Josephan statement which has been touched up with pious Christian additions.[57] There is, of course, disagreement about the extent of the additions, but, as Meier notes, the "first impression of what may be a Christian interpolation may be the correct impression."[58] What seem to be the obvious Christian additions (italic in the translation above), two with a christological bent and the third extolling Jesus' resurrection, are unlikely to have been couched by a non-Christian Jew. When they are removed what remains reads fluently and uses typically Josephan vocabulary and ideas.[59] We can thus with some confidence take this statement as evidence for the way some Jews viewed the founder of the Christian movement toward the end of the first century.

Most interesting is the reference to Jesus as a *wise man* who was both *miracle worker* and *teacher*. These three concepts were closely allied in the Greco-Roman world, and the last two may well be a definition of the first.[60] "Wise man" and "teacher of people who receive the truth with pleasure"[61] were, in Josephus and in the Greco-Roman world in general, usually laudatory or at least neutral epithets. There is some doubt about the third, "performer of startling deeds." Is this simply a report of one of the better-known aspects of Jesus' public activity, singled out perhaps because it coincided with one of the commonly expected attributes of a wise man? Or does it have a negative ring, implying that Jesus was a sorcerer?

In Philo and Josephus the term *paradoxon* was used mainly of abnormal, supernatural acts of God, but it could occasionally be used of actions performed by people inspired by the power of God.[62] It could thus be used as the equivalent of the more common term for miracle, *semeion*. The tradition of Jesus as a performer of miracles could, however, be given a negative twist. This happens early in the Gospel records, in second-century disputes, and in later rabbinic tradition.[63] Some conclude that Josephus is also implicitly hostile in his description of Jesus, but there is no good reason to think this.

Josephus is quite capable of expressing disapproval, usually by calling the offending miracles acts of magic (*mageia*; cf. *Ant.* 2.284–86)—the usual ploy in his day. But the language he uses about Jesus is essentially neutral, and we would expect some other indication of hostility if that was what he wished to convey.[64]

What do we learn from Josephus's statement? Most importantly that a Jew, writing toward the end of the first century, could introduce a notice about Jesus in terms that his fellow Jews would understand, yet without passing judgment. He seems to be neither sympathetic nor hostile. The same can be said of his passing reference to James the brother of Jesus later in the same work. Both notices are brief and are used to illustrate some aspect of the immediate political situation that is the main theme of the narrative—the role of Pilate in the first case and the reprehensible opportunism of some members of the Sanhedrin in the other. Yet, compared with some other Jewish reactions, Josephus's studied neutrality is noteworthy. He knows that Christianity has had success among Jews and Greeks, but can view this with equanimity. This fits well with his generally cosmopolitan tone and follows his own advice that Jews should not blaspheme the gods of other nations nor abuse the gifts offered to them.[65] Of course, Josephus had an unusual career, and it could be argued that he was not typical of the Jews of his day. But he is nevertheless an important example of one way that nonrabbinic Jews could react to the Christian movement.

This leads us naturally to consider some contrasting evidence in the rabbinic tradition. One important strain, in effect the negative version of Josephus's twofold description, accuses Jesus of sorcery/magic and of leading the people astray:

> On the eve of Passover they hung Jeshu. And the crier went forth before him forty days, saying, "He goes forth to be stoned because he has practised magic and deceived and led Israel astray. Anyone who knows anything in his favour let him come and declare concerning him." And they found nothing in his favour. And they hung him on the eve of Passover. (*b.Sanh.*43a)

> And a teacher has said, "Jesus the Nazarene practised magic and led astray and deceived Israel." (*b.Sanh.*107b)

> It is tradition that Rabbi Eliezer said to the sages, "Did not Ben Stada bring spells from Egypt in a cut which was upon his flesh?" They said to him, "He was a fool, and they do not base a proof upon a fool." Ben Stada is Ben Pandira. (*b.Sabb.*104b)[66]

The first of these passages is one of the clearest references to Jesus in rabbinic tradition, and for that reason was deleted in some manuscripts. Like most such material it is a mixture of firm reference and garbled detail. The significance of the forty days of publicity by the herald remains obscure, but the accusation against Jesus is clear and, as noted above, is a good example of the way in which Josephus's view could be given a negative twist. The second, identical accusation comes at the end of a rambling and legendary story about Jesus' excommunication by one R. Joshua ben Perahya who, according to the passage itself, lived some 130 years before Jesus, in the time of Alexander Janneus!

It is often argued that these traditions are so confused and legendary and the connection with Jesus made at such a late stage that they are historically worthless.[67] But even if largely true, this does not mean that they are of no use for our purpose. We can distinguish between the accusation itself and its confused or legendary framework, and we need not assume that something added to the Babylonian Talmud had no prior life in Jewish communal tradition. In fact, there is persuasive evidence to the contrary. Justin reports (*Dial*.108:2; cf.17:1) that when the Jews sent emissaries throughout the world to counter Christianity they announced that it was a godless and lawless sect (*hairesis*) founded by Jesus, a deceiver (*planos*). There is some reason to think that this summary draws on Jewish allegations known to the writer.[68] Elsewhere Justin notes (*Dial*.69:7) that the Jews attribute Jesus' miracles to "magical art" (*phantasian magiken*) and call him a "magician and deceiver of the people" (*magos kai laoplanos*)—in substance (and in another language), precisely the rabbinic allegation. The notion of Jesus as a deceiver is found elsewhere on the lips of Jewish opponents, and the suspicion of sorcery may well go back to his own lifetime. In the apocryphal Acts, Thomas and Philip, followers of Jesus but in each case his alter ego, are likewise accused of magic and deception. Celsus repeatedly attributes to his Jewish informant the view that Jesus was a sorcerer, and it has even been suggested that the early apologist Quadratus emphasizes the long-term success of Jesus' healings and exorcisms precisely to counter the common charge of sorcery.[69] The concurrence of evidence from Christian and Jewish sources, especially the near-identical double accusation of magic and deception, suggests that we are dealing here with a long-standing and familiar reaction to Jesus and his followers on the part of at least some Jews.

The third rabbinic text is more obscure, and the allusion to Jesus much less certain. Most scholars agree that the original ben Stada was a Jewish heretic accused of sorcery, that is, importing spells (perhaps tattooed, perhaps in incisions of the flesh) from one of the most famous ancient sources of the magical arts, Egypt.[70] At some point Jesus was assimilated to ben Stada (cf. *b.Sanh*.67a), but it is not clear when. Was ben Stada a code name for Jesus earlier than the tradition recorded in the Babylonian Talmud? We cannot be sure. The connection with Jesus is sometimes found not only in the accusation of magic but also in the visit to Egypt described in Matthew 2:13–21.[71] This would be tenuous were it not for the supporting evidence in Origen (*Cels*.1.28,38), where Celsus's Jewish informant makes a very similar accusation—that Jesus learned his magical arts in Egypt. There is no reason to doubt that Celsus was, as he claims, following a Jewish source, and this would place the tradition somewhere around 170 CE. [72] This seems to be prima facie evidence that the (albeit later) rabbinic tradition picks up an anti-Christian slur that was already circulating in the second century, that is, a lot earlier than we might otherwise think.

A related, but less specific, reaction has been found in some other rabbinic passages where Jesus is viewed as an outcast and heretic. In one story the dispute is over Jewish use of Christian healing:

> The case of Eliezer ben Dama, whom a serpent bit. There came in Jacob, a man of Cephar Sama, to cure him in the name of Jesus ben Pantera, but R. Ishmael would not allow it. He said, "You are not allowed, ben Dama." He said, "I will bring you a proof that he may heal me." But he had not finished bringing the proof when he died. R. Ishmael said, "Happy are you, ben Dama, for you have departed in peace, and have not broken the ordinances of the wise." [73]

> The case of R. Eliezer, who was arrested for *minuth* [heresy]. And they brought him to the tribunal for judgement. Said the governor [*hegemon*] to him. . . . And when he had been released from the tribunal he was troubled because he had been arrested for *minuth*. His disciples came in to console him, but he would not take comfort. R. Aqiba came in and said to him, "Rabbi, shall I tell you why you are grieving?" He said to him, "Speak on." He said to him, "Perhaps one of the *minim* has spoken to you a word of *minuth* and it has pleased you." He said, "By heaven, you have reminded me! I was once walking along a street of Sepphoris, and I met Jacob of Cephar Sichnin, and he spoke to me a word of *minuth* in the name of Jesus ben Pantiri, and it pleased me." [74]

In these two stories we find a rough parallel to the double accusation we have already observed: in the ben Dama story, healing in the name of Jesus is seen as a form of sorcery, and in the Eliezer story the teaching of Jesus is considered to be heresy, that is, that which leads people astray. Morton Smith finds the first of these accounts essentially credible, dating it ca. 100–130 CE, on the ground that there was no reason for any later sage to invent such a story about one of his predecessors. [75] By somewhat similar reasoning, the tradition of R. Eliezer's temporary lapse into heresy, which also introduces the name of ben Pantiri, can be considered to have an authentic core. He is charged with "heresy" but, oddly, before a Roman official (*hegemon*). A likely explanation is his association with Christians, who were periodically suspect, and Jacob of Cephar Sichnin was probably a prominent Jewish Christian. [76] Yet it is only in the Babylonian Talmud that the identification of Jesus with ben Pantiri is secure—when "Jesus ben Pantiri" is replaced by "Jesus the Nazarene" in *b.Abod.Zar.*16b–17a—and this has led some to doubt any earlier connection between them and to dismiss these traditions as evidence for the Jewish view of Jesus in the first two centuries. [77] Of course it could be that there is an authentic core to the experience of the Jewish protagonists, which originally had nothing to do with Jesus or the

Christians. But there is some slight evidence to suggest that the anti-Christian element was either original or introduced sometime in the second century. The first is that these stories cohere with what we have observed elsewhere in rabbinic and other traditions. The second is that there is some nonrabbinic evidence about the use of the name ben Pantera.

This evidence is found in Origen. The Jew who informs Origen's antagonist, Celsus, makes a number of allegations about Jesus' birth: that his mother was a poor adulteress and his father a soldier named Panthera; that she bore Jesus after being banished by her husband; and that the virgin birth stories were concocted to cover up these disgraceful events (*Cels.*1.28–32, 39, 69). If we give Celsus's informant the sort of credence we accepted above, then the use of the name Panthera suggests that ben Panthera, or its variants, was probably in circulation as a designation for Jesus long before it appeared in the Babylonian Talmud, in fact at least as early as the second half of the second century. In this case the use of ben Pantera in earlier rabbinic traditions may have been a code whose meaning was clear to a Jewish audience and was only being made more explicit in the later rabbinic texts.[78]

The evidence from Origen also introduces us to another theme: Jewish calumnies about Jesus' birth. The chief rabbinic tradition is found in one of the ben Stada stories that we shall look at for other reasons below. It concludes as follows:

> And thus they did to Ben Stada in Lod and they hung him on the eve of Passover. Ben Stada was Ben Pandera. R. Hisda said: "The husband was Stada, the paramour Pandira. But was not the husband Pappos ben Judah? His mother was Stada. But was not his mother Miriam the hairdresser? As we say in Pumpeditha, This one has turned away [Aramaic: *satadah da*] from her husband." (*b.Sanh.*67a)

This is the conclusion to a discussion of the process of entrapment that was used to uncover a particularly egregious and wily heretic, ben Stada. The identification of ben Stada with ben Pandera/Jesus is an addition in the Babylonian Talmud to a tradition that is briefer, though not much clearer, in its earlier manifestations. The mix of legend, anachronism, and misleading wordplay would not encourage much confidence in this material if it stood alone.[79] But the tradition of Jews disputing the Christian account of Jesus' birth had a long history. It is found by implication already in the Gospels—in the insulting "son of Mary" of Mark 6:3, in the more defensive parts of the Matthean genealogy, and perhaps in John 8:41. The *Acts of Pilate*, probably a second-century work, presents the Jewish elders charging that Jesus was "born of fornication," which other devout Jews (presumably Jewish Christians) deny by referring to the betrothal of Jesus' parents (2:3–4).[80]

We also have the account of Celsus's Jewish informant, outlined above, which is indirectly confirmed by Justin. His dialogue partner, the Jew

Trypho, is on this as on other issues unfailingly respectful and polite, eschewing the rougher polemical tone of his fellows. But he nevertheless has
serious questions about the stories of Jesus' birth and the Christian defense
of them, objecting in particular to their use of Isaiah 7:14 on the grounds
that it does not mention a virgin and that it refers to contemporary rather
than distantly future events (*Dial*.43, 67). Trypho does not hint at adultery
or deception, but in the end he wants to make the same point as Celsus's
Jew: that Jesus is human and not divine and that the idea of the incarnation
is both offensive and absurd. In addition, other rabbinic allusions may reflect the same tradition.[81] Thus, while we certainly should be wary of many
of the details in the rabbinic reports, there is evidence that they got one
thing right—that some Jews cast aspersions on Christian accounts of the
birth of Jesus. In so doing they cleverly picked on an item of Christian
teaching that was both inherently weak and readily open to a pejorative
recasting. Indeed, "pejorative" may be the wrong term, since the notion that
Jesus was illegitimate is one of the more plausible explanations for the origin of the nativity traditions.[82]

In considering Jewish reaction to the virgin birth, we have already moved
from things Jesus did and said to the claims that Christians made on his
behalf. If one aspect of the Jewish reaction to Christian claims was incomprehension at the claim that God had taken on human form, and thus skepticism about the virgin birth, there is evidence to suggest that the notion of
the existence of two gods, or a second god, was even more fundamentally
unacceptable. There may be an allusion to Jesus' claims on his own behalf
in *y. Ta'an*.2:1[65b]:

> If a man says to you, "I am a god," he is a liar; If [he says] "I am the son of
> man," he will regret it; If [he says] "I go up to the heavens," he promises but
> will not perform it.

Some have found an allusion to Jesus in a late midrash in which advice is
given on the protection to be found in certain biblical passages "if a whore's
son tells you there are two gods" (*Pesiq.R*.100b–101a). The more interesting
material, however, is found in the earlier versions of this tradition which
deal with heretics who believed in "two powers in heaven." These concern
mostly the angelic or theophany texts or the use of plurals with reference
to God, that is, anything in the biblical text that might suggest the existence
of more than one God. A. Segal has subjected these to a thorough analysis
and argued, firstly, that the issue of a "second god" was known already to
Philo and was discussed in terms that are echoed in later rabbinic tradition
(Philo *Som*.1.227–33; *Q.Gen*.2.62; *Spec.Leg*.3.81). Second, the idea of corresponding or cooperating deities suggests that the original heretics were
speculative apocalyptists, moderate Gnostics, or Christians rather than dualists or radical Gnostics, though the rabbinic discussion was subsequently
broadened to include the latter. Moreover, radical Gnosticism, in which

Yahweh becomes a hostile demiurge arrogating to himself the claim of divinity, ironically finds its most likely roots in forms of speculative Judaism, such as those interested in the "two powers." It is clear, thirdly, that variety in the description of the "two powers" heretics suggests that more than one group was in mind. The rabbis conveniently subsumed several heretical groups under one label, tarring some of the more moderate apocalyptists or Christians with the same brush as the more radical gnostic dualists.[83]

That the assertion of Jesus' divinity was met with resistance is confirmed by the Gospel of John, where Jesus' Jewish opponents consistently justify their opposition to him on the ground that he claimed equality with God (John 5:18; 10:33; cf. 8:39–47). Justin provides further insight into the same tradition when, in the claims he makes about Jesus, he draws on the same biblical texts and echoes the same language found in Philo and others who speculated about a second god (*Dial.*56; 61–65). He appears to draw on earlier Jewish traditions and, like most of his competitors, to twist them to his own (in his case, christological) ends. Most interesting for our purpose is that Justin's debate about Jesus' divinity is ostensibly with a Jew, Trypho, who concedes the puzzling nature of some of his own biblical traditions but insists in the end that the christological claims of the early Christians are an assault on one of the most fundamental of Jewish beliefs—the unity of God. And so it seems that both sides of the earlier debate could be adapted and reused. For if Justin could call on earlier speculation about divine hypostases, or a second god, so could the rabbis call on earlier forms of opposition to it. Although the rabbinic texts that Segal adduces are difficult to date, they follow the pattern of evidence we have found acceptable up to now: rabbinic traditions that are confirmed and mutually illuminated by nonrabbinic sources. Speaking of the rabbinic evidence, Segal concludes:

> Hidden within the texts too is the Jewish witness to the rise of Christianity, even though they date from centuries later. They indicate that the nascent Christian faith began to differentiate and define itself somewhere on the evolving continuum from earlier pluralistic Judaism to radical gnosticism. They also suggest that we can identify diverging attitudes towards monotheism and the "two powers" as one important cause of the separation of Christianity from Judaism—as long as we recognize that in the complex situation of the first two centuries there was divergence both within Judaism and within Christianity on the same issue.[84]

The debate about the nature and manifestations of the divine was complex, and opinions ranged from moderate, pre-Christian Jewish speculation to the later radical, anti-Jewish gnostic dualism. Clearly, too, it was not between Jews and Christians alone. The issue arose before the appearance of the Christian movement, and even afterward they were only one of the participants. The rabbis viewed all forms of "two powers" speculation as dangerous, and they used the label in the same way they used the term *minim:*

as a blanket term for all manner of heretics, only one group of which were the Christians.

Eventually the debate settled into a three-way conflict between rabbis, Gnostics, and Christians. Catholic Christians had the most difficult position to defend, for their increasingly grand Christology made them a legitimate target for the rabbis, and yet, while obliged to defend their core christological conviction, they had to fend off the more extreme dualism of the Marcionites and Gnostics. In addition, they had to defend their position against their fellow Christian Monarchians and modalists, who accused them of compromising Christian monotheism! What is clear, but not surprising, is that the question of Jesus' divine status and thus of the character of God himself was a cause of profound disagreement not only among various Christian groups, but also between Jews and Christians in the early centuries.

We turn our attention finally to a few other alleged rabbinic allusions to Christians. We have to rely on allusions because direct references are scarce indeed. We have already seen that the extremely rare uses of *notzrim* are ambiguous and not always textually secure.[85] Many other allusions are not much more helpful. In *m.Sanh.*10:1–2 we are offered a catalog of groups who have no place in the world to come, several of whom have been connected to the Christians: deniers of the resurrection, detractors of the Torah, those who read "outside books" or utter charms over a wound, and four "commoners" (Balaam, Doeg, Ahithophel, Gehazi). Yet these designations are vague enough to be associated with any number of Jewish groups, and the most that can be claimed is that Christians may have been included in some of them, though which ones remains unclear.[86]

It has recently been argued that the story of the entrapment of ben Stada in Lod, the later additions to which we looked at above, referred originally not to Jesus or to some later Jewish heretic, but to the apostle Peter. Although this might explain, by a process of assimilation, the association of this incident with Jesus in the Talmudic tradition, there is little else in its favor. The only association of Peter with Lod (= Lydda) is a brief spate of missionary activity there (Acts 9:32–35); otherwise there is no more connection with Peter than with most other proposed candidates.[87]

In a continuation of a passage quoted above, the following comment appears: "Our rabbis have taught, Jesus had five disciples—Matthai, Neqai, Netzer, Buni and Thodah" (*b.Sanh.*43a). The misinformation about the number of disciples is analogous to the view of Celsus's Jew that he had ten (*Cels.*1:62; 2:46), and certainly makes both of them useless for information about Jesus. But it has been suggested that the otherwise unknown and inexplicable names refer to Christian martyrs of the Bar Cochba uprising who became confusingly lodged in the tradition as the original disciples of Jesus.[88] This is no more than a conjecture, but, if correct, it would reveal that the rabbis thought that some Christians were executed for legitimate reasons and it would confirm the conclusion we have already come to about the significance of the Bar Cochba rebellion on the Jewish-Christian schism.

It has been conjectured that an obscure note in *b.Sabb*.116a may conceal divergent attitudes toward Christians among the rabbis. In connection with a discussion of the books of the *minim*, it is said that while one rabbi would enter the *Be Abidan* but not the *Be Nitzraphi*, another would enter neither. One way of understanding these two opaque allusions is to see them as corrupt forms of "House of the Ebionites" and "House of the Nazarenes." The indication would then be that some rabbis would associate with some Christians (Ebionites) but not with others (Nazarenes).[89] There is only indirect evidence to confirm such discrimination. Trypho is said to converse with Christians against the instructions of his teachers, and Justin suggests that some Jewish Christians lived more strictly than others and eschewed Gentile Christians—perhaps implying that their fellow Jews would have found them more acceptable. Patristic distinctions between Jewish Christian groups also indicate that some stood closer to Judaism than others. We might surmise, therefore, that some Jews were willing to have contact with some types of Jewish Christians but not with others, or with Christians in general—but it is only surmise.[90]

B. L. Visotzky has suggested a congruence between patristic reports of calumnies against various Christian groups and some late rabbinic traditions. The calumnies commonly include charges of cannibalism, promiscuity, and upsetting the lamp. Justin accuses the Gnostics of precisely this (*I Apol*.26:7; cf. Epiphanius, *Pan*.26:4–5), while Tertullian implies that pagans leveled the same accusation against all Christians (*Apol*.7:1; 8:3; 8:7; cf. Athenagoras *Leg*.3:31ff., Eusebius *Hist.eccl*.5.1.14,26,52. See also chap. 1 above). Uniquely, Origen attributes the calumnies to the malicious rumor-mongering of the Jews (*Cels*.6:27). The problem is, to use Visotzky's own words, that "there is precious little from the Jewish literature of the period which speaks to these charges." There is one late midrash that suggests that certain heretics (not necessarily Christians) were sexually deviant (*Eccl.-Rabb*. 1.1.8). There is no rabbinic evidence for the charge of cannibalism, and the one allusion to overturning the lamp (which in the patristic statements is simply a way of creating darkness for promiscuous deeds) has in the immediate context a meaning that is clear and local, despite the possibly ironic allusions to Matt 5:14–17 (*b.Sabb*.116a–b). There simply is no evidence that the rabbis originally thought "overturning the lamp" meant creating heresy. There is thus no congruence between rabbinic and nonrabbinic sources, such as we have usually sought, because in this case there is nothing to suggest that the rabbinic sources allude to Christians.[91]

It is clear that in general rabbinic evidence provides us with lean pickings, but it is nevertheless not unimportant. By focusing on those traditions that find echoes in nonrabbinic sources some material is eliminated, though not much of importance is thereby lost. The advantage of this procedure is that we can be more confident of being on firm ground and, at the same time, allow the rabbinic and nonrabbinic sources to illuminate each other. The evidence must, of course, be kept in perspective. Even on the most optimistic count, allusions to Jesus and his followers make up only a minuscule portion of the voluminous rabbinic tradition.[92] True, censorship may account for the deletion of some material, but this would not change the balance significantly. It is commonly thought that the paucity of rabbinic evidence shows that Jews were largely unconcerned about Christians in the earlier centuries. This may be a false assumption. What the rabbis put into their writings was not the sum total of their views on all matters, but rather a range of opinion on a selection of narrowly defined issues. Moreover, in the first two centuries CE most Jews probably were not "rabbinic," in the sense that they were ruled by some central rabbinic authority, so that even if it is thought that the rabbis gave little thought to Christianity, it does not follow that other Jews did the same.

What, then, can we conclude about Jewish reactions to Christianity in rabbinic sources? First, that Jesus drew more attention than his followers. He was accused of magic, of misleading the people, and more generally of being a heretic or outcast. Stories about his birth were ridiculed, and he and his mother besmirched. If one objection was to the very idea of a god becoming human, another was to the undermining of divine unity, so that Christians got caught up in the "two powers" debate, which is larger than, but also pointedly includes, them. Other snippets of information hint at the trauma and intensity of the Bar Cochba rebellion and its effects on Jewish-Christian relations, and at the possibility that some Jews, more discriminating in their view of Christians than other Jews, were positively disposed at least toward Christians from Jewish stock.

CONCLUSION

As we glance back over this chapter, a number of things come to light. There is evidence that Jews persecuted and harassed Christians intermittently in a number of locations. This could take the form of synagogue discipline or of persuading Gentile authorities to act on their behalf. Christians nevertheless had a tendency to exaggerate the intensity and extent of Jewish hostility, and this has unduly influenced certain strains of scholarly analysis since.

Christians were included among those targeted by the Jewish authorities at Yavneh. The banning of books, occasional expulsion, and liturgical malediction all appeared in new or revised form during the Yavnean period, and their implementation throughout world Jewry was probably encouraged by roving envoys. From the rabbinic viewpoint, Christians were one of several troublesome groups of nonconformists, but Christians increasingly saw themselves as singled out for rabbinic antipathy. The Bar Cochba uprising may have been an important turning point, precipitating the expansion of the synagogue malediction to include Gentile Christians too. And, as an element of liturgical routine, the more this malediction focused on Christians the greater its influence would have been on popular Jewish attitudes.

Traditions about Jesus as a miracle worker and teacher are prominent in Jewish sources. Josephus, noncommittally, describes him in just these terms, but the rabbis preserve the negative version of the same two traits: that Jesus was a magician and deceiver of the people. The rabbinic view is ascribed more generally to Jews by Justin and Origen. In the stories about Eliezer ben Dama and R. Eliezer there is a hint that some rabbis consorted with Christians until they were challenged by stricter colleagues or came under suspicion by political authorities.

Christology was one of the main obstacles to Jewish-Christian rapprochement. There is nothing surprising about this, nor about the two foci of disagreement that appear in many different sources: messianism and monotheism. The issue of messiahship does not arise explicitly in the rabbinic sources, though the polemical reading of Jesus' role as miracle worker and teacher effectively denies to him activities that some sources expected of the messiah. The assertion of Jesus' divinity met with several objections. One centered around his arrival in the world, about which the rabbis transmitted a polemical (perhaps, unknown to them, historical) line: that Jesus was a bastard and his mother an adulteress. If the idea of God's becoming human was absurd, the idea of a second god was for many Jews blasphemous. To the rabbis, Christians were part of a wider heretical tendency in which the existence of "two powers" in heaven was espoused. This may have made the Christians more difficult to combat, since other Jews were promoting speculations along the same lines.

Overall, Jewish reaction to Christians took many forms: political action, communal discipline, liturgical innovation, exegetical reasoning, and polemical subversion. Variety of action, however, is not matched in the sources by much variety of mood. Most of the evidence we have considered in this chapter suggests that resistance and opposition were the instinctive modes of Jewish response. But even if this reflects the preponderant reality, it is still misleading. Recalling Josephus's statement, and the possible rabbinic references to amicable contact between Jews and Jewish Christians, might seem to be clutching at straws, and it does not do much to balance the account. However, the actions and attitude of Trypho (see chapter 9), as well as the encouragement that some Christian Judaizers were presumably given from the Jewish side, are only two other factors that need to be considered for a fully rounded picture.

GNOSTICS AND MARCIONITES

7

❖

At first sight it might seem strange in a book on Jewish-Christian relations to find a chapter devoted to two movements, one of which may have been only partially Christian and both of which were firmly rejected by what was to become mainstream Christianity. That the two movements were resisted and eventually outlawed is an important observation. Indeed, it might be added, the way in which they were resisted made a significant contribution to the ingraining of negative attitudes toward Judaism in later Christian theology. This, however, is a story that falls largely outside our chronological limits. It is a commonplace observation that during the period we are interested in, especially the second century, Christianity showed great diversity and no settled sense of orthodoxy. It is thus important to recognize that the Marcionites and the various Christian gnostic sects were a significant, widespread, and visible component of the Christian movement. It is not inconceivable that they were as numerous as their Catholic opponents, though it has to be admitted that the demography of the early Christian movement is notoriously difficult to estimate with any precision. It is certain that in some areas they were the main, if not the sole, representatives of Christianity. Their attitude toward Jews and Judaism was therefore, from the perspective of an outsider, either the only attitude of Christianity or the attitude of a significant and vocal element within it. Thus, although both movements were condemned as heretical and subsequently marginalized, in their heyday they were not to be ignored.

We must, of course, recognize that many think that the Gnostics were neither originally nor solely a Christian group. The existence in the Nag Hammadi collection of non-Christian gnostic writings, and of Christian adaptations of some of these, is thought to provide graphic demonstration of the importance of non-Christian Gnosticism and to suggest that Christianity was a secondary rather than a primary influence.[1] Indeed, the origins of

Gnosticism have been one of the most debated issues of the last two or three decades—a debate we shall review briefly below. The most fashionable hypothesis is that Gnosticism originated within Judaism. The matter is, however, not entirely settled. The case for the Christian origins of Gnosticism should not be dismissed out of hand, even if it is currently a minority view.[2] It is sufficient to note that these two hypotheses are the most credible contenders in current discussion and, although each places the anti-Jewish strain in Gnosticism in a somewhat different light, for our purposes they are of equal interest.[3]

It should at any rate be noted that the surviving evidence suggests that the most vibrant forms of Gnosticism in the second century were Christian, often led by prominent and influential figures such as Basilides and Valentinus. This, at least, is what their ecclesiastical opponents imply and what is reflected in the percentage of Christian or Christianized texts in the Nag Hammadi collection. Of course, Irenaeus, Tertullian, and the others were not interested in non-Christian Gnostics, and the Nag Hammadi collection was in all probability deposited by Christian monks.[4] Still, there is no reason to doubt the impression that, wherever and whenever Gnosticism originated, it had by the second century taken root most successfully in Christian communities. Thus, even if gnostic anti-Judaism may have originated among disaffected or disillusioned Jews, by the second century it had become predominantly a form of *Christian* anti-Judaism whose origin was probably as obscure to its contemporaries as it is to us now.

GNOSTICISM

A brief sketch of a typical gnostic system will allow us to place the Jewish and anti-Jewish strains in their appropriate context. It will at the same time provide a point of comparison with Marcion, whose relation to Gnosticism has long been considered enigmatic.[5] It might immediately be pointed out that there is no such thing as a "typical" gnostic system, that the very notion is misleading and refers only to an artificial construct. This is a legitimate warning. A typological sketch that focuses on the elements common to all Gnostics will tend toward two particular distortions: a favoring of the more fully developed and rounded systems, such as we find among the later Valentinians or Sethians, precisely because they are more comprehensive in scope; and an eliding of the extraordinary variety of gnostic speculation in the service of a simplified, bird's-eye view. Some of these (and other) problems were sensed long ago by Irenaeus:

> Let us now look at their unstable opinion—how, when there are two or three of them, they do not say the same things about these matters but express opposite opinions as to contents and names.

Every day each one of them, in so far as he is able, produces some novelty. For no one is perfect among them who is not productive of great lies.

Since they disagree with one another in teaching and in tradition, and the more recent converts pretend to find something new every day and to produce what no one ever thought of, it is difficult to describe the opinions of each.[6]

Even allowing for his antagonism, it is clear that Irenaeus put his finger on an important point—that the unbridled search for novelty among Gnostics led to an array of opinion, often mutually inconsistent, which it is virtually impossible to summarize. Summary sketches, therefore, have their limitations, but they still have heuristic value when we are trying to consider the broad outlines of the gnostic phenomenon.[7]

Fundamental to the more developed gnostic myths is a transcendental, precosmic drama. It is the story of the upper world, the world of the absolute, unknown God and the heavenly beings that emanate from him. In this once perfect world a fatal fissure appears, produced by dark forces from without or, more commonly, by rebellion from within. Thus begins a frequently complex process of devolution, what Jonas has pithily characterized as an "epic of decline."[8]

The fall from the state of heavenly perfection is commonly associated with one of the lowlier divine emanations, often designated Sophia, who then precipitates the creation of the world. Creation is the handiwork of an even lower being, the Demiurge, an inferior deity flawed by ignorance and pretension. The cosmos he fashions is corrupt and evil and is defined by its antipathy to the heavenly world. The same is true of the creation of humankind, but with one critical exception: due to the unexpected success of the Demiurge or the surreptitious incursion of higher powers, humans are infused with the spirit of the supreme, transcendent Deity. This chink in an otherwise catastrophic process of creation eventually provides the one hope of salvation.

Human beings are born into a situation that is profoundly paradoxical. In essence they and the supreme God belong together, but between them stand the world, its creator, and their own corrupt material nature. In their natural state they neither sense the paradox nor see the dilemma, for they are subject to the wiles of a hostile creator, imprisoned by the material world, and blinded to their own true nature. In gnostic myth this paradox is expressed in terms of a series of radical dualisms: the heavenly versus the created order, the transcendent versus the creator god, humanity versus the world, the material versus the spiritual.

This epic of decline can be reversed only through the reception of *gnosis* (knowledge), a knowledge that consists of both subjective spiritual enlightenment and objective information about where we came from, where we are, and where we are going, that is, the whole mythological story in whatever version is being purveyed. Only in this way can the divine essence in human beings and the supreme God be reunited. In principle gnosis is available to all, since all share in the divine essence, but in practice only some will come to know. In some versions gnosis is imparted by a redeemer who descends from and returns to the heavenly world, thus exemplifying the route of the aspiring Gnostic whose ultimate aim is to escape from this world and return to the true, heavenly home. The redemption of the individual is often paralleled by a collective eschatology in which the redemption of all the elect is accompanied by the destruction of the material cosmos and a return to the state of perfection.

Underlying gnostic mythologies lies a deep sense of existential dislocation. Their complexity, as Irenaeus suggests, may in part result from a love of novelty for novelty's sake, but a sense of extreme alienation from this world and its creator never lies far beneath the surface. Indeed, there is a sense in which the more complex the myth, the more desperate is the attempt to explain the gulf between their convictions about divine perfection and the perceived disasters of this world. The sense of alienation from the world led most commonly to asceticism, more rarely to hedonism—both of which are an expression of distance and disdain.[9]

Where did the Jewish element fit into this scheme, and what form did gnostic anti-Judaism take? As two sides of the same coin, they can largely be dealt with together. In many gnostic myths the Demiurge, creator of this world and human beings, is identified with the God of Israel. In line with gnostic logic, he is thus seen as a rebellious, ignorant, flawed, and inferior deity. The names they give him (often playing on biblical names) indicate his character—"Ialdabaoth" (= child of chaos), "Saklas" (= fool) or "Samael" (= blind god)—and his disastrous ignorance is shown in the regular boast that he is the one and only god.[10] The revered and singular god of the Jews is deliberately degraded and dishonored, and so too the world he has created.[11]

In sketching their cosmogonies, with their myriad variations, the Gnostics drew heavily on the biblical stories of creation, especially Genesis 1–9. To these they brought exegetical traditions and methods familiar enough to other Jews and Christians, but from them they drew radical and startling conclusions. For much that was valued in the "mainstream" was devalued by the Gnostics and vice versa. Using a deliberately polemical process of hermeneutical reversal, the traditional order was turned on its head: what was good was now frequently considered evil and what was evil was now considered good. And not only the deity but lesser figures—such as the serpent, Cain, Sophia, Norea—were often subject to the same treatment. The pattern is not entirely consistent. Some texts show a considerable interest in Seth as the progenitor of the "third" race, the elect, while others are as dismissive of Cain as the biblical narratives themselves.[12] Yet there can be no doubting the tenor of hostility and willful perversion of Jewish traditions which pervades many gnostic writings.

By a similar logic the Gnostics challenged the traditional estimation of the Jewish law.[13] They accepted the scriptures as one basis for constructing their own worldview, but only the parts they deemed inspired and only as they interpreted them. Moses and his law are usually dismissed as misleading (*Ap.John* II 13,19–20; 22,22–23; 23,3). The law, of course, springs ultimately from the creator and reflects his control over humanity (*Hyp.-Arch.*II 90,6–10). Those who obey the commandments are slaves of the Demiurge and fated for destruction and death (*Apoc.Adam* V 65,20–21; 72,21–22; *Ap.John* II 21,23–24). The true Gnostics required no such commandments because they had the benefit of superior enlightenment; only the ignorant would enslave themselves to the laws of an inferior god. This attack on Jewish law may not be as pervasive as the attack on the Jewish God, but when it occurs it is equally polemical and equally dismissive.

It is commonly noted that Judaism at the turn of the era was defined more by orthopraxy than by orthodoxy. True as this is, there were nevertheless certain things that were so central to Jewish conviction that they amounted to a sort of core credo. They were few in number, and two of them were a belief in the supremacy of Yahweh and in the centrality and validity of the Mosaic law.[14] These were shared by Jewish groups of all shades of opinion, even though there were differences over their precise definition, and they were two of the most important distinguishing features of the Jew in the ancient world. To deny them, even if one was born Jewish, would in effect have been to place oneself beyond the normally accepted bounds of the Jewish community. Gnostic antipathy to these core elements thus attacked Jewish tradition at two of its most sensitive points.

In the light of this it is remarkable that references to the Jews, as distinct from elements of the Jewish tradition, are extremely rare in both gnostic documents and in patristic reports about the movement. This has led Gager to distinguish it from other forms of anti-Judaism, because its polemic is directed "not against the Jews, or only rarely, but against the heroes, the scriptures, and the god of the Jewish Bible according to the principle of value-inversion. It is thus to be distinguished from anti-Semitism in that its animus is not against Jews as persons, and from Christian anti-Judaism in that it has very little interest in claiming itself as the true Israel." The revolt is not so much against Judaism as against the cosmos and the god who created it, a form of metaphysical anti-Judaism.[15] There is a considerable element of truth in these distinctions, but they require further refinement.

It has recently been suggested that tensions between Christian Gnostics and Jews can be detected in the *Gospel of Philip*, a work that Gager also refers to as an exception to his general view.[16] Siker argues that five occurrences of the term "Hebrew" (51:29 [x2]; 52:21; 55:28; 62:5) refer to nongnostic Christians rather than to Jews, both because they are defined as "apostles and apostolic men" in 55:30 and because elsewhere the gospel refers to "Jews" as a group distinct from Christians (62:26, 75:30–32). On this basis, when in 51:29 it is said that "a Hebrew makes another Hebrew and such a person is called a proselyte," he takes "proselyte" to mean Gentile converts to nongnostic Christianity rather than to Judaism. In a passage contrasting "slaves, non-heirs, the dead" and "sons, heirs, the living" (52:1–24), Gentiles are clearly defined as the former. Taken with the consistently positive references to "Christians" (52:24; 62:32; 64:24; 67:26, etc.), presumably Gnostics, we have the following five groups: Gentiles, Jews, proselytes, Hebrews, and Christians. Siker suggests that they be classified according to the three types of humanity in Valentinian thought: hylic, psychic, and pneumatic. Gentiles are hylic, Hebrews (= nongnostic Christians) and Jews psychic, and gnostic Christians pneumatic, while proselytes are those who move from lower to higher grades.[17]

Elsewhere in the gospel the circumcision of Abraham signifies not the covenant with the Jews but, in line with gnostic asceticism, the benefits of mortifying the flesh (92:26–28), while in two other obscure passages there may be implicit criticism of the Jewish sacrificial system (54:34) and sabbath observance (52:33). From all of this he concludes that the *Gospel of Philip* provides evidence of conflict and competition between a number of different groups—Jews, nongnostic (possibly Jewish) Christians, and gnostic Christians. He surmises the place to be Syria, probably Antioch, and a date toward the end of the second century.

This is a valiant attempt to bring some clarity to the typically oblique and cryptic information in the *Gospel of Philip,* though it is perhaps a little too neat. The term "Hebrew" is used as follows:

A Hebrew makes another Hebrew and such a person is called "proselyte." But a proselyte does not make another proselyte. [Some] both exist just as they [are] and make others like themselves, while [others] simply exist. (51:29—52:1)

Ever since Christ came the world is created, the cities adorned, the dead carried out. When we were Hebrews we were orphans and had only our mother, but when we became Christians we had both father and mother. (52:20–22)

Some said,"Mary conceived by the Holy Spirit." They are in error. They do not know what they are saying. When did a woman ever conceive by a woman? Mary is the virgin whom no power defiled. She is a great anathema to the Hebrews, who are the apostles and apostolic men. . . . And the Lord [would] not have said "My [Father who is in] heaven" unless he had had another father, but he would have said simply "[My Father]." (55:24–36)

He who has not received the Lord is still a Hebrew. (62:5)[18]

An initial step in understanding what the term "Hebrew" means is to ask why it was chosen. It is just possible that it was a sobriquet for all nongnostic Christians (Jewish or Gentile) who retained a positive attitude toward the Jewish God and scriptures. But it more obviously points to their Jewishness in a more specific sense, suggesting that they were Jews or Jewish Christians. Of these Hebrews it is said that they make proselytes, have only one parent, reject the virgin Mary, and fail to receive the Lord; and it is implied that the author was once a Hebrew too. The reference to apostles in 55:30–31 might seem to settle the matter in favor of Jewish Christians, though Jews as much as some Jewish Christians rejected the virgin birth. The reference to making proselytes in 51:29, however, more naturally alludes to Jews.[19] The "father" in 52:22 is probably Christ, who is referred to in the previous sentence, before whose coming Hebrews (most naturally, Jews) had only a mother.[20] Those who have "not received the Lord" could be Jews but also almost anyone of whom the author did not approve. On balance, it seems likely that the basic meaning of "Hebrew" is "Jew," and that 55:30–31 is a case in which a particular kind of Jew, the early Christian Jew, is specified.[21] For what it is worth, the use of "Hebrews" in Tri.Trac. I 110,24; 111,6 clearly has an ethnic sense and in Orig.World II 113,31 it probably refers to Jews rather than Jewish Christians.[22]

If this is so, we can flesh out the only other place where the relationship between Judaism and the Gnostics is broached: "No Jew [was ever born] to Greek parents [as long as the world] has existed. And [as a] Christian [people] we [ourselves do not descend] from the Jews" (75:30–32). In this translation the Christian Gnostics deny any prior connection with Judaism: Jews are one thing, Christians something entirely different.[23] If so, then how does this fit with the implication (52:20–22) that the author and readers were once Hebrews/Jews (or, for that matter, Jewish Christians)? There is, in fact, no contradiction. What is denied is the dependence of the Christian (gnostic) religion on Judaism, not the Jewish background of individual Gnostics. And if they were Jews, this tells us something suggestive about the origins of at least one form of Gnosticism.

There is evidence, therefore, that at least one gnostic author/group, who were formerly Jews, saw Judaism as an inferior form of existence and Christianity as a superior and independent venture. The anxiety about independence and identity may reflect day-to-day tension between Gnostics and Jews, a phenomenon that is rarely suggested elsewhere and may be because the Gospel of Philip represents a Christian form of Gnosticism adhered to by former Jews. But it is an important, if relatively isolated, example of a direction in which Gnosticism could go.[24]

It has been argued recently that there are oblique allusions to the Jews in the First Apocalypse of James.[25] It appears to have a hostile attitude toward Jerusalem, the city that brings bitterness to the sons of light, inhabited as it is by hostile archons and the (Jewish) people they represent (25:16–19;

31:23–26). Eventually the city is destroyed, an act that symbolizes the defeat of the hostile forces as well as their earthly representatives, the Jews. The key passage is 31:15–26:

> The Lord said, "James, do not be concerned for me or for this people. I am he who was within me. Never have I suffered in any way, nor have I been distressed. And this people has done me no harm. But this [people] existed as a type of the archons, and it deserved to be destroyed through them."

The destruction is linked at least temporally with the martyrdom of James (36:16–18; cf. 2 *Apoc.Jas*.60:12–22), and the forces responsible for his death were responsible for the death of Jesus too' (27:13–24; 43:17–21). When it says they did him no harm (31:20–22), this is not an exculpation, but merely reassures James that the inner being was unaffected by the sufferings of the outer person.

In this curious blend of the cosmic and the mundane a number of themes are played out. One is the unsuccessful attempt by the archons to block the ascent of James (and presumably Jesus) to the ultimate God (33:2–5). Another is the connection between the destruction of Jerusalem and the deaths of Jesus and James, a theme that appears elsewhere in early Christian literature (Justin *Dial*.16:4; Origen *Cels*.1:47; 4:22; Eusebius *Hist.eccl*.2.23.18–20). Although the argument is allusive, it would appear to involve both a denigration of the earthly Jerusalem, as the dwelling place not of God but of the hostile archons, and a castigation of the Jews for their role in the deaths of Jesus and James.

The opening words of the *Testimony of Truth*, about those who erroneously seek the truth in the teaching of the Pharisees and scribes and their law and thus fall under the sway of the evil archons, may reflect a situation somewhat like that in the *Gospel of Philip* and the *First Apocalypse of James*. The remarks, while assuming a standard gnostic position, seem more polemical and pointed than many others and may reflect a local conflict with Jews or nongnostic Christians.

The references to the "Pharisees and scribes" and the "Jews" in the *Gospel of Thomas*, according to Gager, merely echo the New Testament.[26] This does not do justice to all the evidence. There is a somewhat casual disregard for Jewish observance—fasting, almsgiving, prayer, and dietary rules (6,14), sabbath (27), circumcision (53)—and some rather dismissive words about the prophets (52). This, together with the allusion to the disciples' incomprehension as being like that of "the Jews," seems to express a degree of distance, if not hostility, uncommon in gnostic texts, whose anti-Judaism normally operates on a more metaphysical plane.

Interestingly, one of the passages we have just discussed goes on to speak of "another people," "the chosen people [of the living God]," "the true man," "this true people" (*Gos.Phil*.75:33—76:6). The choice of language strongly implies that the favored group, the gnostic Christians, saw themselves as the inheritors of Israel's special status even while they were denying any dependence on Judaism. A much more common way for Gnostics to express their privileged standing was through Seth, the third child of Adam and Eve, who became the object of speculation in both Jewish and gnostic traditions. The "seed of Seth" became a designation for the gnostic elect, and Seth himself was seen as a redeemer and revealer.[27] Other gnostic texts adopt common Jewish self-designations, such as "the elect" or "the children of light," thus implicitly usurping the traditional role of Israel. This was not, of course, because they were claiming to be descendants of the Jews, but because they had the true gnosis. But in their exclusivism, their sense of being the privileged elect, they mimic the very Judaism whose influence they disclaim and deny to Jews what the Jews had claimed for themselves.[28] If the Gnostics' attack on the Jewish deity and the Mosaic law struck at two of the more sensitive and central Jewish convictions, then this strikes at a third—the sense of being God's elect.

We have, then, two sorts of evidence about the relationship between the Gnostics and Judaism: denigration of the Jewish God and the Jewish scriptures on a metaphysical level, and conflict arising from competing claims on a mundane level. These two worlds are brought together in the *First Apocalypse of James* when the ramifications of the historical event of the destruction of Jerusalem are projected onto a cosmic plane. In the *Gospel of Philip* it is implied that these particular Christian Gnostics were themselves once Jews. Where and when did these forms of anti-Judaism originate? To ask this is to open up the broader issues of the origins and date of the gnostic phenomenon. There is as yet no consensus on these matters, but for our purposes a brief overview is all that is required.

All are agreed that many developed forms of gnostic speculation, in terms of both their content and their procedures, demonstrate a knowledge of Judaism, which is frequently used to formulate views diametrically opposed to those of most Jews. It is clear too that gnostic intellectuals had eclectic tastes and drew on the vast range of philosophical and religious views circulating in the Hellenistic world, one of which, Neoplatonism, has received particular attention in recent discussion.[29] But it is above all the Jewish element that has fueled recent debate. Was the Jewish/anti-Jewish element in Gnosticism primary or secondary? Did it originate within Judaism, Christianity, or the pagan world? When did it arise—before or after the appearance of Christianity?

It has recently been argued that all the main gnostic themes can be traced to Christian sources, in particular the anticosmic, antilaw views of Paul and the anticosmic, anti-Jewish views of John.[30] The early "Gnostics," Simon and Menander, mark a preliminary stage, but extreme antipathy to the Jewish god, in which he is cast in the role of Demiurge, does not appear until

Saturninus and Basilides. Later, Valentinus attempted to tone down the more extreme elements of his predecessors and to rehabilitate the creator god by allying him more closely with the supreme deity.

That there were currents in early Christian thought that could have evolved in a gnostic direction can be plausibly argued, if only by pointing to the Gnostics' use of Christian writings. The critical point, however, as with the theories of Jewish origins, comes when an attempt is made to explain the extreme turn against Judaism. In Pétrement's view, outlined above, it appears first in Saturninus and Basilides (ca. 130–140 CE). Why just then? Here the argument inevitably gets vague, and reference is made to a growing emphasis on the newness of the Christian revelation and the increasingly bitter separation of Jews and Christians beginning around the turn of the century. These, together with some of the more extreme positions of Paul and John, provided the catalyst for the anti-Jewish lurch. This makes some sense, although it provides a better explanation for hostility toward the Jews than toward their God. In this view, at any rate, gnostic anti-Judaism arose in Christian circles, the result of the confluence of a number of different theological and social factors rather than of any specific crisis, and it took at least some Christians on the road to a metaphysical anti-Judaism virtually without parallel.

Undoubtedly the most influential current view is that Gnosticism arose among disaffected Jews, that is, within but on the outskirts of Judaism.[31] The argument takes several forms, but there are certain observations common to them all. First, there is the sheer obsession with Jewish tradition, which may not demonstrate Jewish provenance but at least shows that gnostic ideas were formulated in close proximity to Judaism. Second, the range of the parallels—with biblical, midrashic, Philonian, apocalyptic, wisdom, and merkavah traditions—strongly suggests the knowledge of insiders rather than outsiders. Third, Jewish content appears in both non-Christian gnostic writings and in the base material of texts that were, it is argued, secondarily and often only lightly Christianized.[32] Fourth, there are traditions in Philo that suggest that at least embryonic forms of gnostic speculation were present in pre-Christian Hellenistic Judaism. At the same time Philo himself resisted more adventurous, possibly gnostic, thinkers who had gutted the law through allegorization or, more significantly, abandoned and ridiculed their ancestral traditions.[33]

These arguments have not gone unchallenged.[34] It has rightly been noted that neither Philo's own speculations nor his information about others provide evidence for pre-Christian Gnosticism. The allusion to those who abandon Judaism in disgust is fascinating but frustratingly cryptic. The Nag Hammadi documents do not help much with dating the rise of Gnosticism—a question that is still unresolved. The knowledge of Jewish traditions, moreover, could have come as easily through Christian as through Jewish circles. The existence of non-Christian or lightly Christianized writings has become a mainstay of the argument, but it remains a matter of judgment whether this is the best way to describe them and, even so, whether they tell us about the origins of the movement. Moreover, while it is likely that behind some of the eccentrics and heretics mentioned in Jewish sources there lurk Jewish Gnostics, others lurk there too.[35] The existence of Jewish Gnostics does not at any rate prove the Jewish origins of Gnosticism. The key objection, articulated in various ways, is that there are no Jewish precedents for the deliberate inversion of Jewish values, that the Jewish material is so often used in such a radically anti-Jewish way that the notion of its arising within Judaism is neither provable nor credible. This is in many ways the nub of the problem, for if the theory of Jewish origins is to be sustained, a plausible explanation of gnostic anti-Judaism must be offered.

A number of suggestions have been made. Some have pointed to theological debates about the anthropomorphic language of the Bible, and the status of God and of secondary divine powers. As the debate sharpened, and the one side insisted on strict monotheism, "some early form of gnosticism was radicalized, and speculative, probably esoteric, Genesis interpretation was turned into a gnostic myth."[36] This debate, in turn, was reflected in rabbinic discussion of the "two powers in heaven" heretics, some of whom were Gnostics. Another view is that gnostic radicalism had its roots in the more extreme forms of skepticism developed in Jewish wisdom circles, with their deep pessimism about the workings of this world and the purposes of God.[37] While intriguing, and while they may point to significant elements in the evolution of gnostic thinking, neither of these views provides us with an explanation of the critical moment when disputes or difficulties within Judaism were transformed into a radical rejection of it.

Attempts have been made to identify more specific factors that explain this radical turn. Green has argued that Gnosticism arose among disaffected Egyptian Jews in the first century BCE who were severely affected by the transformation of the Egyptian economy from state to private ownership under Roman rule. Jews who assimilated could take advantage of these changes and become wealthy and prosperous, but were consistently denied the civic and legal standing of their non-Jewish neighbors. Their social mobility was thus curtailed by their Jewishness, and to compensate for and overcome the ensuing alienation some Jews "rebelled against Judaism and founded spiritualistic sectarian movements which in turn contributed to the development of Gnostic mythology."[38] The metaphysical rebellion against Judaism is thus attributed to socioeconomic causes. The two ends of this thesis—the social and economic changes in Egypt and the characteristic features of Gnosticism—are plausibly reconstructed. The problem lies in the connection between them, between cause and effect. It is possible that Egyptian Jews reacted in the way Green supposes, and it is clear that Jews there and elsewhere aspired to equality with their non-Jewish neighbors. But in only one or two exceptional cases do we know of Jews who abandoned their Judaism to advance their social ambitions or compensate for their frustrations. Many Jews in the Roman Empire experienced a similar status inconsistency without abandoning their tradition. Their frustration was with the social system, not with the God they worshiped, whereas gnostic rebellion was precisely against the God of Israel and his creation. Green's analysis, especially if it is freed from its specifically Egyptian location, opens up new ways of understanding the development, and especially the social structures, of Gnosticism. As an explanation of the root cause it is, however, less successful.[39]

The other major theory of this kind was propounded some time ago by R. M. Grant.[40] He suggested that Gnosticism arose after 70 CE, when the Romans had crushed the Jews and obliterated their eschatological and messianic hopes. Defeated and profoundly disillusioned, some Jews began to reconstruct their worldview out of the debris of apocalyptic speculation, which had in part been the inspiration for their rebellion. There are several advantages to this view. It relates to an event that caused both profound theological questioning and socioeconomic disruption of the sort that might well have led to disillusionment with the Jewish God and his creation. There are also intriguing connections between apocalyptic and gnostic speculation.[41] It is true that 4 Ezra and 2 Baruch show a more positive reaction to the war and that the spirit of rebellion was sufficiently alive to inspire the Bar Cochba revolt some sixty years later. But the authors of 4 Ezra and 2 Baruch may have written precisely because there were those who did not share their view, and the revival of rebellion in the second century merely shows that not all Jews thought alike. If the more extreme anti-Jewish strain appeared in the second century, however, we would require some explanation for the long lapse of time between the Jewish War and its gnostic theological outcome. In fact, we might be moving much closer to the Bar Cochba rebellion, which, as we have seen, was more messianically inspired and in its outcome more traumatic than the Jewish War. Could it have precipitated (or at least exacerbated) the anti-Jewish turn? It is possible, but it is no more than a guess.[42]

What, then, can we conclude? First, that a form of metaphysical anti-Judaism, originating most probably within Judaism but perhaps within Christianity, came to full and varied expression in the second century. If it originated within Judaism, it was in this respect unlike any other form of anti-Judaism in the ancient world—it was Jewish anti-Judaism. Second, by challenging the central affirmations of Judaism, Gnosticism amounted to the most radical rejection of Judaism that we know of, with the possible exception of Marcion. Third, wherever it originated, this anti-Judaism flourished in a significant number of second-century Christian groups. Catholic Christians may have railed against them, but where Gnostics were the dominant, even sole, representatives of the Christian tradition their view would presumably have been identified as the Christian view. In such communities a profound denigration of the biblical God and his law, and thus of the Jews (and other Christians) who adhered to them, would have been the norm. It is likely, too, that these Christian Gnostics blended this metaphysical strain with some of the more traditional forms of Christian anti-Judaism. It is significant, for example, that it is in the *Gospel of Philip* and other Christian gnostic writings that we find the appearance of claims to be the elect, the true people of the true God. In the *First Apocalypse of James* too we find evidence of the anti-Jewish interpretation of the destruction of Jerusalem, even if in symbolic mode. This reminds us, fourthly, that while the distinction between metaphysical and mundane gnostic anti-Judaism is useful, it should not be drawn too firmly. There is evidence, slight but not insignificant, that some Christian Gnostics found themselves in direct conflict with the Jewish (perhaps Jewish Christian) tradition from which they themselves had originally sprung. Their anti-Judaism may have arisen in the context of day-to-day tensions, but it could also have led to broader and more sweeping anti-Jewish claims.

This estimate of gnostic anti-Judaism is not shared by all. It has been suggested that while denigration of the Creator God is anti-Jewish, the rest of the evidence either reflects an earlier, and no longer active, stage of Christian opposition to Judaism or is the expression more of disparagement than of hostility toward the Jews. It is thus akin to the gnostic attitude of superiority to all other religious claimants. In my view this underestimates the extent of gnostic anti-Judaism, which, as we have seen, goes beyond denigration of the Creator God. And while the gnostic claim to privileged and superior knowledge is not in doubt, it is nevertheless striking that Jewish traditions function as the negative pole more often and more obviously than those of any other religious or intellectual system of the time. It may be true, as noted above, that nongnostic Christians were often the immediate target, and it is important to note the degree to which gnostic theorizing is an expression of their own sense of identity. But whatever their immediate objectives, Gnostics did promote a view of Judaism that is almost unrelievedly negative. Whether this "disparagement" (perhaps not a strong enough term) led to hostility we do not know, except perhaps through obscure texts like the *Gospel of Philip*. But that it was anti-Jewish, if largely on a metaphysical level, cannot be doubted.[43]

Put briefly, gnostic anti-Judaism was unique, radical, and deeply embedded in a significant portion of the early Christian movement.

MARCION[44]

Marcion and his followers are sometimes seen as a subgroup of the Gnostics but, for a number of reasons, it is important to treat them separately. It is well recognized, for example, that despite some intriguing overlap, the fit between Gnosticism and Marcionism is not precise. Some key features of

Gnosticism are absent from Marcionism and Marcion held some eccentric views found nowhere else in the gnostic or Christian traditions. One of these was his view of the relationship between Judaism and Christianity, on which he carved out a quite distinct position, and about which he had more to say than was typical of the Gnostics—and for both of these reasons he is for our purposes a significant figure. Moreover, reflection on the origin of Marcion's peculiar views, while no less speculative than the search for the origins of gnostic anti-Judaism, introduces factors unique to him and to his kind of Christian experience.

Marcion, in addition, was a major Christian figure of the second century. Around 160 CE, Justin claimed that Marcion's teaching had spread throughout the whole human race, and about fifty years later Tertullian made much the same observation. The number of tracts written to combat Marcionite influence (most no longer extant), the extraordinary length of Tertullian's *Adversus Marcionem,* and the fact that Celsus knew of only two branches of Christianity, one of them Marcionite, all reinforce the view that during its heyday in the second century the Marcionite church was one of the dominant forms of Christianity, and that beyond the second century its influence continued to be felt. Theodoret, a Syrian bishop in the mid-fifth century, announced with some pride his success in cleaning up pockets of Marcionite resistance in several villages in his diocese.[45] To complete the picture we must remember, too, that the Marcionites, like the Gnostics, in some places and for some time, would have been the main or even the sole representatives of the Christian tradition. For many in the second century, whether Christian believers or outside observers, the word "Christianity" would have meant "Marcionite Christianity."

The attitude of the Marcionites toward Judaism is thus an important component in the relationship between Jews and Christians in the second century. Surprisingly, however, this aspect of Marcion's thought has received little attention. There may be several explanations for this. Perhaps Marcion's anti-Judaism has been considered to be so obvious and so extreme that it scarcely warrants analysis. No other early Christian thinker, it might appear, so openly rejects the Jewish scriptures and denigrates their God. There is some truth, too, in the observation that "the real problem for him is posed not by the Jews but—as he saw it—by Judaizing Christians."[46] That is, Marcion was involved in an intra-church dispute, so that problems such as his connection with Gnosticism, his eccentric Paulinism, and his innovations in the Christian canon have naturally dominated scholarly discussion. It was, moreover, Marcion's opponents who won the day and their attitude toward Jews and Judaism that most influenced the subsequent history of Christianity, and, for this reason, some have concentrated more on the anti-Jewish strain in the Catholic reaction to Marcion's teachings than on the teaching of Marcion himself.[47]

On a more general level it is perhaps pertinent to note that exploring any theme connected with Marcion is a daunting task. All the evidence that has survived is both secondary and hostile, and this makes any discussion of Marcion an uncertain business.[48] His opponents were interested not in being fair but in being victorious, and they wrote on behalf of an increasingly settled orthodoxy, which had begun to propagate its own simplified vision of the past.

In addition, no discussion of Marcion can fail to be daunted by the classic work of modern times published by A. von Harnack in 1921.[49] The result of some fifty years of labor, into which he put more of himself than he did into any other of his voluminous works, it is a brilliant example of collation, synthesis, and sympathetic portrayal. He overshadows the field and cows his successors. In fact, it is difficult to speak of Marcion without speaking of Harnack. His work is, of course, flawed. Inevitably, it reflects the predispositions of both the man and the liberal theology he espoused. There is, for example, a natural affinity between Harnack's view that the simple gospel of Jesus had been obscured by a complex overlay of christological dogmatism and Marcion's notion of a Jewish-Christian conspiracy which had successfully misrepresented the teaching of both Jesus and Paul. It is well known, too, that Harnack went to some lengths to defend his view that while Marcion's rejection of the Old Testament was rightly resisted in the second century, the beginning of the twentieth century was a propitious moment for its revival in modified form—a judgment that was doubtless, in its turn, influenced by the inadequate view of Judaism and its law that prevailed in the scholarship of Harnack's day.[50] The novelty and radicalism of Marcion's teaching, and the heroic individuality that Harnack believed to be rooted in a profound religious experience, also greatly appealed to him, even though he recognized the distortions that resulted. At the same time he consistently refused to allow for any gnostic influence on his hero.[51]

This brief digression on Harnack is of some relevance to our theme, not only for the obvious reason that the image of Marcion in our day is to a large degree filtered through his work, but also because, despite disagreements we might properly have with both Harnack and Marcion, they both raise the issue of the relationship between Christianity and Judaism in a sharp and distinctive fashion. Whether their views have, in some respects, more to be said for them than the solutions adopted by their contemporaries is a matter worthy of some reflection at a later stage.

A brief review of Marcion's life and teaching will set the scene and provide some clues about his unusual view of Judaism.[52] There are a few things about which we can be fairly certain. Marcion was born and raised in Sinope, an important port and trading center on the Black Sea in the province of Pontus. He is described as a *naukleros*—a shipowner, or merchant seaman (Tertullian *Marc.*1.18; 3.6; 4.12; 5.1). We can reasonably assume that he was wealthy, well traveled, and well connected. About the city of Sinope we know little, except for one potentially significant fact: it contained in Marcion's day a flourishing Jewish community, some of whom (e.g., Aquila) were developing a literalist reading of the Jewish Bible as part of a campaign of resistance to Christian use of their scriptures.

Sometime in the thirties or forties of the second century Marcion traveled to Rome and attached himself to the sizable and important Christian community there. One of his first actions was to donate a substantial sum of money to the church—an action that demonstrates his wealth, his generosity, and, no doubt, his ambition.[53] Around 144 CE he tried to persuade the Roman churches to accept and promote his version of the Christian message, but he was firmly rebuffed and his earlier gift returned. Sometime during his stay in Rome, whether before or after the break is not known, Marcion met and was subsequently influenced by the gnostic teacher, Cerdo (Irenaeus Haer.1.27.1–3; Tertullian Marc.1.2; 1.22; 3.21; 4.17). From then until his death (ca. 160 CE) he busied himself with extraordinary energy and a great deal of success in establishing an alternative church.

These are the firm, if sparse, biographical details. Other spicy or salacious tidbits appear at various stages in the anti-Marcionite tradition, but it is hard to assess their worth. The least plausible has him recanting and returning to the "Catholic" side just before his death. In fact it is more probable that he was martyred, like a number of his followers. When traveling from Sinope south through Asia Minor he is said to have met Polycarp, bishop of Smyrna and a well-known bastion of orthodoxy. When Marcion inquired, "Do you know me?" Marcion received the instantaneous reply, "I certainly do, you son of Satan."[54] It sounds a bit like a set piece—notorious heretic decisively put down by famous bishop—but there is perhaps a grain of truth to it. More interesting, because less obviously tendentious, is the tradition that he was the son of the bishop of Sinope and left the church there after a dispute with his father. The reason is not known. One rumor, circulated by his opponents, was that it was because he seduced a young girl and had to leave hurriedly in disgrace; but most prefer to think it was a result of his already eccentric views.

Why was Marcion so successful? We cannot fully answer the question at this stage, but a number of fairly obvious things come to mind. To start with, Marcion must have cut something of a dash in his day. He was wealthy, energetic, ascetical, articulate, and rigorously intellectual—an awe-inspiring and imposing figure. His followers were known for their high moral purpose and their willingness to undergo martyrdom. There was no doubting their sincerity and commitment. Then again, Marcion's business activities would have given him both the influence and the contacts to launch an independent church—a church that was more open and less hierarchical than its competitors, encouraging the participation of women and laypeople, while at the same time sufficiently close to the mainstream in ritual (Baptism/Eucharist) and liturgy to be comfortingly familiar. Beyond personal charisma and organizational advantage, Marcionism exhibited a rigor and clarity of thought that were uncommon in their day. It is no accident that the title of Marcion's major work (no longer extant) was *Antitheses*. He favored clear-cut, decisive solutions to otherwise baffling and murky issues, and this may help to account for his appeal.

This leads us naturally to a consideration of Marcion's teaching. Although it has come down to us only at the hands of his opponents, who focused on different elements according to their own interests and predilections, the outlines are fairly clear. Any summary will, of course, be composite and will telescope developments in Marcionite thinking. Moreover, while some of Marcion's views are marked by what seems to be rigorous logic, not all his positions appear to have been fully thought through. This, at least, is the impression conveyed by Tertullian, and probably has as much to do with the inchoate nature of Marcion's thought as it does with Tertullian's desire to ridicule and rebut him. That this was so is perhaps further indicated by the significant adjustments to Marcion's teaching that his most important pupil, Apelles, later felt obliged to make.[55]

1. There were, in Marcion's view, two gods.[56] The one, creator of the world and all that is in it, was the god of the Jewish Bible—a fickle, temperamental deity who ruled the created order through his law. Sometimes Marcion described him as wretched and petty, capable of vindictive outbursts and favoritism, but he viewed him as an essentially righteous rather than evil god; and while he clearly considered him to be inferior, he was never in any doubt as to his reality and divine status. The special concern of the creator was his favored people, the Jews.

The other, the redeemer deity, was radically different: a god of mercy rather than justice, of love and compassion, utterly separate from the creator god and wholly unknown until revealed by Jesus. He was an alien god, alien, that is, to the creator's world and all that belonged to it. His appearance in the person of Jesus was an unprecedented irruption. He was the god of the Christians rather than of the Jews, the God of the Christian rather than of the Jewish scriptures.

These two deities, entirely distinct in character and attributes, can be further characterized by the principles law and gospel, which not only belong to different documents but also describe two different modes of operation in the world. According to Tertullian this distinction lay at the root of Marcion's system: "The separation of law and gospel is the primary and principal exploit of Marcion" (*Marc.*1.19; cf. 4.6; 5.13).

2. Human beings, as part of the created order, belong wholly to this world and its god.[57] As distinct from most gnostic systems, they have no divine spark, no natural affinity with the savior god, and as a result they cannot be held to account. They are inexorably defined by the creator and the world he has produced. Salvation originates outside both humanity and the world. Gnostic myths were in part designed to preserve, at however distant a remove, a connection between at least some of humanity and the deity who

was the ultimate source of redemption. For Marcion there was no such connection. Hope for salvation rested solely upon the intrusion of an alien and hitherto unknown god.

3. Jesus' irruption onto this scene was unprecedented and unheralded.[58] As the son and revealer of the savior god, he could have no close association with the creator god and his world. He was thus in his earthly existence not a real but a phantom man, appearing only in "the likeness of human flesh." His message about the god of love who cares for the poor and the oppressed (just the way, incidentally, in which Harnack portrays the teaching of Jesus in *The Essence of Christianity*) implicitly undermines the biblical god, though without explicitly attacking him.

Jesus' death, enacted by the Jews but inspired by dark, cosmic forces, provided a ransom (understood, as one would expect, in a quite literal fashion), which brought release for the redeemed from the clutches of the creator god and his world—a more realistic understanding of Jesus' death than is usual among Christian Gnostics, for whom it was a particularly troublesome issue.[59] Precisely how it was that human beings enslaved totally to the creator god could respond to the message of an alien deity, Marcion scarcely makes clear, apart from a few vague references to the impression created by Jesus' words and deeds.[60]

4. Marcion imposed a rigorous asceticism on his followers. Since the body belonged to the created order and did not share in the process of redemption, everything connected with it had to be disciplined and controlled. It was a commonplace of Christian polemics, from the New Testament on, that false belief led directly to immoral behavior. No such charge was made against Marcion (apart from the late seduction rumor) or his followers, and doubtless their high moral purpose, as well as their willingness to suffer martyrdom, in part accounted for their appeal. On the other hand, an ascetically inspired repudiation of sexual intercourse, even within marriage, contributed to their own decline by cutting off the most natural source of new members: their own children.

5. Crucial to Marcion's belief was his understanding of Paul. He believed that his own teaching was neither more nor less than a retrieval of the true Pauline gospel. Paul's letters were the source of much of his terminology, the distinctive twist of many of his "gnostic" ideas, and his conviction that Judaizing Christians had conspired to pervert the message of Jesus and Paul.

Moreover, taking up Paul's references to "my gospel" in Galatians, Marcion concluded that he used one written gospel, and that it was the Gospel of Luke. Since he had abandoned the Jewish scripture along with its god, he needed a replacement; and the combination of Paul's letters and Luke's Gospel, drastically but not always consistently purged, provided it. Together with the no longer extant *Antitheses* written by Marcion, they became the core of the Marcionite tradition, ultimately provoking their opponents into producing an expanded canon of their own.[61]

This rather too orderly sketch should not be taken to presume a solution to the persistent dispute about the roots of Marcion's thought. Was he essentially a Gnostic or a Paulinist, a metaphysician or a biblicist? How much did his literal turn of mind and ascetic inclinations mold him? Was his view of Judaism sui generis, or can it be wholly explained by gnostic or Pauline influence?

There are personal characteristics that certainly help to explain the direction of Marcion's thought.[62] If Marcion was by temperament an ascetic or responding to an ascetic trend of his time, this would explain his revulsion for the natural world and the flesh, and thus his reading of certain biblical and Pauline texts. He was also rather doggedly literal-minded in his reading of Jewish scriptures and of those New Testament writings he chose to use, perhaps in reaction to the kind of unrestrained allegorical exegesis found among some of his contemporaries (e.g., the author of *Barnabas*).[63] Moreover, there is no doubt that he had an antithetical turn of mind, which preferred stark oppositions and clear distinctions to the rather muddled and unthinking compromises that typified much Christian belief of his day. These characteristics do explain Marcion up to a point, but they are only a beginning.

It must be remembered too that Marcion, like the Gnostics, inherited a tradition in which the newness of the Christian revelation and the alien nature of the world were increasingly emphasized (*Diognetus*, Ignatius, *Hermas*).[64] For these Christians, however, the alien world was dominated by Satan or the Roman state, which hardly explains the radical shift in Marcion's thought, where the alien world is linked to an inferior biblical god and the novelty of Jesus with another deity altogether.

The two main options in terms of which the origins of Marcion's thought are usually debated are Gnosticism and Paulinism. That is, was he essentially a Gnostic whose Gnosticism led to an eccentric reading of Paul; or was he an eccentric Paulinist whose brand of Paulinism made certain gnostic notions congenial? The latter was argued by Harnack, who was convinced that Marcion's views sprang from his intense religious experience and exaggerated Paulinism alone.[65] The reverse has commonly been argued,[66] not only because of the striking parallels with Gnosticism but also because it is held that Marcion's eccentric reading of Paul is inexplicable unless he was predisposed to view things in a dualistic fashion. In extreme form neither view is convincing. The notion of an inferior creator god, the deeply pessimistic view of the world and the flesh, and the deliberate reversal of biblical traditions are so close to gnostic ideas that it is difficult to think that there has not been some cross-fertilization. On the other hand, Marcion was a Gnostic but not as one of the Gnostics. The absolute separation of the two deities from each other, and one of them from the world, the contrast between the god of justice/law and the god of compassion/grace, the insistence that humans are defined wholly by their location in this world, and the notion of Jesus' death as a ransom are not typically gnostic and are almost certainly taken from his reading of Paul. Of course the contrast, Gnosticism versus Paulinism, is itself questionable in view of the intense interest in Paul in some gnostic groups, notably the Valentinians. In addition, the issue is partly one of definition. Scholars have recently emphasized the considerable variety of strains within Gnosticism, and it is thus possible to think of Marcion's teaching as one version of Gnosticism among others.[67] But when we compare Marcion and other Gnostics who used Paul it is apparent not only that his reading of Paul was eccentric, even for a Gnostic, but also that no other gnostic thinkers were as profoundly influenced by Paulinism as he was.

In fact, to read Marcion's thought in the light of scanty evidence for his career makes a great deal of sense. Ascetically inclined and with a literal cast of mind, he could well have formed the basis of his views by a concentrated reading of some of Paul's letters. If Christianity in Sinope was essentially Pauline, but of a kind in which the sharp edge and verve of the original Paul had been lost (cf. the Pastoral Epistles, Ephesians, etc.),[68] a reading of some of Paul's letters might well have set him thinking—especially if the letter most familiar to him was Galatians. That the language of Galatians was so influential in his thought, that it stands at the head of his list of the Pauline epistles, and that of all Paul's letters it was addressed to communities closest to Sinope are all things that suggest that this was so. And if the view of Paul that Marcion got from Galatians is exaggerated, distorted, or truncated, then so is any view of Paul that knows him only through this epistle—as is shown by the difficulty some of us have in bringing the views expressed in Galatians into line, for example, with those expressed in Romans.

Marcion edited Galatians as he did all of Paul's epistles but, according to Tertullian (*Marc.*5.13), his editing of Romans was the most drastic of all, which is what we might expect from someone brought up on Galatians, whether he distorted its meaning or not. It may well be, too, that in Asia Minor Marcion had already come across groups who interpreted Paul in a gnostic fashion (cf. the opponents of the author of the Pastorals, 2 Peter 2:15–16, etc.). The likelihood, therefore, is that Marcion began as a Paulinist, but with a brand of Paulinism already open to gnostic influence and profoundly affected by his own eccentric reading of Paul. His sessions with Cerdo in Rome presumably exposed him to ideas that were both congenial and suggestive and that could, with some adaptation, be used to articulate and extend the views he had already formed.

We are now in a position to draw together some of the threads that relate specifically to our theme and dwell on them a little further. It is important, first, to state the obvious: Marcion's teaching in general contains a profound denigration of Judaism and the symbols precious to its life and faith. Whether it is in his view of their god, their scriptures, their law, or in his account of Jesus, Paul, or the Jewish Christian conspiracy, in each case Juda-

ism appears as an inferior religion. In Marcion's system of dualistic oppositions, the things that characterize Judaism always form the darker side of
the contrast. Their god is real and essentially righteous, but also severe,
capricious, and prone to anger (*Marc.*2.16,20,23; Origen *Hom.*vii.i). His
plans for the world are supposedly set out in the law—that is, the scriptures
as a whole—yet many of its regulations are complex and pointless
(*Marc.*2.18–19), and he even arbitrarily encourages people to disregard
them (*Marc.*2.21–22), as Jesus did too (*Marc.*4.12,16,27). And, while the
salvation offered by Jesus might be received by unrighteous Israelites who
were far removed from the creator god by virtue of their misdeeds, righteous
Israelites would be immune to his appeal by virtue of their attachment to
Yahweh (Irenaeus *Haer.*1.27.3; Epiphanius *Pan.*42.4). This latter looks very
much like a mild form of the radical reversal of Jewish beliefs found in some
gnostic systems, although in Marcion's case it may have a different basis,
since it is the logical outcome of his belief that the Jewish god was a real
deity with a special attachment to his chosen people.

Yet a great deal of what Marcion said about Judaism seems to have been
the result of his antithetical turn of mind and his own peculiar form of
Christian self-definition, and there is little to suggest that he was deliberately anti-Jewish. Quite the opposite, in fact, for in a number of places Tertullian reports that Marcion often allied himself with the Jews against received Christian opinion:

> So then, since heretical madness was claiming that the Christ had come who
> had never been previously mentioned, it followed that it had to contend that
> the Christ was not yet come who had from all time been foretold: and so it was
> compelled to form an alliance with Jewish error, and build up an argument for
> itself, on the pretext that the Jews, assured that he who has come was an alien,
> not only rejected him as a stranger but even put him to death as an opponent,
> although they would beyond doubt have recognized him and have treated
> him with all religious devotion if he had been their own. (*Marc.*3.6)

> It is now possible for the heretic to learn, and the Jew as well, what he ought
> to know already, the reason for the Jews' errors: for from the Jew the heretic
> has accepted guidance in this discussion, the blind borrowing from the blind,
> and has fallen into the same ditch. (*Marc.*3.7)

> Let the heretic now give up borrowing poison from the Jew—the asp, as they
> say, from the viper. (*Marc.*3.8)

> [Y]our Christ promises the Jews their former estate, after the restitution of
> their country, and, when life has run its course, refreshments with those be-
> neath the earth, in Abraham's bosom. (*Marc.*3.24)[69]

From these quotations a number of things become apparent about Marcion's
view of Judaism. He did not believe that Jesus was the messiah of Jewish
expectation. The creator, according to him, did not prophesy a suffering

messiah and would not at any rate have subjected him to that cursed form of death, crucifixion (*Marc*.3.18; 5.3). Many of the prophecies used by other Christians as christological proof texts (Isa 7:14, for example) were inapplicable or had already been fulfilled in past events (*Marc*.3.13). For Marcion there were two messiahs and two kingdoms, just as there were two gods (*Marc*.4.16). It is not clear why he reached this conclusion, what Hoffmann has called his "second christology."[70] It could have been the logical outcome of an a priori conviction about the unprecedented nature of Jesus' message and the god he represented, as is suggested by Tertullian in *Marc*.3.6, or it may be that exposure to Jewish arguments about Jesus' messiahship, or even simply a comparison of the discrepancies between the promises and their supposed fulfillment, led Marcion to conclude that Jesus was an unlikely candidate for messianic office. It suited Tertullian's purpose admirably to associate Marcion and the Jews (against whom he also wrote a tract) to their mutual disadvantage, but there is no reason to doubt his report (cf. Justin *I Apol.*38; *Dial.*44, 133, 136).

In addition, Marcion did not berate the Jews for the death of Jesus. That event was ultimately the responsibility of the creator and the principalities and powers working under him (*Marc*.3.24; 5.6), and the Jewish rejection of Jesus was understandable since he was an alien and unprecedented figure who did not fit their messianic expectations (*Marc*.3.6).

Marcion also developed a highly unusual view of the salvation of the Jews. As we noted above, there was some chance that unrighteous Israelites, because more detached from the creator god, would respond to the Christian god, but little chance that righteous Israelites would follow suit. Even more remarkable was Marcion's conclusion that, since Jesus was not the Jewish messiah, then the Jewish messiah had yet to come. When he did so he would bring an earthly kingdom in Judaea that would incorporate Jews and proselytes (*Marc*.3.24, quoted above). Here the future is described in thoroughly Jewish terms: restitution of the land and rest in the bosom of Abraham.

These three convictions thus allied Marcion *with* the Jews and *against* received Christian opinion. The standard view of the day was that Jesus was the prophesied messiah, that the Jews were responsible for his death, and that, as a result, they had been permanently and justly punished by expulsion from their holy land.

Viewed overall, two things are particularly striking about Marcion's view of Judaism:

1. A curious tension: on the one hand, Judaism is often implicitly denigrated and always, by definition, seen to be inferior; and on the other hand, in many crucial respects the Jewish view of Christian claims was conceded and a future for the Jews described in their own terms—even though for Marcion it could not compete with the eternal kingdom brought by Jesus.

2. The promotion of a radical and unprecedented simplification of the

relationship between Judaism and Christianity: they are to be seen as two entirely separate entities. The latter did not, as in most Christian systems, develop from and feed on the former.

In both respects Marcion flew in the face of current Christian opinion. Why? To ask this question will allow us to delve a little deeper into the roots of Marcion's thought. In addition to the factors already brought into play—asceticism, Paulinism, Gnosticism, a literal and antithetical turn of mind—what else drove him?

Blackman, basing himself on one of Tertullian's opening salvos—that Marcion, like many heretics, was unduly obsessed by the problem of evil—thinks that much of Marcion's thought, including his view of the Jewish Bible and its god, sprang from profound disquiet over the problem of theodicy.[71] While he prefers Tertullian's monotheistic solution, he thinks that Marcion may well have had a more profound perception of the problem. There is evidence that some Jews, reflecting on the problems of divine justice and the existence of evil, split God into two aspects, each with its own name: the attribute of justice (Elohim) and the attribute of mercy (Yahweh).[72] This kind of functional dualism could be seen to be moving in the direction of Marcion's two deities, who are described in remarkably similar terms, and it is possible that Marcion was in part motivated by the same issues. But it does not explain why one god is demoted and denigrated, nor does it shed any immediate light on Marcion's ambivalent attitude toward Judaism.

Goppelt suggests that Marcion was intent on rejecting the Jewish god rather than the Jewish people. As a Hellenist, Marcion took a cool, somewhat distant view of Judaism, while at the same time being influenced by certain kinds of Jewish exegetical tradition.[73] This is more a statement of the problem than an explanation of it, and it probably underestimates the degree to which contemporary Jewish-Christian relations affected Marcion's thought. Rengstorf takes a slightly different tack when he argues that Marcion's rejection of Judaism and its scriptures had nothing to do with anti-Semitism, because the Jews with whom he disputed were not the Jews of his time but those of the biblical and early Christian periods, insofar as they were people of the creator god and belonged to him. Quite apart from the logic of this statement, which is not altogether clear and overlooks the obvious denigration of Judaism in Marcion's teaching, there is no evidence that Marcion made such a clear distinction between ancient and contemporary Judaism. Rengstorf goes on to suggest another two, admittedly speculative, reasons why Marcion was fairly favorably disposed toward the Jews.[74] On the one hand, by rejecting Jesus, who was not their messiah, the Jews unwittingly opened up the way for the universal salvation brought by Jesus—against the will of the creator god and despite themselves. On the other hand, Marcion's dispute was not with the Jews as such but rather with (as he saw them) Judaizing Catholic Christians who perpetuated the errors of the earlier false apostles. These observations may be pertinent, but they scarcely explain why Marcion allied himself with the Jews on certain central issues, unless we are to suppose that it was a mere tactical move to procure all available ammunition for the defense of his position.

Harnack takes a somewhat different tack. His tentative explanation is that Marcion came from a family of proselytes and, like his hero Paul, experienced a dramatic conversion to Christianity, which led him to turn on his former religion in anger and disillusionment but without kicking over the traces altogether.[75] Thus Marcion's conception of a Jewish messiah and a Jewish kingdom were merely a hangover from his Jewish past. We need not accept the questionable view of both Paul and Judaism that this implies to concede that it has a certain degree of plausibility, although it is entirely speculative. That Marcion's rejection of Judaism is more radical than his predecessors' is explained, according to Harnack, by his exaggerated Paulinism and, in the light of our knowledge of the way in which Paul's relationship to Judaism has frequently been distorted, we cannot doubt that this could happen. It might have been equally important that, by the time Marcion wrote, church and synagogue were sufficiently distinct that, for a Jew, conversion to Christianity would almost inevitably have led to a more radical break with Judaism than it would have at the time of Paul.

Hoffmann, who also thinks Marcion was from Jewish proselyte stock,[76] gives a different twist to this argument, for he sees Marcion as having a less negative view of Judaism than Harnack does. He emphasizes the Pauline origins of Marcion's view of Judaism—not, as Harnack argued, Paul the model convert and the source of radical ideas, but rather a Paul whose "ambivalent concern for the welfare of the Jews" led Marcion to an unusual empathy for them.[77] Yet there is not the slightest evidence that Marcion came from Jewish or proselyte stock and, even if we allow for the influence of Paul, we must still explain how Marcion's ambivalent attitude toward Judaism came to look so different from Paul's.[78]

Recognition of the complex relationship between church and synagogue in the second century may provide further clues. Grant suggests that Marcion was driven primarily by the need to reassess the relationship of Christianity to Judaism following the disastrous Jewish revolt under Bar Cochba. The hounding of the Christians, the defeat of the Jews, and the immediate Roman oppression would have made any association with Judaism unlikely in principle and a political and social liability in practice.[79] This is not implausible, and we have found considerable evidence elsewhere to indicate that the Bar Cochba rebellion was a critical turning point in Jewish-Christian relations. Marcion was developing his views at precisely this time and may well have been affected.

There are other aspects of church-synagogue relationships that may be pertinent too. If Jews and Christians, in Sinope and elsewhere, had contact with each other, this could have provided material to set Marcion thinking.

We know, for example, of Aquila, an older contemporary of Marcion's from Pontus and a Jewish proselyte, who produced a Greek translation of the Hebrew scriptures, one purpose of which seems to have been to counter Christian use of the LXX, especially with respect to christological proof texts.[80] Most Christians of Marcion's day had appropriated the Jewish god and the Jewish scriptures and had come to think of themselves as the new Israel. For them the old Israel was defunct, passé. Christianity had absorbed and superseded Judaism. That, at least, was the theory.

The problem was that Judaism both continued to thrive and strongly contested these Christian claims. Moreover, when arguing about the meaning of proof texts from the Jewish Bible, Christians were often in a weak position because the texts did not naturally support the conclusions they wished to draw (e.g., the prediction of a crucified messiah). For some Christians this was probably of little concern. Justin, for example, in his *Dialogue,* rode the waves of Jewish-Christian debate with ostensible confidence while fully aware of Jewish counterclaims, although even he seems uneasy on occasions and may have been aware of the difficulty of defending some Christian positions against Jewish opposition. Marcion would certainly have been caught up in this game of claim and counterclaim. Perhaps he was more troubled and less certain. He was undoubtedly convinced of the superiority of Christianity, and yet the continuing success of the Jews and their more persuasive (to his literal mind) interpretation of scripture belied the usual Christian way of expressing this. Could it be that Marcion concluded that the standard Christian claim that Jesus was the messiah and the Christian church the true Israel fitted neither the observable facts nor the ancient predictions? And might this have tempted him to sever the Gordian knot that bound Judaism and Christianity together, cutting through the confusion once and for all?

One more factor has also to be borne in mind. There is some evidence to indicate that some churches in Marcion's day were troubled by Gentile Judaizers, that is, Gentile Christians who found themselves attracted to some of the beliefs and practices of Judaism. Ignatius and the author of Revelation, for example, seem to be aware of and alarmed by the problem.[81] Marcion, we know, was convinced that from the beginning Christianity had been distorted by false, Judaizing teachers. Could it be that a particular kind of contemporary Judaizing, that of Gentile Christians, also pressed him toward extreme solutions? These Judaizers, who transgressed the boundaries between church and synagogue and sometimes defected permanently, blurred the distinction between Judaism and Christianity, causing confusion and a crisis of identity. One way of responding, found in Ignatius, was to sound the alarm, to threaten and cajole. Another might have been to insist upon a clear-cut separation. Where others blurred the boundaries Marcion unambiguously defined them.

We cannot be sure that Jewish-Christian debates and Gentile Christian

Judaizing affected Marcion. But the uncertainty and unease created by them, in all probability exacerbated by the aftermath of the Bar Cochba revolt, do provide a plausible setting for his extreme solution to the problem of Jewish-Christian relations: leave Judaism to the Jews and treat Christianity as a novel and superior venture. Conceding to Judaism their god, their scriptures, their messiah, and their kingdom would have solved in one bold move the dilemmas posed by the survival of Judaism, rival claims to a common scripture, and the attraction of Judaism to some Gentile Christians.

Among Christians there were several solutions to the Jewish-Christian question in the first two centuries. One was the Jewish-Christian option that was rapidly becoming a side stream by Marcion's time. It could be crudely defined as Judaism with Christian additions. Another, perhaps the least consistent, was the Catholic desire to have the best of both worlds and this was to become the dominant Christian position. It involved selective appropriation of facets of Judaism with vilification of the Jews. A third was the radical separation proposed by Marcion, part of the attraction of which, perhaps, was that it solved with one bold stroke what must have been an extraordinarily puzzling situation for many Gentile Christians in the second century who had rubbed shoulders with the Jews. Far from being surprised at the appearance of Marcion, we should perhaps be surprised that his enthusiastic and fairly numerous supporters were alone in coming to the same conclusion.

This leads finally to a brief comparison between Marcion's view of Judaism and that propounded by his Catholic Christian opponents. As Efroymsen rightly points out, the Catholic response to Marcion drew upon the *adversus Judaeos* tradition in order to defend its view of the creator god and his dealings with humanity. In place of Marcion's notion of an inferior god they put the notion of an inferior and disobedient people. The character of God was salvaged, but at the expense of the character of the people. In reply to Marcion's view that the arrival of Jesus was wholly without precedent, Tertullian resorts to a heightened emphasis on the clarity of the biblical predictions, both of Christ and of his rejection by the Jews. And insofar as it is conceded that Jesus and Paul propounded a legitimate sense of the newness of the gospel in their conflict with the Jews, this is seen to be consistent both with the endless tussle between God and his disobedient people and with his intention all along to replace the old covenant with the new. Views that were thus familiar enough in the context of the Christian conflict with Judaism were used in another setting to resolve an internal Christian dispute. The effect is that "Marcion's challenge and threat placed all the anti-Judaic themes in a new apologetic context, appending them to ideas of God and Christ in ways which came perilously close to permanence."[82]

It is clear that both the Marcionite and the Catholic positions involve a denigration of Judaism. Putting it simply, it is as if the Marcionite said to the Jew: "Keep your god, your scriptures, your messiah, and your law; we consider them to be inferior, superseded by the gospel." The Catholic said: "We'll take your God, your Messiah, your scriptures, and some of your law; as for you, you are disinherited, cast into limbo, and your survival serves only as a warning of the consequences of obdurate wickedness." Few would like to be found defending either view of Judaism. It might be argued, however, that the one that more obviously belittles Jewish symbols was, ironically, in practice the lesser of two evils. The Marcionite position left Judaism intact, decidedly inferior though it was considered to be. There was a point, as Marcion seems to have noted, in Jews' continuing to be Jews, keeping their law, and awaiting their messiah. And it is of some interest, though perhaps no more than a coincidence, that there is no record of the persecution of Jews by the Marcionite churches. The Catholic position, imperiously defending its proprietary rights to the Jewish God and scriptures, found mostly negative reasons for the continued existence of Jews. The one involved a radical break, which left Judaism for the Jews; the other took what it wanted and, in effect, left nothing for the Jews. Or, to exaggerate a little, the one attacked the symbols but left the people alone; the other took over the symbols and attacked the people. Judaism was the loser in either case.

CONCLUSION

Gnosticism and Marcionism make an interesting comparison. Some things they share in common. Both may have been influenced by the trauma of the Bar Cochba rebellion: in the one case a Christian who, because of the souring of relations and the opprobrium attaching to Judaism after the war, concluded that Christianity must be seen as an entirely separate entity; and in the other case Jewish thinkers who began to despair of their traditional beliefs as their world collapsed around them. It is possible that the denigration of Jewish symbols in Gnosticism spilled over into Marcionism. Yet the Marcionite view of Judaism seems to have had additional roots, which resulted in a more complex and, in a backhanded sort of way, more positive picture. Debates between Jews and Christians, Gentile Judaizers, and the fallout from the Bar Cochba rebellion all had their part to play. Nor should we forget Marcion's own intellectual predispositions. In most of the important matters over which he fought (the canon, Paul, orthodoxy/heresy, as well as the Jewish-Christian problem), the views of his Christian contemporaries were woolly and ill-defined. Perhaps the single most consistent characteristic of Marcion was his rigor and asperity. With his gimlet eye, his antithetical turn of mind, and his love of plain meaning, he called attention to issues that no one had recognized *were* issues up to that point. We may not like his solution to the Jewish-Christian problem, but he irrevocably contributed to its definition.

PATTERNS OF CHRISTIAN WORSHIP

8

❖

The importance of worship as one context in which the Christian view of Judaism could come to expression in a particularly negative and destructive way was long ago recognized by J. Juster.[1] After considering the origins and content of several aspects of early Christian worship—prayers, hymns, homilies, liturgies, and festivals—he argued that the view of Judaism expressed in them had a powerful and lasting effect on Christian consciousness. Christian liturgical anti-Judaism he describes as vulgar, quotidian, dramatic, and solemn when compared with the more literary, elitist, and abstract pagan critique of Judaism. He may well underestimate populist strains of pagan anti-Semitism, but he points to an important distinction, which can be applied to different kinds of Christian evidence. It is clear that the texts that, precisely because they are extant, loom so large in our reconstructions of early Christian thinking can easily be ascribed an altogether too significant role in their day. Certainly, it is a priori likely that attitudes toward Judaism expressed or implied in the repetitious round of Christian worship would have had a great deal more influence on the thinking of ordinary Christians than tracts such as Justin's *Dialogue with Trypho* or Tertullian's *Adversus Judaeos*. And not only were the liturgies and festivals inherently more significant—because more repetitive, widespread, and accessible—than the musings of the educated elite, they also encouraged the persistence of a largely negative view of Judaism well beyond the time when the Jews were a significant social presence.[2]

The issue is not merely antiquarian. The Christian Easter, whose beginnings we shall consider, is a perfect illustration. It was Jules Isaac who insisted, in the years immediately following World War II, that the prayer for the Jews (*Pro Perfidis Judaeis*) in the Good Friday service of the Roman liturgy had made a fundamental contribution to the development of Christian anti-Semitism.[3] The Jews, as subjects of the prayer, were singled out both by unflattering terminology (*perfidis*, wicked or unbelieving) and by a distinctive liturgical gesture (no kneeling during this prayer). The prayer was banned in 1955, but not before much damage had been done.[4] Even so, Isaac has raised in a modern context an issue with deep historical roots.

It is well known too that the Passion narratives, which form the backbone of the Easter liturgy in most churches, portray the Jews in a particularly negative fashion and often become the basis for deliberate or unwitting anti-Semitism. The well-documented association of the Easter season with the pogroms is more than sufficient to demonstrate the point. The increasingly common celebration of a Christian Passover on Maundy Thursday is a more innocent but further example. Prayers and rituals based on the Jewish rite, but interlarded with supersessionary convictions, reinforce the view of Judaism as a defunct tradition.[5]

In this chapter we shall review a number of different kinds of evidence that bear on the nature of early Christian worship and its relation to Judaism in the first two centuries. We shall first consider a number of ritual and liturgical practices that are thought to depend on Jewish precedents, but that at the same time evince a tendency toward deliberate distancing from Judaism. We shall then assess explanations for the well-known and relatively well-documented transformation of two originally Jewish festivals into distinctly Christian feasts: from Sabbath to Sunday and from Passover to Easter. Finally we shall take a close look at one of the few extensive Christian liturgical texts that has survived, and that is, happily, directly pertinent to our theme: the recently discovered Easter sermon of Melito of Sardis, *Peri Pascha*.[6]

Our task is not altogether straightforward. Christian texts contain little overt liturgical information, presumably because it was familiar, preserved, and reinforced through regular use, and recorded in writing only when in dispute.[7] The problem is compounded when we restrict ourselves to the first two centuries, where the evidence, both Jewish and Christian, is particularly slight. It is noticeable, for example, how many discussions of Christian liturgical practice are based on the *Didascalia*, the *Apostolic Constitutions*, and the *Apostolic Traditions* of Hippolytus, all of which come from the third century or later. In addition, the assumptions that lie behind many earlier attempts to analyze Jewish and Christian liturgical practice have been so severely challenged that one author has concluded that "even the most basic facts about the early liturgical relationship between Jews and Christians must be rethought."[8] R. S. Sarason's comments a few years ago on the state of Jewish liturgiology, many of which apply equally well to Christian scholarship, still hold: the older assumptions—that an urtext could be reconstructed from the extant variant versions, that the shorter versions were more original, and that the development of liturgical phenomena was sequential and monolinear—no longer hold, but more subtle and sophisticated analyses are, with a few notable exceptions, still awaited.[9] It has nevertheless become clear that, like their Christian counterparts, Jewish liturgical practices were not unalterably fixed, that variant versions indicate differences in practice rather than distortions of a single urtext, and that evidence from later centuries (which is often all we have) has to be used with extreme caution in reconstructing the situation in the first two centuries CE. These lessons have not gone unheeded, and a number of recent works consciously attempt to absorb them into their analysis of particular features of Christian worship.[10]

DEPENDENCE AND INDEPENDENCE IN
EARLY CHRISTIAN WORSHIP

In early Christian worship, as in so many aspects of early Christian life, there is clear evidence of substantial borrowing from Judaism. So broad is the evidence for dependence that it led J. Daniélou to conclude that virtually all early Christians were Jewish Christians—a definition, it is now realized, so capacious as to be meaningless.[11] But if the conclusion is false, the phenomenon remains. We shall take a passing glance at some of the evidence, but our attention will be particularly focused on those examples where evidence of Jewish influence goes hand in hand with a conscious distancing from, or even hostility toward, Judaism.[12]

In *Didache* 8:1 the author gives his Christian readers the following advice:

> Let not your fasts be with the hypocrites, for they fast on Mondays and Thursdays, but do you fast on Wednesdays and Fridays.

The days chosen for fasting by pious Jews are as far apart as possible, while at the same time leaving a day free both before and after the Sabbath. As has been noted, we might have expected Christians, if they were celebrating Sunday (14:1), to choose by analogy Tuesdays and Fridays. Why, then, did they choose Wednesday? There are two, not mutually exclusive, suggestions. The first, and more common, is that it was a deliberate attempt by Christians to dissociate themselves from the Jews. More recently Talley has suggested that the valorization of Wednesday and Friday (as well as Sunday) in the Qumran calendar may explain the Christian preference for these days, so that far from expressing a desire to break with Judaism they indicate a rather intimate proximity to at least one form of early Judaism. From this he draws the following general conclusion:

> While some have supposed on the basis of this castigation [*Did*.8:1] that the concern was primarily one of dissociation from Judaism, more recent studies have suggested repeatedly that Christian liturgical origins, although they diverge from the contemporary development of Judaism in the second century, are seldom motivated by deliberate dissociation from inherited patterns. On the contrary, our growing familiarity with sectarian Judaism in the earliest

period has suggested at several points a cultural context for what once seemed only Christian peculiarities.[13]

The general observation is not without interest, but it is not clear precisely how it explains *Didache* 8:1. It is conceivable that Syrian Christianity toward the end of the first century (assuming that is where and when *Didache* originated) was in some distant way influenced by the remnants of an originally small, now inactive, Jewish sect—though this is to assume a lot. But this scarcely diminishes the force of what the author of *Didache* explicitly states: the motive for fasting on Wednesdays and Fridays is to avoid coinciding with the "hypocrites"—clearly in this context the Jews.[14] The choice of language, which like other parts of the *Didache* recalls the Gospel of Matthew, as well as the plain sense of the exhortation, have an undeniably anti-Jewish ring. The fasting itself and its twice weekly performance are almost certainly practices taken over from Judaism, but they are taken over in a manner that anxiously tries to assert their independence and distinctiveness. The combination of proximity to, and antagonism toward, Judaism is one that we shall see again and again.

Immediately following this injunction is another:

> Do not pray as the hypocrites, but as the Lord commanded in his Gospel. [followed by the Lord's Prayer more or less in its Matthean version]. . . . Pray thus three times a day. (*Did.*8:2–3)

Here again we find an injunction that evinces Jewish influence and yet insists on distinguishing Christian from Jewish practice. Moreover, the immediate context (8:1) reinforces the sense of aversion. The recommendation to use the Lord's Prayer could be understood in a number of ways: a general injunction to prefer Christian to Jewish prayers, of which this is a specific example; substitution of the Lord's Prayer for the tephillah or the kaddish;[15] or the addition of the Lord's Prayer to other traditional Jewish prayers that were then in common use.[16] That the Lord's Prayer is thoroughly Jewish in tone and content none would deny, though it is not patterned precisely on any Jewish prayer known to us. The tephillah was not at this time as fixed in form as it was later to be, and it was normal for particular groups to add their own special prayers to the common core. In principle, therefore, the notion of an addition to the tephillah is plausible. While there are verbal parallels with the kaddish, it was essentially a public prayer used in the synagogue, whereas the Lord's Prayer has the marks of brevity and direct address to God that typify Jewish private prayers.[17] We cannot be sure precisely what practice the author of the *Didache* had in mind, but the immediate context and the phrasing of the injunction seem to want to encourage doing things in a publicly different way from the Jews rather than merely adding a distinctive touch to the group's otherwise thoroughly Jewish forms of worship.

That the Lord's Prayer should be recited three times a day seems to imitate Jewish practice, though there is some uncertainty as to what that was. The tephillah appears to have been recited three times a day (Ps 55.17; Dan 6:10; 2 *Enoch* 51:4; Epiphanius *Adv. Haer.*29.9), a practice recommended by early rabbinic sources (*m.Ber.*4:1) and possibly followed at Qumran too.[18] Other fundamental elements of Jewish devotion were the twice daily recitation of the semicreedal Shema, the twice daily times of sacrifice in the Temple, and the three or four times for synagogue worship, mainly on the Sabbath but perhaps on other days of the week too.[19] It is not clear how these different obligations were coordinated, though it seems inherently likely that the various obligations (e.g., tephillah and Shema) were fulfilled simultaneously. In praying three times a day, perhaps following earlier Christian practice,[20] the Christians to whom the *Didache* was addressed probably mimicked the Jews but at the same time diverged from them.

In the tenth chapter of the *Didache* we find an early Christian prayer that exhibits precisely the same sort of relationship to Judaism:

Didache 10
We give thanks to thee, O Holy Father, for thy Holy Name which thou didst make to tabernacle in our hearts, and for the knowledge and faith which thou didst make known to us through Jesus thy child.
To thee be glory for ever. (Vv.1–2)

Thou, Lord Almighty, didst create all things for thy name's sake, and didst give food and drink to men for their enjoyment, that they might give thanks to thee, but us hast thou blessed with spiritual food and drink and eternal light through thy child. Above all we give thanks to thee for thou art mighty.
To thee be glory for ever. (Vv.3–4)

Remember, Lord, thy church, to deliver it from all evil and to make it perfect in thy love, and gather it together in its holiness from the four winds to thy kingdom which thou hast prepared for it.
For thine is the power and the glory for ever. (v.5)

Birkat ha-Mazon
Blessed art thou, O Lord, our God, King of the universe, who feedest the whole world with goodness, with grace, and with mercy.
Blessed art thou, O Lord, who feedest all.

We thank thee, O Lord, our God, that thou hast caused us to inherit a goodly and pleasant land, the covenant, the Torah, life and food.
For all these things we thank thee and praise thy name for ever and ever
Blessed art thou, O Lord, for the land and for the food.

Have mercy, O Lord, our God, on thy people Israel, and on thy city Jerusalem, and on thy Temple and thy dwelling-place and on Zion thy resting-place, and on the great and holy sanctuary over which thy Name was called, and the

kingdom of the dynasty of David mayest thou restore to its place in our days, and build Jerusalem soon.
Blessed art thou, O Lord, who buildest Jerusalem.

The connection between *Didache* 10 and the Jewish grace after a meal (= *Birkat ha-Mazon,* lit., blessing for the meal) has long been noted.[21] The similarities are obvious—a threefold structure and the use of the same key words and themes—and most scholars accept that this is clear evidence of dependence. But equally interesting are the differences. In *Didache* 10, the first two prayers are in reverse order, that is, it begins with a thanksgiving (which is second in the Jewish order) and is followed by a prayer that praises God in and of himself. Compared with its Jewish counterpart, the second prayer does not open with *baruch* ("blessed"), and thus the standard language of benediction is replaced with language of thanksgiving. A further striking contrast is the substitution of spiritual food and drink for physical, of the name for the land, and of the church for the land and temple. The content of the second and third Christian prayers is thus radically altered, even though the indications of a Jewish substratum are unmistakable. Again, dependence and distinctiveness mark the relation of Christian to Jewish forms of prayer. The probable reference to the Lord's Day in 14:1, in the absence of a corresponding reference to the Sabbath, has been taken to be a further sign of the distancing of the community of the *Didache* from contemporary Judaism.[22]

From the end of the first century we turn to the end of the second for our next example. It has long been held that embedded in the *Apostolic Constitutions* 7–8 are Jewish prayers, adapted to their Christian context but still close to their original form.[23] It is widely agreed that the work as it now stands was composed ca. 380 CE in Syria and that it used a number of earlier writings as sources (*Didache, Didascalia,* Hippolytus's *Apostolic Tradition,* etc.). The collection of prayers in *AC* 7:33–39 is more clearly dependent on its Jewish forerunners (the Seven Benedictions) than those in *AC* 8:37–39 and 8:12, which only vaguely resemble the prayers accompanying the Shema and the *Yozer Or* (prayer at dawn) respectively. The prayers in *AC* 7:33–39 show evidence of Semitic origin, and were presumably first translated into Greek by a Jew before being borrowed by Christians. The date at which the borrowing took place has been variously estimated but, although there is no way to pin it down precisely within the agreed range of 150–300 CE, the many primitive elements and the close connection with Judaism perhaps suggest an earlier rather than a later date.[24] Thus we have yet again clear evidence for the liturgical dependence of Christians on Jews, but dependence with a distinctive twist, as in the *Didache.* The prayers are adapted for use in Christian worship, which already indicates an element of distancing. How this could, at least later, take a more negative turn is pointed out by D. A. Fiensy: the fourth-century compiler placed these thoroughly Jewish prayers in a thoroughly anti-Jewish context. To him the Jews were wicked (6.18.3), Christ killers (2.61.1; 6.25.1; 7.38.7), and generally like the ungodly (2.61.3). Christians were to avoid both their synagogues (2.61.1) and their Passover feasts (5.17.1–2). Fiensy concludes: "Thus the compiler must have inherited the prayers and must have been unaware of their origin, since he polemicized against Christians frequenting the synagogue—ironically the very practice which assisted in the compilation of his work by providing him with a source."[25]

In Pliny's letter to Trajan (ca. 110 CE), he makes the following comment about the Christians in Bithynia:

> They were in the habit of meeting on a certain fixed day before it was light, when they sang in alternate verses a hymn to Christ, as to a god, and bound themselves by a solemn oath, not to do any wicked deeds, but never to commit any fraud, theft or adultery, never to falsify their word, nor deny a trust when they should be required to deliver it up. (Ep.10:96)

The allusion to oath taking in the context of communal worship, with its brief paraphrase of the ethical commandments, has been seen as an indication that the Decalogue was recited in early Christian worship and that this is the result of influence from the Shema (in which the Decalogue was recited with the other designated Mosaic passages).[26] A fuller elaboration of ethical commandments, clearly dependent on Jewish precedents, is found in the Two Ways teaching which opens the *Didache*. It concludes with the following exhortation:

> Thou shalt not forsake the commandments of the Lord, but thou shalt keep what thou didst receive, "adding nothing to it and taking nothing away." In Church thou shalt confess thy transgressions, and shalt not take thyself to prayer with an evil conscience. This is the way of life. (4:13–14)

This evidence, together with the echoes of the Shema in AC 8:37–39 and the possibility that the rabbis abandoned recitation of the Decalogue because of its misuse by Christians (y.Ber.1:4; b.Ber.12a), have led some to conclude that this daily Jewish creedal recitation influenced the form and content of early Christian worship.[27] It must be admitted that the lines of connection are tenuous.[28] The Shema was recited twice daily as a form of private devotion, whereas the letter of Pliny envisages communal worship on a limited number of fixed days (weekly?). Moreover there is no evidence that the Shema had any influence on later Christian usage, which, given its content, is hardly surprising. The *Didache* undeniably shows the influence of Jewish ethics but does not associate them with any particular liturgical setting. A stronger case can be made for the influence of Jewish ethical teaching in general and the Decalogue in particular, though it is not clear that in either case this is due to the influence of the Shema rather than the scriptures and/or synagogue instruction. It is nevertheless interesting that the rabbinic traditions, which we have looked at elsewhere, may show that Christian use of the Decalogue had a polemical edge to it, insofar as it was claimed that this alone was the true core of Mosaic teaching.

There are many other hints that Christians were influenced by Jewish patterns of worship. C. W. Dugmore argued that the primary influences on the development of the Christian daily office were the morning and evening prayer times of the synagogue, though in so arguing he has a tendency to simplify both Christian and Jewish practice.[29] It was perhaps the reservation of set times for prayer rather than the times themselves that constitutes the strongest Jewish influence. The postures adopted for prayer, eastward orientation, and the practice of nighttime prayer are reminiscent of Jewish practice;[30] the celebration of the agape retains Jewish features even toward the end of the second century;[31] the use of scripture readings and sermons in communal worship (Justin *I Apol.*67) follows normal synagogue routine; and even liturgical music shows signs of dependence.[32] In many cases the best parallels are to be found in the practices of minority groups, such as the Qumran sect.[33] The evidence from Qumran here, as elsewhere, is invaluable in alerting us to the variety of practice in early Judaism, but there is no reason to suppose that there was direct influence on Christian practice. The similarities should not be overlooked, but they arise partly because we know more about the details of community life at Qumran than we do about other Jewish groups and partly because they and the Christian community shared a similar sectarian status and mentality vis-à-vis Judaism. Thus it is not surprising to find the practice of nighttime praying and a strong eschatological coloring to prayers in two groups who shared the same sort of intense sectarian commitment.

From the evidence we have reviewed a few broad conclusions emerge. First, we see that the influence of Jewish practice was, in one way or another, pervasive. Set times and fasts, liturgical structures and lections, forms of prayer and praise, both private and communal, again and again show that Jewish precedent was fundamental in setting the pattern of Christian worship.[34] This often took the form, secondly, of peaceful borrowing or adaptation by those who felt no particular tension with the Jewish community and were perhaps unaware of the origins of the material they used. Here Jewish influence was freely allowed and transformed in Christian use. In contrast, thirdly, there are a number of prominent instances where Jewish influence is unequivocal but profoundly colored either by a deliberate, sometimes desperate, attempt to differentiate the two traditions or by the blatantly anti-Jewish context in which they appear. On one occasion we get a glimpse of this process from the Jewish side, when the Christian use of the Decalogue accompanied by distinctly Christian claims forces the Jews to revamp their own devotional practices.

FROM SABBATH TO SUNDAY

In considering the origins of Sunday we are not without evidence, some of it quite early. Yet, as so often, it is frequently ambiguous and occasionally obscure. Most important in this regard are the variations between references to "Sunday" and the "Lord's Day," and the understandable confusion between the weekly, and the annual Easter, Sunday. Our task is to review the evidence and then to ask when and where, but above all why, the shift from Sabbath to Sunday occurred.

References to what we call Sunday are expressed as "the first day of the week" or "the eighth day." 1 Corinthians 16:2 is the earliest possible example:

> On the first day of every week, each of you is to put something aside and store it up, as he may prosper, so that contributions need not be made when I come.

A number of things are obscure here. Is the first day of the week mentioned because it was payday, or because it was a day of particular significance for Christians (i.e., Sunday)? Is a regular weekly meeting implied or merely individual action? If a weekly meeting, were the funds to be collected then or privately set aside? That the reference is to a special collection taken at the weekly Sunday gathering of the Corinthians has often been assumed.[35] Yet the text itself mentions neither a public assembly nor the context of Christian worship, and there is nothing else in Paul that helps us fill out his meaning.[36] Colossians 2:16, if it is by Paul, expresses his indifference to Sabbath observation, and Galatians 4:10 could be seen as expressing hostility toward all religious feasts (though the Sabbath is not directly mentioned). Yet Galatians 4:10 must be seen within its polemical setting, and hostility or indifference toward Jewish observation does not afford any certain clues about Paul's likely attitude toward Christian feasts. A reference to Sunday in 1 Corinthians 16:2 seems unlikely but, if present, is singularly uninformative about the origins and meaning of that Christian day.

Several decades later the author of Acts describes Paul's visit to Troas:

> On the first day of the week [mia ton sabbaton], when we were gathered together to break bread, Paul talked with them, intending to depart on the morrow; and he prolonged his speech until midnight. (Acts 20:7)

Many see this as a clear reference to the Christian Sunday and Eucharist, and assume that the casual nature of the allusion suggests a widespread and regular practice.[37] It has also been argued that the choice of a special Christian day for public worship expressed a deliberate repudiation of the Jewish Sabbath, based on the example of Jesus.[38] The text, however, is not without its ambiguities. It is not clear whether the reference is to Saturday evening (Jewish reckoning) or Sunday evening (Roman reckoning).[39] The "breaking of bread" can be associated with the Eucharist (1 Cor 10:16; 11:24), but elsewhere in Acts seems to mean simply "eating together" (Acts 2:42,46), while delaying the meal until after midnight (Acts 20:7,11) suggests a social rather than a cultic gathering.[40] If there is a reference to Sunday it might reflect the practice in Luke's day rather than the apostolic era, and with such uncertainties it would be foolish to draw any far-reaching conclusions from this passage.

We are on somewhat surer ground with Pliny's letter to Trajan (*Ep.*10:96):

> They maintained, however, that this had been the whole of their fault or error, that they were accustomed on a fixed day [*stato die*] to assemble before day-light and recite by turns a hymn to Christ as god and that they bound them-selves by an oath.

This allusion to distinctly Christian practices perhaps suggests that the fixed day was Sunday rather than the Sabbath, though as we have seen the taking of an oath against immoral behavior is thought by some to have been influenced by Jewish precedents.[41]

A further allusion to the Christian Sunday is found in *Barnabas* 15:8–9, where it is contrasted with the Jewish Sabbath, which God has now over-turned:

> The present sabbaths are not acceptable to me, but that which I have made, in which I will give rest to all things and make the beginning of an eighth day, that is the beginning of another world. Wherefore we also celebrate with gladness the eighth day in which Jesus also rose from the dead, and was made manifest, and ascended into heaven.

The author runs a number of themes together here in his anxiety to oppose a literal understanding of the Jewish law—no easy task, since the Sabbath command was part of the Decalogue and difficult to dismiss. First, he dis-misses a literal (i.e., Jewish) understanding of the command, in line with his broad attack on Jewish observance. He suggests, second, that the true sabbath will be a future, eschatological event, the beginning of a new world. At the same time, thirdly, Christians use the eighth day as one of joyful celebration, in memory of Jesus' resurrection on that day and in anticipation of the eschatological rest. The notions of a seventh (six days of the world followed by an eternal sabbath) and an eighth day (the world's week fol-lowed by a new world) are conflated, apparently without causing the author any concern.[42] Justin, writing somewhat later, works with some of the same ideas—the seventh day as the rest after creation, the association with Jesus' resurrection—but also introduces some novel ideas when he associates Sunday with the pagan day of the sun (*I Apol.*67). It is possible to read these as references to Easter Sunday rather than a weekly feast, but in *Barnabas* the contrast with the Jewish Sabbath in the immediate context makes this unlikely.

To summarize so far: the first fairly secure reference to the Christian Sunday comes in the letter of *Barnabas*. That *Barnabas* is the first depends on its date, which, we have mentioned elsewhere, can most plausibly be located ca. 96–98 CE.[43] The earliest evidence (1 Corinthians) is too vague to be of use, and the next (Acts) not much better. Though it is an argument from silence, we would also have expected that the early, even apostolic, substitution of Sunday for Sabbath would have left more obvious traces in the tradition than are currently visible. The evidence of *Barnabas* fits well with that of Pliny some ten years later, and we can conclude that the Christian Sunday became a regular practice in at least some parts of the church toward the end of the first century.

References to the "Lord's day" may confirm this pattern:

I was in the spirit on the Lord's day [*te kyriake hemera,*]. Rev 1:10

On the Lord's day of the Lord [*kata kyriaken de kyriou*] come together, break bread and hold eucharist. (*Did.* 14:1)

. . . no longer sabbatizing, but living according to the Lord's day [*kata kyriaken zontes*], on which also our life arose through him and through his death. (Ignatius*Magn.*9:1)

Now in the night in which the Lord's day [*kyriake hemera*] dawned . . . (*Gos.Pet.*35)

Early in the morning of the Lord's day [*kyriake hemera*] . . . (*Gos.Pet.*50)

Of these five early references we note that only three use the full Greek term *kyriake hemera*, while *Didache* has the obscure "Lord's day of the Lord." Despite the eschatological context of Rev 1:10, it seems unlikely that here or elsewhere the phrase is equivalent to the earlier biblical phrase "Day of the Lord," that is, that it has a primarily apocalyptic sense.[44] The two alternatives are the regular weekly day of worship or the annual celebration of Easter Sunday.[45] Ignatius provides the strongest evidence for a weekly Sunday, since he contrasts living according to the Lord's Day with the sabbatizing of the Judaizers. If the one was a weekly celebration, it is natural to think that the other was too. The peculiar phrase in *Didache* 14:1 may well refer to Easter Sunday, but only if *kyriake* was already known as a term for Sunday.[46] The narrative context of the *Gospel of Peter* 35, 50 makes a reference to Easter Sunday plausible; otherwise here and in Rev 1:10 there are no obvious clues to the meaning. However, a reference to Easter Sunday is for other reasons improbable.[47]

The references to Sunday and the Lord's Day are roughly contemporaneous: *Didache* (ca. 100 CE); Ignatius (ca. 110 CE); *Barnabas* (ca. 96–98 CE); Pliny (ca. 110 CE).[48] The book of Revelation, if included, falls into the same period (ca. 95 CE), while Justin and the *Gospel of Peter* come from somewhat later in the second century. Thus we may conclude that by approximately the end of the first century Christians in some areas had established an alternative or additional day of worship. The early references originate in or reflect the situation in Asia Minor and Syria.[49] This may be fortuitous or it may mean that the Christian Sunday originated, or at least was more widely observed, there. The view that Sunday worship must have spread from Palestine for it to have been so widespread and uncontroversial in the second century is pure speculation.[50] The early evidence for its use in the second century is in fact geographically limited and none of it comes from Palestine; and of the two sorts of Ebionites, one of whom observed the Sabbath and the other Sabbath and Sunday (Eusebius *Hist.eccl.*3.27.5), the former probably reflects the earlier practice, to which Sunday observance was later added.[51]

How the transition from Sabbath to Sunday took place we do not know. For Jewish Christians, observing the Sabbath came naturally but, according to the passage from Eusebius just referred to, for some this was sufficient while others at some stage added Sunday practices too. When they did so, it was probably an expression of their increasing isolation from the synagogue and a desire to bring themselves into line with what was becoming the dominant Christian practice. To what degree Gentile Christians observed the Sabbath cannot readily be ascertained. If many of them were originally God-fearers/sympathizers, they could have been used to various forms of Jewish observance and in no rush to change. And we have to distinguish between keeping the Sabbath in a Jewish way and using the Sabbath as a day of Christian worship. There can be little doubt that the need for regular meetings to focus on the distinctive elements of Christian worship—such as common meals, Christology, and the resurrection—would from an early stage have required them to do some things in a different way from the Jews. The problem is to discover when a different way also became a different day.

It is doubtful that there was a sudden and decisive break, since we would expect that to be reflected somewhere in the sources. When the transition had been made it did, after all, express one of the more radical antinomian decisions of the early Christian movement. The notion of a gradual transition—where Christians extended their Sabbath observance to Saturday evening and eventually to Sunday morning, allowing both Jewish and Gentile Christians to associate their celebration loosely with the Jewish Sabbath—perhaps makes the best sense.[52]

A key question is why the majority of Christians eventually focused their interest on Sunday rather than the Sabbath. We have already considered one motive: the purely pragmatic need for regular, separate gatherings to cater to distinctive Christian needs. That could have been done by replacing the Jewish with a Christian form of the Sabbath, but Jewish Christians and even some Gentile Christians might have been reluctant to give up their deeply ingrained practices. The early texts we have looked at provide a host of associations and rationalizations for observing Sunday—the order of creation, the expected perfect world, pagan worship of the sun—but the most common is association with the day of Jesus' resurrection (Ignatius, *Barnabas,* Justin, *Gospel of Peter*). Apart from the last, however, these are reasons that were later devised to justify an already existing practice. The association with the resurrection is different. It comes to have a major role in Christian reflection, and some consider it a very early influence on the singling out and shaping of Sunday. There is no doubt that the association was natural, powerfully recalled in liturgical repetition, and that it could have motivated the establishment of a separate day of worship in the first few Christian decades. But there is no firm evidence that it did so.

The most extensive, and for our purposes most intriguing, argument about the origin of Sunday has been proposed by S. Bacchiochi. He rejects all purported early references to Sunday and argues that it was introduced to exploit the associations of the pagan day of the sun. This was done in Rome under the bishop Sixtus (ca. 115–125 CE), at the same time as the shift from Passover to Easter. That these two decisions were taken in Rome he surmises on two grounds. First, only the Roman church had the authority to generate and impose such significant changes. Second, there were unique tensions between Jews and Christians in Rome, which were exacerbated by mistrust of the Jews in the Roman government—thus providing the most natural setting for these essentially anti-Jewish moves. Later, after 135 CE, the newly appointed Gentile bishops in Judaea introduced these Roman practices in the wake of the Bar Cochba rebellion, which had soured the relationship of the Jews with both the Christian church and the Roman Empire. The overriding motive for the development of Sunday was thus a conscious desire to separate from Judaism. It had two sources: Jewish-Christian tensions in Rome and, later, hostility following the Bar Cochba rebellion.[53] For the purposes of an argument we have pursued about the significance of the Bar Cochba rebellion, this is an attractive thesis. It is also, unfortunately, flawed.

First, the earliest references to Sunday come before 115 CE, and none of them is associated with Rome. Second, the case for the supremacy of Rome at this stage is entirely without foundation in the historical sources, and there are, further, no grounds for supposing that hostility between Jews and Christians was especially intense there. Moreover, if the Christian Sunday had been peremptorily devised and subsequently imposed by Rome, we would surely have heard about it somewhere. Third, while association of Sunday with the pagan day of the sun eventually provided some exploitable analogies, the first hint of this is in Justin. Fourth, the argument for the substitution of Sunday for the Sabbath by the Jerusalem bishops is wholly an argument by analogy with the shift from Passover to Easter Sunday. But while there is some evidence for the latter, there is none whatsoever for the former.[54]

Bacchiochi has nevertheless incidentally pointed to a number of important issues. His analysis of the situation following the Bar Cochba rebellion concurs with what we concluded in chapter 1, namely, that it had a pronouncedly negative effect on Jewish-Christian relations. This provides an important context for the Passover/Easter conflict, but, in the absence of any other firm evidence we have to be cautious about drawing parallels with the shift from Sabbath to Sunday. Most important, however, is the focus on an anti-Jewish impulse—if not in the origination, then certainly in the justification, of the Christian Sunday. We have already surmised that the origins of Sunday had something to do with the internal needs of the Christian church—they needed time to worship and eat together and to attend to other aspects of their communal life. But this could have been done by revamping the Sabbath, and the insistence on promoting a separate day speaks of something more—a desire to separate or dissociate themselves from Judaism. In the early evidence, this comes through. Ignatius's warning against sabbatizers appears in the context of his profound concern about Gentile Judaizers who blur the boundaries between church and synagogue. The immediate context of the comments of the author of *Barnabas* is a frontal attack on the Sabbath, and these, in turn, are part of his broader polemic against the Jewish law. The less transparent allusion in the *Didache,* whether to a weekly or an annual Sunday, occurs in a document that promotes Christian practices in deliberate opposition to Judaism. When Justin speaks of Sunday worship it is partly to make the practice intelligible to pagan readers and to allay their suspicions about immoral practice in the church, but it is also presented in a context in which the superiority of Christianity over a moribund, ignorant, and politically suspect Judaism is clearly maintained (*I Apol*.32, 47, 49, 53, 63). Thus while we cannot be sure that anti-Judaism was a prime motive in establishing Sunday, because we cannot be sure precisely where or by whom it was done, when references to Sunday begin to crop up in Christian sources they are more frequently than not associated with a desire deliberately to dissociate from Judaism and to assert the superiority of Christian practice. And the conflict was doubtless sharpened by the unavoidable but awkward recognition that in abandoning the Sabbath, Christians were abandoning one of the fundamental Mosaic commands.[55]

FROM PASSOVER TO EASTER

We turn now to a closely allied issue—the recognition of Easter Sunday as a festival separate from the Jewish Passover. The appearance of two different versions of the Christian feast complicates the matter. The Quartodecimans celebrated their version of the Christian Pasch on the same day as Passover (the 14th of Nisan)—which fell on whatever day of the week was indicated by the Jewish lunar calendar—and were heavily influenced by elements of the Jewish feast. Most other early Christians also followed the lunar calendar, but shifted their festival to a fixed day—the Sunday following Passover.[56] Our interest is in where and why these two different forms of the Christian Pasch arose, the conflict between them, and what this indicates about their relationship to Judaism.

It is commonly agreed that the Quartodeciman celebration was the earlier of the two, and that it originated in the Palestinian Christian communities. Toward the end of the second century Polycrates, bishop of Ephesus, writing in defense of Quartodeciman practice in Asia Minor, traces the tradition back to the apostolic age:

> Therefore we keep the day undeviatingly, neither adding nor taking away, for in Asia great luminaries sleep. . . . Philip of the twelve apostles and two of his daughters. . . . John who lay on the Lord's breast. . . . Polycarp at Smyrna . . . . and Thraseas. . . . Sagaris. . . . Papirius and Melito. . . . All of these kept the fourteenth day of the passover according to the rule of faith. (Eusebius *Hist.eccl.*5.24.2–7)

The claim to an apostolic pedigree is clearly apologetic, but nevertheless detailed and impressive. Eusebius seems to take it at face value and knows of no equivalent claim from the proponents of Easter Sunday. That the Quartodecimans followed an ancient practice was recognized by their opponents (Irenaeus in Eusebius *Hist.eccl.*5.24.16; Theodoret in *Haer.Fab.Comp.* 3.4) and, even in the absence of any firm evidence, it is inherently likely that the Christian feast would develop out of the Jewish. It seems probable, therefore, that in the first century the only form of Christian paschal celebration was Quartodeciman, though how widespread it was we cannot tell.[57] Eventually it spread to Asia Minor, perhaps among those who were refugees from Judaea.[58]

A key piece of evidence for the transition from Quartodeciman dating to Easter Sunday is found in Eusebius *Hist.eccl.*5.24.14–17, quoting a letter from Irenaeus to Victor, bishop of Rome, in which he chides him for his precipitate action in excommunicating the Asian churches for their Quartodeciman convictions and points out that more radical disagreements were at an earlier stage peacefully resolved:[59]

> Among these too were the presbyters before Soter, who presided over the church of which you are now the leader, I mean Anicetus and Pius and Telesophorus and Sixtus. They did not themselves observe it, nor did they enjoin it on those who followed them, and though they did not keep it they were none the less at peace with those from the dioceses in which it was observed when they came to them, although to observe it was more objectionable to those who did not do so. . . . And when the blessed Polycarp was staying in Rome in the time of Anicetus . . . neither was Anicetus able to persuade Polycarp not to observe it . . . nor did Polycarp persuade Anicetus to observe it. . . . And they parted from each other in peace, for the peace of the whole church was kept both by those who observed and by those who did not.

The recurring references to observing (*terein*) and not observing (*me terein*) are ambiguous. It seems clear that those who observe are the Quartodecimans and that not observing among the Roman Christians means, at least, that they did not share this practice. The question is whether "not observing" means that they had an alternative to the Quartodeciman Pasch or no celebration at all. Some think the dispute was over the meeting of two different paschal traditions—the Roman Easter Sunday and the Quartodeciman dating from Asia Minor—and they accordingly date the introduction of Easter Sunday in Rome earlier in the second century.[60] This view depends, however, on *terein* and *me terein* being technical terms for the observance or nonobservance of the Quartodeciman feast, a view for which there is little philological support. It seems more likely that Irenaeus is implying that before the time of Soter (i.e., before 165 CE) there was no fixed paschal celebration in Rome, so that when Quartodecimans like Polycarp visited there was a more serious divergence in practice than in the time of Victor when the contrast was merely between two different types of Pasch.[61]

If the observance of Easter Sunday was not known in Rome until late in the second century, it seems unlikely that it originated in the apostolic era, since we would expect it to have been more widely known and more readily accepted as one authoritative tradition in major Christian communities.[62] This points to a relatively late date, sometime in the first half of the second century.[63] The most intriguing piece of evidence in this regard is a statement by Epiphanius:

> The [paschal] controversy arose after the time of the exodus of the bishops of the circumcision and it has continued until our own time. (*Adv.Haer.*70.10)

The change from a Jewish to a Gentile line of bishops in Jerusalem occurred ca. 135 CE, after the banishment of Jews from Jerusalem following the Bar Cochba rebellion. Epiphanius considers 135 CE—or, to be more precise, the period immediately after that—to be a critical date in the paschal controversy, but he does not explain why. He could be suggesting that the retiring bishops took their existing practice (presumably Quartodeciman) out into a world that kept Easter Sunday or no Pasch at all. The problem then would have been the diffusion of Palestinian practice into other parts of the Christian world. Or the allusion may be to the actions of the incoming Gentile bishops, who abandoned the existing Quartodeciman practice in favor of Easter Sunday. But, in that case, was Easter Sunday introduced from elsewhere, or was it first devised in Jerusalem? The need to sever connections with the Jews who were, in Jerusalem, at this point an ignominiously defeated and outlawed people could have provided the motive in either case. We are not told where the Gentile bishops came from: they may have been from the Jerusalem area, since the population was not wholly Jewish, or they may have been brought in from elsewhere. In either case, if they brought the Easter Sunday tradition with them we must assume that the controversy arose in Jerusalem because it was there that the two existing traditions first came into conflict.[64] As we have seen, however, there are few if any secure early references to Easter Sunday.

On the other hand, the notion that the Gentile bishops devised Easter Sunday as an alternative to the Quartodeciman festival in the aftermath of the Bar Cochba rebellion has two advantages: it provides us with a palpable motive for the establishment of Easter Sunday, whose origins are otherwise only vaguely surmised; and it explains why the church in Rome could get well into the second century without any paschal feast: because the form that they were eventually to adopt was only lately devised.[65] Assuming that the weekly Sunday was already known, it would not have been a large step to elevate one Sunday into a distinctly Christian annual festival. It would, of course, have provided an especially appropriate way to celebrate Jesus' resurrection.[66] But in terms of both chronology and content the Quartodeciman celebration made the Christians almost indistinguishable from the Jews, at least to an outsider. A distinctly Christian festival, therefore, had the advantage of clearly marking them off from the Jews—a move that was, in the circumstances, presumably inspired by a mixture of religious antipathy vis-à-vis the Jews and political necessity vis-à-vis the Romans.

When we turn from dating to content, we are less well informed for the early period.[67] In common with the Jews, the Quartodecimans celebrated on the 14th of Nisan, read and expounded the biblical stories of Passover, and, in the early years at least, awaited the arrival—or, as Christians would have it, the return—of the Messiah.[68] At least two things, however, distinguished them: first, during the time of the Passover meal on the 14th of Nisan, a fast (broken early in the morning with a Eucharist), which was both a memorial of the death of Jesus and a vicarious fast for the Jews who put him to death (*Didascalia* 21); and second, a focus on Jesus as the once and for all true paschal lamb (cf. 1 Cor 5:7).[69] In some sources the fast, it should be noted, while associating the Jews with the death of Jesus at the same time speaks of them as brothers and holds out hope for their repentance. The mood is one of sadness and concern, rather than of bitterness and recrimination.

Altogether the Quartodeciman celebration was a curious mix, but one that we have come to expect. There was on the one hand commonality with Judaism in terms of the timing and much of the content of their festival, including a fast that viewed the Jews as erring brothers to be pitied rather than despised. On the other hand the fast laid responsibility on the Jews for Jesus' death, transformed the Jewish meal of rejoicing into a solemn ritual of abstinence, and was followed by a Christian Eucharist, which enhanced the remembrance of Jesus' death. In other words, the Quartodeciman Pasch exhibited both dependence on and differentiation from its Jewish counterpart. Part of the process of differentiation was the willful, often polemical assertion of independence from the parent tradition. This tendency was muted in at least some early forms of Quartodeciman celebration, but a relatively benign tone was not guaranteed—as the example of Melito will soon make clear.

The form of Easter Sunday worship was probably dependent on established Quartodeciman practice to begin with. Three things, however, would immediately have appeared distinctive: first, and most obviously, the choice of a fixed day, dependent on the Jewish calendar but not coinciding with the Jewish feast; second, an increasing emphasis on Jesus' resurrection, which would follow naturally on the change of day, especially if Easter Sunday was designed to be a climactic expression of the themes repeated in the weekly Sunday;[70] and third, the disappearance of the vicarious fast for the Jews, which is nowhere associated with Easter Sunday. These changes would have encouraged divorce in place of a previously intimate relationship. The motives, as we have seen, would have been mixed: the desire to focus on a memorial of Jesus' resurrection; the reaction to religious antipathy engendered by the Bar Cochba conflict; and the pragmatic need to sever connections with Judaism if the Jerusalem community was to survive.

The dispute between Victor and the Christians in Asia Minor was not the end of the matter, and, though it goes beyond the second century, a brief look at subsequent disputes provides a useful perspective. As we move into the third and fourth centuries there is evidence for continuing paschal disputes and an increasing hostility toward those who mingled Jewish and Christian practice. Best known, perhaps, is the decree of the Council of Nicaea (325 CE) and the accompanying letter from Constantine:

> All the brethren who are in the East who formerly celebrated Easter with the Jews will henceforth keep it at the same time as the Romans, with us and with all those who from ancient times have celebrated the feast at the same time as us.[71]

> It appeared an unworthy thing that in the celebration of this most holy feast we should follow the practice of the Jews, who have impiously defiled their hands with enormous sin and are, therefore, deservedly afflicted with blindness of soul. . . . Let us then have nothing in common with the detestable crowd of Jews; for we have received from our Saviour a different way. (Eusebius *Life of Const.*3.18–19)

Whether this and similar evidence refers to a continuing Quartodeciman controversy,[72] or to a new dispute over the use of Jewish and non-Jewish calendrical calculations,[73] remains unclear. More important for our purposes than a precise demarcation of the disputes is the evidence for a persistent entanglement of Passover and Easter and the various anti-Jewish sentiments it provoked. Sometimes this was the result of long-established tradition (Quartodecimans) and sometimes the result of understandable confusion about the relationship of the two among ordinary Christians who lived in close contact with Jews. Thus Aphrahat, speaking of the situation in Syria, notes how "greatly troubled are the minds of foolish and unintelligent folk concerning this great day of festival, as to how they should understand and observe it."[74] The issue could become inflamed, as it did in Chrysostom's Antioch, when Judaizing Christians expressed their attraction to Judaism by following the Jewish calendar and, even more remarkably, attending the synagogue for Jewish feasts.[75] To counter this threat a number of arguments were devised, which range from supersessionary theologies, through denial of the legality of the Jewish Passover, to outright vilification. The following points are typical:

—The true meaning of the Passover is to be found in the sacrifice of Jesus as the Paschal lamb (Justin *Dial.* 40.2,46.2; Aphrahat *Dem.*12; Chrysostom *Adv.Jud.*3; *Chron.Pasch.*6–7).

—Pasch is for Christians a weekly (i.e., eucharistic) as well as an annual feast (Aphrahat *Dem.*12; Chrysostom *Adv.Jud.*3).

—The Jews cannot legally celebrate Passover, because Jerusalem is destroyed (Aphrahat *Dem.*12; Chrysostom *Adv.Jud.*3) and the priesthood gone (Chrysostom *Adv.Jud.*3).

—The precise date of Pasch is insignificant, because for Christians the key day is always Friday in remembrance of Jesus' passion (Aphrahat *Dem.*3) or because it cannot at any rate be securely fixed (Chrysostom *Adv.Jud.*3).

—Christians who follow the Jewish reckoning or, worse still, join in the Jewish feast give prestige to Jewish rather than Christian leaders, confuse and divide the church, and consort with the killers of Christ: "After you have gone off and shared with those who shed the blood of Christ, how is it that you do not shudder to come back here and share his sacred banquet, to partake of his precious blood?" (Chrysostom *Adv.Jud.*2.3.5).

From this brief survey we might draw the following conclusions. Whether we consider the dating, the form, or the rationale for the Christian Easter, there seems to be an underlying anti-Jewish motif. The Pasch, it seems, presented the church with a particularly thorny problem as it strove to establish an identity distinct from Judaism. Chronological coincidence, ritual indebtedness, and supersessionary convictions combined to present a complex situation. The earliest and simplest move, found among the Quartodecimans, was to reverse the ritual pattern—fasting when the Jews feasted and celebrating joyfully when they ate unleavened bread. The shift to Sunday from the 14th of Nisan was a more overt break. True, it may have been natural to combine two feast days that celebrated the resurrection, though early Easter traditions seem to focus more on Jesus' death than on his resurrection, but the desire to disentangle the Christian from the Jewish feast was almost certainly a prominent motive. The third and fourth centuries witness the appearance of conciliar decisions banning association with the Jews and theological schemes that appropriate Passover traditions for the church and deny them to the Jews. Passover/Easter was, at the best of times, a sensitive issue whenever Jews and Christians came into contact, and it could quickly become a cause of bitter dispute and inflamed rhetoric when, as in fourth-century Antioch, it was one of many features of Jewish life that attracted the attention and allegiance of Christians. Hovering all the while was the potentially explosive issue of Jewish responsibility for Jesus' death, recalled sometimes in a vicarious fast and at all times by the Passion stories, and always liable to flare up when relationships soured. And this, quite naturally, leads us to turn our attention to Melito.[76]

MELITO'S PASCHAL HOMILY

"Marred by cavalier and superficial use of evidence, as well as by a deplorable harshness of tone" is one judgment on an article by a Jewish scholar that castigates Melito in no uncertain terms as the author of the accusation of deicide.[77] Harsh words they may be but, as we shall note, scarcely harsher than the words of Melito himself. Moreover, the comment is made by the author of several tightly argued and persuasive articles about Melito and the best modern edition of the *Peri Pascha,* who nevertheless relegates the problem of Melito and the Jews to a passing reference to "the power of the Jewish community in civic life in Sardis," in order to explain the parallels between the *Peri Pascha* and the Jewish Passover Haggadah, and a laconic footnote to the effect that "Melito shares with the *Evangelium Petri* the tendency to attribute the crucifixion directly and exclusively to Israel."[78]

S. G. Hall is not alone in this regard for, as A. T. Kraabel noted in 1971, a whole generation of scholars ignored the anti-Jewish polemic in Melito— a fact for which he could provide no ready explanation.[79] A partial explanation is doubtless to be found in the elementary hermeneutical observation that what is derived from a text depends to a great extent on the questions brought to it. For Christian scholars whose interest has been in the theology and liturgical practices of Melito and his community, and for whom the appropriation of Jewish traditions and the assertion of Jewish obduracy and perfidy are natural and necessary concomitants of Christian self-definition, Melito's view of Judaism was neither an important nor a problematic aspect of his work. Yet, when 72 of the 105 sections of *Peri Pascha* (1–45, 72–99) deal implicitly or explicitly either with the status of Israel or the charge of deicide, the scholarly silence still remains somewhat puzzling. A notable exception is the sensitive discussion by J. Blank of the charge of deicide but, as we shall see below, a neglected but equally important component of Melito's view of Judaism is the typological exegesis of the Passover traditions at the beginning of the homily.[80]

A consideration of Melito's view of Judaism falls naturally into two parts, corresponding to two of the main sections of his work: the typological exposition of the exodus story (1–45) and the charge of deicide (72–99). Our purpose will be to consider both what is explicitly stated and what is implied about the nature and status of Judaism and the Jews. An attempt to explain Melito's position will be reserved for a later section.

Pasches Old and New: From Type to Reality

Melito's homily, preceded by a reading of the story of the exodus,[81] opens with the bold declaration that the mystery of the Pasch is about to be revealed. Superficially the story is clear—"how the sheep is sacrificed, and how the people is saved and how Pharaoh is scourged through the mystery" (lines 3–5)—but its true and deeper meaning is a "mystery." The word *mysterion*, used several times, not only recalls the terminology of the mystery cults but also prepares for the mystagogic flights that characterize Melito's Christian exposition of the Pasch.[82]

For Melito the Passover is, most profoundly, a christological archetype; but Melito's ruminations on this theme, while frequently repetitious, introduce a number of subtle variations designed to reinforce this central message. At the heart of Melito's typological exegesis lies a contrast between the old and the new Pasch, expressed typically in pairs of contrasting terms: *typos/aletheia, parabole/hermeneia, nomos/euaggelion* (or *logos*). His use of terminology is flexible, so that even the pairs do not remain fixed and new terms can be used to express one or the other side of the contrast. Sometimes a distinction is drawn between the events and the words of the past:

> Whatever is said, and done finds its comparison
> What is said, a comparison [*parabole*]
> What is done, a prefiguration [*protyposeos*]
> In order that, just as what is done is demonstrated through the prefiguration
> So also what is spoken may be elucidated through the comparison.
>
> (lines 219–23)

Broadly speaking, as Daniélou notes,[83] this distinction accords with Melito's use of Jewish biblical traditions: events and people are seen as types and words as promises; type is to reality as promise is to fulfillment—much like the distinction found in Justin (*Dial.* 110:2; 114:1, using *typos/logos*).

The key to Melito's exposition of the scriptures is found in a bold and unusually self-conscious statement of hermeneutical principle:

> This is just what happens in the case of a preliminary structure:
> it does not arise as a finished work,
>   but because of what is going to be visible through its image acting as a model.
> For this reason a preliminary sketch is made of the future thing
>   out of wax or of clay or of wood,
> in order that what will soon arise
>   taller in height,
>   and stronger in power,

and beautiful in form,
and rich in its construction,
may be seen through a small and perishable sketch.

But when that of which it is the model arises,
that which once bore the image of the future thing
is itself destroyed as growing useless
having yielded to what is truly real the image of it;
and what once was precious becomes worthless
when what is truly precious has been revealed.

For to each belongs a proper season:
a proper time for the model,
a proper time for the material,
a proper time for the reality.

(lines 224–44)

The analogy between model (*typos*) and reality (*aletheia*), between blueprint and artifact, contains *in nuce* Melito's view of Israel's past and the Christian present. All the things of the past—the great figures and events of Israel's history and the promises of their scriptures—are to Christianity as model is to finished product; and, Melito concludes, when the reality appears or the artifact is made, the model that was once "precious" and "marvellous" becomes worthless, defunct, and void:

The model then was precious before the reality,
and the parable was marvellous before the interpretation;
that is, the people was precious before the church arose,
and the law was marvellous before the gospel was elucidated.

But when the church arose
and the gospel took precedence,
the model was made void, conceding its power to the reality,
and the law was fulfilled, conceding its power to the gospel.

In the same way as the model is made void, conceding the image to the truly
    real,
and the parable is fulfilled, being elucidated by the interpretation,
just so also the law was fulfilled when the gospel was elucidated,
and the people was made void when the church arose;
and the model was abolished when the Lord was revealed,
and today, things once precious have become worthless,
since the really precious things have been revealed.

(lines 266–79)

Melito's claims are confident and remarkably unambivalent. Not for him are the qualms and uncertainties of earlier Christian writers who tried to balance Christian appropriation of Jewish traditions with some sense of their abiding value—the result, no doubt, partly of the different circumstances under which they wrote. The implications for Melito's view of Judaism are to some extent self-evident, but it is worth dwelling on them momentarily.

In his meditation on the stories of Israel's past, Melito concerns himself with the broad sweep of events rather than with minor details and with their plain meaning rather than their allegorical significance. And, though christological typology is at the heart of Melito's understanding, not all the retelling is done with an eye on its typological significance. A certain relish for dramatic embellishment of the biblical narrative is shown in the imaginative portrayal of the horrors that befell the Egyptians (lines 93–212): the swift and implacable grip of Death in the face of desperate but ineffective ploys of the firstborn to evade it, and the bewilderment and grief of mourning parents who, throughout Egypt, become a robe of wailing surrounding the grief-stricken Pharaoh. But this is not merely for dramatic effect. In the sections dealing with the death of Jesus (72ff.) the Jews act out a role roughly analogous to that of the Egyptians in sections 1–42: as salvation was miraculously wrought for the Jews, surrounded by their enemies, by the blood of the Passover lamb, so salvation was miraculously wrought for the Christians by Jesus, surrounded by his enemies, in the true paschal sacrifice. Who were Jesus' enemies? Clearly, the Jews. For Melito the tragedy of the Jews was that in the midst of celebrating their own saving event they were, by an ironic twist, responsible for the death of the true Paschal Lamb. Those who were once the saved become the enemies of salvation. The interplay of these ideas is seen in the following:

> But while the sheep is being slain
> and the Pascha is being eaten
> and the mystery is being performed
> and the people is making merry
> and Israel is being marked,
> Then came the angel to *strike Egypt,*
> the uninitiated in the mystery,
> the non-participating in the Pascha,
> the unmarked with the blood,
> the unguarded by the Spirit,
> the hostile,
> the faithless.

(lines 92–103)

Here, in language that echoes the Christian rites of initiation and unction, Egypt's fate anticipates that of those who do not participate in the Christian mysteries, especially the Jews. Likewise the fate of the Jews who were responsible for Jesus' death is described in a series of couplets which contrast their conscious remembrance of the old deeds of salvation with their ignorance of the new ones being accomplished in their midst. The language is strongly reminiscent of that used to describe the fate of the Egyptians:

So you quaked at the assault of foes;
you were not terrified in the presence of the Lord,
you did not lament over the Lord,
so you lamented over your firstborn;
you did not tear your clothes when the Lord was hung,
so you tore them over those who were slain;
you forsook the Lord,
you were not found by him;
you did not accept the Lord,
you were not pitied by him;
you dashed down the Lord,
you were dashed to the ground.
And you lie dead,
but he has risen from the dead
and gone up to the heights of heaven.

(lines 732–47)

It is not altogether farfetched, therefore, to see an analogy between Melito's view of the "enemies of the Jews" in sections 1–45 and the "enemies of Jesus" in sections 72–99. To some extent the description of the one spills over into the description of the other, and it is one of several links between these two parts of the homily that suggest a degree of interdependence between the claim that Christians rather than Jews are the inheritors of the traditions of Israel and the insistence on Jewish responsibility for Jesus' death.

It is worth noting, secondly, how Melito's Christology affects his assessment of Israel's past. The typological foreshadowing of Jesus in the scriptures is clearly central, but Melito also resorts to a form of modalism in which Christ is seen to be not only prefigured by, but also a participant in, the events of Israel's past. Not only was Abel murdered, Isaac bound, Joseph sold, Moses exposed, and David persecuted (lines 415–24), but Christ too was murdered, bound, sold, exposed, and persecuted with them (lines 479–88). The shift from typological prefiguration to modalist participation in Melito's fluid Christology strengthens the claim to Israel's tradition while it compounds Israel's guilt in rejecting Christ, for he was not just prefigured in their past, he *was* their past.

Thirdly, while the main purpose of *Peri Pascha* is to appropriate Jewish Passover traditions for Christian belief and practice—to show how Christ is the true Lamb and the Christian feast the true Passover—Melito does not stop there. He moves inexorably from a concentration on the foundational saving event of Judaism to sweeping claims about their other distinctive attributes. It is apparent in the lines quoted above (266–79) that the once chosen people have been superseded by the church, and the law by the gospel. The succeeding lines tell a similar story and illustrate the ease with which Melito moves from the one to the others:

Once, the slaying of the sheep was precious,
but it is worthless now because of the life of the Lord;
the death of the sheep was precious,
but it is worthless now because of the salvation of the Lord;
the blood of the sheep was precious,
but it is worthless now because of the Spirit of the Lord;
a speechless lamb was precious,
but it is worthless now because of the spotless Son;
the temple below was precious,
but it is worthless now because of the Christ above.

The Jerusalem below was precious,
but it is worthless now because of *the Jerusalem above;*
the narrow inheritance was precious,
but it is worthless now because of the widespread bounty.

(lines 280–93)

The holy city goes the way of the Passover, the people, and the law—deemed worthless (*atimia*) because superseded. What was once the particular inheritance of the Jews is overtaken by the universal bounty of the Christian faith. And thus the status of the Passover epitomizes the status of Jewish tradition as a whole.

It is worth noting, finally, that Melito's estimation of Jewish tradition is not entirely negative. There is no suggestion, such as we find in *Barnabas,* that the law has no value in itself and was never intended for literal observance or, as in Justin, that the law was given to Israel because they were too wicked to receive a "spiritual law." For the period prior to the Christian revelation Melito assigns positive value to law, Temple, holy city, and people: they were "precious" and "marvellous." When there is nothing but the model or the preliminary sketch, they are to be highly valued. When the reality or artifact appears, however, the model and sketch have no value: they are "abolished" (*luo*), "worthless" (*atimia*), "made void" (*kenoo*), "fulfilled" (*pleroo*), or "useless" (*achrestos*). The terminology is varied but the conclusion is singular: Judaism and all it signifies is defunct. The positive assessment belongs solely to Israel's past, the negative to their present. This stark contrast between two epochs in Israel's history is perhaps less dramatic in practice than in theory, that is to say, not all of the old is discarded out of hand: a reading of Ex.12 is, after all, the setting for the homily and the law can still function as christological promise. But insofar as the attributes of Judaism have continuing value it is by absorption into the Christian reality alone.

Israel and the Death of God

If for no other reason, Melito is notable as the first Christian writer to make an unambiguous accusation of deicide. Between the "mystery of the Pascha" (sections 1–45) and the death of Jesus (sections 72f.), Melito reflects upon

the Fall and the arrival of sin and death in its wake (sections 46–71). We
might expect the meditation on Jesus' death to be related to what precedes,
and, in fact, consideration of the benefits of Christ's death takes up the last
forty lines or so of the homily (lines 763–804). The bulk of it, however,
consists of an impassioned denunciation of the crime of Israel in rejecting
and killing her God (lines 551–762). The proportions reveal where Melito's
real interest lay. The following excerpts are typical of the tone, content, and
powerful rhetorical effects of the final section:

> O lawless Israel, what is this unprecedented crime you committed,
> thrusting your Lord among unprecedented sufferings, your Sovereign,
> who formed you,
> who made you,
> who honoured you,
> who called you "Israel"?
>
> But you did not turn out to be "Israel";
> you did not "see God,"
> you did not recognize the Lord.
> You did not know, Israel,
> that he is the firstborn of God,
> who was begotten *before the morning star,*
> who tinted the light,
> who lit up the day,
> who divided off the darkness,
> who fixed the first marker,
> who hung the earth,
> who controlled the deep,
> who spread out the firmament,
> who arrayed the world,
> who fitted the stars in heaven,
> who lit up the luminaries,
> who *made the angels* in heaven,
> who established the thrones there,
> who formed man upon earth.
>
> (lines 582–607)
>
> An unprecedented murder has occurred in the middle of Jerusalem, in the city
>   of the law,
> in the city of the Hebrews,
> in the city of the prophets,
> in the city accounted just.
>
> And who has been murdered? Who is the murderer?
> I am ashamed to say and I am obliged to tell.
> For if the murder had occurred at night,
> or if he had been slain in a desert place,
> one might have had recourse to silence.

But now, in the middle of the street and in the middle of the city,
at the middle of the day for all to see,
has occurred a just man's unjust murder.

Just so he has been lifted up on a tall tree,
and a notice has been attached to show who has been murdered.
Who is this? To say is hard, and not to say is too terrible.

Yet listen, trembling at him for whom the earth quaked.
He who hung the earth is hanging;
he who fixed the heavens has been fixed;
he who fastened the universe has been fastened to a tree;
the Sovereign has been insulted;
the God has been murdered;
the King of Israel has been put to death
by an Israelite right hand.

(lines 694–716)

The notion that the Jews were responsible for the death of Jesus had a long
pedigree in Christian thinking, stretching back at least to the early accounts
of Jesus' Passion. Prior to Melito, however, no one had made the accusation
with such boldness and dramatic skill, and no one had transformed the
"crime" of the Jews from responsibility for the death of Jesus to responsibility for the death of God. It is this that provokes Melito's incomprehension
and horror and that inspires his denunciation, but he develops a number of
subsidiary themes to vary the rhetorical effect, bolster the accusation against
Israel, and compound her guilt.

Melito uses the term "Israel," for example, without discrimination: it refers to all Jews. No distinction is made between leaders and people or between Palestinian and diaspora Jews as in some earlier Christian writings,
nor apparently between Jews of the past and the present. The crime is the
crime of all Jews. Some take the sting out of Melito's language by supposing
that "Israel" refers solely to Jews contemporary with Jesus, who were responsible for his death: "Nothing would be more mistaken than to reproach
the bishop of Sardis with a low-class and malicious anti-Judaism. . . . The
Jews he has in mind and accuses are not the Jews of his time, much less the
Jews of his diocese, but the Jews of long ago, the Jews of the first Good
Friday in Jerusalem."[84] Despite the confidence of his assertion Rengstorf
provides no evidence to support it. In its favor we might note that most of
what Melito says about "Israel" relates specifically to the events surrounding
Jesus' trial and death, but in view of the subject matter of this section of
the homily anything else would have been anachronistic. Cataloging the
misdeeds of the Jews, especially those surrounding the death of Jesus, is
precisely the point of sections 72f. It might also be argued that, for Melito,
in a sense there was no real "Israel" to address after these decisive events:
she was no longer "Israel" because she did not "see God" (lines 589–91);[85]
she had been "dashed to the ground" and "lies dead" (lines 744–45; cf.

662–64). However, it seems improbable that this theologoumenon would lead Melito or his community entirely to ignore the existence of contemporary Jewish communities, not least in their own city, who were in some senses successors to those who "murdered God," even if he did refuse to grant them the title "Israel." There are, moreover, places where "Israel" is addressed in a manner that suggests something more than a rhetorical flourish aimed at a deceased generation, and in which the direct form of address suggests that the boundaries between past and present are consciously blurred: Ungrateful Israel, come and take issue with me about your ingratitude (lines 634–35; cf. 73–74,519–31).

> Value for me the withered hand
> which he restored to the body;
> Value for me those *blind from birth*
> to whom he brought light with a word;
> Value for me those who lay dead
> whom he raised from the dead *already four days* old.
>
> (lines 651–56)

> Bitter for you is the feast of unleavened bread.
>
> (line 678)

It is unlikely, of course, that Jews are being directly addressed, though it is not impossible that they would have heard reports of the gist of his message. But is it likely that he and his audience would in these moments have thought solely of the Jews of the first century who killed Jesus, and not of their Jewish contemporaries? It is possible but unlikely.

The guilt of the Jews is underlined in a number of other ways. Their malevolence contrasts starkly with the non-Jews who eagerly admired and worshiped the Lord:

> But you cast the opposite vote against your Lord.
> For him whom the gentiles worshipped
> and uncircumcised men admired
> and foreigners glorified,
> over whom even Pilate *washed his hands.*
>
> (lines 671–76)

The action of the Jews is cause not to lament, that they rejected him *despite* his good deeds, but to exaggerate further their strange and perverse behavior: they rejected Jesus *because* he was just, *because* he did works of compassion (lines 505ff., 545ff.). When it came to the point of death, not only did the Jews participate vigorously to inflict the greatest possible agony, they also had the temerity to crucify him in broad daylight in the midst of the holy city (lines 693ff.), while they themselves joyfully celebrated their Passover (lines 566ff.). And lest they should attempt to justify their actions by arguing that they were merely the instruments of divine necessity (cf. Justin

Dial. 95:2–3), Melito counters with the claim that it should have been accomplished by the hands of godless and uncircumcised foreigners and not
by the hands of his elect (lines 537–45).

Finally we can again note the effect of Melito's Christology, which is more
fully developed in sections 82–90 than elsewhere. As before, Jesus is seen
to be a participant in as well as prefigured by the history of Israel. Now,
however, he is identified with the God of Israel. Thus Israel rejects and cru-
cifies not only a Christ, whose significance was deeply embedded in their
own past, but also their God, the author of creation and of their election
and salvation. In rejecting Jesus they eschew their own past and their own
God, and thus forfeit the right to be his people. For their shocking ingratitude (lines 635ff.) they are rewarded with bitterness (lines 680ff.) and, ultimately, death (lines 744ff.). The conclusion is entirely consistent with, and
may well have influenced, the hermeneutic that operates earlier in the
homily.

The first and the third parts of Melito's homily are thus inextricably
linked. In the one we find a radical and rigorous supersessionary claim: the
Jews, as the erstwhile people of God, are no longer; all that survives of their
tradition is of positive value only insofar as it is absorbed into the Christian
reality. In the other we find the explanation: in rejecting Christ, the Jews
had rejected their God and he, in turn, had rejected them. The two parts are
mutually supportive and equally important for Melito's view of Judaism.

The Context

It is no simple matter to explain Melito's views. In part this is because he
writes not only in the context of inherited paschal disputes among Christians but, more importantly, after a lengthy period of Jewish-Christian conflict. When we add to this his personal interests and skills, it makes for a
complex situation that needs to be carefully delineated.

First, it is obvious but necessary to note that a number of the implicitly
anti-Jewish themes are the reverse side of Melito's attempt to articulate his
definition of Christianity. The long-standing adoption of many of the beliefs
and structures of Judaism and, above all, of their scriptures meant that it
was virtually impossible to assert a Christian understanding of salvation
without implicitly denying the Jewish equivalent. Between them there was
bound to be a degree of animus that was lacking in their conflict with other
competitors. Christians and Stoics, for example, despite some common
ground, offered two distinct and discrete views of the world; but Christians
and Jews offered variant interpretations of the same basic tradition. The
closer they were, the more intense was the competition. It is natural, too,
that with the well-established split between most Christians and Jews and
the increasing confidence of the claims of a Gentile church, the ambivalence
and anxiety of a Paul or a Matthew in coming to terms with his Jewish roots
should be replaced by a more explicit and categorical rejection of the claims

of Judaism. What we find in Melito can be partly understood in this context, especially the exegetical procedures in sections 1–45, but there are features of this exegesis as well as the damning charge of deicide that require further explanation.

Second, Melito was also an accomplished writer and orator. Tertullian apparently considered him to have an *elegans et declamatorium ingenium* (Jerome *De viris illustribus*, 24), and the *Peri Pascha* itself provides ample evidence of his rhetorical and dramatic skills.[86] There are clear signs of biblical and Jewish influence in the structure and mannerisms of the homily,[87] but the more telling stylistic parallels are to be found in the writings of the Asian school associated with the "Second Sophistic"—especially in Maximus of Tyre—and from this evidence Wifstrand concludes that "the main impression made by the homily of Melito is that of a genuine Greek rhetorical production."[88] Melito's rhetorical skills contribute significantly to the tone, if not the content, of his work. Scarcely a paragraph of *Peri Pascha* is formulated without resort to a formal rhetorical device designed to dramatize and enhance its effect. Excessive dependence on such devices can create a somewhat cluttered effect, and Melito is occasionally open to this charge, but in general he uses them skillfully and to good advantage. The homily is a work of art as well as a work of theological reflection. Would his contrast between Jewish and Christian Passovers have been so stark without his fondness for antithesis, paronomasia, rhetorical question, and exclamation? And would his denunciation of the Jews for the murder of Jesus have been so insistent and exaggerated without his love of repetition, anaphora, and oxymoron and his imaginative capacity to turn the tables on Jesus' accusers by putting the Jews on trial? In both cases, probably not. His skill with language, rhetorical device, rhythm, and phrasing sometimes runs away with him, with the result that contrasts are often bolder and denunciations more vehement and colorful than they might otherwise have been. Nevertheless, there is more to Melito than mere rhetorical excess.

Melito was, thirdly, a Quartodeciman. Eusebius (*Hist.eccl.* 5.24.2–6) quotes a letter in which Polycrates, the aged bishop of Ephesus, defends (ca. 195 CE) the paschal tradition of the Asian churches.[89] It lists the Asian luminaries who had been faithful to this tradition, among them:

> Melito the eunuch whose whole career was in the Holy Spirit, who lies at Sardis awaiting the visitation from heaven when he shall rise from the dead. These all kept the fourteenth day of the Pascha in accordance with the Gospel, in no way deviating, but following the rule of faith.

From this we can infer that Melito was a celibate (less likely a full eunuch) and a man of notable prophetic gifts. Eusebius assumes (*Hist.eccl.*4.26.1) that he was the bishop, which was probably, but not certainly, the case.[90] Most important for our discussion is that Melito was a Quartodeciman. There are some differences between Melito's *Peri Pascha* and other Quartodeciman traditions that we have looked at. There is little emphasis on eschatological expectation and no hint of a fast for the Jews. Indeed the tone of sections 72ff. moves in quite the opposite direction—loading blame on the Jews rather than longing for their salvation. It is nevertheless clear that while both the Quartodeciman and Roman practices were affected by their association with the weekly and annual festivals of the Jews, the closer association of the Quartodecimans with Jewish practice raised an acute problem: in what way was their Passover to be distinguished from that of the Jews? By insisting on the same dating as the Jews, were they not, in effect, Judaizing (one of the main objections, apparently, of their opponents)? The accusation would be as natural as the response: a paradoxical determination to distance the Christian from the Jewish festival, the new from the old, the church from Israel, in order to show that their ostensibly closer connection with Judaism was a case of the "Christianizing" of Judaism rather than the reverse.

Kraabel has noted that none of the other evidence for Quartodeciman practices provides an analogy to, or a theological motive for, the vituperative attack on Israel in sections 72ff., and suggests that Melito's local circumstances provide the only plausible explanation.[91] Even so, there is no reason to deny the influence of Melito's Quartodeciman commitments on other parts of the homily, especially sections 1–45, where the greater intimacy with Judaism may have led, paradoxically, to a firmer rejection of it. Moreover, our other evidence for Quartodeciman practice is very slight and mostly later than Melito, so that he may not have been atypical in the second century—that is, if we suppose that Quartodecimans necessarily took a uniform view of Judaism.

Fourth, the positive side of Kraabel's assertion is much more important. It is clear both from the reports of Josephus (*Ant.* 14.235; 16.171) and from extensive archaeological excavations "that the Sardis Jewish community was a large one, with a degree of wealth, social status and political power and that the synagogue, on a choice location in the centre of the Roman City, is by far the largest discovered anywhere in the ancient world."[92] The Jewish community was probably active in the rebuilding of Sardis after a disastrous earthquake in 17 BCE, a process that took some one hundred and fifty years, and several of their leaders appear to have been active members of the city council.[93] They were thus a highly visible element in the population, a force to be reckoned with, and it would have been virtually impossible for Christians to ignore them when attempting to establish their own identity and political standing. This provides an additional reason for doubting Rengstorf's conclusion, quoted earlier, that for Melito "Israel" referred exclusively to first-century Jews. Apart from the evidence of the text itself, where the boundaries between past and present are blurred and where appeals are apparently made to contemporary as well as to past generations of Jews, the political and social realities of life in Sardis suggest quite the opposite. Only when the text is read in isolation from its context can an argument like Rengstorf's appear plausible.

We have no explicit evidence to show how Jews and Christians in Sardis viewed each other. Eusebius records (*Hist.eccl.*4.26.14) that Melito paid a visit to Jerusalem in order to obtain precise information about the number and arrangement of the books of the Jewish Bible, partly as a favor for a fellow Christian who was eager both for this information and for a collection of "extracts from both the law and the prophets concerning the Saviour and all our faith."[94] The list Melito gives accords closely with the canon established by the sages at Yavneh. Doubtless natural curiosity and piety also motivated Melito's trip—some call him the first Christian pilgrim to the Holy Land—but it is strange that he should need to travel there for information that presumably was available from the Jewish community in Sardis. Is it possible that they, as a diaspora community, knew only the LXX? This seems unlikely, even if it was the version they used most. More probable is that it indicates a lack of contact with the Jews in Sardis, perhaps due to mutual hostility which discouraged the informal exchange of information—the sort of hostility in fact that, from the Christian side, comes to expression in the homily itself.

It is not improbable that some of the Christians were converts from Judaism or descendants of such. There may also have been traffic in the other direction. As we have seen, there is evidence that Gentile Christians, including those in Asia Minor, were fascinated by and attracted to Judaism.[95] There is no hint of such a problem in the *Peri Pascha,* but a situation where church and synagogue, while separate entities, found occasional traffic flowing in one or both directions, and where there was the additional need to defend Quartodeciman practice yet refute the charge of Judaizing, would go a long way toward explaining Melito's hostility toward the Jews. Quite apart from this, however, it is clear that the very existence of a large, visible, and influential Jewish community in Sardis would implicitly challenge any Christian claims to the traditions of Israel, encourage a strident tone, and make it most unlikely that Melito's communities, unless specifically instructed (which they are not), would exclude from the term "Israel" all Jews except those responsible for Jesus' death in the first century.

A fifth point to consider is that there are a number of hints that Melito, like many of his contemporaries, tried to counter the increasingly popular teachings of Marcion. Blank notes that the titles of many of the sixteen works attributed to Melito have an anti-Marcionite ring to them and, though we can only guess at their contents and even the titles can be differently construed, it seems probable that Melito was conscious of the Marcionite threat.[96] The conscious attempt to clarify the relationship between the two covenants, which shows some points of contact with the gnostic Ptolemaeus,[97] the insistence that the one is fulfilled in the other, the modalist Christology, which identifies Christ with God and sees him as an active participant not only in Israel's history (lines 398ff., 451ff., 582ff.) but also in the creation of the universe (lines 311ff., 590ff., 710ff.), could all have been developed without reference to the Marcionites, but in the context in which Melito worked it seems unlikely that they were.

It has been argued that Tertullian is more anti-Jewish when writing against Marcion than when writing specifically against the Jews,[98] and there is no doubt that Marcion posed some awkward problems, not the least of which was how to justify use of the Jewish scriptures while resisting Marcion's charge of Judaizing—to which, of course, a Quartodeciman would be peculiarly susceptible. Disputes with the Marcionites could have influenced Melito's view of Judaism in two ways: first, by encouraging the preservation of the old covenant by means of its subordination to and fulfillment in the new, with its inevitable denigration of the old and those who continued to live by it; and second, in reaction to Marcion's separation of Jesus from the biblical God, by encouraging a virtual identification of them, which, in turn, transforms the murderers of Jesus into the murderers of God.

This last point, sixthly, deserves separate consideration. Whether reacting to Marcion or not, the fluid and not entirely consistent christological statements contribute significantly to Melito's views of Judaism. The identification of Jesus with the character and attributes of God (lines 41–64), the understanding of the Incarnation as the enfleshment of the Creator (lines 451–504), and the assertion that "God is murdered" (line 715) fully justify Hall's succinct summary: "Melito does attribute to Christ all the acts of God without exception; he rarely uses expressions which imply a personal distinction of the Son from the Father; where the term Logos is used of Christ there is no suggestion of the Middle Platonist ideas which led Justin to think in terms of a second God; and Melito addresses his doxologies to Christ rather than distinctly to the Father."[99] This identification is also at the root of Melito's view that Christ was not only foreshadowed by, but also a participant in, the history of Israel. The effect on Melito's view of the Jews is dramatic. When they rejected Jesus they were rejecting no upstart Messiah, but God himself, the creator and redeemer of Israel. Without this conviction there could be no charge of deicide. The tragedy and guilt of the Jews are compounded because the God they killed was the God of the Jews.

Seventh, conflict between Jews and Christians in Asia Minor was not without precedent. The concern of Ignatius and the author of Revelation with the problem of Judaizing already indicates this, but it is the Gospel of John that provides the better parallel. In this Gospel not only are the Jews seen as representatives of the world, of all that is demonic and at enmity with the gospel, but there is a chronology of Jesus' death that unambiguously associates Jesus with the Passover lamb. We should not make too much of this, since the location of John in Asia Minor, while widely accepted, is not certain, and the association of Jesus with the Passover lamb is suggested, if less precisely, in the Synoptic traditions of Jesus' death, which are equally saturated with Passover symbolism. If the connection is allowed, however, and if it is thought that the Johannine tradition in Asia Minor encouraged the development of a Quartodeciman tradition, it may be that the anti-Jewish polemic of that Gospel in turn influenced Melito's castigation of the Jews.[100]

Finally, in addition to his various theological tracts Melito addressed an apologetic work to the Emperor Marcus Aurelius in response to decrees that had led to persecution of Asian Christians.[101] Melito seems confident that the emperor had not authorized these decrees, a confidence based not only on the proven record of imperial support for the Christian movement (with Nero and Domitian mentioned as notorious exceptions) but on the novel argument that the simultaneous flowering of Christianity and the Roman Empire from the time of Augustus suggested a degree of mutual dependence best nurtured by continuing mutual support:

> Our philosophy first flourished among barbarians, but it blossomed out among your peoples during the great reign of your ancestor Augustus, and became especially for your empire an auspicious benefit.

The surviving fragments of Melito's apology reveal a concern for the public reputation of Christianity as well as the protection of its adherents, which may well in turn have influenced his view of Judaism. Kraabel, for example, suggests that Melito's apologetic efforts would have been made more difficult by the established political status and civic influence of the Jewish community in Sardis, over and against whom the Christians would have had to assert their own identity and standing.[102] We also know that Christians were sometimes accused of being upstarts with no venerable ancestry, and that one response to this was to claim Jewish antiquity for their own. Is this what Melito means when he says, "Our philosophy first flourished among barbarians"? Are the "barbarians" the empires that preceded Rome, under whom the Jews lived, or are they, as Kraabel hesitantly suggests, the Jews?[103] In an apology the former is perhaps more probable, and it would amount to a passing claim for antiquity, which is implicitly and more fully worked out in the reflections on the old and new covenants in sections 1–45 of the homily. It is, therefore, possible that the need for an acceptable pedigree, a distinct identity, and a respectable status contributed to the manner in which Melito attacks the Jews and asserts the Christian claim to the traditions of Israel.

Concluding Reflections

At the beginning of this chapter we raised the question of liturgical anti-Judaism. Juster, we noted, argues that the drama and solemnity of liturgical occasions and their constant repetition ensured a far more lasting effect on the average Christian than many other expressions of anti-Judaism.[104] He concludes that many of the components of early Christian liturgy—hymns, prayers, creeds, scripture readings, and homilies—made a decisive contribution to anti-Jewish sentiment in the early centuries. Melito's text was a sermon, composed and delivered with a rhetorician's skill on a key liturgical occasion. Its effect is likely to have been lasting and profound, even when we allow for the conventions of rhetorical exaggeration. It is a text that confirms in a dramatic way Juster's suspicions, and invites further exploration along the path he has opened up.

In addition, the specific example of Melito's *Peri Pascha* confirms many of the more general observations about the development of Easter traditions, in particular the anti-Jewish strain that seems to go with them hand in hand. Melito may, of course, have been eccentric, and we cannot even be sure he was a typical Quartodeciman. Yet he illustrates one second-century response to the anxiety and confusion caused by the chronological and theological proximity of Passover and Easter. His solution was extreme—an absolute denial of the Jewish celebration of Passover, together with a selective appropriation of some features on behalf of Christianity, and an unrestrained vilification of the Jews for causing the death of Jesus. Further, his paschal reflections become the context for a more sweeping denial of Israel's existence and the charge of deicide. If he is not typical, at least he shows one direction in which paschal disputes could develop. Above all, he alerts us to the potential mischief in the distortions of even the earliest accounts of Jesus' death. For even if we do not go all the way with Paul Winter's seminal work on the trial of Jesus,[105] it can still be said that Melito's claims about Jewish responsibility in the death of Jesus are, with few exceptions, historically indefensible and, without exception, theologically abhorrent.

We cannot read Melito and ignore the dark shadow cast by subsequent Christian vilification of the Jews, in which the accusation of deicide played such a dominant and malicious role. For this Melito cannot be directly blamed, as there is no evidence that his views on this or any other matter were influential for more than a generation or two. A prolific and highly regarded author,[106] his influence was nevertheless short-lived, because he represented a minority strain in Asian Christianity and because his theological views (e.g., Christology) were suspect. Yet he is in some senses a pivotal figure. Partly because he comes at the end of the period we are interested in, but partly because of the peculiar blend of personal, sociocultural, and theological factors that help to explain his extreme position, he emerges as a point of confluence for many of the themes we have uncovered elsewhere. At the same time, he points to the future, to that strain of unrelieved anti-Judaism that was to dominate the Christian movement from this point on.

SUMMARY

From the evidence we have surveyed a consistent pattern emerges. The pattern of early Christian worship—in timing and content, fasts and prayers, private and communal—shows the pervasive influence of Judaism. Sometimes the borrowing was benign, a process of peaceable adaptation. But often the urge to differentiate led to denigration of the Jews.

The appearance of the Christian Sunday around 100 CE probably occurred as the result of a gradual transition from the Jewish Sabbath. It was motivated in part by the need to provide a setting for peculiarly Christian components, not least the celebration of Jesus' resurrection. It may also have been motivated by the need to be publicly distinguished from the Jews, but, while we cannot be sure that anti-Judaism motivated the shift to Sunday, it is nevertheless striking that the earliest witnesses to it appear in decidedly anti-Jewish contexts.

The transition from Passover to Easter occurred later. It is quite possible that it was introduced by the Gentile bishops in Jerusalem after 135 CE, in order both to separate themselves from the Jews and to curry favor with the Romans. The earlier Quartodeciman festival was intimately tied to Passover. It was marked by distinctive traits designed in conscious opposition to the Jewish feast, but it included a fast that expressed deep concern for the salvation of the Jews. The latter disappears in the Christian Easter, and the feast is moved to a new and fixed day.

The emerging pattern, dependence and proximity versus distance and antipathy, reaches an extreme pitch in Melito. As a Quartodeciman in the late second century he was more visibly proximate than most but, for this very reason, more manifestly hostile.

The phenomena we have observed were a response to the internal dynamics of various Christian groups as well as the tense and ambiguous relations they had with the Jews. But they would not have remained an entirely private matter, within or between the two communities. Jewish observance of the Sabbath, their fasts and annual feasts, were the things that publicly marked them off in the ancient world. Deliberate dissociation from them on the part of Christians would not have gone unnoticed by outside observers.

DIALOGUE AND DISPUTE

9

❖

Unquestionably one of the most important and fascinating early texts dealing with Jewish-Christian relations is Justin's *Dialogue with Trypho the Jew*. This is partly for the obvious reason that it is cast in the form of a discussion between a Christian and a Jew which takes place in Asia Minor soon after the Bar Cochba rebellion. Other Jewish-Christian dialogues are known to have existed but are not extant, such as the *Controversy between Jason and Papiscus*, attributed to Aristo of Pella and dating from around the same time as the *Dialogue*. Alternatively, we have texts such as *Barnabas*, Melito's *Homily*, and, toward the end of the period, Tertullian's *Adversus Judaeos*, all of which explicitly or implicitly engage with Judaism and its claims but prefer polemical broadside to reasoned exchange. Justin's *Dialogue* is thus the sole surviving example of a type of conversation between Jews and Christians that, in tone as well as content, may have been as rare then as it has been in subsequent Christian centuries. We shall also explore the interesting parallels between Trypho and the Jew who was purportedly one of Celsus's informants at the time he marshaled his arguments against Christianity (ca. 170 CE)—the only two Jewish voices we hear in this period with any directness, even if they are filtered through Christian and/or pagan tradents.

In itself this would be enough to recommend Justin's *Dialogue*. But apart from the central themes and the way in which they turn almost inevitably on differing interpretations of a common scripture, the *Dialogue* also introduces us to a rich array of incidental data relevant to our theme: Jewish reaction to and persecution of Christians, the effects of the Bar Cochba rebellion, Jewish Christians, Jewish and Christian sectarians, and the relative value of the LXX and the MT, or of different versions of the LXX, in resolving disagreements. These and other themes combine to make the *Dialogue* a text of exceptional interest.

"Dialogue" has become a familiar term in recent consideration of the challenges that arise when two or more major religions confront one another. At issue is not only the question of content—that is, what things are most likely to provide common ground and promote mutual understanding, or even what ineradicable differences can be used for mutual enlightenment—but also that of style. What mode of interaction is most likely to produce positive results? The most favored is dialogue, the firm but sensitive presentation of one's own view together with openness and receptivity to that of the other. Both elements are important: honest statement of a view and a willingness to learn. Jewish-Christian dialogue has been a significant part of this trend, fueled not least by the guilt that some Christians have increasingly felt over the contribution of their tradition to modern anti-Semitism. It is as well to be aware of this and to recognize the natural tendency of those sympathetic to dialogue to transpose the second-century dialogue into a twentieth-century key. While alert to this danger, we must at the same time avoid the opposite reaction, that is, allowing a distaste for or skepticism about modern interreligious dialogue, especially among Jews and Christians, to express itself in an irritable and blinkered survey of the early sources.[1]

Dialogue is a classical form, with its roots in the Socratic debates, but Justin's Dialogue is related only broadly to this genre.[2] Compared with the classical model, in which the conversation was open and exploratory, Justin more rigidly controls the content according to preformed conclusions.[3] Moreover, the normal progression by means of widely accepted norms of philosophical reasoning is usurped by a process of exegetical disputation focused on a scripture sacred to both participants.

Justin's text is thus only loosely tied to its classical predecessors, and has more in common with a Christian work that either precedes or is roughly contemporary with it: the Controversy between Jason and Papiscus. We know frustratingly little about this work: the debate was between a Jewish Christian and a non-Christian diaspora Jew; the chief topic was the application of messianic prophecies to Jesus; and, at the end, the Jew was converted by the persuasive powers of the Christian and the miraculous intervention of the Holy Spirit.[4] The core debate over messianism was judged by Celsus to be pitiful; and even Origen writes about it defensively and admits that it could be misleading. There are differences between the Controversy and the Dialogue: in one the author is not one of the protagonists and in the other he is; in one the Jew converts but in the other he does not; and in one the debate is between two Jews, rather than a Gentile and a Jew.[5] Despite these differences, however, the two works have in common the notion of conveying Jewish-Christian differences in the form of a dialogue and without any sense of profound animosity. If Aristo wrote before Justin, the Controversy could have been the model for the Dialogue.[6] Later Christian writings also resort to the dialogue form, favoring the polemical edge and the opportunity for authoritative exegesis over the reasoned argument established by

Justin's *Dialogue*. But in other respects they differ: Trypho is a layman, remains unconvinced by Justin's arguments, and has a discernible voice in the conversation; later Jewish protagonists are typically rabbis, mere mouthpieces for their Christian authors, and eventually convert—often, as in Aristo's *Controversy*, as a result of miraculous divine intervention rather than of persuasive argument.[7]

This brings us naturally to some of the more controversial judgments on the tone and content of the *Dialogue* and, in particular, the role of Trypho. Goodenough famously dismissed Trypho as "in many respects a straw man who says the right thing in the right place," who "never seriously embarrasses Justin by his replies and is a tool in his hands."[8] In this he was echoing the earlier judgment of Harnack, that the ostensible dialogue is in fact a monologue, the monologue of the victor, who allows his opponent to speak only when and how it suits him.[9] That Trypho is simply a convenient fiction is underlined by the observation that he is too passive, timid, and deferential to be a representative Jew—not at all the sort of robust and tough-minded antagonist who would in reality have engaged in Jewish-Christian dialogue.[10]

There are several issues tangled together here. Whether the debate reflects an actual conversation and whether Trypho was a historical personage—once thought to be significant matters—are of far less interest than a judgment on whether Trypho is a plausible representation of at least one strain of Judaism and whether the *Dialogue* gives a proper sense of the issues and the arguments that would have concerned Jews and Christians engaged in debate in the mid-second century.[11] Even if Trypho and the dialogue are fictional, are they realistic? Increasingly the consensus is that they are, that Justin was well-informed about Judaism, that the issues and arguments are precisely what we would have predicted, and that the voice of the author is not the only one to be heard.[12] Further, while it is true that Justin enjoys the lion's share of the debate and that, enjoying authorial control, he does not wittingly present arguments that would embarrass or disadvantage himself, Trypho nevertheless remains a significant conversational partner as he probes and queries the Christian position with point and skill.[13]

And what of Trypho's wry smile and courteous manner, his willingness to reason, to listen, even to concede? They may be unusual, but they are not inherently implausible. Moreover, if Trypho makes concessions, he does so on minor issues that do not affect his fundamental opposition to the Christian line, and he usually couples them with requests for further evidence, new questions, or a more general statement of opposition.[14] On most of the critical issues Trypho is as firm and as quietly insistent as Justin, and in the end, of course, he does not convert.

Ironically, Trypho's politeness and modesty, his willingness to listen and to learn, and the brevity and pertinence of his arguments convey a far more positive image of him than of Justin, who often appears to be overbearing and condescending, too fond of discursive rambling, and too ready to resort to irritable abuse. There is a sense in which Justin's strategy, which is presumably to demonstrate the superiority of his own view, inadvertently backfires or is subverted from within. This may, in part, be because we respond with modern rather than ancient sensibilities, but not entirely so. By laying out his opponent's view in a clear and plausible form, Justin runs the danger that the reader may find it more persuasive than his rebuttal. Celsus, a pagan, is one example of precisely such a response to Jewish-Christian debates, in that, although he had little time for either, he found the Jewish case superior. In this regard we should also remember that the dialogue has no triumphant ending: Trypho and his friends are charmed and unexpectedly impressed, but in the last resort unpersuaded.

Thus while we cannot deny that Justin, in his capacity as author, has ultimate control, we need not dismiss Trypho and his arguments as implausible fictions, nor need we, any more than Justin's contemporaries, feel obliged to be swept along by his own confident rhetoric. Indeed, while there is a broad structure and progression to the argument, it is often undisciplined, baggy, discursive, and not at all smooth-flowing. This seems to be deliberate in part: it demonstrates Justin's omniscience (50:1)[15] and Trypho's love of contention (64:2); it suits the two-day framework (92:5; 126:5); and it allows Justin to reinforce his views by repetition.[16] Yet the lengthy, rambling, often tangential replies to Trypho may also show us something else. Could it be that Justin was subconsciously aware that his case was not so obvious or persuasive as his superficial confidence would seem to imply?[17]

ADDRESSEES

To whom did Justin address the *Dialogue*? The question is important, not only because it can influence the way we understand some of the detailed arguments, but also because it tells us something about the nature of Jewish-Christian relations in the mid-second century. A number of options have been touted without any consensus being reached. A common view is that the targeted readers were Gentiles,[18] and this is supported by three main observations.

First, it is argued, there are several reasons for thinking that the most obvious alternative—a Jewish audience—is implausible. The arguments come in many forms, and we shall consider them below.

Second, there are suggestions within the text that Gentiles are the intended audience: the formal addressee, Marcus Pompeius, was probably a Gentile (141:5; cf. 8:3); the discussion of philosophy in the prologue (1–8) and the use of the classical dialogue genre were most appropriate for a Gentile audience; and, finally, the rhetorical appeal to Gentiles that surfaces frequently in the course of the argument (23:3; 24:3; 29:1; 32:5, for example).

The last observation brings us, thirdly, to the most popular recent version of this hypothesis, first suggested by T. Zahn: that Justin was addressing God-fearers, that is, Gentiles who sympathized with and were attached to the synagogues but were not yet full converts, and who were natural targets for Jewish and Christian missionaries. Such God-fearing Gentiles are per-sonified in the *Dialogue* by Trypho's friends, who are described as "those wishing to become proselytes" (23:3) and "the fearers of God" (10:4), and who are thus taken to represent Justin's readers.[19]

The attempt to find internal evidence for pagan readers has had little success: the references to Marcus Pompeius may be no more than a token gesture; there is no reason why Jews, including Trypho (1:2–3), should not have been interested in philosophy; and the use of a particular literary form indicates a cultural milieu but not necessarily a particular audience.[20] More-over, while Justin does discuss the meaning of scripture in *I Apol.*32ff., many other themes in that document that are also found in other early Christian apologies are not found in the *Dialogue*. If the *Dialogue* is addressing pagans, then, it would be on a uniquely narrow range of issues.

The third option has more to be said for it. It hinges in part on the mean-ing of *proselytos* and *phoboumenoi ton theon*. The latter is used in a general rather than technical sense, to mean all actual or potential believers, Jew or Gentile (24:3; 98:5; 106:1–2). The use of *proselytos* is less clear. In one pas-sage *proselysis* refers to joining the Christian movement (28:1–2), but this may be a loose, nontechnical use. In another passage Christians are referred to, in contrast to the proselytes of the law, as "proselytes of Christ" (*ton Christon kai tous proselytous autou*, 122:5). Such phrases show that *proselytos* can be used loosely, but not that, unqualified and on its own, it can be taken to mean converts to Christianity rather than to Judaism. All the other uses in the *Dialogue*, as the context in each case makes clear, refer to Jewish proselytes (80:1; 122:1; 122:2; 122:3–4 [twice]; 122:5; 123:1; 123:2). *Dia-logue* 23:3, in many ways the key to Zahn's theory, is ambiguous:

> And when no one answered I added: Therefore to you, Trypho, and to those who wish to become proselytes, I proclaim the divine message which I heard from that man. You see that Nature does not idle nor keep the sabbath. Re-main as you were born. For if before Abraham there was no need of circumci-sion . . . neither in like manner is there any need now.

Stylianopoulos, by referring to 28:1–2, and by noting the way in which Trypho and the others are bracketed together, thinks that Trypho and his companions are Jews who Justin supposes might be interested in becoming proselytes to Christianity.[21] But the analogy with 28:1–2 is not secure, and the immediate context, a discussion of circumcision, together with the phrase "Remain as you were born," surely more naturally implies that at least some of them were Gentiles and that "those who wish to become proselytes" were in the first instance potential converts to Judaism rather than to Christianity.

A number of other passages rhetorically invite the Gentiles (*ta ethne*) to worship God (24:3; 29:1). The term *ta ethne* can be used of believing (25:1; 26:1; 52:4; 122:3) or unbelieving (10:3; 17:1; 95:1) Gentiles and the context alone can decide the sense. In 24:3 and 29:1 Christians would seem to be in mind. And while there is abundant expression of the universal sweep of Justin's vision of salvation (1:2; 8:2; 35:8; and especially 64:2) it does not follow that he was appealing directly to all nations.[22]

Recently it has been argued that Justin was addressing non-Christian Jews.[23] That the dialogue is between a Jew and a Christian might seem to point in this direction, and the earnest appeals and conciliatory tone could be addressed to the unconverted. The section about Jewish Christians (46–47) indicates that there was traffic between the two communities: some of the Jewish Christians may have been contemporary converts, indicating that some were open to persuasion, and Justin mentions that some Christians defected to the synagogue.[24] Certainly Justin seems knowledgeable about Judaism (which presumably implies some sort of connection), and he retains, unusually for his day, a remnant theology which apparently includes some Jews in its vision of future salvation.

Against this it has been argued that Trypho was too compliant to be representative of mainstream Jewish opinion and would scarcely have been to Jews a persuasive model; that the scriptures are quoted at excessive length for a Jewish audience, who would have conceded their authority in general, yet in a translation (the LXX) whose standing was increasingly being questioned by the Jews; and, finally, that Justin gives the impression that Jewish-Christian relations were marked by a mood of competition and conflict, rather than understanding and compromise.[25]

These arguments are not persuasive. The portrait of Trypho and his relationship to other Jews we have already considered, and while it would be difficult for any single figure to represent all Jews, there is every reason to think that Trypho represents at least one kind of Judaism that Christians were likely to have come into contact with. The dominant role that scripture plays accurately reflects its significance for Jews and Christians as well as the disagreements over which versions were authoritative and how they were to be interpreted. The use of different Greek versions of scripture, including the LXX, merely demonstrates the fluidity of textual tradition at that time. And if Justin's text suggests, and rightly so, that there was competition and conflict between Jews and Christians, it also suggests by its very existence as a dialogue, as well as in many incidental details (e.g., 46–47), that contact between the two groups was sufficient to make the Jews a plausible audience.

Yet there are other reasons for doubting that Justin was addressing non-

Christian Jews. The polemical tone of parts of the *Dialogue* may have been common enough in second-century debates, and it is certainly milder than in some later dialogues, but it is scarcely designed to convince the Jews that they are wrong. Indeed, in Justin's *Dialogue* it does not. Trypho and his friends are not persuaded—surely an odd way to end an argument designed to convert Jews. Moreover, Justin's undeniable interest in and knowledge of Judaism does not necessarily indicate a Jewish audience, since Christians had an abiding and profound interest in many of the same issues. In the absence of any direct indication, how would we at any rate distinguish between the interests of a Jewish and a Christian community?

This brings us naturally to the final option—that Justin wrote primarily for Christian readers, to bolster their beliefs in the face of Jewish criticism and/or to arm them with arguments they could use in evangelizing the Jews.[26] As has been noted, "the Church at large is unambiguously addressed in liturgical language and in the first person plural hortatory subjunctive (24:3; 29:1)."[27] Quite apart from such direct evidence, it can scarcely be doubted that Justin intends his work to be read by Christians, even if they are not the only audience he had in mind.

One aspect of the problem is this: To what extent are we justified in identifying those rhetorically addressed in the work with the actual readers? That there is more than one such group should in itself be a warning against presupposing a simple correspondence between the implied and the actual audience. Justin can appeal to the church, to Gentiles at large, to Christians or to God-fearing Gentiles; and if there is no rhetorical appeal to the Jews it remains true that the whole of Justin's argument is ostensibly addressed to Trypho.

Most scholars sensibly allow that more than one audience could have been in mind. But when we turn to more general forms of argument we find little to be said for a pagan audience and problems with a Jewish audience, even though the debate is more relevant to their concerns. God-fearers are more plausible candidates, but the case rests more securely on general considerations than on the one or two allusions to them in the text. Their uncertain status—attached to but never fully part of the synagogue—would make them prime targets for Justin's argument for the superiority of the Christian over the Jewish position, and some of his stronger statements about the Jews would presumably have been less offensive to them.

If Justin was in the first instance addressing Christian readers, then different purposes can be surmised. Trypho's views may represent precisely the sort of arguments that Jews mounted against Christians. According to chapter 47 some Christians, probably Gentiles, defected to the synagogue, no doubt in part because they were persuaded by the Jewish rather than the Christian side of the case. In reality, in debates between Jews and Christians the latter did not always triumph, either by the force of their arguments or by the number of their converts. Sometimes it was the Jews who won, and the *Dialogue* could be in part an attempt to forearm and protect Christians.

Yet Christians would not always have been on the defensive. In the same chapter (47) the existence of Jewish Christians indicates that missionary efforts among Jews had not been entirely unsuccessful, although there is some dispute about whether Justin alludes to a minority group who were a hangover from the past or to Jewish Christians recently recruited. Justin does seem to retain some hope for Jewish conversions in the future, and this may suggest that they were not unknown in his day too.[28]

If we are guided by these passages and by the general content of the *Dialogue*, which is relevant to both situations, it is difficult to differentiate between the aim of shoring up Christian convictions in the face of Jewish propaganda and confronting the Jews with the Christian message with a view to conversion. That Trypho is politely noncommittal at the end may point to the former rather than the latter purpose even if it does not signal that all attempts to convert the Jews will inevitably be in vain.[29]

MAIN THEMES

The Mosaic Law

At the opening of the *Dialogue*, Trypho raises an issue of considerable embarrassment to Christians: Given their claim that they have taken over and submitted to the authority of the scriptures, how is it that they ignore some of the plain commands of Moses (10:2–3)? Why, for example, do they not keep the sabbath and the food laws? This question dominates the first section of the *Dialogue* (9–31), and it is often alluded to later. It also exposes Justin's weakest line of defense. Trypho's arguments are brief but challenging. Trypho does make a few concessions—admitting, for example, that the absence of circumcision among the patriarchs requires some explaining, and that the destruction of the Temple makes fulfillment of parts of the law impossible—but in general he argues uncompromisingly and from a position of strength. The elements of the law that Trypho harps on—circumcision, sabbath, food laws—are precisely those that most clearly distinguished the lifestyle of Jews from pagans and that even ordinary God-fearers acceded to, an observation that Trypho himself quite pointedly makes (10:2–3).

Justin's response, whose rambling, prolix character seems in part to be caused by his inability to come up with a straight answer, takes a number of different tacks. One is to call on scripture, by selectively repeating some of the more savage prophetic criticism of the Israelites (27), for example, or by quoting prophetic promises of a new covenant which is taken to have dissolved many of the obligations of the old covenant (11–12). Another is to marshal historical facts. The patriarchs, for example, were not circumcised and were none the worse for it (19–22). More recent events, the destruction of the Temple and the banishment of Jews from Jerusalem, are seen to be rich in significance: they are a punishment for Jewish obduracy; they demonstrate that the Temple cult is not essential; and (one of Justin's more remarkable and polemical arguments) they show that the ultimate purpose of circumcision was to facilitate enforcement of the ban after 135 CE (16)—an argument whose force is somewhat reduced when Justin notes that circumcision was practiced by other nations as well (28). Further, one can point to contradictions within scripture itself: some commands, like keeping the Sabbath, are undercut by other biblically endorsed practices (sacrifice and circumcision [27]), and this in turn reinforces the view that the law has a hidden purpose—to curb the sinful inclinations of human beings, most especially those of the Jews (18:2,23).[30] Finally, he argues, it is not weakness or lack of discipline that prevents Christians from keeping the law, for they bear up under far greater obligations than this (such as martyrdom, 18–19)—the reverse side of a later argument that Jews do not accept the Christian message for fear of persecution and death (39:6; 44:1).

In this opening section, as often elsewhere, Justin is the dominant voice if we judge by length alone—so much so that at one point he preemptively announces an objection that he supposes Trypho would have to his position, and proceeds to answer it before Trypho has a chance to intervene (20:2). But the imbalance is not only because Justin is the author. It is also because Trypho has, fundamentally, one simple and challenging point, to which Justin has no equally simple reply. And, with regard to the main issue at stake, apart from a few concessions there is little common ground between them.

If it is generally true that Jews were interested primarily in orthopraxy and Christians in orthodoxy, it is of some interest that the issue of halakic observance is raised at all, and that it is raised at the very beginning of the Dialogue. That is, it is precisely the sort of thing that we would expect to have been high on the list of Jewish objections, and to this extent we can say that their agenda has influenced the shape and content of the Dialogue.

Christology

The bulk of chapters 32–110 is taken up with various christological disagreements: the incarnation and the virgin birth; the crucifixion and resurrection; and the divinity of Jesus. Trypho balks chiefly at two things: the claim that Jesus is Messiah and the threat to monotheism that his divinity implies. The two are not unconnected, for, as Trypho argues, if Jesus is the Messiah, then he is human and not divine (49:1; cf. 67–68). Thus the two key Christian claims appear to be mutually incompatible.

With respect to Christian messianic claims Trypho raises a number of objections, but at the heart is his resistance to the notion of a crucified messiah. Whether or not the messianic forerunner had come could be debated

(49:1), and Trypho was willing to concede that scripture predicted two arrivals of the Messiah, one in lowly suffering and one in majesty. But if a suffering messiah was conceivable, a crucified messiah was not (32:1; 36:1; 89–91; 95–97). When countering, Justin was hard pressed to find appropriate proof texts, and the status of many of those he called on was in dispute: he claims that the Jews had deliberately excised them from the scriptures, while Trypho rightly notes that they appeared in neither the Hebrew nor the Greek (71–74).

Trypho's difficulties with Jesus' divinity are multiple: it implies the unprecedented and incredible notion that God could enter the world as a human being; it relies on a weak argument to explain the moment of entry, namely, the virgin birth; and it threatens the unity and singularity of God. The idea of the divine entering the world in human form is to Trypho profoundly puzzling and paradoxical, and even Justin is prepared to concede that it involves the mixing of two normally separate categories—the divine and the human (48; 68). The resort to scripture compounds the issue, for when Justin reinforces his claim by calling on the notorious LXX of Isaiah 7:14, Trypho is quick to note that the Christian interpretation ignores not only the original context but also the plain meaning of the underlying Hebrew (43:8; 67). The delicate matter of defining Jesus' divinity finds them sharing some common ground. Justin is given a hearing by Trypho and his friends only because he argues from scripture and defends the superiority of the creator god (56), while Trypho is willing to concede that scripture indicates the presence of angels or other obscure figures (e.g., Wisdom) when the divine is at critical moments manifested in the world (55–64; 75–76). But while for Justin these become precedents for the Incarnation, for Trypho they have to be understood in the uncompromising context of the unity of God.

In the end, though the subject is Christology the argument is about scripture: Justin and Trypho agree on the facts of Jesus' career such as his teaching, his miracles, and his death, but differ on the degree to which these are foreshadowed or predicted in scripture. As we view it, sometimes Trypho seems to get the better of things (on Isa 7:14), and at other times Justin (when discussing the "second god"). They debate over common ground, but without much common agreement, even though occasionally the discussion flares up into a sharp and lively exchange (see especially 67–68). For, while on a number of matters they can agree—Trypho conceding a number of exegetical points and Justin admitting that the points he is making are difficult to grasp—in the end their paths inexorably diverge. That Christology should be a core issue is entirely understandable, and it is, significantly, the main theme in the *Controversy between Jason and Papiscus*. That the discussion of Christology should focus on two issues—messianism and monotheism—is also precisely what we would have predicted about a conversation between a Christian and a Jew. They are the two areas where early Christians, because of their Jewish roots, had most trouble in bringing their convictions into line with received tradition. Both debates were long-standing, but each of them may have been sharpened by recent events.

We have rightly been warned not to exaggerate the importance of messianism for Jews in this period, and it is easy to allow the central role it plays in Christian conviction to spill over into our picture of Judaism. The paucity of references in the Pseudepigrapha and the virtual silence of the Mishnah are striking. But the Mishnah is a collection with a very narrow range of interests, and the Pseudepigrapha may give only haphazard evidence for normal Jewish beliefs. We should not assume that they represent the full range of Jewish thought in the second century. Even without any intrinsic interest in the subject, it is hardly likely that Jews would have remained wholly unaffected by Christian claims that the Messiah was a roughly contemporaneous figure, now dead, and dead by crucifixion at that. This flies in the face of most Jewish tradition, however it is construed. Further, it is likely that messianic fervor fueled the hope for rebuilding the Temple under Nerva and the revolts during the reign of Trajan, and certain that it played a significant role in the Bar Cochba rebellion.[31] Indeed, Justin himself suggests that the Bar Cochba revolt forms part of the immediate background to the *Dialogue*. Jewish messianic hopes were raised, only to be dashed when the rebels were overrun. Not only had the most recent Jewish claimant thus been removed from the scene (after pressing his claims with some ferocity against those Christians within his aegis), but when Justin announced his millennial vision of a cleansed Jerusalem as the focal point of restoration for the (largely Christian) redeemed, this would only have added salt to the wound.[32]

It has been suggested that some of the messianic beliefs ascribed to Trypho are implausible, in particular the view that the Son of Man in Daniel 7:13 is a messianic figure (*Dial.*32:1) and the notion that there were to be two advents of the messiah, one in humility the other in glory (*Dial.*36:1; 39:7; 89–91).[33] As to the former, this is surely wrong, as *1 Enoch* 48:10; 49:3; *4 Ezra* 13:1–53; and *Sib.Or.*5:414–33 indicate, even if Jews like Trypho would have had difficulty seeing the expectation fulfilled in Jesus.[34] The notion of two messianic advents is commonly used by second-century Christians to get themselves out of a tight corner. It rests on a deeply rooted Jewish notion of the association of humiliation and glory,[35] but there is no evidence that Jews connected the pattern with two advents of the messiah. It is true that the Son of Man in *1 Enoch* 37–71 is connected with the messiah and with the Servant figure in Isaiah, but this composite figure does not take on the suffering of the Servant. In view of the considerable fluidity of messianic expectation in Judaism at this time, I do not think it impossible that, in the course of a debate and on exegetical grounds, a Jew might concede that there were to be two advents of the messiah, if only to press on to the objection (voiced by Trypho) that this cannot be connected with a recent and crucified individual. In this instance, at any rate, Trypho's objections are more plausible than his concession.[36]

The conflict with Gnostics and Marcionites undoubtedly hovered in the background during discussion of the unity of God, and figures like Justin required some fairly nimble moves in order to stake out ground between their Jewish and Christian opponents.[37] Justin's task was not made easier by the existence of Christians who promoted a Christology congenial to his opponents, thus further muddying the issue (48:4). That Jews were concerned about the Christian threat to monotheism can be surmised from some of the later discussions about the "second god" in rabbinic literature.[38] And this was not so rare, since the threat to monotheism was a constant feature of Jewish theology. Emanations, hypostatizations, and various heavenly and angelic beings constantly threatened the stricter boundaries of monotheism.[39] Into this environment Christian claims could slot, even if they were unusually pointed and extreme, and it is not surprising to find a representative of Judaism reacting with alarm.

The True Israel

The bulk of the final chapters (111–42) considers the relationship between the old people of God and the new. That the church is in some sense the new Israel is implied in earlier Christian writings, perhaps as early as Paul, but Justin is the first openly to express and defend the claim with explicit arguments.[40] The universal promises of the scriptures refer to Christ and the Christians and not to diaspora Jews and proselytes (117–18), and thus Christians turn out to be more understanding and religious than the Jews who are reputed to be (but are not) intelligent and lovers of God (118:3). To reinforce his point Justin, in the same manner as many of his predecessors but with greater thoroughness, divides scriptural predictions into threats and promises, whereby Jews inherit the former and Christians the latter. If once there was one people of God, now there are two—the physical and the spiritual (134–42). What once belonged to the physical Israel, the promises and the inheritance, now belongs to the spiritual Israel, the church: "So also we . . . are . . . both called and in fact are Jacob and Israel and Judah and Joseph and David, and true children of God" (123:9; cf. 134:3).

The issue has, of course, hovered in the background throughout the *Dialogue* (11:5; 14:1; 29:1; 55:3; 63:5; 87:5; 116:3), and is implicit in all those passages that casually announce the Christian supersession of Jewish practice and belief (e.g., 29:2; 41:1–4; 42:1–4; 116:1), but in the final section Justin brings it to a climax in a series of triumphal assertions. There is not much of Trypho to be heard here. At one stage he tries to stem the flow, but only just avoids (as on other occasions he does not) the accusation that he was quibbling (123:7), while at the same time Justin's windy repetitions are justified by the presence of newcomers on the second day (118:4; 123:7).

Justin has most of the say, but is this because of a blithe disregard for any view other than his own, or an anxiety that he might not be as convincing as he likes to sound? After all, the old Israel was still fairly securely and visibly in place, and this might well have posed difficulties even for more thoughtful Christians, let alone for outsiders expected to arbitrate between the competing claims.

In his millennial scheme of things, Justin seems to envisage a quite literal return to the holy land and city. The beneficiaries will clearly include Christians, who are, equally clearly, predominantly Gentile (80:5; 81:4; 85:7; 119:5).[41] What it means for the fate of the Jews is a matter to which we shall return.

Scripture

As we have already had cause to note in more than one context, the argument of the *Dialogue* is throughout essentially exegetical. There is a touch of the logical and rational, Christian writings are occasionally introduced under the title of "Memoirs of the Apostles" (98–107), and there are allusions to recent or contemporary events, but in the end the crucial points turn on the meaning of a common scripture.[42] Both participants accept that to win the argument would be largely a hermeneutical victory. The authority of the scriptures is a presupposition, which is assumed but not discussed (34:1), although it is casually mentioned as one of the reasons for Trypho's participation in the debate (56).

But if in this they agreed, in many other things they did not. There was first the question of the text: Which Greek translation was to be used, for example (43:8; 68:1–4; 71:2), and was it the Hebrew or the Greek that took precedence in the case of disagreement (52; 72–73; 120)? Disagreements on this level were enough to encourage mutual recrimination—Justin accusing the Jews of falsifying the text of scripture and Trypho suggesting that Christians indiscriminately chose any version that suited their purpose. Then again, were the prophets addressing their contemporaries or predicting the distant future (33:1; 34:34; 36:2–6; 43:8)? Does Isaiah 7:14, for example, refer to Hezekiah or to some distant messianic figure?[43] Trypho defends the former and Justin, when it suits him, the latter. When the question of the text or the predictive quality of scripture was not in dispute, other disagreements could arise. Was the real message of scripture the plain, literal meaning or some deep, allegorical sense lurking beneath the surface? Justin and Trypho agree that the latter is often the case and that many readers are unable to grasp it (90:2), but that is as far as they can agree. Otherwise Justin accuses Trypho and the Jews of obtuseness and willful blindness (9:1; 12:3; 14:2; 43:8; 68:3–4; 71:2; 72:1; 123:3–4), turning back on them the prophets' earlier castigation of the Israelites, while Trypho accuses Justin of arbitrary selection of (27:1; 79:1), and allegorical imposition on, the biblical text.

Some of these disputes were understandable. The text of the scriptures was not firmly fixed, and there were competing Greek versions vying for attention. Thus, when Christians found the LXX congenial, the Jews, at around this time, authorized Aquila's translation, one of whose aims was probably to undermine Christian exegesis.[44] And at this time few if any Christians knew Hebrew, and so relied heavily on the LXX. In Justin's case, a further complication may have been that he occasionally quoted Samaritan tradition when it suited his purpose.[45] Moreover, there were in all probability collections of testimonies (biblical proof texts) circulating as handbooks in Christian communities of the second century. In these the scriptures were sometimes quoted in conveniently doctored form, which then became the most familiar version to Christian apologists and added a little more mud to the already murky textual stream.[46]

Other disagreements were deeper and more intractable. If above we suggested that the nub of the christological dispute was the meaning of scripture, the reverse is equally true: for Justin the Bible was a Christian book, one whose deep and constant truth could be understood only christologically.[47] Trypho could concede to the Christians some of their proof texts and admit that their exegesis was sometimes fascinating and suggestive, but over the christological hurdle he could not, in the last resort, go.

Other Issues

Up to now we have focused on the issues that were explicitly at the forefront of the debate. There are several other matters, however, that weave in and out of the discussion, two of which are of particular interest to us. The question of miracles crops up in a number of places, not because Trypho expresses any specific opinion on the matter, as if it were an issue between himself and Justin, but because it was more broadly a point of contention between Jews and Christians, and Justin feels obliged to drag it in at certain points. False prophets, Justin's distinction suggests, perform miracles to astound humanity and glorify the demons, whereas true prophets do them only for the glory of God (7:3). Jews may subjugate demons if they do so in the name of the God of Israel, but they tend to resort to the magical arts of the Gentiles (85:2–3). The Jews, on the other hand, attribute Jesus' healings and exorcisms to "magical art" (*phantasian magiken*), calling him a "magician" (*magos*) and "deceiver of the people" (*laoplanos* [*Dial.* 69:7]). Elsewhere it is claimed that the Jews sent envoys throughout the world to announce that Jesus was a "deceiver" (*planos*) who founded a "godless" (*atheos*) and "lawless" (*anomos*) sect (108:2–3). Clearly we have here a classic case of miracle conflict: one person's miracle was another person's magic.[48] That miracles (healings and exorcisms) could be performed by either party is not denied; if Jesus can do them, so can the Jews. The key questions are: By whose inspiration and to what end are they performed? Are they done in the name of God and to glorify him, or do they use magical (i.e., demonic) arts in order to flatter and deceive? It all depends on where you stand. Miracles are important to Justin (11:4), but he is aware that they are open to diabolical counterfeit, and that only the original eyewitnesses have anything better than secondhand testimony (69:6–7). Thus, while he takes a fairly standard line, Justin is aware that it is a slippery subject.

The accusation that Jesus was a "deceiver" is found in Matthew 27:63 and John 7:12,47, but the more interesting parallels are in *T.Levi* 16:3 and two rabbinic passages, *b.Sanh.*43a and *b.Sanh.*107b. In these rabbinic passages the charge that Jesus was a "deceiver" is linked to the charge that he was a "magician," just as in *Dialogue* 69:7. It is probable that these rabbinic passages reflect the type of argument used by Jews to counter Christian claims about Jesus in the early centuries and, if so, they vividly confirm the point that Justin had an accurate knowledge of the kind of objections Jews had to Christianity.[49]

Another issue to consider is that there are a number of passages where Justin considers the ultimate fate of the Jews.[50] Hovering in the background is his down-to-earth chiliasm, which he admits was not shared by other Christians he knew (80).[51] When the salvation of the Jews is envisaged in the *Dialogue,* it is seen as the action sometimes of God and sometimes of Christ.[52] Justin clearly has not abandoned hope for their conversion, which he both urges upon them and prays for.[53] What exactly did he expect? Was it only through conversion that Jews could be saved, or could they be saved simply as Jews? Were all Jews to be saved or only some? It is not always clear. In 64:2–3 Justin refuses to answer the question "whether or not anyone of your race" will be saved. Is this momentary irritation at Trypho's quibbling, or does it reveal a more profound uncertainty? In 25:6–26:2 the following exchange takes place:

> T. Do you indeed intend to say that none of us shall inherit anything on the holy mountain of God?
>
> J. I did not say that . . . but those who have persecuted Christ in the past and still do, and do not repent, shall not inherit anything on the holy mountain. But the Gentiles who have believed in him and have repented for all their sins will inherit with the righteous patriarchs and the prophets and all the righteous descendants of Jacob [*meta ton patriarchon kai ton propheton kai ton dikaion hosoi apo Iakob gegennetai*].

Would Justin have distinguished between those Jews who persecuted Christ and the Christians and those who did not, or were all Jews by implication persecutors? Clearly, one group of Jews were safe—the righteous of Israel's past (cf. 45:2; 67:7; 80:1). But who, then, are the "righteous descendants of Jacob"?

> T. Will those who have lived according to the law instituted by Moses live again together with Jacob, Enoch and Noah in the resurrection of the dead?

J. . . . I also stated that those who obeyed the Mosaic law would equally be saved. . . . Since they who did those things (in the law) which are universally, naturally and eternally good are pleasing to God, they shall be saved through this Christ in the resurrection, together with their righteous forefathers . . . , together with those who recognise Christ, the Son of God. (45:2–4)

Here we seem to have three groups: righteous ancient Israelites, Christian believers (including Jews?), and non-Christians who abide essentially by the law. This last group could include both postbiblical Jews and Gentiles, and it is particularly striking that, although they are to be saved through Christ, this will be not in their lifetime but at the resurrection.

There is at least the germ of an idea here of salvation for non-Christian Jews.[54] Yet even here the clear implication is that this will involve at most only some Jews—those who keep the law and do not persecute. This fits with other passages where Justin introduces the notion of a faithful remnant, which, by definition, includes only some Jews.[55] Moreover, there are a number of passages in which the need to believe and the exclusiveness of salvation through Christ are made quite clear.[56] That some Jews did believe is demonstrated by the existence of Jewish Christians (46–48), and it is elsewhere implied that the conversion of Jews was something that Justin knew about at first hand: "He has not exacted judgement of you, because he knows that every day some of you are forsaking your erroneous ways to become disciples in the name of his Christ" (39:2). Elsewhere Justin is firm in his warning that the time to repent is short (28:2), and that Jews who think they will be saved because they are sons of Jacob according to the flesh are deceived (125:5).

Was Justin inconsistent? Did he, perhaps by extending his acknowledgment of the salvation of ancient worthies, find himself drawn to the notion that other righteous Jews might be saved, even though they were not Christian believers in their lifetime? And did this conflict with his more commonly expressed view that there was no salvation outside of Christ, and with his encouragement of Jews to convert? Perhaps Justin's language is simply a little loose—so that he didn't really think of nonbelieving, law-abiding Jews as a separate and privileged category—or perhaps he accepted them but considered it adequate to assert that they would at any rate be saved in the end only through the intervention of Christ.

It has been noted that there is a similarity between these themes in the *Dialogue* and the sin-exile-redemption pattern found in other, similar texts. In particular a comparison is made between Justin's expression of hope for the conversion of Trypho and his companions and the *Testaments of the Twelve Patriarchs*, in which a hope for the future salvation of Israel is unabashedly maintained.[57] The connection is intriguing and, as we have seen, Justin may go beyond mere expressions of hope. It would remain true that his vision is more cautious and limited than the *Test.XII*: at best only a remnant of Jews will be saved, either because they became Christians or because Christ will intervene on their behalf in the last days. It would be equally pertinent to note that even in this attenuated form Justin's statements about the future of the Jews are not as pessimistic or as polemical as those of most of his immediate predecessors and successors.

Whatever conclusions we draw about Justin's vision of the fate of Israel, these would have to be placed beside the many passages where he unambiguously and enthusiastically asserts the Gentile dominance of Christianity (109; 119; 122, etc.). He sometimes gives the impression that he saw Gentiles as the natural, even the sole, inheritors of God's promises, even though he knew that Jewish Christian groups existed. He appears on occasions to be replacing the old Jewish exclusiveness with a new Gentile exclusiveness.[58] This is in part because he is determined to claim that the church is the true Israel, a conclusion that, in the face of a thriving Jewish community that showed no sign of disappearing or relinquishing its claim, was not self-evident. Indeed, the very difficulty of defending the Christian takeover may have lured Justin into more extreme statements and a more strident tone than a more relaxed and rounded account of his views would require. There are thus several threads running through Justin's work, and it may be that he had not made a coherent pattern of them in his own mind.

BACKGROUND AND SOURCES

The question of the sources of Justin's information about the issues that divided Jews and Christians has been explored frequently. He demonstrably had a considerable knowledge of the biblical tradition and knew which texts to light on when making his case.[59] But it seems unlikely that all the arguments were of his own making. The most recent study suggests that Justin, like his fellow Christians, drew on collections of testimonies that had become so familiar to and authoritative for him that he preferred their (Christian) version of the text to the (Jewish) LXX when the two diverged.[60] That is to say, both the selection of texts and (presumably) some form of interpretative tradition were ready-made. This would not have stifled Justin's creative use of or addition to the tradition, but it indicates a rich strain preceding him.

In addition, there is evidence that Justin gained knowledge of contemporary Jewish beliefs and practices that allowed him to update and reinforce his biblical arguments.[61] Some of this material could have come to him from earlier Christian sources—testimony collections, for example, or works like *Barnabas*. Thus the tradition that the two goats on the Day of Atonement should be identical (40:4) could have come directly from Jewish sources, but it could also have come from *Barnabas* 7:6 or from a testimony collection. But while Christian tradition may account for some of the evidence—

and in many cases there are no parallels in other Christian sources to verify things one way or the other—there is every reason to suppose that Justin learned some of what he knew about Judaism from Jews themselves. This can be denied only if we presuppose complete isolation of the two communities, and this runs up against the very structure of the *Dialogue*, against what Justin tells us about contacts between Jewish Christians and the synagogue, and against his own claim to have had frequent contact with Jewish teachers (50:1). Thus, for example, the backdrop to some of the christological disagreements is not only the biblical text but also the rabbinic tradition of giving a messianic interpretation to many of the texts that Justin also chooses to draw on for the same purpose.[62] The parallels do not have to be precise in every detail for the case to be convincingly made.[63] Yet until this material is given a thorough review using all the available techniques for analyzing rabbinic traditions, something that neither older nor recent works can claim to have done, it remains a persuasive hypothesis rather than a fully demonstrated conclusion.[64]

The most obvious source of Justin's information about Judaism is, of course, the very one he describes: dialogue with Jews. Unless the framework as well as the content of the *Dialogue* is considered to be entirely fictitious, for which there seems little warrant, dialogue would have been the most obvious way to pick up the sort of knowledge that Justin demonstrates. It is for this reason that he can provide a broadly reliable picture of the kind of arguments that Jews would have used against Christians. But his knowledge probably went beyond this, for he not only represents Jewish views but also introduces Jewish material to reinforce his own argument. Dialogue with Jews may have been his most important, but not necessarily his sole, source of information.

If Justin drew in various ways on Jewish material, he had his Christian sources too. There were above all the collections of testimonies. Skarsaune discerns two main blocks of such material: a "kerygma source," related in part to the *Kerygma Petrou*; and a "recapitulation source," identified with Aristo's *Controversy between Jason and Papiscus*. Skarsaune compares these with two other strands of early Christian evidence: the *Anabathmoi Jakobou* and the Christian redactor of the *Testaments of the Twelve Patriarchs*. Most interesting is that three of these, whether designated a direct source or a related tradition, are usually thought to be of Jewish Christian provenance, suggesting that Justin was heir to traditions profoundly influenced by Jewish Christian ideas.[65]

In principle this is plausible. Justin tells us that although some were reluctant to mix with Jewish Christians he was himself quite willing to do so as long as they did not try to impose their ways on other Christians. In the same passage it is implied that there was some traffic between the synagogues and the churches (46–47). Jewish Christians, therefore, were in a position to inform Justin about their own as well as Jewish traditions. The identification of specific sources and contemporary parallels is problematic, but we can with some confidence conclude that Justin was in touch with strains of Jewish Christian thought that influenced his view of both Judaism and Jewish-Christian dialogue.[66]

Skarsaune, in fact, hears two voices speaking in the sources underlying the *Dialogue*. The Jewish Christian voice, addressing the Jews in the aftermath of the Bar Cochba revolt, had the following to say: Jesus is the true and promised messiah; baptism effects cleansing from sin and replaces the sacrificial cult; the devastation of Judaea and the prohibition against entering Jerusalem are punishment for the death of Jesus; believing Gentiles replace, but do not destroy an ultimate hope for, the unbelieving Jews in the people of God. The second, Gentile Christian voice, still in close contact with Jewish exegesis and still concerned about Jerusalem and the land of Judaea, has absorbed the Jewish Christian tradition but with significant alterations: circumcision and other Jewish rites are abandoned or their significance allegorically transformed; there is a new Israel, the church, and it is predominantly Gentile; hope for the old Israel wanes, and they are portrayed as an irretrievably reprobate people. It is a triumphant voice, the voice of success, profoundly symbolized by the Gentile takeover of the Jerusalem church after 135 CE.[67]

This is an intriguing and subtle reading, but in the end suggestive rather than compelling. How, for example, are we to allow for the development of a distinctive Jewish Christian theology in response to the events of 132–35 CE when the Gentile church had already made its profoundly symbolic move in 135 CE by replacing Jewish with Gentile bishops? Presumably neither the creation of the theology nor its absorption by the Gentile church happened overnight. Perhaps the Bar Cochba revolt is being asked to explain too much. It would make more sense to suppose that the Jewish Christian view was largely in place before the revolt, though perhaps touched up somewhat after it. In fact, apart from a few allusions to the messianism of Bar Cochba, which could as easily come from Gentile as from Jewish Christian quarters, everything defined as Jewish Christian could have been developed from the late first century on. And the disputes about messianism themselves do not require the Bar Cochba revolt as a context, since this had been an issue between Jews and Christians from the earliest days. On the other hand, that the conditions imposed on the Jews after 135 CE encouraged Gentile Christian triumphalism is highly probable. Speaking of the takeover by Gentile Christians, Marcel Simon puts it this way:

> It marked the failure of Jewish Christianity, which had been rejected by both Christians and Jews, and it underlined the fundamental incompatibility of Christianity and Judaism. The Gentile Christians made their entry into Zion as part of the trappings of Rome, and, taking advantage of the Jews' misfortune, they filled the place hitherto occupied by that rebellious people.[68]

This is a matter we shall return to below as we turn our attention to the historical background of Justin's thought. Aside from exegetical sources, what else motivated him to develop his line of argument? We have noticed in passing how certain historical realities impressed themselves on him, and how he calls on them to undergird his position. The dispute with gnostic and Marcionite churches—and together they were no mean opposition— hovers in the background, and, even though they are not central to the debate of the *Dialogue*, some of the issues are surreptitiously slipped in.[69] The universal success of the Christian mission impresses Justin, and he turns it into an argument for the superiority of Christianity and confirmation of the Christian inheritance of the promises to Israel (117). Missionary competition between Jews and Christians over God-fearers has been suggested as an important context for the *Dialogue*. This cannot be convincingly demonstrated from the text, but it was doubtless one of the realities of life that evoked the sort of arguments used by Justin and his contemporaries.

Jewish persecution of Christ and the Christians, regular maledictions against them in the synagogues, and the dispatch of anti-Christian envoys throughout the world confirmed for Justin that the rejection by God that most Jews would experience would be fully justified.[70] Justin was able to turn the destruction of the Temple to his advantage by claiming that it was not only a punishment for the wickedness of the Jews but also a proof that the Mosaic law was a temporary dispensation, which could no longer be fulfilled (16; 40; 46).

Above all, however, it is the Bar Cochba rebellion that impinges itself on Justin's consciousness and provides a context for his reflections. Trypho, we are told, was in Ephesus (where the dialogue supposedly took place) because he was a refugee from the rebellion in Judaea. That is, either for pragmatic or principled reasons some Jews were forced to leave their homeland for the relative safety of the diaspora, even though the rebellion continued to be a matter of concern to them (1:3; 9:3). Bar Cochba's claim to be messiah may lie behind Justin's cryptic allusions to the man who has temporary power as king but speaks blasphemous words against God (31:6; 32:3). Refusal to recognize him was the most likely reason for the persecution, and sometimes execution, of Christians mentioned in *I Apol*.31.6ff., a conflict that profoundly damaged Jewish-Christian relations. The banishment of the Jews from Jerusalem after the revolt was particularly significant: it was foretold by the prophets, a just punishment for an unjust people, and even—in a twist of the argument unique to Justin—the explanation why Jews were circumcised (they could be identified if found sneaking into Jerusalem, 16; 17:1–4; 22). It is possible that the breakdown in relations after 135 CE led to a more intense and sharply focused use of the maledictions against Christians in the synagogue which Justin frequently mentions, though it must be said that he does not make this connection. And what of the Gentile Christian triumphalism that Simon hints at? In one passage Justin seems to imply that, since the war was over and the Jews banished, Jerusalem was cleansed and ready to be the focal point in the fulfillment of his remarkably literal and universalist eschatological vision: "Come all nations, let us assemble at Jerusalem, no longer disturbed by war because of the peoples' sins" (24:3).

While Justin sometimes blends his references to the Jewish War and the Bar Cochba rebellion, speaking of them almost without distinction and in the same breath (*Dial*.16; *I Apol*.47), the latter is overwhelmingly the more important. One reason may be simply that it was for Justin the more recent event, something he had lived through rather than something in the relatively distant past. Another is that it was, as argued elsewhere in this book, the more traumatic and significant of the two for Jewish-Christian relations.

Other influences on Justin can be more briefly dealt with. It has been noted that he was born and presumably raised near Judaea. This could explain his knowledge of Judaism, his contact with Jewish Christians, and his Jerusalem-centered millennialism, but this is only speculation.[71] It has been suggested that his early Samaritan environment may account for some of his anti-Judaism,[72] but then Justin seems to see himself as a Gentile rather than a Samaritan. Some attempt has been made to illuminate the *Dialogue* by exploring the important places in Justin's life—Samaria/Palestine where he was born, Ephesus where the debate supposedly took place, Rome where he lived—but we rarely know enough about Jews and Christians in these specific locations to take us far.[73] The one important exception is that we know that there were thriving Jewish communities, and probably therefore contact between Jews and Christians, in at least the last two places.

Finally we should not overlook Justin's own spiritual odyssey. He demonstrably had an unusually wide knowledge of Judaism, Christian tradition, and Hellenistic philosophy, and doubtless this contributed much to his success as a teacher in Rome and an apologist and defender of the Christian view. But for all this knowledge, and the ingenious ways in which he can employ it, Justin remains at heart an axiomatic thinker, one whose certainties spring from his own conversion and the Christian tradition into which he was baptized. For him the truth of his own and the Christian position was self-evident and, as he somewhat disingenuously says on occasions, he needed only to be frank and clear for his arguments to be immediately persuasive (80:2; 120:6; 125:1). He speaks with the confidence of the convert.[74]

JUSTIN'S TRYPHO AND CELSUS'S JEW

Only a few scraps of information about Trypho are volunteered in the *Dialogue*. He learned philosophy at a Socratic school in Argos and retains an interest in it alongside his love of the Jewish tradition. Now a refugee from the war in Judaea, he is forced to live in Greece (1:3). The suggestion that he and his companions discussed the war among themselves implies that it was a matter of deep concern for them (9:3). He claims to have read at least one of the Christian Gospels, and praises the precepts he finds there even though he thinks they express an unobtainable ideal (10:2–3). Trypho participates in the debate in defiance of his own leaders (38:1; 112:4), though not all his companions are prepared to do the same (9:2–3), while Justin encourages him to ignore his Jewish teachers (38:2; 68:7; 71:1–2; 112:4) and to avoid the blaspheming of Christ and the persecution of Christians (137:1–2; 141:2–3).

There is nothing inherently implausible here. That some Jews left Judaea during the revolt, because they disapproved of it or simply to avoid the turmoil and danger, is probable. In the few sources we have, it is implied that the Bar Cochba rebellion was devastating for both Jews and Romans. Whether he was born and raised in Judaea or simply a temporary resident there is not said, but in either case it would explain his knowledge of certain Jewish traditions, just as his philosophical training would explain his broader intellectual sympathies. That there were Jews who had fairly amicable conversations with Christians, Jewish or Gentile, and read some of their basic writings, is not surprising, even if it is generally true that Christians would have shown a great deal more interest in Judaism than vice versa. That Jewish leaders discouraged contact with Christians is as understandable as Christian leaders' lambasting the Judaizers and taking an increasingly cautious and suspicious attitude toward the Jewish Christians. Trypho did not convert, but the danger was always there, and Justin himself tells us that defection took place in the other direction from the church to the synagogue (47). Although Trypho is never given an opportunity to answer the charges about cursing and persecuting Christians, it seems unlikely that he was an active participant. Rather, he is swept up in Justin's judgment that in matters such as these all Jews were to be held responsible.

What, then, of the arguments Trypho uses? As we have noted above, the confluence of Trypho's arguments with other Jewish and Christian sources of the period provides prima facie evidence for the view that many of them are appropriately placed. With the occasional minor exception, not only are they the sort of arguments that we would expect from a Jew, they appear in a sufficient number of diverse sources to suggest that they were precisely the sort of arguments used. Another way of checking is to compare Trypho's viewpoint with that of the Jew whom Celsus claims as an informant in books 1 and 2 of his work called *True Doctrine*.

This treatise, known to us only through Origen's refutation of it about seventy years later, is usually dated somewhere around 175 CE, or very close to the date normally assigned to the *Dialogue*.[75] It is, of course, not the best of evidence, since Celsus's views are filtered through Origen and, before that, the Jew's views through Celsus. Celsus, knowing of the long relationship between Judaism and Christianity and of Christian claims to be the true Israel, cleverly calls on this Jewish interlocutor to reinforce his own arguments against the Christian position. This is for him only a temporary expedient, since in the end he also rejects Judaism as a superstition (Origen *Cels.*1.14; 1.20–26) even if he recognizes that it has some claim to respect because of its antiquity (*Cels.*5.25).

The authenticity of Celsus's Jew is as controverted as that of Justin's Trypho. It has been argued that he, like Trypho, is entirely fictional, a view routinely encouraged by Origen to discredit his opponent (*Cels.* 1: 28,34,49,55,57,67; 2:1,34,53, etc.). Yet neither Origen's assurances nor the content of the Jew's arguments support this conclusion. As with Trypho, the important issue is not whether he was a real person, a single individual whose opinions Celsus repeats verbatim, but whether the arguments attributed to him accurately reflect the sort of things a Jew might have said about Christianity in the second half of the second century. In general, they do, and I would take the arguments of the two figures to be mutually supportive.[76]

Origen, it is often noted, is unusually generous toward, as well as defensive about, Judaism in *Contra Celsum,* his only work addressed directly to pagan readers. He had little choice, since the main objections expressed by Celsus (and they were not peculiar to him) were that Christianity was neither ancient nor the religion of a particular people. This Origen could refute only by claiming the heritage of Israel. But he had to be circumspect—being positive enough about Judaism to make it a worthy predecessor, but not so positive that he could not explain why Christianity had broken free from Judaism.[77] In addition, the negative judgment of pagans on Jews (e.g., that they were secretive and clannish; that they were especially gullible about the miraculous) meant that if he was to defend the one, he had to defend the other. He would have been particularly sensitive, therefore, to "Jewish" charges against Christianity, and even though he may have been convinced that they were ill-founded, even fictitious, we do not have to accept his opinion.

Which brings us to a second factor—that Origen was unusually well connected with the Jews in Caesarea and relied on his conversations with them to form his view of "normal" Jewish opinion. That some of the views ascribed to Celsus's Jew were not shared by Origen's Jewish contemporaries, as he frequently claims, is probable, but this may only be because Celsus's Jew represents a form of Judaism not known to him: "Celsus' acquaintance with Judaism, which is surprisingly thorough in some respects, is with a rather hellenized and syncretistic form of the religion, and Origen, by opposing Celsus' words with statements about the more exclusive Judaism of the rabbis, attempts to ridicule Celsus' knowledge of Judaism."[78] There is no reason to suppose that figures like Celsus's Jew did not exist some seventy years earlier (perhaps in Origen's day too) and in other places than Caesarea.

In fact, in several instances it can be shown that the Jew whom Origen does not recognize was a familiar part of the nonrabbinic world of the second century. In addition, many of the accusations attributed to this Jew sound much more Jewish than those we would expect from a pagan philosopher, and this is particularly evident when there is a discrepancy between Celsus and his Jewish contact.[79] This is not to say that there are no signs of Celsus coloring the argument to suit his interests, which are not always those of his Jewish source, but it does allow us the rare experience of hearing a voice from the other side of the Jewish-Christian debate.

The Jew in *True Doctrine* addresses part of his argument to Jesus and part to Jewish Christians. The Jewish viewpoint, as in the *Dialogue,* is expressed more tersely than the Christian's extensive reply, but it touches on many of the same themes. First, the question of Christian defection from the law is pointedly raised in *Cels.*2.1,4, as it was by Trypho. Origen's response shares one thing with Justin—the claim that Christians have a superior knowledge of the law, which lies deeper than its surface meaning—but otherwise his argument follows a different line.

Second, Christology was a major problem for Trypho on two fronts: that Jesus' career did not fulfill, indeed in some ways contradicted, messianic expectations, especially in the manner of his death; and that his divinity not only implied absurd notions about incarnation but also threatened the unity of God. The same issues arise in *True Doctrine,* but the question of messiahship is not so prominent, partly because, according to Origen, Celsus muddles the concepts of messiah and son of God. He attributes to his Jewish informant beliefs about the son of God when the Jews speak only of a messiah: "Frequently they [Jews] press us with questions on this very title of the son of God, saying that there is no such person, and that the prophets do not mention him" (*Cels.*1.48; cf. 2.31). In this case Origen was probably wrong.[80] Still, the question of messiahship does come up: Jesus cannot be messiah because there is no evidence that he was truly resurrected (*Cels.*2.77–78), his appearance neither demonstrated his kingship nor had universal impact (*Cels.*2.29–30), and the prophecies supposedly applied to him could as easily apply to others (*Cels.*1.51,57; 2.28). The general sense is that Jesus failed to live up to normal messianic expectations—a charge that Origen, like Justin before him, answers by referring to the two advents, one in humiliation and the other in glory (*Cels.*1:56).

There are, on the other hand, repeated attacks on Jesus' divinity: a god could not have been born in the manner that Jesus was, and the birth stories are a fabrication to cover up his illegitimacy (*Cels.*1.28; 69–70); the idea of a crucified divinity is absurd (*Cels.*2.31; cf. 2:68); his behavior toward his immediate followers was distinctly ungodlike (*Cels.*2.6–10), and he did not display any of the conventional features of pagan divinities (*Cels.*2.33–41); his supposed divine foreknowledge is contradicted by the pattern of his life (*Cels.*2.13–29); and his failure to find acceptance, even among the Jews, proves finally that he was a mere man (*Cels.*2.72–79). This is an example of what appears to be a mix of Jewish and pagan objections, but might in fact have as much to do with the sort of Jews Celsus knew as with his own influence on the argument.

The christological arguments of Celsus's Jew thus bear a resemblance to those of Justin's Trypho even though they are not identical. The same two central issues come up, and some of the supporting arguments, especially about Jesus' divinity, are very similar. But other arguments are introduced too, and one of Trypho's main concerns—the threat to monotheism of the concept of two gods—does not arise.

Two other issues are found in common. First, the question of Jesus' purported miracles, dismissed by the Jews as examples of vulgar sorcery (*Cels.*1.67–68). If Jesus predicted that others would employ similar miracles, but would nevertheless be false Christs and wicked sorcerers, what is there about his miracles that is distinctive? To which skeptical question Origen replies that Jesus' miracles are broadly similar to those of biblical figures like Moses, but superior to them in both number and kind (*Cels.*2.48–52). This is essentially the same conflict—between Jew, Christian, and pagan—that appears in the *Dialogue* and frequently elsewhere in second- and third-century literature. Second, disputes over the meaning and fulfillment of scripture, while not so prominent or intense as in the *Dialogue,* nevertheless play a significant role. They arise in discussion of whether the prophecies could refer to events other than the ones Christians suggest (*Cels.*1.51–57; 2.28–30), why the Jews reject Jesus if he is the fulfillment of their expectations (*Cels.*2.8; 2.74–75), and indeed why his life ostensibly did not conform to the common hope (*Cels.*2.30).

On a number of matters, therefore, the arguments attributed to Celsus's Jew provide interesting parallels to those placed on the lips of Trypho. Clearly there are differences—both in specific arguments and in emphasis—but questions of law, Christology, miracles, and scripture clearly rankle Celsus's Jew as well as Trypho. The issue of who is the true Israel does not explicitly arise as it does in the third part of Justin's *Dialogue.* This is partly, no doubt, because it would scarcely have interested Celsus, who considered both Judaism and Christianity to be superstitions. But, as suggested above, implicit in the very choice of a Jewish interlocutor and explicit in his charge that Christians are renegade Jews (*Cels.*2.1–4) is the judgment that there is nothing at all to be said for any Christian claims along these lines. All in all, therefore, the arguments attributed to Celsus's Jew cover many of the same points raised by Trypho and provide at least indirect confirmation that the arguments that Justin attributes to him genuinely reflect the sorts of issues Jews were likely to raise in the second half of the second century.

When we place all these elements together with the characteristics he displays in the debate—a willingness to listen and concede with only rare moments of irritation—is Trypho a plausible figure? On the whole, he is. He doesn't look precisely like a rabbinic Jew or like most of the Hellenistic Jews whom we know anything about. But that would have been true of most of the Jews of his day. Only if we work with limited and cumbersome categories such as "rabbinic" and "Hellenistic," and at the same time suppose that they refer to homogeneous entities, does the figure of Trypho seem problematic. A Jew who had lived in Judaea (whether he was born there is not clear) but had been taught philosophy in a Socratic school in Argos (*Dial.*1:2–3) is just the sort of figure to challenge our familiar categories.[81] And he may not have been so rare. Without pushing the argument too far, perhaps we should recognize that, in terms of both his peculiar blend of Jewishness and his attitude toward Christianity, there may have been rather more Jews like Trypho than we have been inclined to think.

SUMMARY

What, then, does Justin's *Dialogue* tell us about Jewish-Christian relations? It tells us, first, that dialogue between the two took place and that both sides could be reasonably well informed about the other's point of view. Second, such debates could be conducted in a polite and civilized manner despite an occasional outburst of irritation. These conclusions are not insignificant when we place them in a broader context, because there has been a tendency to present the story of Jewish-Christian relations in this period as one of unrelieved gloom and hostility. Justin gives important evidence for another side to the story.[82] Of course, Justin argues for Christian superiority and against the Jews, but he does so without introducing many of the themes that characterize anti-Jewish tracts of this period.[83]

These conclusions should be kept in perspective, and they are thus deliberately expressed in conditional form. For, if it would be misleading to ignore the positive implications of Justin's evidence, it would be equally misleading to treat them as the norm. Justin represented only one Christian approach toward Judaism. His views on the matter could represent a minority viewpoint, as did his tolerance of Jewish Christians. Trypho, too, is presented as something of a maverick, one who defied the advice of his own community leaders and is urged by Justin to continue doing so. It is moreover noticeable that as Trypho is often more polite than his friends, so is he treated more benignly than the Jews and their leaders in general—toward whom Justin can express sweeping hostility, especially when he brings to mind their harassment and persecution of Christians.

Such caveats may qualify, but they do not undermine, the two essential points—that there was informed dialogue and that it was conducted in a civilized tone. And there is, thirdly, a further implication. With due caution we can use Trypho and Celsus's Jew to help build our picture of Jewish approaches to Christianity in the second century.[84] Most of the evidence for this period comes from the Christian side and distorts by its very preponderance, so that any way of seeing things from the Jewish point of view is invaluable. It is as unfortunate that it is filtered through Christian tradents as it is that other material is shaped by the interests of the tannaim. In each case we have to accept the limitations of the evidence and do the best we can. It is a triumph of sorts that there is any evidence at all.

Fourth, we may conclude that while there were some clear disagreements between Jews and Christians on matters of both practice and belief, the means of settling them were often slippery and ill-defined. Neither community, for example, was homogeneous. There were differing Christian groups (Marcionites and Gnostics are obvious examples) as there were Jewish groups (Trypho, his friends, their leaders, and other Jewish sects mentioned in passing). Each tradition had some difficulty in defining an authoritative voice to speak for it, one effect of which was that they presented a constantly shifting target to the opposition. Or again, the meaning of scripture was a nodal point of the debate, but scripture came in different languages and different versions, and even when this was not a problem remarkably similar exegetical techniques could be used in the service of fundamentally different conclusions. Or yet again, while the reality of miraculous occurrences was rarely challenged, their inspiration and meaning were hotly disputed.

It is striking, fifthly, that the more or less predictable disagreements about practice and belief were compounded by immediate historical pressures, most notably the Bar Cochba rebellion and the Jewish War, as well as by certain observable historical realities such as the universal spread of the church. These both provided a context for and introduced additional terms to the more traditional form of the debate.

AN OVERVIEW

10

❖

In chapter 1 we considered the influence of the Jewish War and the Bar Cochba rebellion on Jewish-Christian relations. The focus was on the events themselves, their known and surmised consequences, and the traces they have left in the Jewish and Christian traditions. We are now in a position to pick up the threads of this argument in the light of the intervening chapters. One way of approaching the issue is to ask, as does J. D. G. Dunn, which of them marks the decisive parting of the ways. Using the two events as chronological markers, he surveys the evidence in between in order to locate the point where an originally intramural squabble turned into an extramural confrontation. Evidence for continuing contact, he thinks, shows that 70 CE was not the decisive turning point, but evidence for increasing separation early in the second century shows that 70–135 CE was the decisive era for the parting of the ways. After 135 CE the separation was clear-cut and final.[1]

Dunn has drawn attention to an important question. Some of his arguments complement those offered here, and his analysis warns us that we cannot consider the two events in isolation, ignoring what transpired between them. Yet his approach is too schematic and the body of evidence he surveys too limited to allow an answer to his own question. The New Testament evidence, which is the focus of his inquiry, is important, but there is an equally important body of noncanonical evidence which is touched on lightly, if at all. The *intra muros/extra muros* distinction carries much of the burden of Dunn's argument, even though he is aware of some of its complexities. The distinction has its uses, but it does not always provide the most helpful way of approaching the evidence (see the discussion below). Above all, however, he gives the impression that we can identify a specific point beyond which Jewish-Christian relations were irrevocably altered. Yet, as will become clear below, the evidence suggests that proximity and

distance, coexistence and confrontation, are to be found variously throughout the period we have studied. It is for this reason that we have asked
which of the two events was the more important—a less pointed but more
appropriate way of phrasing the question. Consideration of the political and
social fallout from the two events suggests that the Bar Cochba rebellion
was likely to have been the more traumatic for Jewish-Christian relations.
The Jewish War had two main effects on Christian thinking. It forced them
to recast their eschatological timetables, as can be seen most clearly in Mark
13 and parallels, and it nourished the thought that God had passed judgment on the Jews for their obdurate refusal to receive his messengers (Matt
22:7; Matt 23:37–39 = Luke 13:34–35). Luke, who alludes most clearly and
frequently to this theme, nevertheless conveys a mood of sadness rather
than bitter recrimination (19:41–44; 23:37–41). Mark was the most affected
by the war because he wrote during the maelstrom of events that brought it
to its conclusion, while John, writing at a greater distance, transposes the
issue into an altogether different key by taking the Temple predictions to
refer to Jesus' death and resurrection (2:18–22).

No clear connection is made between the destruction of the city and the
death of Jesus. In Matthew 22:7 the destruction is seen as a punishment,
but for the death of God's servants, not his Son. Luke 23:37–41 links the
death of Jesus with the fate of the city, but not as cause and effect, and there
are no allusions to the destruction in Acts—despite the polemic against the
cult (7:44–50) and the many references to Jewish responsibility for Jesus'
death (including 7:51–52), both of which later tradition connects with the
fall of Jerusalem. Hebrews, as we have seen, does not mention the outcome
of the war despite considerable interest in cultic supersession. The obscure
allusion in Revelation 11:1–2 probably distinguishes between the heavenly
(inner court) and earthly (outer court) temples, in line with reflections on
the heavenly Jerusalem and Temple elsewhere in the work (3:12; 7:15;
11:19; 14:15; 21:2,10). Yet this vision is not so much a reaction to the destruction of the earthly Temple of the Jews as a projection of an ideal heavenly future which counteracts the pressures of living under what was perceived as a hostile Roman state.

If it is correct to connect *Barnabas* with a pro-Jewish turn in Roman policy under Nerva, we have evidence that around the turn of the century the
prospect of a rebuilt Temple could cause Christians considerable alarm, in
part no doubt because post-70 conditions had come to be seen increasingly
as a confirmation of Judaism's rejection and inferior status. At any rate, an
explicit cause of the destruction is, for the first time, suggested: the Jews'
idolatrous attachment to a building (*Barn.*16:1–5). The author's views may
not have been representative—he indicates that other Christians took a different view of Judaism—and their influence may have been limited to the
time of the crisis during which they were written.

Barnabas is at any rate an exception, since the author responds primarily to the prospect of a rebuilt Temple. It is the destruction of the old Temple that is, from this time on, increasingly and explicitly used in anti-Jewish polemic. It is seen as a punishment for the persecution of Christians (Justin *Dial*.16), the death of James (Origen *Cels*.1.47, allegedly quoting Josephus), and the death of Jesus (Justin *Dial*.16; Tertullian *Marc*.3.23; Origen *Cels*.1.47; 4.22,32; 8.42), or as a sign that God wished to bring the sacrificial system to an end (*Ps.-Clem.Rec*.1.39,64). Naturally, too, it was seen as a fulfillment of prophecy (Justin *Dial*.16,110; *I Apol*.47; Tertullian *Marc*.3.23).

It is striking that a number of these passages make no clear distinction between the results of the Jewish War and of the Bar Cochba rebellion (Justin *I Apol*.47; Tertullian *Marc*.3.23; Tertullian *Adv.Jud*.13; *Ps.-Clem.Rec*.1.37). Justin's statement in *Dial*.16 is perhaps the clearest example. Speaking of circumcision, he claims that it was designed "to set you off from other nations and from us Christians. The purpose of this was that you and only you might suffer the afflictions that are justly yours; that only your land be desolate and your cities ruined by fire; that the fruits of your land be eaten by strangers before your very eyes; and that none of you be permitted to enter your city of Jerusalem." The banishment of the Jews from Jerusalem left a particularly strong impression on Justin (*Dial*.17,22) and later on Eusebius (*Hist.eccl*.4.6.3–4). At the same time Justin can use the cessation of the cult as evidence that the Jews were disinherited (*Dial*.40,46), while Tertullian uses their banishment from Jerusalem to make the same point (*Apol*.21). Justin is the first to have had knowledge of both events, and was much affected by the rebellion, in part perhaps because he lived through it; but he started a trend that continued well beyond him.

Equally interesting is that the more explicit and hostile anti-Jewish interpretations of the Jewish War first appear in Christian writings in conjunction with reaction to the Bar Cochba rebellion. This may be fortuitous, a result of the paucity of our evidence, but it seems to indicate a tendency to blend the two together in Christian memory, with the first being seen as a mere prelude to the second. Perhaps the Bar Cochba rebellion spurred Christian thinkers on to recognize that the outcome of the Jewish War was final and God's judgment irrevocable. Earlier, this may not have been so clear. Nerva and Trajan may briefly have made Jewish hopes for a restoration seem more than a dream, and *Barnabas* shows how unsettling this could appear, while during the rebellion a few decades later the fate of Jerusalem hung in the balance again for a time. But with the devastating defeat under Hadrian the future must have seemed, from a Christian perspective, secure. The holy city and its Temple had been once and for all taken from the Jews, and the Christians had taken over.

The effect of the Jewish War on the Jewish view of Christians is more difficult to document. The introduction of the *Birkat ha-minim*, along with other attacks on the *minim* and occasional rabbinic reports of conflict, suggest that Jewish Christians were increasingly seen as a threat by a beleaguered Jewish community. That the traumas of the war led the Yavnean rabbis to attempt to redefine their community and assert control over it is commonly, and rightly, noted. Yet the evidence also indicates that Christians were only one part of a troublesome group of Jewish heretics, and that rabbinic control over Judaism at large had barely begun to take effect.

The significance of the Jewish War should not be belittled, yet a number of the texts we have considered confirm our suspicion that the events associated with the Bar Cochba rebellion had a more dramatic effect on Jewish-Christian relations. The execution of some Christians (Justin), perhaps preceded by their temporary defection to the cause of Bar Cochba (*Apocalypse of Peter*), the suppression and ignominy of the Jews (Hadrian's measures) and their permanent banishment from Jerusalem, and the introduction of Gentile Christian leaders to the Jerusalem church were all potentially divisive events. In addition to hovering in the background of Justin's *First Apology* and *Dialogue,* they appear to have given impetus to, and historical confirmation of, the radical rejection of Israel and her replacement by a new people in the *Apocalypse of Peter, 5 Ezra,* and *4 Baruch.* Moreover, the disastrous failure of the rebellion may have led some Jews to pursue their doubts and speculations in a radically gnostic direction, and the ignominy following the defeat may be part of the explanation for Marcion's decisive separation of Christianity from its Jewish roots. It is possible, too, that it precipitated the move to dissociate Christianity from Judaism by the promotion of Easter Sunday as the Christian pasch. If the rebellion affected the Christian view of Judaism, it may also have done the reverse. It is true that only a few Jews were involved in the harassment and execution of Christians—at any rate, an exceptional action taken during a tense military crisis. Yet the presence of Gentile Christian bishops and a Christian community in Jerusalem after the rebellion must have been galling to Jews banished from their sacred city, and this, in turn, may have been the time that Gentile Christianity impinged itself on the rabbis as a force to be reckoned with, leading to an expansion of the *Birkat ha-minim.* All in all, the evidence suggests that the Bar Cochba rebellion had a significant effect on the way in which Jews and Christians viewed each other, confirming but exceeding the effect of the Jewish War.

Yet the events surrounding the Jewish revolts were only one aspect of the political context of Jewish-Christian relations. The broader picture must take into account the overall standing of Jews and Christians in the Roman world. Here the balance fell heavily in favor of the Jews. They were more numerous, politically and legally more secure, socially more integrated, and able to call on an ancient tradition that gave weight and respectability to their position. To find a niche in the world was thus, for the Christians, an uphill struggle against Jewish superiority and Roman suspicion. The Christian apologists consciously attempted to present their case in terms comprehensible to the outside world, and in the process explicitly contrasted themselves with the Jews. This sometimes involved denigration of the Jews and always involved, in one form or another, appropriation of their heritage. The desire to deflect the charge of novelty probably encouraged others to take over the Jewish tradition as their own, as shown by the *Protevangelium of James* or Melito, for example. Indeed, wherever we find Christians claiming to be the true Israel, we should ask whether enhancement of their political standing was not at least one of their motivations.

A further way of enhancing their position was for Christians to present their own past as politically harmless. This is most obvious in the Passion narratives. The canonical versions increasingly blame the Jews and exonerate the Romans for Jesus' death, a trend that becomes even clearer in the apocrypha, notably in the *Gospel of Peter* and the *Acts of Pilate*, and that finds its most complete expression in Melito's *Paschal Homily.* In this way Christians intended to curry favor with the Romans, to gloss over the embarrassing fate of their founder, and to denigrate the Jews. The Jews, however, did not always stand passively to one side. They periodically put pressure on Christians in the synagogues and fanned the suspicion and hostility to which state authorities were already predisposed.

Yet things were not always so simple. Roman pressure on Christians may have led some of them to return to or seek refuge in the synagogue—the situation that apparently lies behind Hebrews and the actions of the Judaizers in Revelation. The latter, at least, probably occurred in a particularly tense period, which Domitian had complicated by extending the Jewish tax and putting pressure on those who Judaized. The same circumstances may have led Luke to encourage association with Judaism—perhaps in the face of vocal opposition from the Jews—as a means of avoiding more severe pressures from the state. If so, it is interesting to note that Luke's pragmatic compromise was precisely the sort of move that infuriated the author of Revelation when he attacked the Judaizers of Smyrna and Philadelphia. Thus, while we can properly speak in broad terms of the position of Jews and Christians in the Roman world, the evidence alerts us to the way in which local circumstances and changing political fortunes led to different, sometimes contradictory, notions of how best to respond.

When we shift our attention from the political setting, the variety of the responses of Christians and Jews to each other becomes even more pronounced. From the Jewish side the evidence is admittedly slim, but not for this reason to be ignored. That the Jews often reacted with hostility and suspicion to Christians is indicated not only by the evidence for their involvement in public harassment, but also by the generally negative attitude recorded in stray rabbinic traditions, including the introduction of the *Birkat ha-minim.* Yet we can point to Josephus as an example of one who could allude to Christianity in neutral rather than hostile terms, and to Trypho as one who could engage in discussion with genuine curiosity, a knowledge of the rival tradition, and a gracious and equable temperament. That there were others who took the time to learn something about the Christian movement, rather than blindly rejecting it, is also shown by Celsus's Jew.

It is not hard to find expressions of intense rivalry with and hostility toward Judaism in early Christian writings. In addition to some of those mentioned above (5 Ezra, 4 Baruch, Apocalypse of Peter, Gospel of Peter), we might point to the Gospels of Matthew and John, Barnabas, Diognetus, Melito, and apocryphal writings such as 3 Baruch, the Sibylline Oracles, and the Synagogue Prayers. Indeed, the general mood of antipathy toward the Jews in these documents has often been taken to represent the mainstream early Christian position and to show that Jews and Christians were constantly at each other's throats.

Yet this is a simplification that amounts to a distortion. There are examples of a more neutral attitude toward the Jews in the Protovangelium of James and the Acts of Pilate, and in apologists like Aristides and Theophilus, who ascribe a positive (if limited) value to the Jews and their heritage. Justin is a significant witness to the possibility of civilized dialogue based on mutual knowledge and respect, and it may be that Marcion was persuaded by some of the arguments from the Jewish side of the debate in just this sort of context. Jewish Christians are another important piece of the jigsaw because, although they were the focus of Jewish hostility early on and were eventually to be cast adrift by most Jews and Christians alike, they appear to have retained a largely positive view of Jewish practice and belief. And then, above all, we have the Christian Judaizers, whose assessment of Judaism is in marked contrast to that of those who speak in much of the other evidence available to us. They appear in Revelation, Ignatius, Barnabas, Justin, perhaps in Hebrews and in Sibylline Oracle 6, and it is their response to Judaism that may lie behind the thinking of Marcion and Melito. Their reasons for Judaizing varied. Political pressure, Jewish persuasiveness, and reversion to a previous lifestyle are those that can be identified, but there may well have been others—as can be seen in better-documented cases like fourth-century Antioch. Whatever their motives, and despite the fact that in one instance (Dial.47) Judaizing led to defection, these Christians demonstrated that it was possible to relate to Judaism in a far more positive manner than much of the other evidence, which is often thought typical, indicates. They are the other voices we need to listen to, scarcely audible in our evidence but not necessarily so in their day.

This points to a related theme—the salvation of the Jews. There is no shortage of texts, in the New Testament and elsewhere, that project a bleak future for the Jews, and there are a number of others that ignore the issue altogether. Matthew and Luke seem to have come to a similar conclusion, if by different routes: the Jews had no future as a special people of God; they were no longer the elect, and their salvation was no longer secure. The best that individual Jews could hope for was to convert and secure their salvation in Christ. It is possible that, prior to this, Paul envisaged, in Romans 11, salvation for the Jews as Jews, by virtue of their original covenant with God. If so, his view was without influence in the rest of the New Testament and, in the particular form in which he expressed it, in most other early Christian literature too.

Yet there are several other places where we can detect a positive hope for the Jews. The Quartodecimans, according to the *Didascalia,* were exhorted to pray for the salvation of their brethren, the Jews. The Nazarenes apparently did the same, and Theophilus appears to have clung to the hope that they would be saved. *Odes of Solomon* 31 clearly states that Jesus died in order to secure the salvation of his nation (apparently, in this context, the Jews), in line with the promises to the patriarchs. Salvation in these contexts is conceived largely in Christian terms, that is, the Jews were to be saved by conversion—a notion that may not go beyond the views of Matthew and Luke. Marcion, in his eccentric way, conceived of a future for the Jews expressed in their own terms. They would be visited by their messiah and gathered into a restored Jerusalem to enjoy their salvation. Admittedly, in Marcion's overall scheme, this was a decidedly inferior prospect compared with the salvation anticipated for the devotees of the God revealed by Jesus, but it strikes a positive, if curious, note. Justin clearly hopes for the salvation of at least a remnant of Jews—the righteous who kept the law and who did not persecute Christians—and the language in which he expresses it is sufficiently ambiguous as to leave it unclear whether this was to occur through conversion (in an eschatological miracle) or through some residual effect of their original covenant. Perhaps, like the pagan worthies from the past who he also expected would be saved, their salvation rested on the way they fulfilled the terms of their relationship with God apart from the gospel.

If Justin's statements are ambiguous, the same cannot be said for the bold universalism of the *Testaments of the Twelve Patriarchs,* and the covenantal schemes of the author of the *Kerygmata Petrou* and the Judaizers alluded to in *Barnabas.* In the first, the salvation of both Gentiles and Jews is confidently expected and frequently expressed, and there is nothing to indicate that the Jews are not to be saved as Jews. That conviction is clearly announced in the other two texts, with their notions of a shared or double covenant for Jews and Christians. And, if the *Acts of Pilate* 14–16 only hint at such a scheme, they are otherwise clearly optimistic about the future of the Jews.

These reflections on the salvation of the Jews are scattered throughout the evidence from this period and have no apparent connection with one another. They are thus the more impressive. They also vary in the generosity of their vision. Yet, singly and collectively, they are an important witness to a way of viewing things that runs against the grain of that negative view of Judaism which finds ample expression in this period and which was to become the dominant Christian position. Yet again, we have voices that have not often been heard and that illustrate the variety and complexity of early

Jewish-Christian relations. And this, of course, is only another way of saying that there was in this period no single entity that we can label Judaism or another that we can label Christianity. Rather, each of them took many forms and reacted to the others in different ways.

If variety marks the way Jews and Christians related to each other and envisaged their respective futures, it is also the hallmark of the ideological and social tensions that separated them. It is not uncommon for scholars to single out one or two themes as the key areas of disagreement, whether it be messianism, the unity of God, the Torah, the Temple, the heritage of Israel, or the meaning of scripture. The impulse is understandable, and it makes sense to presuppose that the distinctive practices and central convictions of Judaism and Christianity were likely to have been the areas of greatest disagreement. The problem is that what we presuppose is what we usually find, and this leads us to pattern and grade the evidence in a way that belies its rich variety—the changes over time, the appearance and disappearance of themes, and the peculiar emphases of particular texts. If in some texts a solitary issue appears, in others, like Justin, they come in droves. It is true that some themes are more widespread and prominent than others in the surviving evidence, but none of them can be said to stand alone as the sole explanation for the Jewish-Christian schism. Far more helpful than grading them is to list them in all their shapes and sizes.

We have noted more than once the truism that Judaism was more concerned with orthopraxy than with orthodoxy. Like all truisms it is, as we have also noted, an exaggeration. Nevertheless, it is hardly surprising that disputes arose over the law. The Gospels, the earliest evidence we have considered, show marked differences. In Matthew the tension and the level of engagement are at their greatest, and we get the impression that the Jews called the shots. Yet for Matthew, as a representative of a Christian group that was intimately related to (and recently part of) the local Jewish community, the law was no small issue either. He tries to deflect the charge of antinomianism and yet hold on to two convictions: that the law remains intact, but that it is to be interpreted by Jesus rather than the Jewish experts. Mark and the Gospel of Luke show much less interest in the issue, probably because they represented Gentile Christians for whom it was not a pressing matter. They seem content to record the disputes and settle for Jesus as the authoritative voice, a tendency that is even more marked in John. In Acts, conflict with the Jews over the law focuses on Jewish rather than Gentile Christians, and especially on the controversial reputation of Paul. The apostolic decree, however precisely understood, leaves Gentile Christians with the most minimal of requirements and shows why the issue of the law was largely a matter of indifference to them.

The common thread of Jewish Christian groups, by all accounts, was their commitment to keeping the law, even if a slightly reduced one (as in the "false pericopes" notion of the *Kerygmata Petrou*). For this they were ridiculed by other Christians, but it drew them closer to the Jews. They were, however, an exception. For most other groups in the second century the law posed questions that were more hermeneutical than practical. That is, they had to explain to themselves and their Jewish opponents why they no longer observed commands that were an integral part of the Jewish scriptures they had taken as their own. Their tactics varied. In some cases they attacked (*Gospel of Thomas, Barnabas*), or ridiculed (*Diognetus*) Jewish observance based on the law, or declared it impossible in the light of recent events, such as the destruction of the Temple (Justin). Faced with pointed queries from those such as Trypho and Celsus's Jew, and no doubt from within their own communities too (e.g., Judaizers), they were more defensive, justifying their position by theories of supersession (Hebrews, *Synagogue Prayers*, Melito) or by allegorical maneuvers, which allowed them to interpret the law along moral or christological lines (*Barnabas*, Justin).

The fate of the Temple and of the city of Jerusalem are recurring themes in the earlier period. The destruction of the Temple was undoubtedly traumatic for the Jews, yet they came to terms with it as they had with similar tragedies in the past. Writings like *4 Ezra* and *2 Baruch* show how this was done, in the immediate aftermath of the war, by placing it in the broad context of convictions about the justice of God and the covenant with his people. Nor was the destruction considered irrevocable. During the time of Nerva, and later Bar Cochba, hope for its rebuilding remained high. The Mishnah, in its own curious mode, continued to regulate for an ideal, transformed Temple, even though in reality it had been physically replaced by a temple of Jupiter. Much of this reflection remained internal to the Jews and did not affect their view of Christians. The one exception was in the time of Nerva, when hope for a rebuilt Temple briefly flared and provoked considerable alarm and antipathy in the author of *Barnabas*.

From the Christian side, as we noted above, the initial reaction to the destruction of the Temple was also mostly internal, a question of rewriting their eschatological schemes. Jewish speculation on a heavenly or future Temple was later to be christologically transmuted into a peculiarly Christian vision of a spiritual or heavenly temple, which implicitly or explicitly excluded the Jews and any aspirations they may have had (John, Hebrews, Revelation, *Barnabas*). If a theological takeover was one reaction, another was to point to the harsh reality of historical experience. There are hints in the Gospels of the theme of judgment, but it becomes increasingly prominent after the Bar Cochba rebellion, starting with Justin. The outcome of the Jewish War, and more importantly of the Bar Cochba rebellion, are presented as an unambiguous sign of God's judgment and the vanity of hopes for the restoration of city and Temple. Marcion is an exception to this, but Justin, with his literal chiliastic vision of a return to Jerusalem in the last days, rubs salt into an already open wound.

There is clear evidence, too, for a dispute over miracles. As is commonly noted, the dispute did not usually turn on whether or not exceptional deeds had been performed, but rather on the question of their source or inspiration. Were they a sign of divine or of demonic influence? The answer depended on prior conviction, for one person's miracle was another's sorcery. Occasionally an attempt was made to inject an element of reason into the issue—by pointing to the obvious benefits or the lasting effects of a healing or exorcism, for example—but by and large it remained an unsubtle dispute, amounting to little more than the assertion of claim and counterclaim. The signs are already there in Mark and the Gospel of Luke, where the issue of Jewish miracle workers is brought in obliquely in the Beelzebul controversy, yet on the whole their portraits of Jesus as an impressive performer of miracles served other apologetic and christological purposes than this. Matthew brings us closer to Jewish-Christian disputes in the accusation that Jesus was a deceiver and magician, an accusation that later finds echoes in rabbinic tradition. Acts is in many ways the most interesting source, since there Luke brings the issue out into the open. He does not merely defend the reputation of Jesus and his followers, but directly contrasts the miraculous powers of Christians and Jews on the public stage. After this the most informative witness is Justin, who reacts strongly to accusations by Jews (but not, apparently, Trypho and his friends), which echo those we find in Matthew. Rabbinic literature picks up the issue and dismisses Jesus as a magician and sorcerer, while Celsus's Jew makes a number of skeptical observations about his purported talents. The evidence is a little patchy, but sufficient to indicate a dispute of continuing significance, which would have been neither arid nor arcane in a world where magic and miracle were commonplace, rarely questioned, and expected of any competent religious aficionado. Stories of magical or miraculous power would have impressed the general populace far more than convoluted theological disputes, and what circulated in legend and rumor was likely to have had a wide and significant effect.[2]

Christology has understandably been seen as one of the key issues that divided Jews and Christians.[3] It appears, not surprisingly, in most of the evidence we have considered. It is a divisive and major point of contention in all the canonical Gospels and Acts, and it becomes the overwhelmingly dominant theme in John. It is said in some sources to have been the only serious point of disagreement between Jewish Christians and other Jews, and in some of the Christian adaptations of Jewish apocrypha the addition of brief christological formulas is the only significant change made. From Hebrews and *Barnabas* through Justin, Celsus, Melito, rabbinic literature and the Christian apocrypha, it runs like a continuous thread, though it is not for that reason the sole, nor always the most important, issue.

The middle section of Justin's *Dialogue* circles around the two main issues: messianism and monotheism. As to the first, Jesus' birth, and more particularly his death, were deeply problematic, and Jews like Trypho and the rabbinic tradents lost no time in pointing this out. At the same time, the Christian tendency to make increasingly grandiose claims for Jesus and to expand his divine status ran up against the rabbis' deep suspicion of anything that tampered with the unity of God. It is probable that Jesus' messiahship initiated the dispute and his divinity brought it to a climax, and some think that precisely these two stages can be traced in the Gospel of John.

In both cases it is significant that the grounds of dispute were not clearcut. Jewish messianic expectations were remarkably varied, in fact capacious enough to support at least some aspects of the Christian claim; and defense of the unity of God took place in the context of Jewish speculations that came dangerously close to the kinds of things asserted about Jesus. The debate was intricate and the terms slippery. Jews may have been more concerned with praxis than belief, but belief was important to them too; and when they ran up against Christian assertions (among others) that challenged their traditional convictions, it appears to have whetted their theological appetites.

Related to all this was the death of Jesus. We know little of the Jewish view of this matter, except that Josephus records it as a matter of fact and a few rabbinic traditions consider his death to be deserving of a sorcerer and deceiver of the people. In the Christian tradition the Jews were, from the start, apportioned the lion's share of the blame. The canonical writings make issue of it by whitewashing the Romans and increasingly bringing all contemporary Jews, leaders and people, into the act. The same trend is evident in the *Gospel of Peter* and the *Acts of Pilate,* even if their overall view of the Jews is not the same, and Justin thinks their due reward came in the destruction of the Temple. In the *Synagogue Prayers* and *Sibylline Oracles* 1, the responsibility of the Jews for Jesus' death is vividly and dramatically portrayed. For Quartodeciman Christians the association of Jesus' death with the actions of the Jews was recalled each year, but, in some circles, led to prayers for their repentance rather than relentless castigation. With Melito, however, there comes an ominous change: the Jews were responsible for the death not only of Christ, but of God—ironically, though they did not know it, their own God.

The Christian claim to be the true people of God is, to begin with, muted, suggested rather than stated, as in Matthew and Luke-Acts. In Christian apocrypha, like the *Protevangelium of James* and the *Apocalypse of Peter,* the same thing is implied, as it is when we imagine how Christians would have read some of the originally Jewish apocrypha which they adopted for their own use (*4 Baruch, Apocalypse of Abraham, Synagogue Prayers*). In none of these writings do we find formulations such as "new Israel" or "new people," but the absence of formulas does not necessarily signify the absence of the idea, even if in inchoate form. Marcion is as usual an exception, but some of the Gnostics, who otherwise distance themselves from Judaism, have their own way of expressing a sense of being a peculiar and chosen people (the "seed of Seth," etc.). As time went by, however, Christians became bolder and more forthright in their claims. *Barnabas* makes it quite clear that the Jews had never inherited the covenant, having lost it from the very start. The covenant belonged to Christians, as God had always intended. Equally bold claims are made in *5 Ezra,* where Christians are called God's "new people," and in the *Kerygma Petrou,* where they are called a "third race," who are neither Jews nor Greeks and who worship God in an entirely new way. That Christians had taken over the heritage of Israel is implied in Melito's wholesale christological appropriation of their history, and, in the third section of the *Dialogue,* Justin makes a sustained and open argument that Christians were the "new Israel"—the first recorded use of this term in early Christian literature.

This line of argument probably met with resistance from the Jews, but we have no record of this, unless it is to be found in rabbinic assertions of the permanence of Israel's election. Trypho protests haltingly but is given little chance to speak in the last part of the *Dialogue.* Christian motives were complex. A need to express their own sense of identity, distinct from Jews (but also from pagans), was one. Another and related purpose was to locate themselves in the grand sweep of salvation history, primarily what we might think of as a theological urge. There was, thirdly, the political value of claiming an ancient heritage to avert the charge that they were a novel and upstart religion. All of these coincided to push Christian claims in a certain direction. Yet they ran into one massive obstacle: the old Israel was alive and well, more numerous, more visible, and more secure. When Celsus accused Christians of being a bastard offspring of Judaism, he would have hit a raw nerve. And if, in view of this, the Christian claim to be the true Israel met with some skepticism in the outside world, this is hardly surprising, since there is some evidence—from the Judaizers and the proponents of a joint or double covenant—that they failed to convince some of their own community too.

If some Gnostics expressed their sense of being an elect and special people in terms that vaguely echoed those used in Judaism, this was part and parcel of a philosophy that was frequently and deliberately anti-Jewish. Their radical denigration of Israel's god and law moved beyond the general run of anti-Jewish arguments and shifted the dispute onto a quite different plane—what has often and appropriately been called metaphysical anti-Judaism. A unique feature of this form of anti-Judaism, according to one currently popular theory, is that it was initially generated within Judaism before it was taken over by the Christian Gnostics who most concern us. If so, it is interesting evidence for the interaction of Jews and Christians at the periphery of their respective communities. There are a few other hints in Christian gnostic texts of a more direct engagement between Gnostics and Jews on a communal level, but quite apart from this it would be a mistake to suppose that metaphysical anti-Judaism had only limited mundane consequences. In one form or another, it was the view that most Christian Gnostics took of Judaism, and such Gnostics made up a not-insignificant percentage of the Christian movement in the second century. The same can be said of the Marcionites, whose scheme allowed a space for Jews that was expressed in terms they might themselves have used, but whose broader parameters demoted the god of the Jews and his creation to a decidedly inferior position, even if it did so in a manner that was not so unrelentingly negative as that of many Gnostics. The views of the Gnostics and Marcionites known to us may have been produced by a handful of intellectuals, but we must suppose that in some form—maybe bowdlerized, and therefore the more dangerous—they were also the views of the bulk of those who made up their communities.

In this summary of ideological disputes, we turn finally to scripture, a shared possession and for that reason the focus of endless disagreements. All the issues mentioned above were at one time or another debated in terms of scriptural precedents and proof texts, and virtually all the Christian texts we have considered contain arguments along these lines. Scriptural argument was undoubtedly used by Christians to bolster their sense of identity or settle internal disputes. Matthew and *Barnabas* in particular, however, convey a sense of how intense, strenuous and rancorous the debate could become when Jews were the imagined, if not the real, disputants. Melito's wholesale takeover of the scriptures, too, may well have been an attempt to counteract the advantages that the Jews of Sardis otherwise enjoyed. Justin, in more measured tones, gives the fullest account of the sort of give-and-take that we can imagine was more common than our evidence explicitly displays. Ignatius generally avoids arguments from scripture, but he probably does so precisely because the Judaizers (and behind them the Jews?) insisted on basing their views on scripture and in a way that he found difficult to refute.

It is possible that the use of scripture in Jewish-Christian debate became formalized, so that Christians like *Barnabas* and Justin relied as much on testimony collections as on the full biblical text. If Jews and Christians shared the scriptures and many of the hermeneutical procedures used to interpret them, they shared little else. Justin, who gives the fullest picture, indicates that there were disputes over texts (Hebrew or Greek) and versions (which LXX), authenticity (deletion/addition of sayings), the predictive reach of prophecies (to the immediate or distant future), and the level where the true meaning lay (literal, typological, or allegorical). In addition, a common and insidious move by Christians was to apply the predictions of doom and judgment to the Jews and the promises of hope to themselves. The arguments were inherently irresolvable, since their purpose was mainly to prove or disprove prior convictions; and for clever exegetes, Jewish or Christian, there was always a hermeneutical procedure that allowed evasion of the plain sense of, or extraction of unlikely meanings from, virtually any text in dispute. It is thus probable, as Justin inadvertently indicates, that the debates were more evenly matched and inconclusive than the Christian evidence would often have us believe.

J. T. Sanders has recently drawn a distinction between the ideological and the pragmatic levels of Jewish-Christian dispute, between what he calls attitudes and relations. The former, he suggests, are not necessarily expressed in the latter, and it is the latter that he particularly wishes to explore. His distinction is in principle correct. It is possible to think one thing and do another. It is also not uncommon, however, for ideological conviction to lead to pragmatic action, and in the ancient sources the two are often conflated. When the Jews introduced the *Birkat ha-minim*, for example, they were expressing an attitude (Christians are *minim*) and a relation (Christians are to be cursed). And when the author of *Barnabas* claimed that Jews had never possessed the covenant because God had reserved it for Christians (an attitude), he also meant to discourage Christians from consorting with the Jewish community (a relation). It may be that in some circles, among Christian Gnostics, for example, the attitude of the one group toward the other remained largely just that, a metaphysical rather than a mundane phenomenon—though even in this case we cannot be sure. Often the evidence is silent, but I suspect that there was a congruence between attitude and action more often than not. We do not know from Melito how Christians and Jews got along in Sardis, but I doubt that their relationship was a happy one. Thus I prefer to include in the concept "relations" both ideological and pragmatic interaction.[4]

When we turn to the social and mundane level, we can identify several factors that created tension between Christians and Jews. Proximity and size were two of them. The closer the two communities, the greater the tension was likely to have been. This was as true for a Jewish Christian community (e.g., Matthew) in the first century as for a Gentile Christian community (Melito) in the second. In both these cases the Christians were probably in a minority, in the one case to Yavnean Jews and in the other to the flourishing diaspora community in Sardis. The smaller group was likely to have felt beleaguered, to have been tenacious in defending its patch and vitriolic in its polemic. This can be shown from the Christian side, but we have less direct evidence for the Jewish response. Throughout this period the Jews were more numerous and more securely established, and this may be one reason why Christians appear so infrequently in what is admittedly a parlous body of Jewish evidence: Jews had less need to engage with Christians than did Christians with Jews. This may partly explain, for example, the absence of allusions to Christians in the Mishnah, recalling too that, in second-century Galilee, Christians were probably an almost imperceptible presence. Yet, though this now-common observation is pertinent, the extent of Jewish response to Christians should not be underestimated. It may well have been greater than the sources directly indicate. There is evidence, as we have seen, that Jews harried Christians in synagogues and public forums. The intensity of Matthew's engagement with Judaism strongly suggests that the Jews were actively involved too, and the same might be said of texts like John or *Barnabas*. It is probable that Jewish Christians, who were closest to the Jews, presented the most immediate problem, although there may have been occasions when the unwelcome proximity of other Christians, as may have been the case in Luke's situation, provoked a sharp response.

Richly polemical language, it is often argued, should not be given undue weight, since rhetorical conventions in the Roman world encouraged the use of extreme and colorful language, which contained more bark than bite. Moreover, such language was often the expression of social tensions which were more in the nature of family squabbles, *intra muros* rather than *extra muros*. The first observation is correct, but not always relevant, since the effect of rhetorical language differed according to the context. The formal jousting of rhetoricians or the disparagement of imaginary or distant opponents was one thing. The use of heated and abusive language by groups fighting over common ground or in close proximity was another.

The *intra/extra muros* distinction is also not without value, but it is relevant to only a few of the earlier texts in our period, particularly those produced by Jewish Christians. The Qumran community provides a useful analogy, though we do not know much about how other Jews viewed their more extreme and dismissive claims. Even so the distinction is overused, often with the curious implication that intramural abuse is more excusable and less damaging than that which comes from outside. Yet, from a Jewish point of view, it would hardly have mattered whether the polemic of Matthew or Melito was, from a Christian viewpoint, being delivered from inside or outside the Jewish fold. That is to say, a distinction that, retrospectively, we may find useful for heuristic purposes may not have meant much, if anything, to those engaged on the ground level in the first and second centuries. Moreover, the distinction often cannot be applied with any precision and is dependent on the point of view of both participants and observers. There is no self-evident way of defining the boundaries in the first place, nor of deciding when an internal dispute transgressed the boundaries and became an external one. And what one group saw as an intramural tussle, the other could have seen as an extramural conflict, as may well have been the case with Matthew, John, and others. Thus to argue that all Christians in the first and early second centuries can justifiably be called Jewish Christians (and fell broadly within the Jewish fold) draws a line that is as arbitrary as it is problematic.[5]

Part of the problem is that ideological claims that convey the impression of an internecine dispute would often, except perhaps for Jewish Christians, have been belied by everyday social realities. Most Christians, even before 70 CE, gathered in communities separate from Judaism. They met in churches, the Jews in synagogues (and the pagans in temples). From the end of the first century they also increasingly worshiped on different days and in different ways. These two things alone would have given them a strong sense of distinct identity, as much publicly observable as privately felt. That these boundaries mattered, and from a fairly early stage, can be seen in the fierce reaction to those who transgressed them.

For, though there were boundaries that generally marked off Jews and Christians as discrete communities, they did not go unchallenged. Public preaching, such as is described in Acts, was probably possible in the synagogues during the early years, though it would have been increasingly unwelcome within and dangerous without. The initial spurt of converts from Judaism eventually dried to a trickle, though exactly when we cannot say. The increasingly blurred contrast between leaders and people in the Gospel narratives may indicate a lingering hope for Jewish conversions, a hope that as late as Justin had not disappeared. Other Jewish Christian groups, often with their roots in the first century, survived in pockets throughout the period we have studied. Christians also recruited God-fearers, an accessible and amenable target to whom Christianity could be presented as a kind of reformed Judaism that lacked some of the more off-putting requirements of other forms of Judaism. Doubtless this caused resentment from the other side. Not only did the Jews lose adherents who were a source of pride and credibility, but, insofar as they were well placed or even eminent, they lost a conduit to the outside world. Their loss was the Christians' gain.

The boundaries were broached in the other direction too by defectors and Gentile Judaizers. The latter caused particular offense, since they implicitly challenged distinctions that other Christians used to flesh out their sense of unique identity. To them Judaizing was a puzzling and alarming phenomenon, and it evoked some of the more hostile and absurd statements about Judaism that we find in early Christian literature. We should remember too that, while those involved in this sort of two-way traffic may have been numerically small, their symbolic potential for proving the superiority of, or fostering pride in, one or the other community was disproportionately large.

This picture is consistent with what we find elsewhere. Christians, with their strong missionary impulse, actively sought adherents, which in itself would have been a likely cause of friction. Jews probably welcomed Christian Judaizers, as they did other non-Jewish sympathizers, but they showed little interest in active recruitment. There is evidence, particularly in rabbinic sources and in Justin, that some Jewish leaders attempted to ban contact with Christians, but that very same evidence indicates that they were not always successful: rabbis were castigated for contact with Christians that had already occurred, if inadvertently, and Trypho defies the recommendation of his teachers that Christians and their literature were to be avoided.

This in turn alerts us to the official slant of much of our evidence. As generally with religions in the ancient world, we are better informed about the views of the leaders and the educated elite. Except for an occasional glimpse in the surviving evidence of those who swam against the official tide, we are largely bereft of evidence for interaction on the more popular level. Stories of the miraculous and disputes over their significance are one exception. Another is the evidence for liturgical innovation, whether it is the *Birkat ha-minim* on the Jewish side, or the patterns of devotional life, weekly feasts, and annual festivals on the Christian side. Here we can imagine that official action had widespread influence, for what was repeated in liturgical routine was likely to have buried itself deeply in the consciousness of ordinary members of the two communities.

There is no doubt that the period we have surveyed nurtured many of the elements of Christian anti-Semitism that were later to become standard fare. The way in which they were beginning to coalesce, as well as the complex reasons why they did so, can be seen in figures like Justin and Melito. This points the way to the period when the relations between Jews and Christians were to settle into a more rigid and predictable pattern. Yet when we stand back from the detail, our survey of this crucial century suggests a story of considerable complexity. Even toward the end, we find an array of attitudes and motives that resist any simple definition. Reducing the story to a single issue, trend, or cause not only misleads, but also hides the rich and subtle variations to which the evidence points. And this is perhaps the only overarching conclusion we can draw.

NOTES

Introduction

1. M. Simon, *Verus Israel: A Study of the Relations between Christians and Jews in the Roman Empire (135–425)* (Oxford: Oxford University Press, 1986).

2. The best summary is to be found in A. J. Saldarini, "Jews and Christians in the First Two Centuries: The Changing Paradigm," *Shofar* 10(1992) 16–34, which, despite its title, goes well beyond the first two centuries. For the patristic period see also L. M. McDonald, "Anti-Judaism in the Early Church Fathers," in C. A. Evans and D. A. Hagner, eds., *Anti-Judaism and Early Christianity. Issues of Polemic and Faith* (Minneapolis: Fortress, 1993) 215–52.

3. R. Ruether, *Faith and Fratricide. The Theological Roots of Anti-Semitism* (New York: Seabury, 1974).

4. J. T. Sanders, *Schismatics, Sectarians, Dissidents, Deviants. The First One Hundred Years of Jewish-Christian Relations* (Valley Forge, Pa.: Trinity, 1993), makes a clear distinction between relations and attitudes and focuses his attention on the former. I use the term relations in a broader way. I doubt the utility of his distinction in connection with much of the ancient evidence and, according to his own conclusions, narrowing the discussion in this way leads to rather meager results.

Chapter 1: The Political and Social Context

1. Many issues touched on in this chapter will subsequently be discussed more fully (in this case, chap. 9). See indexes.

2. For discussion and bibliography, see B. Isaac, "Judea after A.D.70," *JJS* 35 (1984) 44–50, and the fundamental work by S. Applebaum, *Prolegomena to the Study of the Second Jewish Revolt (A.D. 132–135)* (Oxford: British Archeological Reports, Supplementary Series, 7, 1976).

3. See M. E. Stone, "Reactions to the Destruction of the Second Temple," *JSJ* 12(1980) 195–203; R. Kirschner, "Apocalyptic and Rabbinic Responses to the Destruction of 70," *HTR* 78(1985) 27–46.

4. E. M. Smallwood, *The Jews under Roman Rule* (Leiden: Brill, 1976) 371–76. The contrary view expressed by S. Mandell, "Who Paid the Temple Tax When the Jews Were under Roman Rule?" *HTR* 77(1984) 223–32, is based on too many false assumptions (e.g., that only the Pharisees prosecuted the war in 66–73 CE) and ignores too much contrary evidence (e.g., Josephus, Dio) to have any weight.

5. G. Alon, *The Jews in Their Land in the Talmudic Age* (Jerusalem: Magnes, 1980) vol.1, esp. 1–17. See also Isaac, "A.D.70"; Smallwood, *Jews,* 327–71.

6. Isaac, "A.D.70," 49–50; Smallwood, *Jews,* 340–42 (with references), against the view of Th. Mommsen (followed by many others).

7. Isaac, "A.D.70," 45–48. Smallwood, *Jews,* 340–41, calls it "unthinkable."

8. Smallwood, *Jews,* 341, with reference to rabbinic evidence. See also the long discussion in Applebaum, *Prolegomena,* 9–15, with more pessimistic conclusions.

9. K. W. Clarke, "Worship in the Jerusalem Temple after A.D.70," *NTS* 6(1959–60) 269–80; contrast Smallwood, *Jews,* 347–48.

10. Alon, *Jews,* vol.1, 70–76, speaks of persecution of Jews, but his evidence is late and weak. There is a Eusebian tradition that Vespasian hunted down descendants of the line of David, but we know nothing further about this.

11. For a critical account of the traditions, see P. Schäfer, "Die Flucht Johanan ben Zakkai aus Jerusalem und die Gründung des 'Lehrhauses' in Jabneh," *ANRW* II.19.1, 43–101.

12. On the Pharisee-rabbi connection, see S. D. Cohen, "The Significance of Yavneh: Pharisees, Rabbis and the End of Jewish Sectarianism," *HUCA* 55(1984) 27–53. Many have used J. Neusner's notion of Pharisaic transference of the Temple cult to the home to suggest that they had inadvertently prepared themselves for the loss of the Temple. See J. Neusner, *The Rabbinic Traditions about the Pharisees before 70* (Leiden: Brill, 1971) 3 vols.; idem, *Judaism: The Evidence of the Mishnah* (Chicago: Chicago University Press, 1981) and often repeated elsewhere. Recently followed, for example, by A. J. Avery-Peck, "Judaism without the Temple: The Mishnah," in H. W. Attridge and G. Hata, eds., *Eusebius, Christianity and Judaism* (Leiden: Brill, 1992) 326–54. This view has now been challenged by E. P. Sanders, *Jewish Law from Jesus to the Mishnah* (London and Philadelphia: SCM/Trinity, 1990) 131–254.

13. Alon, *Jews,* vol.1, 119–31, dates it ca. 100 CE (but thinks it was lost, and then only slowly regained, after the Bar Cochba revolt). Similarly B. S. Jackson, "On the Problem of Roman Influence on the Halakah," in E. P. Sanders with A. M. Baumgarten and A. Mendelson, eds., *Jewish and Christian Self-Definition* (Philadelphia: Fortress, 1981) vol.2, 157–203, here 161–65. J. Maier, *Grundzüge der Geschichte des Judentums im Altertum* (Darmstadt: Wissenschaftliche Buchgesellschaft, 1981) 111, dates it after 138 CE.

14. Jackson, "Problem," 163; Alon's term "collaborators" (*Jews,* vol.1, 76) is unnecessarily loaded.

15. T. D. Barnes, "Trajan and the Jews," *JJS* 40(1989) 145–62, argues that the revolt took place in 116–17 CE and (reversing the normal assumption) that it began in Mesopotamia and spread west from there. He suggests that they were defending their lifestyle in Mesopotamia against a Roman takeover.

16. So S. Applebaum, *Jews and Greeks in Ancient Cyrene* (Leiden: Brill, 1979) 335. His discussion of the revolts (269–344) is one of the most thorough. See also M. Hadas-Lebel, *Jérusalem Contre Rome* (Paris: Editions du Cerf, 1990) 151–60.

17. See further Smallwood, *Jews,* 371–76; Meier, *Grundzüge,* 99–100; M. Hengel, "Messianische Hoffnung und politischer 'Radikalismus' in der jüdisch-hellenistischen Diaspora," in D. Hellholm, ed., *Apocalypticism in the Mediterranean World and the Near East* (Tübingen: Mohr [Siebeck], 1983) 655–86. There is a suggestive allusion to a "king" (Lukuas in Eusebius *Hist.eccl.*4.2.4; Andreas in Dio 68.32.1), but Hengel fills out the picture largely by analogy with the two other rebellions. See further D. Frankfurter, "Lest Egypt's City Be Deserted: Religion and Ideology in the Egyptian Response to the Jewish Revolt (116–17 C.E.)," *JJS* 43(1992) 203–20, a fascinating attempt to reconstruct the view from the Egyptian side (but see 205–6 on the Jewish position).

18. Especially useful are the discussions by P. Schäfer, *Der Bar-Kokhba Aufstand* (Tübingen: Mohr [Siebeck], 1981); idem, "Hadrian's Policy in Judea and the Bar Kokhba Revolt: A Reassessment," in P. R. Davies and R. T. White, eds., *A Tribute to Geza Vermes: Essays on Jewish and Christian Literature and History* (Sheffield: JSOT Press, 1990) 281–303; and M. Hengel, "Hadrians Politik gegenüber Juden und Christen," *JANESCU* 16–17(1984–85) 153–82. See also the standard works: Smallwood, *Jews*, 428–80; E. Schürer, *The History of the Jewish People in the Age of Jesus Christ (175 B.C.–A.D. 135)*, rev. G. Vermes and F. Millar (Edinburgh: T. & T. Clark, 1973) vol.1, 535–53; and Maier, *Grundzüge*, 106–10. Further, H. Mantel, "The Causes of the Bar Cochba Revolt," *JQR* 58(1967–68) 224–42, 274–96; G. L. Bowersock, "A Roman Perspective on the Bar Cochba War," in W. S. Green, ed., *Approaches to Ancient Judaism* (Chico, Calif.: Scholars Press, 1980) vol.2, 131–41. An interesting analysis of a wide range of views is found in B. Isaac and A. Oppenheimer, "The Revolt of Bar Kokhba: Ideology and Modern Scholarship," *JJS* 36(1985) 33–60.

19. D. Rhoads, *Israel in Revolution 6–74 CE* (Philadelphia: Fortress, 1976) 150–73, is a good summary. The way in which the Bar Cochba revolt (and the earlier diaspora revolts) was a reaction to, and a continuation of the spirit of, the Jewish War is emphasized by H. Schwier, *Tempel und Tempelverstörung: Untersuchungen zu den theologischen und ideologischen Faktoren im ersten jüdisch-römischen Krieg (66–74 n.Chr.)* (Göttingen: Vandenhoeck & Ruprecht, 1989) 338–62.

20. Smallwood, *Jews*, 443–44, thinks it was taken; Schäfer, *Bar Kokhba*, 78–88, thinks not.

21. This is a complex matter. Dio (69.11.15) gives the building of Aelia as a cause, Eusebius as a result (*Hist.eccl.* 6.6.1–4). The *Hist.Aug.Hadr.* 14.2 is the only source for the ban on circumcision as a cause. Some think one or both are more plausible as consequences than causes of the rebellion (Mantel, "Causes," 226–36). See the thorough and contrasting assessments in Hengel, "Hadrians," 171–75, and Schäfer, "Reassessment," passim. Hengel suggests that the ban on circumcision may have been a war measure, introduced after the rebellion had begun.

22. Schäfer, *Bar Kokhba*, 47–51; "Reassessment," passim. His general case for hellenized, assimilated, mostly urban Jews who welcomed Hadrian's policies is strong. That some took things as far as epispasm rests on his largely persuasive interpretation of *t.Sabb.*15.9.

23. There is some dispute over the character of Hadrian: some think he was an intolerant, hellenizing activist (Israel and Oppenheimer, "Bar Kokhba," 47), others that he was a moderate and enlightened ruler (Mantel, "Causes," 226–31; Smallwood, *Jews*, 434–35; Hengel, "Hadrians").

24. As argued by A. Reinhartz, "Rabbinic Perceptions of Simeon Bar Kosiba," *JSJ* 20(1989) 171–94. She argues that it was probably made by his followers after his initial military success and that traditions that emphasize only his strength and military prowess were another way of accounting for the same phenomenon.

25. Maier, *Grundzüge*, 108–9; Schäfer, *Bar Kokhba*, 51–55. Apparently for the same reason rabbinic traditions about Akiba concentrate on his martyrdom rather than on his recognition of Bar Cochba.

26. R. A. Horsley and J. S. Hanson, *Bandits, Prophets & Messiahs* (Minneapolis: Winston, 1985) 118–26.

27. Justin *I Apol.*31.6; cf. *Dial.*16; repeated in Eusebius *Hist.eccl.*4.6.2.

28. Justin's reliability: Maier, *Auseinandersetzung*, 133–34; Schäfer, *Bar Kokhba*, 59–60. Bar Cochba's rigorous legalism: Isaac and Oppenheimer, "*Bar Kokhba*, 59–60".

Bar Cochba's ruthlessness: Schäfer, *Bar Kokhba,* 59–60. Epispasm: *t.Sabb.*15.9; *y.Sabb.*19.2; *b.Yeb.*62a.

29. The translation and the commentary are from D. D. Bucholz, *Your Eyes Will Be Opened: A Study of the Greek (Ethiopic) Apocalypse of Peter* (Atlanta: Scholars Press, 1988) 283–89, 408–12.

30. Smallwood, *Jews,* 457–66.

31. Schäfer, *Bar Kokhba,* 194–235, esp. 234–35. He is reacting to uncritical accounts that give maximal weight to the rabbinic evidence. Alon, *Jews,* vol. 2, for example, thinks that Jews were forced to participate in pagan worship (as in the Maccabean period). Hadas-Lebel, *Jérusalem,* 181–82, has a useful chart of the evidence.

32. Schäfer, *Bar Kokhba,* 38–50; Mantel, "Causes," 231–36; and Smallwood, *Jews,* 428–31, discuss the ambiguities of this report.

33. See Maier, *Grundzüge,* 109; Isaac and Oppenheimer, "Bar Kokhba," 53–55.

34. Maier, *Grundzüge,* 108–9.

35. A. von Harnack, *The Mission and Expansion of Christianity in the First Three Centuries* (New York: Harper & Row, 1962) 63. S. G. F. Brandon, *The Fall of Jerusalem and the Christian Church* (London: SPCK, 1968), has developed the argument in a number of ways; on pp. 12–14 he lists representative opinions on the matter. G. Lindeskog, *Das jüdisch-christliche Problem: Randglossen zu einer Forschungsepoche* (Stockholm: Almqvist & Wiksell, 1986) 43–44, described it as "eine endgültige Katastrophe."

36. M. Simon, *Verus Israel: A Study of the Relations between Christians and Jews in the Roman Empire (135–425)* (Oxford: Oxford University Press, 1986) 3–65. He thinks that for the Jews (but not for Jewish-Christian relations) the consequences of the Jewish War were more devastating than those of the Bar Cochba rebellion. See also P. Richardson, *Israel in the Apostolic Church* (Cambridge: Cambridge University Press, 1969) 33–38; L. H. Schiffman, *Who Was a Jew? Rabbinic and Halakhic Perspectives on the Jewish-Christian Schism* (Hoboken, N.J.: Ktav, 1985) 75–78.

37. J. D. G. Dunn, *The Partings of the Ways between Christianity and Judaism and Their Significance for the Character of Christianity* (Philadelphia: Trinity, 1991) esp. 230–53—but it is the question that controls his discussion throughout. Despite a number of disagreements and a difference of approach, I take his conclusion and some of his arguments as complementary to mine.

38. See chap. 5.

39. G. W. H. Lampe, "A.D. 70 in Christian Reflection," in C. F. D. Moule and E. Bammel, eds., *Jesus and the Politics of His Day* (Cambridge: Cambridge University Press, 1984) 153–71, here 153. See also H. J. Schoeps, "Die Tempelverstörung des Jahres 70 in der jüdischen Religionsgeschichte," in *Aus frühchristlicher Zeit: religionsgeschichtliche Untersuchungen* (Tübingen: Mohr [Siebeck], 1950) 143–83; E. Fascher, "Jerusalems Untergang in der urchristlichen und altkirchlichen Überlieferung," *TLZ* 89(1964) 82–98; R. Kampling, "Neutestamentliche Texte als Bausteine der späteren Adversus-Judaeos Literatur," in H. Frohnhofen, ed., *Christlicher Antijudaismus und jüdischer Antipaganismus: ihre Motive und Hintergründe in den ersten drei Jahrhunderten* (Hamburg: Steinmann & Steinmann, 1990) 121–38, here 124–30; S. Heid, "Auf welcher Seit kämpft Gott? Der Anspruch Jerusalems und Roms auf die Waffenhilfe Gottes in frühchristlicher Apologetik," *ZKG* 104(1993) 1–22.

40. Lampe, "A.D.70," 156.

41. Alon, *Jews,* vol.1, 18–38. He recognizes the need for caution in handling rabbinic tradition, but still tends to accept their own romanticized view of the past.

42. Most recently S. Schwarz, *Josephus and Judean Politics* (Leiden: Brill, 1990). A useful summary can be found in L. I. A. Levine, "Judaism from the Destruction of the Temple to the End of the Second Jewish Revolt: 70–135 CE," in H. Shanks, ed., *Christianity and Rabbinic Judaism. A Parallel History of Their Origins and Early Development* (Washington, D.C.: Biblical Archeology Society, 1992) 125–49.

43. Schwarz, *Josephus,* 209–22. He distinguishes between the upper priests and the high-priestly aristocracy. Josephus belonged to the former and is consistently positive about them. It is probably from their ranks that the priestly support for the rabbis came. The rabbis, he notes, shared much with the Pharisees but were not identical with them.

44. That proselytes were eligible for the tax is argued by Smallwood, *Jews,* 376–78; M. H. Williams, "Domitian, the Jews, and the 'Judaizers'—A Simple Matter of Cupiditas and Majestas?" *Historia* 39(1990) 196–211, here 199. Williams also argues that proselytes and no others are referred to.

45. J. J. Walsh, "On Christian Atheism," *VC* 45(1991) 255–77, argues that the charge of atheism was not common until the second half of the second century.

46. See P. Keresztes, "The Imperial Roman Government and the Christian Church. I. From Nero to the Severi," *ANRW* II.23.1, 247–315, here 257–72. P. Lampe, *Die stadtrömischen Christen in den ersten beiden Jahrhunderten* (Tübingen: Mohr [Siebeck], 1987) 166–72, draws two conclusions from these confused accounts. Either there was a Christian Domitilla who was banned and whose pagan husband was executed for political reasons; or there was a Christian Domitilla who was banned, and Clemens and his wife (not Domitilla) were Jewish sympathizers. Either way, Clemens was not a Christian.

47. Suetonius *Dom.*10,12,14–15; Tacitus *Agric.*2–3; Pliny *Pan.*33:3–4; 42:1; Dio 67.13.2–14.5. But see L. L. Thompson, *The Book of Revelation: Apocalypse and Empire* (New York and Oxford: Oxford University Press, 1990) 107–9, for a more positive view.

48. Smallwood, *Jews,* 377–83, and Williams, "Domitian," 206–11, agree that political and financial factors came into play, but Smallwood uses it to exonerate Domitian while Williams does not (next note). Both Williams and B. W. Jones, *The Emperor Domitian* (London: Routledge & Kegan Paul, 1992) 119, note the tension between the *fiscus judaicus* and charges of Judaizing, and explain the fate of Flavius Clemens and his wife by their social position.

49. Williams, "Domitian," 202–6, with good bibliographies. Her comments are astute, but her conclusion—that this amounts to persecution of the Jews—goes a step too far.

50. Josephus *Vit.*76. The class distinction mentioned above, plus his favored role with Vespasian and Titus, may partially explain why Josephus received Domitian's protection. He was something of a court poodle. Note that it is other Jews who are punished for accusing him. Another (probably second-century diaspora) Jewish supporter of Domitian gives a positive summary in *Sib.Or.*12:124–42.

51. S. Mandell, "The Jewish Christians and the Temple Tax," *SecCent* 7(1989–90) 76–84, suggests that *m.Šeqal.*1:5 reflects a rabbinic ban on Jewish Christians' paying the Temple tax. The argument depends on an implausible series of links to define the "Cutheans" and the "servants of the stars," not to mention the (undefined) tax.

52. Thompson, *Revelation,* 95–115, but also throughout. See also H-J. Klauck, "Das Sendschreiben nach Pergamon und der Kaiserkult in der Johannesoffenbarung," *Bib* 73(1992) 153–82; P. J. Botha, "The Historical Domitian—Illustrating

Some Problems of Historiography," *Neot* 23(1989) 45–59; A. Y. Collins, *Crisis and Catharsis: The Power of the Apocalypse* (Philadelphia: Westminster, 1984) 69–73. Thompson's arguments are extensive and thorough, but in the end they protest (and ignore) too much. A more balanced assessment is given by Jones, *Domitian,* 114–25, and J. T. Sanders, *Schismatics, Sectarians, Dissidents, Deviants. The First One Hundred Years of Jewish-Christian Relations* (Valley Forge, Pa.: Trinity, 1993) 166–69.

53. F. G. Downing, "Pliny's Prosecution of Christians: Revelation and 1 Peter," *JSNT* 34(1988) 105–23, here 107, suggests cautiously, but implausibly, that Pliny's conviction about previous trials is genuine but misinformed. There were none. It depends in part on his view that 1 Peter and Revelation are to be dated to the time of this correspondence rather than the reign of Domitian.

54. For discussion and bibliographies see Keresztes, "Imperial," 252–72; D. L. Jones, "Christianity and the Roman Imperial Cult," *ANRW* II.23.2, 1023–54, here 1032–35. Their conclusions, however, need to be treated with caution. For a somewhat different angle see G. Krodel, "Persecution and Toleration of Christianity until Hadrian," in S. Benko and J. J. O'Rourke, *The Catacombs and the Coliseum* (Valley Forge, Pa.: Judson, 1971) 255–67, here 260–62.

55. On these three texts see K. Wengst, *Pax Romana and the Peace of Jesus Christ* (Philadelphia: Fortress, 1987) 89–136.

56. Thompson, *Revelation,* 158–64, gives a good description of the imperial cult and its possible effects on Christians.

57. M. Goodman, "Nerva, the *Fiscus Judaicus* and Jewish Identity," *JRS* 79(1989) 40–44, suggests that, since the only workable way of identifying Jews under Nerva's policy would have been by their own confession, he inaugurated a tendency to define Jews by their religion rather than their birth.

58. P. Richardson and M. B. Shukster, "Barnabas, Nerva and the Yavnean Rabbis," *JTS* n.s.34(1983) 32–55; idem, "Temple and *Beth ha-Midrash* in the Epistle of Barnabas," in S. G. Wilson, ed., *Anti-Judaism in Early Christianity* (Waterloo: Wilfrid Laurier University Press, 1986) 17–32. See chap. 5.

59. Discussion and bibliography in Keresztes, "Imperial," 247–57.

60. The conclusion of Keresztes, "Imperial," 273–87; Krodel, "Persecution," 262–64; and D. Lührmann, "Superstitio—die Beurteilung des frühen Christentums durch die Römer," *TZ* 42(1986) 193–213.

61. Eusebius *Hist.eccl.*4.9.1–3; Justin *I Apol.*68.6–10. Justin was addressing a situation in which persecution of Christians was based precisely on confession of the name, and this probably accounts for his more optimistic reading, though the text of the rescript is ambiguous. For discussion and bibliography see Hengel, "Hadrians," 163–70. The classic modern essay is E. Bickerman, "Pliny, Trajan, Hadrian and the Christians," *RFIC* 96(1968) 290–315.

62. Hengel, "Hadrians," 161–62.

63. A useful survey of Christians and Rome in the second century is R. M. Grant, *Augustus to Constantine. The Rise and Triumph of Christianity in the Roman World* (San Francisco: Harper & Row, 1990) 77–100.

64. Keresztes, "Imperial," 287–309; Jones, "Christianity," 1035–43.

65. *Sib.Or.* 5:44. See G. Stemburger, "Die Beurteilung Roms in der rabbinischen Literatur," *ANRW* II.19.1, 328–96, here 358–61; Smallwood, *Jews,* 393–412.

66. See chap. 5.

67. *Sib.Or.* 5:46–50; Stemburger, "Beurteilung," 361–64 (pp.364–67 present the negative strain). I am most dependent on Hengel, "Hadrians," 155–60.

68. Apart from the standard works see L. I. Levine, *The Rabbinic Class of Roman*

Palestine in Late Antiquity (Jerusalem and New York: Yad Izhak Ben-Zvi/Jewish Theological Seminary of America, 1989), who can only infer the situation in the second century from changes that apparently took place in the third; and Alon, *Jews*, vol.2, 641–81. A good recent survey, fully alert to how little we know, is provided by S. D. Cohen, "Judaism to the Mishnah: 135–220 CE," in Shanks, ed., *Christianity*, 195–223.

69. Alon, *Jews*, vol.2, 647–48, thinks the persecution continued well after 135 CE.

70. M. Goodman, *State and Society in Roman Galilee, A.D.132–212* (Totowa, N.J.: Rowan & Allanheld, 1983), is a vivid and unrivaled account. See also Alon, *Jews*, vol.2, 647–74.

71. Maier, *Grundzüge*, 98, dates this before 132 CE, while Smallwood, *Jews*, 473; Alon, *Jews*, vol.2, 461–64; and S. W. Baron, *A Social and Religious History of the Jews* (New York: Columbia University Press, 1952) vol.2, 122–23, date it after 135 CE.

72. Goodman, *State*, 91–117; for the earlier period see S. Freyne, *Galilee from Alexander the Great to Hadrian* (Wilmington: Notre Dame University Press, 1980).

73. Levine, *Rabbinic*, 23–42.

74. S. J. D. Cohen, "Pagan and Christian Evidence on the Ancient Synagogue," in L. I. Levine, ed., *The Synagogue in Late Antiquity* (Philadelphia: American Schools of Oriental Research, 1987) 159–81, here 170–75, argues that patriarchal involvement in the diaspora did not begin before the fourth century.

75. Smallwood, *Jews*, 475.

76. Goodman, *State*, 111–18, dates Roman recognition as late as the fourth century, but recognizes the wide influence of Rabbi Judah I in his day.

77. J. Gager, *The Origins of Anti-Semitism* (Oxford: Oxford University Press, 1983) 35–112, has made this case persuasively. For other views see J. N. Sevenster, *The Roots of Anti-Semitism in the Ancient World* (Leiden: Brill, 1975) and J. Meagher, "As the Twig Was Bent: Antisemitism in Greco-Roman and Early Christian Times," in A. T. Davies, ed., *Anti-Semitism and the Foundations of Christianity* (Paramus, N.J.: Paulist, 1975) 1–26. Z. Yavetz, "Judeophobia in Classical Antiquity. A Different Approach," *JJS* 44(1993) 1–22, argues (against Gager, but with little detail) that ancient anti-Semitism was neither trivial nor insignificant, at least as important as Christian anti-Semitism, and more pointed than the familiar Greco-Roman xenophobia (anti-barbarianism).

78. Estimates vary. These figures are taken from R. Wilken, *The Christians as the Romans Saw Them* (New Haven, Conn., and London: Yale University Press, 1984) 113–14.

79. M. Avi-Yonah, *The Jews under Roman and Byzantine Rule* (New York and Jerusalem: Schocken/Magnes, 1984) 19, estimates them at one quarter of the population in Judaea and three quarters in Galilee.

80. For discussion and bibliographies see E. M. Meyers and A. T. Kraabel, "Archeology, Iconography, and Nonliterary Remains," in R. A. Kraft and G. W. E. Nickelsburg, eds., *Early Judaism and Its Modern Interpreters* (Atlanta: Scholars Press, 1986) 175–210; P. R. Trebilco, *Jewish Communities in Asia Minor* (Cambridge: Cambridge University Press, 1991) is a very useful recent survey. L. V. Rutgers, "Archeological Evidence for the Interaction of Jews and Non-Jews in Late Antiquity," *AJA* 96(1992) 101–18, deals mostly with the third and fourth centuries, but his evidence for Jewish integration into the Roman world is important.

81. M. P. Bonz, "The Jewish Community of Ancient Sardis: A Reassessment of Its Rise to Prominence," *H.St.Class.Philol.* 93(1990) 343–59, makes the interesting

argument that the heyday for Jews in Sardis did not come until the middle of the third century, due to changes in imperial policy and local circumstances. H. Botermann, "Die Synagoge von Sardes: Ein Synagoge aus den 4.Jahrhundert?" ZNW 81(1990) 103–21, pushes the date into the fourth century on archaeological grounds. The more interesting evidence often comes from the third and fourth centuries, but there is enough to suggest that the Jews were a significant force in the second century too. It is nevertheless all too easy to skip back 200 years or so as if the intervening period was insignificant.

82. J. Reynolds and R. Tannenbaum, *Jews and Godfearers at Aphrodisias: Greek Inscriptions with Commentary* (Cambridge: Cambridge Philological Society, 1987), is the fundamental work. In an unpublished talk (Society for New Testament Studies, Dublin, 1988) Joyce Reynolds suggested that the God-fearers may have made up one third of the total synagogue membership—a strikingly large proportion. The existence of Gentile God-fearers (sometimes Jews are called the same) finds ample testimony, literary and epigraphic. See Trebilco, *Communities,* 145–66. I see no reason why Luke's usage in Acts should not be used as additional evidence, and even less reason to suppose that he invented the term or the class of people designated by it.

83. See the stimulating discussion by M. H. Williams, "The Jews and Godfearers Inscription from Aphrodisias—A Case of Patriarchal Interference in early 3rd Century Caria?" *Historia* 41(1992) 297–310. She clearly demonstrates the unlikelihood that it shows the beginnings of control over the diaspora by the rabbinic patriarchy. The relations between Jews and God-fearers are not much affected either way.

84. J. M. O'Connor, "Lots of Godfearers? Theosebeis in the Aphrodisias Inscription," *RB* 99(1992) 418–22, argues that only two Gentiles, those in the Torah-study group (the *dekania* of the *philomathon*), were God-fearers in the full sense. The rest were merely donors. This follows Reynolds and Tannenbaum for the meaning of the text. In Williams's interpretation they would be part of the group who first funded the project. See also the interesting classification of Gentile sympathizers by the degree of their attachment to Judaism by S. J. D. Cohen, "Crossing the Boundary and Becoming a Jew," *HTR* 82(1989) 13–33.

85. See L. H. Feldman, "Proselytism by Jews in the Third, Fourth and Fifth Centuries," *JSJ* 24(1993) 1–58; idem, "Jewish Proselytism," in Attridge and Gata, eds., *Eusebius,* 372–408, for a chronologically broader survey. The evidence for God-fearers is better than that for proselytes. Simon, *Verus Israel,* 271–305, gives a similar (and somewhat exaggerated) account of the successes of Jewish recruitment. In fact, while many Jews welcomed sympathetic Gentiles into various forms of association, there is no evidence that they actively recruited them, at least not before the third century CE. See M. Goodman, "Proselytizing in Rabbinic Judaism," *JJS* 40(1989) 175–85; idem, "Jewish Proselytizing in the First Century," in J. Lieu, J. North, and T. Rajak, eds., *The Jews Among Pagans and Christians in the Roman Empire* (London and New York: Routledge & Kegan Paul, 1992) 53–78; S. McKnight, *A Light among the Gentiles: Jewish Missionary Activity in the Second Temple Period* (Minneapolis: Fortress, 1991).

86. A. T. Kraabel, "Unity and Diversity among Diaspora Synagogues," in Levine, ed., *Synagogue,* 49–60.

87. P. W. van der Horst, "Jews and Christians in Aphrodisias in the Light of Their Relations in Other Cities of Asia Minor," *NedTTs* 43(1989) 106–21, with reference to Sardis and Aphrodisias.

88. The standard work is M. Hengel, *Judaism and Hellenism* (London: SCM,

1974) vols. 1 and 2. He has recently extended his argument to include the first century CE in *The "Hellenization" of Judaea in the First Century after Christ* (Philadelphia: Trinity, 1989). L. H. Feldman, "How Much Hellenism in Jewish Palestine?" *HUCA* 57(1986), 83–111, has a good discussion.

89. See, for example, Cohen, "Pagan," 165–66.

90. The major work on the Mishnah is J. Neusner, *Judaism*. A useful nontechnical summary can be found in J. Neusner, *From Testament to Torah: An Introduction to Judaism in Its Formative Age* (Englewood Cliffs; N.J.: Prentice-Hall, 1988). Questions have been raised about the way Neusner isolates the various strands within the Mishnah and about some aspects of his comprehensive account of the aims of the compilers of the Mishnah. But if we do not use Neusner there are few serious competitors.

91. J. Neusner, *Formative Judaism: Religious, Historical and Literary Studies* (Chico, Calif.: Scholars Press, 1982) 114.

92. The lack of interest in proselytizing in rabbinic sources prior to the third century shows the same thing.

93. Neusner, *Formative Judaism,* 261.

94. In recent years, Neusner has attempted to undergird his claim that the Mishnah is properly called a philosophical work. The most convenient summary is in *Judaism as Philosophy: The Method and Message of the Mishnah* (Columbia, S.C.: University of South Carolina Press, 1991). He likens its obsession with definitions and hierarchical classifications, its taxonomic urge, with aspects of Aristotelian philosophical method, and its implicit demonstration of the "Unity of Being" from the multiplicities of quotidian existence with aspects of Neoplatonism. He insists that this is not a claim for influence or deliberate mimicking and that the overlap does not necessarily touch on what was most important for Aristotelian or Neoplatonic philosophies. It merely shows that the Mishnah, in both its method and its substance, is properly called "philosophy." The purpose, he suggests, might be to counter pagan philosophies in which the multiplicity of artifacts in the world points to a multiplicity of deities. By using the scriptural account of the cosmos to generate its categories of quotidian existence, the Mishnah aspires to demonstrate the Unity of Being, the existence of one God. The argument in this work (and its precursors in the eighties) makes heavy weather of an original, but not complex, point.

95. E. P. Sanders, *Jewish Law,* 308–31.

96. Sanders, ibid., makes a number of other points too: that repeated use of the present tense is typical legalese and has no profound implications; that Neusner ignores parts of the Mishnah that contradict his theories (e.g., *Berakot, 'Abot*); and that the Mishnah cannot confidently be associated with any identifiable social group, and certainly not exclusively so. Several of these criticisms are repeated by C. A. Evans, "Mishna and Messiah 'in Context': Some Comments on Jacob Neusner's Proposals," *JBL* 112(1993) 267–89; replied to—sometimes effectively, sometimes evasively—in the same volume by J. Neusner, "The Mishna in Philosophical Context and out of Canonical Bounds," 291–304.

97. Neusner's recent suggestion (and he would not claim any more for it) that the Mishnah implicitly combats pagan philosophical pantheism (n.94 above) would put a different complexion on things, showing a greater degree of "engagement" with the outside world. It would not, even so, be equivalent to the Christian apologists' direct and aggressive engagement with pagan worldviews. Neusner's own description of the backcountry Galilean "philosophers" independently, and almost inadvertently, doing what other philosophers were doing on another plane does not

provide much support for his suggestion at any rate, and the Mishnah itself provides none. I find myself more persuaded by aspects of his earlier account.

98. I am using here some of the more recent, if reluctant, attempts to put a number on the early Christian population. See R. MacMullen, *Christianizing the Roman Empire (A.D.100–400)* (New Haven, Conn., and London: Yale University Press, 1984) 109–10, 135 n.26; R. Lane Fox, *Pagans and Christians* (San Francisco: Harper & Row, 1986) 271–72, and the works they cite.

99. Origen *Cels.*3.55.

100. Pliny *Ep.*10:96. Central to the discussion of the social makeup of the early church are W. A. Meeks, G. Theissen, and P. Lampe. For a good review see Lane Fox, "Pagan," 293–312, and n.103 below.

101. Lane Fox, "Pagan," 308–11. This may have been truer of the first than the second century. It is clear that women could play a prominent role in the synagogue, but less clear how common this was. See the basic work of B. J. Brooten, *Women Leaders in the Ancient Synagogues* (Chico, Calif.: Scholars Press, 1982); more recently, Trebilco, *Communities,* 104–26.

102. That converted God-fearers could be a political and social asset (as they were to Judaism) has been pointed out by a number of writers, including H. Güzlow, "Soziale Gegebenheiten der Trennung von Kirche und Synagoge und die Anfänge des christlichen Antijudasimus," in Fronhofen, ed., *Antijudaismus,* 95–120, here 108–18.

103. A number of recent studies have taken up this issue. See W. A. Meeks, *The First Urban Christians: The Social World of the Apostle Paul* (New Haven, Conn.: Yale University Press, 1983) 74–110; J. E. Stambaugh and D. L. Balch, *The New Testament in Its Social Environment* (Philadelphia: Westminster, 1986); H. J. Klauck, *Hausgemeinde und Hauskirche im frühen Christentum* (Stuttgart: Katholisches Bibelwerk, 1981); R. Banks, *Paul's Idea of Community: The Early House Churches in Their Historical Setting* (Grand Rapids: Baker, 1980); on architectural questions see the review by P. C. Finney, "Early Christian Architecture: The Beginnings (A Review Article)," *HTR* 81(1988) 319–39.

104. The parallels between churches and collegia, or voluntary associations, are discussed by Meeks, *Urban,* 77–80. I have learned much from a number of as yet unpublished papers given at the 1989 meetings of the Canadian Society of Biblical Studies seminar on Voluntary Associations in the Ancient World.

105. See Meeks, *Urban,* 80–81.

106. Most helpful are S. Benko, "Pagan Criticism of Christianity during the First Two Centuries," *ANRW* II.23.2, 1055–1118; idem, *Pagan Rome and the Early Christians* (Bloomington, Ind.: Indiana University Press, 1984). See also R. L. Wilken, *Christians,* passim; Lührmann, "Superstitio," 206–13.

107. Jones, "Imperial," passim.

108. Athenagoras *Leg.*3.1; 31–32; Minucius Felix *Octavius* 9.5–6.

109. On the argument from antiquity among Greeks, Romans, Jews, and Christians see P. Pilhofer, *Prebyteron Kreitton: Der Altersbeweis der jüdischen und christlichen Apologeten und seine Vorgeschichte* (Tübingen: Mohr [Siebeck], 1990). The essence was: old is good, older is better; new is bad, newer is worse. H. Conzelmann, *Gentiles, Jews, Christians: Polemics and Apologetics in the Greco-Roman Era* (Minneapolis: Fortress, 1992) 275–316, is the best survey of the apologists relevant to our study, but it is unhelpfully shaped by his own convictions about kerygmatic theology and his obsession with the theme of salvation history.

110. Justin *I Apol.*1–4; Athenagoras *Leg.*1–2.

111. *Diogn*.5–6; Justin *I Apol*.11.

112. Translation by W. R. Schoedel, *Athenagoras: Legatio and De Resurrectione* (Oxford: Clarendon, 1972) 87.

113. Athenagoras *Leg*.1–12, esp. 4; Justin *I Apol*.6; 13. For the trinitarian argument, see Athenagoras *Leg*.10.

114. On the prophets see Athenagoras *Leg*.7.3; 9.1; Theophilus *Autol*.2.9,30,33. On the use of pagan writers see Athenagoras *Leg*.5–6; 23–28; Justin *I Apol*.44.

115. *Diogn.* 2; Theophilus *Autol*.2–3; Athenagoras *Leg*.13–30; Aristides *Apol.* 3–13.

116. See especially H. Remus, *Pagan-Christian Conflict Over Miracle in the Second Century* (Cambridge, Mass.: Philadelphia Patristics Foundation, 1983). Also A. Segal, *Rebecca's Children: Judaism and Christianity in the Roman World* (Cambridge, Mass.: Harvard University Press, 1986) 143–46.

117. For the former see Justin *I Apol*.30; *II Apol*.6; Theophilus *Autol*.2.30–33. For the latter see Justin *II Apol.* 6; Quadratus in Eusebius *Hist.eccl*.4.3.2.

118. Athenagoras *Leg*.31–36; Aristides *Apol*.15–16; Justin *I Apol*.26,65–67; Theophilus *Autol*.3.9–15.

119. Justin *I Apol*.14; Theophilus *Autol*.3.6–8.

120. See A. Marmorstein, "Jews and Judaism in the Earliest Christian Apologies," *Expositor* 8(1919) 104–9.

121. *Diogn*.3–4, quotation from chap. 4, Loeb edition.

122. P. H. Poirier, "Éléments de polémique anti-juive dans l'*Ad Diognetum*,'" *VC* 40(1986) 218–25. Reading *koine* in 5.7 he suggests another possible contrast: Christians, as distinct from Jews, keep a "common" table, i.e., undiscriminating in both food and people.

123. J. Rendel Harris, *The Apology of Aristides on Behalf of the Christians* (Cambridge: Cambridge University Press, 1891) 13.

124. So R. M. Grant, *Greek Apologists of the Second Century* (Philadelphia: Westminster, 1988) 39.

125. S. Laeuchli, *The Language of Faith* (New York: Abingdon, 1962) 165.

126. Grant, *Apologists*, 166.

127. So W. A. Meeks and R. L. Wilken, *Jews and Christians in Antioch* (Missoula, Mont.: Scholars Press, 1978) 21–22.

Chapter 2: Jews and Judaism in the Canonical Narratives

1. It should be remembered that, while Jerusalem fell in 70 CE, the rebellion continued spasmodically until the destruction of Masada in 73/74 CE.

2. W. Wrede, *The Messianic Secret* (Greenwood, S.C.: Attic Press, 1971). See the recent review, critique, and extension of Wrede's thesis by H. Räisänen, *The "Messianic Secret" in Mark* (Edinburgh: T. & T. Clark, 1990).

3. See, however, the recent work by C. Dahm, *Israel im Markusevangelium* (Frankfurt: Lang, 1991), and the studies on Jewish leaders and on Mark's view of the law cited below. Further, see R. A. Guelich, "Anti-Semitism or Anti-Judaism in Mark?" in C. A. Evans and D. A. Hagner, eds., *Anti-Semitism and Early Christianity. Issues of Polemic and Faith* (Minneapolis: Fortress, 1993) 80–101. The terms "Israel" and "Jews" are of course very rare in Mark. In the interests of brevity and of the need to take a bird's-eye view in the context of my overall theme, I shall restrict myself to more recent studies that I have found particularly interesting—where extensive bibliographies can be found. My primary interest is in the final form of the

Gospels, which allows me to take advantage of some of the more persuasive literary interpretations without eschewing the history of the traditions or the historical context in which the Gospels appeared.

4. The dividing lines are in all cases somewhat arbitrary, though they do help us to grasp the broad outlines of the story. M. A. Tolbert has recently suggested three sections: 1:1–13; 1:14–10; 11–16—mainly on the ground that while the Jerusalem phase is anticipated in chaps. 8–10 it does not begin until chap. 11. She suggests that the parable of the sower (4:1–9) anticipates the themes of the Galilean period as the parable of the tenants (12:1–11) does of the Jerusalem period, and that whereas in the first phase Jesus shuns publicity and commands humans and demons to silence, in the second he precipitates public debate and conflict. The attractiveness of this proposal is an indication of the flexibility of all our narrative divisions. See *Sowing the Gospel* (Philadelphia: Fortress, 1989) 108–26.

5. See especially J. D. Kingsbury, "The Religious Authorities in the Gospel of Mark," *NTS* 36(1990) 42–65; idem, *Conflict in Mark* (Philadelphia: Fortress, 1989) 63–88; E. S. Malbon, "The Jewish Leaders in the Gospel of Mark: A Literary Study of Markan Characterization," *JBL* 108(1989) 259–81; D. Lührmann, "Die Pharisäer und die Schriftgelehrten im Markusevangelium," *ZNW* 78(1987) 169–85; Dahm, *Israel*, 81–96. Earlier studies tend to focus on the historical reliability of Mark's portrait. So J. C. Weber, "Jesus' Opponents in the Gospel of Mark," *JBR* 34(1966) 214–22; M. J. Cook, *Mark's Treatment of the Jewish Leaders* (Leiden: Brill, 1978). On the portrait of the crowds see L. Schenke, *Das Markusevangelium* (Stuttgart: Kohlhammer, 1988) 95–98; and Dahm, *Israel*, 37–64, both of which are nicely nuanced.

6. Räisänen, *"Messianic Secret,"* 76–166, has argued forcefully that the parable theory of Mark 4 and the commands to silence which the people disobey are not integral to Mark's messianic secret. The latter applies only to the commands to the demons and disciples that concern the identity of Jesus.

7. The similarities between the crowds and the disciples in their response to Jesus are convincingly demonstrated by E. S. Malbon, "Disciples/Crowds/Whoever: Markan Characters and Readers," *NT* 28(1986) 104–30. She notes that both groups present to the reader plausible models of the vagaries of Christian discipleship. See also Schenke, *Markusevangelium*, 97–98; Dahm, *Israel*, 64–81.

8. There is no denying that the portrait of the disciples is fairly unflattering (though not uniformly so, cf. 1:16–20; 3:13–19; 6:7–13), but I am not persuaded that Mark wishes us to see them in an entirely negative light, even though T. J. Weeden's implausible thesis along these lines at least has an ostensible basis in the text. See *Mark: Traditions in Conflict* (Philadelphia: Fortress, 1971). Part of the explanation lies, I suspect, in the tradition (their doubts and uncertainties are historically plausible), part in the paraenetic possibilities (see note above), and part in the situation for which Mark wrote (see Räisänen, *"Messianic Secret,"* 195–222). Working along different lines but with some astute comments is R. Tannehill, "The Disciples in Mark: The Function of a Narrative Role," in W. R. Telford, ed., *The Interpretation of Mark* (Philadelphia: Fortress, 1985) 57–95.

9. "Those who passed by" (15:29) presumably refers to the people in general as distinct from the priests and scribes of 15:31.

10. In 2:16 we should probably read "the scribes of the Pharisees" as the more difficult reading. The Herodians remain an obscure group. For Mark, and probably in actuality too, they represented political forces from the court of Herod Antipas.

11. Malbon, "Leaders," 270–72; Kingsbury, "Authorities," 42–46. This is contrary to Lührmann's argument ("Pharisäer") that Mark distinguishes the Pharisees

and scribes and that he was, at the time of writing, more engaged with the issues raised by the scribes (Jesus' authority) than by the Pharisees (foods, fasting, sabbath, marriage, and so on). See also Lührmann's commentary, *Das Markusevangelium* (Tübingen: Mohr [Siebeck], 1987) 50–51, 60–61.

12. Kingsbury, "Authorities," 50–57.

13. On the narrative escalation in chaps. 11–15 see Kingsbury, "Authorities," 273–75. M. Kähler's famous description of the Gospel of Mark as a Passion narrative with a lengthy introduction is apt, though for him this had more to do with the theology of the final chapters than their length and dramatic force. See *The So-Called Historical Jesus and the Historic, Biblical Christ* (Philadelphia: Fortress, 1964; 1st German ed. 1892) 80 n.11.

14. Kingsbury, "Authorities," 48–50, prefers this solution.

15. Tolbert, "Sowing," 169–71, suggests in addition that the second soil characterizes the disciples, the third Herod and the rich young man, and the fourth those healed or saved by their faith.

16. H. Sariola, *Markus und die Gesetz: Eine redaktionskritische Untersuchung* (Helsinki: Suomalainen Tiedeakatemia, 1990), I have found particularly useful and his conclusions generally congenial. I am in principle doubtful about identifying Marcan redaction, but he is duly cautious too. Dahm, *Israel*, 148–73, is more inclined to think that Mark is addressing issues pertinent to his community and that the radical break is not with Israelite tradition but with current Jewish leaders (see also 194–97). He agrees, however, that the main emphasis is on following Jesus and his teaching, which relativizes, but does not dismiss, the authority of Moses.

17. R. A. Guelich, *Mark 1–8:26* (Dallas: Word Books, 1989) 363–64, suggests that "all the Jews" is an inaccurate but understandable generalization, referring to *Ep.Arist.*305 and the loose use of "all" (*pas*) in 1:5,22,33; 6:33; 11:11. He thinks the whole complex, including the asides, arose in a pre-Marcan, Gentile Christian setting, and that it tells us nothing about the author of the Gospel. This is a curious way of having one's cake and eating it, and seems designed mainly to retain the tradition of John Mark as author.

18. This is contra Schenke, *Markusevangelium*, 32–35, who thinks it indicates a mixed community of Jews and Gentiles where the issue of common meals was still a problem. It is certainly correct to take Mark's asides to the reader seriously, since they provide valuable insight into what the author was consciously trying to convey. But the aside in Mark 7:19 does not necessarily imply either that the community was mixed or that foods were a pressing problem. It could merely be dominical confirmation of a well-established Gentile Christian position, for which the community might occasionally have been criticized by Jews or Jewish Christians. On Mark 7:1–23 I am largely following Sariola, *Gesetz*, 21–73, especially the summary on pp.72–73. Lührmann, *Markusevangelium*, 125–29, agrees that the question of food rules was long settled. Other potentially "legal" issues (sabbath, fasting, divorce) could have been pertinent to Gentile Christians as matters of common Christian practice

19. A weakness of Schenke's book (*Markusevangelium*) is a tendency to interpret every detail in the Gospel as if it related to the immediate experience of Mark and his community and to overlook the influence of the historical tradition. To a lesser extent I would say the same of Dahm, *Israel*.

20. See Sariola, *Gesetz*, 239–47. As he notes, one can (and he does) formulate the various principles implicit in Mark's account in a systematic way as long as one does not assume that this was the way Mark thought about them. On pp.12–16 he

summarizes earlier discussions which, whether they think Mark attacked or defended the law, tend to be overly systematic.

21. This is so notably by Weeden, *Mark*; similarly U. Luz, "Das Geheimnissmotiv
und die markinische Christologie," *ZNW* 56(1965) 9–30.

22. The observation that *theios aner* may not have existed as a technical term is
routinely trotted out, but it is of only marginal interest. When the term is applied to
Jesus it refers to his exceptional divine powers, including the ability to perform
miracles, and that this phenomenon was familiar to everyone in the ancient world,
whatever they called it, is clear. See Räisänen's shrewd comments, *"Messianic Secret,"*
64–68, including the observation, contra Weeden and others, that composing a Gospel in which about 30 percent of the stories are about Jesus' miraculous powers is a
very odd way of attacking the notion of Jesus as miracle worker!

23. *Synedria* and *synagogai* are obviously Jewish; *hegemones* and *basileis* could
be Jewish or Roman (cf. 6:14–27).

24. E. Schweizer, *The Good News According to Mark* (Richmond: Knox, 1970)
233, rightly emphasizes the universalism but misconstrues it as an attack on the
principle of legalism.

25. The quotation from Jer 7:11 in v.17 is from a prophecy about the destruction
of the Temple. That the cursing of the fig tree alludes to the fate of Israel is commonly argued, for example by Schweizer, *Mark*, 233, and J. Gnilka, *Evangelium nach
Markus* (Zürich: Benziger, 1978–79) vols.1 and 2, 122–25. Lührmann, *Markusevangelium*, 190–91, denies a connection between the fig tree and Israel. But it is the
context rather than any traditional association that suggests the connection here. Of
course, Mark also wished to emphasize Jesus' miraculous power (11:23–24). On
Mark's view of the Temple, see further Dahm, *Israel*, 174–84.

26. The rending of the Temple curtain (15:38) might put another slant on this
if, as is commonly supposed, it signifies that the destruction of the Temple was associated with the death of Jesus. If this is the right interpretation, it could point to a
future rather than an immediate result. See Lührmann, *Markusevangelium*, 264.

27. See commentaries ad loc. G. Theissen, in his fascinating recent discussion,
argues that the original allusion was to Caligula's actions in 39–40 CE and that Mark
has reinterpreted it with reference to Vespasian in the turbulent times that followed
the destruction of the Temple. See *The Gospels in Context: Social and Political History
in the Synoptic Tradition* (Philadelphia: Fortress, 1991) 125–65.

28. The best case for a date before 70 CE is made by M. Hengel, *Studies in the
Gospel of Mark* (London: SCM, 1985) 14–28, and for a date after 70 CE by Theissen,
Gospels, 258–81. Both try to make their case by referring to known events. Both take
v.14 to refer to the future—Hengel to an antichrist, perhaps a Nero redivivus, and
Theissen to Vespasian, who, it was feared, might desecrate the Temple site as he had
synagogues elsewhere. On the connection between Mark and the Jewish War see
also W. Kelber, *The Kingdom in Mark* (Philadelphia: Fortress, 1974) 129–47; Lührmann, *Markusevangelium*, 6; Schenke, *Markusevangelium*, 35–49; and the interesting
argument by J. Marcus, "The Jewish War and the *Sitz im Leben* of Mark," *JBL*
111(1992) 441–62.

29. Schenke, *Markusevangelium*, 56–57, 159–65, thinks that Mark's Gospel reveals an intense concern with Judaism, the evidence for which is every pericope that
might conceivably be concerned with the matter. He does not follow up on his own
shrewd observation that the question of Judaism is rarely a topic in its own right,
but usually arises in contexts that deal with the teaching of Jesus, discipleship, or
some other topic.

30. This is contra Schenke, *Markusevangelium,* 160–61, who thinks it provoked for Mark and his readers profound questions about the future of Judaism.

31. Dahm, *Israel,* 255–58, notes that there is no denial of Jesus' Jewish roots or rejection of Israel as a whole. Jesus affirms the great commandments (12:28–34) and chooses the Twelve, and it is only certain groups (especially the authorities) who reject him. Dahm takes 12:28–34 to indicate that salvation is open even to the enemy (scribes). Equally well, 12:9 and much of chap. 13 might point to a wider rejection of Israel. Mark does not seem to be clear one way or the other.

32. Papias's Mark may be John Mark or another. Not much can be based on Papias at any rate, as even defenders of the traditional ascription agree, and Papias is the basis for most later patristic speculation. We are left with internal evidence. Chapter 7 suggests, as we argued, a Gentile author. Gentiles knew Aramaic and could have translated it for unilingual readers (e.g., 5:41; 7:34; 14:22; 15:34)—see Theissen's comments on the languages spoken in the lands bordering Galilee (*Gospels,* 68–70). The interest in preaching to the Gentiles fits naturally, but not inevitably, with this view. Lührmann, *Markusevangelium,* 6, makes the point that Mark is well informed about Judaism when his sources are; otherwise he is vague and imprecise. The case I am arguing would not be seriously affected if the author was Jewish and the audience Gentile. S. Sandmel, *Anti-Semitism in the New Testament* (Philadelphia: Fortress, 1978) 25–48, assumes a Gentile context and thinks that is why Mark is much less clear about Judaism than he might have been.

33. See particularly Theissen, *Gospels,* 236–49. Marcus, "Jewish War," 460–62, suggests one of the Hellenistic border cities, maybe Pella, which had been attacked by Jews at the beginning of the war. Syrian provenance is increasingly defended: Lührmann, *Markusevangelium,* 7; H. C. Kee, *Community of the New Age* (London: SCM, 1977) 100–105; Dahm, *Israel,* 277–81. Hengel, *Mark,* 28–30, makes the best of a not very strong case for Rome. Galilee, often loosely defined, is defended by E. Lohmeyer, *Galiläa und Jerusalem* (Göttingen: Vandenhoeck & Ruprecht, 1936); W. Marxsen, *Mark the Evangelist* (Nashville: Abingdon, 1969) 93–107.

34. Schenke, *Markusevangelium,* 41, and Marcus, "Jewish War," 451–53, 461, make the connection with the breakdown of Jew-Gentile relations in the border towns during the war. According to Josephus the Jews were often victims, but frequently enough the aggressors too. Thus the Jews of the narrative are equivalent to Jews at the time of writing and not, as E. Trocmé argues, conservative Jewish Christians—*The Formation of the Gospel according to Mark* (Philadelphia: Westminster, 1975) 107–19. N. A. Beck, *Mature Christianity: The Recognition and Repudiation of the Anti-Jewish Polemic of the New Testament* (Cranbury, N.J.: Associated University Presses, 1985), recognizes the influence of the eschatological crisis on Mark's portrayal of Jewish authorities.

35. The latter point I have taken from W. A. Meeks, "Breaking Away: Three New Testament Pictures of Christianity's Separation from the Jewish Communities," in J. Neusner and E. S. Frerichs, eds., *"To See Ourselves as Others See Us": Christians, Jews, "Others" in Late Antiquity* (Chico, Calif.: Scholars Press, 1985) 93–115. He notes (pp. 98, 111, 113) that in Matthew the Jewish opponents and the issues under dispute recall the emerging rabbinate of Yavneh and the issues of praxis that they debated—as compared with John, in which they focus on matters of belief. A similar but less pointed contrast between legal issues (Matthew) and christological issues (John) is made in the same volume by S. Freyne, "Vilifying the Other and Defining the Self: Matthew's and John's Anti-Jewish Polemic in Focus," 117–43, here 123. S. MacKnight, "A Loyal Critic: Matthew's Polemic with Judaism in Theological

Perspective," in Evans and Hagner, eds, *Anti-Semitism*, 55–79, thinks theological principles were more decisive.

36. Meeks, "Breaking Away," 111, notes the absence of precise parallels. While questioning W. D. Davies's detailed arguments (p.109), he approves of his fundamental insight that Matthean traditions were developed in parallel (and partly in reaction) to those produced by the scribes at Yavneh. See W. D. Davies, *The Setting of the Sermon on the Mount* (Cambridge: Cambridge University Press, 1966). In response to Davies, K. Stendahl, *The School of St. Matthew* (Philadelphia: Fortress, 1968), 2nd ed., xii, followed by G. N. Stanton, *A Gospel for a New People: Studies in Matthew* (Edinburgh: T. & T. Clark, 1992) 122, make what I consider to be a false distinction between ethics and exhortation (Matthew) and halakah (Yavneh) based, perhaps, on too close an identification of Yavneh with the Mishnah. The problem with Davies's argument is, rather, that many of the suggested parallels are unconvincing and that he works with a too-narrow definition of "Yavneh" (or, as he has it, "Jamnia").

37. P. Perkins, "Gender Analysis: A Response to Antoinette Clark Wire," in D. L. Balch, ed., *Social History of the Matthean Community* (Minneapolis: Augsburg Fortress, 1991) 122–28, here 122, suggests that Matthew is mainly Haggadah. Stanton, *New People*, 169–91, notes that christological tensions are part of the picture in Matthew.

38. See the discussion in chapter 6. D. A. Hagner, "The *Sitz im Leben* of the Gospel of Matthew" in K. H. Richards, ed., *Society of Biblical Literature 1985 Seminar Papers* (Atlanta: Scholars Press, 1985) 244–70, here 251–54, observes that emphasis on the date 85 CE telescopes and gives undue precision to what was a complex and drawn-out process. J. A. Overmann, *Matthew's Gospel and Formative Judaism* (Minneapolis: Fortress, 1990) 48–56, makes the important point that, in addition to other problems, the standard view presents us with a sociological improbability—i.e., such radical and widespread change would almost certainly not have happened overnight.

39. It is interesting that there is nothing in the Gospel where we might most expect it. Luke-Acts and John at least have hints, even if the connection has turned out to be something of a blind alley. This either confirms the limited influence of the *Birkat ha-minim* or suggests that Matthew was written before it was introduced. Stanton, *New People*, 142–45, notes that we can be more confident in associating Matthew with Yavnean Judaism than with the *Birkat ha-minim*.

40. I tend still to use "Yavneh" as convenient shorthand for them; others prefer terms such as "formative Judaism." The term is less important than how we define it.

41. See the helpful recent summary by A. J. Saldarini, "Delegitimation of Leaders in Matthew 23," *CBQ* 54(1992) 659–80, here 662–67. I am following his argument that neither Matthew nor his Yavnean rivals were dominant in Judaism as a whole, but that in the Matthean setting the rivals had the upper hand.

42. We shall return later to the question of how precisely Matthew's group related to the synagogue. For now it is sufficient to say that the evidence that the Gospel was written by and for Jewish Christians seems to me overwhelming. For an assessment of this and the theories of Gentile Christian origin see W. D. Davies and D. C. Allison, *A Critical and Exegetical Commentary on the Gospel according to Saint Matthew* (Edinburgh: T & T Clark, 1988) vol.1, 7–58; U. Luz, *Das Evangelium nach Matthäus* (Zürich: Benziger, 1985) vol.1, 62–65; Stanton, *New People*, 131–39; B. Przybylski, "The Setting of Matthean Anti-Judaism," in P. Richardson [with D.

Granskou], eds., *Anti-Judaism in Early Christianity* (Waterloo: Wilfrid Laurier University Press, 1986) vol.1, 181–200, here 184–92.

43. On Matthew's language see Luz, *Matthäus*, 31–56; Davies and Allison, *Matthew*, 72–86.

44. On Matthew and the law see recently I. Broer, *Freiheit vom Gesetz und Radikalisierung des Gesetzes: Ein Beitrag zur Theologie des Evangelisten Matthäus* (Stuttgart: 1980); A. Segal, "Matthew's Jewish Voice," in Balch, ed., *Social History*, 3–37; Overmann, *Matthew's Gospel*, 78–90; G. Barth, "Matthew's Understanding of the Law," in G. Bornkamm, G. Barth, H. J. Held, *Tradition and Interpretation in Matthew* (London: SCM, 1963) 58–164. A lucid and balanced discussion is given by K. Snodgrass, "Matthew and the Law," in D. J. Lull, ed., *Society of Biblical Literature 1988 Seminar Papers* (Chico, Calif.: Scholars Press, 1988) 536–54.

45. The case for Matthew's using Mark and Q as sources is, I think, persuasive despite niggling uncertainties. At any rate, most of the time a simple comparison of the Gospels is enough to make our case.

46. When Matthew adds to Jesus' apocalyptic speech the advice to "pray that your flight may not be in winter or on a Sabbath" (24:20), this might imply commitment to sabbath observance, but other explanations make equally good sense. E. K. C. Wong, "The Matthean Understanding of the Sabbath: A Response to G. N. Stanton," *JSNT* 44(1991) 3–18, argues that it implies a commitment to Sabbath observance. A common explanation is that Sabbath travel in disregard of the law would make them altogether too obvious in a community that generally kept the Sabbath. Stanton, *New People*, 192–206, thinks the point is to avoid giving offense to Jews who did keep the Sabbath (leaving open whether Matthean Christians routinely kept it).

47. Segal, "Voice," 7, apparently gives more force to 15:11, since it implies that Matthew did not value biblical purity injunctions, though he could still be part of Hellenistic Judaism, broadly conceived. This would be a more accurate rendering of Mark than of Matthew. I cannot understand Overmann's conclusion (*Matthew's Gospel*, 83–84) that according to Matthew, Jesus and his disciples violate neither the law nor the "traditions."

48. V. P. Furnish, *The Love Command in the New Testament* (Nashville: Abingdon, 1972) 74–84; Barth, "Law," 76–78; Snodgrass, "Law," 541–45; Overmann, *Matthew's Gospel*, 84–85; Segal, "Voice," 7–8.

49. See the useful summaries by Broer, *Freiheit*, 42–81; Barth, "Law," 64–71; Snodgrass, "Law," 545–52; Luz, *Matthäus*, 231–43; Davies and Allison, *Matthew*, 481–503. The last three present particularly clear discussion of the issues. They uniformly reject the second interpretation, which has recently been promoted by J. P. Meier, *The Vision of Matthew* (New York: Paulist, 1979) 229–35; R. A. Guelich, *The Sermon on the Mount* (Waco, Tex.: Word Books, 1982) 134–74; L. Gaston, "The Messiah of Israel and the Teacher of the Gentiles," *Int* 29(1975) 24–40. I also assume that, whether he inherited or created them, Matthew thought he was saying something coherent in these four verses.

50. Recently, A. J. Saldarini, "The Gospel of Matthew and Jewish-Christian Conflict," in Balch, ed., *Social History*, 38–67, here 49 n.38; in the same volume L. M. White, "Crisis Management and Boundary Maintenance: The Social Location of the Matthean Community," 211–47, here 241 n.100; A. J. Levine, *The Social and Ethnic Dimensions of Matthean Salvation History* (Lewiston, N.Y.: Mellen, 1988) 182–85. Luz, *Matthäus*, 241–43, has some interesting reflections on the "liberalizing"

potential in Matthew's christological thrust and the sort of adjustments that would
have been necessary if and when Gentiles joined their community.

51. Following Jesus: Matt 4:25; 8:1; 14:13; 15:30; 19:2; 20:29; 21:9. Witnessing
miracles: 8:1–4; 9:1–8; 12:22–30; 15:30–31; 17:14–18. Public declarations: 7:28;
9:8,33; 12:23; 15:31; 21:8–11; 22:33.

52. On the crowds see P. Minear, "The Disciples and the Crowds in the Gospel
of Matthew," *ATR,* Supplementary Series 3 (1974) 28–44; D. E. Garland, *The Intention of Matthew 23* (Leiden: Brill, 1979) 36–41. It is easy enough to see what the
disciples and the hostile authorities might have stood for in Matthew's day (see below). What, if anything, the crowds signified is less clear. Some think they represent
actual or potential Jewish converts, so J. C. Fenton, *Saint Matthew* (London: Penguin, 1963) 197. S. van Tilborg, *The Jewish Leaders in Matthew* (Leiden: Brill, 1972)
160–61, rather oddly, thinks they stand for crowds of believing Gentiles. J. D. G.
Dunn, *The Partings of the Ways between Christianity and Judaism and Their Significance for the Character of Christianity* (Philadelphia: Trinity, 1991) 155–56, thinks
Matt 27:25 is ameliorated by positive references to the people elsewhere and the
distinction between leaders and people in 27:64.

53. The appearance of Sadducees in Matt 3:7; 16:1–12, which seems to be the
author's doing (compare Mark), and the tacit assumption that Pharisees and Sadducees held the same views, have struck many as odd. As to the second, nothing in the
passage obliges us to suppose that the Pharisees and Sadducees shared anything
apart from the request for a sign. We know that despite disagreements the two
groups held many things in common, including in all probability their opposition
to Jesus. Why Matthew introduces them is more puzzling—on the assumption that
they were a spent force at the time of writing. Perhaps Matthew desired a touch
of verisimilitude, or a comprehensive list of opponents. Perhaps, too, some Sadducees continued to be influential after 70 CE—a period about which we know
virtually nothing at any rate. See Stanton, *New People,* 136–37; Davies and Allison,
Matthew, 32.

54. See R. Walker, *Die Heilsgeschichte im ersten Evangelium* (Göttingen: Vandenhoeck & Ruprecht, 1967) 38–74; Luz, *Matthäus,* 148; Garland, *Intention,* 44; van
Tilborg, *Leaders,* 1–6; J. D. Kingsbury, *Matthew as Story* (Philadelphia: Fortress,
1988) 16–23; idem, "The Developing Conflict between Jesus and the Jewish Leaders
in Matthew's Gospel: A Literary-Critical Study," *CBQ* 49(1987) 57–73, here 58–64,
which is the fullest discussion of the narrative role of the Jewish leaders.

55. Pharisees: Matt 30; Mark 12; Luke 27. Scribes: Matt 23; Mark 21; Luke 14.
Scribes and Pharisees: Matt 11; Mark 3; Luke 5.

56. The inclusion of Matt 23:3 has understandably baffled commentators: "Do
whatever they teach you and follow it; but do not do as they do, for they do not
practice what they teach." Some see it as a sop to the synagogue authorities, soften-
ing the tirade that follows, others as a realistic recognition of their influence at the
time of writing. In either case it implies a close relationship with the contemporary
synagogue and its leaders. The effect is short-lived, for the modestly positive introduction is rapidly swamped by devastating and vituperative criticism which leaves
the image of the scribes and Pharisees in tatters. See Garland, *Intention,* 46–55. Also
on Matthew 23 see Saldarini, "Delegitimation," 668–78; G. M. Smiga, *Pain and Polemic: Anti-Judaism in the Gospels* (Mahurah, N.J.: Paulist, 1992) 61–65; Overmann,
Matthew's Gospel, 114–47.

57. There are clear indications that problems within the church are being tackled
too (23:8–12), but nothing to suggest that these were primary, contra Garland, *Inten-*

tion, 210–15; Gaston, "Messiah," 34–37. For further references see Saldarini, "Delegitimation," 661 n.4; B. Viviano, "Social World and Community Leadership: The Case of Matt 23.1–12, 34," *JSNT* 39(1990) 3–21; H. J. Becker, *Auf der Kathedra des Mose: Rabbinische und theologisches Denken und antirabbinisches Polemik im Matthäus* (Berlin: Institut Kirche und Judentum, 1990) passim. That the scribes and Pharisees are a polemical construct, as Gaston suggests, is at least partially correct; but they could also stand for contemporary Jews. The notion that they were simply a relic of the historical past leaves unexplained the polemical energy expended on them. On the broader issue of internal and external problems tackled by Matthew see White, "Crisis Management," 227–28.

58. See especially J. Neusner, "The Formation of Rabbinic Judaism: Yavneh (Jamnia) from A.D.70 to 100," in *ANRW* II.19.2, 3–42, which summarizes the view he argues for in many other places. With respect to Matthew he is followed by Meeks, "Breaking Away," 109; Saldarini, "Delegitimation," 662–63.

59. The patterns are not without exception. Thus the elders turn up in the question of hand washing (15:2), and the Pharisees can be involved in the Passion (22:15; 27:62). This serves to bind the leaders together and does not seriously affect the different emphases observed above. On the dispute over signs (16:1–12; cf. 9:34; 12:34) and Davidic messiahship (22:41–46) see below.

60. White, "Crisis Management," 242. Of course not all disagreements, especially christological ones, were marginal. But it is a useful insight to much else.

61. Mark 1:23,39 and Luke 4:15 use the same phrase. Stanton, *New People,* 128–29, notes that the argument [see G. D. Kilpatrick, *The Origins of the Gospel According to St. Matthew* (Oxford: Oxford University Press, 1946) 110] for omitting the pronouns is textually weak. There is therefore a precedent for Matthew. But he has made much more of the phrase than Mark who, at any rate, uses it more in a local or geographical than in a polemical sense. See White, "Crisis Management," 215 n.17.

62. Overmann, *Matthew's Gospel,* 104–5. I am most dependent in this section on Overmann's chapter on the social development of the Matthean community, which is the heart of his book (72–149). See also Stanton, *New People,* 126–31.

63. Overmann, *Matthew's Gospel,* 126–30.

64. Luz, *Matthäus,* 134–41, has a full discussion. Cf. Overmann, *Matthew's Gospel,* 74–78, 115–17. For the rich associations of "scribe" and the suggestion that the disciples (and Jesus before them) represent the true scribes, see D. E. Orton, *The Understanding Scribe* (Sheffield: JSOT Press, 1988) esp. 161–76.

65. K. Pantle-Schreiber, "Anmerkungen zur Auseinandersetzung von *ekklesia* und Judentum im Matthäusevangelium," *ZNW* 80(1989) 145–62, here 146–52.

66. Stanton, *New People,* 180–91. For the two-parousias scheme he refers to Justin (e.g., *Dial.*14:8), Origen (*Cels.*I.56), and *Ps.-Clem.Rec.*I.49. Cf. Smiga, *Pain,* 75–78.

67. Stanton, *New People,* 171–80. The evidence is discussed more fully in chap. 6.

68. Dunn, *Partings,* 155, notes that "Jews" in 28:15 is anarthrous, but draws the implausible conclusion that it is purely descriptive and conveys no sense of separation.

69. Noted by R. T. France, *Matthew: Evangelist and Teacher* (Grand Rapids: Zondervan, 1989) 214–15.

70. France, *Matthew,* 215, thinks that Matthew may be distinguishing the two witnesses for this charge from the previously mentioned false witnesses. What this implies he does not say—presumably that Matthew thought the accusation justified.

This does not fit the impersonal form of the statement in 24:2. Similar to France: E. Schweizer, *The Good News According to Matthew* (London: SPCK, 1976) 498; A. Sand, *Das Evangelium nach Matthäus* (Regensburg: F. Pustet, 1987) 540–41.

71. The "sign of the Son of Man" in 24:30 may be a deliberate allusion to the "sign of your coming" in 24:3. If so, the events in between, including the laying waste of the Temple (24:15ff.), are clearly separated from the parousia itself. So, for example, F. Hahn, "Die eschatologische Rede Matthäus 24 und 25," in L. Schenke, ed., *Studien im Matthäusevangelium: Festschrift für Wilhelm Pesch* (Stuttgart: Katholisches Bibelwerk, 1988) 107–26, here 118–19, 125. On the other hand, the introduction of "immediately" (*eutheos*) in 24:30 pulls them close together.

72. The ambiguity has often been noted. In favor of the more positive sense is that the passage cited (Ps 118:36) is an expression of joyful praise; in favor of the second is the surrounding context of judgment. D. Allison, "Matt 23.29 = Luke 13.35b as a Conditional Prophecy," *JSNT* 18(1983) 75–84, favors the first; also Stanton, *New People*, 249–50, on the basis of the biblical sin-exile-redemption pattern. Luke's placement of the saying (Luke 13:35) allows for its fulfillment when Jesus entered Jerusalem (Luke 19:38), rather than at the parousia.

73. Schweizer, *Matthew*, 215, draws attention to this, but rightly does not make too much of it. Levine, *Social*, 105–30, does not successfully establish her view that Jews and Gentiles are included in both the "heirs" and the "many."

74. Stanton, *New People*, 151–52, suggests that the rejected stone (21:42,44) is the church rather than Jesus. White, "Crisis Management," 224 n.48, correctly notes that "nation" is not the same as "the nations," that it includes Jew and Gentile, and that the whole concept is cast in Jewish terms. The contrast between this "nation" and the old Israel nevertheless stands, whether we call it a new/true Israel or something else. Matthew may not have been thinking as precisely as we might wish.

75. The former view was argued most forcibly by D. R. A. Hare and D. J. Harrington, "'Make Disciples of All the Gentiles' (Matt 28:19)," *CBQ* 37(1975) 359–79, and most forcibly refuted by J. P. Meier, "Nations or Gentiles in Matt 28:19?" *CBQ* 39(1977) 94–102. Following Meier recently are Segal, "Voice," 24; Stanton, *New People*, 137–38, 214; Saldarini, "Matthew," 42–43, nn.14,16; Davies and Allison, *Matthew*, 22–25; Sand, *Matthäus*, 496.

76. Levine, *Social*, 182–90, suggests that *ethne* in 28:19 means Gentiles alone, specifically to extend the earlier mission (10:5), but that their inclusion does not mean the Jews' exclusion. T. L. Donaldson, *Jesus on the Mountain* (Sheffield: JSOT Press, 1985) 281 n.74, notes that whatever 28:19 means, the command to preach to the Jews (10:6) is not revoked.

77. Matthew 27:25 lays the blame for Jesus' death squarely on the Jews. Its notorious extension to include all Jews of all times was surely not Matthew's intention. D. J. Harrington, "Polemical Parables in Matt 24–25," *USQR* 44(1991) 287–98, finds a polemic against the Jews (written from the inside) in 24:45–25:30. These parables are surely aimed at the church. Being made to share the same fate as the hypocrites (= Jews, 24:51) does not mean that it is the hypocrites who are being addressed.

78. Several scholars have noted that Matthew's defensiveness and colorful polemic suggest a beleaguered minority. It may be that another group (the Yavnean rabbis) were more successful in persuading other Jews to follow them, or simply that the Matthean group were outnumbered by Jews whom they could not persuade.

79. It is uncertain how far the Matthean church had gone in fulfilling the final commission. Many think it had begun to recruit Gentiles but only recently and only few in number. The situation of the church would then be analogous to the pattern

of the Gospel: universalism is known in the present but it projects primarily into the future. J. T. Sanders, *Schismatics, Sectarians, Dissidents, Deviants: The First One Hundred Years of Jewish-Christian Relations* (Valley Forge, Pa.: Trinity, 1993) 154–59, relates this evidence to stages in the composition of Matthew.

80. There is no need to relate the range of opinion on this topic, so well set out by Stanton, *New People,* 113–45; idem, "The Origin and Purpose of Matthew's Gospel: Matthean Scholarship from 1945–1980," *ANRW* II.25.3, 1885–1951. Stanton argues for separation, recent and traumatic; Saldarini, "Delegitimation," thinks they were "functionally Jewish," competing from within even if officially expelled; Overmann, *Matthew's Gospel,* 148–49, hovers between the two. They read the evidence in substantially the same way but give differently nuanced reconstructions, hobbled in each case by our lack of information. It goes without saying that whatever claims Matthew made about his community and Israel would have been absurd, perhaps incomprehensible, to non-Christian Jews.

81. L. Gaston, "Anti-Judaism and the Passion Narrative in Luke and Acts," in P. Richardson, ed., *Anti-Judaism,* vol.1, 127–53, quotations from pp.127, 153. This would explain why Sandmel, *Anti-Semitism,* 73, thinks Luke presents a "subtle, genteel anti-Semitism" (which becomes a bit more aggressive in Acts), while Beck, *Mature,* 207, judges Luke to be the most anti-Jewish of all New Testament writers.

82. Generally on the leaders in the Gospel see the useful study by M. A. Powell, "The Religious Leaders in Luke: A Literary-Critical Study," *JBL* 109(1990) 93–110.

83. This is commonly argued. See commentaries ad loc. J. T. Sanders, *The Jews in Luke-Acts* (Philadelphia: Fortress, 1987) 164–68, is representative.

84. R. L. Brawley, *Luke-Acts and the Jews: Conflict, Apology, and Conciliation* (Atlanta: Scholars Press, 1987) 6–27. He cautions against finding any programmatic theme other than the identity of Jesus.

85. S. G. Wilson, "The Jews and the Death of Jesus in Acts," in P. Richardson, ed., *Anti-Judaism,* vol.1, 155–64; Gaston, "Anti-Judaism," passim; F. J. Matera, "Responsibility for the Death of Jesus according to the Acts of the Apostles," *JSNT* 39(1990) 77–93; Sanders, *Jews,* 3–16; E. J. Via, "According to Luke, Who Put Jesus to Death?" in R. J. Cassidy and P. J. Sharper, eds., *Political Issues in Luke-Acts* (Maryknoll, N.Y.: Orbis, 1983) 122–45.

86. Acts 9:23,29; 13:45,50; 14:2,4,5,19; 16:3; 17:5–9,13; 18:12; 20:2,19; 21:11,21,27; 22:30; 23:12,27; 24:5,9,18,27; 25:7,9,10,24; 26:2,7,21; 28:19. They are set out in Gaston, "Anti-Judaism," 137–38, and commented on by Sanders, *Jews,* 71–72. Of the seventy-four uses of *Ioudaioi* in Luke-Acts, sixty-six occur after Stephen's martyrdom and the vast majority are pejorative. It is noteworthy that the people (*laos*), in the sense of Israel (26:17; 28:26–27; cf. 12:11) or the common folk (21:30,36), are consistently at enmity with the church from Acts 6:8 on.

87. See Wilson, "Jews," 162–63; also implied in the way Gaston, "Anti-Judaism," structures his discussion, starting with Acts.

88. Blasphemy: Luke 5:21; 19:39. Halakic matters: Luke 5:30,33; 6:2,7; 7:39; 11:37–38; 14:1; 15:2. These are Sanders's distinctions, *Jews,* 88–93. He thinks it possible that 5:26 shows a change of mind from 5:21 and that 19:39 might be a friendly warning like 13:31. All the remaining disputes are halakic, i.e., questions of interpretation. This is his term, not Luke's, and (contra Sanders) it is significant that Luke does not explicitly distinguish law and tradition (as Mark 7 and Matthew 15 do), Torah and practice. These are our categories which may (or may not) describe what is going on in Luke. See S. G. Wilson, *Luke and the Law* (Cambridge: Cambridge University Press, 1983) 35. Sanders's observation (pp.88–89) that Luke reduces the

evidence for Pharisaic hostility in Mark and Matthew should be balanced by Gaston's point ("Anti-Judaism," 141) that Luke makes every one of the controversy stories in 5:17–6:11 refer to the Pharisees (in comparison with Mark 2:1–3:6), and the probability that Matthew adds (rather than that Luke omits) hostile references to their common material. Sanders rightly notes that Luke often has "some Pharisees" or "a/the Pharisee" where the others use the more comprehensive "the Pharisees" (Luke 6:2; 19:39; 7:37–39; 11:37–38). Of course, a moment's reflection would have told an alert reader/listener that "the Pharisees" could scarcely have meant "all the Pharisees."

89. Luke 11:42–44; 12:1; 16:14.

90. Sanders, *Jews*, 85–131, esp. 96–98, 110–12. He has some difficulty (pp.112–14) with the fact that the Pharisees in Acts 15:5 are Christians. Gaston even suggests ("Anti-Judaism," 136) that they are introduced to endorse the eventual outcome of the conference! The conflict in Acts 15 is not just over matters of halakah (as in the Gospel), but over the imposition of the law in toto. Paul also presents something of a problem. The positive side of the Gospel portrait Sanders explains as follows: as representatives of Jewish Christianity, they can be friendly to Jesus and are not involved in his crucifixion, but ultimately stand under Jesus' blanket condemnation of Pharisees. It is not so clear to me, as it is to Sanders, that Luke dislikes Jewish Christians. Brawley, *Jews,* 84–106, raises similar objections. It is difficult to find a coherent explanation for Luke's disparate evidence. See also J. A. Ziesler, "Luke and the Pharisees," *NTS* 25(1979) 146–57; J. T. Carroll, "Luke's Portrait of the Pharisees," *CBQ* 50(1988) 604–21; and my own sketchy comments in *Law,* 113–14. J. D. Kingsbury, "The Pharisees in Acts," in F. van Segbroek, C. M. Tuckett, G. van Belle, and J. Verheyden, eds., *The Four Gospels 1992: Festschrift für Frans Neirynck* (Leuven: Peeters, 1992) vol.2, 1497–1512, is a useful corrective to the tendency to exaggerate the positive image in Acts, but his nuanced attempt to reverse the trend is not wholly successful.

91. J. Jervell, *Luke and the People of God* (Minneapolis: Augsburg, 1972) 133–51; Wilson, *Law*; C. Blomberg, "The Law in Luke-Acts," *JSNT* 22(1984) 53–80; A. Seifrid, "Jesus and the Law in Acts," *JSNT* 30(1987) 39–57; P. F. Esler, *Community and Gospel in Luke-Acts* (Cambridge: Cambridge University Press, 1987) 110–30; Sanders, *Jews,* 124–28; M. Klinghardt, *Gesetz und Volk Gottes: das lukanische Verständnis des Gesetzes nach Herkunft, Funktion und seinem Ort in der Geschichte des Urchristentums* (Tübingen: Mohr [Siebeck], 1988); and most recently K. Salo, *Luke's Treatment of the Law: A Redaction-Critical Investigation* (Helsinki: Suomalainen Tiedeakatemia, 1991).

92. See Wilson, *Law,* 20–23; Esler, *Community,* 111–14. Jesus' teaching will be considered below. The curious exception in Acts when Peter is driven to do something that Luke thought was illegal—treating Gentiles, and perhaps all foods too, as clean—plays no role outside the story of the first Gentile convert (Acts 10, esp. v.28). It is difficult to know what to make of this, though it may indicate that Luke was a lot more concerned about the reputation of Paul than that of Peter.

93. The obvious examples are Acts 16:1–3; 18:18; 21:24; 22:3; 23:1–5; 24:14,17–18. The exceptions noted by Esler, *Community,* 128, etc., in which Paul supposedly abandons the Levitical food laws, are barely significant in view of the overall thrust. Acts 16:17; 18:7 involve God-fearers, a special case, and the second does not speak of eating. This leaves 16:35, and it does not say what food was eaten. Esler's view of the mixing of Jews and Gentiles is at any rate flawed. See E. P. Sanders, "Jewish Association with Gentiles and Galatians 2:11–14," in R. T. Fortna and B. R.

Gaventa, eds., *The Conversation Continues: Studies in Paul and John* (Nashville: Abingdon, 1990) 170–88; C. C. Hill, *Hellenists and Hebrews. Reappraising Division within the Earliest Church* (Minneapolis: Fortress, 1992) 118–22.

94. Wilson, *Law,* 12–58. Blomberg, "Law," largely agrees.

95. Esler, *Community,* 128. The discussion of Gospel material is on pp.111–22. If Luke includes (and presumably approves of) material where Jesus transcends or challenges the law, even if he was constrained by the shape of the tradition or current Christian practice, the resulting view can hardly be called conservative. A mixed or balanced view would better describe it. Further, to argue (p.116) on the basis of Luke 23:56; Acts 1:12 that Luke supported Sabbath observance is rather desperate. The other example he quotes, Acts 20:7–12, might show the exact opposite. He rightly (pp.117–18) links Luke 9:60 with other statements about renunciation of family ties (Luke 12:51–53; 14:26), but this provides no backing for his insistence that Luke was aware of their legal implications. Jervell had already argued that Luke had an extremely conservative view of the law (the most conservative in the NT), based on his generally unpersuasive argument that Luke held that the church had joined Israel and was thus bound to her law. His views are discussed in Wilson, *Law,* 12–58. Sanders's assessment of the theme of law (*Jews,* 124–28) is linked with his view of the role of the Pharisees which, I think, he misconstrues (see above n.88).

96. Esler, *Community,* 121. Esler's view of the Lucan community has been criticized on other grounds (n.93 above). There is a difference of opinion about whether intensifying (rather than liberalizing) the Mosaic rules on divorce would count as undermining or undergirding them. It would at least run against the grain of Jewish practice, which the Jews believed had Mosaic authorization.

97. Klinghardt, *Gesetz.* Almsgiving (pp.41–68) is connected with purity on the basis of Jewish precedents. The ruling on divorce (pp.85–96) is connected with purity because it is akin to regulations for priests in the Jewish tradition and pagan cult officials in the Hellenistic tradition. On the Sabbath see pp.238–40. He notes that any charge of abrogation of the law springing from their attitude toward the Temple is met by reversing the accusation; cf. Acts 7 (pp. 303–5).

98. Klinghardt, *Gesetz,* 310–13.

99. Thus Klinghardt has some trouble (p.311) explaining why scribes and Pharisees are often mentioned together and not always distinguished. The presentation of the Pharisees, as is well known, is not uniform (see above nn.88,90). Note how Sanders, *Jews,* 132–37, connects the tax collectors and sinners in the Gospel with the Gentiles in Acts, and presumably with Gentiles in Luke's community!

100. Luke 3:10–14; 10:25ff.; 11:41; 12:33; 14:12–14; 16:1–18,19–31; 18:18–25; 19:1–10; Acts 2:44–45; 4:32; 5:1–11; 10:2–4. See also Esler, *Community,* 164–200; and the intriguing sociopolitical analysis of H. Moxnes, *The Economy of the Kingdom: Social Conflict and Economic Relations in Luke's Gospel* (Philadelphia: Fortress, 1988).

101. Klinghardt, *Gesetz,* 306–13, insists on calling this (and the Gentile obligations in the decree) "ritual"—presumably as distinct from ethical—requirements.

102. Salo, *Law,* 295–301, thinks Luke addresses both Jewish and Gentile Christians (the former keep the whole law, the latter only minimum requirements), but is not sure whether they belong to mixed or separate communities.

103. J. Jervell, "The Church of Jews and Godfearers," in J. B. Tyson, ed., *Luke-Acts and the Jewish People* (Minneapolis: Augsburg, 1988) 11–20, is correct to note that most of the Gentile converts in Acts are God-fearers, but wayward in his conclusion that they were "semi-Jews" and the only sort of Gentile converts Luke was interested in. J. T. Sanders, "Who Is a Jew and Who Is a Gentile in the Book of Acts,"

NTS 37(1991) 434–55, here 443–52, argues that Jervell is wrong to equate *ta ethne* with God-fearers. If that is what Jervell means, Sanders is right. But Jervell seems to recognize (p.13) that it means Gentiles in general, and to argue only that the sort of Gentiles Luke was interested in were God-fearers. Sanders (pp.451–53) rightly dismisses the argument of M. Salmon ("Insider or Outsider? Luke's Relationship with Judaism," in Tyson, ed., *Jewish People*, 76–82) that Luke was a Jew.

104. Wilson, *Law*, 68–102. Sanders, *Jews*, 115, suggests that the puzzling term *pniktos* ("strangled things," Acts 15:20; 21:25) in the decree alludes to the hunted (i.e., snared) animals in Lev 17:13 and to "what dies of itself or what has been torn by wild animals" (Lev 17:15; cf. Philo *Spec.Leg.*4.122). But neither Leviticus nor Philo mentions snaring nor do they use *pniktos* of what is snared, torn by beasts, or dies of itself. To say that Acts 15:29; Lev 17:13–15; Philo *Spec.Leg.*4:122 "all have in common that something killed in the hunt might not be properly drained of blood" blends the three texts by assertion rather than by careful argument. Sanders's conclusion that Gentiles are obliged to keep the Mosaic laws appropriate to them gives him problems when he tries to refute Jervell (p.117). Sanders seems to want to hold that the decree is both Mosaic and Christian. That Luke could have seen some Gentile obligations (e.g., loving one's neighbor) in this way is possible, though I doubt if that is the way he would have put it. The point would be stronger if the connection with Leviticus were firmer. That the LXX assumes that the rules of Lev 17–18 were for proselytes (Wilson, *Law*, 86) is not a problem for Sanders, who thinks that Luke does not clearly distinguish proselytes from God-fearers and likens Gentile Christians to proselytes (pp.116, 137–40; similarly Klinghardt, *Gesetz*, 181–85). This is a lot to build on the admittedly ambiguous "worshiping [*sebomenoi*] proselytes" in Acts 13:43. Klinghardt (*Gesetz*, 202–4) thinks Philo may have been the first to connect *pniktos* and Lev 17:15. He admits that it is not clear exactly what it means in Acts 15, even if it refers in some way to improperly bled meat. His suggestion (pp.186–200) that only these four prohibitions appear in the decree because only they were accompanied in Lev 17–18 by the threat of being cut off makes an interesting observation about Lev 17–18. What it tells us about Luke and the Christians of his day is much less certain. See now the interesting attempt to revive the view that the original purpose of the decree (and one that Luke understood) was to preserve Gentiles from idolatrous and magical practices: A. J. M. Wedderburn, "The 'Apostolic Decree': Tradition and Redaction," *NT* 35(1993) 362–89.

105. Salo, *Law*, 297, comes to a similar conclusion.

106. Wilson, *Law*, 1–11. Other motives have been ascribed to Luke. Seifrid, "Law," 51–53, suggests that he condones observation of the law by Jewish Christians out of a concern for Christian unity and a desire to maximize the chance of converting Jews. Blomberg, "Law," 71–80, suggests on the other hand that readers would conclude that even Jewish Christians were free from the law.

107. Of course the point would be resolved if we could accept the Western reading that omits *pniktos;* but that is problematic. See Wilson, *Law*, 99–101. J. H. Neyrey, "The Symbolic Universe of Luke-Acts," in J. H. Neyrey, ed., *The Social World of Luke-Acts: Models for Interpretation* (Peabody, Mass.: Hendrikson, 1991) 271–304, considers Luke's view of the law, Temple, and related matters within the broader context of a system of "purity" or order. Jesus and his followers, he concludes, both depended on and broke free from the Jewish way of ordering the world. From a Jewish perspective they had abandoned Judaism; from their perspective they had reformed it.

108. The almost identical wording in 19:38 (cf. 13:35) has led some to find the

fulfillment of Jesus' prediction in the triumphal entry. This is possible, but it is hard to know what the forsaking of the house then refers to.

109. See especially D. Tiede, *Prophecy and History in Luke-Acts* (Philadelphia: Fortress, 1980) 92–95; J. Bradley Chance, *Jerusalem, the Temple and the New Age in Luke-Acts* (Macon, Ga.: Peeters, 1988) 127–38; Brawley, *Jews*, 125–32; E. Franklin, *Christ the Lord. A Study in the Purpose and Theology of Luke-Acts* (London: SPCK, 1975) 128–30. For a different view see C. H. Giblin, *The Destruction of Jerusalem according to Luke's Gospel. A Historical-Typological Model* (Rome: Biblical Institute, 1985), though his focus is mainly on other issues. Understandably, the future of city and Temple is for many tied to the fate of the Jews, but they are separate issues. The latter will be dealt with in a subsequent section.

110. Chance, *Jerusalem*, 134–38. He also alludes to Luke 19:11 but admits that in neither case is Luke explicit.

111. This last argument is Brawley's, *Jews*, 127–32.

112. See C. K. Barrett, "Attitudes to the Temple in the Acts of the Apostles," in W. Horbury, ed., *Templum Amicitiae: Essays on the Second Temple Presented to E. Bammel* (Sheffield: JSOT Press, 1991) 345–67. He notes that overall the evidence of Acts is ambiguous, but the final judgment is negative.

113. Sanders, *Jews*, 32: "Jerusalem, in Luke-Acts, is characterized primarily by enmity towards God and his purposes and messengers, by judgement, and by destruction."

114. W. Stegemann, *Zwischen Synagoge und Obrigkeit* (Göttingen: Vandenhoeck & Ruprecht, 1991) 21–26, 34–36, argues that the claim for continuity with Israel coincided with the separation of church and synagogue. The claim for continuity was thus belied by the sociological reality. F. Bovon, "Israel, die Kirche und die Völker im lukanischen Doppelwerk," *TLZ* 108(1983) 403–14, makes much the same point (p.408). A sketch of the manifold ways Luke undergirds the claim to Israel's heritage is found in the shrewd discussion by M. J. Cook, "The Mission to the Jews in Acts: Unravelling Luke's 'Myth of the Myriads,'" in Tyson, ed., *Jewish People*, 102–23.

115. A point also made by Cook, "Mission," 105.

116. Jervell, *Luke*, 41–74. Jervell correctly notes that in Acts the Christian message causes a division within Israel. The same theme was traced in the Gospel by A. George, "Israël dans l'oeuvre de Luc," *RB* 75(1968) 481–525. Jervell makes two other major points: that Jewish belief rather than Jewish unbelief motivated the Gentile mission; and that Gentile converts joined, not some new entity, but Israel, in which they linked up with believing Jews. This distinctive theology of Israel and church is then seen to permeate Luke's work. The second argument is flimsily based and the first flies in the face of plain statements in the text. See S. G. Wilson, *The Gentiles and the Gentile Mission in Luke-Acts* (Cambridge: Cambridge University Press, 1973) 219–33.

117. See n.86 above.

118. These arguments are most clearly stated by Brawley, *Jews*, passim, but especially pp.28–50, 68–83, 133–54. Similar, but differently nuanced, are D. Tiede, "Glory to thy People Israel: Luke-Acts and the Jews," in Tyson, ed., *Jewish People*, 21–34, and earlier in *Prophecy and History;* D. P. Moessner, "Paul in Acts: Preacher of Eschatological Repentance to Israel," *NTS* 34(1988) 96–104; idem, "The Ironic Fulfilment of Israel's Glory," 35–50, also in the Tyson volume; B. J. Koet, *Five Studies on Interpretation of Scripture in Luke-Acts* (Leuven: Leuven University Press, 1989) esp. 150–53; idem, "Simeon's Worte (Lk 2,29–32. 34c–35) und Israel's Geschick,"

in van Segbroek et al. (see n.90), *Four Gospels,* vol.2, 1549–69; F. Bovon, "Studies in Luke-Acts: Retrospect and Prospect," *HTR* 85(1992) 175–96, here 189–90; idem, "Schon hat der heilige Geist durch den Propheten Jesaja zu euren Vätern gesprochen," *ZNW* 75(1984) 345–50; Dunn, *Partings,* 149–51; see also n.109 above, and the discussion in Smiga, *Pain and Polemic,* 126–30. The sixth argument is that of K. Haacker, "Das Bekenntnis des Paulus zur Hoffnung Israels nach der Apostelgeschichte des Lukas," *NTS* 31(1985) 437–51, based on the overall message of Luke-Acts and on the observation that in Acts the "hope of Israel" is associated with the resurrection and in Jewish thought resurrection often includes the salvation of Israel. R. Tannehill, "Israel in Luke-Acts: A Tragic Story," *JBL* 104(1985) 69–85, further expanded in his two-volume commentary, *The Narrative Unity of Luke-Acts* (Philadelphia: Fortress, 1986, 1990), finds a lingering hope for the Jews that runs up against the reality of Jewish rejection which, he thinks, creates a tragic mood. Rather, like many, I detect a note of antipathy.

119. Sanders, *Jews,* 366 n.245, and the scholars quoted there. See also the careful analysis of H. J. Hauser, *Strukturen der Abschlusserzählung der Apostelgeschichte (Apg.28,16–31)* (Rome: Biblical Institute, 1979) 62–66.

120. The abrupt transition from the Jews' debating among themselves to Paul's scathing condemnation was noted by an early editor, who added v.29 to soften the effect: afterward the Jews continued to dispute among themselves.

121. For a summary of earlier views along these lines (Overbeck, Haenchen) see Sanders, *Jews,* 39–42. More recently see Jervell, *Luke,* 62–64; Wilson, *Gentiles,* 219–38; Sanders, *Jews,* 37–83, 296–99; J. B. Tyson, *Images of Judaism in Luke-Acts* (Columbia, S.C.: University of South Carolina Press, 1992) 158–80; Cook, "Mission," passim; D. Juel, *Luke-Acts: The Promise of History* (Atlanta: John Knox, 1983) 109–12; J. L. Houlden, "The Purpose of Luke," *JSNT* 21(1984) 53–65; D. Slingerland, "The 'Jews' in the Pauline Portion of Acts," *JAAR* 54(1986) 305–24; Smiga, *Pain and Polemic,* 132–33.

122. The first is from E. Haenchen, "The Book of Acts as Source Material for the History of Early Christianity," in L. E. Keck and J. L. Martyn, eds., *Studies in Luke-Acts* (London and Philadelphia: SPCK/Fortress, 1966) 258–78, here 278; the second is from Brawley, *Jews,* 152–53.

123. An interesting distinction observed by Sanders, *Jews,* 37–83. The speeches, he thinks, give Luke's ultimate judgment. In the narrative the Jews progressively become what they in essence always were, and at the end of Acts speech and narrative coincide. This, however, presupposes a particular reading of the end of Acts.

124. Thus, for example, it has often been argued that Luke's particularly conservative view of Jewish Christian obedience to the law had only to do with the past and had no practical consequences in his communities.

125. That Luke would have objected to Jewish Christians who meddled with Gentile Christians or undercut the reputation of Paul seems certain. Whether this would have led to what Sanders (*Jews,* 131, 316–17) calls an almost indiscriminate "disgust" with Jewish Christians, placing them on a par with nonbelieving Jews, is less clear. Many scholars make the distinction between a future for individual Jewish converts and the Jewish people as a whole. See especially Tyson, *Images,* 177–78. Even Sanders, *Jews,* 129, grudgingly accepts this, but his comment is, typically, overstated: "'We Gentiles,' thinks Luke, 'are in charge here and you Jews can just sit down and shut up.'"

126. See the lucid analysis by S. R. Garret, *The Demise of the Devil: Magic and the*

Demonic in Luke's Writings (Philadelphia: Fortress, 1989), which includes reflections on the Jewish-Christian conflict implicit in some of the stories.

127. Recently noted by R. F. Stoops, "Riot and Assembly: The Social Context of Acts 19:23–41," *JBL* 108(1989) 73–91, here 89; L. M. Wills, "The Depiction of the Jews in Acts," *JBL* 110(1991) 631–54, here 653–54; V. Robbins, "The Social Location of the Implied Author," in Neyrey, ed., *Social World,* 305–32, esp. 327–32, moves in much the same direction. W. Stegemann's *Zwischen Synagoge und Obrigkeit* (n.114 above), as the title indicates, is about precisely this theme and will be discussed below.

128. Wills, "Depiction," 651–52, makes the interesting observation that the Roman rulers who were viewed unfavorably by Romans (Felix, Festus) are viewed unfavorably in Acts, and those viewed positively in Acts (e.g., Gallio) were held in high regard by Romans. He also thinks that the view of Herod Agrippa I (negative) and Herod Agrippa II (positive) accorded with Roman sentiment. He concludes, nevertheless, that Luke was concerned with "a construction of a self-image for Christians as legitimate citizens of the Roman Empire" (p.652).

129. This applies whether or not Theophilus was Luke's patron, indeed, whether or not he was real or fictional. Other elements that point in this direction are noted by Wills, "Depiction," 651, summarizing E. Plümacher, *Lukas als hellenistischer Schriftsteller* (Göttingen: Vandenhoeck & Ruprecht, 1972) 16–27: the location of the story in the chronology of world history (Luke 3); favorable official Roman comments; engagement with Hellenistic philosophy (Acts 17); peaceable and orderly Christian behavior; Christian expressions of loyalty to Rome (Acts 25:11). See also H. Conzelmann, *The Theology of St. Luke* (London: SCM, 1961) 138–44, and others quoted by Wills. The most extensive argument against any notion of political apology, addressed to Romans or Christians, is made by R. J. Cassidy, *Jesus, Politics and Society: A Study of Luke's Gospel* (Maryknoll, N.Y.: Orbis, 1978); idem, *Society and Politics in the Acts of the Apostles* (Maryknoll, N.Y.: Orbis, 1987).

130. See R. Maddox, *The Purpose of Luke-Acts* (Edinburgh: T. & T. Clark, 1982) 91–99; P. W. Walaskey, *"And so we came to Rome": The Political Perspective of St. Luke* (Cambridge: Cambridge University Press, 1983) passim; Esler, *Community,* 217–19; Wills, "Depiction," 651–53.

131. The consistency with which Luke establishes this pattern can be seen by listing all the appropriate passages in Acts, as is done conveniently by Wills, "Depiction," 640–42.

132. This is a bald summary of a complex and fascinating argument. Stegemann, *Zwischen,* 268–80, gives a very useful summary.

133. That is, the message was aimed at Christians rather than Romans, and at Gentile Christians rather than Jewish Christians (of which there were none in Luke's community). Stegemann, *Zwischen,* 143–44, 278–80, likens the situation to Rev 2:9; 3:9, where the blasphemers "who say that they are Jews and are not" are called in turn a "synagogue of Satan." These he seems to identify as Jews (not Christians) who insisted on their Jewishness in order to avoid state harassment. They were thus able to avoid the pressures placed on Christians by such things as the emperor cult. They are condemned because in effect they bowed to imperial authority by asserting their Jewishness. This, Stegemann thinks, shows how much more secure the position of Jews was under Domitian. This is an odd argument. Why would a Christian worry about what Jews did and condemn them so savagely? And why would he say that these Jews were not Jews? At any rate, in this view Luke would seem to

recommend a form of behavior—association with the Jews to avoid political pressure—that greatly agitated the author of Revelation. A more convincing interpretation, and one that provides a better analogy with Luke, understands the blasphemers to be Jewish or Gentile Christians who associate with the synagogue in order to avoid state harassment. See chap. 5.

134. I am not sure which of these Stegemann prefers. Did Luke's readers know of Jewish opposition such as is described in Acts, as Stegemann suggests? Sanders, *Jews,* 306–13, thinks not: Luke's target was contemporary Jewish Christianity, but this led him to defame the Jews in general. I think it likely that harassment by Jews was known in Luke's day, as at least Matthew and John would seem to confirm. For further consideration of Stegemann's argument see now Sanders, *Schismatics,* 180–86.

135. Stegemann, *Zwischen,* 34–36, is inclined to doubt that Jewish-Christian conflict is ever for Luke an entirely internal matter.

136. It is clear by now, I hope, that singling out a dominant and distinctive characteristic is not meant to be exhaustive or exclusive. As noted above, Matthew is also interested in christological belief, perhaps to a greater degree than John overtly is in Christian halakah. It will also become clear below that the beliefs propagated by John are at least loosely analogous to theological speculations favored by some Jews and attacked by others in his day (which also shows that Jews were not indifferent to questions of belief).

137. It will be clear to any knowledgeable Johannine scholar that I am simplifying some complex arguments. The seminal versions are those of J. L. Martyn, *History and Theology in the Fourth Gospel* (New York: Harper & Row, 1968, rev. ed. 1979), and R. E. Brown, *The Community of the Beloved Disciple: The Life, Loves and Hates of an Individual Church in New Testament Times* (New York: Paulist, 1979), which also summarizes earlier views on pp.171–82. See also J. L. Martyn, "Glimpses into the History of the Johannine Community," in M. de Jonge, ed., *L'Evangile de Jean: Sources, rédaction, théologie* (Gembloux: Duculot, 1977) 149–76, now also in J. L. Martyn, *The Gospel of John in Christian History* (New York: Paulist, 1978). See also B. Lindars, *Behind the Fourth Gospel* (London: SPCK, 1971). Good examples of the blending and adaptation of these theories are found in the recent works by J. Ashton, *Understanding the Fourth Gospel* (Oxford: Clarendon, 1991), esp. 160–98, and J. Painter, *The Quest for the Messiah: The History, Literature and Theology of the Johannine Community* (Edinburgh: T & T Clark, 1991) esp. 40–62. I have abbreviated and adapted these attempts to integrate compositional and communal history with the particular problem of John's view of Judaism in mind—a problem that is, of course, central to such reconstructions. An analysis of John's view of Judaism and his Christology is not, in the last resort, dependent on such views. Some scholars remain skeptical and believe that sense can be made of the text in its current form (usually with the exception of chap. 21) by taking account of the subtle and dialectic thought of the author: C. K. Barrett, *Essays on John* (London: SPCK, 1982); J. Lieu, *The Second and Third Epistles of John* (Edinburgh: T & T Clark, 1986) 168, 205–8, 214–16; M. Hengel, *The Johannine Question* (London: SCM, 1989) 99.

138. John 12:42–43 is the best evidence and 8:30–31 may be read this way. See Brown, *Community,* 71–73; Painter, *Quest,* 102–3. S. J. Tanzer, "Salvation Is for the Jews: Secret Christian Jews in the Gospel of John," in B. A. Pearson, ed., *The Future of Early Christianity: Essays in Honour of Helmut Koester* (Minneapolis: Augsburg Fortress, 1991) 285–300, argues that one purpose of John's Gospel was precisely to persuade such secret believers to leave the synagogue and openly join the church.

139. I say "toward ditheism" because it can be argued that John remains a monotheist, even if he comes perilously close to undermining it. Dunn, *Partings*, 220–29, has a useful discussion. He suggests that John might have thought he was still a monotheist, even if most Jews would certainly have thought he was not. Martyn, "Glimpses," 162, thinks that the more advanced Christology grew out of the situation following the rupture; similarly, Sanders, *Schismatics*, 40–47. I am, broadly, following Ashton, *Fourth Gospel*, 167, 170–73, who suggests high Christology as the cause. Brown, *Community*, 40ff., 166, agrees, but ascribes this specifically to an influx of Samaritan believers whose Mosaic speculations, when applied to Jesus, led in the direction of "descent from above" and "preexistence." W. A. Meeks, "The Man from Heaven in Johannine Sectarianism," *JBL* 91(1972) 44–72, here 71, rightly notes that the high Christology was probably both a cause and an effect of the rupture.

140. Whether the dualistic patterns of thought, so pervasive in the final version of the Gospel, belong to the second or third stage is unclear. As a way of recasting christological assertions and expressing the self-understanding of the community, they could belong to either. Martyn, "Glimpses," 169, thinks that dualism emerged in the second period but flowered fully in the third. The article by Meeks, "Man from Heaven," is still in many ways the best attempt to relate the symbolic world of John to the social world of the community.

141. Brown's case for Jewish Christians with whom the author did not agree is strongest at 6:60–66 and 8:30–31 (*Community*, 73–81). See the comments of W. A. Meeks, "'Am I a Jew?' Johannine Christianity and Judaism," in J. Neusner, ed., *Christianity, Judaism and Other Graeco-Roman Cults: Studies for Morton Smith at Sixty* (Leiden: Brill, 1975) vol.1, 164–85, here 183.

142. Martyn, *History*, 31–41, has made the strongest case for the connection between John's *aposynagogos* and the synagogue curse, but it is not essential to his theory. See the recent assessment by D. M. Smith, "Judaism and the Gospel of John," in J. H. Charlesworth, ed., *Jews and Christians: Exploring the Past, Present and Future* (New York: Crossroad, 1990) 76–96, here 83–88. For further discussion see chap. 6.

143. This raises the question of the provenance of John where the theories are, as in other respects, complex. It is widely held that the founding figure (the apostle John? the Beloved Disciple? John the Elder?) migrated, perhaps with some followers, from Palestine to Ephesus. This would explain both the Palestinian ethos of parts of the Gospel and the strong ecclesiastical tradition about Ephesus as the place of composition. The case for Galilee or Batanaea is discussed by W. A. Meeks, "Breaking Away: Three New Testament Pictures of Christianity's Separation from the Jewish Community," in J. Neusner and E. S. Frerichs, *"To See Ourselves as Others See Us": Christians, Jews, "Others" in Late Antiquity* (Chico, Calif.: Scholars Press, 1985) 93–115, here 96–104.

144. I do not get the sense (contra Dunn, *Partings*, 159) that the Johannine Christians and the Jewish authorities were locked in a struggle for control over the Jewish people. If anything, that lay in the past. The argument for a wholly Jewish community is made, for example, by Martyn, "Glimpses," 170–74. Hengel, *Question*, 119–24, argues for a predominantly Gentile ethos, but is inclined to exaggerate the evidence in his favor. The mediating position is close to Brown, *Community*, 55–58. See also Painter, *Quest*, 54–55.

145. These various uses are conveniently listed in U. C. von Wahlde, "The Johannine 'Jews'; A Critical Survey," *NTS* 28(1982) 33–60, here 46.

146. The statistics are those of von Wahlde. He proceeds by analyzing the results of ten previous studies. They unanimously agree on thirty-one: 1:19; 2:18,20;

5:10,15,16,18; 6:41,52; 7:1,11,13,15; 8:22,48,52,57; 9:18,22a,22b; 10:24,31,33; 13:33; 18:14,31,36; 19:7,31,38; 20:19. To these he adds 7:35; 11:8; 18:12,38; 19:12,14, but not seven others which are disputed: 3:25; 8:31; 10:19; 11:54; 18:20; 19:20, 21a. To catch their distinctive flavor von Wahlde, like others, somewhat confusingly labels this the "Johannine use."

147. On the pattern of occurrences see A. Culpepper, "The Gospel of John and the Jews," *RevExp* 84(1987) 273–88, here 276–80; earlier in *Anatomy of the Fourth Gospel: A Study in Design* (Philadelphia: Fortress, 1983) 125–32. He has a harder time showing that the hostility of the Jews is progressive. Chapter 8 is much discussed, recently, for example, by J. S. Siker, *Disinheriting the Jews. Abraham in Early Christian Controversy* (Louisville, Ky.: Westminster/John Knox, 1991) 128–43.

148. The addition of the Pharisees to the list of Jerusalem authorities (7:45; 11:47; 18:3; cf. 1:19,24) and their appearances elsewhere outside the Passion narrative might seem to counteract this, but probably springs from the same circumstance. On the one hand, when he uses "the Jews" John means the Jews in general and of his day; on the other hand, one of the leading groups after 70 CE were the successors of the Pharisees, whose role as representative contemporary authorities John might naturally reflect. M. J. Cook, "The Gospel of John and the Jews," *RevExp* 84(1987) 259–71, emphasizes the breadth and flexibility of John's use of *hoi Ioudaioi*. See further J. D. G. Dunn, "The Question of Anti-Semitism in the New Testament Writings of the Period," in J. D. G. Dunn, ed., *Jews and Christians. The Parting of the Ways A. D. 70–135* (Tübingen: Mohr [Siebeck], 1992) 175–211, here 177–87, 195–203.

149. J. Bassler, "'The Galileans': A Neglected Factor in Johannine Community Research," *CBQ* 43(1981) 243–57, here 253, summarizes her argument as follows: "Galileans (and on one occasion the Samaritans) symbolize those who receive the Word, Judeans symbolize those who reject it." See also Meeks, "Breaking Away," 96–104. John 4:44 is particularly striking, where the *patris* that rejects Jesus is Judaea and not, as in the Synoptics, Galilee. John 4 is more likely to reflect past success among the Samaritans than a present mission (rightly, Painter, *Quest*, 96–98). J. W. Pryor, "Jesus and Israel in the Fourth Gospel: John 1:11," *NT* 32(1990) 201–18, makes the following connection in John 1:11: his own (*ta idia*) = Galileans = Israel. Thus Galilee/Israel and the world (John 1:10) are connected in their rejection of Jesus. Here the Galileans symbolize rejection. The term *idia* in John 1:11 is, however, too vague to hang much on.

150. S. Pancaro, "The Relationship of the Church to Israel in the Gospel of St. John," *NTS* 21(1974–75) 396–405. In view of the occasional references to believing Jews, the contrast between believing Israelites and unbelieving Jews is not as precise as Pancaro makes out.

151. On 8:30–31 and other possible allusions to Jewish believers see nn. 138, 141 above. Several scholars emphasize the more positive strain: Painter, *John*, 100–104; Culpepper, "Jews," 282; J. T. Townsend, "The Gospel of John and the Jews," in A. T. Davies, ed., *Anti-Semitism and the Foundations of Christianity* (New York: Paulist, 1979) 72–97, here 74–75, 81. This needs to be done, but it remains a matter of judgment how much this counteracts the otherwise largely negative strain. Not much, I think.

152. M. Lowe, "Who were the Ioudaioi?" *NT* 18(1976) 101–30.

153. Meeks, "Breaking Away," 95–96; developed by J. Ashton, "The Identity and Function of the *Ioudaioi* in the Fourth Gospel," *NT* 27(1985) 40–75, here 43–46,

who in general gives Lowe a sympathetic hearing. See also Ashton, *Fourth Gospel*, 131–37.

154. Von Wahlde, "Johannine 'Jews,'" 41–46. F. Hahn, "'Die Juden' im Johannes-evangelium," in P. G. Müller and W. Stenger, eds., *Kontinuität und Einheit: für Franz Mussner* (Freiburg: Herder, 1981) 430–38, thinks most hostile references refer to leaders, but still thinks they stand generally for those Jews who reject Jesus. Smith, "Judaism," 82, is inclined to follow von Wahlde.

155. The distinction between reference and sense follows Ashton, "Identity," 55, 57. See further Culpepper, "Jews," 275–76. Meeks, "Breaking Away," 96, also insists on taking account of the real world in which the Gospel circulated. He thinks that a Christian community outside of Judaea might have spoken about Judaeans doing this or that, but would agree that this does not take account of the contemporizing and symbolic elements in John's usage. Further, once the synagogue authorities who expelled the Johannine group are in mind at certain points in the narrative, we have already moved beyond the world of the narrative to the world of contemporary Judaism. This then affects all other uses in the Gospel. Sanders, *Schismatics*, 232–33, also notes that deviants typically react to those so labeling them in general and negative terms. The symbolic dimension will be taken up at a later point.

156. I am following S. Pancaro's *The Law in the Fourth Gospel* (Leiden: Brill, 1975). It is true that John usually attacks the misunderstanding of the Jews rather than the law per se (though 1:17 comes close). But I do not detect a positive view of the law in John that gives it any permanent or central value, as does R. A. Whitacre, *Johannine Polemic: The Role of Tradition and Theology* (Chico, Calif.: Scholars Press, 1982), esp. 25–69. Nevertheless, he rightly stresses the polemic against the Jews. See the discussion of Smiga, *Pain and Polemic*, 140–48, who rightly concludes: "John does not mention the law or Jewish feasts because he wishes to reinterpret them as abiding values, but only because they serve as a basis of comparison with Christ, who in his person renders them irrelevant" (p.148). On the supersession of Jewish feasts see Pancaro, *Law*, 452–87.

157. On the refusal of John to engage with the Jews on their own terms see Freyne, "Vilifying," 124, 135. For John, everyday observance of the law seems not to have been a problem. This could be because, as Jewish Christians, they kept it or were confident of christological authorization for ignoring it. It could also point to a predominantly Gentile community for whom such disputes lay far in the past. Painter, *Quest*, 50–51, suggests that the Sabbath was a point of conflict known to the Johannine community. This could be so, or it could be that these traditions were selected to set up the christological dispute (which he recognizes as fundamental). Much depends on the makeup of the Johannine group.

158. Meeks comments astutely: "The contours of the Jewish expectations are so transformed by the peculiar christology of the Christian group that some aspects of the Johannine presentation become virtually a parody" ("'Am I a Jew?'" 172, also 173). See also Martyn, "Glimpses," 153–60; Painter, *Quest*, 148–54; Dunn, *Partings*, 220–29; and especially Ashton, *Fourth Gospel*, 251–66. For Painter the messianic category is so important that it becomes the controlling theme of his book. For our purposes a detailed discussion of John's Christology would take us too far afield. The different christological themes are, of course, present whether or not we connect them with theories of literary and communal development.

159. See especially Martyn, *History*, 78–119; idem, *Gospel* (chap. 1); Ashton, *Fourth Gospel*, 273–78; Painter, *Quest*, 8–13.

160. Ashton, *Fourth Gospel,* 137–51. Son of God has here moved from a weaker to a stronger sense.

161. I am alluding, of course, to the formative work of A. Segal, *Two Powers in Heaven: Early Rabbinic Reports about Christianity and Gnosticism* (Leiden: Brill, 1977).

162. This is not to underplay the emphasis on the incarnation and humanity of Jesus or the significance of his death and resurrection—or, indeed, any other of the strands in John's Christology. It is, rather, to concentrate on those themes that arise specifically in debate with the Jews in the Gospel. We know, for example, that the notion of a crucified messiah was to many Jews a contradiction in terms, but this does not become an issue with the Jews in John except in the sense that they are held responsible for his murder.

163. As noted above, some connect this stage intimately with rejection by the synagogue. Ashton, *Fourth Gospel,* 237, thinks the author may once have been an Essene. Many have pointed to a connection with the world of Qumran. See the recent reflections of Ashton, *Fourth Gospel,* 199–237, and Painter, *Quest,* 29–38.

164. R. Bultmann, *The Gospel of John* (Philadelphia: Westminster, 1971) 86, often and with good reason approvingly quoted. Recently on the Jews and the "world" in John see W. Wiefel, "Die Scheidung von Gemeinde und Welt im Johannesevangelium," *TZ* 35(1979) 213–27. On dualism and Christology in John see Ashton, *John,* 199–237; Painter, *Quest,* 256–60. Further on the connection between dualism, Christology, and anti-Judaism in John see J. E. Leibig, "John and 'the Jews': Theological Antisemitism in the Fourth Gospel," *JES* 20(1983) 209–34, here 221; Smiga, *Pain and Polemic,* 15–52, 171–73; R. Kysar, "Anti-Semitism and the Gospel of John," in Evans and Hagner, *Anti-Semitism,* 113–27.

165. Far from mitigating John's view of the Jews, in the sense that they are no longer really Jews but ciphers for the unbelieving world, this compounds the anti-Judaism and pushes it in a disastrous direction.

Chapter 3: Apocrypha

1. J. H. Charlesworth, "Christian and Jewish Self-Definition in Light of the Christian Additions to the Apocryphal Writings," in E. P. Sanders, A. I. Baumgarten, and A. Mendelson, eds., *Jewish and Christian Self-Definition* (Philadelphia: Fortress, 1981) vol.2, 27–55.

2. The recent article by B. Dehandschutter, "Anti-Judaism in the Apocrypha," *StPatr* 19(1987) 345–50, sets the issue up well but is brief and selective in its comments on specific texts. R. Wilde, *The Treatment of the Jews in the Greek Christian Writers of the First Three Centuries* (Washington, D.C.: Catholic University of America Press, 1949) 216–25; H. Conzelmann, *Gentiles, Jews and Christians: Polemics and Apologetics in the Greco-Roman Era* (Minneapolis: Fortress, 1992) 263–68; and G. Kretschmar, "Die Kirche aus Jude und Heiden," in J. van Amersfoort and J. van Oort, eds., *Juden und Christen in der Antike* (Kampen: Kok, 1990) 9–43, here 31–35, comment very briefly on only a few of the relevant texts. The article by M. Lowe, "Ioudaioi of the Apocrypha," *NT* 23(1981) 56–90, looks promising, but in fact the focus is quite narrow—variations in the use of the terms Jew/Judaean/Israel in selected texts and what this may tell us about their provenance. See now J. R. Mueller, "Anti-Judaism in the New Testament Apocrypha: A Preliminary Survey," in C. A. Evans and D. A. Hagner, eds, *Anti-Semitism and Early Christianity. Issues of Polemic and Faith* (Minneapolis: Fortress, 1993) 253–68, whose sketch is

more thematic and covers a broader chronological span than this chapter. His preliminary methodological observations should also be noted.

3. J. H. Charlesworth, ed., *The Old Testament Pseudepigrapha* (Garden City, N.Y.: Doubleday, 1983) vols. 1 and 2. These volumes use the notations BC and AD rather than BCE and CE.

4. For the text see O. Cullmann, in W. Schneemelcher, ed., *New Testament Apocrypha* (Louisville, Ky.: Westminster/John Knox, 1991) rev. ed., vol.1, 421–39. H. R. Smid, *Protoevangelium Jacobi: A Commentary* (Assen: Van Gorcum, 1965) 14–20, has a discussion of the apologetic, dogmatic, and biographical interests of the text. Further, H. Koester, "Überlieferung und Geschichte der früchristlichen Evangelienliteratur," *ANRW* II.25.2, 1463–1542, here 1483–84.

5. P. Vielhauer, *Geschichte der urchristlichen Literatur* (Berlin: De Gruyter, 1975) 667–72, calls it a "garland of legends," but accepts the label "infancy gospel" despite the concentration on Mary. Vielhauer and Cullmann suggest a date ca. 150–200 CE. Justin (*Dial.*70:1–2; 78:5; 76:6) has parallels to Jesus' birth in a cave and the Davidic descent of Mary. Koester, "Überlieferung," 1484, thinks that chaps. 22–24, on the death of Zechariah, were probably a later addition. Dehandschutter, "Apocrypha," 348–49, refers to numerous accounts of the *Dormitio Mariae* (the death, burial, and assumption of Mary), but they are chronologically beyond the limits of this study.

6. John L. Allen, Jr., "The *Protevangelium of James* as an *Historia*: The Insufficiency of the 'Infancy Gospel' Category," in E. H. Lovering, ed., *JBL Seminar Papers 1991* (Atlanta: Scholars Press, 1991) 509–17. On the position of Christianity in Roman society see chap. 1.

7. There is little elsewhere in the text to encourage the anti-Jewish interpretation that some find in chap. 17, since the two groups Mary sees, one lamenting and one rejoicing, probably represent believers and unbelievers rather than Jews and Christians. So correctly Dehandschutter, "Apocrypha," 346.

8. For the text see F. Scheidweiler and A. de Santos Otero, in Schneemelcher, ed., *Apocrypha*, vol.1, 501–34. They date it in the second century (125–150 CE), arguing that there are signs of dependence on early tradition—in particular that Mary is accused of fornication rather than the later charge of adultery (as in Celsus). A similar date is suggested if the *Acts of Pilate* are identified with the Pilate documents first mentioned by Justin, *I Apol.*35:8–9, 48:2–3. Koester, "Überlieferung," 1485–86, thinks that Justin knew an early form of the *Acts of Pilate*.

9. See O. Cullmann, in Schneemelcher, ed., *Apocrypha*, vol.1, 439–53, who dates it toward the end of the second century, but notes that it is difficult to provide an authoritative text for this early version. It is ostensibly written by "Thomas the Israelite" (1.1) but Cullmann thinks (p.450) the author was a Gentile who "betrays no knowledge of Judaism." A second-century date is also suggested by Wilde, *Treatment*, 218–19, Vielhauer, *Geschichte*, 673, and Koester, "Überlieferung," 1484–85. See also the references in Dehandschutter, "Apocrypha," 346–47. He notes, as does H. Schreckenberg, *Die christlichen Adversos-Judaeos-Texte und ihre literarisches und historisches Umfeld (1.–11 Jh)* (Frankfurt and Bern: Lang, 1982) 404, the anti-Jewish twist given to this gospel in the later Syriac version and the *Arabic Infancy Gospel*.

10. Lowe, "Ioudaioi," 88. He thinks the point is to show Jewish leaders acceding to the Christian claim and locates it firmly in the second century.

11. Scheidweiler and de Santos Otero, in Schneemelcher, ed., *Apocrypha*, vol.1, 501–2.

12. For the text see C. Maurer and W. Schneemelcher, in Schneemelcher, ed., *Apocrypha*, vol.1, 216–28, who date it around 150 CE and place it in Syria. The

fragment is usually assigned to the *Gospel of Peter,* which Serapion of Antioch (ca. 200 CE) claimed he got from "the successors of those who compiled it" (Eusebius, *Hist.eccl.*4.12.3–6). See further Koester, "Überlieferung," 1487–89; idem, *History and Literature of Early Christianity* (Philadelphia: Fortress, 1982) vol.2, 162–64; Vielhauer, *Geschichte,* 641–48. There has been considerable debate about the relation of this fragment to the canonical Gospels. Vielhauer and Koester recognize both early and secondary features, and Koester thinks it contains very old oral tradition which the Synoptic writers depended on too. But see Maurer and Schneemelcher, 219–21. J. D. Crossan, *The Cross That Spoke: The Origins of the Passion Narrative* (San Francisco: Harper & Row, 1988), has the most complex theory along these lines: *Gos.Pet.* contains within it the earliest written form of the Passion narrative, which influenced the canonical accounts but was then in turn influenced by them to produce the version we now have. His arguments are as intriguing as they are circular. Our concern is at any rate with the second-century text.

13. Maurer, in Hennecke and Schneemelcher, eds., *Apocrypha,* 1963 ed., vol.1, 182. He contrasts John 19:28–30 (the fulfillment of scripture) with *Gos.Pet.*17 (the fulfillment/accomplishment of the sins of the Jews), and the use of Deut 21:23 in John 19:31 (Jesus as the Passover lamb) with *Gos.Pet.*5,15 (Jewish legalism).

14. Crossan, *Cross,* 394–403, makes much of the division among the Jews. Lowe, "Ioudaioi," 85–86, thinks the author blames the Jewish leaders rather than the masses. Dehandschutter, "Apocrypha," 347–48, makes mention of this but recognizes that it "remains on the precarious level of interpretation."

15. J. Denker, *Die theologiegeschichtliche Stellung des Petrusevangeliums* (Bern and Frankfurt: Lang, 1975) 78–92. He connects *Gos.Pet.* with the views of the opponents of Ignatius (pp.126–30). Response to Jewish polemic could explain some things, if there were other grounds for suspecting it, but the explanation is not required. A good example of false deduction at every turn is on pp.89–91: *Gos.Pet.*27 mirrors the fasting practices of the community, which were like the fasts in *Did.*8:1, which, like fasts in the *Didascalia,* were observed on behalf of the Jews. *Gospel of Peter,* therefore, reflects a fast on behalf of the Jews! See the criticism in Maurer and Schneemelcher in Schneemelcher, ed., *Apocrypha,* 221.

16. In this respect the same can be said of L. Vaganay, *L'Evangile de Pierre* (Paris: Gabalda, 1930) 103–4, 201, who proposes that the author had no personal animus against Jews but saw them as mere puppets in the inexorable divine plan. He reflected the common Christian perception about Jewish responsibility for the death of Jesus and may have had a few unhappy experiences at their hands himself. He may still, however, have hoped for their conversion. Wilde, *Treatment,* 216–18, follows Vaganay.

17. See P. Vielhauer and G. Strecker, in Schneemelcher, ed., *Apocrypha,* vol.1, 134–78; idem, *Geschichte,* 648–62; Koester, "Überlieferung," 1498–1500; idem, *History,* 201–3, 223–24. *ANRW* II.25.5 contains three useful discussions: S. Gero, "Apocryphal Gospels: A Survey of Textual and Literary Problems," 3969–96; A. F. J. Klijn, "Das Hebräer—und das Nazoräerevangelium," 3997–4033; G. Howard, "The Gospel of the Ebionites," 4034–53. J. Kloppenborg kindly sent me his work on these gospels which is scheduled to appear in the new edition of the early Christian apocrypha. See also chap. 5 below.

18. Koester, *History,* 202, says that "nothing indicates that they [sayings of *Gos. Naz.*] maintained any special Jewish Christian doctrines."

19. Kloppenborg's suggestion. He notes that in general the arguments for Jewish Christian provenance of this gospel are not strong.

20. Vielhauer, in Hennecke and Schneemelcher, eds., *Apocrypha,* 1963 ed., vol.1, 159. In Schneemelcher's rev. ed., 1991 (p.172) this is related to an antidocetic aim.

21. Kloppenborg notes this particularly with respect to *Gos.Heb.*

22. For the text see B. Blatz, in Schneemelcher, ed., *Apocrypha,* 110–33. F. T. Fallon and R. Cameron, "The Gospel of Thomas: A Forschungsbericht and Analysis," in *ANRW* II.25.6, 4195–4251, give a lucid account of current discussion.

23. Associated chiefly with G. Quispel, "'The Gospel of Thomas' and 'The Gospel of the Hebrews,'" *NTS* 12(1965–66) 371–82; idem, "The Gospel of Thomas Revisited," in B. Barc, ed., *Colloque international sur les textes de Nag Hammadi (Québec, 22–25 août 1978)* (Quebec: Presse de l'Université Laval, 1981) 218–66. The other sources he identifies are an encratite gospel and a hermetic anthology. He is latterly reluctant to connect the Jewish Christian gospel with any of those mentioned in our preceding discussion. One of the arguments against a Jewish Christian connection is precisely the anti-Jewish strain we are considering, which Quispel tends to ignore.

24. The Jewish Christian connection has attracted far more attention than the attitude toward Judaism which, in fact, seems rarely to have been discussed, though see J. Ménard, *L'Evangile selon Thomas* (Leiden: Brill, 1975) 97–98, 143–44. It is of less interest to us to decide whether it was first or second century, gnostic or nongnostic. Some, of course, would have discussed it in the chapter on gnostic anti-Judaism (chap. 7).

25. Quispel, "Revisited," 243–44, gives his list of Jewish Christian sayings in *Gos.Thom.* He argues, intriguingly, for a reference to the flight to Pella (saying 68) and the curse against the *minim* (saying 72), but his reading of the evidence is somewhat forced. Dehandschutter, "Apocrypha," 345 n.5, dismisses the anti-Judaism of *Gos.Thom.* too quickly.

26. The *Odes of Solomon,* trans. J. H. Charlesworth, in Charlesworth, ed., *Pseudepigrapha,* vol.2, 725–71. He dates them ca. 100 CE. Koester, *History,* 216–18, and Vielhauer, *Geschichte,* 750–57, recognize gnostic traits but do not think them gnostic overall or identifiable with any known gnostic group.

27. See chap. 1 for the Bar Cochba allusion. See C. Maurer, in Hennecke and Schneemelcher, eds., *Apocrypha,* vol.2, 663–83, but above all now the edition of D. D. Buchholz, *Your Eyes Will Be Opened: A Study of the Greek (Ethiopic) Apocalypse of the Apocalypse of Peter* (Atlanta: Scholars Press, 1988).

28. I am following the excellent article by G. N. Stanton, "5 Ezra and Matthean Christianity in the Second Century," *JTS* n. s. 28(1977) 67–83, here especially 69–73, to which I am merely adding a few details. M. A. Knibb, in M. A. Knibb and R. J. Coggins, *The First and Second Books of Esdras* (Cambridge: Cambridge University Press, 1979) 78, finds a setting in the time of Bar Cochba attractive but uncertain. R. A. Kraft, "Towards Assessing the Latin Text of '5 Ezra': The 'Christian' Connection," in G. W. E. Nickelsburg and G. W. McCrae, eds., *Christians among Jews and Gentiles* (Philadelphia: Fortress, 1986) 158–69, thinks we have too readily assumed Christian provenance. T. Bergren, *Fifth Ezra: The Text, Origin and Early History* (Atlanta: Scholars Press, 1990) 313–28, argues cautiously for Christian authorship on the grounds of the ultimate rejection of Israel and the dependence of 1:30–33 on Matt 23:34–38. He dates it anywhere from 130 to 250 CE. The theme of radical rejection is emphasized by all the scholars mentioned above as well as J. M. Meyers, *I and II Esdras* (Garden City, N.Y.: Doubleday, 1974) 140–58. For translation and commentary see B. M. Metzger, in Charlesworth, ed., *Pseudepigrapha,* vol.1, 516–59.

29. Knibb, *Esdras,* 89, 93, thinks that the mother is Jerusalem in vv.2–4, but the church in vv.15ff. He favors a Jewish Christian author.

30. For the text see W. Schneemelcher, in Hennecke and Schneemelcher, eds., *Apocrypha*, vol.2, 94–102. It is preserved by Clement of Alexandria. I shall refer to the fragments using Schneemelcher's numbering. The most extensive and informative discussion is by H. Paulsen, "Das *Kerygma Petri* und die urchristliche Apologetik," *ZKG* 88(1977) 1–37, who dates it 100–120 CE and places it in Egypt. Koester, *History*, 163–64, dates it ca. 100 CE.

31. Paulsen, "*Kerygma*," esp. 30–37. He notes that the term apologetic is also open to more than one definition. He notes too that many now think much Jewish, as well as Christian, apologetic is aimed at insiders rather than outsiders. One of Paulsen's aims is to deny too strict a separation of early Christian preaching (kerygma) and later apologetics.

32. Paulsen, "*Kerygma*," 16, thinks Clement overinterprets the *Kerygma Petrou* at this point. On the anti-Jewish use of Jewish antipagan rhetoric see pp.14–19.

33. A. von Harnack, *A History of Dogma* (New York: Beacon, 1961) vol.1, 179, made this observation which has been repeated by many others. P. Richardson, *Israel and the Apostolic Church* (Cambridge: Cambridge University Press, 1969) 22–23, recognizes that it is an important step toward a broader conception.

34. On the mission of the Twelve—restricted sometimes to Jews and sometimes to Gentiles—in other early Christian literature see W. Bauer in Hennecke and Schneemelcher, eds., *Apocrypha*, vol.2, 44–45.

35. Paulsen, "*Kerygma*," 23–26, rightly sees *nomos* as an allusion to the christological fulfillment of Judaism and its scriptures rather than the notion of Christ as a new lawgiver.

36. Charlesworth's survey (n.1 above) is intentionally selective and can be supplemented from, among other things, the two-volume edition of the Pseudepigrapha that he edited (see n.3).

37. That is, the first two and the last two chapters of what is now *4 Ezra*. See Stanton (n.28 above); Charlesworth, "Self-Definition," 46–48.

38. If the texts were conflated in the third century, the problem may not have been evident in the period we are considering.

39. See J. Schreiner, *Das 4.Buch Esra* (Gütersloh: Mohn, 1981) [pp.301–6 in W. G. Kümmel et al., *Jüdische Schriften aus hellenistischer–römischer Zeit* (Gütersloh: Mohn, 1973–), vol.5].

40. Stanton, "5 Ezra," 76–77, emphasizes these two themes and notes that the author does not call Christians a "new" people. It should also be noted that he does not take over the titles Jacob/Judah/Israel for Christians, which breaks the continuity somewhat.

41. Stanton, "5 Ezra," passim, works this out in detail and draws parallels with the gnostic *Apocalypse of Peter*. We have noted above the parallels in theme and setting with the other *Apocalypse of Peter*. The identification of the community of *5 Ezra* to some extent hinges on the reading of 1:24. If the original was plural (other nations) rather than singular (another nation) it might suggest Gentile rather than Jewish Christians (see n.29 above). Stanton, "5 Ezra," 73–74, argues that the original reading in 1:24 was singular (*gens altera*), as does Kraft, "Assessing," 165.

42. S. E. Robinson in Charlesworth, ed., *Pseudepigrapha*, vol.2, 413–25, provides the most recent translation and commentary. See also Nickelsburg, *Literature*, 313–16. The text is otherwise known as *The Paraleipomena of Jeremiah*. The only argument for seeing chaps. 1–8 as Christian is the possible allusion to baptism in 6:25.

43. C. Wolff, "Irdisches und himmlisches Jerusalem—Die Heilshoffnung in den Paralipomena Jeremiae," *ZNW* 82(1991) 447–58.

44. Robinson, in Charlesworth, ed., *Pseudepigrapha,* vol.2, 414.

45. J. Rendel Harris, *The Rest of the Words of Baruch* (London: Clay, 1889) 13–17.

46. P. Bogaert, *Apocalypse de Baruch* (Paris: Le Cerf, 1969) 216–21.

47. For a translation and commentary see R. Rubinkiewicz and H. G. Lunt, in Charlesworth, ed., *Pseudepigrapha,* vol.1, 681–705; and B. Philonenko-Sayar and M. Philonenko, *Die Apokalypse Abrahams* (Gütersloh: Mohn, 1982) [pp.415–55 in Kümmel, *Jüdische Schriften,* vol.5]. Also Nickelsburg, *Literature,* 297–98; J. J. Collins, *The Apocalyptic Imagination* (New York: Crossroad, 1984) 180–86.

48. I am following R. G. Hall, "The 'Christian Interpolation' in the *Apocalypse of Abraham,*" *JBL* 107(1988) 107–10. Rubinkiewicz, in Charlesworth, ed., *Pseudepigrapha,* vol.1, 685, thinks the Christian interpolation might be by the Bogomils.

49. Collins, *Apocalyptic,* 185.

50. For a translation and commentary see H. E. Gaylord, in Charlesworth, ed., *Pseudepigrapha,* vol.1, 653–79; also Nickelsburg, *Literature,* 299–301; Collins, *Apocalyptic,* 198–201. Gaylord (pp.655–56) suggests Syria, and Collins (p.198) Egypt, as the likely place of origin.

51. Collins, *Apocalyptic,* 200.

52. Ibid.

53. Nickelsburg, *Literature,* 143–45, dates the Jewish material to the time of the founding of Qumran.

54. N. Hammershaimb, *Das Martyrium Jesajas* (Gütersloh: Mohn, 1973) [pp.15–34 of Kümmel, *Jüdische Schriften,* vol.2], suggests the last third of the first century. Knibb, in Charlesworth, ed., *Pseudepigrapha,* vol.2, 143–76, here 149, notes the following arguments for a second-century date for the Christian material (though he dates the combination of Jewish and Christian material to a later date): the allusion to Nero redivivus (4:2–4) must come after the time of Nero; church corruption (3:21–23) parallels the situation in the Pastorals, 2 Peter, and *1 Clement;* the empty tomb story (3:17) is close to *Gos.Pet.*39; and *4 Bar.* 9:18,20 seems to know chaps. 1–5 in their Christian form. R. G. Hall, "The Ascension of Isaiah: Community Situation, Date and Place in Early Christianity," *JBL* 109(1990) 289–306, draws persuasive parallels with the prophetic activities described in Revelation, Ignatius, and the *Odes of Solomon,* and dates the completed work to the end of the first century or the beginning of the second.

55. This is a bald summary of the subtle analysis of Hall, "Ascension."

56. See Charlesworth, "Self-Definition," 41–46, for this and other themes.

57. For translation and commentary see D. A. Fiensy and D. R. Darnell, in Charlesworth, ed., *Pseudepigrapha,* vol.2, 671–97. Charlesworth's discussion, "Self-Definition," 31–35, is important. For the connections with Jewish liturgical forms see chap. 8.

58. Fiensy and Darnell note that prayer 2:14 knows Aquila's LXX and must come after ca. 135 CE. They suggest a date anywhere between 150 and 300 CE.

59. Charlesworth, "Self-Definition," 35, notes that they would have had about the same effect as the *Birkat ha-minim* on Jewish Christians.

60. Fiensy and Darnell, in Charlesworth, ed., *Pseudepigrapha,* vol.2, 680, n. c.

61. Charlesworth, "Self-Definition," 35, thinks they show that the community who used them saw themselves as thoroughly Jewish—which is not quite the way I would express things.

62. For translation and commentary see J. J. Collins, in Charlesworth, ed., *Pseudepigrapha*, vol.1, 317–472. Also Charlesworth, "Self-Definition," 48–54.

63. "A vile hatred for Israel" (Charlesworth, "Self-Definition," 50) is perhaps a little strong, but captures the general sense.

64. Collins, *Apocalyptic,* 192.

65. Collins, in Charlesworth, ed., *Pseudepigrapha,* vol.1, 381.

66. Ibid., 383.

67. Ibid., 406–7, dates it sometime before 33 CE. See also Charlesworth, "Self-Definition," 51.

68. Charlesworth comments that it reveals "a type of Christianity that has moved far away from Judaism and is perhaps dangerously on the verge of many tendencies and ideas associated with Marcion" ("Self-Definition," 51). The first half of his statement may be true, but there is no warrant for the second.

69. Collins, in Charlesworth, ed., *Pseudepigrapha,* vol. 1, 408–4; J. Gager, "Some Attempts to Label the Oracula Sibyllina," *HTR* 65(1972) 91–116, here 91–96; Charlesworth, "Self-Definition," 51–52.

70. Ibid., 409.

71. Wilde, *Treatment,* calls them "Judaizers," but he probably means by this Jewish Christians.

72. Collins, in Charlesworth, ed., *Pseudepigrapha,* 415–29; Charlesworth, "Self-Definition," 53–54. Collins dates 1–216 to 175 CE, Charlesworth more vaguely to 180–300 CE.

73. For translation and commentary see H. Kee, in Charlesworth, ed., *Pseudepigrapha,* vol.1, 773–828. See also Charlesworth, "Self-Definition," 35–41; Collins, *Apocalyptic,* 106–13. For our purposes the two most important discussions are by J. Jervell, "Ein Interpolator interpretiert: Zu der christlichen Bearbeitung der Testamente der zwölf Patriarchen," in W. Eltester, ed., *Studien zu der Testamenten der Zwölf Patriarchen* (Berlin: Töpelmann, 1969) 30–61; and M. de Jonge, "The Future of Israel in the Testaments of the Twelve Patriarchs," *JSJ* 17(1986) 196–211.

74. Jervell, "Interpolator," 54–55.

75. M. de Jonge, "The Main Issues in the Study of the Testaments of the Twelve Patriarchs," *NTS* 26(1979–80) 508–24. De Jonge's views have developed over the years. His article on the future of Israel (n.73 above) abandons his original perception of this material as a loose collection of traditions that did not present a live issue for the writer. Kee, pp.777–78, dates the Jewish stage of composition to ca. 150 BCE. A second-century date for the Christian additions is suggested by Charlesworth, "Self-Definition," 36, and J. Becker, *Die Testamente der Zwölf Patriarchen* (Gütersloh: Mohn, 1974) [pp.1–163 in Kümmel, *Jüdische Schriften*], vol.3, 24–25. See also his earlier study, *Untersuchungen zur Entstehungsgeschichte der Testament der Zwölf Patriarchen* (Leiden: Brill, 1970). For our purposes a second-century date is sufficient and Jewish or Christian origin immaterial.

76. Jervell, "Interpolator," 47–49, argues that this is the Christology of the earliest interpolators, subsequently bolstered by more "orthodox" expressions.

77. *T.Sim.*7:2; *T.Levi*2:11; 4:4; *T.Jud.*24:6; *T.Zeb.*9:5–8; *T.Dan*6:1–7; *T.Naph.*8:1–3; *T.Ash.*7:3; *T. Benj.*3:8; 11:2–5.

78. Jervell, "Interpolator," 41–43. This judgment is largely impressionistic and could easily be reversed. Becker, *Testamente,* 28, thinks that salvation of the nations is not that important for a work that is "streng innerisraelitisch ausgerichtet."

79. A number of other texts show signs of Christian adaptation, but they are usually dated later than the second century. They can all be found in Charlesworth,

ed., *Pseudepigrapha*, vols.1 and 2: *Questions of Ezra; Testament of Abraham; Testament of Solomon; Apocalypse of Elijah; Ladder of Jacob; Lives of the Prophets; History of the Rechabites*.

80. Birth: *Asc.Isa., Syn.Pray.* Death: *Asc.Isa., Syn.Pray., Sib.Or., Test.XII*.

81. *Sib.Or., Test.XII*.

82. Strongly expressed in *5 Ezra., 4 Bar., Apoc.Abr., Syn.Pray.;* less clearly stated in *Sib.Or.* In *3 Bar.* Israel is rejected but no new collectivity put in her place.

83. *Sib.Or., Test.XII, Syn.Pray., 5 Ezra.* Jewish Christians might seem the natural candidates to be involved in the transmission and adaptation of Jewish writings. They are commonly thought to have been responsible for *4 Bar., Sib.Or.,* and *Test.XII*.

Chapter 4: Supersession: Hebrews and *Barnabas*

1. S. Lehne, *The New Covenant in Hebrews* (Sheffield: JSOT Press, 1990) 124. Many others have proposed an overarching theme to sum up the message of Hebrews. The result is often that important material is either neglected or artificially subsumed. Lehne's scheme is more comprehensive and more naturally capacious than most.

2. W. Klassen, "To the Hebrews or against the Hebrews? Anti-Judaism and the Epistle to the Hebrews," in S. G. Wilson, ed., *Anti-Judaism in Early Christianity* (Waterloo: Wilfrid Laurier University Press, 1986) vol.2, 1–16, here 15–16.

3. The survey by E. Grässer, "Der Hebräerbrief 1938–1963," *TR* 30(1964) 138–236, is fundamental; more recently, idem, "Neue Kommentare zum Hebräerbrief," *TR* 56(1991) 113–39.

4. H. Attridge, *The Epistle to the Hebrews* (Philadelphia: Fortress, 1989) 9–13, warns that the author may have assumed more about the readers than he knew.

5. It is frequently noted that there is some tension between passages that chide the readers for needing basic instruction all over again (5:11–14) and those that suggest that they leave behind the basic teaching and move on to a more mature understanding (6:1–3).

6. Two key terms, *hypostasis* and *elenchos* (here translated "assurance" and "conviction" as in NRSV), are obscure. See the discussion in Attridge, *Hebrews,* 307–14, where he suggests the following translation: "Faith is the reality of things hoped for, the proof of things unseen." Recently on faith in Hebrews see Th. Söding, "Zuversicht und Geduld im Schauer auf Jesus: Zum Glaubensbegriff des Hebräerbriefes," *ZNW* 82(1991) 224–41.

7. See commentaries ad loc.

8. On Jewish persecution of Christians see chapter 6. The commentators are almost unanimous in finding a reference to Roman action. One exception is B. Lindars, *The Theology of the Letter to the Hebrews* (Cambridge: Cambridge University Press, 1991) 4–14, on which see below. It is just possible that the language would fit a situation where Jews had taken over complete judicial authority, as in Jerusalem during the Jewish War (64–70 CE), and we should not exclude the possibility that persecution by Romans in the past is used as a paradigm for persecution by Jews in the present.

9. Attridge, *Hebrews,* 299, notes that "plundering" in 10:34 could refer to mob violence or to judicial confiscation.

10. W. L. Lane, "Hebrews: A Sermon in Search of a Setting," *SWJTh* 28(1985) 13–18, ties the two together: past persecution refers to 49 CE (Claudius), present persecution to the early sixties (Nero).

11. Suetonius's comment that the Jews were expelled from Rome because of riots instigated by a certain Chrestus (*Claud.* 25.4) has often been taken to refer to disturbances resulting from the introduction of Christianity to Rome ca. 49 CE. That Christians, even if not responsible for the disturbances, would have been involved in the expulsion is implied by Acts 18:2. Note that this verse implies that Aquila and Priscilla were expelled because they were Jews, not because they were Christians. See recently D. Slingerland, "Chrestus: Christus?" in A. J. Avery-Peck, ed., *New Perspectives on Ancient Judaism* (Lanham, Md.: University Press of America, 1989) vol.4, 133–44.

12. Could this be because they were Jewish Christians, i.e., they had enjoyed some protection from their association with Judaism?

13. Attridge, *Hebrews,* 299. It is strange that in the same paragraph he rules out an allusion to the persecution under Nero!

14. Attridge, *Hebrews,* 171 n.58, compares the use of *apostenai* ("turn away") in 3:12 with *parapesontas* ("fall away") in 6:6. Similarly, R. Mcl. Wilson, *Hebrews* (Grand Rapids and London: Eerdmans/Marshal Morgan & Scott, 1987) 109. G. E. Rice, "Apostasy as a Motif and Its Effects upon the Structure of Hebrews," *Andrews University Seminary Studies* 23(1985) 29–35, makes too much of the apostasy theme.

15. Living "outside the camp" could refer to an existence on the margins of society as part of a despised and rejected minority. It is sometimes taken, more specifically, to refer to leaving the Jewish community—an interpretation that hinges on the sense made of a great deal else in Hebrews.

16. E. Schüssler-Fiorenza, "Der Anführer und Vollender unseres Glaubens. Zum theologischen Verständnis des Hebräerbriefes," in J. Schreiner and G. Dautzenberg, eds., *Gestalt und Anspruch des Neuen Testaments* (Würzburg: Echter, 1969) 262–81.

17. Translation in this case from Attridge, *Hebrews,* 390, which captures the nuances of the Greek.

18. Attridge, *Hebrews,* 394–96, has a thorough discussion.

19. O. Holtzmann, "Der Hebräerbrief und das Abendmahl," *ZNW* 10(1909) 251–60; J. Moffat, *A Critical and Exegetical Commentary on the Epistle to the Hebrews* (New York: Scribner's, 1924) 234–35. For recent discussion see R. Williamson, "The Eucharist and the Epistle to the Hebrews," *NTS* 21(1975) 300–12; O. Knoch, "Hält der Verfasser des Hebräerbriefs die Feier Eucharistischer Gottesdienste für Theologisch Unangemessen?" *Liturgisches Jahrbuch* 42(1992) 166–87. Knoch thinks that the recipients suffered from hypersacramentalism, which they used as a means of retreating from the world and from other Christians. The author, in reality a moderate sacramentalist, took a virtually antisacramentalist position as a rhetorical ploy to jolt his readers.

20. To see in this an oblique allusion to a form of Christian sacramentalism which the author denigrates by association with the old tabernacle is a bit too subtle, although we know that the Eucharist was understood in a considerable variety of ways in the early Christian world (1 Cor 11:29; *Did.*9:3; Ignatius *Eph.*20:2; *Phld.*4:1; *Smyrn.*7:1). For those who go this route, v.10 can be taken to imply that the author objected to all sacramental meals and focused entirely on the heavenly sacrifice of Christ (see previous note). In general, we would expect an attack on so central a feature of Christian worship to be less casual and oblique. In the bulk of the letter it is Jewish, not Christian, cultic activities that are seen to be superseded, and it is misleading to jump from the one to the other without further ado. On the other

hand it is odd that the most obvious Christian substitute for the Jewish cultus, the Eucharist, is not mentioned, especially in view of the language used in 13:15–16.

21. The Passover meal is another possibility, though it took place only once a year. The sacred meals of the Essenes and the Therapeutae are a more remote but interesting part of the backdrop.

22. Attridge, *Hebrews*, 394; Wilson, *Hebrews*, 242; H. Braun, *An die Hebräer* (Tübingen: Mohr [Siebeck], 1984) 461–62.

23. Son (1:2,5,8; 3:6; 4:14; 5:5,8; 6:6; 7:3,28; 10:29); Christ (3:6,14; 6:1; 9:11,14,24,28; 10:10; 13:8,20–21); Lord (2:3; 7:14; 13:20); firstborn (1:6).

24. Most commentators take the "descendants of Abraham" (2:16), like the "heirs of the promise" (6:17), to be Christians. G. W. Buchanan, *To the Hebrews: Translation, Comment and Conclusions* (Garden City, N.Y.: Doubleday, 1972) 36, thinks they are Jews in 2:16; Wilson, *Hebrews*, 115, thinks Christians and Jews could be included in 6:17.

25. For example, O. Michel, *Der Brief an die Hebräer* (Göttingen: Vandenhoeck & Ruprecht, 1966) 105; H. W. Montefiore, *A Commentary on the Epistle to the Hebrews* (London and New York: Black/Harper, 1964) 35; P. E. Hughes, "The Christology of Hebrews," *SWJTh* 28(1985) 19–27. Attridge, *Hebrews*, 52, is more inclined to see the angels as a foil that allows the author to develop his own complex Christology.

26. Especially emphasized by E. Käsemann, *Das wandernde Gottesvolk: Eine Untersuchung zum Hebräerbrief* (Göttingen: Vandenhoeck & Ruprecht, 1938). Like many studies of Hebrews it suffers from focusing too closely on one part of the text. See the comments in W. G. Johnsson, "The Cultus of Hebrews in Twentieth-Century Scholarship," *ET* 89(1978) 104–8; idem, "The Pilgrimage Motif in the Book of Hebrews," *JBL* 97(1978) 239–51.

27. Notably at Qumran (11QMelch), in the Nag Hammadi collection, and in *2 Enoch*.

28. See recently J. M. Scholer, *Proleptic Priests: Priesthood in the Epistle to the Hebrews* (Sheffield: JSOT Press, 1991).

29. Attridge, *Hebrews*, 216.

30. G. W. MacCrae, "Heavenly Temple and Eschatology in Hebrews," *Semeia* 12(1978) 179–99. More generally on eschatology see C. K. Barrett, "The Eschatology of the Epistle to the Hebrews," in W. D. Davies and D. Daube, eds., *The Background of the New Testament and Its Eschatology: C. H. Dodd Festschrift* (Cambridge: Cambridge University Press, 1954) 363–93; B. Klapper, *Die Eschatologie des Hebräerbriefes* (Munich: Kaiser, 1969); Attridge, *Hebrews*, 27–28.

31. See H. W. Attridge, "The Use of Antitheses in Heb 8–10," *HTR* 79(1986) 1–9.

32. Adapted from Lehne, *Covenant*, 98–99, who in turn adapted it from W. G. Johnsson, *Defilement and Purgation in the Book of Hebrews* (Ph.D. dissertation, Vanderbilt University, 1973) 293, 337.

33. This paragraph draws on Klassen, "Hebrews," 6–13, quotation 7.

34. For example, Wilson, *Hebrews*, ad loc.; and G. Hughes, *Hebrews and Hermeneutics* (Cambridge: Cambridge University Press, 1979) 24–31; M. Rissi, *Die Theologie des Hebräerbrief* (Tübingen: Mohr [Siebeck], 1987) 18–19. See further Lehne, *Covenant*, 97 n.98.

35. Whether these heroes were to join in the new covenant, as might be implied in this verse, is not clear. If so, it would appear that they would do so as in some sense Christians. That the original promise remained unfulfilled until the coming of

Christ is emphasized by C. Rose, "Verheissung und Erfüllen: zum Verständnis von *epaggelia* im Hebräerbrief," *BZ* 33(1989) 60–80, 178–91. His insistence that the new covenant is not better than, but simply the fulfillment of, the old takes insufficient account of the more negative strain.

36. E. Grässer, "Hebräerbrief," 149, trans. and quoted by Klassen, "Hebrews," 3. In view of the rest of his paper I am not sure why Klassen endorses this comment so completely. Similar to Grässer's view is that of R. W. Wall and W. L. Lane, "Polemic in Hebrews and the Catholic Epistles," in C. A. Evans and D. A. Hagner, eds., *Anti-Semitism and Early Christianity: Issues of Polemic and Faith* (Minneapolis: Fortress, 1993) 166–98.

37. Hughes, *Hebrews*, 54–55.

38. The view that the recipients face two problems, an outer and an inner threat, is common, though explicated with different nuances. See Attridge, *Hebrews*, 13–14; Lehne, *Covenant*, 100, 103–4, 116, 120.

39. P. Richardson has pointed out to me that it could mean those originally from Italy, now living abroad, greeting the recipients wherever they may be. That is, it might tell us nothing about the whereabouts of the greeters or the recipients.

40. In R. E. Brown and J. P. Meier, *Antioch and Rome* (Ramsey, N.J.: Paulist, 1983) 140–57, Brown gives as full a case for Rome as can be mustered.

41. Brown, *Antioch*, 152–57, quotation 156. Accordingly, Brown thinks the author of Hebrews represents a more radical, Hellenist form of Jewish Christianity (cf. Acts 6–8). Lehne, *Covenant*, 103, 115, finds Brown's reconstruction attractive. The connection with Stephen, often noted since Moffat, *Hebrews* (see recently L. D. Hurst, *The Epistle to the Hebrews: The Background to Its Thought* [Cambridge: Cambridge University Press, 1990] passim), is interesting but not especially illuminating.

42. Brown notes, *Antioch*, 155, that "apostasy" does not mean returning to another religion, and that it might be hyperbole. But the term is one thing, the surrounding descriptions (6:6; 10:29) another. This would be exceptionally strong language for one Jewish Christian to use of another who moved to a different Jewish Christian group or outlook.

43. This part of Lindars's reconstruction (see n.8) is not dissimilar to W. Schmithals's suggestion, *Neues Testament und Gnosis* (Darmstadt: Wissenschaftliche Gesellschaft, 1984) 138–44, that the readers were refugees from the synagogue during the post-70 reorganization (partly because of the *Birkat ha-minim*), simultaneously losing the political protection provided by Judaism and provoking its hostility. Oddly, Schmithals seems to think these were primarily Gentile God-fearers. Wilson, *Hebrews*, 14–15, suggests that they must have included Jewish Christians too, but otherwise finds the suggestion attractive. Schmithals assumes that association with Judaism is no longer a live option, but in this he may be underestimating the urgent calls to perseverance, etc., and the allusions to current pressure.

44. Lindars, *Theology*, 4–14, further developed in his essay in W. Horbury, ed., *Templum Amicitiae: Essays on the Second Temple Presented to E. Bammel* (Sheffield: JSOT Press, 1991) 410–33. He assumes a date before 70 CE and thinks that references to the tabernacle would have been immediately understood as applying to the Temple and its cult. W. G. Übelacker, *Der Hebräerbrief als Appell* (Stockholm: Almqvist & Wiksell, 1989) 234, also emphasizes the importance of doubts about forgiveness. H. Hegermann, "Christologie im Hebräerbrief," in C. Breytenbach and H. Paulsen, eds., *Anfänge der Christologie: Festschrift für F.Hahn zum 65.Geburtstag* (Göttingen: Vandenhoeck & Ruprecht, 1991) 337–51, esp. 350–51, also emphasizes

the attraction of spiritual forms of worship in the diaspora synagogues, before or after 70 CE.

45. Lindars refers to E. Schürer (rev. and ed. G. Vermes, F. Millar, and M. Goodman), *The History of the Jewish People in the Age of Jesus Christ* (Edinburgh: T. & T. Clark, 1986) vol. 3,1, 144–45, whose evidence tells us that Jews prayed, studied the scriptures, and sometimes gathered for communal meals in the synagogue. But these were regular activities and not special to the Day of Atonement. It is probable that the day was marked by a fast and extra prayers, and that it was considered one of the most important of the year (Philo *Spec.Leg.*2.193–97; *m.Yom.*), but there is no firm evidence for this period. See *EJ*, 5.1376–89 (Jerusalem: Keter, 1971).

46. It will soon be apparent that much of this is merely combining the well-known pieces of the jigsaw into a slightly different configuration. Brown and Lindars are two of the more helpful recent attempts to make sense of the situation behind Hebrews. I do not find convincing the view, still being propounded by Grässer and others, that the only issues were a general weariness with Christian life and belief at the end of the first century which the author combats with a piece of creative theological thinking drawing on Philonic/gnostic strains of thought. It ignores too much evidence that stares one in the face.

47. This is expressed in a deliberately vague way. Knoch, "Hebräerbriefs," 172, suggests that the readers saw Jesus as a mere man, subordinate to the angels, Moses, and Aaron, whose role as savior and coming judge was seriously questioned. It is hard then to see what made them Christians at all, or how this accords with the strong, Christ-centered sacramentalism that he later attributes to them as well. It is disputed how much of the Christology of Hebrews was new to the readers and how much an expansion of existing confessions/titles, etc. Did they initially have a notion of Jesus as high priest which the writer dramatically extends? We cannot be sure.

48. It would be tempting to add: an appreciation of the benefits of Jewish cult and/or fellowship as a means of dealing with sin (understood mainly as a problem of defilement). This would make sense, as Lindars argues, of certain emphases in the cultic chapters. One might surmise that Christian teaching had engendered among Jewish Christians a more piquant sense of sin but no ritual means of dealing with it. But unless Hebrews was written when the Temple still stood, it is hard to know (because the evidence is lacking) what advantage the synagogue could have offered in this regard (n.45 above). Rissi, *Hebräerbrief*, 1–25, explains the cultic emphasis by arguing that the recipients were a small Roman house church of Christian ex-priests, originally from Judaea (pp.11–12). He thinks their earliest experience was intensely charismatic but that they had lapsed into spiritual quietism, cutting themselves off from other Christians and the world.

49. As noted above, it is highly likely, though not certain, that Christian Jews who apostasized returned to Judaism.

50. Hughes, *Hebrews*, 26–28, argues against the relapse theory on two grounds: there is no reference to Jewish "seducers," and the arguments would have been completely unpersuasive to non-Christian Jews. But there need not have been "seducers"; the movement could have come from the other side. Also, the addressees were surely Christian, not non-Christian, Jews. Later, Hughes rightly draws the conclusion that the readers were Christians (pp.54–56), thus undercutting his own objections.

51. D. Guthrie, *Hebrews* (Grand Rapids: Eerdmans, 1983) 32, compares the bare, nonritual worship in early house churches with the rich ritual tradition of Judaism.

As contrasted with the Temple this makes sense, but most synagogues probably had no more ritual than the average church and many synagogues were based in a household.

52. H. Feld, "Der Hebräerbrief: Literarische Form, religionsgeschichtlicher Hintergrund, theologische Fragen," in W. Haase, ed., *ANRW* II.25.4, 3522–3601, argues for Jewish Christian readers and an early date (ca. 60 CE). If any passage suggests a pre-70 date, it is 9:8–10, which is often passed over all too briefly by those arguing for a later date. Unfortunately it is too ambiguous and cryptic to settle the matter decisively. Does the "first tabernacle" represent the first covenant (Judaism), the Temple, or "this age" in an eschatological scheme that anticipates "the age to come"?

53. See particularly E. Käsemann's influential book, *The Wandering People of God: An Investigation of the Letter to the Hebrews* (Minneapolis: Augsburg, 1984), originally published in 1938 (see n.26 above). Käsemann attributed gnostic inclinations to the author; others attribute them to the readers (e.g., H. Koester, *Introduction to the New Testament* [Philadelphia: Fortress, 1982] vol.2, 272–76). There seems to me little to encourage either view, though Käsemann's view (with some updating) has recently been endorsed by H. Braun, *An die Hebräer* (Tübingen: Mohr [Siebeck], 1984) 1; and Grässer ("Neue Kommentare") says more than once that he finds a gnostic understanding of Hebrews increasingly persuasive.

54. Lehne, *Covenant,* 103 n.94.

55. See chap. 5.

56. Jewish Christians and ex–God-fearers could, of course, have been part of the same group. I am distinguishing Jews and Gentiles here for heuristic purposes, attempting to imagine where the majority lay. For Gentile readers see Moffat, *Hebrews,* xvi–xvii; H. Windisch, *Der Hebräerbrief* (Tübingen: Mohr [Siebeck], 1931) 48; Braun, *Hebräer,* 2. See also the discussion in F. F. Bruce, "Hebrews: A Document of Roman Christianity," in W. Haase, ed., *ANRW* II.25.4., 3496–3521, here 3505–6, and in Attridge, *Hebrews,* 9–13. It is usually argued that "to fall away from the living God" (3:12) or to "purify your conscience from dead works and serve the living God" (9:14; cf. 6:1) would more likely be used of Gentiles than of Jews. From a Jewish perspective perhaps; but from a Christian perspective Jews were equally capable of doing works that led to death or rebelling against and abandoning their God, as the surrounding context of chaps. 6 and 9 makes clear. The outline of basic teaching in 6:1–2, it has often been noted, could as easily be Jewish as Christian and refers to the sort of things Gentiles (not Jews) would need to be instructed in. But if, as the context suggests and the terms allow, they have a specifically Christian content, Jews would need instruction in them just as much as Gentiles.

57. Attridge, *Hebrews,* 6–9, who in the end, however, sets an approximate limit of 100 CE (because of the reference to Timothy).

58. P. Lampe, *Die stadtrömischen Christen in den ersten beiden Jahrhunderte: Untersuching zu Sozialgeschichte* (Tübingen: Mohr [Siebeck], 1987) 53–78.

59. That is, the "weak" of Romans 14 may have been Gentile Judaizers rather than Jewish Christians.

60. The urge to locate *Barnabas* in Egypt is understandable since we otherwise know very little about early Christianity there. The arguments are concisely set out by M. B. Shukster and P. Richardson, "Temple and *Bet Ha-Midrash* in the Epistle of Barnabas," in S. G. Wilson, ed., *Anti-Judaism in Early Christianity: Separation and Polemic* (Waterloo: Wilfrid Laurier University Press, 1986) vol.2, 17–31, here 17–20. I have learned much about *Barnabas* in subsequent discussions with P. Richardson. R. S. MacLennan, *Early Christian Texts on Jews and Judaism* (Atlanta: Scholars Press,

1989) 21–48, bases his interpretation on the assumption that Alexandria was the context for *Barnabas*, which then becomes an excuse for haphazard references to almost anything that can be said about Alexandrian Judaism and Christianity over a 200-year period. Even if he were correct about the city of provenance, his indecisive catalog of secondary opinion functions more as an assertion than as an argument. See, for example, his attempt to interact with Shukster and Richardson and with Lowy (below, n.63) on pp.44–48.

61. As argued by K. Wengst, *Tradition und Theologie des Barnabasbriefes* (Berlin and New York: De Gruyter, 1971) 103–4. In the last resort this is a matter of judgment and, for the case we wish to make, of indifference. In the absence of any tangible evidence, I prefer to take the text at face value in this regard.

62. The Sinaitic reading in 3:6, *epelutoi* for *proselytoi*, does not substantially change the meaning. *Epelutos* means an "imitator" or "one who has come lately" (Bauer, 285) and the two terms are apparently synonymous in Philo (Loeb edition 348 n.1). The translations here and elsewhere, unless specified, are from the recently revised edition of the translation of J. B. Lightfoot and J. R. Harmer by M. W. Holmes (Grand Rapids: Baker Book House, 1989). Contrast L. W. Barnard's argument that the author was a converted rabbi, *Studies in the Apostolic Fathers and Their Background* (Oxford: Blackwell, 1966) 41–55.

63. S. Lowy, "The Confutation of Judaism in the Epistle of Barnabas," *JTS* n.s. 8(1960) 1–33, here 1–3, emphasizes this too. See now the excellent discussion of *Barnabas* by W. Horbury, "Jewish-Christian Relations in Barnabas and Justin Martyr," in J. D. G. Dunn, ed., *Jews and Christians: The Parting of the Ways A.D. 70–135* (Tübingen: Mohr [Siebeck], 1992) 315–45. He also notes the use of pairing pronouns, and the connection between 3:6 and 4:6 and the problem of Christian defectors. He also makes the pertinent observation that the rejection of fasting relates to the prominence this had in contemporary Judaism beyond scriptural requirements.

64. H. Schreckenberg, *Die christlichen Adversus-Judaeos Texte und ihr literarisches und historisches Umfeld (1.–11. Jh.)* (Frankfurt and Bern: Lang, 1982) 177, notes the tension.

65. It should not be overlooked that the author makes positive use of Jewish ethical teaching in 18–20, but these chapters tell us nothing specific about the author's origins or view of Judaism.

66. Lev 26:41; Deut 10:16; 30:6; Jer 4:4; 6:10; 9:26; Philo *Spec.Leg.*1.304ff.; Q.Gen.3.46–52; Justin *Dial.*29:1; 41:4.

67. See the concise and helpful discussion by J. N. B. Carleton-Paget, "Barnabas 9:4: A Peculiar Verse on Circumcision," *VC* 45(1991) 242–54. He argues, rightly, against the view that the verse is an interpolation, and thinks it may be a reaction to successful Jewish proselytizing and renewed hope for a rebuilt Temple. Kraft's statement that the author "is neither rejecting the idea of circumcision nor substituting a Christian rite such as baptism for it" is, with respect to the first half, astonishing, but part of what I find to be a consistent misreading of the epistle. See R. A. Kraft, *Barnabas and the Didache: The Apostolic Fathers,* vol.3 (New York: Thomas Nelson & Sons, 1965) 106–7.

68. For this mollifying interpretation see, among others, H. Windisch, *Die apostolischen Vater III: Der Barnabasbrief* (Tübingen: Mohr [Siebeck], 1920) 357.

69. *Ep.Arist.* 142–71 gives a spiritual/ethical interpretation but still insists on literal observance. Philo, of course, extensively does the same. *Barnabas* goes one step farther.

70. The burden of Wengst's argument, *Barnabasbriefes,* passim.

71. Barnabas, like Justin, seems to know extra-biblical traditions that derive from either pre-70 practice or later rabbinic circles.

72. L omits this statement. If it is included, it is exceedingly obscure. It must presumably allude to present catastrophes of the Jews or to their future fate. See commentaries, ad loc.

73. Shukster and Richardson, "Temple," 24–27, suggest a polemic against the Temple throughout the work. See, in addition to the passages we discuss, 1:7; 6:3,15; 11:1–4; 16:6–10.

74. Note that in his eagerness to make this point he defines the apostles as those "sinful beyond measure"!

75. A. L. Williams, "The Date of the Epistle of Barnabas," *JTS* 34(1933) 337–46, here 342–43, mentions (with no great enthusiasm) the possibility that v.4 refers to the first Temple and its rebuilding and v.5 to the destruction of the second Temple.

76. *Barn.*16:3 omits Isaiah's reference to the destroyers' departing. This could be because it was no longer relevant, although the more we allow for the author's use of testimonies already shaped for Christian use, the less we can ascribe to his conscious rewriting. The author's interpretation (v.4) of his own form of the Isaiah passage (v.3) is clearly significant.

77. See the full discussion in P. Richardson and M. B. Shukster, "Barnabas, Nerva, and the Yavnean Rabbis," *JTS* n.s. 34(1983) 32–55, here 34–37.

78. Windisch, *Barnabasbrief*, 388–90, like most others supports the first meaning for S (but eventually opts for the omission of the second *kai*). Schäfer, *Bar Kokhba*, 32–34, allows for the second. The second could have been more neatly expressed (for example, *kai hoi auton hyperetai* instead of *kai hoi ton echthron hyperetai*), but the construction, with or without the second *kai*, is clumsy whichever translation we choose. The omission of *ginetai* in S and C, as many have observed, does not change the sense in the light of the emphatic *nyn*. See Richardson and Shukster, "Barnabas," 35 n.10.

79. Richardson and Shukster, "Barnabas," 37, note that the term usually means voluntary helpers, and think it is used here pejoratively of the Jews—and thus explain the switch from "enemies" in v.3 to "servants of the enemies" in v.4. It is more commonly taken to refer to Roman workers. In part the meaning depends on which temple is being alluded to. D. R. Schwarz, "On Barnabas and Bar Kokhba," in *Studies in the Jewish Background of Christianity* (Tübingen: Mohr [Siebeck], 1992) 147–53, here 152 n.21, suggests that a reference to Roman underlings would add to the humiliation of the Jews. That the servants were Roman converts to Christianity (slaves or even aristocrats) who became part of the spiritual temple discussed in vv.6ff. runs into the many objections to interpreting vv.1–5 in the light of the following verses. For this view see Williams, "Date," 343; J. J. Gunther, "The Epistle of Barnabas and the Final Rebuilding of the Temple," *JSJ* 7(1976) 143–51. The objections are most succinctly laid out by Windisch, *Barnabasbrief*, 390. See also Schwarz, "Barnabas," 150–51.

80. Perhaps on the same site, but see G. W. Bowersock, "A Roman Perspective on the Bar Kochba War," in W. S. Green, ed., *Approaches to Ancient Judaism*, vol.2 (Chico, Calif.: Scholars Press, 1980) 131–42, here 137, who argues that Dio Cassius's report (*Hist.*69.12.1) means that it was in place of, not on the place of, the Jewish Temple.

81. A. von Harnack, *Geschichte der altchristlichen Literatur bis Eusebius* (Leipzig: Hinrich, 1897) II/I, 410–18; Windisch, *Barnabasbrief*, 389–90; Schäfer, *Bar Kokhba*,

32–34; Wengst, *Barnabasbriefes,* 111–13; Schwarz, "Barnabas," 151–53; Schreckenberg, *Adversus-Judaeos,* 176–77.

82. Wengst, *Barnabasbriefes,* 113, proposes precisely these dates. He thinks that Dio Cassius's report (*Hist.*69.12.1) that the construction of the Jupiter temple was a cause of the rebellion and Eusebius's report (*Hist.eccl.*4.6) that it was a result can be blended: one refers to the announcement of the plan, the other to its execution. Schwarz, "Barnabas," 153, argues that the evidence of *Barn.*16, as well as the discussion of circumcision in *Barn.*9, favor the view that the building of the Jupiter temple and the ban on circumcision were causes rather than results of the rebellion.

83. Windisch, *Barnabasbrief,* 390.

84. A. Schlatter, *Synagoge und Kirche bis zum Barkochba-Aufstand* (Stuttgart: Calwer Verlag, 1966) 64–68, made most of these observations long ago (the essay appeared originally in 1897). Windisch, *Barnabasbrief,* 389–90, recognizes their force, yet concludes that an allusion to a Jewish temple is improbable, if not impossible. He suggests that the use of "rebuild" is justified by the association of the Jewish Temple with pagan temples in v.2, but that is a rather unconvincing leap. Wengst, *Barnabasbriefes,* 112 n.53, trying unsuccessfully to refute Schlatter, thinks an allusion to a pagan temple shows how radical the author's cult critique was, but this hardly explains the deliberate choice of words in v.4b which is, in the end, the most significant evidence. Schwarz, "Barnabas," 152, evades the issue by loosely paraphrasing the statement as "build another temple in its stead."

85. Wengst, *Barnabasbriefes,* 108, makes this point. But the argument works both ways. Despite Windisch (n.83 above), would not a replacement pagan temple have invited a much more prominent notice than the obscure allusion here?

86. On the messianic nature of the rebellions see M. Hengel, "Messianische Hoffnung und politischer Radikalismus in der jüdisch-hellenistischen Diaspora," in D. Hellholm, ed., *Apocalypticism in the Mediterranean World and the Near East* (Tübingen: Mohr [Siebeck], 1983) 655–86. It has recently been suggested that *Sib. Or.*5:414–33, which seems to be messianic in tone and clearly expects the restoration of the Temple, dates from around 115 CE and expresses the sort of hope that inspired the rebels. See A. Chester, "The Sibyl and the Temple," in Horbury, *Templum Amicitiae,* 37–69, here 47–62; and in the same volume C. C. Rowland, "The Second Temple: Focus of Ideological Struggle?" 175–98, here 183–84; W. Horbury, "Herod's Temple and Herod's Days," 103–49, here 112 n.12. See the earlier discussion by L. Gaston, *No Stone on Another* (Leiden: Brill, 1970) 148; Lowy, "Barnabas," 13, 32–33, thinks that *Barnabas* reacts to a form of Jewish messianism that promised a rebuilt Temple, but declines to be more specific. MacLennan, *Early,* alludes frequently to the Egyptian revolts, implying that they were a significant part of the background to *Barnabas,* but then denies (p.44) that they were important at all.

87. Hadrian is the more common. See, for example, J. G. Muller, *Erklärung des Barnabasbriefes* (Leipzig: Hirzel, 1869) 334–40; Schlatter, *Synagoge,* 64–67; H. Bietenhard, "Die Freiheitskriege der Juden unter den Kaisern Trajan und Hadrian und der messianische Tempelbau," *Judaica* 4(1948) 95–102; L. W. Barnard, "The Date of the Epistle of Barnabas," *Journal of Egyptian Archeology* 44(1958) 101–7; G. Alon, *The Jews in Their Land in the Talmudic Age* (Jerusalem: Magnes, 1983) vol.2, 448–52; Smallwood, *Jews,* 435. The case for Nerva has been impressively collated by Richardson and Shukster (nn. 60, 77 above).

88. See especially Schäfer, *Bar Kokhba,* 28–32; Wengst, *Barnabasbriefes,* 108–11. The anonymous emperor who granted (and then revoked) permission to build a

third temple according to *Gen.Rabb.*64.10 is often associated with Hadrian, but could as well be Nerva or Trajan. *Sib.Or.*5:46–50, 414–33 are too vague to be associated with Hadrian, and the latter at any rate refers to a heavenly savior. The reference to Hadrian's visit to Jerusalem in Epiphanius *Mens.Pond.*14 expressly excludes a rebuilding of the Temple, and Chrysostom's allusion (*Adv.Jud.*10–11) to the Jews' attempt to rebuild the Temple under Hadrian is, in context, an allusion to the Bar Cochba rebellion, and presumably refers to the rebels' (unfulfilled) ambitions.

89. Richardson and Shukster, "Barnabas," 41–44, make the most of the well-known coin inscription *fisci Iudaici calumnia sublata,* but admit that all that can be certainly surmised is that Nerva reformed the tax. This, as we saw in chap. 1, would have been more beneficial to "peripheral" Jews and Gentile sympathizers (including perhaps some Christians) than to the Jews as a whole.

90. It has often been noted that Vespasian is an equally plausible candidate, but he scarcely comes into play in the present context.

91. Richardson and Shukster, "Barnabas," 44–53, handle this evidence with sensitivity and aplomb, but the association of Nerva and Temple rebuilding is even so a surmise. *Gen.Rabb.*64.10 implies that the same government/emperor ordered and then effectively quashed permission to rebuild. This could have been Trajan, extending the policies of his predecessor at the beginning of his reign (and thus the origin of Trajan's Day?), though there is nothing else in his career to suggest he was so well-disposed toward the Jews.

92. Richardson and Shukster, "Barnabas," passim. They note that Lowy, "Barnabas," has a similar argument but without being specific about the historical context. Windisch's view, *Barnabasbrief,* 388, is entirely (and unconvincingly) the opposite: "Das es sich hier um eine brennende Frage und um den Schlussel zum Barn. handele, tritt absolut nicht hervor und ist wenig einleuchtend."

93. Harmer and Lightfoot emend the text to read: "Our covenant remains to them also. Ours it is, but . . ." This gives the same sense as L.

94. Shukster and Richardson, "Temple," 24; idem, "Barnabas," 41, tend to see 4:6 as an allusion to those who have been affected by the change of Roman policy toward the Temple, i.e., they are part of the Temple issue. They may well be right to connect the two, but the appearance of the covenant theme in three separate chapters suggests that it was a significant problem in its own right.

95. Shukster and Richardson, "Temple," 31 n.36, note that there was some discussion among the tannaitic rabbis about the place of Gentiles in the covenant, though they take those who made the claim in 4:6 to be members of the Christian community. In "Barnabas," 38–39, they assume that they were Jewish Christians.

96. Windisch, *Barnabasbrief,* 323.

97. Wengst, *Barnabasbriefes,* 101–4.

98. P. Vielhauer, *Geschichte der urchristlichen Literatur* (Berlin: De Gruyter, 1975) 606: "Die Eröterung über das Judentum ist völling akademisch."

99. As Vielhauer, ibid., correctly notes, though he rather vaguely describes the opponents' view as "traditional covenant theology."

100. The same objections can be raised to the view of K. H. Rengstorf and S. von Kortzfleisch, *Kirch und Synagoge: Handbuch zur Geschichte von Christen und Juden* (Stuttgart: Klett, 1968) vol.1, 61, who argue that the author is not concerned about a lapse into Judaism but only with establishing the unique Christian position.

101. This can be translated as "finally" or "completely."

102. Taking "the greater" in v.3 as the Jews removes one inconsistency but creates another: "this people" in v.3 then become the Jews. Alternatively, if we take the

unlikely view that "this people" in vv.1,3,6 were the Jews, and also "the greater" in vv.2,3,6, they would be the "first" people in v.6 but not in v.1. In view of the general tenor of the work, it is unlikely that the Jews are the "lesser" in v.5 and, therefore, are to share in the blessing.

103. We can perhaps detect behind 6:18–19 an element of doubt caused by the disjunction between Christian claims and a reinvigorated and officially supported Judaism. The rule and authority of Christians, part of the promised inheritance, is projected into the future probably because it was not manifest in the present.

104. On the use of testimonies in *Barnabas* see P. Prigent, *Les testimonia dans le christianisme primitif: L'Epître de Barnabé et ses sources* (Paris: LeCoffre/Gabalda/Cie, 1961). The discussion of testimonies has recently been taken up in connection with Justin and *Barnabas* by O. Skarsaune, *The Proof From Prophecy. A Study in Justin Martyr's Proof Text Tradition: Text-type, Provenance, Theological Profile* (Leiden: Brill, 1987) 47–92. Both Wengst, *Barnabasbriefes,* and Kraft, *Barnabas,* emphasize the dependence of the author on well-developed Christian traditions.

105. Shukster and Richardson, "Temple," 27–31. *Barn.*10:10–11 is particularly interesting in this regard.

106. Horbury, "Jewish-Christian," 335, suggests that the numerical dominance of Judaism, Christian dependence on Jewish culture, and Jewish anti-Christian propaganda may also have contributed to the author's anxiety. MacLennan's view, in *Early,* that *Barnabas* was a moderate voice opposed to Jewish and Christian messianic/Temple fanatics, and that he thus opposed only one extreme form of Judaism, is well-intentioned but not based on the text.

107. K. Thieme, *Kirche und Synagoge: Die erste nachbiblischen Zeugnisse ihrens Gegensatzes im Offenbarungverständnis: Der Barnabasbriefe und der Dialog Justins der Märtyrers* (Olten: Walter, 1945) 32, 225, 228, 231, 233. See the ensuing dialogue between J. Oesterreicher and K. Thieme, "Um Kirche und Synagoge im Barnabasbrief," *ZKT* 74(1952) 63–70.

108. The amazement of those who hear the Lord speaking through believers and the church (16:10) does not necessarily refer to conversion and, even so, cannot control the meaning of 7:10.

109. The phrase is omitted by L, and Lightfoot and Harmer suspect that the text is corrupt (so also the Loeb editor).

110. See the summary in the final chapter.

111. G. Strecker, *Das Judenchristentum in den Pseudklementinen* (Berlin: Akademie Verlag, 1981) is the standard modern work. Cf. pp.70, 165, 257. He locates this passage in the *Grundschrift* and in the *Kerygma Petrou.* Some older works have full and perceptive consideration of this passage. See A. Schliemann, *Die Clementinen nebst den verwandten Schriften und der Ebionitismus: Ein Beitrag zur Kirchen—und Dogmengeschichte der ersten Jahrhunderte* (Hamburg: Friedrich Werthes, 1844) 135–36, 215–19, 270–72; A. Hilgenfeld, *Die clementinischen Recognitionen und Homilien, nach ihrem Ursprung und Inhalt dargestellt* (Jena: J. G. Schreiber, 1848) 154–55, 229–30.

Chapter 5: Jewish Christians and Gentile Judaizers

1. Basic material is found in A. F. J. Klijn and G. Reinink, *Patristic Evidence for Jewish Christian Sects* (Leiden: Brill, 1976). See also A. F. J. Klijn, "The Study of Jewish Christianity," *NTS* 20(1974) 419–31; S. K. Riegel, "Jewish Christianity: Definitions and Terminology," *NTS* 24(1978) 410–15; G. Strecker, *Das Judenchristentum in den Pseudoklementinen* (Berlin: De Gruyter, 1958); idem, "Judenchristentum," *TRE*

17(1988) 310–25, with an extensive bibliography; H. J. Schoeps, *Jewish Christianity* (Philadelphia: Fortress, 1969); idem, "Das Judenchristentum in den Parteienkämpfen der Alten Kirche," in *Aspects du Judéo-Christianisme* (Strasbourg: Publication of Centre d'Etudes Supérieures Spécialisés d'Histoire des Religions, 1965) 53–75; in the same volume M. Simon, "Problèmes du Judéo-Christianisme," 1–17; G. Lüdemann, *Opposition to Paul in Jewish Christianity* (Minneapolis: Fortress, 1989) esp. 1–32; J. D. G. Dunn, *Unity and Diversity in the New Testament* (London: SCM, 1977) 239–66; G. Kretschmar, "Die Kirche aus Juden und Heiden," in J. van Amersfoort and J. van Oort, eds., *Juden und Christen in der Antike* (Kampen: Kok, 1990) 9–43. T. Callan, *Forgetting the Root: The Emergence of Christianity from Judaism* (Mahwah, N.J.: Paulist, 1986), is a useful sketch for the general reader. He divides Jewish Christians into conservative and liberal camps. B. L. Visotzky, "Prolegomenon to the Study of Jewish-Christianities in Rabbinic Literature," *AJS* 14(1989) 47–70, has a good summary of the problems but no solutions. Two important recent works which have helped to reopen some of the issues are R. Pritz, *Nazarene Jewish Christianity: From the End of the First Century Until Its Disappearance in the Fourth Century* (Jerusalem and Leiden: Magnes/Brill, 1988), and R. E. van Voorst, *The Ascent of James: History and Theology of a Jewish-Christian Community* (Atlanta: Scholars Press, 1989).

2. L. Gaston, "Paul and Jerusalem," in P. Richardson and J. C. Hurd, eds., *From Jesus to Paul* (Waterloo: Wilfrid Laurier University Press, 1984) 61–72, here 62. He thus anticipates S. C. Mimouni, "Pour une définition nouvelle du judéo christianisme ancien," *NTS* 38(1992) 161–86, who suggests that a definition must accommodate both sides of the equation—a belief in Jesus as Messiah (which may include belief in his divinity), and observance of the law. J. E. Taylor, "The Phenomenon of Early Jewish Christianity: Reality or Scholarly Invention?" *VC* 44(1990) 313–34, here 314–15, insists that the term "Jewish Christian" be reserved for those who upheld the praxis of Judaism, in order to distinguish them from Christian Jews (like Paul and others) who thought Jewish customs and observance obsolete. This is more applicable to the early decades.

3. On the question of defining Jewish Christianity see Gaston, "Jerusalem," 61–63 and literature cited; R. E. Brown and J. P. Meier, *Antioch and Rome: New Testament Cradles of Catholic Christianity* (Ramsey, N.J.: Paulist, 1983) 1–9. Earlier discussions are found in B. J. Malina, "Jewish Christianity or Christian Judaism: Toward a Hypothetical Definition," *JSJ* 7(1970) 46–57; S. K. Riegel, "Jewish Christianity: Definitions and Terminology," *NTS* 24(1978) 410–15.

4. Many early Christian documents—e.g., Matthew, *Didache*, Revelation—are thought to be Jewish Christian. They are discussed in other chapters (though, for convenience, James is included in this chapter). If their Jewish Christian provenance is accepted, they can be seen broadly as representatives of the more "orthodox" stream, whereas in this chapter we are concerned with the more "heterodox." It is not clear that the *Discourse of Barnabas* is either Jewish Christian or from the second century. Its typological interpretation of biblical figures is not, at any rate, distinctively Jewish Christian. But see F. Manns, "Une nouvelle source littéraire pour l'étude du Judéo-Christianisme," *Henoch* 6(1984) 164–80; P. M. van Esbroeck, *Discours de saint Barnabé, archevêque de Jérusalem, au sujet de notre Seigneur Jésus Christ, des Eglises et des chefs des prêtres* (Turnhout: Brepols, 1982). Rabbinic allusions to Jewish Christians will be discussed in chap. 6. The so-called archaeological evidence for Jewish Christians tells us little or nothing about our period—see J. E. Taylor, "The Bagatti-Testa Hypothesis and Alleged Jewish Christian Archeological Remains,"

Mishkan 13(1990) 1–26; idem, *Christians and Their Holy Places: The Myth of Jewish-Christian Origins* (Oxford: Clarendon, 1993); Kretschmar, "Kirche," 29–30.

5. Schoeps, *Jewish Christianity,* esp. 13–18; idem, "Judenchristentum," 1–4; Strecker, *Pseudoklementinen,* is more cautious and he is followed by A. Stötzel, "Die Darstellung der ältesten Kirchengeschichte nach den Pseudo-Klementinen," *VC* 36 (1982) 24–37.

6. See J. Wehnert, "Literarkritik und Sprachanalyse: Kritische Anmerkungen zum gegenwärtigen Stand der Pseudo-Klementinen-Forschung," *ZNW* 74 (1983) 268–301; followed by Lüdemann, *Opposition,* 169–70. A useful review of critical opinion on the Pseudo-Clementines is given by F. Stanley-Jones, "The Pseudo-Clementines: A History of Research," *SecCent* 2 (1982) 1–33, 63–96.

7. Such arguments are put forward persuasively by W. Pratscher, *Die Herren-bruder Jakobus und die Jakobustradition* (Göttingen: Vandenhoeck & Ruprecht, 1987) 121–26. Lüdemann, *Opposition,* is the other outstanding example of tradition-history, tracing the evolution of a single theme. He doubts that we can isolate sources in the Pseudo-Clementines with any certainty, but agrees that this does not settle questions about the date and provenance of particular traditions.

8. The fullest discussion is by Klijn and Reinink, *Jewish-Christian,* passim.

9. Pritz, *Nazarene.* Despite the apparent skepticism of her title, Taylor, "Phenomenon," agrees that various groups can be identified. Her main point, shared by many others, is that we should resist the tendency of patristic writers both to use the terms "Jew" and "Judaize" indiscriminately and to amalgamate disparate evidence under broad labels such as "Ebionite."

10. The classic formulation is found in A. von Harnack, *The Mission and Expansion of Christianity in the First Three Centuries* (Gloucester, Mass.: P. Smith, 1972) 44–72; followed more recently by R. Lane Fox, *Pagans and Christians* (San Francisco: Harper & Row, 1986) 265–336. The absence of any discussion of Jewish Christianity in W. Bauer's *Rechtgläubigkeit und Ketzerei im ältesten Christentum* (Tübingen: Mohr [Siebeck], 1934) led to the addition of a chapter by G. Strecker in the English edition (see next note).

11. See H. Koester and J. M. Robinson, *Trajectories Through Early Christianity* (Philadelphia: Fortress, 1971) 115; W. D. Davies, "Paul and the People of Israel," *NTS* 24(1977) 4–39, here 19; H. Conzelmann, *History of Primitive Christianity* (Nashville: Abingdon, 1973) 134–38; G. Strecker, "On the Problem of Jewish Christianity," appendix to W. Bauer, *Orthodoxy and Heresy in Earliest Christianity* (Philadelphia: Fortress, 1971) 241–85.

12. F. Wisse of McGill University has argued this in at least two as yet unpublished papers, which we shall consider further below: "The Pseudo-Clementines and Jewish Christianity," read at the 1987 Canadian Society of Biblical Studies annual meeting; and "A Critical Evaluation of the Literary and Archeological Evidence for Jewish Christianity," read at the 1989 Society of Biblical Literature conference in Copenhagen. He is currently in the process of enlarging them into a full-length study.

13. G. Lüdemann, "The Successors of Pre-70 Jerusalem Christianity: A Critical Evaluation of the Pella Tradition," in E. P. Sanders, ed., *Jewish and Christian Self-Definition* (Philadelphia: Fortress, 1980) vol.1, 161–73; idem, *Opposition,* 200–13; J. Verheyden, *De vlucht van de christenen naar Pella. Onderzoek van het getuigenis van Eusebius en Epiphanius* (Brussels: Brepols, 1988)—not accessible to me (a German translation is forthcoming). A brief statement of his argument is found in "The

Flight of the Christians to Pella," *ETL* 66(1990) 368–84. His book is carefully analyzed by J. Wehnert (see next note). See also Brandon, *Fall*, 167–84; Strecker, *Pseudoklementinen*, 230–31, 283–86; J. Munck, "Jewish Christianity in Post-Apostolic Times," *NTS* 6(1959–60) 103–16; G. Lindeskog, *Das jüdisch-christliche Problem: Randglossen zu einer Forschungsepoche* (Stockholm: Almqvist & Wiksell, 1986) 81–82. Munck's main aim is to deny any connection between pre-70 and post-70 (heretical) Jewish Christians. Brandon (p.172) thinks the Pella Christians were Gentile, possibly of Galilean origin.

14. B. C. Gray, "The Movements of the Jerusalem Church during the First Jewish War," *JEH* 24(1973) 1–7; S. Sowers, "The Circumstances and Recollection of the Pella Flight," *TZ* 26(1970) 305–20; J. J. Gunther, "The Fate of the Jerusalem Church: The Flight to Pella," *TZ* 29(1973) 81–94; M. Simon, "La migration à Pella: Légende ou réalité?" *RSR* 60(1972) 37–54; Pritz, *Nazarene*, 122–27; and C. Koester, "The Origin and Significance of the Flight to Pella Tradition," *CBQ* 51(1989) 90–106. See now the incisive argument of J. Wehnert, "Die Auswanderung der Jerusalemer Christen nach Pella—historisches Faktum oder theologische Konstruktion?" *ZKG* 102(1991) 321–55.

15. Translation of Eusebius from K. Lake in the Loeb edition (Cambridge, Mass.: Harvard, 1926), and of Epiphanius from Lüdemann, "Pella," 164.

16. I am here combining the arguments of Lüdemann and Verheyden in particular. Lüdemann (following Strecker) thinks it is an etiological legend emanating from a Jewish Christian community in Pella that wished to claim descent from the Jerusalem church. Verheyden thinks it is a theological construct of Eusebius, which explains the timing of God's punishment of the Jews in 70 CE (a prominent Eusebian theme): it was delayed until God's true people, the Christians, had left the land. Such explanations are only necessary, of course, if the historicity of the tradition is denied.

17. Wehnert, "Auswanderung," 235–45, who includes Luke 21, especially v.39; Koester, "Pella," 91–103, includes Epiphanius, but he is not at any rate a crucial witness.

18. Pritz, *Nazarene*, 123–27. On the rebel raids see *Bell*.2.457–80, and on escapees see 5.420ff., 446ff., 551ff.; 6.352, 383–86. Josephus's reference to the sack of Pella by Jewish rebels (*Bell*.2.458) is widely agreed to be an exaggeration, though as the haven of Jewish Christian defectors it might have been a prime target. After 68 CE the Romans controlled Pella and it would have been a safe refuge, especially if it already contained Christians.

19. Wehnert, "Auswanderung," 248–49 (alluding to Rec.1.70.1–5), like Simon, "Pella," 44, suggests the period between 62 and 66 CE. Gunther, "Fate," suggests 66 CE; Josephus's evidence (note above) suggests that flight was possible even up to 70 CE. Wehnert notes too that Eusebius speaks of a "departure," not a "flight"—a term he suggests came in with the conflation of Eusebius and the synoptic apocalypses. He also speculates that the departure may have become an item of Jewish-Christian polemic and apologetic, used as early as the *Dialogue of Jason and Papiskos* (ascribed to Aristo of Pella).

20. The problem is, of course, that there is little hard evidence for this reasonable assumption. On the early Galilean mission see R. Bauckham, *Jude and the Relatives of Jesus* (Edinburgh: T. & T. Clark, 1990) 57–70.

21. Lüdemann, "Pella," 162–63, 173; *Opposition*, 201–3.

22. Wehnert, "Auswanderung," 250–51, dates this event to 70 CE. Bauckham, *Jude*, 93, thinks it took place in 62 CE and that Eusebius was at this point (*Hist.*

*eccl.*3:11) affected by Hegesippus's view that the destruction of Jerusalem followed immediately upon the death of James.

23. Even a date early in Trajan's reign, say 99–100 CE, would not leave much time for thirteen successors in thirty-five years. Some think the list contains names of elder-bishops who overlapped, others that it includes bishops from elsewhere in Palestine, or that it is the list from Pella but in reality stretches well beyond 135 CE. Recently it has been suggested that the list originates in a Jewish Christian tradition which named twelve elders who worked under James and who were later mistakenly taken to have been bishops—see R. van den Broek, "Der Brief de Jakobus an Quadratus," in T. Baarda, A. Hillhorst, G. P. Luttikhuizen, and A. S. van der Woude, eds., *Text and Testimony* (Kampen: J. H. Kok, 1988) 56–65, esp. 63–65. Bauckham, *Jude*, 70–79, has developed this suggestion: the first three names are the three bishops up to 135 CE, the following twelve are the council of elders who worked with James and include surviving apostles, other disciples, and perhaps even other relatives of Jesus. Lüdemann, *Opposition*, 119–20, suggests that even if Simeon was martyred the date is unreliable. Taylor, "Phenomenon," 315–16, thinks the bishop list is an independent (and more reliable) tradition than the story of the flight.

24. Tertullian *Haer.*33.11; cf. Hippolytus *Haer.*7.35.1.

25. Taylor, "Phenomenon," 324, notes the similarities with Qumran, the Elkesaites, and the Pseudo-Clementines.

26. Taylor, "Phenomenon," 321–24, makes the same point.

27. The view of Klijn and Reinink, *Jewish Christian*, 43, 69–70.

28. I am adapting Pritz's argument (*Nazarene*, 20) in his discussion of the Nazarenes. He rightly suggests that, whether we read "of your [*humeterou*] race" or "of our [*hemeterou*] race," in context the reference must be to Jewish Christians. J. T. Sanders, *Schismatics, Sectarians, Dissidents, Deviants: The First One Hundred Years of Jewish-Christian Relations* (Valley Forge, Pa.: Trinity, 1993) 54, thinks they are non-Christian Jews.

29. Contra Pritz, *Nazarene*, 9, who sees this as a late development.

30. See especially L. E. Keck, "The Poor among the Saints in the New Testament," *ZNW* 56(1965) 100–29; idem, "The Poor among the Saints in Jewish Christianity and Qumran," *ZNW* 57(1966) 54–78. The term seems to refer to a group within the Jerusalem community rather than to all of them.

31. See generally F. Hauck and E. Bammel, *ptochos, TDNT* 6.885–915. Most striking is the use of the phrase "congregation of the poor" as a common self-designation at Qumran. See also Matt 5:3; 11:5; James 2:5.

32. There is no need to be more specific, tying them in for example with the "circumcision party" of Acts 15:5. "Ebionite" may have been a self-designation of Jewish Christians who wished to claim a connection with Jerusalem even though they had none; so Taylor, "Phenomenon," 322—though she does not dismiss the possibility of an early origin (p. 323).

33. The best discussions are in Klijn and Reinink, *Jewish Christian*, 54–67; G. Strecker, "Elkasai," in *Eschaton und Historie* (Göttingen: Vandenhoeck & Ruprecht, 1979) 320–33; Lüdemann, *Opposition*, 129–39; G. P. Luttikhuizen, *The Revelation of Elchasai* (Tübingen: Mohr [Siebeck], 1985).

34. Lüdemann, *Opposition*, 135–37; Strecker, "Elkasai," 330–31.

35. See Klijn and Reinink, *Jewish Christian*, 66–67, who speak vaguely of contact with other groups around the River Jordan without specifying a date. Luttikhuizen, *Elchasai*, provides the most detailed discussion and concludes that most of the Christian traits are third-century additions.

36. See Strecker, "Problem," 252–70; *Judenchristentum,* passim. He reconstructs the document by looking for passages that parallel and expand the notions expressed in the *Epistula Petri* and *Contestatio,* but is coy about delineating KP in any precise way. It should be noted that he specifically dissociates it from the Ebionites—because the author does not use the term Ebionite, the ideal of poverty is absent, and a sectarian mentality is not apparent. These are not strong arguments, and at any rate would not disallow a loose clustering of them with other Ebionites.

37. See n. 6 above.

38. On the Petrine bias of *KP* see T. V. Smith, *Petrine Controversies in Early Christianity: Attitudes towards Peter in Christian Writings of the First Two Centuries* (Tübingen: Mohr [Siebeck], 1985) 59–61.

39. According to the two associated documents, the *Epistula Petri* (1:1) and the *Contestatio* (1:1; 5:1,4; cf. *Hom.*XI.35.4 = *Rec.*IV.35.1), James has the critical role of carrying out Peter's instructions for preserving and protecting his writings. This could be used to argue that it belongs as much to the Jacobite as to the Ebionite cluster (or that the clusters are of doubtful value!). Pratscher, *Jakobus,* 135–43, gives a maximal view of James' role; but I think Strecker, *Judenchristentum,* 195, is nearer the mark in emphasizing Peter's clear priority in this part of the Pseudo-Clementines.

40. Strecker, "Problem," 265–71, is anxious to distinguish Ebionite ideas from those of groups like the Elkesaites. On the question of baptism and lustrations, he describes the Ebionite view as moralistic and fundamentally Jewish as distinct from the magical-sacramental view of the Elkesaites. This is partly to counter the view that the Ebionites were a minority sect associated with other baptizing sects of the day, but it leads to some distinctions that are finer than the evidence suggests.

41. Strecker, *Judenchristentum,* 164–65, 257; idem, "Problem," 261. He notes that it is fully congruent with the views expressed in the *Epistula Petri.* Some older works have full and perceptive consideration of this passage. See A. Schliemann, *Die Clementinen nebst den verwandten Schriften und der Ebionitismus: ein Beitrag zur Kirchen-und Dogmengeschichte der ersten Jahrhunderte* (Hamburg: Friedrich Werthes, 1844) 135–36, 215–19, 270–72; A. Hilgenfeld, *Die Clementinischen Recognitionen und Homilien, nach ihren Ursprung und Inhalt dargestellt* (Jena: J. G. Schreiber, 1848) 154–55, 229–30.

42. Van Voorst, *Ascent,* 78–80, summarizes the evidence for date and provenance. There is some discussion about how much of *Rec.*1.33–71 is to be included. Lüdemann, *Opposition,* 237–40, excludes *Rec.*1.55–65 as redactional. Unlike Strecker he does not conflate the two versions, but rather suggests that Epiphanius and the author of *Recognitions* used a common source (which he calls *RI*). In addition to Strecker and Lüdemann see Stötzel, "Darstellung." Pratscher, *Jakobus,* 124–26, following Strecker, considers 44:3—53:4 to be an insertion by the author of the *Grundschrift.*

43. I am assuming that the author of *AJ* was Jewish Christian, though he could have been a Gentile Christian using Jewish Christian sources. It is as facile to assume that every text that has a universalist strain is Gentile Christian as that every appearance of anti-Paulinism is necessarily Jewish Christian.

44. The Pseudo-Clementine *Grundschrift* (probably third century) takes the final step and makes James into the supreme authority, the bishop of bishops and head of the worldwide church (*Ep.Clem.*1:1; *Rec.*1.68.2)—the aptly called "pope of Ebionite fantasy."

45. Van Voorst, *Ascent,* 163–65, notes that Jesus provides a substitute for sacri-

fice (i.e., baptism 36.1–2; 39.2), and chooses disciples (40.4) and performs miracles (41.4; 58.3) just like Moses.

46. Van Voorst, *Ascent,* 163–65, thinks it is implied, if undeveloped. Lüdemann, *Opposition,* 182–83, earlier argued for the presence of a preexistence Christology.

47. In Epiphanius, Paul is more clearly marked as an antinomian.

48. Van Voorst, *Ascent,* 167–70, finds the closest parallels in Acts 7 and in *Sib.Or.*4.

49. Lüdemann, *Opposition,* 182, argues that they did not practice circumcision or follow the purity laws; van Voorst, *Ascent,* 174–76, argues the opposite, and the evidence favors his view even though, as he recognizes, it is only implicit. Similar to van Voorst is the conclusion of Sanders, *Schismatics,* 55–58, 161–63.

50. See Lüdemann, *Opposition,* 140–49; Pratscher, *Jakobus,* 208–20; Lindeskog, *Problem,* 67–70; S. Laws, *A Commentary on the Epistle of James* (London: A & C Black, 1980) 26–37.

51. Lüdemann, *Opposition,* 144–45, thinks the author of the letter knew some of Paul's writings and deliberately caricatured them. I am inclined to think, with Pratscher, *Jakobus,* 213–14, that he knew oral traditions in which the distortion had already occurred. In neither case is there any proof.

52. See the discussion in Laws, *James,* 111–18.

53. Thus some have concluded that the author has lightly adapted a Jewish homily for his Christian purposes. This is something of an exaggeration, given the allusions to the Gospel tradition and the confrontation with what was thought to be Pauline tradition.

54. See James 1:5/Matt 7:7ff.; James 1:22ff./Matt 7:24ff.; James 2:5/Matt 5:3; James 4:9; 5:1ff./Luke 6:24ff.; James 3:1ff./Matt 12:36ff.; James 4:11ff./Matt 7:1ff.; James 5:12/Matt 5:23ff.

55. It has been argued that the author of the letter was a Gentile Christian. I am not persuaded, but even if true it does not mean that the author did not know and use Jewish Christian traditions. Pratscher, *Jakobus,* 219–20, suggests the following date and location: the end of the first century in Syria.

56. The letter is addressed to "the twelve tribes in the Dispersion" (1:1). This could refer to Jewish Christians, but more likely expresses the church's claim to be the ideal and true Israel (cf. 1 Pet 1:1; 2:9ff.; *Hermas Sim.*9.17.1ff.). If so, it presumably includes Gentiles.

57. See the discussion of this material in Pratscher, *Jakobus,* 103–21; Lüdemann, *Opposition,* 155–77. On the status of Hegesippus see Lüdemann, ibid., 166–67; W. Telfer, "Was Hegesippus a Jew?" *HTR* 53(1960) 143–53. They are both inclined to doubt Eusebius's conclusion that Hegesippus was a Jewish Christian with access to early Palestinian traditions. Eusebius's reasoning seems to be that Hegesippus knew the following: Jewish Christian traditions, a Jewish Christian gospel (*According to the Hebrews*), Semitic languages, and oral traditions of the Jews (*Hist.eccl.*4.22.4–9). It is true that knowledge of Jewish Christianity does not make someone a Jewish Christian, but I would take Eusebius's guess to be as good as any. At any rate, the important thing for us is the recognition that Jewish Christian traditions, in which James played a prominent role, were circulating in the mid to late second century.

58. Here I am dependent on Pritz, *Nazarene,* 29–47. See also Klijn and Reinink, *Jewish Christian,* 44–50. W. Kinzig, "'Non-Separation': Closeness and Co-operation between Jews and Christians in the Fourth Century," *VC* 45(1991) 27–53, here 30–32, notes how careful we have to be with Epiphanius's information.

59. See Pritz, *Nazarene,* 48–52, based on A. F. J. Klijn, "Jerome's Quotations from a Nazorean Interpretation of Isaiah," *RSR* 60(1972) 241–55.

60. Eusebius gives a rather muddled account of the second group, claiming that they accepted the virgin birth but not the preexistence of Jesus.

61. Pritz, *Nazarene,* 19–28.

62. The NT has variant spellings of "Nazarene": *Nazoraioi* (Matt, John, Acts) and *Nazarenoi* (Luke). The former reflects Semitic, and the latter Greek, usage— much like the two terms *Essaioi* (Semitic sources) and *Essenoi* (Greek sources). Whether the allusion was originally to Jesus' hometown (i.e., Nazareth) or to the messianic prophecy in Isa 11:1 (i.e., the branch [*netzer*] springing from the root of Jesse, cf. Matt 2:23) remains uncertain. Some prefer the term "Nazoreans" to "Nazarenes."

63. Pritz, *Nazarene,* 102–7. Further discussion of the rabbinic references to Christianity and the *Birkat ha-minim* can be found in chap. 6.

64. So Pritz, *Nazarene,* passim, and Klijn and Reinink, *Jewish Christian,* 50. Pritz, ibid., 44–45, points out the similarities between the Nazarenes and the Jewish Christians described in the early chapters of Acts. He also makes the interesting suggestion that when Epiphanius says that Ebion "came out of" the Nazarenes (*Pan.*30.2.1) he might be alluding to a split between the Ebionites and the Nazarenes which took place after the move to Pella, perhaps over Christology, perhaps over other matters (the Pauline mission? the return to Jerusalem?). Also supporting the origins of the Nazarenes in the early church are Taylor, "Phenomenon," 326, and Kinzig, "'Non-Separation,'" 34.

65. F. Wisse, of course, notes the evidence I have quoted against him, but his attempts to dismiss it are not persuasive. In particular his argument that Justin is speaking hypothetically and tells us nothing about the Jewish Christians of his day is unconvincing (see the discussion under Gentile Judaizers below).

66. It is at any rate probable that Gentile Christians were in the majority well before 70 CE and it is not clear how long the Jerusalem church was able to retain its original authority, especially in the sixties.

67. Van Voorst, *Ascent,* 177, draws too much from this and concludes that "the community of the *AJ* has undergone persecution at the hands of Jewish authorities."

68. Disputes over messiahship are the gist of Hegesippus's reports about the work of James among his fellow Jews, though precisely how the differences were defined is not made clear (Eusebius *Hist.eccl.*2.23.4–18). Further on Hegesippus see above, n.57.

69. I realize, of course, that my heuristic clusters are loose and that the connection of *KP* with the Ebionites is tenuous. The parallel with *Barnabas,* voicing the view of Gentile Judaizers, could spur interesting speculations about the origins of the Pseudo-Clementines.

70. J. G. Gager, *The Origins of Anti-Semitism* (Oxford: Oxford University Press, 1986).

71. L. Gaston, "Judaism of the Uncircumcised in Ignatius and Related Writers," in S. G. Wilson, ed., *Anti-Judaism in Early Christianity* (Waterloo: Wilfrid Laurier University Press, 1986) vol.2, 33–44. Gaston draws his evidence from Ignatius and Revelation. When he discusses Cerinthus or the "heretics" who lie behind the Pastorals he is more concerned to show that they were not Jewish Christians than to show that they were Gentile Judaizers.

72. Of which the best account is now R. Wilken, *John Chrysostom and the Jews* (Berkeley, Calif.: University of California Press, 1983).

73. The view of M. Barth, *Ephesians 1–3* (New York: Doubleday 1974) 242–52, for which, on the face of it, the writing itself offers little evidence. Colossians is more interesting. The Gentile Colossians (3:5–7) are warned off various practices (2:8–23), probably Jewish, that others (Jews? Jewish Christians?) are urging them to observe (2:16). The authenticity and date of Colossians, however, remains uncertain and I have left it to one side.

74. Gager, *Anti-Semitism*, 117–18; M. Simon, *Verus Israel: A Study of the Relations between Christians and Jews in the Roman Empire (135–425)* (Oxford: Oxford University Press, 1986), 306–7, speaks of Judaizers in the chapter heading but of Jewish Christians in the text.

75. Gaston, "Judaism," 35–36. He notes that Josephus *Bell.*2.454 and Esther 8:17 LXX speak of forced conversion to Judaism, while Josephus *Bell.*2.463, Plutarch *Cic.*7:6, *Acts Pil.* 2:1, and Ignatius *Magn.*10:3 speak only of the adoption of certain Jewish customs. Gal 2:14 implies an element of compulsion, but it is at any rate the Gentiles and not the Jews who Judaize.

76. These texts, their manuscript variants, and their setting in the epistle as a whole are discussed fully in chap. 4.

77. See chap. 7.

78. H. Kraft, *Die Offenbarung des Johannes* (Tübingen: Mohr [Siebeck], 1974) 60–61.

79. Collins, "Insiders," 206–7. See n. 80.

80. The most extensive recent argument for this view is made by A. Y. Collins, "Insiders and Outsiders in the Book of Revelation and Its Social Context," in J. Neusner and E. S. Frerichs, *"To See Ourselves as Others See Us": Christians, Jews, "Others" in Late Antiquity* (Chico, Calif.: Scholars Press, 1985) 187–218, here 204–10; idem, "Vilification and Self-Definition in the Book of Revelation," in G. W. E. Nickelsburg and G. W. MacRae, *Christians among Jews and Gentiles* (Philadelphia: Fortress, 1986) 308–20, here 310–14. Page 310 n.5 lists many of the scholars who have taken this view. Also recently H-J Klauck, "Das Sendschreiben nach Pergamon und der Kaiserkult in der Johannesoffenbarung," *Bib* 73(1992) 153–82, here 163–64; P. Borgen, "Polemic in the Book of Revelation," in C. A. Evans and D. A. Hagner, eds, *Anti-Semitism and Early Christianity: Issues of Polemic and Faith* (Minneapolis: Fortress, 1993) 199–211; Sanders, *Schismatics*, 169–80.

81. Some have taken 7:1–8 to refer to Jewish Christians and 7:9–17 to Gentile believers; but it is more common to see 7:9–17 as a comment on the preceding passage. The number 144,000 is at any rate symbolic.

82. Noted by Collins, "Vilification," 312. In some ways a fuller treatment of Revelation would be pertinent to my overall argument. But, like some texts (e.g., the *Didache*) and in contrast to others (Hebrews, *Barnabas*), with the exception of a few obscure asides the argument with Judaism is neither explicit nor hostile. For a good overview see O. Böcher, "Israel und die Kirche in der Johannesapokalypse," in idem, *Kirche in Zeit und Endzeit. Aufsätze zur Offenbarung des Johannes* (Neukirchen-Vluyn: Neukirchener Verlag, 1983) 28–55.

83. The similar phrase in Rev 2:2—"those who call themselves apostles but are not"—does not help much, because the characteristics of an apostle were neither as clear nor as public as those of a Jew.

84. Dio 66.1.4., cf. 37.17.1. Mentioned by S. D. Cohen, "Crossing the Boundary and Becoming a Jew," *HTR* 82(1989) 13–33, here 20–21. See further R. S. Kramer, "On the Meaning of the Term 'Jew' in Greco-Roman Inscriptions," *HTR* 82(1989) 35–53, here 51. Kramer contends that the inscriptional evidence suggests that

Ioudaios was applied *especially* to Gentiles who adopted Jewish ways, i.e., it could have an ethnic ("Jew"), geographic ("Judaean"), or an affiliate ("Gentile sympathizer") sense—the latter as a self-designation, or even a proper name for a child, where the Jewishness of the individual, though not immediately apparent, was being publicized.

85. Gaston, "Judaism," 42–43; Gager, *Anti-Semitism,* 132. A few scholars had anticipated them in part: M. H. Shepherd, Jr., "The Gospel of John," in C. M. Laymon, ed., *The Interpreter's One-Volume Commentary on the Bible* (New York: Abingdon, 1971) 708, thought they were a Christian Judaizing movement but one that was open to Jews and Gentiles alike. Kraft, *Offenbarung,* 60–61, agrees that they were Christians but thinks they were Jewish Christians.

86. Collins's arguments ("Vilification," 311–12) against the use of Ignatius's evidence repeat the standard reservations. See the discussion below.

87. Kraft, *Offenbarung,* 62, gives this as the motive for the (Jewish) Christians associating with the synagogue.

88. Admittedly some of these arguments could apply equally well to "ordinary" (as distinct from Kraft's "syncretistic") Jewish Christians. But why would the author describe them as "those who say that they are Jews and are not" when they were Jews? Is he merely railing against their convenient switching of labels ("For this purpose, I'm a Jew"), when he thought they should have described themselves as Christians and not Jews? Perhaps. The evidence about Philadelphia in Ignatius also tips the balance in favor of Gentile Judaizers.

89. As noted in another context by Simon, *Israel,* 106–7, there is later evidence for the synagogue's being used as a sanctuary in times of persecution. He points to the defection of Domnus during a local persecution in the early third century (Eusebius *Hist.eccl.*6.12.1), the solicitations of the Jews during the Decian persecution (*Passio Pionii* 13), and he suggests that Tertullian may have had something similar in mind when he attempts to refute the view that Christianity sheltered under the shadow of the more famous and licit religion (*Apol.*21.1). We should not, of course, assume that the offer of shelter by the Jews was an opportunistic attempt to best the church (the way *Passio Pionii* presents it). It may have been motivated by empathy and compassion.

90. H. Paulsen's revision of W. Bauer, *Die Briefe des Ignatius von Antiocha under der Polykarpbrief* (Tübingen: Mohr [Siebeck], 1985) 64–65. J. L. Sumney, "Those Who 'Ignorantly Deny Him': The Opponents of Ignatius of Antioch," *JECS* 1(1993) 345–65, suggests a number of protocols for assessing the evidence for opponents which introduce a proper note of caution. However, I think he underinterprets the evidence in *Magnesians,* even though, as (p.365) and I would agree, the discussion in *Magnesians* may well have been affected by Ignatius's experience in Philadelphia. Note, however, that Ignatius had met with representatives of the Magnesian church (15:1; cf. 2:1), so that his knowledge of the situation there was not based entirely on supposition.

91. So Gaston, "Judaism," 37 (and 38 n.30 for a list of those supporting this view); Gager, *Anti-Semitism,* 127–29; J. Speigl, "Ignatius in Philadelphia. Ereignisse und Anliegen in den Ignatiusbriefen," *VC* 41(1987) 360–76, here 370; Taylor, "Phenomenon," 318–19, is hesitant, but thinks they may have been Gentiles; similarly idem, "Apocalypse, Ignatius, Montanism: Seeking the Seeds," *VC* 43(1989) 313–38, here 323–25; W. Horbury, "The Benediction of the *Minim* and Early Jewish-Christian Controversy," *JTS* n. s. 33(1982) 19–61, here 54 n.2, thinks they were non-Christian

Gentile sympathizers with Judaism "who might be uncircumcised but were 'plus royalistes que le roi' in opposing Christianity."

92. Barrett, "Judaizers," 234; W. Bauer, *Orthodoxy and Heresy in Earliest Christianity* (Philadelphia: Fortress, 1971) 88; V. Corwin, *St. Ignatius and Christianity in Antioch* (New Haven, Conn.: Yale University Press, 1960) 58; P. J. Donahue, "Jewish Christianity in the Letters of Ignatius of Antioch," *VC* 32(1978) 81–93; R. G. Hall, "Epispasm and the Dating of Ancient Jewish Writings," *JSP* 2(1988) 71–86, here 80. R. J. Hoffmann, *Marcion: On the Restitution of Christianity* (Chico, Calif.: Scholars Press, 1984) 57–63, makes the eccentric proposal that those who "expounded Judaism" were Marcionites offering their negative view of it—a suggestion that can be sustained only by ignoring what Ignatius says elsewhere about the Judaizers.

93. W. R. Schoedel, *Ignatius of Antioch* (Philadelphia: Fortress, 1985) 202–3. His discussion of this passage is, unusually, obscure.

94. This is the opposite of Barrett's suggestion, "Judaizers," 234: Ignatius wanted to say, "It is better to hear Christianity from a circumcised man," got trapped in his own rhetoric, and had to invent a contrasting clause—about the uncircumcised expounding Judaism. Sanders, *Schismatics*, 159–61, 186–89, thinks the Christian Judaizers were Jewish in Magnesia and Gentile in Philadelphia.

95. Donahue, "Jewish Christianity," 89, recognizes this but seems oblivious to the way in which it undercuts his thesis that Ignatius's opponents were Jewish Christians.

96. This touches on the vexed question whether Ignatius is addressing one or two groups of opponents. Were there Judaizers and Docetists/Gnostics, or only Judaizers who were also Docetists/Gnostics? Gaston, "Judaism," 36–38, inclines to the latter view, along with many others. E. Molland, "The Heretics Combatted by Ignatius of Antioch," *JEH* 5(1954) 1–6, is the classic statement of this view, and Speigl, "Ignatius," 364–69, has reinforced it with some detailed observations. Donahue, "Jewish Christians," 82–87, is the fullest argument for two groups. I am inclined to think of a single group, though Schoedel's supposition that the Docetism of the Judaizers existed only in the mind of Ignatius needs to be considered (*Ignatius*, 202). We are at any rate dealing with the more tangible group, for the Judaizers are mentioned specifically whereas the Docetists/Gnostics are merely alluded to. Recently C. Trevett, "Prophecy and Anti-Episcopal Activity: A Third Error Combatted by Ignatius?" *JEH* 34(1983) 1–18, has tried to isolate yet another group—charismatic rebels who challenged Ignatius's claim to prophetic authority and his imposition of episcopal rule.

97. Justin does not state specifically that the defectors of 47:4 were Gentile Christians, but the context favors this view and, if he had Jewish Christians in mind, we might have expected him to say that they "returned to" rather than "switched over to" (*metabaino*) the Jewish community.

98. I refer here to the argument forwarded by F. Wisse in the unpublished paper "Pseudo-Clementines," above, n.12.

99. Cohen, "Crossing," passim.

100. Note Justin's liberal attitude (*Dial.*46–47), but also the fact that others took a less generous view.

Chapter 6: Jewish Reactions to Christianity

1. J. Maier, *Jesus von Nazareth in der talmüdischen Überlieferung* (Darmstadt: Wissenschaftliche Buchgesellschaft, 1978) 11–13, is the best discussion. He notes

among other things that Christian censors were often hypersensitive and excised passages that did not allude to them. Thus we cannot assume that where there is now a gap in the text a reference to Christians originally stood.

2. Among Neusner's many discussions of this issue see *Rabbinic Traditions about the Pharisees before 70* (Leiden: Brill, 1971) vols. 1–3; *Judaism: The Evidence of the Mishnah* (Chicago: University of Chicago Press, 1981); *Formative Judaism: Religious, Historical and Literary Studies* (Chico, Calif.: Scholars Press, 1983); *Major Trends in Formative Judaism: The Three Stages in the Formation of Judaism* (Chico, Calif.: Scholars Press, 1985); *Judaism in the Beginning of Christianity* (Philadelphia: Fortress, 1984). Sometimes his views are more clearly set out in book reviews: see, for example, *Ancient Judaism: Debates and Disputes* (Chico, Calif.: Scholars Press, 1984). Neusner provides a useful bibliography of his own works in *From Testament to Torah: An Introduction to Judaism in Its Formative Age* (Englewood Cliffs, N.J.: Prentice-Hall, 1988) 174–81, and a review of his career in "After Forty Years: Epilogue to a Career," *Rel.St.Th.* 10(1990) 19–42. Further on the problem of using rabbinic traditions see A. J. Saldarini, "Reconstructions of Rabbinic Judaism," in R. A. Kraft and G. W. E. Nickelsburg eds., Early Judaism and Its Modern Interpreters (Atlanta: Scholars Press, 1986) 437–77. The state of the text of rabbinic sources is discussed by P. Schäfer, "Research into Rabbinic Literature: An Attempt to Define the Status Quaestionis," *JJS* 37(1986) 139–52; idem, "Once Again the Status Quaestionis of Research into Rabbinic Literature: An Answer to Chaim Militowsky," *JJS* 40(1989) 89–94; C. Militowsky, "The Status Quaestionis of Research into Rabbinic Literature," *JJS* 39(1988) 210–11.

3. The best discussion of Neusner's approach is now a series of fine critical studies in E. P. Sanders, *Jewish Law from Jesus to the Mishnah* (London and Philadelphia: SCM/Trinity, 1990) passim. It is no mean feat to analyze the voluminous writings of Neusner. Sanders notes (pp.111–15, etc.) that Neusner does not always abide by his own critical strictures and frequently voices opinions that are inconsistent with each other. Neusner is not alone in this. It is extremely rare, for example, to find among even the most critical of scholars anyone who denies that Samuel the Small had a significant role in shaping the *Birkat ha-minim* sometime toward the end of the first century CE. They may disagree about what exactly he did, but most accept the gist of the report of the Babylonian Talmud without further ado.

4. Maier, *Jesus*, 268ff., and *Jüdische Auseinandersetzung mit Christentum in der Antike* (Darmstadt: Wissenschaftliche Buchgesellschaft, 1982) 206–8. Generally he dates the Christian allusions as late as possible, often to the sixth or seventh centuries and beyond. As such he stands in a line of Jewish apologists who have held much the same view and have denied that there was any serious vilification of Christians by the Jews. This is not to impugn his scholarship. His two books provide far and away the most thorough and critical overview available. But see now the judicious discussion by P. S. Alexander, "The 'Parting of the Ways' from the Perspective of Rabbinic Judaism," in J. D. G. Dunn, ed., *Jews and Christians: The Parting of the Ways A.D. 70–135* (Tübingen: Mohr [Siebeck], 1992) 1–25; and J. T. Sanders, *Schismatics, Sectarians, Dissidents, Deviants. The First One Hundred Years of Jewish-Christian Relations* (Valley Forge, Pa.: Trinity, 1993) 58–67.

5. Sanders, *Jewish Law,* 167–71, here 168. On Qumran see J. M. Baumgarten, "Recent Qumran Discoveries and Halakah in the Hellenistic-Roman Period," in S. Talmon, ed., *Jewish Civilization in the Hellenistic-Roman Period* (Sheffield: JSOT Press, 1991) 147–67; and in the same volume L. A. Schiffman, "Qumran and Rabbinic Halakah," 138–46.

6. The name most commonly associated with this view is W. H. C. Frend, *Martyrdom and Persecution in the Early Church* (Oxford: Oxford University Press, 1965) 189–91; idem, "The Persecutions: Some Links between Judaism and the Early Church," *JEH* 9(1958–59) 141–58. Frend was in turn following in the footsteps of A. von Harnack in *The Mission and Expansion of Christianity in the First Three Centuries* (New York: Harper & Row, 1962) 58: "Unless the evidence is misleading, they [the Jews] instigated the Neronic outburst against the Christians; and as a rule whenever bloody persecutions are afoot in later days, the Jews are either in the background or the foreground."

7. A recent exponent is R. S. MacLennan, *Early Christian Texts on Jews and Judaism* (Atlanta: Scholars Press, 1989) 75–78. Essentially the same view was expressed by J. Parkes, *The Conflict of the Church and the Synagogue. A Study in the Origins of Antisemitism* (London: Soncino, 1934) 137.

8. E. M. Smallwood, *The Jews under Roman Rule* (Leiden: Brill, 1976) 507–9, 543; M. Simon, *Verus Israel: A Study of the Relations between Christians and Jews in the Roman Empire (135–425)* (Oxford: Oxford University Press, 1986) 115–25; D. R. A. Hare, *The Theme of Jewish Persecution of Christians in the Gospel According to St. Matthew* (Cambridge: Cambridge University Press, 1967) esp. 19–79.

9. Rumors (*Dial.*17:1–3; 108:2–3; 131:2); killing Jesus (*Dial.*16:4; 133:6; 136:2); killing and persecuting Christians (*Dial.*96:2–3; 109:1–3; 133:6; 137:1ff.; *I Apol.* 31); proselyte persecutors (*Dial.*122); Roman constraints (*Dial.*16:4); praying for the Jews (*Dial.*108:3; 136:2); and vigorous expansion despite persecution (*Dial.*109:1–3).

10. The references to killing in *Dial.*96:2–3, 109:1–3 are vague and could easily be to the Bar Cochba period.

11. See the discussion in Hare, *Persecution*, 20–43. Simon, *Israel*, 119, suggests that Tertullian's famous statement—*Synagogas Judaeorum fontes persecutionum*—may refer primarily to the situation in the early church rather than to his own day. In that case, says Simon, it is not inaccurate even if *persecutionum* is not quite the correct term to use.

12. See Simon, *Israel*, 116–17. Hare, *Persecution*, 36–38, speculates that some Christians may have suffered death during the Jewish War and that this may have been one reason for the flight to Pella, but he knows that this can be only speculation. The allusion in Rev 2:10–11 to Christians being "faithful until death," which is closely associated with a warning against "those who say that they are Jews and are not" in the preceding verse, has often been taken to imply Jewish connivance in Christian persecution and execution. But, as we have seen above, the meaning of these verses is not at all self-evident. The author at any rate attributes responsibility to the devil.

13. Gospel predictions of death at the hands of the Jews will be dealt with below.

14. Simon, *Israel*, 124–25.

15. See Simon, *Israel*, 120–22; Parkes, *Conflict*, 137.

16. E.g., stoning, 14:19; imprisonment, 8:3; 22:19; temporary detention, 4:3; 5:18; 12:4; flogging, 5:40; reviling Paul, 13:45; 18:6; poisoning the minds of Gentiles, 14:2; 19:33. Hare, *Persecution*, 43–64, carefully defines these various actions. He notes that many of them are passing references and may be overtranslated by terms such as "persecution." In general, he wishes to minimize their significance and is inclined not to see them as part of an official or organized anti-Christian policy on the part of Judaism.

17. Hare, *Persecution*, 61–62, 78.

18. There is, of course, more to be said about Matthew and Luke. See chap. 2. Whether persecution by the Jews, which is Matthew's main concern, was primarily a thing of the past depends largely on an assessment of the proximity of his community to Judaism. The obscure excerpt from 1 Thessalonians has been taken as an interpolation. I am not convinced, but if not from Paul it still tells us what some later Christian believed (and perhaps knew) to be the case. See J. C. Hurd, "Paul Ahead of His Time: 1 Thess 2:13–16," in P. Richardson, ed., *Anti-Judaism in Early Christianity* (Waterloo: Wilfrid Laurier Press, 1986) vol.1, 21–36. I will also leave aside *1 Clem.* 6, since it seems to refer to factions internal to the Christian movement rather than to Jewish or Roman pressure. See O. Cullmann, *Peter: Disciple-Apostle-Martyr* (Philadelphia: Fortress, 1953) 102–4; R. E. Brown and J. P. Meier, *Antioch and Rome: New Testament Cradles of Catholic Christianity* (Ramsey, N.J.: Paulist, 1976) 124–25; J. Taylor, "The Love of Money Will Grow Cold: Matt 24:9–13 and the Neronian Persecution," *RB* 96(1989) 352–57.

19. Whether the expulsion was a recent, even current, experience or something that occurred in the past but still rankled in the present is disputed.

20. Simon, *Israel,* 124–25. Distorted readings of the evidence can occur in more than one way. If Harnack and those who followed him were too ready to accept and exaggerate Jewish opposition, others have been too eager to dismantle the evidence piecemeal until nothing is left.

21. Probably the most extensive account along these lines is found in W. D. Davies, *The Setting of the Sermon on the Mount* (Cambridge: Cambridge University Press, 1963) 256–315, which is now routinely cited as exemplary.

22. R. Kimelman, "*Birkat ha-minim* and the Lack of Evidence for an Anti-Christian Jewish Prayer in Later Antiquity," in E. P. Sanders, ed., with A. I. Baumgarten and A. Mendelson, *Jewish and Christian Self-Definition* (Philadelphia: Fortress, 1981) vol.2, 226–44; in the same volume E. E. Urbach, "Self-Isolation or Self-Affirmation in Judaism in the First Three Centuries," 269–98; also in that volume L. Schiffman, "Tannaitic Perspectives on the Jewish-Christian Schism," 115–56; S. T. Katz, "Issues in the Separation of Judaism and Christianity after 70 CE: A Reconsideration," *JBL* 103(1984) 43–76; Maier, *Auseinandersetzung,* 130–41; P. Schäfer, "Die sogennante Synod von Jabne," in *Studien zur Geschichte und Theologie des rabbinischen Judentums* (Leiden: Brill, 1978) 45–64; A. Finkel, "Yavneh's Liturgy and Early Christianity," *JES* 18(1981) 231–50. Katz and Maier apparently worked independently toward the same conclusions. See now also Alexander, "Parting," 6–11; Sanders, *Schismatics,* 58–61.

23. Katz, "Issues," 53–63. Sanders, *Schismatics,* 64–65, takes "books of the *minim*" to be primarily a reference to Christian books.

24. Urbach, "Self-Isolation," 291; earlier K. G. Kuhn, "Giljonim und Sifre Minim," in W. Eltester, ed., *Judentum Urchristentum, Kirche* (Berlin: Töpelmann, 1960) 24–61. One could argue that the margins were the spaces used for interpretative notes.

25. Maier, *Auseinandersetzung,* 19–114, is the most extensive discussion. He concludes that *gilyonim* refers to a single (probably leather) folio containing part of one or several biblical texts. For some older interpretations see M. Goldstein, *Jesus in Jewish Tradition* (New York: Macmillan, 1950) 53.

26. E.g., G. F. Moore, "The Definition of the Jewish Canon and the Repudiation of Christian Scriptures," in S. Leiman, ed., *The Canon and Masorah of the Hebrew Bible* (New York: Ktav, 1974) 115–41, here 121–22, 139; S. Liebermann, *Tosefta ki-Fshutah* (New York: Jewish Theological Seminary, 1955–73) vol.3, 206–7 (quoted

in Katz, "Issues," n.56); R. Gibbs, D. Jacobsen, and J. Diamond, "Empty Margins," *Cons.Jud.* 42(1989–90) 21–33; Alexander, "Parting," 11–15.

27. Katz, "Issues," 59.

28. See L. Ginzberg, "Some Observations on the Attitude of the Synagogue toward Apocalyptic Writings," *JBL* 41(1922) 115–26. That is, it is not a synonym for *sifre minim* ("heretical books") as Moore (n.26) argued.

29. Katz, "Issues," 59–61.

30. Moore, "Canon," 122ff.

31. Katz, "Issues," 55; Schäfer, "Synod," 56–64; Maier, *Auseinandersetzung,* 3–4. Katz relies in part on S. Leiman, *The Canonization of Hebrew Scripture: The Talmudic and Midrashic Evidence* (Hamden, Conn.: Archon Books, 1976). G. Veltri, "Zur traditionsgeschichtlichen Entwicklung des Bewusstseins von einem Kanon: die Yavneh-Frage," *JSJ* 21(1990) 210–25, argues that among the early rabbis there did not exist the concept of authority that would have produced canonical decisions.

32. See the discussion below under liturgical maledictions.

33. Katz, "Issues," 44–45—opposing Frend, *Martyrdom,* 192. W. Horbury, "Jewish-Christian Relations in Barnabas and Justin Martyr," in J. D. G. Dunn, ed., *Jews and Christians: The Parting of the Ways A.D. 70–135* (Tübingen: Mohr [Siebeck], 1992) 315–45, here 326–27, 344–45, argues for an organized Jewish response to Christianity.

34. Katz, "Issues," 47; and the discussion below.

35. Katz, "Issues," 46, following Davies, *Sermon,* 295–96, alludes to rabbinic traditions about the frequent travels of the leading tannaim. This does not imply that the rabbis dominated Judaism; it perhaps implies the opposite.

36. Katz, "Issues," 47; Maier, *Jesus,* 6–7.

37. Katz, "Issues," 48ff.

38. Katz, "Issues," 53; W. Horbury, "The Benediction of the *Minim* and Early Jewish-Christian Controversy," *JTS* n.s. 33 (1982), 19–61, here 58–59; and Sanders, *Schismatics,* 63–64, note the connection between *t.Hul.*2.20–21 and 22–24. See also Alexander, "Parting," 15–16. Maier, *Auseinandersetzung,* 264ff., thinks the Christian connection is post-Talmudic.

39. The two translations are from Katz, "Issues," 63–64. The first he takes from the Soncino edition of the Babylonian Talmud and the second from S. Schechter, "Genizah Specimens," old series *JQR* 10(1898), 197–206, 654–59.

40. Davies, *Sermon,* 276ff; Hare, *Persecution,* 54–56, 65–66; Simon, *Israel,* 198; Alon, *Jews,* 29; E. Lerle, "Liturgische Reformen des Synagogengottesdienstes als Antwort auf die judenchristliche Mission das ersten Jahrhunderts," *NT* 10(1968) 31–42; J. L. Martyn, *History and Theology in the Fourth Gospel* (Nashville: Abingdon, 1979) 37–63.

41. Schäfer, "Synode," 46–47; Urbach, "Self-Isolation," 288; Kimelman, "*Birkat,*" 226; Katz, "Issues," 67–69. D. Flusser, "Das Schisma zwischen Judentum und Christentum," *EvT* 40(1980) 214–39, here 229–33, thinks that the pre-Yavnean malediction already referred in some versions to heretics as well as outside political forces ("the arrogant"). The Yavnean change was to combine the two and place the reference to heretics first, partly because Jewish Christians were at this time the most troublesome of that group.

42. See Katz, "Issues," 64–69; Kimelman, "*Birkat,*" 232ff.; Schiffman, "Perspectives," 151–52; Maier, *Auseinandersetzung,* 136–41; Schäfer, "Synode," 46–48.

43. See Schäfer, "Synode," 42; Katz, "Issues," 72–74. Maier, *Auseinandersetzung,* 113–14, points out too that the characteristics of *minim* according to rabbinic

literature (idolatry, Hellenistic lifestyle, etc.) are not those associated with Jewish Christians. Finkel, "Liturgy," 234–35, independently makes the same point. They are reacting to the older view that virtually all references to *minim* in rabbinic literature are to Christians—see for example T. Herford, *Christianity in Talmud and Midrash* (New York: Ktav, 1903) 97–343.

44. W. A. Meeks, "Breaking Away: Three New Testament Pictures of Christianity's Separation from the Jewish Communities," in J. Neusner and E. S. Frerichs, eds., *"To See Ourselves as Others See Us": Christians, Jews, "Others" in Late Antiquity* (Chico, Calif.: Scholars Press, 1985) 93–115, here 102–3. Some think the Johannine expulsion was in effect before the introduction of the malediction: J. A. Overman, *Matthew's Gospel and Formative Judaism* (Minneapolis: Augsburg Fortress, 1990) 54; Horbury, "Benediction," 52, thinks this possible.

45. S. J. D. Cohen, "The Significance of Yavneh: Pharisees, Rabbis and the End of Jewish Sectarianism," *HUCA* 55(1984) 27–53, emphasizes the variety of opinion that prevailed in post–70 Judaism. The gradual articulation and implementation of Yavnean reform is emphasized on sociological grounds by Overman, *Formative*, 48–56.

46. A. Segal, "Ruler of the World: Attitudes about Mediator Figures and the Importance of Sociology for Self-Definition," in Sanders, Baumgarten, and Mendelson, eds., *Self-Definition*, vol.2, 245–68, here 245–57; idem, *Rebecca's Children: Judaism and Christianity in the Roman World* (Cambridge, Mass.: Harvard University Press, 1986) 151–60.

47. Horbury, "Benediction," passim. The article is immensely learned and subtle but often tangential, not to say odd. He suggests, for example (pp.52–53), that evidence for the presence of Christians in the synagogues is not contradicted by the existence of the malediction. The malediction, he suggests, could have been for the Jews a necessary precondition for allowing Christians there in the first place. By confirming the exclusive and universal claims of Judaism it would remove any threat to their community caused by the Christian presence. This somewhat contorted logic might make some sense from the Jewish point of view, but none at all from the Christian point of view.

48. These observations are made by Katz, "Issues," 70–71; Kimelman, *"Birkat,"* 233–36.

49. Maier, *Auseinandersetzung*, 132.

50. I prefer this to Horbury's view, "Benediction," 27, that Jewish Christians under suspicion would have been required to curse Christ as a test of loyalty. The ambiguous 1 Cor 12:3 is scarcely adequate support for this reading of Justin.

51. This raises the complex question of the meaning of Nazarenes/*notzrim*. Do they refer to Jewish Christians or Christians at large? That "Nazarenes" could refer to Christians in general is implied by Acts 24:5. Tertullian *Marc*.4:8, Epiphanius (*Pan*.29) and, in places, Jerome (e.g., *Ep*.112:13, where "Nazarenes" are, intriguingly, equated with *Minae*) use it of Jewish Christian sectarians, though it could be that they misunderstood the earlier usage. Epiphanius, in addition, confirms that in his day the term "Nazarenes" was included in the synagogue prayer. The uses of *notzrim* are rare (as distinct from several uses of *ha-notzri* to refer to Jesus) and even less helpful. There are no tannaitic references and few from the amoraic period. The one clear reference (*b.Ta'an*.27b) could refer to Christians in general, but might mean only "Jewish Christians." The fullest discussion is in Kimelman, *"Birkat,"* 241–44, who prefers the reading *natzrim* and finds reference to Jewish Christians alone. The evidence for both terms together makes best sense if we assume a development from

a broad (all Christians) to a narrower (Jewish Christians) sense. I assume, therefore, as Katz apparently does too, that *notzrim* could have referred to all Christians in the second century. The difficulty of supposing that *notzrim* referred only to Jewish Christians and was a late addition to the malediction (so Kimelman) lies in explaining why what had become an obscure, insignificant Christian group should have been considered important enough to be mentioned in the daily liturgy—see D. Halperin's review of Kimelman in *RSR* 11(1985) 136. There was the reverse shift in the meaning of *minim* in rabbinic tradition. In tannaitic usage it alludes to Jewish heretics, but in later traditions includes Gentile heretics too.

52. Horbury, "Benediction," 26–28, 38, 44. He dates the addition of *notzrim*, not always very precisely, to the turn of the first or the early second century. I would disagree mainly on the early date.

53. R. Pritz, *Nazarene Jewish Christianity: From the End of the First Century until Its Disappearance in the Fourth Century* (Jerusalem and Leiden: Magnes/Brill, 1988) 106–7. His geographical limitation works best if we exclude Justin, though which area Justin's view most closely mirrors is uncertain (Samaria, Asia Minor, Rome?).

54. Schiffman, "Perspectives," 155–56; idem, *Who Was a Jew? Rabbinic and Halakhic Perspectives on the Jewish-Christian Schism* (Hoboken, N.J.: Ktav, 1985) 60–61; Katz, "Issues," 72, 76. I am adapting Katz's argument since he seems to prefer a date after Justin for the addition of *notzrim*, thus explaining its absence in Justin's reports. But the term may be less significant than the overall sense of Justin's allusions. Finkel, "Liturgy," 242–43, also argues that 135 CE was a critical date, but in a different way and for different reasons. In his view, what was added to the malediction at that time was not a reference to Nazarenes but to "removers of the yoke, rescinders of circumcision, and those who pervert the interpretation of the Torah," i.e., Jewish Christians (cf. *t.Sanh.*12:9; *y.Sanh.*27c), since before that they had not been rejected by the Jewish community. He credits this move to Eliezer of Modein, the priest who worked closely with Bar Cochba, and finds the primary cause in the split over the latter's messiahship. Justin, he thinks, was mistaken in thinking there was a reference to Gentile Christians in the *Birkat ha-minim*. There is, however, no version of the malediction that supports this interpretation.

55. Urbach, "Self-Isolation," 288.

56. We note in passing the possibility that *notzrim* may have been added with specific reference to Jewish Christians (to distinguish them from the general run of *minim*) but understood by some, like Justin, to refer to all Christians. On the possible shift in meaning of Nazarenes/*notzrim* see n.51 above.

57. J. P. Meier, "Jesus in Josephus: A Modest Proposal," *CBQ* 52(1990) 76–103, who argues clearly and succinctly while at the same time providing extensive bibliographic information. W. Bienert, in Scheemelcher, ed., *Apocrypha*, 489–91, agrees that the statement is a mixture of authentic material and Christian redaction. He thinks the references to resurrection and messiahship are probably redactional.

58. Meier, "Josephus," 87.

59. Meier, "Josephus," 90–92, 100–103, notes not only the Josephan tone of the "authentic" core but also the absence of typical NT language. The Christian additions tend in the other direction, though not consistently so. Meier (pp.88–97) also uses the following arguments: the manuscripts unanimously include the passage: the implied theological content suits a first-century Jew much better than a second- or third-century Christian; and the later, casual reference to James the brother of "Jesus the so-called messiah" (*Ant.* 20.200) implies an earlier allusion to Jesus. He notes (p.93 n.46) that the Christian interpolations may be marginal glosses from

different hands. G. Vermes, "The Jesus Notice of Josephus Reexamined," *JJS* 38(1987) 1–10, here 3–5, also notes that some of the language is typical of Josephus and atypical of the New Testament.

60. Meier, "Josephus," 88.

61. It has been noted that this phrase refers to the good faith and receptivity of the audience rather than the truth of the message—Meier, "Josephus," 92 n.43.

62. Supernatural acts: cf. Philo *Vit.Mos.*1.143, 203; 2.213; *Migr.Abr.*47; *Decal.*46; Josephus *Ant.* 2.7–48; 3.30. Human acts: cf. Josephus *Ant.*3.37–38; 9.182.

63. Mark 3:20–30 and parallels; Origen *Cels.*1.6.17–18; *b.Sanh.*43b. These are the examples quoted by Vermes, "Jesus Notice," 9–10. He notes the language attributed to Celsus: "It was by magic that he was able to perform the *paradoxa* which he appeared to have done." In addition, he suggests that the comment in *b.Sanh.*43b is simply the pejorative way of describing the attributes of Jesus according to Josephus: "He practised sorcery and he seduced and led Israel astray" is the reverse of the statement that he was a "wise man" and "miracle worker." It might be seen more precisely as the reverse of "miracle worker" and "teacher of the people," which are a sort of definition of "wise man." See further the discussion in chap. 1 on the apologists and chap. 9.

64. This is the conclusion of both Vermes, "Jesus Notice," 8–9; and Meier, "Josephus," 96–97. Those who think Josephus's statement is hostile include S. G. F. Brandon, *Jesus and the Zealots* (Manchester: Manchester University Press, 1967) 359–68; M. Smith, *Jesus the Magician* (New York: Harper & Row, 1978) 45–46; E. Bammel, "Zum Testimonium Flavianum (Jos Ant 18, 63–64)," in O. Betz, K. Haacker, and M. Hengel, eds., *Josephus-Studien. Untersuchungen zu Josephus, dem antiken Judentum und dem Neuen Testament* (Göttingen: Vandenhoeck & Ruprecht, 1974) 9–22. The argument often depends on emending the text of Josephus.

65. See S. G. Wilson, *Luke and the Law* (Cambridge: Cambridge University Press, 1983) 1–12. Josephus's advice on foreign gods is found in *Ant.*4.207; *Ap.*2.237. Not everyone would have seen Christianity as the equivalent of a foreign nation at this stage, but Josephus may imply something like this when he calls the followers of Jesus the "tribe [*phylon*] of Christians." The term *phyle* usually means tribe, nation, people.

66. Translations in this section are from Herford, *Christianity.*

67. See J. Z. Lauterbach, "Jesus in the Talmud," in *Rabbinic Essays* (Cincinnati: Hebrew Union College Press, 1951) 473–570, here 490–500; Maier, *Jesus,* 29–38.

68. The best recent discussion is G. N. Stanton, "Aspects of Early Jewish-Christian Polemic and Apologetic," *NTS* 31(1985) 377–92, here 379–84. He notes that the accusation of magic and deception reverses the order in the basic biblical text (Deut 13:6–11, deception; Deut 13:9–14, magic).

69. On Jesus as deceiver see Matt 27:63; John 7:12,47; *T.Levi*16:3. The allegation of sorcery is clearest in Mark 3:20–30 and parallels but probably lurks in the background elsewhere too, even if not as prominently as Smith, *Magician,* 45–67, argues. On Thomas and Philip see *Acts of Thomas* 96, 102; *Acts of Philip* 69 [Greek]. Stanton notes that Philip (but not Thomas) is accused by the Jews. Celsus makes his point in *Cels.*1:6; 1:28,38, etc. on Quadratus see Eusebius *Hist.eccl.*4.3.2.

70. Cf. *t.Sanh.*10:11; *y.Sabb.*12:4[13d]; *y.Sanh.*7:16[25c-d]; *y.Yebam.*16:5[15d].

71. Smith, *Magician,* 48, even suggests that the Matthean story may be an apologetic account of an innocent stay in Egypt designed to counter the rabbinic slander.

72. M. Goldstein, *Jesus in the Jewish Tradition* (New York: Macmillan, 1950) 36–37, thinks that Celsus concocted the views of his Jewish informant, but provides no

real evidence for this judgment. Celsus may not have been using a single written source (*pace* M. Lods, "Etudes sur les sources juives de la polémique de Celsus contre les Chrétiens," *RHPR* 21(1941) 1–33, or a single informant, but this does not mean that his report of Jewish views is unreliable. Smith, *Magician*, 58–59, notes that the content of the Jew's remarks, and the fact that he is represented as speaking to Jewish rather than Gentile Christians and uses arguments designed to appeal to them, suggest that Celsus was using a Jewish source and not simply making things up. He recognizes, as we must, that the evidence is doubly filtered—through Celsus and then Origen—but thinks it reliable in essence. See the discussion in chap. 9.

73. *t.Hul.*2:22–23. Later versions elaborate some of the details: *y.Sabb.*14:4[14d]; *y. Abod.Zar.*2:2[40d]; *b.Abod.Zar.*27b.

74. Smith, *Magician*, 178. *t.Hul.*2.24b; cf. *b.Abod.Zar.*16b–17a; *Midr.Qohelet Rabba*1.8.3. Variants for Pantera are Pandera/Pantiri/Pantira. That they are oral variants rather than the names of different figures is argued by R. Bauckham, *Jude and the Relatives of Jesus in the Early Church* (Edinburgh: T. & T. Clark, 1990) 114, 119.

75. Smith, *Magician*, 48–49; similarly Schiffman, *Jew*, 69–71. Smith suggests that the story is later connected to the story of the son of a famous rabbi who is healed by a word "in the name of ben Pandera": *y.Abod.Zar.*2.2[40d]; *y.Sabb.*14.4[14d]. Simon, *Israel*, 183–84, accepts the essential authenticity of these stories.

76. See the interesting discussion of Bauckham, *Jude*, 106–21, here 110–11. He notes that the story is significant even if fictitious. Schiffman, *Jew*, 71–73, accepts the core story and dates the charge of associating with Christians to Trajan's rule. Sanders, *Schismatics*, 62–63, associates it with Trajan and the persecution of Christians at the time of the death of Simon, bishop of Jerusalem (Eusebius *Hist. eccl.*3.32).

77. Lauterbach, "Jesus," 532–37. See esp., Maier, *Jesus*, 130–82, who concludes that the original story about Eliezer was itself probably legendary, originating sometime before the Bar Cochba rebellion, and that the association with Jesus appeared much later. He argues similarly that ben Dama originally had no connection with Jesus or the Christians. When the reference to Jesus was added later, the transmitter of heretical words, one Jacob of Cephar Sichnin, was taken to be a Christian.

78. The meaning of ben Pantera remains obscure. Some have seen it as a play on the Greek word for "virgin" (*parthenos*), but there is no compelling linguistic argument for this. Others think it was simply a family name, perhaps that of Jesus' family. The Jewish usage that Origen knew from Celsus may explain why he apparently thought that Jesus' family name was *Panther* (Epiphanius *Adv. Haer.*78). See R. E. Brown, *The Birth of the Messiah* (Garden City, N.Y.: Doubleday, 1977) 535. The name was not uncommon and was often borne by soldiers. Smith, *Magician*, 47, notes one contemporary gravestone with the name of a soldier called Pantera on it (CIL XIII, ii.1.7514) and suggests somewhat mischievously that it may be the sole surviving hard evidence for the holy family.

79. See J. Schaberg, *The Illegitimacy of Jesus* (New York: Crossroad, 1990) 173. Maier, *Jesus*, 238–48, is predictably skeptical. He notes that the name of Jesus is not even mentioned and concludes that the tradition is hopelessly muddled, that there is no connection with Celsus's Panter, and that ben Pandera was an illegitimate, second-century magician/idolater who was assimilated to Jesus much later.

80. "Son of Mary" contrasts implicitly with "son of Joseph" and probably implies that Jesus is illegitimate (Mark 6:3 parallels), though contemporary parallels are hard to come by. In Matt 1:1–17 the inclusion of four strange women is often thought to foreshadow the oddity of the virgin birth, and the identification of Joseph

as the "husband of Mary" shows that arguing for Jesus' Davidic descent through the line of Joseph raised some rather awkward questions. When in John 8:41 the Jews say to Jesus, "We were not born of fornication" they may be implying that he was. The fullest and most recent discussion is found in Schaberg, *Illegitimacy*, 156–69. The saying in the *Gospel of Thomas*, 105, that "He who knows the father and the mother will be called the son of a harlot" is too obscure to be used with any confidence.

81. *Pesiq.R.*100b–101a advises the reader what biblical verses can be called on "if a whore's son tells you there are two gods." Smith, *Magician*, 49, thinks this is an allusion to Jesus, though "whore's son" may simply mean "heretic" rather than "illegitimate." An obscure reference in *b.Sanh.*106a to an unnamed woman who "was the descendant of princes and rulers, [who] played the harlot with carpenters," may be part of the same tradition, though it is in one of the Balaam passages which are generally not very useful for uncovering the rabbinic view of Jesus—see Smith, *Magician*, 49, and Lauterbach, "Jesus," 503–13, in contrast to Herford, *Christianity*, 63–78. Some rabbinic traditions speak, in a discussion of Levirate marriage, about a "certain man" who was considered illegitimate (*m.Yebam.*4.13; *t.Yebam.*3.3.4; *b.Yoma* 66d). The Mishnaic passage could be a rare tannaitic reference to Jesus, but there is no reason to take it this way since it makes perfectly good sense in its context. See Lauterbach, "Jesus," 539–43; Herford, ibid., 43–50; Schaberg, *Illegitimacy*, 170–71. When Schaberg (pp.174–77), following scholars like E. Bammel, calls on the late, anti-Christian *Toledoth Yeshu* (Life of Jesus) woven together by medieval Jewry, eagerness to find supporting evidence has overcome scholarly prudence.

82. Schaberg, *Illegitimacy*, 73–77, 138, thinks that even Matthew and Luke knew about this tradition and were less concerned to cover it up than to give it a theologically uplifting interpretation.

83. A. Segal, *Two Powers in Heaven: Early Rabbinic Reports about Christianity and Gnosticism* (Leiden: Brill, 1977). The argument is summarized and extended in the later essay "Judaism, Christianity and Gnosticism," in S. G. Wilson, ed., *Anti-Judaism in Early Christianity* (Waterloo: Wilfrid Laurier University Press, 1986) vol.2, 133–61. Essentially the same essay is found in A. Segal, *The Other Judaisms of Late Antiquity* (Atlanta: Scholars Press, 1987) 1–40. The identification of the "two powers" heretics is a longstanding issue in rabbinic scholarship, but Segal's work is far and away the most thorough and suggestive (as well as the most recent) study of the problem. The primary texts he uses are the Mekilta of R. Simeon b.Yohai (*Bashalah* 15) and of R. Ishmael (*Bahodesh* 5/*Shirta* 4). It is clear that Segal supports, and with some detailed argumentation, the increasingly common view that Gnosticism is a speculative/mystical/heterodox form of Judaism. His concern with the notoriously complex question of the origins of Gnosticism is not immediately of interest to us in this chapter. This whole section on "two powers" is little more than a summary of Segal. For an earlier discussion, see Simon, *Israel*, 193–96.

84. Segal, "Judaism," 161.

85. See Lauterbach, "Jesus," 567–68, and above n.51.

86. The best discussion is Maier, *Jesus*, 51–130. The tradition is developed in *t.Sanh.*12:9–11; *y.Sanh.*10:1–2[27c–29b]; *b.Sanh.*90a–107b. Christians could be included among those who detract from the Torah, read outside books, and use healing charms, but so could many other nonrabbinic Jews. The later versions make a connection with Christianity clearer, but this may not reflect the intent of the compilers of the Mishnah.

87. J. Schwartz, "Ben Stada and Peter in Lydda," *JSJ* 21(1990) 1–18. The suggestion that Stada may derive from the Greek *stadios* (stand firm or fast) and thus con-

nect with the Christian tradition of Peter/Cephas (= rock) shows how difficult the identification is. The rabbinic use would then have to be seen as ironic, because ben Stada did not, from their point of view, stand firm. Here (p.10 n.40), as elsewhere, Schwartz effectively undermines his own case by honestly exposing the discrepancies between the rabbinic and Petrine traditions. If there were more to be said for the Petrine connection, then Schwartz's explanation of it would make sense: it is designed to counter Christian claims to antiquity and primacy in Lydda and bolster the standing of the Jewish community there. Smith, *Magician,* 47, thinks ben Stada was an otherwise unknown heretic in Lydda. See also Maier, *Jesus,* 203–48, who (p.248) concludes that the traditions originated in some sort of execution in Lydda during the Bar Cochba uprising. See also Herford, *Christianity,* 82–85.

88. Herford, *Christianity,* 92–94; Lauterbach, "Jesus," 554–60, both of them apparently following H. Laible, *Jesus Christus im Talmud* (Berlin, 1891), 68ff. [not available to me].

89. Herford, *Christianity,* 161–71, mentions this view which goes back to the nineteenth century. He accepts the interpretation of *Be Nitzraphi* (as a reference to Jewish Christians) but thinks *Be Abidan* refers to an odeum or theater which was used, among other things, for philosophical discussions. The exact distinction would further depend on the meaning given to "Nazarene" (see n.51 above).

90. The notion that the rabbinic development of the *Akedah* (the binding of Isaac) in terms of the salvific benefits of the near-sacrifice of Isaac was designed to counter Christian belief in the atoning death of Jesus has been refuted most recently by C. T. R. Hayward, "The Sacrifice of Isaac and the Jewish Polemic against Christianity," *CBQ* 52(1990) 292–306. He shows that the development can be explained entirely by the internal needs of Judaism. The argument at any rate deals largely with amoraic sources which are too late for our purposes. His article contains a full bibliography.

91. B. L. Visotzky, "Overturning the Lamp," *JJS* 38(1987) 72–80; quotation p.76.

92. The most detailed (and skeptical) discussion of other possible allusions to Christians is Maier, *Auseinandersetzung,* passim. Some later rabbinic texts have been understood as a defensive reaction to Christian claims. See E. Mihaly, "A Rabbinic Defense of the Election of Israel: An Analysis of Sifre Deuteronomy 32:9," *HUCA* 35(1964) 103–43; L. H. Silberman, "Challenge and Response: Pesiqta DeRab Kahana, Chapter 26 as an Oblique Reply to Christian Claims," *HTR* 79(1986) 247–53. B. L. Visotzky, "Prolegomenon to the Study of Jewish-Christianities in Rabbinic Literature," *AJS* 14(1989) 47–70, suggests that rabbinic denigration of the ten lost tribes is a covert attack on Jewish Christians. There is no external evidence to confirm this.

Chapter 7: Gnostics and Marcionites

1. In principle two conclusions are possible: that there was a de-Christianizing of Christian Gnosticism or a Christianizing of non-Christian Gnosticism. Most scholars support the latter, though a case can be made for the former (see next note). A typically clear formulation is found in G. W. McRae, "Nag Hammadi and the New Testament," in B. Aland et al., eds., *Gnosis: Festschrift für Hans Jonas* (Göttingen: Vandenhoeck & Ruprecht, 1978) 144–57. A useful and well-documented summary of the discussion is found in H. A. Green, *The Economic and Social Origins of Gnosticism* (Atlanta: Scholars Press, 1985) 174–209, esp. 177–82.

2. That Gnosticism was an offshoot of Christianity was essentially the view of their patristic opponents. It has recently been defended at great length by S. Pétrement, *A Separate God: The Christian Origins of Gnosticism* (San Francisco: Harper & Row, 1990). Prior to this the fullest defense was that of F. C. Burkitt, *Church and Gnosis* (Cambridge: Cambridge University Press, 1932), and the best-known formulation that of A. von Harnack that Gnosticism expressed "the acute hellenization of Christianity" (*History of Dogma* [London: Williams & Norgate, 1897] vol.1, 226).

3. Though see nn.30,34 below.

4. The disparate nature of the Nag Hammadi writings (Christian gnostic, non-Christian gnostic, even nongnostic) has made it difficult to surmise how and by whom they were used. It is not clear that they are a coherent, rather than a haphazard, collection. They could have belonged to Christian Gnostics or to the heresiologists who opposed them. See A. Veilleux, "Monasticism and Gnosis in Egypt," in B. A. Pearson and J. E. Goehring, eds., *The Roots of Egyptian Christianity* (Philadelphia: Fortress, 1986) 271–306; in the same volume, J. E. Goehring, "New Frontiers in Pachomian Studies," 236–57. Further, F. Wisse, "Gnosticism and Early Monasticism in Egypt," in Aland, ed., *Gnosis,* 431–40; and in the same volume, M. Krause, "Die Texte von Nag Hammadi," 216–43.

5. The main features of gnostic mythology can be found in any of the standard accounts, the fullest of which is now K. Rudolph, *Gnosis: The Nature and History of Gnosticism* (San Francisco: Harper & Row, 1983) 53–274. Still unsurpassed for its lucidity and penetration is the essay by H. Jonas, "Delimitation of the Gnostic Phenomenon—Typological and Historical," in U. Bianchi, ed., *Le Origini Dello Gnosticismo* (Leiden: Brill, 1970) 90–108.

6. Irenaeus *Haer.*1.11.1, 1.18.1, 1.21.5. Translations taken from R. M. Grant, *Gnosticism and Early Christianity* (New York: Columbia University Press, 1959) 11.

7. Some of the anti-Jewish themes are sketched by K. W. Troeger, "The Attitude of the Gnostic Religion Towards Judaism as Viewed in a Variety of Perspectives," in B. Barc, ed., *Colloque international sur les textes de Nag Hammadi* (Quebec: Presse de l'Université Laval, 1981) 86–98. See now the interesting essay by R. M. Wilson, "Anti-Semitism in Gnostic Writings," in C. A. Evans and D. A. Hagner, eds., *Anti-Semitism and Early Christianity. Issues of Polemic and Faith* (Minneapolis: Fortress, 1993) 269–89.

8. Jonas, "Delimitation," 97.

9. Further discussion of the cultic and social life of the Gnostics is not essential for our purposes. See further Rudolph, *Gnosis,* 204–74; Green, *Origins,* 210–60.

10. Ialdabaoth: *Ap.John* II 24,12; *Hyp.Arch.* II 95,11; *Trim.Prot.* XIII 39,27. Saklas: *Ap.John* II 11,17; *Hyp.Arch.* II 95,7; *Gos.Eg.* III 57,16; *Apoc.Adam* V 74,3. Samael: *Ap.John* II 11,18; *Hyp.Arch.* II 87,3; *Trim.Prot.* XIII 39,27. The claim to be the sole god (cf. Isa.45:5; 46:9) is found in *Ap.John* II 11,19–21; *Hyp.Arch.* II 86, 27–87; *Gos.Eg.* III 58,23–59, etc. Cf. B. A. Pearson, *Gnosticism, Judaism and Egyptian Christianity* (Minneapolis: Fortress, 1990) 124–35, here 128–30.

11. The gnostic view of the biblical deity is explored by N. A. Dahl, "The Arrogant Archon and the Lewd Sophia," in B. Layton, ed., *The Rediscovery of Gnosticism* (Leiden: Brill, 1981) vol.2, 689–712. It may be that, like Marcion, not all Gnostics saw the creator as evil or ignorant, but they do consider him inferior. Wilson, "Anti-Semitism," 274–75, notes that denigration of the biblical god is less prominent in the Nag Hammadi texts than in patristic reports about the Gnostics, and that this could mean either that the patristic sources exaggerated, or that later Gnostics phased out, this element.

12. The figure of Cain in Gnosticism is puzzling. The heresiologists thought there was a Cainite sect, but the Nag Hammadi texts give only slight support for this. Pearson, *Gnosticism*, 95–107, has reviewed the evidence thoroughly and concludes that the sect was a figment of the church fathers' imagination.

13. Pearson, *Gnosticism*, 128–29, emphasizes the attack on the biblical god and the Jewish law as critical elements in gnostic self-definition (though there were exceptions, e.g., Ptolemy's *Letter to Flora*).

14. I have chosen the phrase "the supremacy of Yahweh" in the light of P. Hayman's essay, "Monotheism—A Misused Word in Jewish Studies," *JJS* 42(1990) 1–15, in which he argues that most forms of Jewish belief are more accurately described as "cooperative dualism" than as "monotheism." The former consists of a supreme creator god together with a secondary divinity (variously named as Michael, Melchizedek, Metatron, Logos, Wisdom, etc.) who is active in running the world. Even the rabbis, he claims, who opposed the belief in "two powers in heaven," themselves resorted to dividing God into two aspects: the Attribute of Justice and the Attribute of Mercy. They were theoretical monotheists but functional dualists. The case is somewhat overstated. Certainly Jewish angelology provided rich soil for the development of secondary divine figures, but it is not clear that the magical strain in Judaism (another source of dualism, even polytheism) is weightier evidence than the strain of rabbinic monotheism, nor that the latter should be universally described as functional dualism. Still, if we accept that there was a dualistic strain in Judaism, the gnostic challenge would have been less to their belief in the unity of God than to their estimation and ranking of the two deities: in the Jewish system the supreme God is creator and works hand in glove with his subordinate; in Gnosticism the two gods work against each other, and creation is assigned to the ignorant god who is also the god of the Jews.

15. J. Gager, *The Origins of Anti-Semitism* (Oxford: Oxford University Press, 1983) 167–73, quotation on p.170.

16. J. S. Siker, "Gnostic Views on Jews and Christians in the *Gospel of Philip*," *NT* 31(1989) 275–88. Gager, *Anti-Semitism*, 169, notes that "Only in the *Gospel of Philip* is there a conscious effort to separate the community of the gospel from the Jews." He refers to 52:21ff. and 75:30–34, apparently assuming that "Hebrew" in the first passage is equivalent to "Jew" in the second. Siker expands and refines Gager's brief allusion.

17. Siker is not quite as clear as this. Having argued that "Hebrews" were non-gnostic Christians, he defines them as "Jews or non-gnostic Christians" on p.280, and on the same page speaks of "Hebrews and non-gnostic Christians" as if they were two different groups.

18. Translation taken from W. W. Isenberg in J. M. Robinson, *The Nag Hammadi Library* (San Francisco: Harper & Row, 1977) 131–51.

19. Siker, "Gnostic," 279 n.7, notes that Justin *Dial*.122:5 seems to use "proselyte" as a term for Christian converts. See the discussion in chap. 9.

20. The "mother" could be the Spirit (*pneuma*), or Sophia. Siker, "Gnostic," 277, suggests that the mother was Spirit and the father God himself.

21. It might be noted that whereas "Hebrew" is always a pejorative term, all the other references in the gospel to apostles are positive (52:8–15; 66:30; 67:25; 74:18–20).

22. Siker, "Gnostic," 277 n.4, calls this last "an interesting parallel" to the use in *Gos.Phil.*, but does not clearly say why. In context "Hebrews" is contrasted with "Greeks," which makes a reference to Jews the more likely.

23. The reconstruction of the text is uncertain. Some reverse the sense and assume the author is claiming Jewish patrimony, i.e., that the author and readers were
formerly Jews or Jewish Christians. It would then be an interesting claim about the
origins of at least one form of Christian Gnosticism. See the discussion and references in Siker, "Gnostic," 278–79; Wilson, "Anti-Semitism," 275–77. In context the
argument of the paragraph seems to be that "like begets like," and this would favor
a denial that Christians descend from Jews.

24. Siker's late-second-century date is earlier than most and, while most accept
Syrian provenance, some prefer Edessa to Antioch.

25. W. Schoedel, "A Gnostic Interpretation of the Fall of Jerusalem: The First
Apocalypse of James," NT 23(1991) 153–78, on which this paragraph is dependent.
He effectively refutes the view that the apocalypse is of Jewish Christian provenance
(pp.155–65). The translation of 35:15–26 is also his, in Robinson, ed., Nag Hammadi, 245. Wilson, "Anti-Semitism," 282–83, emphasizes the transmutation of the
Jews into evil archons and is less inclined to find an anti-Jewish element. He rightly
notes (pp.281–86) that in several other allusions to Jesus' death there is no mention
of the Jews (1Apoc.Jas. V 4,28–30; 5,9–20; Great Pow. VI 41,7–25; 2 Treat.Seth VII
55,9–56,19; Gos.Truth I 18,17–26). Similarly, when opponents are mentioned in language that recalls the canonical Gospels they are often not specified as Jews but
rather as various opponents of the Gnostics, including "orthodox" Christians (Gos.-
Truth I 19,18–30; Auth.Teach. VI 33,4–34,34; Apoc.Pet. VII 7,3).

26. Gager, Anti-Semitism, 170. See further chap. 3. Wilson, "Anti-Semitism,"
277–81, 288, notes that the Gospel of Thomas, like other texts (see n.25 above),
reflects an earlier conflict between Jesus or Jewish Christians and the Jews and may
not, in Gnostic circles, have been anti-Jewish in intent. He thus approves (p.288)
Hans Jonas's claim: "The more archaic the source, the more vehement the anti-
Judaism." The observation is pertinent, but I doubt that it nullifies the anti-Jewish
strain of the Gospel of Thomas, as Wilson to some degree recognizes. Further on his
view, see n.43 below.

27. See especially G. Strousma, Another Seed: Studies in Gnostic Mythology
(Leiden: Brill, 1984).

28. See Pearson, Gnosticism, 130–32, for Gnostic and Jewish use of the terms for
the elect. Gager's comments (n.15) thus need to be qualified. The Gnostics do claim
biblical predecessors and privileges analogous to those of Israel. The implicit denial
of Jewish claims is not so very different from that found in other Christian evidence either.

29. See Pearson, Gnosticism, 148–64, and the literature cited there.

30. This is a brief and simplified version of Pétrement's lengthy argument (Separate God), which originally appeared in 1984. It is a curious blend of the plausible
and the eccentric, which raises as many questions as it purports to answer. Some of
the problems are discussed by B. A. Pearson, "Early Christianity and Gnosticism: A
Review Essay," RSR 13(1987) 1–8, here 4–6.

31. The arguments are found most readily in Pearson, Gnosticism, passim; Green,
Origins, 174–210. See also G. Quispel, Gnostic Studies (Istanbul: Nederlands
historisch-archaeologisch Instituut, 1974) vol.1, part 2; Strousma, Seed; McRae,
"Nag Hammadi."

32. Examples of what, in this view, are non-Christian gnostic texts are Eugnostos,
The Paraphrase of Shem, and The Apocalypse of Adam. Lightly Christianized works
are said to be Sophia of Jesus Christ, Gospel of the Egyptians, Hypostasis of the Archons,
and On the Origin of the World.

33. For the allegorizers see *Migr.Abr.*86–93; and for the apostates see *Conf. Ling.*2ff. The connection with Philo and Alexandria was long ago argued by M. Friedländer, *Der vorchristliche jüdische Gnosticismus* (Göttingen: Vandenhoeck & Ruprecht, 1898), a thesis that has been reviewed and expanded by Pearson, *Gnosticism*, 10–28. He argues that Friedländer is essentially correct about Jewish, but not necessarily about Alexandrian, origins. He cautiously favors a pre-Christian date. Green, *Origins*, has recently taken up the case for the Alexandrian/Egyptian origin of Gnosticism. On Philo and Gnosticism see also R. M. Wilson, *The Gnostic Problem* (London: Mowbray, 1958).

34. See W. C. van Unnik, "Gnosis und Judentum," in Aland, ed., *Gnosis*, 65–86; Jonas, "Delimitation," 101–3; Tröger, "Attitude," 86–98; G. P. Luttikhuizen, "The Jewish Factor in the Development of the Gnostic Myth of Origins: Some Observations," in T. Baarda, A. Hilhorst, G. P. Luttikhuizen, and A. S. van der Woude, eds., *Text and Testimony* (Kampen: Kok, 1988) 152–61; I. Gruenwald, *From Apocalypticism to Gnosticism* (Frankfurt: Lang, 1988). Naturally there are variations in the argument, to some extent dependent on when the work was published. Thus, for example, Gruenwald freely admits that Gnosticism contains a significant Jewish element but denies that this implies Jewish origin. He also argues that key concepts of apocalyptic may have provided grist for the gnostic mill even if they were used in an un-Jewish fashion.

35. It is ironic that while others have argued that the rabbis' concern with Christian heretics (*minim*) has been overplayed, and that other Jewish heretics (including Gnostics) were in mind (see chap. 6), Gruenwald plays down their concern with Gnostics and suggests that Christians were the more important!

36. Dahl, "Arrogant Archon," 701. I am blending here the views of Dahl and A. Segal, *Two Powers in Heaven: Early Rabbinic Reports about Christianity and Gnosticism* (Leiden: Brill, 1977).

37. Rudolph, *Gnosis*, 280–82.

38. Green, *Origins*. Pages 261–65 are a good summary. See also the less geographically specific reflections of Rudolph, *Gnosis*, 288–94.

39. It should be noted that many prefer a Syro-Palestinian to an Egyptian provenance for Gnosticism. Green's analysis of the social ethos of Gnosticism necessarily relies heavily on Valentinian sources, and there is some considerable distance between Valentinianism in the second and third centuries CE and the Jewish apostates he identifies in Egypt of the first century BCE. The gap between cause and effect that I have noted is common in sociological explanations of cultural phenomena and touches on some complex debates about the relationship between ideology and society. It may be true that there is often a connection between an ideology and the socioeconomic experience of its adherents of which they are unaware and therefore do not speak, and it could be that gnostic mythology is merely the expression of social alienation. In this case, however, I think the explanation does not dig quite deep enough.

40. Grant, *Gnosticism*, passim. It is, in my view, an underrated thesis. Pearson, *Gnosticism*, 28 n.50, concedes its value, but rejects the specific connection with the Jewish War—as apparently has Grant himself.

41. Noted by Grant and subsequently by others, for example Gruenwald, *Apocalypticism.*

42. This is suggested by E. Yamauchi, "Jewish Gnosticism? The Prologue of John, Mandaean Parallels and the Trimorphic Protennoia," in R. van der Boek and M. J. Vermaseren, eds., *Studies in Gnosticism and Hellenistic Religions* (Leiden: Brill,

1981) 467–97, here 490–91. It is interesting that Dahl, "Arrogant Archon," 701 n.27, speculates that the most likely time when the "two powers" heretics revolted and became radical Gnostics was between 70 and 135 CE, the period in which he would place the rabbinic polemic against them. He also notes that the more extreme attacks on the biblical deity are not attested for the earlier Samaritan and Syrian Gnostics.

43. I am here arguing against Wilson, "Anti-Semitism," 271–75, 288–89, also n.26 above. That the metaphysical anti-Judaism was aimed at an audience that understood its implications, Jews as well as nongnostic Christians, is argued by Gruenwald, Apocalypticism, 226–28, 231.

44. An earlier version of this section was published as "Marcion and the Jews," in S. G. Wilson, ed., Anti-Judaism in Early Christianity (Waterloo: Wilfrid Laurier University Press, 1986) vol.2, 45–57. It has been revised in the light of other chapters in the current work and discussions of Marcion that have become available in the meantime. Most important are G. May, "Marcion in Contemporary Views: Results and Open Questions," SecCent 6(1987–88) 129–51, and the full-scale, but eccentric, book by R. J. Hoffmann, Marcion: The Restitution of Christianity (Chico, Calif.: Scholars Press, 1984), which has one of the few discussions of Marcion's view of Judaism. Less useful for our purposes is Hoffmann's essay, "How Then Know This Troublous Teacher? Further Reflections on Marcion and His Church," SecCent 6(1987–88) 171–91.

45. Justin I Apol.20.5–6; Tertullian Marc.5.19; Celsus in Origen Cels.2.6; 5.54; 6.57; 7.25–26; Theodoret Ep.81, 113. See further W. Bauer, Orthodoxy and Heresy in Earliest Christianity (Philadelphia: Fortress, 1971) chap. 1, on Edessa, and the corrections by H. Koester, "Gnomai Diaphoroi: The Origin and Nature of Diversification in the History of Early Christianity," in H. Koester and J. M. Robinson, Trajectories Through Early Christianity (Philadelphia: Fortress, 1971) 114–57.

46. K. H. Rengstorf and S. von Kortzfleisch, Kirche und Synagoge: Handbuch zur Geschichte von Christen und Juden (Stuttgart: E. Klett, 1968) vol.1, 82 n.139. The term "Judaizing Christians" here seems to refer to the false apostles and their followers whom Marcion accused of distorting the gospel. We shall consider later whether Judaizers of another sort may have influenced Marcion.

47. D. P. Efroymsen, "The Patristic Connection," in A. T. Davies, ed., Antisemitism and the Foundations of Christianity (New York: Paulist, 1979) 98–117, esp. 100–108.

48. See the comments of Hoffmann, "Troublous," 173–76; May, "Marcion," 132–34.

49. A. von Harnack, Marcion: Das Evangelium vom Fremden Gott (Leipzig: J. C. Hinrichs, 1921) TU 45. In Neue Studien zu Marcion (Leipzig: J. C. Hinrichs, 1923) Harnack reviewed some of his reviewers. Some of this material was later incorporated into a second edition (1924), now available in translation (without the lengthy appendices): Marcion: The Gospel of the Alien God (Durham, N.C.: Labyrinth Press, 1990). The major studies since then are R. S. Wilson, Marcion: A Study of a Second-Century Heretic (London: Clarke, 1933); J. Knox, Marcion and the New Testament (Chicago: University of Chicago Press, 1942); and E. C. Blackman, Marcion and His Influence (London: SPCK, 1948). See also J. von Walter, Christentum und Frömmigkeit (Gütersloh: Bertelsmann, 1941) 41–62; U. Bianchi, "Marcion: Theologien biblique ou docteur gnostique?" VC 21(1967) 141–49; B. Aland, "Marcion: Versuch einer neuen Interpretation," ZTK 70(1973) 420–47; K. Beyschlag, "Marcion von Sinope," in M. Greschat, ed., Gestalten der Kirchengeschichte (Stuttgart: Kohlhammer, 1984) 69–81; E. Muehlenberg, "Marcion's Jealous God," in D. F. Winslow, ed., Disciplina

Nostra: Essays in Memory of Robert E. Evans (Cambridge, Mass.: Philadelphia Patristic Foundation, 1979) 93–114. The only comprehensive book in recent years is Hoffmann's *Marcion* (n.44 above) which, like the curate's egg, is good in parts.

50. Harnack, *Marcion*, 247–54 [ET 133–38; see n.49].

51. It scarcely need be added that the study of Gnosticism has changed beyond all recognition since Harnack's day. Harnack, ironically, was far from comfortable when the closest thing to a Marcionite revolution took place in his own day with the publication of Barth's commentary on Romans. Noted by Aland, "Marcion," 421–22. Further on Harnack see D. L. Balas, "Marcion Revisited: A 'Post-Harnack' Perspective," in W. E. March, ed., *Texts and Testaments: Critical Essays on the Bible and the Early Church Fathers* (San Antonio: Trinity University Press, 1980) 95–108; May, "Marcion," 129–30.

52. Harnack, *Marcion*, 1–27 [ET 15–21]; Blackman, *Marcion*, 1–14. May, "Marcion," 134–37, is the best (if unduly skeptical) recent discussion of the biographical sources. I am following the standard chronology, which places Marcion's birth ca. 100 CE. Hoffmann, *Marcion*, 44–74, argues for dates some thirty years earlier. He thinks the patristic dating shows only that they wished to demonstrate that Marcion was a latecomer. He dates his birth to ca. 70 CE and thinks he was active early enough to have founded a heretical tradition that was opposed by Polycarp, Ignatius, and the author of the Pastorals. The argument is somewhat circular, for it is the identification of the obscure heretics opposed by Ignatius et al. as Marcionites that proves that Marcion came earlier. The dates are not, at any rate, of critical significance to us.

53. G. May, "Der 'Schiffsreeder' Marcion," *StPatr* 21(1987) 142–53, here 148–49, surmises that Marcion sold his shares in the shipping business to pay for this gift.

54. Irenaeus, *Haer.* 3.3.4.

55. Harnack, *Marcion*, 213–29 [ET 99–123], 323–39. Further on the sources for Marcion's thought see May, "Marcion," 137–43.

56. Harnack, *Marcion*, 135–59 [ET 67–81]; Blackman, *Marcion*, 60–80; H. Jonas, *The Gnostic Religion* (Boston: Beacon, 1953) 137–46. Aland, "Marcion," 425–29, has useful corrections of Harnack; and see most recently Hoffmann, *Marcion*, 185–208.

57. Aland, "Marcion," 433–37, is especially good on this; also Hoffmann, *Marcion*, 212–20.

58. Harnack, *Marcion*, 160–80 [ET 81–93]; Blackman, *Marcion*, 98–102; Aland, "Marcion," 437–40.

59. As Aland, "Marcion," 438, points out, Marcion's docetism and his view of the death of Jesus were perfectly suited to his view of the body in the economy of salvation.

60. H. J. W. Drijvers, "Christ as Warrior and Merchant: Aspects of Marcion's Christology," *StPatr* 21(1987) 73–85, notes how little we know about Marcion's Christology. Based on the fourth-century Ephrem of Syrus, he explores the notions of military combat and commercial bargaining (for the purchase of souls) between Jesus and the creator god.

61. By far the best account of Marcion's view of scripture is in H. von Campenhausen, *The Formation of the Christian Bible* (Philadelphia: Fortress, 1972) 73–102, 149–67.

62. P. Lampe, *Die stadtrömischen Christen in den ersten beiden Jahrhunderten: Untersuchung zu Sozialgeschichte* (Tübingen: Mohr [Siebeck], 1987) 209–12, suggests that Marcion projected his disgruntlement as a trader with the Roman authorities onto his image of the creator god. May, "'Schiffsreeder,'" 152–53, thinks the

uncertain life of a sailor and trader, subject to arbitrary forces, may have led him to emphasize the reliable and wholly loving God of love. Both acknowledge that they are speculating.

63. May, "Marcion," 146–47, argues the reverse, i.e., that Marcion rejected the Jewish Bible as uninspired and, since allegorical interpretation was to be applied only to sacred and revelatory texts, as a result would not countenance allegorical interpretation of it. M. Enslin, "The Pontic Mouse," *ATR* 27(1945) 1–16, here 14–15, notes Marcion's lack of cant, opposition to muddleheaded syncretism, and objections to the grotesque allegorization of scripture among his contemporaries.

64. Beyschlag, "Marcion," 72–73.

65. Harnack, *Marcion*, 135–36 [ET 21–24]. Hoffmann, *Marcion*, mounts essentially the same argument in updated form (pp.155–84, for example, but also passim). He admits that Marcion must have known of the Gnostics' use of Paul but thinks he was not significantly influenced by them. Rather it was Marcion's pupil, Apelles, who later revised Marcionism in a gnostic direction.

66. See the list in A. Lindemann, *Paulus im ältesten Christentum* (Tübingen: J. C. B. Mohr, 1979) 387, and the comments of Harnack on several of his reviewers in *Neue Studien*, 1ff.

67. See also May, "Marcion," 144–46, who notes that whether we see Marcion as a Gnostic or not depends on our definition of Gnosticism and does not much affect our description of Marcion. Earlier forms of Gnosticism, Samaritan and Cerinthian for example, do not radically reject the biblical god, who is seen as inferior without being evil. Valentinus was also more nuanced than some. Occasionally, too, gnostic writings speak of Jesus' suffering and his death as a ransom (*Gos.Phil.*52:35–53:14), at least for some. The more we recognize variety in Gnosticism, the easier it is to fit Marcion in, even though that is not the only significant thing to be said about him.

68. Hoffmann, *Marcion*, 239, plausibly suggests that Marcion was in part reacting against the watered-down Paulinism of his day.

69. The translation here and elsewhere is that of E. Evans, *Tertullian Adversus Marcionem* (Oxford: Clarendon, 1972).

70. Hoffmann, *Marcion*, 226–33. He makes some astute comments on Marcion's attitude toward Judaism and is one of the few who address this issue. There is much to be said for his view (p.231) that "there is no compelling evidence to support the judgement that Marcion's theology is anti-Jewish in design, and the familiar view that the 'rejection' of the Old Testament made him the arch-antisemite of the ancient church is uninformed." He does, however, tend to neglect the negative side of Marcion's view of Judaism.

71. Blackman, *Marcion*, 71–73; similarly G. Filoramo, *A History of Gnosticism* (Oxford: Blackwell, 1990) 164–65.

72. Hayman, "Monotheism," 12–14; idem, "Rabbinic Judaism and the Problem of Evil," *SJT* 29(1976) 461–76.

73. L. Goppelt, *Christentum und Judentum im ersten und zweiten Jahrundert* (Gütersloh: Bertelsmann, 1954) 272–73.

74. Rengstorf, *Kirche*, 65–66, 81 n.139.

75. Harnack, *Neue Studien*, 15–16 [ET 15].

76. Hoffmann, *Marcion*, 29, asserts this almost as if he has taken Harnack's speculation as documented fact.

77. Hoffmann, *Marcion*, 227. He even suggests (pp.231–32) that Marcion may have excised anti-Jewish statements from his edition of Romans—a remarkable re-

versal of the traditional picture of Marcion removing pro-Jewish statements from his canon!

78. Paul's view of Judaism is, of course, much debated, but however construed it does not look much like Marcion's. A minority think Paul believed in two covenants, one of which guaranteed salvation for the Jews as Jews, and this comes closest to providing a parallel; but, in this view, whereas Paul considered the covenants to be equal, Marcion viewed one of them as superior.

79. Grant, *Gnosticism*, 121–28; followed by Balas, "Marcion," 98–99.

80. Noted by Harnack, *Marcion*, 22.

81. Ignatius *Phld*.6:2; Rev 2:9, 3:9. See the discussion of Gentile Judaizers in chap. 5.

82. Efroymsen, "Patristic," 100–108, quotation on p.105.

Chapter 8: Patterns of Christian Worship

1. J. Juster, *Les Juifs dans l'empire romain* (Paris: P. Guenther, 1914) vol.1, 304–37, here 335–37. M. Simon, *Verus Israel: A Study of the Relations between Christians and Jews in the Roman Empire (135–425)* (Oxford: Oxford University Press, 1986) 232–30, picks up and develops some of Juster's comments, especially as they apply to the later evidence.

2. G. Kretschmar, "Early Christian Liturgy in the Light of Contemporary Historical Research," *SL* 16(1986–87) 31–53, here 50–52; idem, "Die Kirche aus Juden und Heiden," in J. van Amersfoort and J. van Oort, eds., *Juden und Christen in der Antike* (Kampen: Kok, 1990) 9–43, emphasizes the role of liturgy as an identity marker and an expression of Jewish-Christian separation.

3. J. Isaac, *Jésus et Israel* (Paris: A. Michael, 1948) 364–65; and in *Genèse de l'antisemitisme* (Paris: A. Michael, 1956) 296–305.

4. Simon, *Israel*, 488–90, has argued that an annual prayer in an obscure language (Latin) could scarcely be credited with such influence. That may be so, but the force of the words and the distinct liturgical gesture should not be underestimated.

5. See the reflections on this issue by W. S. Adams, "Christian Liturgy, Scripture, and the Jews: A Problematic in Jewish-Christian Relations," *JES* 25(1988) 39–55.

6. The text was thus not available to Juster and plays no role in Simon's discussion.

7. W. Rordorf, *Sunday: The History of the Day of Rest and Worship in the Earliest Centuries of the Christian Church* (London: SCM, 1968) 177–78.

8. S. C. Rieff, "Jewish Liturgical Research: Past, Present, Future," *JJS* 34(1983) 161–70, here 168. See further the survey by P. F. Bradshaw, "The Search for the Origins of Christian Liturgy: Some Methodological Reflections," *SL* 17(1987) 26–34; idem, "Ten Principles for Interpreting Early Christian Liturgical Evidence," in P. F. Bradshaw and L. A. Hoffman, eds., *The Making of Jewish and Christian Worship* (Notre Dame, Ind.: Notre Dame University Press, 1991) 3–21.

9. R. S. Sarason, "On the Use of Method in the Study of Jewish Liturgy," in W. S. Green, ed., *Approaches to Ancient Judaism: Theory and Practice* (Missoula, Mont.: Scholars Press, 1978) 97–172; idem, "Recent Developments in the Study of Jewish Liturgy," in J. Neusner, ed., *The Study of Ancient Judaism 1* (New York: KTAV, 1982) 180–87. The notable exception referred to by most scholars is J. Heinemann, *Prayer in the Talmud: Forms and Patterns* (Berlin: De Gruyter, 1977). See also T. Zahavy, "A New Approach to Early Jewish Prayer," in B. M. Bokser, ed., *History of Judaism: The*

Next Ten Years (Chico, Calif.: Scholars Press, 1980) 45–60, and his two more recent works (n.26 below).

10. See the works by Talley, Bradshaw, Beckwith, and Taft referred to below.

11. J. Daniélou, *The Theology of Jewish Christianity* (London: Darton, Longman & Todd, 1964).

12. It is for this reason that I have omitted discussion of Christian practices that arose in a Jewish matrix but very early took on a distinctive Christian shape and where the Jewish connection is at any rate disputed. Thus baptism was probably as much influenced by John's baptismal mission as by proselyte baptism (whose date is uncertain). The Eucharist had roots in Passover but quickly outgrew them. In Justin's invaluable account (*I Apol.*65–67), only the elements of scripture reading and prayers look, in a general way, like regular synagogue worship. He admits himself that pagan readers would have likened it to Mithraic worship. See A. Cabannis, *Patterns in Early Christian Worship* (Macon, Ga.: Mercer University Press, 1989) for a discussion of these traditions. The Jewish background of early ecclesiastical offices is defended by J. T. Burthcheall, *From Synagogue to Church: Public Services and Officers in the Earliest Christian Communities* (Cambridge: Cambridge University Press, 1992). He takes insufficient account of the parallels in Greco-Roman voluntary associations, but even if he is right, the degree of neither dependence nor deviance is sufficiently clear-cut to help with our argument.

13. T. J. Talley, *The Origins of the Christian Year* (New York: Pueblo, 1986) 27–31, quotation on p.28; idem, "The Eucharistic Prayer of the Ancient Church According to Recent Research: Results and Reflections," *SL* 11(1976) 138–58, here 148–49.

14. Perhaps specifically Pharisees—see J. A. Draper, "Christian Self-Definition against the 'Hypocrites,'" in E. Lovering, ed., *SBLSP* (Atlanta: Scholars Press, 1992) 362–77, here 366–68; idem, "Torah and Troublesome Apostles in the *Didache* Community," *NT* 33/34(1991) 347–72. He argues that *Didache* 1–6 was originally formulated for Jewish Christians to encourage separation from Gentiles. At a later stage (indicated by 8:1–2 et al.) the material is expanded and used to encourage separation from other Jews. That the reference is to Jews rather than Jewish Christians is also argued by G. Schöllgen and W. Geerlings, *Didache, Traditio Apostolica* (Freiburg: Herder, 1991) 47–49; K. Niederwimmer, *Die Didache* (Göttingen: Vandenhoeck & Ruprecht, 1989) 165–66.

15. For the Lord's Prayer as a substitute for the tephillah (later known as *Shemoneh Esreh* or Eighteen Benedictions), see R. T. Beckwith, "The Daily and Weekly Worship of the Primitive Church in Relation to Its Jewish Antecedents," in R. Beckwith, J. Luyten, G. Rouwhorst, and H. Wegmen, *Influences juives sur le culte chrétien* (Leuven: Abbaye du Mont César, 1981) 89–122, here 106 [authors' names have different initials on the book cover]; also found in *Quest.Lit.* 62(1981) 5–20, 83–101. See also Draper, "Christian Self-Definition," 369–70. That the Lord's Prayer borrows from and thus, in effect, replaces the kaddish (a synagogue prayer associated with the public exposition of scripture) is suggested by Heinemann, *Prayer,* 191–92, 251ff. On the tephillah and kaddish see the recent account in C. Di Sante, *Jewish Prayer: The Origins of Christian Liturgy* (Mahwah, N.J.: Paulist, 1991) 78–106, 171–73.

16. For the Lord's Prayer as a Christian addition to the tephillah see P. F. Bradshaw, *Daily Prayer in the Early Church* (London: SPCK, 1981) 27.

17. Bradshaw, *Prayer,* 27.

18. The Qumran texts are ambiguous; see the full discussion of 1QS 10:1–3a; 1QH 12:4–7 by Bradshaw, *Prayer,* 4–7, who also concludes (pp.9–11), after a careful review of the evidence that the practice of praying morning, noon, and evening was

widespread, though not necessarily universal, among Jews. Some think the Qumran covenanters prayed only twice a day, like the Therapeutae (Philo, *Vit.cont.*27)—see G. Vermes, *The Dead Sea Scrolls in English* (London: Penguin, 1975) 89, 188.

19. The Shema combined Deut 6:4–9, 11:13–21; Num 15:37–41, and recited them together with various benedictions. Cf. *Ep.Arist.*; Josephus *Ant.*4:212ff. See the recent exposition of the Shema in Di Sante, *Prayer,* 49–77. That synagogue worship took place on days other than the Sabbath is mentioned in *m.Meg.*1:3; 3:6–4:1, though how far back this practice goes is not known. For further discussion see Beckwith, "Worship," 95–98. Bradshaw, *Prayer,* 1–21, and R. Taft, *The Liturgy of the Hours in East and West* (Collegeville, Minn.: Liturgical Press, 1986) 3–9, are both sensible of the difficulties in creating a clear and uniform picture from the scattered and inconsistent evidence.

20. Evidence for early Christian practice is to be found largely in Acts (2:1,15; 3:1; 10:3,9,30), but it is not unambiguous.

21. The most thorough study is by L. Finkelstein, "The Birkat ha-Mazon," *JQR* 19(1928) 211–62. For further discussion see Talley, "Eucharistic Prayer," passim; Beckwith, "Worship," 115. The translation of the *Didache* is from the Loeb edition. The text of the *Birkat ha-Mazon* is taken from Finkelstein, which he in turn reconstructed from a tenth-century witness. For a recent discussion see Di Sante, *Prayer,* 141–49.

22. On the meaning of the obscure Greek in *Didache* 14:1 see below. The pattern of dependence and distancing can be seen in the nonliturgical sections of the *Didache* too. The Two Ways teaching (1–6) is entirely Jewish in content and may only be Christianized to the extent that it is lodged in a Christian context (though "Lord" in the subtitle may be Jesus rather than God). The instructions on food (6:3) seem to recommend the pattern of Jewish observance, yet allow for some laxity. The rules for baptism (7:1–4) may reflect similar Jewish practices (Draper, "Christian Self-Definition," 363), but are distinguished by their trinitarian formula. The pattern appears to be consistent throughout.

23. Far and away the most thorough discussion (with full bibliography) is to be found in the recent book by D. A. Fiensy, *Prayers Alleged to Be Jewish: An Examination of the Constitutiones Apostolorum* (Chico, Calif.: Scholars Press, 1985), and I am heavily dependent on his conclusions.

24. Commonly the date has been given as 150–200 CE, and that is the justification for including it in this discussion. Fiensy, *Prayers,* 220–28, prefers a date ca. 250 CE.

25. Fiensy, *Prayers,* 222.

26. On the early history of the Shema and the Amidah see the interesting recent work of T. Zahavy, *Studies in Jewish Prayer* (Lanham, Md.: University Press of America, 1990); summarized in P. F. Bradshaw and L. A. Hoffman, eds., *Making,* 42–68. He argues that in the post-70 period the Shema was promoted by the scribes and the Amidah by the priests.

27. Beckwith, "Worship," 116–17. W. O. Oesterley, *The Jewish Background of the Christian Liturgy* (Oxford: Clarendon, 1925) 121–25, while noting the lack of direct evidence for its influence thinks the use of the Shema might have fueled the reluctance of some early Christians to develop a high Christology.

28. Bradshaw, *Prayer,* 27–28, notes the absence of clear evidence in either the earlier or later periods. C. W. Dugmore, *The Influence of the Synagogue upon the Divine Office* (London: Faith, 1964) 102–4, thinks that the Jews were banned from using the Shema in 135 CE and that by the time they could use it again Christians

would have had no incentive to borrow from them. He seems to assume that at least some Christians (probably Jewish Christians) recited the Shema before the Bar Cochba rebellion.

29. Dugmore, *Influence,* 10, 47, 70, 112. Bradshaw, *Prayer,* 47ff., notes some of the problems with Dugmore's argument. Taft, *Liturgy,* 6–9, emphasizes the confusion in the Jewish evidence and questions whether we can draw anything certain from it. The later addition of three minor hours of prayer (the "third," "sixth," and "ninth" hours) by the end of the second century, as shown by Tertullian (*On Prayer* 25) and Clement of Alexandria (*Stromata* 7.7.40), probably stems from the general significance of these hours as markers dividing the day—which Dugmore, *Influence,* 66–67, thinks were publicly announced. J. H. Walker, "Terce, Sext and None: An Apostolic Custom?" *StPatr* 5(1962) TU 80, 206–12, thinks they originate as a memorial of the Passion, a view that is adapted by Bradshaw, *Prayer,* 59–62, who sees their origin in the services that concluded the twice-weekly fasts. Certainly there appears to be no clear Jewish precedent. Bradshaw, *Prayer,* 47–50, has rightly noted that this pattern was not universal and that an earlier pattern in Alexandrian Christianity was prayer at morning, noon, evening, and night.

30. For the various Jewish parallels see especially Bradshaw, *Prayer,* 47–71.

31. Bradshaw, *Prayer,* 51. Cf. Tertullian *Apol.*29.

32. On the influence of synagogue music see E. Werner, "The Doxology in Synagogue and Church: A Liturgico-Musical Study," *HUCA* 19(1945–46) 276–328. See further A. A. R. Bastiaensen, "*Psalmi, hymni,* and *cantica* in Early Jewish-Christian Tradition," *StPatr* 21(1987) 15–26.

33. Bradshaw, *Prayer,* 47–71, constantly refers to the Qumran parallels.

34. G. W. Buchanan, "Worship, Feasts and Ceremonies in the Early Jewish-Christian Church," *NTS* 26(1979–80) 279–96, has a useful summary on p.92 but, in general, the title of the paper promises more than it delivers. P. Sigal, "Early Christian and Rabbinic Liturgical Affinities," *NTS* 30(1984) 63–90, finds some interesting parallels but they are not directly relevant (because usually too late) for us. For further detail see Oesterley, *Background,* 111–54; Dugmore, *Influence,* passim. The recent discussion by S. Cavaletti, "The Jewish Roots of Christian Liturgy," in E. J. Fisher, ed., *The Jewish Roots of Christian Liturgy* (Mahwah, N.J.: Paulist, 1990) 7–40, covers a lot of ground but only lightly. In emphasizing Jewish influence there is no intention of belittling the development of uniquely Christian elements that appeared from a very early stage, though they are of less interest for our theme. In some instances the Christian elements become so dominant that the Jewish roots rapidly become almost invisible—as in the Eucharist, with its distant connection to the Passover meal.

35. See commentaries on 1 Corinthians, and especially Rordorf, *Sunday,* 193–96, who argues the case cautiously. He notes that if the churches had begun to structure their week around Sunday, there is no suggestion why they did so. Similarly, D. R. De Lacey, "The Sabbath/Sunday Question and the Law in the Pauline Corpus," in D. A. Carson, ed., *From Sabbath to Lord's Day: A Biblical, Historical and Theological Investigation* (Grand Rapids: Zondervan, 1982) 160–95, here 184–86.

36. See especially S. Bacchiochi, *From Sabbath to Sunday* (Rome: Pontifical Gregorian University Press, 1977) 90–95.

37. For example F. F. Bruce, *The Acts of the Apostles* (London: Tyndale, 1952) 372; H. Conzelmann, *Acts of the Apostles* (Philadelphia: Fortress, 1987) 169. See also M. M. B. Turner, "The Sabbath, Sunday and the Law in Luke-Acts," in Carson, ed., *Sabbath,* 100–57, esp. 129.

38. Rordorf, *Sunday,* 196–205.

39. Bacchiochi, *Sabbath,* 101–11, argues for Saturday evening. Talley, *Origins,* 14–16, agrees and suggests that the transition from Sabbath to Sunday may have been eased by Christians' starting their celebrations after the end of the Sabbath (i.e., Saturday evening), so that initially there was a degree of proximity and overlap—a view that Rordorf, *Sunday,* 178–79, disputes. Along the same lines as Talley see M. H. Shepherd, *The Paschal Liturgy and the Apocalypse* (London: Lutterworth, 1960) 31; and H. Riesenfeld, "Sabbat et jour du Seigneur," in A. J. B. Higgins, ed., *New Testament Essays* (Manchester: Manchester University Press, 1959) 210–17. Turner, "Sabbath," 129, thinks Luke's Gentile readers would automatically have used Roman reckoning.

40. Bacchiochi, *Sabbath,* 106–10. Turner, "Sabbath," 129, notes that the alternatives—social versus cultic meal—may be too rigid, certainly for the apostolic period. But are we to think of the apostolic era or the time of writing?

41. Rordorf, *Sunday,* 202–3, argues for Sunday. Bacchiochi, *Sabbath,* 95–99, suggests the Sabbath or, even more implausibly, that the day was not always the same but was fixed week by week.

42. See R. J. Bauckham, "Sabbath and Sunday in the Post-Apostolic Church," in Carson, ed., *Sabbath,* 252–98, here 262–64.

43. See P. Richardson and M. B. Shukster, "Barnabas, Nerva, and the Yavnean Rabbis," *JTS* n.s. 34(1983) 32–55; idem, "Temple and *Bet ha-midrash* in the Epistle of Barnabas," in S. G. Wilson, ed., *Anti-Judaism in Early Christianity* (Waterloo: Wilfrid Laurier University Press, 1986) vol.2, 17–32. The later dates commonly given, ca. 117–19 or 128–30 CE, would shift the argument only slightly.

44. So earlier J. B. Lightfoot, *The Apostolic Fathers* (London: Macmillan, 1889–90) part 2, vol.2, 129; more recently Bacchiochi, *Sabbath,* 123–31, who thinks the author proleptically experiences the eschatological Lord's Day when he receives his vision. But why use "Lord's Day" instead of the more familiar "Day of the Lord," especially when the former was beginning to get a different technical sense in roughly contemporaneous writers (Ignatius)? See the thorough discussion in R. J. Bauckham, "The Lord's Day," in Carson, ed., *Sabbath,* 221–50, here 225–27, 232–33.

45. Favoring the weekly Sunday are Rordorf, *Sunday,* 205–15; and Bauckham, "Lord's Day," 225–27, 232–33. Bauckham rightly disputes Rordorf's conflation of the reference to the Lord's Supper in 1 Cor 11:20 with Rev 1:10, a circuitous route by which he argues that the "Lord's Day" in fact meant the "Lord's Supper Day." Favoring Easter Sunday are A. Strobel, "Die Passa—Erwartung als urchristliches Problem in Lc 17:20f.," *ZNW* 49(1958) 185; C. W. Dugmore, "Lord's Day and Easter," in *Neotestamentica et Patristica* (Leiden: Brill, 1962), Cullmann, *Festschrift,* 272–81; and K. A. Strand, "Another Look at 'Lord's Day' in the Early Church and in Rev. I.10," *NTS* 13(1967) 174–81. All of them recognize the ambiguity of the evidence.

46. See Bauckham, "Lord's Day," 228–29.

47. Bauckham, "Lord's Day," 230–31, is the best discussion. He notes that the normal argument is that the weekly Sunday developed out of Easter Sunday. But the best evidence for Easter Sunday is later than the best evidence for the weekly Sunday. At any rate it is not clear, as we shall see below, that Easter Sunday was established by the early second century. Moreover, the texts that most likely refer to the weekly Sunday come from areas (Asia Minor and Syria) that were largely Quartodeciman, i.e., they celebrated Easter on the same day as the Jewish Passover, which did not occur on a fixed day of the week. This makes the derivation of the weekly from the annual festival unlikely.

48. J. P. Audet, *La Didaché* (Paris: Gabalda, 1958), is virtually alone in dating parts of the *Didache* as early as 50–60 CE. J. A. Draper has recently advanced the interesting hypothesis that Matthew was dependent on the *Didache* rather than vice versa: "Troublesome Apostles," 347–72. On the date of *Barnabas* see above n.43. Ignatius's letters are traditionally dated between 100 and 118 CE.

49. Noted by Rordorf, *Sunday*, 214–15; Bauckham, "Lord's Day," 230–31.

50. Contra Bauckham, "Lord's Day," 236–38. Rordorf, *Sunday*, 218ff., thinks of a Palestinian origin for different reasons—its early development for celebration of the resurrection and the weekly Eucharist. On Bacchiochi's argument for Rome as the place of origin see below.

51. Bauckham, "Lord's Day," thinks the original practice was to celebrate both and that Sunday worship was abandoned after 70 when Jewish-Christian relations worsened!

52. See n.39. A sense of overlap could have occurred if Gentile Christians reckoned the day from sunrise to sunrise rather than sunset to sunset as did the Jews. Acts 20:7, read in one way, could refer to Saturday evening as the time for Christian worship, but Pliny seems to envisage early morning worship followed by a meal on the same day. It is notable that Sunday is not defined as a day of rest for some considerable time.

53. See Bacchiochi, *Sabbath*, passim. He provides the best brief discussion (pp.38–52) of the significance of 135 CE in Jewish-Christian relations.

54. These arguments are slightly different from, but move in the same direction as, those used by Bauckham, "Sabbath," 269–75.

55. Another way of dealing with this problem was to treat the Sabbath command allegorically, where the Sabbath rest is understood as a permanent rest or ceasing from sin. See *Gos.Thom.*27; Justin, *Dial.*12:3; Epiphanius *Pan.*33.3.5 (on Ptolemaeus). This could be allied to the trend we have been discussing—the establishment of an alternative Christian day.

56. T. C. G. Thornton, "Problematical Passovers: Difficulties for Diaspora Jews and Early Christians in Determining Passover Dates during the First Three Centuries A.D.," *StPatr* 20(1987) 402–8, notes that due to the vagaries of lunar observation and the difficulties of communication, Jews and Christians may unwittingly have celebrated different days, even different months.

57. Talley, *Origins*, 18–20. Generally on the Quartodecimans see B. Lohse, *Das Passafest der Quartodecimaner* (Gütersloh: C. Bertelsmann, 1953); W. Huber, *Passa und Ostern* (Berlin: Töpelmann, 1969). Huber (pp.33–37) thinks that the letter of Polycrates is fictitious, but still opts for a Palestinian origin. R. T. Beckwith, "The Origin of the Festivals of Easter and Whitsun," *SL* 13(1978) 1–20, argues (pp.8–9) that Easter Sunday was established ca. 110 CE and that the Quartodeciman form grew out of this in a desire to coordinate more closely with the Jewish dates.

58. Some suggest a time after 70 CE, or even 135 CE. It is not uncommon to suppose that the Johannine community originated in Palestine but migrated to Asia Minor in the first century. This would explain both the Palestinian features of the Johannine writings and the tradition that connects them with Ephesus. Talley's argument, *Origins*, 7–9, that around the early second century the Asia Minor Christians gave up the lunar calendar in favor of the Julian solar calendar, is based on the comments of a fifth-century writer about an obscure group of Montanists (Sozomen *H.E.*7.18).

59. Victor's problem may have been exacerbated by the presence of Quartodeci-

mans in Rome. He seems to have been motivated more by the desire to assert the will of Rome and impose uniformity than by any special anti-Jewish bias.

60. So Bacchiochi, *Sabbath*, 45–52; Lohse, *Passafest*, 113–18; C. Mohrmann, "Le conflit pascal au IIe siècle: note philologique," *VC* 16(1962) 61, thinks the point is that since the Quartodecimans brought their practice to Rome to Soter and were tolerated, Victor should now tolerate them in distant Asia Minor.

61. Huber, *Passa*, 56–61; Talley, *Origins*, 18–27; K. Holl, "Ein Bruchstück aus einem bisher unbekannten Brief des Epiphanius," in *Gesammelte Aufsätze zur Kirchengeschichte*, II: *Der Osten* (Tübingen: Mohr [Siebeck], 1927) 204–24; H. Lietzmann, *A History of the Early Church*, II: *The Founding of the Church Universal* (London: Lutterworth, 1938) 135–36. H. von Campenhausen, "Ostertermin oder Osterfasten? Zum Verständnis des Irenäusbriefs an Viktor," *VC* 28(1974) 114ff., suggests that the divergence prior to Soter was over the practice of fasting rather than the date of Pasch.

62. Rordorf, *Sunday*, 218–20, tentatively suggests an apostolic origin; Talley, *Origins*, 25, treats it as one option; Beckwith, "Origin," 4–7, argues against it.

63. Bacchiochi, *Sabbath*, 45–52, suggests ca. 115 CE in Rome. The date is possible but, as we have seen, the location is doubtful. Beckwith, "Origin," 9–17, argues for a date ca. 110 CE in Antioch, but the case is made only through broad inferences.

64. So Bacchiochi, *Sabbath*, 45–52, who thinks the Gentile bishops imposed a recently established Roman practice.

65. A date around this time is also suggested by Talley, *Origins*, 24–25; Huber, *Passa*, 43–55; Kretschmar, "Kirche," 37–38.

66. Emphasized by Huber, *Passa*, esp. 54–55.

67. For Easter Sunday in the first two centuries there is little to go on but surmise. For the Quartodecimans we rely on later witnesses: the *Didascalia*, Eusebius (*Hist.eccl.*5.24–26), Epiphanius (*Pan.*50,70), and Melito's *Peri Pascha*. Huber and Lohse disagree not only on the interpretation of the evidence but also on what counts as evidence. For example, Huber thinks Melito was not a Quartodeciman and includes the *Epistula apostolorum* as evidence for Quartodeciman practice (*Passa*, 12–14, 33–37). Lohse is more liberal in identifying sources. In general I am persuaded by Huber's more restrained use of the sources, except when he denies that Melito was a Quartodeciman.

68. According to Melito, Exod 12 was read at the Jewish Passover. According to rabbinic tradition (*m.Pesah*10:4) Deut 26:5–11 was recited. See Huber, *Passa*, 3–11; S. G. Hall, "Melito in the Light of the Jewish Haggadah," *JTS* 22(1971) 229–46.

69. Lohse, *Passafest*, 62–74, emphasizes the fast, while Huber, *Passa*, 16–18, argues that the fast and the memorial of the Passion were equally significant originally with the latter becoming more prominent after the separation from Judaism.

70. It is unlikely that the resurrection of Jesus was ignored in Quartodeciman celebrations, but it seems to have been secondary to the emphasis on Jesus' death.

71. Translation from Bacchiochi, *Sabbath*, 86 n.256.

72. Lohse, *Passafest*, 17–21.

73. Huber, *Passa*, 64ff.

74. J. Neusner, *Aphrahat and Judaism* (Leiden: Brill, 1971) esp. 123–27.

75. R. Wilken, *John Chrysostom and the Jews* (Berkeley: University of California Press, 1983) passim.

76. Anti-Judaism was not, of course, the only motivation for paschal disputes. As mentioned before, the natural drive to develop a festival expressing Christian

realities played its role. An avoidance of unseemly public disagreement is mentioned by Epiphanius. The assertion of Rome's primacy may have motivated Victor as much as a concern for church unity, while the disruption that Judaizing created in the church was a major theme of Chrysostom.

77. The comment is by Hall, "Haggadah," 29, on the article by E. Werner, "Melito of Sardis: The First Poet of Deicide," *HUCA* 37(1966) 191–210.

78. S. G. Hall, *Melito of Sardis "On Pascha" and Fragments* (Oxford: Clarendon, 1979), quotations from xxvii and 39 n.40. All references to and quotations from the *Peri Pascha* in the following pages are based on Hall's edition. The text is referred to either by section or by line.

79. A. T. Kraabel, "Melito the Bishop and the Synagogue at Sardis: Text and Context," in D. G. Mitten, J. G. Pedlen, and J. A. Scott, eds., *Studies Presented to George M. A. Hanfmann* (Mainz: von Zabern, 1972) 72–85, here 81 n.25.

80. Noted by Kraabel, "Melito," 85 n.35. See J. Blank, *Meliton von Sardes* Vom Passa: *Die älteste christliche Österpredigt* (Freiburg: Lambertus, 1963) 77–86. Also K. W. Noakes, "Melito of Sardis and the Jews," in *StPatr* 13(1975) TU 166, 244–49; R. Wilken, "Melito and the Sacrifice of Isaac," *TS* 37(1976) 53–69.

81. Presumably in Greek and not, as some have suggested, in Hebrew. See S. G. Hall, "Melito *Peri Pascha* 1 and 2," in P. Granfield and J. A. Jungmann, eds., *Kyriakon* (Münster: Aschendorff, 1970), *Festschrift* for J. Quasten, vol.1, 236–48.

82. Blank, *Meliton*, 46–51.

83. J. Daniélou, "Figure et événement chez Méliton de Sardes," in van Unnik, ed., *Neotestamentica*, 282–92; Blank, *Meliton*, 60–65.

84. K. H. Rengstorf and S. von Kortzfleisch, *Kirche und Synagoge: Handbuch zur Geschichte von Christen und Juden* (Stüttgart: E. Klett, 1968) vol.1, 73.

85. On this false etymology of the word "Israel" see Hall, *On Pascha*, 45 n.50.

86. Detailed analysis can be found in T. Halton, "Stylistic Device in Melito, *Peri Pascha*," in *Kyriakon* (n.81 above) 249–55. See also J. Smit Sibinga, "Melito of Sardis: The Artist and His Text," *VC* 24(1970) 81–104; C. Bonner, *The Homily on the Passion by Melito Bishop of Sardis and Some Fragments of the Apocryphal Ezekiel* (London and Philadelphia: Christophers, 1940) 20–27.

87. Noted by Werner, "Melito," and Hall, "Haggadah."

88. A. Wifstrand, "The Homily of Melito on the Passion," *VC* 2(1948) 201–23, quotation on p.214.

89. See the discussion of Passover and Easter above.

90. Hall, *On Pascha*, xii.

91. Kraabel, "Melito," 82–83; though on p.84 he does seem to allow for the added pressure of Melito's Quartodeciman views.

92. Kraabel, "Melito," 77 and n.5 for literature. As we noted in chap. 1, the date for the period of greatest Jewish prominence, based on the archaeological evidence, has recently been pushed into the third or fourth century. See H. Botermann, "Die Synagoge von Sardes: Eine Synagoge aus dem 4.Jahrhundet?" *ZNW* 81(1990) 103–21; M. P. Bonz, "The Jewish Community of Ancient Sardis: A Reassessment of Its Rise to Prominence," *H.St.Class.Philol.* 93(1990) 343–59. But while their heyday may have come later, it is not unlikely that they were a significant presence in Melito's day too, more so than the Christians he represented.

93. Kraabel, "Melito," 83.

94. The *Extracts* may be one of the sixteen books listed by Eusebius, or a separate work altogether.

95. See chap. 5.

96. Blank, *Meliton*, 15–17; Werner, "Melito," 206–7; Hall, *On Pascha*, xli.

97. B. Lohse, "Meliton von Sardes und die Brief des Ptolemaus an Flora," in E. Lohse, ed., *Der Ruf Jesu und die Antwort der Gemeinde* (Göttingen: Vandenhoeck & Ruprecht, 1970) 179–88.

98. D. P. Efroymsen, "The Patristic Connection," in A. T. Davies, ed., *Antisemitism and the Foundations of Christianity* (New York and Toronto: Paulist, 1979) 98–117.

99. Hall, *On Pascha*, xliii, also the notes on xliii–xliv; Bonner, *Homily*, 27–28.

100. Notably Blank, *Meliton*, 35–38.

101. Identification of the decrees has remained difficult. Melito says that they affected Asia, which need not mean that they affected Asia alone. The confident request for imperial support and the suggestion that the emperor had not authorized the decrees suggest a local phenomenon.

102. Kraabel, "Melito," 83–84.

103. Ibid., 84.

104. Juster, *Juifs*, vol.1, 304–37.

105. P. Winter, *On the Trial of Jesus* (Berlin: de Gruyter, 1961).

106. Eusebius (*Hist.eccl.*4.26.14) attributes sixteen works to him, but, apart from the *Peri Pascha*, only a few fragments have survived and their attribution both to Melito and to specific works in Eusebius's list is often uncertain. It is uncertain whether *Peri Pascha* is to be identified with Eusebius's references to "two books on the Pascha." For full discussion of the list and the fragments see Hall, *On Pascha*, xiii–xxii, xxviii–xxxix and the translation on 62–96. Also Blank, *Meliton*, 15ff.; O. Perler, *Méliton de Sardes sur la pâque et fragments* (Paris: Les éditions du Cerf, 1966) 11–15.

Chapter 9: Dialogue and Dispute: Justin

1. I have in mind here the work of H. Conzelmann, *Gentiles, Jews, Christians. Polemics and Apologetics in the Greco-Roman Era* (Minneapolis: Fortress, 1992) 290–303. Conzelmann's blinkered discussion focuses on Justin's concept of *Heilsgeschichte*, its strengths and weaknesses, and what is retrievable for today. This, together with his running polemic against those engaged in Jewish-Christian dialogue, leads him to overlook much important material in the *Dialogue*.

2. I am relying here primarily on M. Hoffmann, *Der Dialog bei den christlichen Schriftstellern der ersten vier Jahrhunderte (1.–11 Jh.)* (Berlin: Akademie Verlag, 1966) 2–28; B. R. Voss, *Der Dialog in der frühchristlichen Literatur* (Munich: W. Fink, 1970) 23–39. On intra-church dialogue see W. Schneemelcher, *Reden und Aufsätze* (Tübingen: Mohr [Siebeck], 1991) 214–35; and on gnostic dialogues see P. Perkins, *The Gnostic Dialogue: The Early Church and the Crisis of Gnosticism* (New York: Paulist, 1980).

3. S. Denning-Bolle, "Christian Dialogue as Apologetic? The Case of Justin Martyr Seen in Historical Context," *BJRL* 69(1986–87) 492–510, notes that Justin does not use dialogue to discover truth; he assumes that he already knows it.

4. Our information is confined to a brief report in Origen *Cels.*4.52, and a preface that falsely attributes the work to Cyprian (*CSEL* 3.3.119–32). The work is normally attributed to Aristo of Pella. It is commonly dated before Justin's *Dialogue*, but this remains uncertain. Since, according to Eusebius (*Hist.eccl.*4.6.3), Aristo reported on the Bar Cochba rebellion, some connect the debate with the situation following the Jewish defeat. But it does not say in which work his report appeared, and we cannot

assume it was the *Controversy*. It is often noted that the choice of the dialogue format indicates common ground between Jews and Christians. When addressing the Romans, Justin uses the apology, though even here the meaning of Scripture can form a significant part of the argument (*I Apol*.32ff.).

5. Justin seems to think of himself as a Gentile even though he was born in Samaria.

6. The relationship between these two writings will be discussed further below. On the face of it, it seems more likely that the simpler work of Aristo was the source for Justin than the reverse.

7. On the relationship of Justin's *Dialogue* to later texts see Voss, *Dialog*, 325; A. B. Hulen, "The Dialogues with the Jews as Sources for the Early Jewish Argument Against Christianity," *JBL* 51(1932) 58–71.

8. E. R. Goodenough, *The Theology of Justin Martyr* (Jena: Frommanische Buchhandlung, 1923) 92.

9. A. von Harnack, *Judentum und Judenchristentum in Justins Dialog mit Trypho* (Leipzig: J. C. Hinrichs, 1913) TU 39:1, 47–98, here 54.

10. Hoffmann, *Dialog*, 20–21.

11. *Dial*.80.3 suggests that the text is the record of a real debate. This is hardly plausible, unless a stenographer was present. L. W. Barnard, *Justin Martyr, His Life and Thought* (Cambridge: Cambridge University Press, 1967) 23–24, 39, argues that Justin elaborates on an actual debate and he tends to take all the information in it at face value. Goodenough, *Theology*, 90, who thinks that the *Dialogue* does not report an actual discussion, nevertheless recognizes that the arguments are precisely the sort that would have arisen in such circumstances. That Justin conflates his (generally accurate) knowledge of Jewish arguments without necessarily recording one particular discussion is argued by G. Archambault, *Justin. Dialogue avec Trypho* (Paris: Picard, 1909) vol.1, 112–16; A. L. Williams, *Justin Martyr: The Dialogue with Trypho* (London: SPCK, 1930) xxiv–xxxiii; and L. Goppelt, *Christentum und Judentum im ersten und zweiten Jahrhundert* (Gütersloh: Bertelsmann, 1954) 289, though Goppelt puts more emphasis on the "Gentile" flavor of the argument.

12. On Justin's knowledge of Judaism see L. W. Barnard, "The Old Testament and Judaism in the Writings of Justin Martyr," *VT* 14(1964) 394–406; idem, *Justin*, 39–52; P. Sigal, "An Inquiry into Aspects of Judaism in Justin's *Dialogue with Trypho*," *AbrN* 18(1978–79) 74–100; H. Remus, "Justin Martyr's Argument with Judaism," in S. G. Wilson, ed., *Anti-Judaism in Early Christianity* (Waterloo: Wilfrid Laurier University Press, 1986) vol.2, 59–80, esp. 66–80. G. N. Stanton, "Aspects of Early Jewish-Christian Polemic and Apologetic," *NTS* 31(1985) 337–92, esp. 377–78, rightly emphasizes that Justin is a valuable source for Jewish-Christian debate in the second century. See now also W. Horbury, "Jewish-Christian Relations in Barnabas and Justin Martyr," in J. D. G. Dunn, ed., *Jews and Christians: The Parting of the Ways A.D. 70–135* (Tübingen: Mohr [Siebeck], 1992) 315–45, here 337–45; and J. T. Sanders, *Schismatics, Sectarians, Dissidents, Deviants: The First One Hundred Years of Jewish-Christian Relations* (Valley Forge, Pa.: Trinity, 1993) 49–55. See also n.61 below.

13. Hoffmann, *Dialog*, 14, counts the following: Justin speaks 117 times, Trypho 81 times, and his friends 6 times. But he notes that Justin's speeches tend to be long, while Trypho is restricted to short answers or objections. He also notes (pp.15–16), as have others, that the conversation between Justin and the old man in chaps. 1–8 is, because of the juxtaposition of question and answer, closer to a genuine dialogue. It has also been noted that the dialogue between Justin and Trypho is more lively

and balanced in some places (especially the christological sections, e.g., 45ff.; 56ff.; 69ff.) than in others: Voss, *Dialog*, 36–37; Hoffmann, *Dialog*, 15–16.

14. A point made by D. Trakatellis, "Justin Martyr's Trypho," in G. W. Nickelsburg with G. W. MacRae, *Christians among Jews and Gentiles* (Philadelphia: Fortress, 1986) 287–97, here 294–95, in what is by far the most glowing summary of Justin's portrait of Trypho. He also makes the significant observation (p.297) that even if the entire *Dialogue* is fictional "it is important that a central place in this vision is a Jew, that the creator of the vision is a Christian, and that the setting of the vision is a dialogue."

15. All references in parentheses are to the *Dialogue* unless otherwise specified. Translations are adapted from Williams, *Justin*; Greek text from Archambault, *Justin*.

16. These points are collected in O. Skarsaune, *The Proof From Prophecy. A Study in Justin Martyr's Proof Text Tradition: Text-type, Provenance, Theological Profile* (Leiden: Brill, 1987) 165–66. This excellent book covers far more ground than the title indicates.

17. This would mean qualifying H. Chadwick, "Justin Martyr's Defence of Christianity," *BJRL* 47(1963) 275–97, here 278, who speaks of Justin's "sunny open-heartedness" and "innocent optimism," suggesting that "nothing could be less haunted than Justin's mind and conscience."

18. So, in one form or another, Harnack, *Judentum*, 51 n.2, though he allows for Jews and Christians as part of the audience; Goodenough, *Theology*, 96–100; Voss, *Dialog*, 38. J. C. M. van Winden, *An Early Christian Philosopher: Justin Martyr's Dialogue with Trypho the Jew* (Leiden: Brill, 1971) 26, 114, argues that Gentiles as well as Jews would have been interested in the argument of the *Dialogue*. J. Nilson, "To Whom Is Justin's *Dialogue with Trypho* Addressed?" *TS* 38(1977) 538–46, here 541–42, provides arguments against a Jewish audience. N. Hyldahl, *Philosophie und Christentum. Eine Interpretation der Einleitung zum Dialog Justins* (Copenhagen: Munksgaard, 1966) 18, notes that if Justin's aim was to convert Jews, it is unlikely that he would have succeeded.

19. T. Zahn, "Studien zu Justinus Martyr," *ZKG* 8(1886) 1–84, here 57–61 (though he doesn't think they are the only group in view); he is followed by Skarsaune, *Proof*, 258–60; Hyldahl, *Philosophie*, 19–20; H. Schreckenberg, *Die christlichen Adversus-Judaeos Texte und ihr literarisches und historisches Umfeld* (Frankfurt: P. Lang, 1982) 182–83. Nilson, "*Dialogue*," makes the same connection but thinks Trypho's friends were committed Jews.

20. I am summarizing the arguments of T. Stylianopoulos, *Justin Martyr and the Jewish Law* (Missoula, Mont.: Scholars Press, 1975) 168–95.

21. Stylianopoulos, *Justin*, 174–76.

22. I am here following Stylianopoulos, *Justin*, 176–87.

23. Stylianopoulos, *Justin*, 35–44, is the most sustained case. R. Wilde, *The Treatment of the Jews in the Greek Christian Writers of the First Three Centuries* (Washington, D.C.: Catholic University of America Press, 1949) 106–7, thinks it was addressed to Jews who were disillusioned by the collapse of Judaism after 135 CE, who chafed under rabbinic laws, and who had strong messianic hopes. Hyldahl, *Philosophie*, 17–18, offers (but then rejects) some arguments for presupposing a Jewish audience.

24. See chap. 5.

25. Nilson, "*Dialogue*," 541–42.

26. Stanton, "Aspects," 378. Stylianopoulos, *Justin*, 32–33, allows that, in

addition to any more specific purposes, the *Dialogue* was written within and for a Christian community—a view that is implicit but not always clearly stated in many discussions of the matter. In addition he makes the important observation (*Justin*, 20–32) that while Marcionites and Gnostics may not have been the readers that Justin had immediately in mind, some of the arguments he uses against Trypho were developed in previous confrontations with these two groups (and were presumably included in his no longer extant *Syntagma against All Heresies*).

27. Stylianopoulos, *Justin*, 32.

28. See chap. 5.

29. R. S. MacLennan, *Early Christian Texts on Jews and Judaism* (Atlanta: Scholars Press, 1990) 49–88, here 53–54, suggests that Justin's main concern is with Christian self-definition. This is asserted rather than argued, but points no doubt to one of Justin's motives. The text, however, points to other motives too.

30. Stylianopoulos, *Justin*, esp. 51–68, argues that in these chapters and elsewhere Justin proposes a tripartite division of the law: the ethical portions, which are universally and permanently binding (e.g., 93:1–3); the predictions, both words and deeds, which foretell the coming of Christ and his church (e.g., 40–42); and the historically limited commands given to and for the sinful Jews. Such a clear threefold structure hinges on the meaning of 42:2, and Stylianopoulos's scheme may be neater than anything Justin consciously worked with. Rather, Justin gives the impression of grasping for any argument that can become grist for his mill.

31. On Nerva and Barnabas see chap. 4; on the diaspora and Bar Cochba revolts see chap. 1. See also the perceptive articles by W. Horbury, "Messianism among Jews and Christians in the Second Century," *Anton* 29(1988) 71–88, here 82–87; and A. Chester, "Jewish Messianic Expectations and Mediatorial Figures and Pauline Christology," in M. Hengel and U. Heckel, eds., *Paulus und das antike Judentum* (Tübingen: Mohr [Siebeck], 1991) 17–89, here 40–47.

32. Skarsaune, *Proof*, 272–73, 287–88, thinks it may have been seen as an opportune moment to present to the Jews an alternative vision of messiahship.

33. A. J. B. Higgins, "Jewish Messianic Belief in Justin Martyr's *Dialogue with Trypho*," *NT* 9(1967) 298–305. My general impression is that the more we get to know about the varieties of Jewish belief in the second century, the more plausible the picture of Trypho (and Celsus's Jew) becomes.

34. See D. Juel, *Messianic Exegesis* (Philadelphia: Fortress, 1988) 165–67; W. Horbury, "The Messianic Associations of 'the Son of Man,'" *JTS*, n.s. 36(1985) 34–55; see also n.59.

35. E. Ferguson, "The Disgrace and the Glory: A Jewish Motif in Early Christianity," *StPatr* 21(1987) 86–94. He notes that Jews (Passover) and Christians (Jesus' death and resurrection) could associate it with one event, but it was a Christian apologetic move to apply the pattern to two advents (*Ps.-Clem.Rec.*1:49–50; Tertullian *Adv.Jud.*14; Origin *Cels.*1:56).

36. The variety of messianic speculation is a major theme of the essays in J. H. Charlesworth, ed., *The Messiah: Developments in Earliest Judaism and Christianity* (Minneapolis: Fortress, 1992).

37. Stylianopoulos, *Justin*, 20–32, is the clearest statement.

38. A. Segal, *Two Powers in Heaven: Early Rabbinic Reports about Christianity and Gnosticism* (Leiden: Brill, 1977) esp. 221–24; idem, "Judaism, Christianity and Gnosticism," in Wilson, ed., *Anti-Judaism*, 133–62. He connects the rabbinic debates with the evidence of Justin. As Segal notes, much of the rabbinic argument could also be directed against (Jewish?) Gnostics.

39. See P. Hayman, "Monotheism—A Misused Word in Jewish Studies," *JJS* 42(1990) 1–15, and the discussion in chap. 7.

40. P. Richardson, *Israel in the Apostolic Church* (Cambridge: Cambridge University Press, 1969) passim, but on Justin, pp.9–13.

41. See J. S. Siker, *Disinheriting the Jews: Abraham in Early Christian Controversy* (Louisville, Ky.: Westminster/John Knox, 1991) 176–78, who sees the notion of the dispossession of the Jews as a prelude to the return (*Dial.*16:2; 25:5; 40:2; 92:2).

42. See W. A. Shotwell, *The Biblical Exegesis of Justin Martyr* (London: SPCK, 1965)—a useful if unimaginative summary of earlier work—which has now been superseded in all respects by Skarsaune, *Proof.*

43. Jewish questions about Jesus' birth appear in other Jewish and Christian sources too. See chap. 6.

44. Aquila's translation is renowned for its literalism. To what degree it is aimed at Christian use of the Jewish Bible is disputed. See S. Jellicoe, *The Septuagint and Modern Study* (Oxford: Oxford University Press, 1968) 76–83; more recently, with bibliography, O. Munnich, "Le Texte de la Septante," in G. Dorival, M. Harl, and O. Munnich, eds., *La Bible Grecque des Septantes du judaïsme héllenistique au christianisme ancien* (Paris: Editions du Cerf, 1988) here 143–47. The main "anti-Christian" texts are usefully set out by F. Field, *Origenis Hexaplorum quae supersunt; sive Veterum interpretum graecorum in totum Vetus Testamentum Fragmenta* (Hildesheim: G. Olms, 1964) vol.1, xix–xx. Justin's account of the dispute between Christians and Jews over essentially the same version of the LXX is treated in detail by M. Hengel, "Die Septuaginta als von den Christen beanspruchte Schriftensammlung bei Justin und den Vätern vor Origenes," in Dunn, ed., *Jews,* 39–84.

45. Stylianopoulos, *Justin,* 97; P. R. Weis, "Some Samaritanisms of Justin Martyr," *JTS* 45(1944) 199–205.

46. This is the conclusion on the fullest, most recent and persuasive discussion of the scriptural traditions in the *Dialogue:* Skarsaune, *Proof,* 25–242.

47. See the useful discussion by Schreckenberg, *Adversus-Judaeos,* 188–94.

48. Generally on this issue see H. Remus, *Pagan-Christian Conflict over Miracle in the Second Century* (Cambridge, Mass.: Philadelphia Patristic Foundation, 1983). As the title indicates, the conflict over miracles arose as much with pagans as with Jews. See also Chadwick, "Justin," 281.

49. Stanton, "Aspects," 379–82. See further chap. 6.

50. See Harnack, "Judentum," 82–84; Schreckenberg, *Adversus-Judaeos,* 184; Conzelmann, *Polemics,* 302–3, who distinguishes between collective and individual salvation for Jews; M. de Jonge, "Pre-Mosaic Servants of God in the Testaments of the Twelve Patriarchs and in the Writings of Justin and Irenaeus," *VC* 39(1985) 157–70, here 165–66. The best discussion of the remnant passages is Stylianopoulos, *Justin,* 39–44.

51. Yet Irenaeus, Tertullian, and Origen, as well as a number of Jews, expressed the same hope for a literal restoration of Jerusalem in the last days. See R. L. Wilken, "Early Christian Chiliasm, Jewish Messianism, and the Idea of the Holy Land," in Nickelsburg and MacRae, *Christians,* 299–307; and, in relation to Jewish and earlier Christian writings, W. D. Davies, *The Gospel and the Land: Early Christianity and Jewish Territorial Doctrine* (Berkeley: University of California Press, 1974); idem, *The Territorial Dimension of Judaism* (Berkeley: University of California Press, 1982).

52. *God:* 25:6–26:2; 32:2; 45:2; 55:3; 64:2–3; 67:7; 80:1. *Christ:* 35:8; 39:2; 44:2–4; 92:6; 108:3; 125:5; 134:3.

53. 35:8; 96:3; 58:1; 133:1; 137:1–2; 142:2–3.

54. 32:2; 55:3 could be interpreted along the same lines. Note too the obscure comment in 134:3 about Jacob and Laban's daughters: "Now Leah represented your people and the synagogue, while Rachel was the figure of our church. And Christ still serves for these and for his servants that are in both."

55. 120:2 is the clearest example, but compare 32:2; 55:3; 80:1–2; and perhaps 25:1 (variant reading).

56. 35:8; 44:2–4; 45:2; 46:1; 92:6; 120:2; 125:3–5.

57. Stanton, "Aspects," 385–89; and Skarsaune, *Proof,* 252–59.

58. Richardson, *Israel,* 10.

59. See Shotwell, *Biblical,* passim; Barnard, "Old Testament," passim. Skarsaune, *Proof,* is by far the most extensive discussion to date.

60. Skarsaune, *Proof,* 47–92.

61. See n.12 above. Also the older and still valuable studies of A. H. Goldfahn, "Justinus Martyr und die Agada," *MGWJ* 22(1873) 49–269; M. Friedländer, "Justins Dialog mit dem Juden Trypho," in *Patristische und Talmudische Studien* (Vienna: Hölder, 1878) 80–137. See further H. F. Schneider, "Some Reflections on the Dialogue of Justin Martyr with Trypho," *SJT* 15(1962) 64–75; Skarsaune, *Proof,* 248–49. Goldfahn restricts himself to material that Justin reports as being Jewish; others add rabbinic parallels to the content and the method of Justin's own exegesis.

62. Skarsaune, *Proof,* 260–72. He is properly cautious in view of the difficulties in dating rabbinic traditions.

63. Goldfahn, "Justinus," passim, makes some particularly detailed comparisons and concludes that, despite some minor slipups, Justin generally presents Jewish traditions with considerable accuracy.

64. I would exempt Skarsaune from this comment, though he himself notes that he does not have the expertise to explore the matter properly. Part of the dilemma is that we now know a lot about the problems but not much about how to proceed in the light of them.

65. Skarsaune, *Proof,* 135–242, 252–69. The "kerygma source" (*Dial.*11–47, 108–41; *I Apol.*31–36, 48–68) contained the following: proof that Jesus, with his two advents (one in suffering, one in glory), is messiah; proof that the rule of the risen Christ was foretold in Scripture; a promise of messianic salvation in Jerusalem (largely excluding the Jews); and an anticultic polemic. The "antihistorical" or "recapitulation source" (*Dial.*48–107) contained arguments about whether certain prophecies refer to the historical past (Jewish kings) or the messianic future (Jesus). In both instances, Skarsaune supposes, these originally Jewish Christian sources have passed through the hands of Gentile Christians before reaching Justin.

66. The *Controversy between Jason and Papiscus* is of uncertain date and origin and its contents virtually unknown; and the *Kerygma Petrou* shows as many, if not more, differences than similarities. The comparison with roughly contemporaneous documents also reveals considerable differences on such questions as circumcision, the law, and the fate of the Jews. Moreover, some of the supposed links—Christology and an interest in baptism as a substitute for the cult—need not be part of a specifically Jewish Christian heritage. Skarsaune, it must be said, scrupulously points all these things out, but still wants to tip the balance in favor of his view. His dates for the *Anabathmoi Jakobou* (ca. 150 CE) and the *Testaments of the Twelve Patriarchs* (ca. 100 CE) are earlier than many would allow, but few would doubt that they are roughly contemporaneous with the *Dialogue* (ca. 160 CE). He further notes that it is an indication of the virility and influence of Jewish Christian traditions that they

survived, if in truncated form, in an overwhelmingly Gentile movement of the second century.

67. Skarsaune, *Proof,* 371–73, and the summary chapter 423–34. He also notes the parallels with NT writers, especially Paul and Luke, but notes that they are an indirect influence at best.

68. M. Simon, *Verus Israel: A Study of the Relations between Christians and Jews in the Roman Empire (135–425)* (Oxford: Oxford University Press, 1986) 67. My attention was drawn to this statement by Skarsaune, *Proof,* 67.

69. Stylianopoulos, *Justin,* 20–32, notes how Justin turns his arguments against the Gnostics against the Jews as well.

70. For a fuller discussion see chap. 6.

71. Skarsaune, *Proof,* 373. We might note that Neapolis, where Justin was born (120:6), was not far from Pella. On the other hand, there were many other places to meet Jews and Jewish Christians—Rome, for example. Justin's chiliasm could have come from prophetic sources rather than any particular attachment to Judaea.

72. MacLennan, *Early,* 56–58. Weis, "Samaritanisms" 199–205, has some bold things to say about Samaritan influence on Justin. Shotwell, *Biblical,* 85–88, is more cautious.

73. MacLennan, *Early,* 49–88, proposes reading each of the three places as a "text," but his rather grand statement of intention is followed by a distinctly lean outcome. It works best with Samaria/Judaea, which allows him to speak of such things as the Jewish Christians and the Bar Cochba revolt. But none of the subjects listed under Ephesus (Hellenistic Judaism and Philo, the LXX, Jewish persecution of Christians, the silence on Paul) have any specific connection with that city, and he rather lamely implies that what we can find out about Justin in Rome (mainly his death!) tells us more about his relation with the Romans than with the Jews.

74. Remus, "Justin," 59–66, is the best discussion.

75. For recent discussion see R. Wilken, *The Christians as the Romans Saw Them* (New Haven, Conn., and London: Yale University Press, 1984) 94–125; and, more briefly, R. M. Grant, *Greek Apologists of the Second Century* (Philadelphia: Westminster, 1982) 133–38.

76. I do not discount the possibility that Celsus is reporting the opinions of a Jew he knew, but this is not important. Generally the discussion focuses properly on the arguments rather than the individual. The fullest recent case for the authenticity of the "Jewish" arguments is made by E. Bammel, "Der Jude des Celsus," in *Judaica* (Tübingen: Mohr [Siebeck], 1986) 265–83, which includes (pp.265–66) a representative sample of earlier, dismissive views. A useful collection of disparate evidence is provided by M. Lods, "Etude sur les sources juives de la polémique de Celsus contre les chrétiens," *RHPR* 21(1941) 1–33, though he implausibly wants to trace a number of them back to a written source used by Celsus. See E. V. Gallagher, *Divine Man or Magician: Celsus and Origen on Jesus* (Chico, Calif.: Scholars Press, 1982) 51. M. Smith, *Jesus the Magician* (New York: Harper & Row, 1978) 58–59, also defends the authenticity of the Jews' arguments.

77. L. H. Feldman, "Origen's *Contra Celsum* and Josephus' *Contra Apionem:* The Issue of Jewish Origins," *VC* 44(1990) 105–35, emphasizes this (pp.106–7) and notes the many ways in which Origen's defense of Judaism parallels that of Josephus. See also H. Remus, "Outside/Inside: Celsus on Jewish and Christian *Nomoi,*" in J. Neusner, P. Borgen, E. S. Frerichs, and R. Horsley, eds., *New Perspectives in Ancient Judaism II* (Lanham, Md.: University Press of America, 1987) 132–50.

78. N. R. M. de Lange, *Origen and the Jews: Studies in Jewish-Christian Relations in Third-Century Palestine* (Cambridge: Cambridge University Press, 1976) 41–43, 63–73, here 41, whose judgment is similar to that of Bammel. When he says that "Celsus' Jew is unconvincing as a Jew" (p.69) I take him to be giving Origen's view rather than his own.

79. Bammel, "Jude," 276.

80. Ibid., 267–68; de Lange, *Origen*, 43.

81. E. R. Goodenough, *Jewish Symbols in the Greco-Roman Period*, 13 vols. (New York: Pantheon, 1953–68) vol.1, 53 n.117, rightly notes that the mix of Hellenistic and halakic traditions in Trypho was something that would have been found to a greater or lesser degree in many Jews of the period.

82. Contrary to L. Goppelt, *Christentum*, 300–301, who argues that the *Dialogue* reveals two communities entirely separate and distinct, between whom traffic has virtually ceased.

83. For a discussion of the supposed anti-Judaism of the *Dialogue* see Remus, "Justin," 74–80.

84. Barnard, *Justin*, 40, states: "The *Dialogue* with Trypho is an important source for Jewish knowledge of Christianity as well as for Christian knowledge of Judaism and implies a closer intercourse between Christians and Jews in the first half of the second century than has usually been supposed."

Chapter 10: An Overview

1. J. D. G. Dunn, *The Partings of the Ways between Christianity and Judaism and Their Significance for the Character of Christianity* (Philadelphia: Trinity, 1991) esp. 230–43.

2. On the importance of miracles in Christian propaganda see especially R. Mac-Mullen, *Christianizing the Roman Empire (A.D. 100–400)* (New Haven, Conn.: Yale University Press, 1984).

3. The burden of R. Ruether's seminal work, *Faith and Fratricide: The Theological Roots of Anti-Semitism* (New York: Seabury, 1974).

4. J. T. Sanders, *Schismatics, Sectarians, Dissidents, Deviants. The First One Hundred Years of Jewish-Christian Relations* (Valley Forge, Pa.: Trinity, 1993). Like him, I would like to know more about how things worked out in practice. There is some evidence, more perhaps than he concedes, but, as he recognizes, it is slight. Whether his intelligent exploration of conflict and deviance theory leads in the end to new knowledge, rather than a recasting of the already familiar, I doubt—but that is a bigger debate. See my review in the *Toronto Journal of Theology* 11(1995) 99–101.

5. Dunn, *Partings*, 234, reviving the view of J. Daniélou, *The Theology of Jewish Christianity* (London: Darton, Longman & Todd, 1964).

MODERN AUTHOR INDEX

❖

SUBJECT INDEX

❖

ANCIENT SOURCES INDEX

❖